T0377111

ROUTLEDGE HANDBOOK OF PRIMARY ELECTIONS

Primary elections have been used for the past century for most U.S. elective offices and their popularity is growing in other nations as well. In some circumstances, primaries ensure that citizens have a say in elections and test the skills of candidates before they get to the general election. Yet primaries are often criticized for increasing the cost of elections, for producing ideologically extreme candidates, and for denying voters the opportunity to choose candidates whose appeal transcends partisanship. Few such arguments have, however, been rigorously tested.

This innovative *Handbook* evaluates many of the claims, positive and negative, that have been made about primaries. It is organized into six sections, covering the origins of primary elections; primary voters; U.S. presidential primaries; U.S. subpresidential primaries; primaries in other parts of the world; and reform proposals. The *Routledge Handbook of Primary Elections* is an important research tool for scholars, a resource guide for students, and a source of ideas for those who seek to modify the electoral process.

Robert G. Boatright is a Professor of Political Science at Clark University and the Director of Research at the National Institute for Civil Discourse (NICD) at the University of Arizona. His research focuses on the effects of campaign and election laws on the behavior of politicians and interest groups, with a particular focus on primary elections and campaign finance laws and practices.

"With partisan polarization rising, political parties beset by factions, and a complete outsider gaining a major-party nomination for president, the workings of primary elections are back in the news – and on research agendas. Boatright has assembled a distinguished set of scholars to take us through the experience of the past, the issues of the present, and the options for the future. *Routledge Handbook of Primary Elections* is bound to be an essential guide as we work to understand the way 'democracy,' in selecting party nominees, ramifies through elections and government."

John Mark Hansen, *University of Chicago*

"Primary elections have not received the robust scholarly attention they merit due to their importance in picking political leadership in the US and abroad. The *Routledge Handbook of Primary Elections*, edited by Robert Boatright, addresses this critical gap. A group of outstanding scholars cover a broad range of topics in a manner that is both lucid for students and insightful for scholars. Boatright's volume sets the table for scholarship on primaries over the next decade."

Ray La Raja, *Professor of Political Science, U Mass Amherst*

"There are few topics in U.S. politics more important to study than the dynamics of primary elections. Yet political scientists have largely dropped the ball in illuminating the dynamics of this unique and critical feature of the American electoral system. That is, until now. With this volume, Robert Boatright, the foremost authority on U.S. primary elections, has assembled an impressive group of scholars to provide a comprehensive treatment of this underexplored terrain of American politics. Anyone who cares about the forces shaping the contemporary political environment will want to read this book and will benefit from doing so."

Nate Persily, *James B. McClatchy Professor of Law, Stanford Law School*

ROUTLEDGE HANDBOOK OF PRIMARY ELECTIONS

Edited by Robert G. Boatright

Routledge
Taylor & Francis Group

NEW YORK AND LONDON

First published 2018
by Routledge
711 Third Avenue, New York, NY 10017

and by Routledge
2 Park Square, Milton Park, Abingdon, Oxon, OX14 4RN

Routledge is an imprint of the Taylor & Francis Group, an informa business

Library of Congress Cataloging-in-Publication Data
Names: Boatright, Robert G, editor.
Title: Routledge handbook of primary elections / edited by
    Robert G. Boatright.
Other titles: Handbook of primary elections
Description: New York : Routledge, [2018] | Includes
    bibliographical references and index.
Identifiers: LCCN 2017044267 | ISBN 9781138684089 (hardback)
    | ISBN 9781134841707 (webpdf) | ISBN 9781134841776
    (epub) | ISBN 9781134841844 (mobipocket/kindle)
Subjects: LCSH: Primaries—United States. | Elections—United
    States. | Political candidates—United States. | Political
    participation—United States. | Primaries—Case studies. |
    Elections—Case studies. | Political candidates—Case studies. |
    Political participation—Case studies.
Classification: LCC JK2071 .R67 2018 | DDC 324.273/0154—dc23
LC record available at https://lccn.loc.gov/2017044267

ISBN: 978-1-138-68408-9 (hbk)
ISBN: 978-1-315-54418-2 (ebk)

Typeset in Bembo Std
by Swales & Willis Ltd, Exeter, Devon, UK

MIX
Paper from
responsible sources
FSC   FSC® C013985
www.fsc.org

Printed in the United Kingdom
by Henry Ling Limited

CONTENTS

FIGURES

Figures

TABLES

CONTRIBUTORS

Robert G. Boatright is Professor of Political Science at Clark University and Director of Research at the National Institute for Civil Discourse (NICD) at the University of Arizona. His research focuses on the effects of campaign and election laws on the behavior of politicians and interest groups, with a particular focus on primary elections and campaign finance laws and practices. He is the author or editor of seven books, including *Getting Primaried: The Causes and Consequences of Congressional Primary Challenges* (University of Michigan Press, 2013); *Interest Groups and Campaign Finance Reform in the United States and Canada* (University of Michigan Press, 2011); and the edited volume *The Deregulatory Moment? A Comparative Perspective on Changing Campaign Finance Laws* (University of Michigan Press, 2016).

Kathleen Bruhn is Professor of Political Science at the University of California, Santa Barbara. Her interests lie at the intersection of political parties and social movements. She has written about partisan alliances and protest, elections and democratization in Mexico, and the implications of party primaries. Her most recent book is *Urban Protest in Mexico and Brazil* (Cambridge University Press).

Barry C. Burden is Professor of Political Science and Founding Director of the Elections Research Center at the University of Wisconsin-Madison. His research focuses on U.S. elections, representation, and public opinion. His recent studies have centered on various aspects of state election administration such as early voting as well as the personal and institutional factors that affect citizen participation. He is the author of *Personal Roots of Representation*, co-author with David Kimball of *Why Americans Split Their Tickets*, and co-editor with Charles Stewart of *The Measure of American Elections*. Burden has also published articles in a wide range of scholarly journals including the *American Political Science Review*, *American Journal of Political Science*, and *Journal of Politics*. Burden earned his Ph.D. at The Ohio State University and was on the faculty at Harvard University for seven years.

Jamie L. Carson is Professor of Political Science at the University of Georgia. He received his Ph.D. from Michigan State University in 2003, where he was a fellow in the Political Institutions and Public Choice Program. Carson's research focuses primarily on congressional politics and elections, separation of powers, and American political development. His work has appeared in such journals as the *American Political Science Review*, *American Journal* *of Political Science*, *Journal of Politics*, *Legislative Studies Quarterly*, *Political Analysis*, and *Political Research Quarterly*. His most recent book is the ninth edition of *The Politics of Congressional Elections*, co-authored with Gary Jacobson.

Marty Cohen received his Ph.D. from the University of California at Los Angeles in 2005. His research interests are varied. His main focus is on the growing electoral influence of the religious right in the Republican Party. To that end, he is working on a book entitled *Moral Victories* which looks at how evangelical Christian activists aided the GOP in taking control of the House of Representatives in the early 1990s. He is also interested in political parties and is a co-author of *The Party Decides: Presidential Nominations Before and After Reform*, published by the University of Chicago Press in 2008. He is co-author of the 2011 *Perspectives on Politics* article "A Theory of Parties" which won the Jack Walker Award for its outstanding contribution to research on political organizations and parties. Marty regularly teaches classes on religion and politics, as well as the introductory American government course and a class on political parties. He also has more than a passing interest in the politics and culture of the 1960s.

Michael H. Crespin is Associate Director of the Carl Albert Congressional Research and Studies Center and Professor of Political Science at the University of Oklahoma. He earned his Ph.D. from Michigan State University in 2005 and served in the office of U.S. Representative Dan Lipinski as an APSA Congressional Fellow from 2005 to 2006. Crespin's research focuses on legislative politics, congressional elections, and political geography. Some of his work has appeared in the *American Journal of Political Science*, *Journal of Politics*, *Legislative Studies Quarterly*, *Political Analysis*, and *State Politics and Policy Quarterly*.

Marino De Luca is Adjunct Professor of Public Policy at the Department of Social and Institutional Science (University of Cagliari, Italy). His main research interests concern political parties, elections, and political communication. Among his latest publications are "The Effects of Primaries on Electoral Performance: France and Italy in Comparative Perspective" (*French Politics*, 2017), "The Role of the People in the Characterization of Populism: Evidence from the Press Coverage of the 2014 European Parliament Election Campaign in Italy" (*Italian Political Science Review*, 2017), and "From the Communist Party to the Front de Gauche: The French Radical Left from 1989 to 2014" (*Communist and Post-Communist Studies*, 2016).

Casey B. K. Dominguez is Associate Professor of Political Science at the University of San Diego. She received her Ph.D. in Political Science from the University of California, Berkeley, in 2005. She researches and teaches undergraduate courses about political parties, congressional elections, and the presidency. Dr Dominguez studies the ways that interest groups relate to political parties in campaigns and in government. Her current book project examines the ways that partisanship and other factors affected the political construction of presidential war powers in the nineteenth century. She has also published research on presidential honeymoons.

Matthew J. Geras is a Graduate Fellow at the Carl Albert Congressional Research and Studies Center at the University of Oklahoma. His research interests include Congress, American elections, and political participation. He previously interned in the office of U.S. Representative Ileana Ros-Lehtinen.

Reuven Y. Hazan is Professor in and former Chairperson of the Department of Political Science at the Hebrew University of Jerusalem. His research interests are elections and electoral systems, political parties and party systems, and legislative studies. He is the co-author of *Democracy within Parties* (Oxford University Press, 2010) and co-editor of *Understanding Electoral Reform* (Routledge, 2012). His articles have appeared in *Comparative Political Studies, Electoral Studies, International Political Science Review, Legislative Studies Quarterly, Journal of Legislative Studies, Journal of Peace Research, Journal of Theoretical Politics, Party Politics, Political Geography, Political Studies, Representation, Scandinavian Political Studies* and *West European Politics*, among others. He is on the editorial board of the *International Political Science Review, Journal of Legislative Studies* and *Party Politics*, and is also on the Executive Committee of the European Consortium for Political Research (ECPR). He has taught at Emory University, Columbia University and at Harvard University.

Shigeo Hirano is Associate Professor of Political Science at Columbia University. His research focuses on issues related to elections and representation. His work has appeared in various journals, including the *American Political Science Review, American Journal of Political Science*, and *Journal of Politics*. Several of his articles and book chapters have focused on primary elections in the United States.

David A. Hopkins is Associate Professor of Political Science at Boston College. He is the author of *Red Fighting Blue: How Geography and Electoral Rules Polarize American Politics* (2017); *Asymmetric Politics: Ideological Republicans and Group Interest Democrats* (with Matt Grossmann, 2016); and *Presidential Elections: Strategies and Structures of American Politics*, 14th edition (with Nelson W. Polsby, Aaron Wildavsky, and Steven E. Schier, 2016). He also serves as a frequent expert commentator in the news media and blogs regularly about current events at honestgraft.com.

Nahomi Ichino is Assistant Professor in the Department of Political Science and a Faculty Associate of the Center for Political Studies and the African Studies Center at the University of Michigan, Ann Arbor. Her research centers on ethnic politics, voter behavior, and political parties in developing democracies, with a regional specialization in sub-Saharan Africa. She also has a research interest in methodology for using qualitative information in small- and medium-n comparative studies. Her work has been published in *American Political Science Review, American Journal of Political Science, Journal of Politics*, and other outlets. She is a member of the research network Evidence in Governance and Politics and her research in Ghana has been supported by the National Science Foundation. She holds a Ph.D. in Political Science from Stanford University and was previously on the faculty in the Department of Government at Harvard University.

Indriði H. Indriðason is Professor of Political Science at the University of California, Riverside and Adjunct Professor of Political Science at the University of Iceland. He received his Ph.D. from the University of Rochester. His research interests include the politics of government coalitions; the formation of government coalitions; and how policy disagreements between coalition partners are settled, for example, through the use of coalition agreements and junior ministers. Other research focuses on various aspects of electoral politics, for example, the use of negative advertisements and campaign sentiment in multiparty elections, primary elections, coalitional voting, and the consequences of economic crisis on voter behavior. His research has appeared, for example, in *American Journal of Political Science, Journal of Politics, British Journal of Political Science, Political Science Research and Methods, Journal of Theoretical Politics*, and *Legislative Studies Quarterly*.

Reut Itzkovitch-Malka is Assistant Professor in the Department of Sociology, Political Science and Communications at the Open University of Israel. Prior to joining the academic faculty of the Open University, she was a Postdoctoral Fellow at Stanford University's Center on Democracy, Development and the Rule of Law. Her research interests include gender and politics, legislative studies, political representation, electoral systems, and candidate selection methods. Her articles have appeared in journals such as *Political Studies*, *European Journal of Women's Studies*, and *Representation*. She is the co-author of *The Representation of Women in Israeli Politics: A Comparative Perspective* (The Israel Democracy Institute, 2016).

Caitlin E. Jewitt is Assistant Professor of Political Science at Virginia Tech. She received her Ph.D. from the University of Minnesota. Her research interests include electoral rules, presidential primaries and caucuses, congressional primaries, and campaigns and elections. She is particularly interested in the institutional features of elections and their effects on voters, electoral outcomes, candidates, candidate strategy, and political elites. Additionally, she has examined the role of the Tea Party in recent congressional elections, particularly when the presence of a Tea Party candidate creates a divisive and competitive Republican primary. Her research has been published in *Electoral Studies*, *Public Choice*, and *American Politics Research*. She is currently working on a book manuscript exploring the effects of the electoral rules and the balance of power between citizens and party elites in presidential nominations in the post-reform era.

Michael S. Kang is the Thomas Simmons Professor at Emory Law School and a nationally recognized expert on campaign finance, voting rights, redistricting, judicial elections, and corporate governance. Professor Kang's work has been published widely in leading law journals, including the *Yale Law Journal*, *NYU Law Review*, and *Stanford Law Review*, and featured in the *New York Times*, *Washington Post*, and *Forbes*, among others. His most recent research focuses on partisan gerrymandering; the influence of partisanship and campaign finance on elected judges; the de-regulation of federal campaign finance following *Citizens United*; and so-called "sore loser" laws that restrict losing primary candidates from running in the general election. He clerked for Judge Michael S. Kanne of the U.S. Court of Appeals for the Seventh Circuit and worked in private practice at Ropes & Gray in Boston before joining the Emory Law faculty. Professor Kang received his B.A. and J.D. from the University of Chicago, where he served as technical editor of the Law Review and graduated Order of the Coif. He received an M.A. from the University of Illinois and a Ph.D. in government from Harvard University.

Kristin Kanthak is Associate Professor of Political Science at the University of Pittsburgh. A former staffer with U.S. House Ways and Means Committee Chair Dan Rostenkowski's personal office, she received her Ph.D. from the University of Iowa. Prior to coming to the University of Pittsburgh, she was Assistant Professor of Political Science at the University of Arizona. Her research centers on questions of political representation, legislatures, parties, and elections in the United States. Her work has appeared in *American Political Science Review*, *American Journal of Political Science*, and other publications. She is co-editor (with Chris W. Bonneau) of *State Politics and Policy Quarterly*. Her book (co-authored with George A. Krause) *The Diversity Paradox: Political Parties, Legislatures, and the Organizational Foundations of Representation in America*, was published by Oxford University Press and received the Legislative Studies Section's Alan Rosenthal Prize in 2013.

Gunnar Helgi Kristinsson is Professor of Political Science at the University of Iceland. His main research interests include democracy, politics of the executive, political parties, and the legislative process. His publications have appeared in the *European Journal of Political Research, Party Politics, West European Politics, Scandinavian Political Studies* and several other peer-reviewed journals as well as edited volumes published by international publishers. Professor Kristinsson's publications also include ten books published by Icelandic publishers and he is founding editor of the *Icelandic Review of Politics and Administration*. He has long standing experience in advising local and national governments in Iceland on constitutional matters and administrative reforms.

Jeffrey Lazarus (B.A. University of California, Los Angeles 1998; Ph.D. University of California, San Diego 2004) is Associate Professor of Political Science at Georgia State University. His area of research is Congressional behavior and elections, with the broad theme of exploring how members of Congress use their powers of office to help win re-election. In that vein, he has published work on distributive spending, revolving door lobbying, parties and partisanship, gender and politics, and the decision of whether or not to run for office. He is co-author *of Gendered Vulnerability: How Women Work Harder to Stay in Office* (University of Michigan Press, 2018), which examines the diverse ways in which female members of Congress face stronger obstacles than men when running for re-election, and how this results in women's legislative activity being more constituent-focused than men's activity. He has also authored and co-authored articles which have appeared in *American Journal of Political Science, Journal of Politics, Legislative Studies Quarterly, Political Research Quarterly*, and others.

Eric Loepp completed his Ph.D. in Political Science at the University of Pittsburgh and is currently Assistant Professor of Political Science at the University of Wisconsin, Whitewater, where he teaches courses in American government, political behavior, and research methods. His research focuses on candidate evaluation and electoral decision-making, particularly in primary elections. His dissertation, *Confounding Cues: How Policy Signals Condition the Impact of Racial and Gender Information in Primary Elections*, considers how voters assess men and women differently based on whether or not the candidate is in a Republican or Democratic primary. His work has appeared in *Electoral Studies* and the edited volume *Law and Election Politics: The Rules of the Game, Volume 2*, another Routledge publication.

Seth C. McKee is Associate Professor of Political Science at Texas Tech University. Previously, McKee taught at the University of South Florida St. Petersburg. He received his Ph.D. in Government from the University of Texas in 2005, a Master's degree in Economics (1998), and a Bachelor's degree in Political Science (1996) from Oklahoma State University. His primary area of research focuses on American electoral politics and especially party system change in the American South. He has published numerous articles on such topics as political participation, public opinion, vote choice, redistricting, party switching, minority representation, and strategic voting behavior. McKee is the author of *Republican Ascendancy in Southern U.S. House Elections* (Westview Press, 2010), the editor of *Jigsaw Puzzle Politics in the Sunshine State* (University Press of Florida, 2015), and author of the forthcoming textbook, *The Dynamics of Southern Politics: Causes and Consequences* (CQ Press).

Vincent G. Moscardelli is a political scientist (Ph.D. Emory University) at the University of Connecticut, where he currently serves as Director of the Office of National Scholarships and Fellowships and Coordinator of the Holster Scholars Program. His research and teaching interests include the U.S. Congress, congressional elections, and political leadership. His work on these topics has appeared in *Journal of Politics, State Politics and Policy Quarterly, American Politics Research, Polity, Congress and the Presidency, Social Science Quarterly, Social Networks*, and other outlets, and has been supported by grants from the Dirksen Congressional Center, the JEHT Foundation, and the Hewlett Foundation. In 2003 to 2004, he served as an American Political

Science Association Congressional Fellow in the office of Senator Richard J. Durbin of Illinois. That same year, he was named "Best Chapter Advisor" by Pi Sigma Alpha, the national political science honor society. Before joining the UConn faculty in 2008, he was Assistant Professor of Political Science at the University of Massachusetts-Amherst.

Noah L. Nathan is Assistant Professor of Political Science at the University of Michigan and completed his Ph.D. in Government at Harvard University. He studies political behavior, the development of political parties, and the political effects of urban growth in new democracies in Africa.

Barbara Norrander is Professor in the School of Government and Public Policy at the University of Arizona. She frequently writes about primary elections, including her two books: *Super Tuesday: Regional Politics & Presidential Primaries* and *The Imperfect Primary: Oddities, Biases, and Strengths of U.S. Presidential Nomination Politics*. Her research on primary elections published in academic journals demonstrates that presidential primary voters are similar to other partisans who vote in general elections but not primaries; that primary participation rules (e.g., open versus closed primaries) have very little effect on the ideological composition of the primary electorate; that primary participation rules do influence the proportion of partisans and independents in a state; and that the "attrition game" is a useful tool for understanding the dynamics of presidential nomination politics. Professor Norrander's other research focuses on the gender gap in public opinion and partisanship.

Ian O'Grady is currently reading for his MPhil in Government (Comparative Politics) at the University of Oxford on a Marshall Scholarship. As a Research Associate for the Rose Institute of State and Local Government and NYU Wagner School of Public Service, Ian has analyzed and assessed a variety of elections and political reforms but has focused primarily on the effects of nonpartisan primary systems. He received his B.A. at Claremont McKenna College in Philosophy, Politics, and Economics, and has most recently worked in Arizona politics and as a Research Fellow for the California Local Redistricting Project before moving to England.

Scott Pruysers is a Social Sciences and Humanities Research Council of Canada (SSHRC) postdoctoral fellow at the University of Calgary. His current research interests include party organization, intra-party democracy, and political psychology. His research has been published in a variety of national and international journals such as the *Canadian Journal of Political Science, Representation, Regional and Federal Studies*, and *Politics & Gender*. He is co-author of *The Promise and Challenge of Primary Elections: A Comparative Perspective* (McGill-Queens University Press, 2016).

John F. Reynolds is Professor Emeritus of History at The University of Texas at San Antonio. He majored in history as an undergraduate at Michigan State University and earned his doctorate from Rutgers University in 1980. His research focuses on voting patterns and election laws especially during the Gilded Age and Progressive Era. *Testing Democracy: Electoral Behavior and Progressive Reform in New Jersey, 1880–1920* appeared in 1988. His second major research monograph, *The Demise of the American Convention System, 1880–1911*, was published in 2006. His essays have appeared in *Journal of American History, Social Science History, The Journal of Gilded Age and the Progressive Era*, and *Historical Methods*. His methodological expertise is in applying statistics to historical data; for a few summers he taught this skill at the InterUniversity Consortium for Political and Social Research. He now divides his time in retirement between Texas and his native Massachusetts.

Anthony Sayers is Associate Professor of Political Science at the University of Calgary. He has written widely on political parties, elections, and representation, is author of *Parties, Candidates, and Constituency Campaigns in Canadian Elections* (UBC Press, 1999), the *Canadian Elections Database* (http://canadianelectionsdatabase.ca, 2017), and articles in journals such as *Party Politics, Electoral Studies,* and the *Canadian Journal of Political Science.* In addition to analyzing data from the *CED,* he is completing a book length manuscript on Alberta politics with David Stewart and is involved in projects dealing with party organization and financing and politics in federal states.

Dante J. Scala is Associate Professor of Political Science at the University of New Hampshire and a Faculty Fellow at the Carsey School of Public Policy. He is the author of two books on presidential primaries, *Stormy Weather* (Palgrave, 2003) and, with Henry Olsen, *The Four Faces of the Republican Party* (Palgrave, 2015). His work on campaigns and elections, political demography, and campaign finance has appeared in numerous journals and scholarly volumes, including *Political Geography* and *Annals of the American Academy of Political and Social Science.* National and international media regularly seek out his commentary on the New Hampshire presidential primary and its role in the nomination process.

Gilles Serra is Associate Professor of Politics at CIDE in Mexico. He received his Ph.D. from Harvard University (in the Political Economy and Government program) and was a postdoctoral fellow at Oxford University (in Nuffield College). His formal models of political parties and electoral competition have appeared in *Journal of Politics, Journal of Theoretical Politics* and edited books in Springer. His research on political institutions, elections, and reforms in Latin America and the United States has been published in *Electoral Studies, Journal of Politics in Latin America,* and handbooks by Oxford University Press.

J. Andrew Sinclair is Clinical Assistant Professor at NYU's Wagner Graduate School of Public Service, where he teaches courses in public policy and quantitative methodology. He conducts research on public policy, electoral institutions, political behavior, and democratic accountability in the United States and in Britain. In addition to academic articles, he is the co-author of *Nonpartisan Primary Election Reform: Mitigating Mischief,* focused on the nonpartisan top-two primary in California. He holds a Ph.D. and M.S. in Social Science from the California Institute of Technology and a B.A. in Mathematics and Government from Claremont McKenna College.

James M. Snyder, Jr. is the Leroy B. Williams Professor of History and Political Science at Harvard University. Professor Snyder's primary research and teaching interests are in American politics, with a focus on political representation. He has written on a variety of topics, including elections, campaign finance, legislative behavior and institutions, interest groups, direct democracy, the media, and corruption. He is a Research Associate at the National Bureau of Economic Research, and a Fellow of the American Academy of Arts and Sciences. His articles have appeared in *American Political Science Review, American Journal of Political Science, Journal of Politics, American Economic Review, Journal of Political Economy, Econometrica,* and many other journals and edited volumes. He is co-author of *The End of Inequality: One Person, One Vote and the Transformation of American Politics.* Professor Snyder taught for six years in the Department of Economics at the University of Chicago, and for eighteen years in the Departments of Political Science and Economics at the Massachusetts Institute of Technology.

Wayne Steger is Professor of Political Science and Distinguished Honors Faculty at DePaul University. His books include *A Citizen's Guide to Presidential Nominations: The Competition for*

Leadership and *Campaigns and Political Marketing*. Previously he was an editor of *Journal of Political Marketing*. He has published over 40 articles, chapters, and essays on campaigns, elections, Congress, and the American presidency. His current research focuses on the relation between competition in presidential and congressional elections and the empowerment of citizenry over the political system. He is also working on a book on the social, cultural and economic forces that have contributed to the rise of populist sentiment in the major political parties.

Danielle M. Thomsen is Assistant Professor of Political Science in the Maxwell School of Citizenship and Public Affairs at Syracuse University. Her research focuses on Congress, campaigns and elections, and women's representation. She is author of *Opting Out of Congress: Partisan Polarization and the Decline of Moderate Candidates*. Her articles have appeared in *Journal of Politics*, *Legislative Studies Quarterly*, *Political Research Quarterly*, and *State Politics & Policy Quarterly*. She has received financial support from the National Science Foundation, the American Association of University Women, and the Dirksen Congressional Center. She received the E.E. Schattschneider Award for the best dissertation in American politics in 2015.

Sarah A. Treul is Associate Professor of Political Science at the University of North Carolina at Chapel Hill, specializing in American political institutions. Her general focus is on the effect of institutional design and rules on political outcomes. Her research frequently focuses on how institutions affect decision-making—and more broadly—representation in the U.S. Congress. Her recent book *Agenda Crossover: The Influence of State Delegations in Congress* was published with Cambridge University Press and analyzes how members in Congress utilize their state delegation to stay abreast of changing policy preferences. She teaches classes on American government, the U.S. Congress, and political parties. She is the recipient of the Tanner Award for Excellence in Undergraduate Teaching at the University of North Carolina at Chapel Hill.

Alan Ware is Emeritus Fellow of Worcester College, Oxford University. Previously he was a Tutorial Fellow of the College and a Professor in the University's Department of Politics; before moving to Oxford in 1990 he taught at the University of Warwick for 18 years. He is the author of many academic articles and of ten books including *Political Conflict in America* (2011), *The Democratic Party Heads North, 1877–1962* (2006), *The American Direct Primary* (2002) and *Political Parties and Party Systems* (1996). Translated versions of this 1996 book have now been published in both Spanish and Chinese. In (so-called) retirement he continues to publish regularly on American politics and also on British educational policy, especially in *The Political Quarterly*.

Ryan D. Williamson received his Ph.D. from the University of Georgia in 2017. Prior to that, he received his B.A. from the University of Alabama at Birmingham. During the 2017–2018 academic year, he will serve on Capitol Hill as a member of the American Political Science Association's Congressional Fellowship Program. His research interests include congressional elections, legislative procedure, election law and administration, separation of powers, and institutional development. His work on these topics has been published in journals such as *Journal of Politics* and *State Politics & Policy Quarterly*.

INTRODUCTION

Robert G. Boatright

"Democracy is not to be found within the parties but between the parties."
E. E. Schattschneider (1942, 60)

"Party leadership is democratic in appearance and oligarchic in reality."
Maurice Duverger (1954, 133)

"To deny the citizen the right to select candidates and to confine his suffrage rights solely to a decision as between candidates after they have been selected is, in reality, at least a partial denial of the right of suffrage."
Senator George W. Norris (1923)

On April 18, 2017, many Americans eagerly anticipated the results of an eighteen-candidate special primary election to fill an open seat in the U.S. House of Representatives. The seat in question, a suburban Atlanta district that had reliably voted for Republican candidates but had been closer than expected in the 2016 presidential race, had been vacated by Republican Representative Tom Price, following his appointment to serve as Donald J. Trump's Secretary of Health and Human Services. Just five months earlier, Price had won reelection in this district by 23 percentage points. Yet the top vote-getter in the primary was Democrat Jon Ossoff, a thirty-year-old political neophyte. Ossoff received 48 percent of the vote. Eleven Republicans, four Democrats, and two independents vied for the remaining votes; Ossoff's closest competitor was Karen Handel, a veteran of Georgia Republican politics, who finished with slightly under 20 percent of the vote. Handel touted her Republican bona fides, but also pointedly declined to discuss Donald Trump during the campaign. According to Georgia law, Ossoff's failure to secure fifty percent of the vote meant that Ossoff and Handel would face off again, in a run-off election.

This election took on outsized significance, in part because Democratic activists throughout the country rallied behind Ossoff's campaign for the purpose of presenting the election as a referendum on public support for Trump's fledgling presidency. Ossoff raised the staggering sum of $8.3 million – an unheard-of sum for a Democrat running in such a reliably Republican district, and more than five times what was raised by the average victorious 2016 House candidate.

Although this election was not a typical primary election – it featured candidates of both parties running on the same ballot, and had Ossoff cleared 50 percent, there would have been no subsequent election – for all practical purposes it was treated by both parties as if it was. It was assumed that it would likely be followed by a contest between a Democrat and a Republican; Democrats rallied behind Ossoff and discouraged his Democratic competitors, and the national Republican Party vowed to support the leading Republican vote-getter in the run-off election. Like most American primaries, voter turnout was low, and those voters who did turn out were not necessarily representative of less politically engaged Georgia voters in their political views or demographic characteristics. Like most primaries, much of the intrigue surrounding the election had to do with whether the party leadership would coalesce behind one candidate before the voters had their say. And like most primaries, the results were arguably influenced by quirks of state election law – rules regarding who could vote and what format the contest would take. After the election, Democrats celebrated their candidate's strong showing, while Republicans responded that Ossoff's failure to clear 50 percent meant that the election did not necessarily say anything about public support for Trump or for the Republican Party.

The Georgia special election is but one of many examples of how the U.S. primary process works. Almost exactly a century ago, the United States was the first major democracy to adopt primary elections. The spread of the "direct primary" throughout the states in the early decades of the twentieth century was swift, and primaries were touted by Progressive reformers as a salutary development.[1] Primaries, according to their proponents, would loosen the grip of undemocratic party bosses, giving the rank and file voters more of a say in choosing candidates. Opponents of the primary protested that voters were not necessarily qualified to determine who would best represent the parties – primaries would become a battle between competing media titans, rather than party leaders, and would result in the nomination of wealthy candidates, candidates who had no particular allegiance to the parties whose banners they flew, or who would be less competitive in the general election than would candidates carefully vetted by party leaders.

It is safe to say that primaries in the United States have neither lived up to the promises of their advocates nor lived down to the fears of their opponents. One major study of primary competition across time has shown that after an initial period of turbulence in the 1910s and 1920s, primaries steadily became less competitive (Ansolabehere, Hansen, Hirano, and Snyder 2010). Voter enthusiasm about primaries also declined precipitously during this time outside of the South. For those who thought primaries would revolutionize American politics, this was certainly a sobering development. On the other hand, for those who feared that primaries would irreparably harm American democracy, this was certainly reassuring. The history of primary elections in the United States is largely a story of the resilience of political parties. Yet hopes and fears about primaries remain with us, and may in fact have grown more salient in recent years.

Primaries have also been treated with some skepticism by other democratic nations. Although, as we shall see in Part V, primary elections have become more common in other nations in recent years, they do not necessarily have anything to do with citizen perceptions of what democracy is. In most indices of the level of democracy, the five Scandinavian countries tend to monopolize the top spots. Depending on which index one uses, the top ten tends to be rounded out by other European nations (Germany, the Netherlands, Switzerland), Canada, New Zealand, or Costa Rica. Some of these countries (for instance, Iceland and Canada, which we will consider later in this book) do use primary elections, but most do not. And none of these countries have used primaries as long, or as extensively, as has the United States. Clearly, a country can be democratic without primaries.

There is also no *a priori* reason why democracy should require that the voters have a say in choosing party nominees, or in otherwise winnowing the field. The chaos of the Georgia special election suggests that it is wise to find a way to reduce the number of competing candidates, lest a multi-candidate race yield a victor who is unacceptable to a large majority of the electorate. Yet it is not at all clear that voters should do the winnowing. Few people vote in primaries; the voters who do show up tend to be unrepresentative of the population; and there is no guarantee that in a multi-candidate race the plurality winner will be ideologically representative of the party, will be the candidate voters would have wanted in a two-candidate match-up, or will be the most competitive general election candidate. Primaries can also contribute to voter fatigue – having too many elections can reduce voter turnout and increase citizens' cynicism about politics.

One the other hand, however, there are numerous examples of primary elections that have arguably advanced democracy. Primaries are popular. During the twentieth century, some American states sought to repeal their primary laws, but more often than not, citizens objected. During the 1920s and 1930s, for instance, some state legislatures repealed the direct primary only to see citizens reinstate it by referendum (Morlan 1955, 301). In addition, some primary campaigns can increase citizens' engagement with politics and create an aura of excitement that lasts well past the election. The most obvious example here is Barack Obama's stunning primary win in 2008; Obama entered the race with little support among Democratic Party elites, and he certainly would not have been the Democratic nominee had it not been for his campaign's skillful exploitation of some of the arcana of different states' primary laws. It is certainly plausible that the excitement generated by Obama's victory prompted other democracies to consider whether they, too, might find more dynamic leaders if they used primaries.

A Brief History of Primary Elections, and of Scholarship about Primary Elections

The Origins of Primary Elections

No one is exactly certain when the first U.S. primary election took place; some studies locate it in Crawford County, Pennsylvania (1842) while others point to the use of the primary by the Union Party in California, in 1866 (Ware 2002, 26; Delmatier, McIntosh, and Waters 1970, 33). By the time Wisconsin adopted the first mandatory statewide primary in 1902, however, there were advocacy movements for the primary in most states. Between 1902 and 1920, all but three states adopted some form of the primary. The last three states established primaries some years later – Rhode Island in 1947, New Mexico in 1953, and Connecticut in 1955. Although some states that had adopted the primary in the first two decades of the twentieth century were to later cut back on the use of primaries, it had become an expected feature of American elections.

There are two competing theories about why the direct primary spread so quickly. The standard account, which can be traced back to Charles Merriam's (1908; Merriam and Overacker 1928) definitive work on primaries, is simple – they were popular. Primary elections were championed by Progressive reformers as a means of giving citizens more control over elections, but they do not play a major role in the larger statements about Progressive goals.[2] They were certainly less controversial than other Progressive reforms; Progressives also championed non-partisan municipal elections, allowing voters to place referendums and initiatives on the ballots, and enabling recall elections for public officials. Some states adopted these, but only the direct primary found near-universal adoption.

Modern political scientists, however, have been skeptical of Merriam's account. Alan Ware (2002) and John Reynolds (2006), for instance, have noted that primaries solved many problems for political parties. As Reynolds notes, candidates were already beginning to engage in informal campaigns for office, so the establishment of the primary was not as big a change as Progressives proclaimed it to be. For much of the late nineteenth century states had been moving to shoulder more of the costs of elections, so assumption of the costs of choosing party nominees also lifted a burden from the parties. Lawrence, Donovan, and Bowler (2013) have compared the Merriam argument and the Ware argument, and found some support for each.

Whichever account one believes, it is clear that the introduction of primaries may well have been advantageous for political parties and for voters. The people who stood athwart the Progressive tide during the 1910s and 1920s, arguing against primaries, sound, to the contemporary reader, somewhat like cranks. In some cases they were. Yet in some cases, their warnings may have been prophetic. In his book entitled *Repeal the Direct Primary*, Bernard Freyd (1926) wrote that "if the direct primary succeeds in accomplishing anything, it merely creates a new and artificial organization which disguises itself by usurping the name of the old organization. This is all that it ever does or ever can do." The Russian political scientist Moisei Ostrogorski (1982 [1902], 113–118), upon his Tocqueville-esque visit to the United States in the 1900s, opined that the primary had completely failed to eliminate fraud and corruption.

In other cases, they were raising legitimate objections to the pace at which reform was proceeding. Former President William Howard Taft, for instance, lamented in 1914 that "the initiative, the referendum, and the recall, together with a complete adoption of the direct primary as a means of selecting nominees and an entire destruction of the convention system are now the sine qua non of the real reformer. Everyone who hesitates to follow all of these or any of them is regarded with suspicion and is denounced as an enemy of popular government and of the people" (White and Mileur 2002). And many writers of the time cautioned that even if one supported the direct primary, there were valid reasons to limit its use or to ensure that only voters who sincerely cared about the party's well-being could vote in it.

It would be oversimplifying matters, however, to merely distinguish between political systems that have primaries and systems that do not. Early primary elections took many different forms; today, as well, there are many different ways of conducting primaries, and small differences in primary laws can have major implications for the types of candidates selected, the choices that voters have, or the ability of party leaders to control the process. Typically, a distinction is made between closed primaries, which are limited to registered members of a political party, and open primaries, where any voter can choose to vote in either party's primary. Numerous variations exist, as we shall see; for instance, in some states voters may change their party registration on the day of the election, in some states voters are limited to voting exclusively in one party's primary or the other, while in others voters may choose to vote in one party's primary for one office and another party's primary for another, and so on. There has also been variation over time and across states in voter registration laws, in the process by which candidates file to have their names on the ballot, and in the number of offices for which primaries must be held. States also vary in their responses to primaries in which no candidate receives more than fifty percent of the vote; some (mostly southern) states hold run-off elections between the top two candidates, as was the case in the Georgia races described above. Other states allow for plurality winners, and still others allow party conventions or party leaders to choose the candidate in such circumstances.

As with any political reform, then, there are subtle distinctions between reforms that might improve the functioning and reforms that were designed to limit its use or effectiveness. It is not always easy to distinguish between these proposals. In nations that do not use primaries, or have only adopted them recently, it may still be appropriate to debate whether there should be primaries at all. In the United States, however, the long history of primaries and the variation in primary laws, suggest that it is just as important to ask what kind of primaries we would like to have. And in order to ask such questions, we must draw on the past century's worth of research on primaries, as well as the best contemporary work on the subject.

Research on Primaries

Many research questions were raised by the advent of primaries; many of these questions are still with us today. Primary elections provide us with the opportunity to understand how multi-stage elections proceed – how, for instance, to effectively winnow the number of candidates, how candidates campaign in low-turnout elections, how political parties and interest groups seek to shape outcomes, how easy it is for candidates to "pivot" from an election in one constituency to an election in another, and how different laws regarding who can vote shape results. There have been many distinct periods of scholarship on primary elections – they have been periodically discovered, forgotten, and rediscovered by academics.

The study of primary elections was an integral part of early twentieth-century American political science. There were thirty-three articles on primaries published in the two leading U.S. political science journals between 1902 and 1931, including evaluative work, advocacy for different types of primary laws, and reports on how primaries were being implemented in the different states. The discipline of political science was itself a logical venue for Progressive scholarship, and the notion that an orderly expansion of public involvement in politics could curb corruption and enhance democracy was a common theme in this early work.

With the demise of the Progressive movement, and subsequently the advent of the Great Depression and World War II, American scholars largely lost interest in exploring the effects of different primary rules. There was also an emerging consensus that primaries had not lived up to reformers' early goals. From roughly the 1940s to the 1960s, American scholarship on primary elections largely had to do with how they had been adapted to fit the politics of different regions of the country. Most consequentially, V. O. Key's *Southern Politics in State and Nation* (1949) provided case studies of how the one-party South increasingly used primaries and primary run-off elections to resolve conflicts between different factions within the Democratic Party. The tendency for primary elections to be followed by uncompetitive general elections resulted in the rise of informal pre-primary nominating procedures, and in the rise of an issue-less politics that occasionally rewarded demagoguery. Other studies of the time also focused on legal maneuvering designed to prevent African-Americans from voting in southern primaries (Alilunas 1940; Overacker 1945).

Other regions of the United States also developed distinctive patterns of primary competition. Duane Lockard (1959) wrote an extended study of elections in New England, experts on the politics of the Plains states explored the way that primaries were used by agrarian reform movements (e.g. Morlan 1955), and many state-specific studies considered particular features of primaries. Yet for the most part these were not works *about* primary elections. Primary elections took on features that were characteristic of the culture of the states. Overall, literature on American politics during this time suggested that political parties had adapted primaries to suit their own ends. Although there was no one book of that era that definitively made this case, it seemed that even in an era where political parties did not take distinctive ideological positions, they exerted enough control to deter the sort of anti-party movements that had characterized the Progressive Era.[3]

All of this changed, however, with the advent of presidential primary elections in 1972. The presidential primary system – as we shall see in Part 4 – bears only a passing resemblance to the direct primary. Presidential primaries had been introduced in some states during the Progressive Era, but they tended to be referred to as "preference primaries" – they allowed voters to state their views but were not binding on the parties. As part of a comprehensive overhaul of presidential candidate selection procedures, however, the Democratic Party established a system of binding primaries and caucuses in which voters chose delegates to attend the party convention; these delegates would be bound to support the candidate for whom they were pledged on the first ballot, as long as that candidate was still in the race. A presidential primary is an election where voters cast ballots throughout the state; a caucus entails an evening of meetings in which voters discuss their thoughts on the nominees before undertaking one (and in some cases, more than one) round of public balloting to determine the sense of the people assembled on which candidates to support. There are many consequential differences in who participates in primaries and caucuses, and successful candidates learn how to modify their strategies accordingly (Panagopoulos 2010).

While the national parties were able to use their power to seat state delegations to compel the states to hold primaries or caucuses to select their delegates, they were unsuccessful in efforts to tell states when to hold their primaries or caucuses. Over time, a sequential order emerged in which four states – Iowa, New Hampshire, South Carolina, and Nevada – chose their delegates before all of the others. Although the sequence of primaries and caucuses was largely an accidental consequence of different states' choices, some scholars and political professionals contended that this sequence was beneficial to citizens – it enabled different regions of the country to have a say in candidate selection, it compelled candidates to campaign before diverse constituencies, and it provided the possibility that "dark horse" candidates might emerge as legitimate contenders over the course of the primary season. In addition, until the 2000s this sequential system worked in tandem with the nation's presidential public financing laws to ensure that the candidate with the most money did not have a decisive advantage over other candidates. States have moved the dates of their primaries and caucuses about, at times changing the rules in ways that have been said to disadvantage the parties, their nominees, or the fortunes of other candidates as they seek to plan their path to the nomination. Literature on American presidential primaries is replete with discussions of how a national primary, or a set of regional primaries, might influence candidate selection (e.g. Kamarck 2016; Norrander 2015).

Whatever merits this system may have, it is certainly quite distinctive from primaries for other offices. In order to reduce the number of elections, however, many states held their presidential primaries on the same day as their primaries for other state and federal offices. This major change to the administration of American primaries fostered a wave of new scholarship on primary elections. Much of this research concerned the characteristics of primary voters and the ability of individual presidential candidates to shape the composition of the primary electorate.

Over the past decade, the increasing ideological distance between the two major parties has fostered a new era of scholarship on primary elections.[4] American political parties have historically had diverse, and at times overlapping, constituencies. As the two parties have moved further apart in their ideological views, and as more and more congressional districts have become reliably Democratic or Republican, some primary elections have become more competitive than general elections, and more important as venues for conflicts between moderate and ideologically extreme candidates. It has been argued that the threat of a primary challenge has become more of a concern for members of Congress than the threat of general election competition, and primary elections have been blamed for a rise of extremism in both political parties. Although these claims have not always been accurate, researchers have documented a rise in interest group activity in primary elections and an increase in campaign spending in some high-profile primary elections. These changes have led to renewed interest on the part of political scientists in primary elections. They have also prompted efforts to develop new forms of primary elections aimed at reducing polarization. The most notable of these have been the nonpartisan "top-two" primary format that has been used in California since 2012 and the adoption following the 2016 election of ranked choice voting in Maine. Innovations such as these may influence primary competition, although if past work in primaries is any indication, they may not change primary elections as substantially as their proponents have forecast.

Primary Elections in Comparative Perspective

The arguments that American Progressives and their critics made about primaries are of relevance to any democratic nation. Holding primaries absolves political party leaders of making difficult decisions that may antagonize some party members or factions. Primaries can provide voters with a sense of inclusion, a sense that their voices are being heard. They can allow individual candidates to improve their ability to speak to the public. And they often reward charismatic candidates who have a talent for speaking to the public, yet who might not be the first choice of party leaders. Such benefits (and the perils that might come from them) are of relevance in a wide variety of different types of electoral systems.

Until recently, primary elections were a rarity outside of the United States. France began using a two-stage presidential election process in 1965, and as Kathleen Bruhn notes in her chapter here, primary elections were discussed as an option in Latin American countries during the 1980s. It is only in the 2000s, however, that they have become, if not commonplace, at least a recognized option for political parties in Europe, Latin America, and to a lesser extent in other democracies.

One might argue that primaries today are particularly attractive to political parties struggling to bridge the "democratic deficit." The relative stability of democratic institutions in much of Europe has, paradoxically, bred a sense on the part of the public that regular citizens have no real say in government. Some have attributed this sentiment to rising populist movements in these nations. Primary elections can give citizens a stake in governance and can compel politicians to explain their plans to rank and file party voters. As Alan Ware notes in his contribution to this volume, it is debatable whether all of these things are, in fact, primary elections. Systems where registered party members vote for their leaders may provide some choice, but they are not the same as the mass elections that currently exist in the United States.

Another key difference between American primaries and other countries' elections is that most American primaries are compulsory. In contrast, as Kathleen Bruhn argues in her chapter here, Latin American political parties are often able to choose whether it is in their interest to have a primary or not. While in a compulsory primary system parties can sometimes endorse candidates or work to winnow the primary field, they usually cannot decide to do away with the primary altogether. An optional primary can be a means for parties to adjust to novel circumstances or to selectively reach out to new voters when they benefit from doing so. That is, when parties can choose primaries, they become strategic tools rather than obstacles.

Finally, the chapters in this book make it clear that the conduct and consequences of primary elections are quite different in different types of electoral systems. As Indriði H. Indriðason and Gunnar Helgi Kristinsson note, most American studies of the consequences of primaries consider changes in ideology or voting activity, but in strong party parliamentary systems such effects are not evident. Indriðason and Kristinsson argue that the threat of primary competition may lead legislators to procure more benefits for their constituents and become more visible in parliament. Nahomi Ichino and Noah L. Nathan show in their chapter here, as well as in previous work (2012, 2014) that primaries with a small electorate feature far more of a transactional, one-on-one approach on the part of candidates than do larger American-style ones.

Despite these differences, it is clear that primary elections do have many similarities across nations and across party systems, and that we are beginning to acquire a body of knowledge about primaries that is relevant across borders. As Hazan and Rahat (2010) note, the decision to hold primaries often rests with the parties, not the governments – the establishment of primaries is thus in itself a political or partisan action, or a way for parties to differentiate themselves from each other. Once primaries are established, however, they set in motion an individual-based, or personality-based, politics that is difficult to reverse. There have been a few major efforts in Europe and in other democratic nations to synthesize knowledge about primaries (see, e.g. Sandri, Seddone, and Venturino 2015). As that volume shows (and perhaps this one as well), we have not yet reached a point where we can consider the U.S. experience and the experience of other countries within a common framework.

Unanswered Questions

Despite a century of research on primary elections, there is still much that we do not know. In fact, many of the arguments made for and against the direct primary in the early years of the twentieth century still are with us. The development of primaries in other nations has, for certain, raised a host of new questions.

The Early Twentieth-Century Research Agenda for Primaries

Many early analyses of primaries raised questions that still have not been answered. Then, as now, researchers focused upon both the causes and consequences of primary elections.

Most studies of the time explored the motivations different states had to enact primaries, or to enact particular types of primaries. In this introduction I have already discussed the debate over whether the establishment of primaries was driven by Progressive reformers or by the quest for advantage on the part of political parties. Chapters in this volume by John Reynolds and by Jamie Carson and Ryan Williamson explore some of these early debates. Similar logics apply today – what drives the quest to limit or expand the use of primaries? Many of the chapters here on other countries' establishment of primaries explore the strategic choices here, and chapters by Andrew Sinclair and Ian O'Grady and by Michael Kang and Barry Burden explore political conflict over current proposals for change in primary laws.

Questions such as these have much to do, of course, with the consequences of primary elections. One obvious consequence is the composition of the electorate. There are both empirical and normative questions here. Is it advantageous to allow anyone, regardless of his or her past voting history, to vote in a party's primary? In such circumstances, do some voters "cross over" in an attempt to sabotage the party, supporting a weak nominee, or were they likely to be sincere converts? In short, who votes in primaries, and how do primary rules shape the composition of the primary electorate? Early researchers focused on distinctions between urban and rural voters, or simply on the percentage of voters who turned out (e.g. Hormell 1923). More recent work, as we shall see in this book, pays particular attention to characteristics of the voters. Are primary voters demographically unrepresentative of the population, in terms of age, race, gender, income, and other such features? Are they ideologically more extreme than the population or than general election voters (Ranney 1968, 1972; Boyd 1989; Kenney 1986). In this volume, chapters by Seth McKee, Barbara Norrander, and Matthew Geras and Michael Crespin discuss what we know about contemporary differences in the characteristics of primary voters.

Questions also arose about the characteristics of the election itself. Do primaries, or certain types of primaries, cost more money? Do they influence interest group activity? The establishment of primary elections was an initial catalyst for campaign finance regulation – some early primary races convinced observers that wealthy individuals could now effectively buy nominations. And most consequentially, throughout the century many political scientists have asked whether the conduct of primary campaigns influences general election results; Jeffrey Lazarus provides a summary of these studies in his chapter here. There have been several studies of spending in primaries and of party and group efforts to shape primary election campaigns (to name just a few: Ware 1979; Born 1981; Herrnson and Gimpel 1995; Lazarus 2005; Johnson, Petersheim, and Wasson 2010). Here, a chapter by Casey Dominguez explores the role of parties in primaries, and chapters by Shigeo Hirano and James Snyder, and Robert Boatright and Vincent Moscardelli explore the connection between primaries and general elections.

A third type of concern had to do with which candidates would be advantaged by primary elections. A common fear was that the candidates who won would be demagogues (Key 1984 [1949], 146). Demagoguery is difficult to measure, but other studies sought to determine whether the "best" candidates won nominations – whether the people who won were less qualified than those selected through other means, or whether they were at all loyal to the party's agenda (e.g. Meyer 1902, Millspaugh 1916). Contemporary studies have continued to measure characteristics of primary nominees, including their ideological positions and their past political experience (e.g. Gerber and Morton 1998). Political scientists have arguably become better at measuring candidate characteristics; there are now widely accepted measurement tools for candidate quality (Jacobson 1989) and candidate ideology (Poole and Rosenthal 1985; Bonica 2014). Chapters here by Kristin Kanthak and Eric Loepp, Caitlin Jewitt and Sarah Treul, and Danielle Thomsen explore what we know about the types of candidates who succeed in primaries.

All of these questions may have been catalyzed by the U.S. experience with state elections and congressional races, but they have played a major role in our efforts to understand other sorts of elections as well. Presidential elections are very different in terms of the primary rules and, of course, in their consequences for American politics, but many of the same kinds of questions remain. Presidential elections have also proven to be easier to study. For many years, we knew more about presidential primary voters than we did about voters in other types of primaries. Barbara Norrander (1986, 1989, 1991) was instrumental in debunking many myths about the ideological extremity of presidential primary voters. Although today we tend not to expect presidential primary voters to be ideologically extreme or to otherwise be that out-of-step with the rest of the electorate, there are many permutations to presidential primaries that can influence the selection process. Dante Scala and David Hopkins explore some of the characteristics of the primary calendar here.

There is, in addition, a longstanding debate about the extent to which political parties get the candidates they want in presidential primaries. As Nelson Polsby (1983), Elaine Kamarck (2016), and Barbara Norrander (2015) have documented, both parties have deliberately tinkered with the primary process to prevent surprising outcomes. Perhaps the best-known work on presidential primaries of the past decade, *The Party Decides* (Cohen, Karol, Noel, and Zaller 2008), concluded that the two parties have been successful in ensuring that once the primaries are over the candidate favored by party elites before the primaries began has received the nomination. This story did not predict Donald J. Trump's nomination in 2016. In this volume, Marty Cohen (one of the coauthors of *The Party Decides*) explains why Republicans failed to choose a more conventional candidate, and Wayne Steger provides a contrasting account of candidate selection in presidential primaries.

Similarly, as Alan Ware notes in his chapter here, the questions that are currently being raised in European countries, in Canada, and in other democratic nations are not new. Yet they are newly relevant given the expansion of primaries. In addition to the aforementioned Bruhn, Indriðason and Kristinsson, and Ichino and Nathan chapters here, this volume includes a chapter on Canada by Scott Pruysers and Anthony Sayers, and a chapter by Reuven Hazan and Reut Itzkovitch-Malka that provides a more general overview of where primaries have been established and how they have affected legislative behavior.

What Shall We Do with Primary Election Research?

It is tempting (and not entirely unreasonable) to blame primary elections for many of the ills that plague contemporary democracies. Political polarization, political corruption, the democratic deficit, citizen disengagement from politics – all have something to do with the choices citizens are given at the ballot box, and in nations where primaries are used, the primary is, of course, either one of those choices itself or the precursor to subsequent choices. Yet U.S. history clearly tells us that primary elections, even when they are flawed, are simply too popular to abandon.

The research presented here provides us with a sort of paradox. Many studies of primary election rules indicate that changing the rules will not necessarily solve some of the problems that have been identified in primaries. Chapters in this book by Barbara Norrander and by Matthew Geras and Michael Crespin explore some of the differences in primary types. There is little evidence, however, that open and closed primaries are so dramatically different from each other that changing from one type to the other will solve the problems contemporary reformers worry about. At the presidential level, there may be slight differences in voting behavior in caucuses and primaries – and according to some accounts, Barack Obama won the 2008 Democratic nomination in part because his campaign was better at using different states' primary laws to its advantage (Plouffe 2009, ch. 8–9). But these differences should not be overstated. The research presented here does not suggest that political polarization, spiraling campaign costs, or boorish and uncivil behavior by politicians can be remedied by changes in primary laws.

Contemporary conservatives often list instances of Progressive reforms that they claim have harmed American politics. Bradley C. S. Watson (2009), for instance, is representative of conservative critics of the toll Progressivism has been said to have on American political institutions, yet he devotes most of his attention to direct democracy efforts such as the referendum and says little about the primary. Yet few conservatives have taken aim at primaries. A handful of recent appreciations of parties as political institutions have lamented the effect that the primary has had on parties; books by, among others, Bruce Cain (2015) and Nancy Rosenblum (2008) have made the case that parties have lost the informal control over primaries that they maintained for much of the twentieth century. These are not, of course, arguments for abandoning them entirely, and they come from writers who would certainly not ally themselves with the most vocal conservative critics of Progressivism. They do suggest, however, that the fears of early twentieth-century Cassandras have begun to be realized. Prominent journalists such as Jonathan Rauch (2015) have recently argued for limiting the use of primaries. It may be politically unrealistic for Americans today to argue that primaries have failed, but such arguments may well appear in the coming years. And in other countries considering the establishment of primaries, arguments against them may be more feasible.

Organization of this Handbook

Each individual section of this book contains a brief introduction explaining how the chapters fit together. Here, however, let us briefly consider the organization of the full handbook. We begin in Part I with a discussion of some major theoretical issues in the study of primaries and a consideration of the origins of primary elections. Part II of this handbook presents new research on voting behavior in primaries. The section contains two pieces on the effects of primary rules on turnout and two on candidate ideology. Part III of the handbook looks at subpresidential primaries – primaries for the U.S. House and Senate, and primaries for state office. Part IV of this handbook concerns presidential primaries. Part V explores the growth and characteristics of primary elections in other countries, and Part VI explores contemporary reform proposals.

As editor, I have given the contributors to this volume substantial latitude in developing their arguments; that is, I have sought to emphasize quality research at the expense of covering some subjects that might have merited inclusion. There are a few subjects that certainly merit researchers' attention but are not well represented here. To briefly name some of these, I regret that I was not able to include more work on the effects different primary election systems have on the electoral fortunes of women and racial minorities. Good articles on these subjects have been published in the past (e.g. Branton 2009 on circumstances in which racial minorities are advantaged by primaries; Kitchens and Swers 2016 on the fortunes of women candidates in primaries; and Lamis 1984 and Bullock and Smith 1990 on the primary election candidacies of African-Americans in the U.S. South). There is a growing interest in primary elections for lower-level offices; McGhee, Masket, Shor, Rogers, and McCarty (2014), for instance, have begun work on state legislative primaries. There is also a growing interest in the United States in qualitative research on how perceptions about primary elections shape political strategies, and I would have liked to include some work in this vein. I have sought to provide a comprehensive overview of some of the best work being done right now on primaries, but it is important to note some of the research that will be done in the next few years or that remains for scholars to consider.

A major goal of this handbook is to show just how difficult it is to find "democracy" in the internal workings of political parties. As the quotes at the outset of this chapter suggest, we need not assume that democracy is enhanced by including citizens in the candidate selection process; there are legitimate reasons why academics and political elites have warned about the undemocratic consequences of primaries. On the other hand, citizens have consistently approved of the establishment of primaries – even when they have not taken advantage of their opportunity to vote in them. In the eyes of many (perhaps most) rank and file voters, democracy is improved by allowing and encouraging citizens to play a role in candidate selection. This compendium seeks to show some of the complexities entailed in our efforts to determine where democracy should and should not exist.

Acknowledgment

I wish to thank the Francis A. Harrington Fund at Clark University for providing financial support for the editing of this book.

Notes

1 The term "direct primary" is used to distinguish elections where voters choose among candidates from delegate selection primaries (such as U.S. presidential primaries), in which voters choose delegates who will in turn attend a convention where candidates are chosen.
2 For instance, there is no sustained discussion of primaries in the major works of Progressive intellectuals such as Walter Weyl, Walter Lippmann, or Herbert Croly, nor do histories of Progressive intellectual thought (e.g. Forcey 1961) include the direct primary among the major electoral reform achievements of the movement.
3 The closest any author came to providing an overview of primary elections of the time was V. O. Key's (1956) *American State Politics*.
4 For summaries, see Brady, Han, and Pope (2007); Boatright (2013); Hall (2015); Hill (2015).

References

Alilunas, Leo. 1940. "The Rise of the 'White Primary' Movement as a Means of Barring the Negro from the Polls." *Journal of Negro History* 25 (2): 161–172.
Ansolabehere, Stephen, John Mark Hansen, Shigeo Hirano, and James M. Snyder, Jr. 2010. "More Democracy: The Direct Primary and Competition in U.S. House Elections." *Studies in American Political Development* 24 (2): 190–205.

Boatright, Robert G. 2013. *Getting Primaried: The Changing Politics of Congressional Primary Challenges.* Ann Arbor: University of Michigan Press.

Bonica, Adam. 2014. "Mapping the Ideological Marketplace." *American Journal of Political Science* 58 (2): 367–386.

Born, Richard. 1981. "The Influence of House Primary Election Divisiveness on General Election Margins, 1962–1976." *Journal of Politics* 43 (3): 640–661.

Boyd, Richard W. 1989. "The Effects of Primaries and Statewide Races on Voter Turnout." *Journal of Politics* 51 (3): 730–739.

Brady, David W., Hahrie Han, and Jeremy C. Pope. 2007. "Primary Elections and Candidate Ideology: Out of Step with the Primary Electorate?" *Legislative Studes Quarterly* 32 (1): 79–105.

Branton, Regina. 2009. "The Importance of Race and Ethnicity in Congressional Primary Elections." *Political Research Quarterly* 62 (3): 459–473.

Bullock, Charles S., and A. Brock Smith. 1990. "Black Success in Local Runoff Elections." *Journal of Politics* 52 (4): 1205–1220.

Cain, Bruce E. 2015. *Democracy More or Less: America's Political Reform Quandary.* New York: Cambridge University Press.

Cohen, Marty, David Karol, Hans Noel, and John Zaller. 2008. *The Party Decides.* Chicago: University of Chicago Press.

Delmatier, Royce D., Clarence F. McIntosh, and Earl G. Waters. 1970. *The Rumble of California Politics, 1848–1970.* New York: John Wiley and Sons.

Duverger, Maurice. 1954. *Political Parties: Their Organisation and Activity in the Modern State.* New York: John C. Wiley.

Forcey, Charles. 1961. *The Crossroads of Liberalism: Croly, Weyl, Lippmann, and the Progressive Era, 1900–1925.* New York: Oxford University Press.

Freyd, Bernard. 1926. *Repeal the Direct Primary.* Seattle: McKay Printing Company.

Gerber, Elizabeth R., and Rebecca B. Morton. 1998. "Primary Election Systems and Representation." *Journal of Law, Economics, and Organization* 14 (2): 304–324.

Hall, Andrew B. 2015. "What Happens When Extremists Win Primaries?" *American Political Science Review* 109 (1): 18–42

Hazan, Reuven Y., and Gideon Rahat. 2010. *Democracy Within Parties: Candidate Selection Methods and Their Political Consequences.* London: Oxford University Press.

Herrnson, Paul S., and James G. Gimpel. 1995. "District Conditions and Primary Divisiveness in Congressional Elections." *Political Research Quarterly* 48 (1): 117–134.

Hill, Seth. 2015. "Institution of Nomination and the Policy Ideology of Primary Electorates." *Quarterly Journal of Political Science* 10 (4): 461–487.

Hormell, Orren Chalmer. 1923. "The Direct Primary Law in Maine and How It Worked." *Annals of the American Academy of Political and Social Science* 106: 128–141.

Ichino, Nahomi, and Noah L. Nathan. 2012. "Do Primaries Improve Electoral Performance? Clientelism and Intra-Party Conflict in Ghana." *American Journal of Political Science* 57(2): 428–441.

Ichino, Nahomi, and Noah L. Nathan. 2014. "Primaries on Demand? Intra-Party Politics and Nominations in Ghana." *British Journal of Political Science* 42 (4): 769–791.

Jacobson, Gary C. 1989. "Strategic Politicians and the Dynamics of U.S. House Elections, 1946–86." *American Political Science Review* 83 (3): 773–793.

Johnson, Gregg B., Meredith-Joy Petersheim, and Jesse T. Wasson. 2010. "Divisive Primaries and Incumbent General Election Performance: Prospects and Costs in U.S. House Races." *American Politics Research* 38 (5): 931–955.

Kamarck, Elaine C. 2016. *Primary Politics.* Washington, DC: Brookings Institution.

Kenney, Patrick J. 1986. "Explaining Primary Turnout: The Senatorial Case." *Legislative Studies Quarterly* 11 (1): 65–73.

Key, V. O. 1984 [1949]. *Southern Politics in State and Nation.* Knoxville, TN: University of Tennessee Press.

Key, V. O. 1956. *American State Politics: An Introduction.* New York: Knopf.

Kitchens, Karin E., and Michele L. Swers. 2016. "Why Aren't There More Republican Women in Congress? Gender, Partisanship, and Fundraising Support in the 2010 and 2012 Elections." *Politics and Gender* 12 (3): 648–676.

Lamis, Alexander P. 1984. "The Runoff Primary Controversy: Implications for Southern Politics." *PS: Political Science and Politics* 17 (4): 782–787.

Lawrence, Eric, Todd Donovan, and Shaun Bowler. 2013. "The Adoption of Direct Primaries in the United States." *Party Politics* 19 (1): 3–18.

Lazarus, Jeffrey. 2005. "Unintended Consequences: Anticipation of General Election Outcomes and Primary Election Divisiveness." *Legislative Studies Quarterly* 30 (3): 435–461.

Lockard, Duane. 1959. *New England Politics*. Princeton, NJ: Princeton University Press.

McGhee, Eric, Seth S. Masket, Boris Shor, Steven Rogers, and Nolan McCarty. 2014. "A Primary Cause of Partisanship? Nomination Systems and Legislator Ideology." *American Journal of Political Science* 58 (2): 337–351.

Merriam, Charles. 1908. *Primary Elections*. Chicago: University of Chicago Press.

Merriam, Charles, and Louise Overacker. 1928. *Primary Elections*. Chicago: University of Chicago Press.

Meyer, Ernst Christopher. 1902. *Nominating Systems*. Madison, WI: author.

Millspaugh, Arthur C. 1916. "The Operation of the Direct Primary in Michigan." *American Political Science Review* 10 (4): 710–726.

Morlan, Robert L. 1955. *Political Prairie Fire: The Nonpartisan League, 1915–1922*. Minneapolis: University of Minnesota Press.

Norrander, Barbara. 1986. "Measuring Primary Turnout in Aggregate Analysis." *Political Behavior* 8 (4): 356–373.

Norrander, Barbara. 1989. "Ideological Representativeness of Presidential Primary Voters." *American Journal of Political Science* 33 (3): 570–587.

Norrander, Barbara. 1991. "Explaining Individual Participation in Presidential Primaries." *Western Political Quarterly* 44 (3): 640–655.

Norrander, Barbara. 2015. *The Imperfect Primary*, 2nd ed. New York: Routledge.

Norris, George. 1923. "Why I Believe in the Direct Primary." *Annals of the American Academy of Political and Social Sciences* 106: 22–30.

Ostrogorski, Moisei. 1982 [1902]. *Democracy and the Organization of Political Parties*. New Brunswick, NJ: Transaction Books.

Overacker, Louise. 1945. "The Negro's Struggle for Participation in Primary Elections." *Journal of Negro History* 30 (1): 54–61.

Panagopoulos, Costas. 2010. "Are Caucuses Bad for Democracy?" *Political Science Quarterly* 125 (3): 425–442.

Plouffe, David. 2009. *The Audacity to Win*. New York: Penguin.

Polsby, Nelson. 1983. *Consequences of Party Reform*. Berkeley, CA: Institute for Governmental Studies Press.

Poole, Keith T., and Howard Rosenthal, Howard. 1985. "A Spatial Model For Legislative Roll Call Analysis." *American Journal of Political Science* 29 (2): 357–384.

Ranney, Austin. 1968. "The Representativeness of Primary Electorates." *Midwest Journal of Political Science* 12 (2): 224–238.

Ranney, Austin. 1972. "Turnout and Representation in Presidential Primary Elections." *American Political Science Review* 66 (1): 21–37.

Rauch, Jonathan. 2015. *Political Realism*. Washington, DC: Brookings Institution.

Reynolds, John F. 2006. *The Demise of the American Convention System, 1880–1911*. New York: Cambridge University Press.

Rosenblum, Nancy L. 2008. *On the Side of the Angels: An Appreciation of Parties and Partisanship*. Princeton, NJ: Princeton University Press.

Sandri, Giulia, Antonella Seddone, and Fulvio Venturino, eds. 2015. *Party Primaries in Comparative Perspective*. Surrey, UK: Ashgate.

Schattschneider, E. E. 1942. *Party Government*. New York; Holt, Rinehart, and Winston.

Ware, Alan. 1979. "'Divisive' Primaries: The Important Questions." *British Journal of Political Science* 9 (3): 381–384.

Ware, Alan. 2002. *The American Direct Primary*. New York: Oxford University Press.

Watson, Bradley C. S. 2009. *Living Constitution, Dying Faith: Progressivism and the New Science of Jurisprudence*. Wilmington, DE: Intercollegiate Studies Institute Books.

White, John Kenneth, and Gerald Mileur. 2002. "In the Spirit of their Times." In *Responsible Partisanship: The Evolution of American Political Parties Since 1950*, ed. John C. Green and Paul S. Herrnson. Lawrence: University Press of Kansas, pp. 61–82.

PART I

The Origins of Primary Elections

In the introduction to this book, we considered some aspects of the history of primary elections. As noted there, one of the most interesting aspects of this history is its relative obscurity. Many Americans have some understanding of the development of the current presidential nominating system, but there have been few detailed treatments of the development of the direct primary, of the establishment of primary elections for offices other than the presidency.

This lack of knowledge is reflected in the relative paucity of historical work on primary elections between the late 1920s and the early 2000s. Although there were some regional histories of elections published during this time, there were no book-length treatments of primary elections written between the publication of Charles Merriam and Louise Overacker's *Primary Elections* in 1928 and Alan Ware's *The American Direct Primary* in 2002. As Ware pointed out in his book, primaries were widely studied in the 1910s and 1920s, but in any generation, historians will bring their own biases and perspectives to the study of historical events. This means that there is much room today for a revisiting of questions regarding why primaries developed and why they spread.

The first section of this book provides examples of some of the best contemporary scholarship on the development of primaries. In each case, the scholars here bring to their analyses distinctly modern ideas about the motivations of politicians.

In Chapter 1 of this handbook, Alan Ware discusses difficulties in defining what a primary is. His chapter was chosen to lead off this book, in part because of his pioneering work in describing the origins of primaries, and in part because Ware, who has spent most of his teaching career in the United Kingdom, brings a different perspective to the study of primary elections than do many Americans. Ware's intent in this chapter is not only to elaborate upon debates among early twentieth-century Americans to determine what a primary election should be, but also to question whether the "primaries" that have been adopted in many Western democracies over the past twenty years – and which are the subject of Part V of this book – are really analogous to the American direct primary.

Chapter 2 is by John Reynolds, the author of *The Demise of the American Convention System, 1880–1911*, published in 2006. As the title of that book suggests, Reynolds has studied the period immediately before the adoption of the direct primary, and his chapter shows that, for Reynolds, the adoption of the direct primary was not necessarily as radical a change to American politics as some have alleged. The seeds of the direct primary lay in part in changes in how candidates campaigned for office and in part in the increasing difficulty political parties had in placating different factions. Both Reynolds and Ware emphasize the strategic significance of adopting primaries; they were not as much a "good government" reform, as some Progressives would have had it, as they were a means for parties and party supporters to resolve disputes.

Another perspective on the adoption of primaries is offered by Jamie Carson and Ryan Williamson in Chapter 3. Carson's approach to the direct primary has been less that of a pure historian and more that of a political scientist studying the development of Congress as a political institution. In his 2013 book *Ambition, Competition, and Electoral Reform: The Politics of Congressional Elections Across Time* (co-written with Jason Roberts), Carson explored the effects of changes in election laws in the nineteenth and twentieth centuries on the development of the incumbency advantage and of changes in general election competition. In the chapter here, Carson and Williamson describe some of the successes and failures of the direct primary. Contrary to the goals of Progressives, the primary did not make elections more competitive, but it did reduce the power of political parties and arguably made candidate selection more democratic.

Finally, it is worth noting that much of what we know, or at least expect, about primaries stems from assumptions about candidate and party behavior in multi-stage elections. That is, the winnowing process for which primaries are employed in the U.S. and elsewhere has a firm grounding in economic theories about how democratic choices are made. Formal models of candidate selection have been used for several decades now to explain what *should* happen in primaries, and many of these formal claims were rather informally stated even in the early years in which primaries were used. Chapter 4 presents a summary of many of the formal claims about the logic of primary elections. Gilles Serra develops a spatial model of the candidate selection process, and then explores the conditions under which political polarization might result from primary competition. He concludes that if voters rationally seek to help their party to win elections, polarization is unlikely. Serra's theory provides a means of using some of the early claims about primary elections, addressed in the earlier chapters of this section, to inform the link between primaries and polarization that will be addressed in the empirical chapters of Parts II and III of this handbook.

1

WHAT IS, AND WHAT IS NOT, A PRIMARY ELECTION?

Alan Ware

Like many political concepts, the idea of a "primary election" has changed over time. As with both "liberal" and "conservative," for instance, the transformation has been so great that a time traveler from the nineteenth century might struggle to comprehend its usage in some contexts today. Equally important, it has now become more open-ended in its application than in the earlier period, when its meaning was quite specific. The aim of this chapter is to explain how and why different meanings of the term "primary" or "primary election" developed over time, both within the United States and, much later, in other democracies. Unlike some American inventions, such as basketball, the original American model was subject to further modification once it was "imported" by other countries. However, and arguably more important, many changes had occurred within the United States itself before the use of primaries elsewhere. For that reason, the initial discussion here is exclusively about the U.S.

In the contemporary United States to speak of a primary election could be to refer to one of three rather different institutional arrangements:

1   For the historian of nineteenth-century America, it could be the first stage in a multi-stage process for selecting candidates in one of the two major parties. The term "primary election" was not used universally during that century, however, and in some regions of the U.S. primary elections were called either primaries (in the Mid-West and most of the West) or caucuses (in New England and a few western states). Yet they were "primary elections" in Pennsylvania and the South, as well as in the statute books of most states except those in New England (Dallinger 1897, n53). This concept of a primary is discussed in the first section of the chapter, along with the pressures that led to a radically different system of nominating candidates emerging form the subject of the first two sections.

2   From the early twentieth century onwards this meaning was largely abandoned, and primaries were now any formal election in the process of candidate selection by a party. Usually, speaking of a primary was to refer to a direct primary – that is, one in which the winner of the primary automatically became the party's candidate. This was because direct primaries had become by far the most common method for nominating candidates. However, in some states, and especially for presidential nominations, a "primary" retained its original meaning of being the first stage in a nomination process. These and related matters form the subject of the third, fourth, and fifth sections.

3   From the second decade of the last century yet another meaning came into use when political parties in several states, mainly in the West, were barred from nominating candidates for some public offices. In the absence of direct party nominations to the ballot, a "primary" came now to refer to no more than the first election in a double-ballot electoral system. The primary is the election preceding a run-off election between the two candidates receiving the most votes in that initial election. This is discussed in the penultimate section of the chapter.

Until the last decades of the twentieth century primary elections were understood as an essentially American phenomenon. When, from that period onwards, parties in various other countries started to introduce what they sometimes called primary elections the term was reserved exclusively for direct primaries – that is, procedures for nominating candidates involving an election, the result of which determined who would be party's nominee for some office. When confronted by it, which is rarely, Europeans and others usually find the third meaning of "primary election" (above) incomprehensible since there are other ways of describing the procedures identified. As for the original American meaning (1), non-Americans would normally find this usage confusing too. However, exporting the idea of a primary election overseas has also been accompanied by some extension beyond the core American notion that the purpose of such elections was to produce nominees for a general election. It is now starting to be applied to the selection of individuals to positions of leadership in a political party, a role that is both broader and more significant than their being candidates for public offices. These issues are examined in the final section.

Primaries in the Nineteenth Century

A simplified account of the emergence of primary elections would be that they developed from three sources during the 1830s. First, there was the much older New England tradition of direct democracy involving men taking decisions for their communities in town meetings. Second, during the 1820s there was a major decline of long-established social deference in much of America, deference that had survived the Revolution but which would persist only in a few places later, including Rhode Island (Silbey 1991). Finally, there was the impact of the Jacksonians whose conception of democracy was that its practice was made possible by people engaging with the activities of political parties. The parties became rejuvenated between the mid-1820s and the late 1830s with a large mass base of participation. In this regime, nominating candidates was a process that began, and in the case of local offices ended, in the lowest level of governmental structures. Anyone eligible to participate in a party nomination, with eligibility usually being defined broadly for white adult males but with others usually excluded, was encouraged to do so at the first stage of candidate selection. (To use the term increasingly popularized by political scientists today, the parties' "selectorates" were large.[1]) For higher-level offices, participation would entail them being involved in electing delegates to subsequent stages in the nomination process.

As noted earlier, there were regional differences in what that first stage was called, but functionally they were identical. Although caucuses in New England had originally lived up to their name, and involved prior discussion and not mere voting for candidates, this had to be abandoned later. In the decades after the Civil War debating the merits of possible candidates necessarily fell into disuse in most places. The reason for this was quite simple: attendances at caucuses grew so much especially in urban areas, because of massive increases in population, as to render the processes more complex and often chaotic. Streamlining them entailed a reduction in function, so that the caucus had to become merely the location where votes were cast in the first stage of candidate selection.[2] By the later nineteenth century caucuses, primaries, and primary elections were merely different names for the same activity.

That the term was first applied to political parties, and to America's highly decentralized parties, shaped how the concept of primary election could evolve. Yet, in assessing the analysis presented here subsequently, it is important to recognize that a primary election is a procedure that could be deployed in other organizations where the views of participants at lower levels are considered relevant in making a final decision. However, it is only relevant when the organization seeks to provide for representation of views, rather than for direct participation by all in decision making. Presbyterian churches are one arena where a primary election structure is appropriate. As one Arizona Presbyterian church notes:

> There are various types of church government, such as "hierarchical" – the Roman Catholic, Episcopal and Methodist churches; "congregational" – Baptist and Congregational churches; and "representative" – Presbyterian Churches. The Presbyterian Church is a representative form of church government in which the congregation elects church officers to lead the congregation. The Presbyterian Church is representative at every level – Congregations elect elders to on the Session, Sessions elect commissioners to go to Presbytery meetings, and Presbyteries elect commissioners to go to Synod and General Assembly meetings.[3]

The Code of the Presbyterian Church of Ireland outlines the Presbyterian principle of representation by identifying two permissible methods through which new Elders of the Church may be selected. The first method is that:

> Members of the congregation put forward names by means of a vote. The Kirk Session form a list of those who received the most votes up to the number of new elders being sought. Each person on the list must have received a minimum of a third of the votes cast. The Kirk Session must approve each person on the list (and therefore can choose not to approve a person on the list).[4]

The initial stage of the process described here is akin to a primary election (as that was understood in the nineteenth century), even though members of the Church might well not use that term in describing it.

First introduced by the Democrats, the multi-stage model of selection would spread not just to other parties (first the Whigs and then, in the 1850s, to the newly founded Republican Party), but would also become the standard model throughout the country. Thanks to canals, and then from the 1830s railways, internal communication within the U.S. had greatly improved since the Republic's early years, facilitating the rapid dispersal of political ideas as well as goods. Migrants from the East took with them to the new territories in the West well-established notions of the purpose of politics and of how to organize for it. The caucus, or primary election, became central to the predominant belief that political parties were the key instrument of "democracy," and that involvement by the many in the activities of parties entailed some form of participation at the most local of levels.

Yet uniformity of practice in candidate selection was never complete. As early as the mid-1840s the Democrats of Crawford County, Pennsylvania began using a procedure that, in later decades of the nineteenth century, would become known as the Crawford County System, and which from the early twentieth century would be called the direct primary. Pennsylvania was unusual in that different models of candidate selection came to be deployed in several counties, though only Crawford County's would subsequently gain widespread favorable attention and publicity. Nevertheless, generally, experimentation in methods of candidate selection remained limited, and until the late 1890s use of the Crawford County System was mostly confined to counties in the vicinity of western Pennsylvania. Yet by that time there was a widespread perception within America of serious weaknesses in the nominating procedures of major parties. That concern led to a national conference on the subject in early 1898.[5] Although the problems were not confined to the procedures' initial stage – the primary – it was most evident there. The problem can be summarized quite simply – as chaos.

Chaos is not endemic to multi-stage selection procedures, and with full justification members of Presbyterian Churches, for example, would probably protest that they do not experience it. However, several important aspects of the context in which primary elections were used by American parties meant that for them, unlike the churches, nominations constituted the proverbial "accident waiting to happen."

The first has already been mentioned: population expansion. The New England party caucuses had drawn on the experience of those communities that had held town meetings in which all – at least all men – could participate. In this face-to-face world in which the lives of most usually depended on various forms of co-operation with others, coming together for discussion and decision making provided a means of restricting and reducing conflict. Not only did the increased size of communities preclude widespread discussion in meetings, it also meant that those who could vote might not even know each other, and hence appreciate why others understood their own interests in the way they did.

Second, for too many people, electoral defeat for their party had adverse consequences. They had a material stake not just in their party winning, but often in the candidates they had backed initially becoming their party's nominees. While parties needed enthusiastic supporters, too many of them committed to particular candidates could pose a threat to the orderliness of party procedures. The spoils system had helped bind a party together but was also the source of internal disruption, because the scope of an older American tradition, "to the victor the spoils," had been greatly extended throughout the country after Andrew Jackson's victory in 1828. The country's original party system had already sustained the principle that the victorious party in an election could choose whom to appoint to public offices, something which, in its masterful circumnavigation of that point, the U.S. Supreme Court had helped to legitimate in *Marbury v. Madison*. However, from the 1830s, and at all levels of government, winning parties also started awarding contracts to key supporters on a large scale. (Although patronage is popularly associated with the distribution of jobs it was contracts, and the money they generated for a party, that were the real engine of that party system.) While this intensified competition between the major parties it was equally present within them because there were too few rewards to satisfy every supporter of a victorious party. Being the backers of your party's nominees from the beginning often mattered more than merely being a known supporter of the winning party.

Third, the Jacksonians expanded the range of governmental offices filled through election rather than appointment, and especially at the local level. Through their family connections and friends many Americans were drawn into the fight for a party's nominations for these offices, with the result that those seeking to vote in a primary could be large in relation to the resources available for imposing order. Not only were rival groups seeking to obtain nominations, usually they were in competition with each other to control proceedings at meetings in which either nominations were made or delegates were selected to a higher-level meeting. That the Jacksonians also favored short terms of office – not for them the six years the Founding Fathers had provided for in the case of U.S. Senators, but more often one or sometimes two years – primaries were an annual intra-party battleground. Indeed, given that the territorial boundaries of some offices might not coincide with others, there could well be several rounds of caucuses and conventions each year when the politically active were in conflict with their fellow party supporters.

Fourth, in America's decentralized parties order could not be imposed effectively from above. Even parties at the state level lacked both the resources and the perceived legitimacy to intervene in providing discipline. At best, in cases where rival delegations were contesting the right to be represented at the State Convention, all a state party could do was decide between their respective claims – and that too was often based on political considerations rather than the merit of a claim. Typically, you backed those on whose support you could rely at the Convention. Those holding party offices could sometimes do little other than deploy physical force to overcome others determined to use whatever means were necessary to ensure the nomination of their preferred candidates. By the end of the 1880s this problem of chaos was becoming widely acknowledged, though it would be another decade before information and ideas as to how to resolve it resulted in the convening of the National Conference on Practical Reform of Primary Elections.

In part, impetus for that initiative was created by the seeming success of reform in a related area of electoral politics – balloting. Until the later 1880s balloting in all states involved parties supplying their supporters with voting papers, stating for whom they were voting in the various elections, and with each supporter then taking their ballot paper to the polling station. A public voting system was open to both abuse and some fraud, and the subsequent introduction of a secret ballot, administered by government agencies and known widely in America as the Australian Ballot, had eliminated most of these problems. Thereby between 1888 and 1891 the situation was transformed in nearly every state. Not only did ballot reform provide a stimulus for tackling the equally chaotic situation in the primaries, but it also raised an important question: if the ballot was administered by a public agency, what should be the criteria for qualifying to be a candidate on the ballot? Under the earlier procedures, someone who had failed to secure the "official" party nomination for a particular office could simply paste his name over that of the "official" candidate, and then have the amended ballot paper taken by a supporter to the polls as their vote. These so-called "pasters" had been a major element in elections, especially for the lowest level of public office, but under the new arrangements there would have to be rules governing how someone got onto the ballot.[6] Changing how primaries worked thus became a still more pressing problem from the early 1890s onwards.

All of these factors helped pushed America down a radically different path from other countries. Its major parties' internal procedures and their conduct of their own nominations would, in part, become directly subject to law. Unable to control effectively their constituent parties at lower levels, state parties would voluntarily – because the relevant laws were enacted by party politicians – subject those procedures to control by government. The idea that parties were merely some, possibly peculiar, form of private association would be abandoned. However, for our purposes an equally important change was that in just a few years it would lead to a transformation in the meaning of "primary" within the concept of a "primary election."

Legal Control of Party Nominations

In virtually all democracies parties are subject to some forms of legal control, as indeed are most organizations in any society. The range of their procedures embraced by law has led some political scientists to argue that America's parties have a peculiar status in its political system compared with those elsewhere, and that it is a response to especially strong anti-party sentiments within American society. However, no one has ever produced any evidence that hostility to, or ambivalence about, political parties has been more widespread in the U.S. It is mere assertion, and a superficial comparison of opposition to parties among the longer established democracies indicates that the assertion is probably not true (Ware 2002, ch. 1).

A separate, though often linked, claim, that from the end of the nineteenth century American parties became more akin to public agencies, a point first made by Austin Ranney (1975, 79), has more substance. The range of a party's *internal activities* that are subject to state regulation, or are carried out by the state on its behalf, is much greater in America than elsewhere. There were two reasons why there was more acceptance in America of a need for the major parties' organizational forms to be enshrined in public law. The first could conceivably be interpreted as an attempt to ensure they conform with the public interest. As noted already, from Jackson's presidency until the twentieth century, parties were widely understood as the key instrument of democracy; they were the means by which people could exercise control over their governments. While they remained private associations, they were unlike other kinds of associations because they were especially crucial for the survival of popular government – or so it was widely believed. Their role in maintaining access by the people to their governments was sufficiently important that eventually, in the 1890s, changes in the legal environment in which they operated became subject to debate. The second reason has been mentioned briefly already. The parties' decentralized structures would always preclude effective policing of party activities at lower levels, which regarded themselves as self-governing and not subordinate to other party bodies within their state. While some anti-party reformers undoubtedly were making more complaints about parties during that decade, the real driving force for legal regulation of party nomination procedures was the party politicians themselves. They were the ones for whom the adverse effects of chaos were most persistent and pressing. Moreover, they were in a position to initiate change, since, whether Democrat or Republican, they controlled the state legislatures in which relevant legislation would be initiated and passed.

By the early 1890s it was the party organizations at the county level that were directly faced with the problem primary elections were posing. Having been slowly adopted by some other county parties, the Crawford County System was then introduced for the first time in a major urban area, by the Republican Party in Cleveland, Ohio, which ran the selection process itself. The results were deemed a complete failure, not least by one of the main reform organizations in the city (the Cleveland Municipal Association) and the reform was abandoned. Any prediction then, that twenty years later and throughout America, the Crawford County System would be the most widely used method for nominating candidates would have been dismissed as improbable. However, as a reform it had one major advantage. It dealt with the problem of primary elections by the simple expedient of just abolishing them. Furthermore, in their place were substituted a procedure that government agencies could organize fairly easily and inexpensively, and at various governmental levels, and without much of the disruption evident in primaries and some party conventions. By about 1910 the institution that in the nineteenth century had been known as a caucus, primary, or primary election had largely disappeared. Their replacement, now widely called the direct primary, was an election to nominate a party's candidate. For elected county officials, these were elections held throughout their county with the winners being the party's nominees; similarly, for the state legislature and for Congress there was just one process – involving self-identified party supporters voting in each electoral district. Statewide gubernatorial candidates and those for other state offices were also nominated without the multi-stage complexities of caucuses and conventions. The primary election was largely exterminated, yet its name lingered on despite the fact that logically only in a multi-stage nomination procedure could there be a *primary* election (or a secondary one for that matter.)

From our own era, it appears as if it would have been more appropriate for it to have been called the Candidate Nomination Election, or the Direct Nominating Election or something similar, given that retaining the earlier "Crawford County System" name was too parochial for general application. Why then was it called the "direct primary" instead?

The context of the reform's introduction is important in understanding this. Only in a few states, including Wisconsin and others mainly in the western half of America, were all the older nominating procedures abolished at the same time. Often there were piecemeal reforms so that the new arrangements, eliminating the multi-level process for some public offices, were operating alongside multi-level nominations for others. Those turning up to vote could be voting directly to nominate some candidates and also voting for delegates to attend the next stage of the process. They were attending primaries operating under various nominating structures. This conjunction facilitated the temporary survival of the older notion of a "primary." However, it also made it possible to think of the Crawford County System as a kind of primary, despite the direct primary not being, in the original sense of the term, a primary at all. Equally important though was an ambiguity in the meaning of "primary" in the electoral process that the transformation of how voting in candidate selections was organized helped to propagate. The switch from selections being the responsibility of private organizations (the parties) to governmental administration meant that direct primaries could be understood as the first of two public elections leading to the filling of public offices. Once it became a public election the Crawford County System could therefore be comprehended as "primary" in a wholly different way from the system it was replacing. It preceded a different second stage, the general election, whereas originally primaries preceded other levels of a nomination process within a party. This linguistic shift had much wider significance than as a mere detail for etymologists. In the future in America there could, and would, be primaries where those contesting the resulting general election were not the nominees of an organization, a major political party. This development is discussed further in the next-to-last section of the chapter.

What Precisely Is a Direct Primary?

Austin Ranney, who wrote authoritatively about the circumstances that led to the reform of the presidential nominating system in the 1970s was one political scientist who made the mistake of assuming that the direct primary was uniquely American, and that key characteristic of its primaries would have to be present in arrangements elsewhere for them to really count as primaries. In 1975 he claimed that:

> The direct primary remains almost exclusively an American institution. Occasionally some parties in other Western nations decide on their own to choose parliamentary candidates by secret votes of the local party members, but no law forces them to do so.
>
> *Ranney 1975, 123*

Unfortunately, he confused at least three separate issues: what is a direct primary election, what are the contexts in which a party is likely to introduce it, and what are the consequences of that context for the form that the primary takes? The American model was shaped by three unusual factors already identified: (a) the widespread acceptance of the Jacksonian principle that mass participation in parties was the cornerstone of democracy; (b) the extreme decentralization of party structures, so that both reforming and, subsequently, the policing of party activities would always be difficult for the parties themselves; and (c) the massive number of elective public offices. Between them, they ensured that abolishing chaos in candidate selection, through the adoption of the direct primary, went hand in glove with making these elections subject to state law and administration.

Consequently, when asking the question "what precisely is a direct primary?" it is important not to try to answer it by discussing instead the characteristics of direct primaries in America. Indeed, as will become apparent, a wide range of nomination procedures can properly be described as being direct primaries, especially now since it has been imported by parties in other countries. However, it is possible to identify three main conditions that must be met for a procedure to count as a direct primary.

1   A direct primary leads directly to the nomination of the victor(s) in that election. There is no further stage at which the result could be reversed or modified by anyone in the party, leaving aside cases where fraud or corruption on the part of the victor can be proved. A direct primary is neither advisory nor merely the construction of a short-list from which party officials (or anyone else) must select the eventual nominee.
2   The result must be determined by the casting and counting of votes. Yet these votes do not necessarily have to be cast secretly. In Crawford County the direct nomination of candidates by parties was conducted for more than three decades before the introduction of the Australian Ballot (the secret ballot) for general elections. Providing those eligible to vote are sufficiently few, a direct primary could be held by a show of hands or by using ballot papers that were open for inspection when the votes were being cast. Obviously, this limiting case is not to be found in contemporary democracies. To prevent fraud an open ballot is hardly ever used now, as a constraint on bribery and corruption. Similarly, the scale of modern democracies will normally prevent voting in any form other than by balloting – whether with paper ballots, on voting machines or electronically.
3   It must be possible for someone to choose to join the list of eligible voters, rather than having to be selected as voters by those currently eligible to vote. In other words, a party organized on the lines of the original European parties – what Duverger perhaps confusingly in this context had labeled "caucus parties" – in which the participants in the party were self-selected could not hold a direct primary.[7] Even if its membership is formally balloted, when choosing candidates for public office, such a small cabal is not conducting a direct primary. For it to have been one it must be the case that at some specified time before the nomination process begins someone can apply to join the list of selectors, and not be subject to rejection on ad hominem grounds.

Although this method of nominating party candidates would spread throughout the United States, replacing other methods, there was one public office for which it did not and could not be used – the Presidency.

Presidential Primaries

In the selection of presidential candidates by the two major parties the original notion that a "primary" was the first stage in a nominating procedure would survive, though not in name. While the solution to chaos introduced for most other public offices in America might conceivably have been used for nominating presidential candidates, its introduction would have depended on circumstances that, both then and now, have been politically impossible to create. A direct nomination would require a national primary with all states binding themselves to hold balloting on the same date. Before the 1970s the obvious objection to such a reform would have been that it would reduce a state's influence in any negotiations over the nominee that could, and frequently did, occur at National Conventions. While the subsequent downgrading of the two Conventions to mere spectacles removed this potential problem, states with small populations will continue to object that the potential candidates would never choose to visit them in the pursuit of votes nationally. Having their own primaries means that at least some lip service, and perhaps more, must be paid to them in the run-up to their selecting Convention delegates. In addition, it brings in some income to, and publicity for, the state with the presence of national media employees and others. While a tiny political lever for small states today, it matters nonetheless.

The history of presidential primaries can be stated briefly. Beginning in 1912 several states began introducing primary elections to select National Convention delegates, thereby abolishing the use of caucuses and various levels of prior conventions within the state. The number of state parties using such primaries increased up to 1920, and then declined again. Between then and 1968 typically only about 12 or 13 states used a presidential primary, with the remainder continuing to use their version of a caucus-convention system. First in 1972 with the Democrats, and then from 1976 in both parties the number of presidential primaries increased dramatically, as did the proportion of delegates selected in primaries. By comparison with the earlier period, and, with the arguable exception of the Democratic nomination in 2008, the identity of the nominee became certain well in advance of the last primaries. The National Convention was thereby transformed from a decision-making arena into a ritual or spectacle. States that retained caucuses as the first stage in nominating their delegates were, of course, persisting with the model of party nominations used throughout the country from the Jacksonian era onwards. However, as noted earlier, the term "caucus" had been used only in some states, with others calling them the "primary" or the "primary election"; with the advent of the direct primary they were all called caucuses. So, in a sense the nineteenth-century notion of a primary survived the subsequent century, but from about 1912 onwards a "presidential primary" nearly always meant an election involving the direct selection of a state party's National Convention delegates. But the linguistic switch is merely a minor curiosity compared with another development that occurred during the years between 1920 and the 1970s. To understand this, it is necessary to discuss the dynamics of presidential candidate selection in that period.

With presidential primaries generating only a minority of Convention delegates in total, securing selection depended far more on winning over support from party elites in the states, and especially a state's governor. Many were able to control their delegations and thus exercise considerable bargaining power when there was no clear frontrunner before the Convention. For a would-be candidate entering, and winning, primaries could demonstrate popularity among some of the party's core voters, but by no means did a clear demonstration guarantee being nominated. In 1952 Estes Kefauver swept the board in the Democratic primaries, but the party still nominated Adlai Stevenson. Candidates chose which primaries to enter and which to avoid because they were unlikely to do well there. Sometimes, as with the Catholic John Kennedy, in predominantly protestant West Virginia in 1960, winning a particular primary would show party elites elsewhere that this was a candidate who could have wide electoral appeal. (In fact, it is now widely accepted that it was his father's money that, in effect, bought the primary victory for Kennedy.) Consequently, having delegates selected in a primary had relatively few advantages for a state, given that it gave little bargaining power to the state party leadership.

Because of that there developed a type of primary that was just a "beauty contest," the term by which they became called popularly known, in which delegate selection was separated from the primary, the latter being little more than a state-run mass opinion poll of the self-identified supporters of a particular party. Despite usually being called presidential primary elections, nobody is selected to be or do anything. In 2016 the Democratic Party in Washington held such a primary, won by Hillary Clinton, although the earlier allocation of the state's Convention delegates had favored her rival Bernie Sanders. From the 1970s such contests have become anachronistic, something noted in Washington, where there had been a move to cancel the 2016 contest on grounds of expense, as there was no prospect of converting the primary into one in which delegates were selected. Earlier their main purpose had been to draw candidates into a state to campaign publicly, when they might otherwise have confined their pursuit of that state's voters to direct contact with the party's political elite there.

Preserving or Reducing the Role of Parties in Direct Primary Elections

Although those who wanted to change, restrict or even minimize the role of political parties in American politics were a minority force during the era when the direct primary was widely adopted, their influence on nomination reform varied greatly between states. One of the main respects in which their views conflicted with those of most party regulars was on how a direct primary should be structured. There were two main components of a primary where that conflict was most obvious. The first, and more widely known subsequently, was whether the vote in a party's primary should be restricted to those who identified with or supported that party or whether anyone who wanted to should be allowed to vote in it. In practice, however, the effects of which of the two arrangements a state opted for had rather limited effects on the ability of party elites and organizations to control nominations in their party. There were several reasons for this. The traditional openness of American parties, dating from the 1830s, meant that any attempt to unduly restrict the primary electorate would be confronted by a consensus against it. In the absence of fee-paying membership-based participation, parties could not try to exclude from primaries those whom they thought might not be loyal to the eventual nominee. The most they could do was require party supporters to register in advance as primary voters, at the same time as they were registering to vote in the next general election; this required stating that they had either supported the party previously or intended to vote for it at the forthcoming one. Since the Australian Ballot was a secret ballot there was no possibility of ever enforcing such requirements effectively. All that could be achieved with a closed primary, by comparison with an open one, was a reduction in the likelihood of the result being affected by defectors from the other party, who were trying to secure the selection of weak candidates by the party they opposed.

Voter raiding of this kind would occur, but was relatively uncommon, and open primaries only occasionally produced perverse results for a party. Nevertheless, at the beginning of the direct primary era most parties had opted for closed primaries, with only nine percent of states opting for open primaries. (By the beginning of this century its usage had risen to over 50 percent of states.) Raiding was more likely, however, when voters were permitted to vote in the primary of one party for some elective offices but in the other party's primary for different offices. The arrangement was permissible until 2002, though until the end of the twentieth century it had been used only in Washington. When California adopted this so-called blanket primary by initiative referendum in 1998 the U.S. Supreme Court rejected it (*California Democratic Party v. Jones*, 2002), the grounds being that it violated the First Amendment's guarantee of a right to freedom of association.

The second way of affecting the role party elites and organizations can play relates to how easy it is for any would-be candidate to get onto the primary ballot. Obviously, those seeking to weaken elite influence wanted to set the barrier very low, and this could be achieved by requiring that a potential nominee obtain only a small number of signatures from eligible voters in support of the candidacy. One response to this from parties was to make that threshold higher, but even when they do not, ballot access can still be denied because of technical mistakes made in the gathering of signatures. In 1985, for example, 16 out of 143 candidates in the Democratic primaries for various offices in New York were disqualified (Schuelke 1989). Usually in the past, party organizations had greater resources than individual candidates to challenge their access to the ballot on technical grounds, and, especially, in New York in the early twentieth century judges were partisan appointees who tended to side with the organizations. However, in many states where party organizations still remained relatively strong, judges could not necessarily be relied on to always act in an overtly partisan manner. A supplementary, and less controversial method, of limiting who could get onto a primary ballot was to deploy what was initially called the Hughes Plan.

Originating as an idea first in New York, but subsequently adopted in a handful of other states including Colorado, it preserved party influence over nominations by having caucuses and conventions *precede* the direct primary. Thus, as with the presidential primaries, it inverted the nineteenth-century arrangement (in which the party caucus or primary was the first stage in the nomination process) with the ultimate stage in a multi-stage process now being a direct primary. The real significance of the Hughes Plan is not this linguistic point, but that it provided an alternative to the original Crawford County model which was a single-stage system of nominating. A direct primary could be multi-stage, therefore, providing there was an election at the ultimate stage from which the winner automatically became the party's candidate.

Adopted in a handful of states, the Hughes Plan, or as it came to be known in some states, the Pre-Primary System (PPS), was a flexible tool in relation to the power it actually gave party elites. Rules could be constructed to make it more (or, alternatively, less) difficult for outsiders in a party to secure nomination. In Colorado candidates were placed on the primary ballot by a convention only if they had received 15 percent of the vote at the convention. Typically, only two, or at most three, candidates were thus eligible to enter the primary ballot by this means. Moreover, the order of names on the ballot paper was determined by the number of votes received at the convention; ballot position mattered because it was presumed, correctly in fact, that some voters typically voted for the candidate at the head of a ballot no matter what.[8] Yet, at the same time, Colorado also weakened party control over the nomination process through an alternative route onto the ballot paper: a candidate could submit a specified number of signatures on an official petition to the state Elections Board.

With the Pre-Primary System the primary is always the secondary stage in the nomination process, and with some offices, including the state governorship, it could even be the tertiary stage. (This is something that might have confused older Colorado voters in the inter-war years who had spent their youth in those states where a caucus was known as a primary or a primary election!) Functionally, however, the primary election under PPS plays exactly the same role as does a party primary in states where the direct primary is the only stage in choosing a party's candidate. The winner automatically becomes the party's candidate at the general election and is unquestionably *the party's* candidate.

This first point is also true of a very different method for influencing party control while the second is true only on one interpretation, although arguably the most important one, of what is meant by "a party's candidate." This is the now abandoned cross-filing primary.

Cross-filing, permitted in California from 1913 to 1959, allowed a candidate to contest the primary of both major political parties and, if they were won, then become the candidate of both. In the absence of independent candidates or candidates there would be no need for a general election. The main effect of any cross-filing system is to strengthen the position of some candidates, especially incumbents, who can use the publicity their office gives them to weaken opposition to themselves – both from within their own party and the other. Since, absent independent candidates, there will be no general election, an incumbent who cross-files and wins both primaries will have reduced the level of financial and other costs. However, the incentive to cross-file is present only when a candidate's personal popularity gives him or her a realistic chance of winning. Thus, there is an advantage to popular incumbents that tends to increase over time, and extend political careers. In California the main effect on the parties was to strengthen further the position of public office holders from the then majority party, the Republicans. Only the Democrats had any incentive to abolish cross-filing, which they duly did in 1959, following the nationwide electoral landslide they enjoyed in the midterm elections the previous year.

While cross-filing is a mechanism tending to weaken partisan politics, this primary system is still a party primary even though each of the major parties has nominated the same candidate. That an incumbent who in previous elections ran only in the Republican primary is not really a Democrat is irrelevant; that party's primary is still a Democratic primary, and that is an important respect in which cross-filing differs from so-called nonpartisan primaries, which are discussed in the penultimate section of the chapter.

Run-Off Primaries in the South

The "directness" of a direct primary relates to the result automatically leading to the winner becoming the party's candidate, and not to there being merely a single procedure in the process of conducting it that leads automatically to the nomination. Just as a direct primary can follow from a pre-primary convention, the process can involve a run-off between the two leading candidates in the first round, or indeed there could be a more complex multi-round of elections; the latter arrangement would still be a direct primary. Again, a direct primary can be structured in various ways, either to retain party power or alternatively to weaken parties, so the form a primary election itself takes can result from trying to promote other objectives. This was the case in the South from the 1890s where a Double Ballot was used on its introduction. After the first round there would be a subsequent round in which only the two leading candidates from the former were on the ballot. (If the leading candidate had received more than a majority of the votes, a second round was not required.) In the run-off round the winner would necessarily receive more than 50 percent of the vote. However, use of a Double Ballot system was not just confined to primaries; nine southern states, and Oklahoma, mandated its use in both primaries and other elections.[9] The origins of this lie in the distinct electoral history of the South following the Civil War (Kousser 1984).

In that region two factors prompted the deployment of run-off elections. Requiring that a majority of those voting must have voted for the winner (whether of a primary or a general election) reduced the likelihood that the minority black population could play a major role in determining the winner. A majority white population could unite against them. Together with other, more obvious, means – disenfranchisement, intimidation, and so on – it reduced the possibility of black influence in the South in all kinds of electoral processes. However, a run-off could also serve another purpose. With the complete collapse of the Republican Party in the 1890s in all but a few areas of the southern Appalachians, nearly all general elections in the region were reduced to a mere formality. The only arena of real competition was during nominations for the Democratic Party. The primary election – whether with a run-off requirement or not – became the functional equivalent of a general election throughout most of the South. Especially in states where the party was not organized into well-defined factions, it was entirely possible that, in a multi-candidate field, the leading candidate in the Democratic primary might receive less than a quarter of the total vote in that election. (Florida was perhaps the most extreme example of the atomization of the vote.[10]) Under such conditions the notion that that candidate could in any sense be described as the "popular choice," even of an exclusively white electorate, was absent. The obvious solution for this was the Double Ballot election in the primary, which thereby increased the incentive for all – whether independents or the small number who might otherwise be attracted to the Republican Party – to enter the Democratic primary.

Thus, one result of the run-off was to virtually eliminate any possibility that minority factions within a southern state might develop and organize outside the Democratic Party (or more accurately the Democratic Party label), rather than inside it, so that new major parties never formed. For more than 60 years, until the early 1950s, the Republican Party provided no serious alternative to the Democrats, with the Double Ballot system helping to solidify the monopoly role enjoyed by the label "Democratic Party," which was scarcely a party at all organizationally.[11] Not until economic development in the 1950s, followed by African-American re-enfranchisement in the 1960s, was party competition resumed. Nevertheless, despite its effects in undermining party politics in the earlier period, the Double Ballot primary was nonetheless, like the cross-filing primary, still a procedure for determining the nominees of a *political party*. In this respect it remained fundamentally different from two other procedures that would be described from the outset as primaries, but which lacked the fundamental feature of being a *nomination procedure for an office*, as opposed to one element of an electoral process for an office.

Primaries as Double Ballot Election Systems

As an electoral system, and certainly in Europe, the Double Ballot (Run-Off Ballot) system pre-dated the advent of the direct primary in America – for example, it was used in the French Third Republic (1871–1914), a regime in which political parties were both weak and highly decentralized.[12] In Europe this kind of electoral system, reintroduced and still used in the Fifth Republic, is never referred to as a kind of primary. However, it has precisely the same structure as so-called Nonpartisan Primaries in the United States. The latter were introduced in many western states during the Progressive era in attempts to eliminate the role of political parties in elections for many local public offices. A Nonpartisan Primary is no more and no less than the first round of a Double Ballot electoral system, with the subsequent election being the second round. (Given its origins, it might seem a curiosity of linguistic usage that the term "primary" should ever have been appropriated for a reform that eliminated parties from the electoral process, as run-off elections had been used in America for two decades before the movement for nonpartisanship developed.) Except for Nebraska and Minnesota (1913–1974), which provided for nonpartisan elections for their state legislatures, the move to exclude parties from electoral politics was confined to county level government and below. In particular, support for nonpartisanship was especially strong in relation to local school board elections.

Nonpartisan requirements typically prohibit political parties from formally endorsing candidates and from using resources in support of their campaigns. The candidates do not identify themselves as being a Republican or Democrat, nor, of course, do the names of a party appear on ballot papers. Nevertheless, typically party activists and public officials elected in partisan elections are involved in support of particular candidacies in nonpartisan elections, though not in a partisan capacity. Paradoxically, therefore, nonpartisan contests can be more partisan in substance than were Double Ballot primaries in the South, with its formally partisan primaries, but which of course were functioning in an era when party organization had largely collapsed. The relevant point here is that with nonpartisan elections there is a significant, and alternative, meaning of "primary" in the United States. It no longer refers to the process of *nominating* candidates (by a party) but to the first stage of a two-stage electoral system in which there are no parties.

A second procedure in which nominating through a party election has been abolished is the nonpartisan blanket primary. First introduced in Louisiana for congressional elections in 1978, candidates can, and do, identify themselves as Democrats or Republicans when campaigning and on the ballot paper itself. Consequently, partisanship is not formally abolished in the electoral process, but the "primary" is not a party primary because the two candidates who end up contesting the run-off election could both be Democrats (or both Republicans). In the former case, therefore, no Republican candidate has been selected for the second ballot. Like a nonpartisan primary, this sort of primary is not an element in a nomination process, but, the first part of a two-stage election system. Like the Progressives' invention of the nonpartisan primary, nomination for election is merely self-nomination by a candidate, involving the acquisition of the required number of signatures of eligible voters to enter the primary ballot. Consequently, the French presidential election of May 1995 can be considered a good example of what in America would be called a nonpartisan blanket primary, although the French would undoubtedly regard that description of it as puzzling. In the first round there were nine candidates, including two who were members of the Gaullist Party – Jacques Chirac and Edouard Balladur – both having served as prime minister during the previous ten years. Three months before, the election opinion polls indicated that the run-off election would be between the two of them, though eventually the Socialist Party's Lionel Jospin finished second to Chirac in the first round. The mechanics of this election were the same as the Louisiana primary, in that there was nothing in the electoral rules themselves to prevent more than one candidate from a single political party contesting the first-round election, and nothing to prevent those two contesting the run-off, were they to win most votes initially.

"Exporting" Primary Elections Outside the United States

Like the United States, many countries have long regulated the activities of their political parties, and in many respects more extensively than America has, especially with respect to the funding of electoral activities. Generally, though, state regulation of the nomination of their own candidates has been absent. There are exceptions. Since 1997 Uruguay has required all its parties to nominate their candidates in a primary election.[13] This might be a precursor for further changes in presidential systems, especially in Latin America which has always looked more closely to the U.S. for its political models, but it is an unlikely development in parliamentary regimes.

Uruguay apart, the "exporting" of primaries abroad so far has taken place without any element of the state regulation that accompanied the switch to direct primaries in early twentieth-century America. Nevertheless, from the end of the last century, and continuing in the present one, parties in various types of democratic systems have started to use primary elections when selecting not just candidates for election, but also party leaders. Several different kinds of procedures have been introduced, but they share two features which distinguish them from some of the extended range of procedures to which the word "primary" has become attached in the United States.

First the primary is used only to select someone who will become a party's nominee. In other words, as noted previously, the third of the three American notions of primary, that nonpartisan primaries can be considered a type of primary, has been absent in European and other democracies. Second, the result of the primary determines directly who will be that candidate. Thus, the original American notion, that a primary election was the first stage in what could be a multi-stage process of selection is absent as well. For non-Americans, it is some form of the direct primary that is their model. However, were they to look at primaries outside the U.S., many Americans would probably regard them as rather primitive or unformed versions of the American model of a direct primary. And they would have good reasons for thinking this.

Explaining this requires understanding both the legal and the cultural contexts in which the American direct primary developed. This is best done by examining three respects in which the operation of primaries elsewhere usually differs from the American original.

(i) Incumbents in America can always be challenged in a primary, providing a challenger meets certain pre-set requirements when doing so, whereas this kind of compulsory reselection is rare elsewhere.

(ii) With the exception of "white-only" primaries in the South before the 1960s, the right to vote in American primaries has been broadly defined, whereas in other countries there are widespread variations in this right.

(iii) In the U.S. the function of a primary is just to nominate a candidate for a public office, but in some other democracies they are used to select party leaders whose candidacies for a public office are only one component of their role.

With all three of these differences it is important to understand why the American model took the form it did, as well as why the context there may be irrelevant for some other democracies' deployment of primaries.

Compulsory Reselection

Typically, primaries are used in other countries only when there is a vacancy to be filled as a party's candidate. They are used far less commonly in reselecting incumbent public officials, and only infrequently are there requirements for incumbents to face reselection automatically. In the U.S., the incumbent might not face a primary opponent in advance of any particular general election, but the possibility that an opponent could emerge and has a right to face that incumbent on the primary ballot is always present. While most American incumbents do enjoy longevity in office, frequently many face primary challengers from time to time. They cannot avoid compulsory reselection, therefore, when someone wants to challenge them in a primary. This difference between America and other countries is linked to the context in which the direct primary emerged in the former.

For three reasons, there was never any possibility of American incumbents being given a free-ride in remaining a party's candidate. First, by abolishing pasters, the Australian Ballot removed an important route for party outsiders to challenge party elites – in a political system that highly valued parties as central to democracy. Within such a polity the idea that incumbents should be afforded any special protection had always been alien. In part, this was because, even among a party's elites, holding any particular elective public offices was not seen as a career. Many offices, especially in state legislatures and Congress, were occupied for much of the nineteenth century by lawyers who, far from seeking a long career in them, were using them to establish useful contacts to advance their legal practices. They left office after only one or two terms, although most would remain active in their party.

Second, in locating the administration of direct primaries in government, any reformed system required there had to be some means for those responsible to determine when a primary ballot had to be held. With the abandonment of parties' distributing their own ballot papers and of pasters, procedures were needed for those officials to determine who was entitled to be on the ballot paper in a general election under the banner of the Democratic Party or the Republican Party. While it might have been possible to find some compromise in the case of Office Block types of ballot, it was with the more commonly used Party Column type where there *could* be only one candidate designated to use the party's name on the ballot paper.[14] Logically one solution was that, in the case of incumbents, the parties themselves could inform the relevant officials that a primary would be unnecessary. Where there was only one office to be contested, this might be relatively straightforward, though still create complications should an incumbent decide late not to run again. Moreover, it increased opportunities for manipulation and corruption. Yet the main problem was the vast number of offices that had to be filled at each election, in marked contrast with most other democracies then or later. Administratively, the easiest solution was to provide for primary elections for every office, although obviously there would never be a contest when only one candidate had submitted a valid nomination form.

Third, under the changed conditions of the early twentieth century incumbents themselves had relatively little interest in being protected from intra-party challengers. From the 1880s onwards there had emerged in America a new kind of political actor – the hustling candidate (Reynolds 2006). Being elected to a public office was less likely to be a short interlude early in a career, and more likely to be the first stage of a longer-term career. Indeed, one important explanation for the demise of a convention-based system of party nominations, and the rise of the direct primary, is that the "hustling candidate" was a key factor in facilitating the transformation. These candidates were operating in a wholly different context than would their counterparts in other countries, because the number of rungs on the career ladder was greater in the former. Careers were built not by being elected to one office – such as a legislature – and remaining there, but using that as a launch pad to a higher level of elective office. Abolishing the convention system weakened the role of others in the party who, previously, could frustrate their ambitions, while the new availability of primaries opened opportunities for hustling candidates to further their careers. Although the possibility of having to face compulsory reselection to maintain their own offices could pose problems for them, as incumbents they often had access to greater campaigning resources than any opponents. The emergence of the hustling candidate into an institutional structure, composed of the many layers of elective offices that the Jacksonians had created in the 1830s, generated a very different set of incentives than those that would become evident elsewhere later. Moreover, at the heart of this growth in political careerism were state legislators, who not only had an incentive to create nomination arrangements that facilitated career progression, but who constituted the membership of the institutions responsible for legislating their introduction.

Of course, a successful primary challenger could put an end to an incumbent's political career; that was the price of having a career ladder where it was possible to progress upwards with a combination of party support and one's own resources and political skills. In the long run – between three and five decades – the direct primary would be a major contributory factor in the weakening of traditional party organizations, and especially in their relationships with their own candidates. Those kinds of relationships were very different in most other democracies. Too many challenges from within a party to its incumbents was potentially destabilizing for the party and unwanted by most incumbents themselves. In general, only "out" groups in a party become advocates of compulsory reselection and, in the rare circumstances when they take over from the "ins," they too may then want to benefit from being exempt from compulsory reselection in the future. Moreover, the extended political career ladder that developed in the U.S. is less evident in other democracies because there are fewer sequential levels of office there. In the absence of such a ladder in a federal system, career progression from state to federal offices can be unusual. In contrast with the U.S., this is the case in Canada; members of Canadian provincial parliaments rarely regarded running for a seat in the federal parliament as career progression.

Wide Variations in Eligibility to Vote in Primary Elections

When the direct primary was established in early twentieth-century America, registering to vote in it was usually done a mere few months before the election itself, and was undertaken at the same time as the annual registration of voters for the general election. There are variations in this between states, but these are not as great as in the countries that have "imported" the direct primary.

Open primaries of the American kind, or even quasi-open primaries, were slow to develop. As late as 1996 in her study of German and British parties Susan Scarrow was analyzing countries in which there were still no open primaries, but she argued that this was a reform that might readily be enacted outside America: "Instituting either open primaries, or closed primaries where the barriers to entry are very low, would be a radical response, but it is a change which could be implemented in many countries" (Scarrow 1996, 209). Nevertheless, even in those countries where all parties restrict voting in primaries to party members, the variations in how long a person must be a member before qualifying to vote in a primary are massive. One comparative study of Belgian and Israeli parties revealed that all the parties using primaries confine voting to party members, but the qualifying period for a primary vote varies from a few weeks to over a year (Wauters, Rahat, and Kenig 2016, 90). The American tradition of having an agency of government responsible for registering eligibility to participate in an intra-party election has had no direct counterpart elsewhere. American parties are structured differently and, consequently, have had a different culture about rights to participate in a party's activities; this is a major factor in explaining one aspect of American political exceptionalism. Yet how parties have been structured in other countries has also varied – both by country and by type of party – so that there are major differences between them as well as between those parties and the major American parties.

Some parties, primarily social democratic parties in northern Europe, formally enrolled individual members who acquired various rights in relation to decision making within the party. With membership came responsibilities, and a failure to observe them could, *in extremis*, lead to expulsion. Not all social democratic parties followed the model of individual membership pioneered by the German SPD in the late nineteenth century. Other left-of-center parties were allied to social organizations – such as trade unions – whose members too could be deemed to be party members, even though the party usually prioritizes recruiting individual dues-paying members. The British Labour Party was an example of this. Still others had a much-diluted notion of a "member" involving relatively few enforceable rights with respect to control over the party and its activities, but also not open to all in quite the way that American parties have been. The British Conservative Party has members of that kind. A still looser notion of party membership became more attractive to party elites later in the twentieth century when some parties had experienced intra-party conflicts over party goals and policies. Thus, when Silvio Berlusconi founded Forza Italia in 1993 he sought to recruit members who would have the same kind of relationship to their party as football supporters did to their team. While wanted for their support, they obtained no control over the organization recruiting them.

Across the wide spectrum of organizational structures there have been parties adopting direct primary elections in recent decades; some use them to select party candidates as in the United States, but others also to select party leaders, a development to be discussed shortly. At one extreme, there is the example of Canada, where formerly the Liberal Party had a structure that scarcely operated at all between election campaigns but now has formal enrolment of members. They have relatively few formal powers over party elites, but primaries are used at both the local level and in selecting its leader. At the other extreme, in countries such as Belgium and Israel, where there was always a much stronger notion of formal membership entailing some rights and responsibilities, primaries have now been used by some, though not all, parties. The constraints imposed by their specific histories and present circumstances affect how willing they are to extend the right to vote in a primary. Yet, overall, the present century has been an age of experimentation in candidate selection in many parties, experiments that can be quickly discontinued because of their uncertain consequences. In 2009 the British Conservative Party encouraged its local party organization in Totnes to select its parliamentary candidate for the next general election in a primary in which any eligible voter could vote. The winner was a local doctor who had scarcely been involved in the Conservative Party previously but who defeated other candidates who had; this experiment has not been widely repeated by the party since then, partly because it might produce candidates who would prove less open to party control later. However, the most interesting aspect of the experiment is that it had happened at all in a party which for much of the last century was dominated by its elite.

The primary has become attractive outside the U.S. in an era when voter loyalty to parties has been eroding, and where primaries are perceived as having two advantages in countering the effects of this. One is that the impression of a candidate or party leader being selected through more open processes, and by larger sets of selectors, could link a party more directly to the idea of democracy itself, and hence increase the perceived legitimacy of those selected. Then there is the greater publicity that a primary might generate for a party compared with other methods of selection. Of course, this was one of the reasons that between 1968 and 1976 state Republican parties had followed their Democratic counterparts in moving to using presidential primaries; persisting with the original caucus-convention system would have given an advantage to the Democrats, because television coverage would focus mainly on the more telegenic method of primary selection.

For those parties whose members had traditionally possessed formal rights over the party's public policy objectives greater flexibility in modifying them to broaden their electoral appeal was needed. As their loyal electorates were shrinking, new objectives had to be pursued to attract other voters. Reducing control by the members over policies, thereby strengthening the ability of party elites to modify them, was required. However, current activists could be pacified, and new members attracted, only if there were some compensating new roles for them. Primaries could provide a suitable forum for that – by opening up candidate selection. Yet there is an obvious tension here. If activists are to be recruited to perform some tasks in the party, and be "rewarded" by being able to choose candidates or the party's leadership, then they (and not non-members) must have the privilege of doing so. When primaries are closed in this way, their role in increasing the legitimacy or popularity of those selected will be limited by comparison with a more open primary. This tension is part of the explanation for there being no pronounced movement towards, nor away from, open primaries outside the U.S.

Of course, even in this new, heterogeneous universe of primaries opposition to proposals for including more people in the selection of candidates for public office and public leaders is difficult to mount. A primary system can always be promoted as being *more* participatory than what has preceded it; this is its great selling point. It becomes therefore a *relative* concept; a primary may still involve only a minority entitled to participate, but, so long as there is a wider potential selectorate than previously, a reform can be presented as, and described publicly as, a primary. Of course, some non-American primaries have been as open as American primaries, with virtually anyone who wants to participating in them. But part of the appeal of primaries for some party reformers is that they do not have to be.

Thus, the American conjunction of a formal election process in nominating candidates and open access to participate in the process is far from universal. Thus, the idea of a primary becomes arguably more elusive even than in America. This open-ended quality of the concept of a primary means that all kinds of selection procedures can be publicized as being primaries, arrangements that bear little resemblance to how the American direct primary itself operates. If, as a minimum, all that it takes for a procedure to be a primary is for a candidate to be selected by means of an election, as opposed, say, to consensus in a small group, then old-style meetings of membership parties to choose a candidate could constitute a primary, just as much as a primary election open to all. There is no identifiable cut-off point or boundary, in relation to eligibility to vote, between a primary and some other form of selection. That is why "primary election" can be understood as a relative concept. In the current era, where widening eligibility has become attractive to politicians, the concept of a primary election has been embraced and understood outside the United States in ways that many Americans would regard as odd: "You might think of that as a primary, but I wouldn't call it one."

Primaries and Leadership Selections

One significant respect in which the domain of the direct primary has expanded on its exportation abroad is its use in the selection of party leaders. Nevertheless, the adoption of more inclusive procedures of selection does not necessarily mean that the parties themselves, the mass media, or communicants on social media will use the word "primary" regularly when referring to them. Both the Canadian Liberal Party in 2013 and the British Labour Party in 2015 used leadership selection procedures that have features necessary to qualify as primaries, but in both cases "leadership contest" remains how they are still typically described. Indeed, it is political scientists and analysts who are often the main promoters now of the term "primary," rather than its usage following from what politicians say. (For example, three political scientists used the term "semi open primary," to describe the leadership contest in 2016 between British Labour leader Jeremy Corbyn and his challenger Owen Smith, even though it had not been described as such in the mass media.[15]) Arguably one reason for this is the slow, long-term, transformation in how leaders have been selected, rather than there being a sudden, and massive, shift towards expanding the selectorate that might prompt the use of new political language. The British Labour Party provides a good illustration of this point. For decades the choice lay entirely in the hands of the party's MPs. By the last decades of the twentieth century this method was replaced by an electoral college, comprising MPs, trade unions and individual members. After the 2010 contest, when there was some concern that the unions' vote had been pivotal in the selection of Ed Miliband, a commission was established to propose how future leaders should be selected. The electoral college was abolished subsequently, with members of trade unions joining individual members in the selectorate. Clearly, the process had now become a primary election but, with the emphasis on evolution rather than a sharp break with the past, there was no advantage, and possibly some disadvantages to, publicizing it as a primary.[16]

In an obvious sense the U.S. president and state governors are also the leaders of their parties. Yet, not only are they selected specifically to contest an election for a public office, how much power they can exercise over their parties has varied greatly. Both the president and some state governors have always had limited power over other actors in their party. In the president's case, federalism and the separation of powers restrict the scope of their power. With state governorships, separation of powers has limited it in all cases, but in some states other factors, including constitutional limits on how many terms a governor could serve, and specific powers assigned to other elected public officials, have reduced their intra-party influence further. This dispersal of power is generally less evident even in presidential systems elsewhere – in France and Latin America, for example – where the party's presidential candidate (and the president) typically are not merely head of the party ticket, but able to exercise control throughout the party. The result is that there is a broader notion than in the U.S. that candidacy and leadership of the party are equal roles that a nominee combines.

In parliamentary regimes the situation is more complicated still. Although the purpose of selecting a leader via a primary election is to recruit someone who will be competing to become prime minister at an election, the role of party leader is not confined to this. In contemporary parliamentary systems the party leader performs at least three roles: fronting the party's campaign in advance of a general election, leading the party in the parliament, and keeping extra-parliamentary factions and groups within the party united. Performance in the last two roles can affect how the party will be perceived by potential voters during the next election campaign. Consequently, how the leader is selected can influence the likelihood that all these roles can be performed competently. Failure in doing so can result in attempts to remove the leader from office in advance of the general election itself; in Britain an attempt to dislodge the Conservative leader Iain Duncan Smith in 2003 was successful, but it failed against Labour's Jeremy Corbyn in 2016. On the other hand, defeat in a general election does not directly result in the demise of the erstwhile party leader, as it does for a defeated presidential candidate in America, although increasingly such failure is followed by the leader's resignation.[17]

These additional roles of parliamentary leaders affect how primary selection procedures are constructed, and then often reconstructed. In presidential systems a broad selectorate, consisting of likely party voters, is feasible since the main objective is to choose a candidate whose electoral appeal is likely to be greatest. For parliamentary leadership contests the risk in enfranchising a broad selectorate is that, while the voters may be able to exercise judgement on the possible electoral appeal of a potential leader, they may have limited knowledge on two other crucial matters: how he or she could perform as a parliamentarian, and in minimizing factional intra-party conflict. This is why in parliamentary regimes there has been considerable variation in the introduction of primaries for party leaderships, and also changes in the rules as to how precisely the primary is to operate. There have been some spectacular miscalculations in this regard. Jeremy Corbyn, selected in 2015 with a view to contesting the 2020 general election, was faced a year later with three-quarters of the party's MPs declaring publicly that they had no confidence in him. Despite this Corbyn did not resign, won reselection again, with much the same selectorate that had chosen him in the first place.

This experience helps to explain why there is some ambiguity about whether elections of parliamentary leaders should be regarded as party primaries or not. What the original nineteenth-century notion of a primary (in America) and the American direct primary had in common was that their purpose was to select a candidate to contest an election for an office. While these procedures might be similar to those of Presbyterian churches, mentioned earlier, the latter were not selecting anyone to contest an election. That is one obvious reason why the churches' procedures are rarely referred to as primaries. Parliamentary leadership contests lie midway between the two cases. It is expected that the leader will be spearheading an election for control of government, but that is not a leader's only function. To call these leadership elections "primaries" is to stretch the notion of a primary still further, although arguably not without good reason.

Conclusions

When discussing primary elections in America years ago, political scientists typically stated that there were different types of primary election which could be identified. It is perhaps more accurate to say that the term "primary election" has several rather different meanings. Moreover, the concept is a rather elastic one because there are so few conditions that must be met for a selection process to be considered a primary, even when discussion is confined to direct primaries. Of course, a direct primary must lead directly to the nomination of a candidate who has won a formal election to be the nominee of a single party, or an alliance of several parties, or some organized group. But that election process might:

(a) be mandated by law, or alternatively have been voluntarily adopted by the party;

(b) be organized and conducted by state institutions or entirely by parties themselves;

(c) have been preceded by earlier processes in which the candidates permitted to contest the primary were selected, or require merely that would-be nominees secure the signatures of a specified number of eligible voters;

(d) allow virtually anyone to vote in the primary, or alternatively restrict the vote to those meeting certain conditions – such as being a party member for a specified period;

(e) be confined solely to the purpose of selecting candidates to contest a specified public office at a general election, or be used as well to select party officials or leaders.

Consequently, many ways of nominating candidates could count as primaries. In addition, the concept has also been hijacked to describe the first round of certain kinds of double-ballot election systems, and has been further deployed to describe selection procedures that are more inclusive than their predecessors, but which still restrict access to the selection process. If asked to answer the question "Is this particular selection procedure a primary election or not?" it is perhaps safest to invoke the spirit of Professor C.E.M Joad, a philosopher who appeared each week on a popular, but educational, BBC radio program in the 1940s. In answer to nearly every question under discussion in the program Joad began with the words "It all depends what you mean by . . .".[18] It does indeed "all depend."

Notes

1 One of the first studies to popularize the term "selectorate" was Norris and Lovenduski 1995.

2 One alternative solution, discussed in 1875 but not implemented, was to make electoral districts smaller; see Ware 2002, 69.

3 http://www.scfaith.org/history/.

4 "Electing Ruling Elders: A Resource for Kirk Sessions," Committee for Training and Resources and Board of Christian Training of the Presbyterian Church in Ireland. Online, https://www.presbytriareland.org/getmedia/a65746fd-d759-44bb-935f-56d7878b0f78/CT-Electing-Ruling-Elders.pdf.aspx?ext=.pdf (page 5).

5 Its proceedings were published and provide a crucial insight into widespread concerns about the problems of nominating candidates; National Conference on the Practical Reform of Primary Elections 1898.

6 The prevalence of pasting was one reason why ticket splitting was so high in the 1880s despite the strength of political parties at the local level; see Reynolds and McCormick 1986.

7 For Duverger (1954, 18), "a caucus consists of a small number of members and seeks no expansion . . . membership is achieved only by a kind of tacit co-option or by formal nomination." It was one of four types of basic unit from which a party could be composed. Definitionally, therefore, it is a different notion of a "caucus" than was commonplace in American political life.

8 That ballot position matters has been reaffirmed several times by political scientists; see for example, Koppell and Steen 2004.

9 See McDonald 1985. The one southern state that did not use run-offs was Virginia, which of all the states in the region had the most highly structured factions within the Democratic Party.

10 On varieties of party factionalism in the South, the best source remains Key 1949.

11 One of the few exceptions to this generalization was Republican success in winning a few southern states in the 1928 presidential election, after the Democrats had nominated a Catholic, Al Smith.

12 A separate run-off election is not the only version of this type of voting system, another being the Alternative Vote (sometimes known as Instant Run-off Voting). Under this arrangement a voter's second preference is expressed on the ballot paper at the same time as the first preference, thus obviating the need for an entirely separate second election.

13 On Uruguay see Buquet 2011. On the issue of why parties in Latin America hold presidential primaries see Kemahlioglu, Weitz-Shapiro, and Hirano 2009.

14 The designs of the two types of ballot differ significantly. The Office Block lists each office in order, with all candidates for any given office being identified under that heading. Should there be a dispute as to who was entitled to be a party's candidate for any office, the overall appearance of the ballot would not be disturbed by including the names of all disputants on it; voters could then be allowed to vote for whichever of a party's putative candidates they wished to. By contrast the Party List type is a kind of grid, with the horizontal axis consisting of the names of each party, and with the vertical axis listing each office being contested. Were an attempt made to include all disputants on the ballot, its appearance would be odd and could cause additional voter confusion. Moreover, in states that were already using voting machines it would have been impossible to print Party Column ballots that could be used on the late 19th and early 20th-century machines.

15 See https://constitution-unit.com/2016/09/06/the-2016-labour-leadership-election-in-comparative-perspective/.

16 The structure of the system used in 2015 resembled a Preprimary Convention because access to the ballot was possible only with support of a stated number of the party's MP's; collectively the MPs were the functional equivalent of a Convention. However, when Jeremy Corbyn's leadership was challenged in 2016, with a new ballot held, he was permitted under the rules to be on the ballot even though he was unable to gain the required support from MPs that his opponents had to obtain.

17 The last leader of one of the two major parties in Britain to hold onto the leadership after an electoral defeat was Neil Kinnock in 1987.

18 The weekly program, *The Brains Trust*, began in 1941 and featured a panel of three experts – always the same three – who tried to answer questions submitted by listeners. Joad was one of the original experts with his catchphrase becoming well known nationally.

References

Buquet, Daniel. 2011. "Participation and Effects of Primary Elections in Uruguay." Paper presented at IPSA-ECPR Joint Conference, São Paulo, Brazil.

Dallinger, Frederick W. 1897. *Nominations for Elective Office in the United States*. New York: Longmans, Green.

Duverger, Maurice. 1954. *Political Parties*. London: Methuen.

Kemahlioglu, Ozge, Rebecca Weitz-Shapiro, and Shigeo Hirano. 2009. "Why Primaries in Latin American Presidential Elections?" *Journal of Politics* 71 (1): 339–352.

Key, V.O. 1949. *Southern Politics in State and Nation*. New York: Alfred A. Knopf.

Koppell, Jonathan G.S., and Jennifer A. Steen. 2004. "The Effects of Ballot Position on Electoral Outcomes." *Journal of Politics* 66 (2): 267–281.

Kousser, J. Morgan. 1984. "The Origins of the Run-Off Primary." *The Black Scholar* 15 (5): 23–26.

McDonald, Laughlin. 1985. "The Majority Vote Requirement: Its Use and Abuse in the South." *The Urban Lawyer* 17 (3): 429–439.

National Conference on the Practical Reform of Primary Elections. 1898. *Proceedings of the National Conference on Practical Reform of Primary Elections*, January 20 and 21, 1898. Chicago, IL: W. C. Hollister.

Norris, Pippa, and Joni Lovenduski. 1995. *Political Recruitment: Gender, Race and Class in the British Parliament*. Cambridge, UK: Cambridge University Press.

Ranney, Austin. 1975. *Curing the Mischiefs of Faction: Party Reform in America*. Berkeley: University of California Press.

Reynolds, John F. 2006. *The Demise of the American Convention System, 1880–1911*. Cambridge, UK: Cambridge University Press.

Reynolds, John F., and Richard L. McCormick. 1986. "Outlawing 'Treachery': Split Tickets and Ballot Laws in New York and New Jersey, 1880–1910." *Journal of American History* 72 (3): 835–858.

Scarrow, Susan B. 1996. *Parties and their Members: Organizing for Victory in Britain and Germany*. Oxford, UK: Oxford University Press.

Schuelke, Katherine E. 1989. "A Call for Reform of New York State's Ballot Access Laws." *New York University Law Review* 64: 182–231.

Silbey, Joel. 1991. *The American Political Nation*. Stanford, CA: Stanford University Press.

Ware, Alan. 2002. *The American Direct Primary: Party Institutionalization and Transformation in the North*. Cambridge, UK: Cambridge University Press.

Wauters, Bram, Gideon Rahat, and Ofer Kenig. 2016. "Democratizing Party Leadership Selection in Belgium and Israel." In *Party Primaries in Comparative Perspective*, ed. Giulia Sandri, Antonella Seddone and Fulvio Venturino. London: Routledge.

2

THE ORIGINS OF THE DIRECT PRIMARY

John F. Reynolds

The United States Constitution holds the states mainly responsible for administering elections. Consequently, it was the state legislatures that ushered in direct primary laws stipulating that political parties hold government supervised elections whereby voters determined their respective party nominees. Prior to that time, candidates commonly won their party's endorsement in conventions of party officials meeting at the local, state, and national levels. The direct primary was one of a number of changes in electoral procedures dating from the Progressive Era (1890–1920): the Australian ballot, women's suffrage, the direct election of United States Senators, the initiative and referendum, and campaign finance laws. The collective impact of these changes in the rules of the game was soon apparent. A party-dominated political system dating back to Jacksonian times evolved into a candidate-centered political process marked by waning partisanship and diminished voter turnout.

Scholars have long singled out the direct primary as one of the more consequential electoral changes of the Progressive Era. One noted political scientist deemed the direct primary "the most radical of all party reforms adopted in the whole course of American history" (Ranney 1975, 18). But the reform's causes and consequences remain a source of contention. Like many of the measure's initial proponents, early scholarly assessments characterized the shift from the convention to the primary as a democratizing trend that empowered the electorate at the expense of self-serving political bosses (Merriam et al. 1928; Lovejoy 1941; Noble 1946). By the latter half of the twentieth century, many academics were less enamored with the reform; they blamed the direct primary for the relatively weak state of political parties in the United States that had rendered them less "responsible" once in power (Key 1964; Sorauf 1972). From this perspective, the party leaders conferring in "smoke filled rooms" could more reliably be trusted to come up with competent nominees who shared their party's values and principles (Wicker 1992). When the choice devolved upon a more fickle electorate, a candidate's positions and qualifications might be lost sight of as voters responded to his or her personal appeal. Whatever their opinion about the effects of the measure, historians and political scientists generally viewed the direct primary as something that was imposed on political parties from without. Progressives adhered to a long anti-party tradition in American political culture in this view. The direct primary was one of many measures they promoted in hopes of curbing the influence of political parties and promoting a more independent political outlook among the electorate.

The historical perspective framing this chapter offers a more nuanced understanding of the direct primary's origins and impact on the American polity. The direct primary was neither as deleterious to the electoral process as was once thought, nor was it unpopular among party elites. To understand how the direct primary came to be and what its effects were on the political order, it is necessary to first understand how the nominating system operated at the end of the nineteenth century. Party leaders – elective office seekers in particular – had their own set of grievances with the candidate selection process during the convention's heyday. Ideally, the parties' councils were supposed to promote harmony by working up a slate of nominees that promised something for all the party's constituent parts. The system worked best when candidates at least appeared to take a "hands off" approach to its workings and awaited their party's call. When candidates became more active in promoting their interests around 1900, the added pressure they brought to bear was more than the convention system could endure. Chaos and controversy disrupted the informal, locally run caucuses and indirect primaries selecting the delegates that overflowed on to the convention floor and lingered on. Parties and their standard bearers suffered at the polls when the nominating process gave rise to disharmony and ill will. The Democratic and Republican parties implemented rules governing their nominating procedures to adjust to these more contentious circumstances, but they soon turned these duties over to the state. The transition to the direct primary might best be understood as an accommodation to a new form of electioneering emerging in the Progressive Era. Consequently, the direct primary is best understood as a response to a more candidate-centered political regime, rather than the other way around.

The Convention System

Political parties invented the nominating convention early in the Jacksonian Era. The recurring party conferences played a key role in the emergence of the Whig and Democratic organizations during what historians refer to as the "party period" (circa 1840–1900; see Silbey 1991; McCormick 1966; Dallinger 1903, 4–45). The Greenbackers, Prohibitionists, Populists, and other minor parties arranged their nominations following a similar format. The advantages a formal nomination bestowed on a party and its candidates were readily apparent. First and foremost, it helped mobilize a party's vote behind a single candidate rather than see it scattered across several aspirants. Moreover, in an age when political ambition was rated as a vice rather than as a virtue, the convention could maintain the useful fiction that a nomination had come unsought and unbidden. The convention itself served to promote party unity. The consultation and negotiation among the party elite assured that the party's choices would be more acceptable to its voting base.

Nineteenth-century political parties were solely responsible for administering their affairs. The nomination process began with an announcement from a national, state or county committee calling for a convention to meet at a given date or place (Dallinger 1903, 63). Given the multilayered framework of the nation's electoral system, several calls were issued over the course of the year for several different conventions selecting candidates for multiple office levels. In the spring the major and minor party state committees might summon a state convention to select delegates to go to the national convention. In the summer the state committee might schedule another party congress to pick candidates for statewide offices. Party organizations representing counties and legislative districts (federal and state) and judicial districts and municipalities might call yet more conventions to fill out a portion of the party ticket to be voted on in the spring or fall. The party's numerous subdivisions responded to each of these appeals by arranging for a set of caucuses or primaries in their townships or wards. Here they might select delegates to the county convention, whose duty it was to appoint delegates to state or congressional conventions. In presidential years the beleaguered voter might be implored to attend a half dozen such caucuses to select delegates to attend multiple nominating bodies (Lovejoy 1941, 17).

Because election laws varied from state to state, and because party organizations were so decentralized, the rules and traditions that governed the nominating process varied considerably from place to place. When it came to local offices, the voters might select the candidates themselves under what was called the "Crawford County System." Administering a primary election was an expensive proposition, however, and it did not guarantee that the result would be satisfactory to all elements of the party. Party-run direct primaries were also popular across much of the South where they were designed "in order to keep the white men united" (Kousser 1974, 76). Far more common was an "indirect primary" where voters selected delegates to act for them. In a medium-sized town a meeting – or caucus – to pick a delegate or two might convene in a local law office or saloon. In other times or places the choice of delegates might be done by ballot at voting places open an hour or two in the evening. Many rural residents could not be bothered traveling miles over rutted roads just to designate someone to attend the state convention; they left that choice with the county committee. In urban areas the party's voters might be convened in a mass outdoor rally where they formally gave their assent to some slate of representatives to attend the state convention (Ware 2002, 57–63; Merriam et al. 1928). Although delegates were commonly appointed just weeks or even days before their nominating body was scheduled to meet, many failed to attend. Perhaps as many as one-fifth of the men participating in the typical convention were never formally selected for the role but held "proxies" they secured from a duly elected delegate (Reynolds 2006, 121).

However organized and administered, primaries and caucuses were rarely well attended. Roughly one in five or perhaps one in ten of the party's loyal followers chose to participate in these wholly internal party affairs. In New York City, for example, it was established that less than 8 percent of Republican voters took part in the party's primaries in the late 1880s (Keller 1977, 533; Bernheim 1888, 112–115). Explanations for the low voter turnout are not hard to come by. First and foremost, there simply was not a whole lot for a voter to do at these local functions. In the interests of "harmony," factions typically agreed on a full slate of delegates ahead of time. The partisan press encouraged the formation of such consensus coalitions, hailing them as harbingers of party unity in the general election. The citizen was left to endorse a single list of delegates whose candidate preferences for the array of offices up for grabs was wholly unknown to him. Voters were left in the dark because it was not always clear who was running – or "available" – for elective office in any case. Moreover, caucuses and primaries occurred at different dates and times for different offices and were often not well advertised. The local party establishment might abruptly call "snap caucuses" before any local opposition could get organized (Dallinger 1903, 121). The abysmally low voter participation rates should come as no surprise, especially after one multiplies these obstacles to grassroots governance by the four to six primaries or caucuses a dedicated Democrat or Republican was supposed to attend in a single election cycle.

Yet, if the system did not welcome input from the party's electoral contingent, it did accord some citizens the occasional opportunity to participate more fully in party governance. Apportionment rules typically set aside a delegate seat at the county convention for one out of every 25 votes cast for the party in a previous election; at the state convention the ratio might be raised to one for every 100 or 300 votes. Given these voter/delegate proportions and the numerous party nominating bodies convened during a political campaign, it can be supposed that many voters attended one or more nominating bodies over a span of a very few years. Here they had an opportunity to frame a platform and select party officials in addition to deliberating over the candidates vying for a place on the ticket. Caucuses and conventions surely helped reinforce the intense partisan feeling that we have come to associate with the "party period" (Silbey 1991).

While formats for citizen input varied, there was much more uniformity across political and partisan boundaries when it came to the workings of their nominating bodies (Bryce 1891, II, 170–179). The chair of the respective party committee called the session to order and introduced a temporary secretary and chair. The latter favored his audience with a rousing speech lambasting the opposition and appealing for unity. At this point, the delegates took a break for lunch while newly appointed committees on credentials, platform, and permanent organization set to work. When the body reconvened, the credentials committee suggested how best to resolve any disputed delegations in a report that the full convention might vote up or down. The committee on permanent organization issued a roster of officers and rules to guide the proceedings. A platform or set of resolutions appeared articulating a set of sentiments or policies that the organization was for or against. The prominence accorded the platform in their proceedings allowed the parties to reaffirm their devotion to "principles not men." The authors of the partisan manifestos took their duties seriously even if the opposition would routinely dismiss their handiwork as flypaper to catch the unwary voter. References to liquor control or free silver could spark an intense debate in the committee and on the convention floor, exposing internal divisions that needed to be addressed.

Finally it was time for the nominating speeches to elaborate on the many virtues of an array of potential nominees, starting with the top of the ticket. As practical politicians, the delegates desired chiefly to settle on men who would draw in the most votes. They rarely touched on a candidate's record or qualifications for any given office (Bryce 1891, 239). The balloting that followed continued until one individual had amassed a majority of the delegates' votes. (The national Democratic Party and many southern states set the bar at a still higher level, requiring two-thirds of the vote to make a choice.) A motion to make the vote unanimous usually followed the emergence of a winner. If the victor was in the vicinity he might be called upon to make a few remarks briefly expressing his thanks. Losing candidates might also be expected to make another short address reassuring one and all of their full cooperation in the coming campaign. Conventions generally did not have time for so much of the hoopla and speechifying that we associate with national party conventions today. A long-winded acceptance speech was neither solicited nor desired. The delegates were anxious to get back to work filling out the rest of the ticket.

The Quest for Harmony

Throughout the convention's proceedings the goal of harmony remained paramount. It manifested itself in the requirement that the winner secure a majority or more of the vote, in the subsequent motion to officially label the choice unanimous, and in the gracious concession speeches from the also-rans. The major parties relied on additional strategies to secure unity in their ranks. One was to require that the loaves and fishes be widely distributed among the faithful. Nineteenth-century political parties functioned as confederations of locally organized political organizations. Arranging for a ticket with geographical balance was an imperative to incentivize all its constituent parts. "It is very necessary that the Republicans of Delta County should nominate a ticket this fall that is fairly representative throughout the different sections of the county," one Colorado newspaper admonished. "It is but fair – to both the people and the party – that a ticket be selected that the entire Republican organization of the county can feel an interest in and support" (*Delta Independent*, Aug. 12, 1904). Under the "claim of locality" each of the political subdivisions within an election district could expect to nominate one of its own in due time. For each election, a different county within a congressional district might choose a favorite son to go to the nation's capital. Some states had their own unique guidelines that recognized special geographical or political domains. Michigan Republicans for a time awarded the lieutenant governorship to men hailing from its upper peninsula. After women achieved suffrage in Colorado, Democrats and Republicans reserved the post of State Superintendent of Instruction for female candidates (Reynolds 2006, 136, 218). But no political subdivision could expect more than its fair share of offices up for consideration. Much of the discussion taking place on and off the convention floor revolved around achieving this geographical balance. Candidates and their surrogates worked out "trades" whereby delegates backing different candidates for different offices from different regions of the state agreed to mutually support one another. The men cast as political bosses or "wire pullers" at party functions were consummate practitioners in this art of vote swapping. Trading in public offices offended some political observers but was perhaps the surest method for building a winning coalition under the convention system.

The principle of rotation in office was another mechanism for widely disseminating the spoils of victory. Andrew Jackson lauded the practice of term limits as a "leading principle in the republican creed." Officials holding an electoral office with a two-year term might expect to be re-nominated to a second term as a matter of course, but thereafter they were usually expected to step aside and let someone else enjoy the privileges of a public trust (Struble 1979). No political figure was subjected to more ridicule in the press or on the stump than the "chronic office seeker." One Colorado politician allegedly grew "dangerously ill if out of office for ten days at a stretch" (*Rocky Mountain News*, Sept. 10, 1886). The sum effect of conventions attempting to achieve balance and enforce term limits was to bring an abrupt end to many promising political careers. Turnover in the U.S. House of Representatives, state legislatures, and other elective offices was high; few members served more than two terms (Bogue et al. 1976; Kernell 1977). Incumbents desiring an extended stay in elective office had to make their case to a skeptical body of partisans with political aspirations of their own.

Would-be candidates hoping to run under the Democratic or Republican banner in the general election consequently faced an assortment of obstacles and circumstances beyond their control as the convention loomed. The political culture imposed further constraints on ambitious office seekers. A lingering legacy of republican ideology still viewed political ambition as a vice rather than as a virtue. Hence, canvassing for support for a nomination was a low-key affair in most states. Presidential aspirants in particular needed to maintain an aloof indifference to the workings of the nomination process; they would not attend the convention where their name was under consideration. In many northern states would-be governors and other state officials maintained a similarly low profile during the nomination process. They were not expected to appear at the nominating bodies where their names were under consideration. Southern states, on the other hand, appear to have suffered fewer qualms about candidates for major offices making speeches and openly soliciting support. These regional differences in campaign styles may date back to the colonial era (Dinkin 1989, 37–38). When it came to more local offices, however, it was not regarded as unseemly for northern or southern candidates to openly appeal for support. This might be accomplished in the local newspaper with a letter to the editor or perhaps a paid announcement. An 1880 edition of South Carolina's *Charlotte Democrat* included fourteen announcements from men interested in serving in the state legislature, eleven postings from men putting themselves forward for sheriff, and twelve notices from Democrats ready to serve as county commissioner. "Citizens" signed this typically terse communication: "Please suggest as a candidate for coroner the name of C. S. Sturgeon, who is a one legged ex-Confederate soldier and deserves the suffrage of the people" (July 30).

The aloof stance assumed by candidates for offices at the top of the ticket did not necessarily indicate a more virtuous or disinterested mindset. The multi-tiered nominating process severely hampered a candidate's efforts to influence state or national conventions. Delegates to these bodies were customarily selected by other delegates in county or state conventions. The latter set of decision makers were generally much more interested in the local nominations they controlled than in the state or national offices they did not. (This assumes they had no plausible favorite son of their own for one of the coveted state offices.) As noted, the convention system also made it difficult for voters to make their preferences known in the way of candidacies, especially when local party organizations only served up a single unity slate to vote on. Thus, whatever support an office seeker could generate at the grassroots tended to get filtered and diluted at each stage of the delegate selection process. An aspirant for a major party office would be better advised to wait until the caucuses and conventions had concluded. Thereafter he might write friendly letters to the delegates or to persons who might influence them. A different dynamic unfolded for local offices where only one layer of delegates stood between the voters and the candidates. Even here, however, the vox populi could emerge if public attention focused on a specific office, but it was much harder to make itself heard across multiple offices. A single voter was unlikely to find a delegate who concurred on all his choices for the range of offices up for consideration in the county convention. Of course, all this assumes the voter had such preferences and shared them with his party representative. In short, the system was not well designed to allow voters to make their candidate preferences known, and many politicos would have regarded this feature of the convention system as one of its strengths rather than as a weakness.

The nominating process worked best, so it was maintained, when the delegates were untrammeled. A delegation to a county or state convention might still be expected to find a place on the ticket for one of their own, but the matter of which office and which prospective office holder would depend on developments taking place on the convention floor. Thus, candidates during the party period tended to leave their fates "in the hands of their friends." "Your friends can do far more for you than you can do for yourself," James Garfield was advised as the 1880 Republican National Convention approached (Evans 1960, 39). Candidates at all ranks were urged not to meddle with the delegate selection process; let the voters or the county conventions appoint as delegates the wisest and most public spirited and knowledgeable citizens from their ranks. New Jersey's *Burlington Gazette* urged the friends of the various candidates to refrain from interfering with the work of the 1883 county convention. "Enough good men may be found in the Democratic Party of Burlington County who may be sent to the state convention entrusted with the duty of selecting a candidate that shall not only command the vote of every Democrat but shall also gather in those of many Republicans . . . Men have tried to make [the convention] hew wood and draw water for them, but that time, we hope, has passed forever . . . The individual is nothing; party, in a true sense, is everything" (Sept. 1, 1883). The partisan press generally extolled the high caliber of men sent to deliberate at the party's official gatherings and predicted that their collective wisdom and knowledge would elevate men worthy of public trust. Under the convention system, the welfare of the ticket as a whole took precedence over the interests of any one candidate.

The quest for harmony could prove elusive. The source of discord was often the informal, decentralized, loosely administered nominating process itself. Many complaints arose about the poorly publicized "snap caucuses" called on short notice or scheduled for inconvenient times or places. Charges of participation in the primaries and caucuses by persons not affiliated with the party were rife. Alternatively, disappointed office seekers might claim that a convention violated time honored practices or simply ran roughshod over the opposition and did not allow for a fair distribution of the spoils of victory. The rules governing rotation in office or balanced tickets were rarely written down; indeed, as late as 1895 the major parties in about half the states had no written rules at all regarding their nomination practices (Remsen 1895, 38–39). What one side labeled "a time honored custom" might be dismissed by the other as a random pattern of no particular consequence. The major parties did not put much faith in procedural measures to resolve or avoid the controversies that inevitably led to defections on election day. Democrats and Republicans relied instead on outcomes – on the negotiations among the interested parties – to work out a deal that gave everybody a reason to back the ticket.

An aggrieved candidate might successfully appeal the convention's decision to the voters in the general election. Voters arriving at the polls might be presented with two different Democratic tickets to cast, each claiming to be "regular." Since political parties enjoyed no official status in the electoral process for much of the nineteenth century, they were in no position to brand such maverick candidates as apostates. Any enterprising politico could print up a facsimile of his party's ticket and insert his name for any office under consideration. The effect of these independent, partisan candidacies was often to divide the party vote sufficiently to allow a minority party candidate to squeeze in. During the 1880s, at least 21 contests for New Jersey's sixty-seat state assembly contained two or more candidates running under the same party label; bolting candidates amassed on average 12.7 percent of the vote. A disgruntled Democrat might fuse with a third party, such as the Greenback or Labor parties, or even the opposition party. Dissatisfaction with the nomination process often surfaced in the form of split ticket voting, aided and abetted by men at the polls who handed out the ballots or party tickets. While voters displayed strong party loyalty when it came to the top of the ticket, they exhibited a more independent streak when it came to more local races for state representative or county clerk (Reynolds and McCormick 1986). The dominant party had the most to lose when a nomination lost legitimacy, but the dominant party was also in the best position to call on the state's help to address the problem.

The convention system surely had its drawbacks, but it did sustain the major parties throughout most of the nineteenth century. The many conventions required to furnish candidates for numerous elective offices in frequent elections over multiple venues renewed and reinvigorated the party organizations. The debate and passage of resolutions and platforms affirmed that the major parties represented something more than mechanisms to carry elections in the interest of local elites. The convention system was less effective at injecting public opinion into the candidate selection process. The voter's role was to select honest, knowledgeable, and intelligent representatives to participate in the party's deliberations; it was the latter's responsibility to select the candidates. (In this respect, the party convention fulfilled a role the framers of the Constitution had assigned to the Electoral College.) Candidates found their roles severely constrained, especially when it came to prestigious offices at the top of the ticket. Again and again they were reminded to keep their ambitions in check – or at least out of public view; the contest was not supposed to be about them but about the fate of the party and its principles.

The Transition to the Direct Primary

The decision to turn the selection of party candidates over to the voters was a consequence of several developments altering the electoral environment at the close of the nineteenth century. It was the political parties, not the reformer types, who bore chief responsibility for these changes. The shift began when Republicans and Democrats each sought to bring more order to their often disorderly and discordant proceedings. The major parties developed a heightened appreciation for rules and an administrative apparatus to make them stick. In areas characterized by one-party rule there was a movement to leave the selection of local candidates with a party-run primary rather than a county convention. Eventually, when the major parties found the new procedures too unwieldy or costly they turned to the state to shoulder some of the burden of administering these affairs. Elements of the direct primary appeared in bits and pieces beginning in the 1890s. Changes in the delegate selection process made it easier for some candidates – those running for the most visible offices – to manipulate the system on their own behalf. Candidates cast an ever larger shadow over the nomination process.

The earliest state laws governing the nomination process appeared shortly after the Civil War. Informal party practices that worked well enough in rural communities proved unsatisfactory in congested, impersonal, and heterogeneous urban centers, giving rise to numerous complaints of irregularities if not outright fraud (Ware 2002, 204–207). Much of this early legislation was enacted with overwhelming bipartisan support and without much public pressure or controversy. Typically, early statutes criminalized vote fraud in the party-run primaries. California's Republican legislature passed the first such statute bearing on the nomination process in 1866 in the wake of a bitterly contested and even violent sequence of caucuses and conventions. The "Porter Law" established guidelines regarding how primaries and caucuses should be conducted and threatened penalties for party officials who violated them. Like much of the pioneering legislation of its kind, the law was optional, but, significantly, both major parties invoked it when announcing their primaries and conventions for some years to come. Enforcement, however, was notably lax and a source of much complaint in California and elsewhere (Dallinger 1903, 173–198; Merriam et al. 1928, 7–14; Sarasohn 1953, 30). Any charges filed or arrests made before the election were generally dropped thereafter. Lacking much teeth, the laws nonetheless represented an important milestone; here was the first indication that the doings of political parties were not to be viewed as purely private affairs but as actions serving a public purpose and warranting official oversight.

The advent of the official or so-called "Australian" ballot in most states around 1890 put added pressure on the major parties to further delineate their nominating practices (Ware 2002, 31–56). In almost all states the new ballot laws automatically assigned space on the ballot for the nominees of the major parties. Many states stipulated that only "regular" candidates could run with the party's label attached to their name; the names of maverick candidates appeared as "Independent Republicans" or without any partisan designation at all (Reynolds and McCormick 1986). In this respect, the state-printed ballot allowed party officials to protect their brand. But candidates who wished to pass themselves off as the official nominee needed to satisfy county clerks and secretaries of state or perhaps the courts that they had come by their title legitimately. The major party organizations came under pressure to implement standard procedures and to see that they were obeyed.

The evidence of more careful supervision of the nomination process appears in the convention calls published by the state and county committees. Prior to the Progressive Era, announcements merely reported when and where the state and county conventions were to be held. The party organizations in the townships or wards were free to choose their delegates however and whenever they pleased. During the 1890s, the calls became more detailed and uniform in their application. They might dictate that all the delegates to the county convention should be selected at a particular date and time and even identify the schoolhouses or stores or private residences where the voting or caucusing would take place. The proclamations further specified who was authorized to participate in the electoral contests, often requiring a voter to swear that he backed the party's choices in the previous election. The practice of county committees appointing the delegates was officially proscribed. Party rules also cracked down on the custom of delegates bestowing their proxies on whomever they pleased; now the delegation as a whole usually chose any replacements in its ranks unless alternates had already been provided for (Reynolds 2006, 110–123).

The most portentous change for the nominating system came with the demise of the indirect primary. In more and more localities, especially in urban areas, the county convention was dispensed with entirely. The citizenry selected both the nominees for more local offices and the delegates going to the state convention. The elections where these officials were selected were still supervised by the party organizations (Ware 2002, 100–105). Although solid data on voter turnout is scarce, the public appears to have been drawn to these more spirited primary proceedings. The hours for voting expanded over time as did the number of voting sites within wards or townships: all were indications of greater mass participation. A party-run primary was an expensive undertaking: voting places needed to be rented, election officials paid, ballot boxes secured, ballots printed up, and votes counted. Candidates who wished to have their names appear on the primary ballot might be assessed for some of these costs. Leaving the final decision about local candidacies in the hands of the voters provided some measure of protection from charges of "fraud," "foul play," or "machine rule." The system had been in place some half dozen years in Newark, New Jersey when the local Republican leader explained its appeal in 1902: "When the present system was adopted it was a question of expense, but it was decided to do it and save the cost in reducing the expenditures in meetings, parades and such demonstrations. We felt that if we satisfied the people that they had fair and honest primaries it would do more good than the parades." The change proved satisfactory to the citizenry. "It is a fact that we wouldn't go back to the old system if we wanted to," he averred (*Newark Evening News*, Oct. 29, 1902).

As political scientists have long suspected, the appearance of the direct primary was also associated with the greater sectionalism and the reduced party competition that we associate with the "system of 1896" (Schattschneider 1960; Key 1964, 373–377). Factionalism threatened to upend the one-party control that Democrats exercised across the southern states and Republicans exerted elsewhere. Majority parties consequently evidenced greater interest in relying on the direct primary to resolve their internal contests. One-party regimes had both greater means to administer a party-run primary and more to lose when a contentious nomination struggle opened a split in their ranks. Majority parties, as a rule, were more financially secure than their competition and could shoulder the extra costs of organizing an election. Bolters were more likely to appear within the dominant party within a given jurisdiction than the minority. Consequently, we tend to find the early experiments with the party-run direct primary in areas of one-party rule. In Iowa, for example, a survey in 1902 found that Democrats employed primaries in only three of the state's 99 counties; the GOP, which captured 58 percent of the vote for president in 1900, employed the system in 34 counties. Iowa counties relying on the party-run direct primary were also much less competitive than those that adhered to the caucus and convention format (Crossley 1903). A similar pattern unfolded in Republican controlled Michigan where GOP voters selected their local officials in 58 of its 83 counties in 1909 while Democrats did so in only seventeen (Reynolds 2006, 217). Democrats in the Solid South readily took up the reform while their Republican opponents retained the convention. In the states of the former confederacy the primary winner needed to secure a majority of the vote to avoid a run-off election. The second primary effectively served as the general election, rendering the state GOP further impotent (Kousser 1974, 73). Given the sorry state of the Republican Party in the region after 1890, this second, run-off primary effectively substituted for the general election. The laws in the southern states granted the Democratic Party maximum authority in the conduct of their primaries, especially when it came to deciding who could participate. In keeping with the party's racist appeal, the Democratic primary was for whites only in the South, a policy the Supreme Court only overturned in 1944 (Weeks 1948).

As parties dispensed with a layer of organization separating elective office seekers from the electorate, candidates redirected their appeals from a roomful of party notables to the electorate.

The individuals who blazed a new path toward the nomination were those vying to head the ticket. Where it had once been possible for gubernatorial candidates to remain above the fray, the new rules encouraged – and soon demanded – a more active canvas. It was possible now for candidates to field slates of loyal state delegates for the voters to approve, especially in the delegate-rich major cities. Oftentimes these candidate-endorsed tickets competed against an uncommitted slate representing the local party organization. Slates pledged to a specific candidate enjoyed an edge in these contests. What the local party organizations learned again and again was that voters attending a primary were more interested in registering a choice on the head of the ticket than leaving this matter to a bunch of uncommitted delegates. "Everyone has known that I am an aspirant for Governor," asserted California's state treasurer in 1894. "I have made my canvas in the San Joaquin valley and the southern portion of the State. In some of the counties I know that entire delegations could not have been elected had they not been pledged to me." Where the slate backed by the local organization might be studded with various local notables and old wheel horses of the party, the men who appeared on a candidate backed slate were distinguished only for their loyalty and reliability. They were persons prepared to vote at their candidate's command when it came to any issue coming before the convention and more especially on "trades" with candidates for lesser offices. "In regard to the delegates to the state convention," California Governor George C. Pardee advised one local supporter in 1906, "it might be well to get together lists of reliable men in each district, who will 'make good' and 'stay put' . . . [E]verybody who goes on the delegation should understand that he must 'programme' for the head of the ticket clear down the line" (Reynolds 2006, 79, 91).

The fates of candidates for lesser state offices were lost sight of as the primary boiled down to one man's determination to elect a slate of delegates wholly and solely committed to his gubernatorial quest. Under the convention system, it was difficult for a prospective secretary of state or county clerk to elect a slate of devoted delegates outside his own bailiwick. Because they could rarely hope to make their candidacy a priority for the voters, the fate of the many aspirants for places lower on the ticket would be decided at the convention. Here the rules governing geographical balance and rotation might prove decisive. The introduction of the direct primary would have a liberating effect on candidates for lesser offices. It was still difficult for candidates for down-ballot positions to get the voters' attention, but at least they did not have to compete for delegates against candidates for more visible offices. The number of elective office seekers knocking on doors, showing up at social events and posting advertisements increased dramatically. A California newspaper reported how local office seekers "were compelled to be in their buggies almost day and night" during the week preceding Orange County's Republican primaries in 1902 (Reynolds 2006, 73).

There were fewer changes made in the workings of the nominating convention itself, but a subtle shift occurred in its image and function. A deliberative body was becoming a more purely representative one. The delegates were less likely to be lauded for their political acumen or independence and more likely to be dismissed as political hacks. "In practice the delegates to nominating conventions are generally mere pieces on the political chess board," derided New York Governor Charles Evans Hughes, "and most of them might as well be inanimate so far as their effective participation in the choice of candidates is concerned" (Beard 1910, 190). There is evidence that the social status of convention delegates also declined over time (Reynolds 2006, 94). Given their role in sending a body of loyal followers to the proceedings, gubernatorial nominees were in a decidedly stronger position to dictate the rest of the slate. Consequently, conventions became shorter and more perfunctory. Office seekers dominated the proceedings to a degree that would have struck an earlier generation as unseemly. Gubernatorial candidates now attended the convention and delivered a more elaborate acceptance speech. (Still, the taboo proscribing presidential candidates from attending the national convention was not broken until Franklin D. Roosevelt captured the Democratic nomination in 1932.) In short, the outlines of a candidate-dominated electoral order had begun to eclipse the party-centered proceedings of the past.

The key change in nomination practices in the 1890s was the decision to dispense with the county convention in many localities under one-party rule. Candidates for county or municipal offices had to secure the nomination by winning a party administered primary. Prospective gubernatorial nominees challenged the local party establishment with a slate of loyal followers. The decisive battles for the nomination were taking place in the primaries – especially in the major cities – rather than on the convention floor. Competition was rising and the major political parties were not well equipped to respond. The informal rules and customs governing the conduct of primaries and caucuses could not handle the added pressure. The number of disputed delegations showing up at state and county conventions increased even as more and more regulations bearing on the nomination process piled up (Reynolds 2006, 154–155). Voter participation was on the upswing and the electorate was developing a sense that they should have a say at least when it came to selecting the individuals whose names would appear at the top of the ticket. By 1900, the need for a major overhaul of the nomination process was evident to party officials as well as more independent-minded reformers.

The Adoption of Direct Primary Legislation

A fully realized direct primary system had three elements that did not come together until the Progressive Era: (1) it was administered by the government rather than the political parties; (2) it was mandatory for all major parties; and (3) it was statewide in coverage and applied to most elective offices. By this standard, Wisconsin is properly credited with enacting the first such statute in 1903 (Lovejoy 1941). By the time the nation entered World War I, hardly more than a decade later, all but a handful of states had followed suit (Wolfe 1966, 1). What popular support primary reform enjoyed among the general public could be attributed to the earnest efforts of intellectuals, journalists, and political gadflies. For many of its warmest advocates, the appeal of the direct primary was less rooted in its democratic tendencies than its promised "purifying" effect on the body politic. A direct primary, in their view, would draw more of the "better element" to the polls and ensure the selection of a higher caliber of public official. But it would be easy to exaggerate the amount of influence reformers exerted on public opinion, much less on the individuals who actually crafted and passed the legislation. Close observers of the movement for the direct primary have characterized its support among the citizenry as broad but not deep (Sarasohn 1953, 161). Former Wisconsin Governor Emanuel L. Philipp firmly denied there was any pressing public demand for the measure. He characterized the direct primary as a necessary measure given "the impossibility of continuing to do party business in an orderly manner in mass caucuses in congested municipal wards" (Philipp 1973, 10). Other party leaders, and elective office holders in particular, had reasons of their own to endorse the direct primary, and they were in a better position than the reformers to make sure it worked to their advantage.

"A decade ago the ballot reformer was much in evidence," noted one political commentator in 1898. "To-day his younger brother proclaims the need of pure primaries. Then, an officially regulated election was announced as the harbinger of our political millennium. Now, with that millennium as far away as before, we are told that the trouble was not with the election, but with the caucus" (Hotchkiss 1898, 583). The convening of the "National Conference on the Practical Reform of Primary Elections" in 1898 marks the inception of the public crusade for the direct primary (Ware 2002, 81–84). The Chicago Civic Federation issued the call for the conference after concluding that any change it wished to see in municipal administration could only be accomplished "through the purification and utilization of the party primaries." It invited municipal officials as well as "practical and political reform workers." Participants shared their experiences and frustrations with their diverse systems of party nomination. Most attendees expected the political parties to take the necessary steps to amend their candidate selection processes, but some proposals envisioned a larger role for the public sector. There was considerable interest in the system of direct nominations already in place in Cleveland and elsewhere, but no guidelines or best practices emerged from the event.

A twin set of concerns expressed at the conference reflected the different perspectives of partisan-minded political operatives versus more independent mugwump types. The latter group might be described as democratic in their approach only to the extent to which they wished to see more respectable, middle- and upper-class citizens participating in the process. Immigrant and working-class voters dominated the caucuses and primaries, so it was claimed, because so few of the "better element" turned out for these events. Corrupt political machines employed fair means and foul through their control of the nomination process to fend off challengers. Civic-minded citizens knew that the system was rigged, reformers averred, hence their decision not to participate was entirely understandable. The same citizens would flock to the polls if they knew their votes would be honestly counted by election officials who were not beholden to a corrupt political boss. A telegram to the conference from Assistant Secretary of the Navy Theodore Roosevelt nicely framed the issue from the reformers' perspective: "The problem . . . is very largely how to stir reputable citizens up to their duties, and to make those duties easy to perform, while at the same time depriving the less reputable portion of the community both of the chance to commit frauds in politics" and the chance to be rewarded for doing so. Party officials and elective office holders, on the other hand, expressed their own unhappiness with a system that generated ill will and internal division. They were in search of a cure for "the mischiefs of faction." Significantly, all sides agreed that the end result of reforming nominating practices would be to rejuvenate the major parties. A former Republican County committeeman from New York City expressed the sentiment that had brought many career politicians to the conference:

> I say, as a party man, that it is the true interest of each party to make honest, straight primaries the possibility, and to render it impossible . . . to accomplish any result by fraud. The cleaner the primary the stronger the organization.
> *National Conference on the Practical Reform of Primary Elections 1898, 86, 30, 109*

In the years that followed, the direct primary won swift and relatively uncontroversial approval from state to state. What opposition the direct primary encountered inside state legislatures chiefly aligned along an urban/rural axis. Rustic legislators understood that the apportionment rules in state conventions gave them greater clout than they could expect if governors or members of congress were selected by counting votes. "Should this bill become law," warned one countrified Michigan legislator in 1903, "Detroit, Grand Rapids and one or two other cities in the lower peninsula could and would dominate state politics" (Reynolds 2006, 220). Given the suspicions of many rural legislators, it often proved easier to inaugurate direct nominations for county and local races, leaving district and state offices to be covered later. In many states the earliest legislation applied only to a specific municipality after one or both of its local political parties requested it (Merriam et al. 1928, 61–68; Hein 1957; Pollock 1943, 1). The progress of the reform from state to state could be slowed by numerous weighty matters entailed in its implementation. What restrictions beyond suffrage should be imposed for participating in a party primary? Should the procedure apply to U.S. Senate seats? What proportion of the vote did the winner need to secure? While intense negotiations over these vital "details" sometimes stymied passage here and there for a time, no-one doubted that the nominating convention was a relic of the past.

Perhaps the most controversial issue associated with the direct primary concerned the criteria for certifying a winner. One of the saving graces of the convention system was its requirement that the victor amass a majority of the vote. Some politicians worried that requiring only a plurality of the vote in a primary might saddle a party with a candidate lacking sufficiently broad appeal. Setting the bar at 40 percent of the vote to qualify as the nominee satisfied some of these skeptics, while others required a convention or run-off primary when no candidate outpolled all his opponents combined (Horack 1921, 94; Dunn 1912, 439). The run-off feature was especially popular in the South (Merriam et al. 1928, 74). Ten states sought to ascertain the wishes of a majority of the electors through a preferential primary whose ballot allowed voters to rank their candidate preferences for each office. When no candidate had the support of a majority of the voters, their second-choice selections were tabulated, and if no majority winner emerged there, it was on to their third choice, etc. The preferential primary epitomized the reformers' vision of a discerning citizenry eager to fully exercise their suffrage rights. Experience with the proviso proved disappointing; few voters took the opportunity to rank their preferences for anything more than their top choice for any office. The provision was soon abandoned everywhere it was tried (Martin 1947, 114). The principle of "first past the post" was the most common selection device in the earliest legislation, and it became more popular in time.

Later scholars would wonder why the major party organizations, most fully embodied by the nominating convention, allowed direct primary legislation to put them out of business (Ware 2002, 196–199). Of course, it was not as if these ephemeral conclaves had much of a say in the matter. But more importantly, a state takeover of their nominating functions had tangible benefits for the major parties themselves. Government responsibility for conducting the primaries lifted a sizeable financial burden off their shoulders. Other features of the laws took aim at the maverick candidates who sowed havoc in the general election. Some states enacted "sore loser" rules that prohibited candidates who lost in the primary from running for the same office in the general election (Petersen 1972, 373; Argersinger 1984, 507). Most of the early direct primaries stipulated that they be closed to all but party members, a policy that became more widespread over time (Merriam et al. 1928, 74). This principle had not been strictly observed when political parties ran their own primaries, in part because there were no clear guidelines conferring party membership. Now, new laws on the statute books required voters to declare a party affiliation when they registered or else forfeit their opportunity to participate in the nomination process. Independent-minded voters were greatly annoyed to find themselves frozen out of the nomination process. In short, state regulation offered an opportunity for the major parties to better control their membership and resist assaults from outsiders.

Democratic and Republican legislators and political incumbents in general found even more to their liking in the new statutes. Some states delegated authority for framing the party platform to their certified nominees instead of a body of party officials; the party stood for whatever its candidates said it did (Boots 1922). Longstanding party practices aimed at countering the influence of incumbency did not make it into the statute books. No effort was made to institutionalize the principles of term limits or rotation in office. Nor was there any requirement for geographical balance that had previously brought an end to many promising political careers. Office holders could exploit the many advantages of incumbency, which explains both the popularity of the direct primary in legislative circles and the decline in turnover of elected officials at about this time (Bogue et al. 1976). Now name recognition reinforced with a steady stream of advertising provided officeholders with formidable weapons to ward off challengers. "Direct primaries liberated the congressman from the caucus and allowed him to employ proven campaign skills and the resources of office to maximum advantage," notes one scholar. "Campaign experience, recognition, franking privileges, and diligent constituent service gave the incumbent . . . a competitive edge . . ." (Kernell 1977, 677). As one Illinois politician remarked with some hyperbole in 1912: "Under this primary law it is practically impossible to defeat the governor . . . if he uses his office to renominate himself" (Pegram 1992, 170). State primary laws would be constantly revised in the years to come to serve the short-term interests of influential public officials (Merriam et al. 1928, 68; Pollock 1943, 5). This pattern coincided with a general trend lengthening the terms of governors and other state officials from to two to four years (Argersinger 1984, 496). A measure ostensibly designed to empower the voters was quickly put to use to protect the interests of elective office holders.

Several states introduced a presidential primary during the Progressive Era, but early experiments with the device were not so encouraging. Consequently, the presidential primary system took longer to take hold. Only half the states had a presidential primary by 1916, and over the next 40 years eight states abandoned the feature (Argersinger 1984, 508). The bitterly contested Republican presidential primaries in 1912 between Theodore Roosevelt and William Howard Taft did little to unify the party. When another series of contentious Republican contests ensued in 1920 the front runners met with widespread condemnation for the very considerable sums of money necessarily spent on their behalf (Baker 2012, 147). But the most important factor limiting the impact of the presidential primary was the reluctance of state leaders to surrender control of the national delegation to an outsider. Thus many of these early presidential primaries were purely "beauty contests" – where the delegates were not bound to support the winner. The question of who attended the national convention and who the attendees voted for was still left largely in the hands of the state party organizations. It was only in the 1960s that candidates began using victories in the New Hampshire or Wisconsin primaries as springboards to the White House.

Given the exorbitant hopes many invested in the direct primary, it was inevitable that some would express disappointment with its workings. This was especially the case among the reform elements who placed so much faith in the civic spirit of the "better citizens." They proved largely willing to assume the duties of discerning convention delegates. Voter turnout plainly did increase under the direct primary, but this was largely a response to the heightened competition that pushed parties to adopt the measure. No-one pretended that the caliber of elected officials had improved much or that government had become notably less corrupt or more efficient. Other developments, like the disappointing experience with the preferential primaries, indicated that voters were not so very engaged in the electoral process. This was especially the case with down-ballot races. Political observers noted how candidates whose names appeared first on the primary ballot for a given office reaped a bigger share of the vote; election officials attempted to mitigate the effect by rotating the candidate listings (Merriam et al. 1928, 80). But this was not the first nor the last electoral reform that failed to live up to expectations. Soon the reform press moved on to tout the virtues of the short ballot or the direct election of United States Senators.

One new preoccupation of the political intelligentsia would be campaign finance reform – a problem the direct primary greatly exacerbated, even if it did not invent it. In retrospect, it is astonishing to come across predictions that a state-administered primary would put the man of modest means on equal footing with an opponent with deep pockets. But the vexing problem of money in politics pre-dated the direct primary. After all, pursuing a nomination under the convention system always entailed some not inconsiderable costs. Prospective candidates were hounded by newspapers and local politicos demanding a hand out in one form or another. Delegates were known to have a soft spot for the rich candidate who was prepared to donate lavishly to party coffers. The *Detroit Free Press* complained in 1882:

> If a candidate for governor is to be selected – in either party – the first question is, "Can he afford to run?" If he has no money to spend or no moneyed friends to spend it for him, and thereby establish a lien on him, he is set aside, no matter what his qualifications may be or even what his availability in a partisan sense may be . . . It is the same thing on a smaller scale if the office in question is that of alderman.
>
> *Aug. 11, 1882*

Public concern over the use of money in elections only mounted when the hustling candidate arrived on the scene. In 1902 the Republican delegates attending their Barry County Convention in Michigan denounced "the use of money to pack caucuses or control conventions in the interest of any candidate for office." Such practices were "unjust, unfair, un-Republican, accomplishing the debauchery of the citizenship and the degradation of our public life." The solution, they concluded, was the direct primary (*Detroit Free Press*, June 10, 1902).

Advertising would drive up the costs of campaigning under the new nomination system, but this problem was not readily apparent to the reform's early supporters. At the 1898 national convention called to consider changes in nominating practices, a Cleveland politician with some experience with the direct primary warned that the system

> gives an opportunity for an immense use of money . . . Candidates seem to proceed upon the theory that the people are only waiting to vote for any person for any position, without regard to fitness or ability, and that ready success lies in a vigorous advertising campaign.
>
> *National Conference on the Practical Reform of Primary Elections 1898, 101*

The import of his comments did not register with his listeners. "It is only when candidates get to spending money freely with leading party workers that the cost grows," one apostle of the direct primary assured the National Municipal League, "and this is not a necessary expense nor is it a fault peculiar to the system" (Hempstead 1901, 206). It took a little time for the law's repercussions to become apparent. When Missouri's direct primary was introduced in 1908, many candidates did not know how it worked or how to adapt their canvassing practices accordingly. Some scorned the expense of newspaper advertising and confined their efforts at publicity to "a modest card or portrait." Most office seekers mounted a conventional "man to man canvass, day and night, in streetcars, on street corners, in offices, lodge meetings, [and] public picnics . . ." Three years later, however, a political observer reported a notable change in campaign tactics whereby "the first thing sought is publicity" (Blair 1911, 428). States sought to curb runaway election expenses with corrupt practices acts and other legislation seeking to impose limits on campaign expenditures (Baker 2012). Whatever good these laws accomplished was undermined by the hard fact that candidates had to raise funds for two elections instead of one. The intractable problem of money in politics was arguably the most significant of the "unintended consequences" that attended the adoption of the direct primary.

The Aftermath

While there was a palpable movement to revive the nominating conventions in a few states during the 1920s (Merriam et al. 1928, 95), the direct primary endured. It flourished because it allowed the "hustling candidates" coming to the fore in the 1890s to design a nominating process that best accommodated their more proactive style of electioneering. In later years scholars would blame the direct primary for fostering the more candidate-centered campaign style of the twentieth century. For better or worse, the focus on personalities rather than parties is regarded as one of the distinguishing features of the American electoral system. It is certainly true that the multi-tiered convention system of the nineteenth century made it more difficult for office seekers to dominate the nomination process. But the convention system was starting to break down well before Wisconsin did away with it. Various steps the parties took during the 1880s and 1890s to stamp out vote fraud and bring some order to their decentralized and disorderly nominating practices paved the way for intervention from the state. Given the control the major parties exercised over the governmental apparatus, state regulation amounted to little more than self-regulation in the interests of office holders or at least office seekers. The shift to the direct primary is best understood as an accommodation to an electoral environment where candidates for the most visible offices were taking center stage. The one group that clearly most benefitted by the new nomination system were incumbents – the very people who enacted the laws in the first place.

The direct primary was part of a broader restructuring of the electoral system that amounted to "cutting out the middle man." The adoption of the official or Australian ballot around 1890 put an end to the small army of ticket peddlers who manned the polls on election day. The mobilization campaigns that called for a vast network of party committees to get out the vote would be replaced by "educational" or advertising campaigns relying instead on the mass media (McGerr 1986; Dinkin 1989, 95–126). Like the direct primary, the direct election of United States Senators starting in 1914 represented a transfer of power from the party elite (state legislators) to its electoral base. Civil service reform removed another incentive for lower level politicos to find employment for the party organization's most loyal warriors. The consequence of these measures was to shift power from the party organization to its elected office holders. The roots the major parties had embedded in the electorate withered somewhat in the Progressive Era. Nonpartisan or independent political movements flourished. But thanks to the direct primary and similar legislation, the major parties and their candidates were now more deeply entrenched in the electoral apparatus than ever before.

References

Argersinger, Peter H. 1984. "Electoral Processes." In *Encyclopedia of American Political History*. Ed. Jack P. Greene. 489–512. New York: Charles Scribner's Sons.

Baker, Paula. 2012. *Curbing Campaign Cash: Henry Ford, Truman Newberry, and the Politics of Progressive Reform*. Lawrence, KS: University Press of Kansas.

Beard, Charles A. 1910. "The Direct Primary in New York." *Proceedings of the American Political Science Association* 7: 187–198.

Bernheim, A. C. 1888. "Party Organizations and Their Nominations to Public Office in New York City." *Political Science Quarterly* 3 (1): 99–122.

Blair, Emily Newell. 1911. "Every Man His Own Campaign Manager." *The Outlook*, Feb. 25, pp. 426–33.

Bogue, Alan G., Jerome M. Clubb, Carroll R. McKibbin, and Santa A. Traugott. 1976. "Members of the House of Representatives and the Process of Modernization, 1789–1960." *Journal of American History* 63 (3): 291–305.

Boots, Ralph Simpson. 1922. "The Trend of the Direct Primary." *American Political Science Review* 16 (3): 412–431.

Bryce, James. 1891. *The American Commonwealth.* 2 Vols. 2nd Edition. London: Macmillan and Co.

Crossley, James Judson. 1903. "The Regulation of Primary Elections by Law." *Iowa Journal of History and Politics* 1 (1): 165–192.

Dallinger, Frederick W. 1903. *Nominations for Elective Office in the United States.* New York: Longmans, Green, and Co.

Dinkin, Robert J. 1989. *Campaigning in America: A History of Election Practices.* New York: Greenwood Press.

Dunn, Arthur Wallace. 1912. "The Direct Primary: Promise and Performance." *Review of Reviews* 46 (3): 439–445.

Evans, Frank B. 1960. "Wharton Barker and the Republican Convention of 1880." *Pennsylvania History* 27 (1): 28–43.

Hein, Clarence J. 1957. "The Adoption of Minnesota's Direct Primary Law." *Minnesota History* 35 (2): 341–351.

Hempstead, Ernest A. 1901. "The Crawford County or Direct Primary System." In *Proceedings of the Rochester Conference for Good City Government and the Seventh Annual Meeting of the National Municipal League.* Ed. Clinton Rogers Woodruff. Philadelphia, PA: National Municipal League, pp. 197–217.

Horack, Frank Edward. 1921. "The Operation of the Primary Election Law in Iowa." *The Iowa Journal of History and Politics* 19 (1): 94–124.

Hotchkiss, William H. 1898. "The Movement for Better Primaries." *Review of Reviews* 17 (2): 583–589.

Keller, Morton. 1977. *Affairs of State, Public Life in Late Nineteenth Century America.* Cambridge, MA: Belknap Press.

Kernell, Samuel. 1977. "Toward Understanding Nineteenth Century Congressional Careers: Ambition, Competition and Rotation." *American Journal of Political Science* 21 (4): 669–693.

Key, V. O. Jr. 1964. *Politics, Parties and Pressure Groups.* 5th ed. New York: Crowell.

Kousser, J. Morgan. 1974. *The Shaping of Southern Politics, Suffrage Restriction and the Establishment of the One-Party South, 1880–1910.* New Haven, CT: Yale University Press.

Lovejoy, Allen Fraser. 1941. *Robert M. LaFollette and the Establishment of the Direct Primary in Wisconsin, 1890–1904.* New Haven, CT: Yale University Press.

Martin, Boyd A. 1947. *The Direct Primary in Idaho.* Stanford, CA: Stanford University Press.

McCormick, Richard P. 1966. *The Second American Party System: Party Formation in the Jacksonian Era.* Chapel Hill, NC: University of North Carolina Press.

McGerr, Michael E. 1986. *The Decline of Popular Politics: The American North, 1865–1928.* New York: Oxford University Press.

Merriam, Charles Edward, Harold F. Gosnell, and Louise Overacker. 1928. *Primary Elections.* Chicago, IL: University of Chicago Press.

National Conference on the Practical Reform of Primary Elections. 1898. *Proceedings of the National Conference on the Practical Reform of Primary Elections, January 20 and 21, 1898.* Chicago: W. C. Hollister.

Noble, Ransom E. 1946. *New Jersey Progressivism Before Wilson.* Princeton, NJ: Princeton University Press.

Pegram, Thomas R. 1992. *Partisans and Progressives: Private Interest and Public Policy in Illinois, 1870–1922.* Urbana: University of Illinois Press.

Petersen, Eric Falk. 1972. "The Adoption of the Direct Primary in California." *Southern California Quarterly* 54 (4): 363–378.

Philipp, Emanuel L. 1973. *Political Reform in Wisconsin: A Historical Review of the Subjects of Primary Election, Taxation, and Railway Regulation.* Madison: State Historical Society of Wisconsin.

Pollock, James K. 1943. *The Direct Primary in Michigan 1909–1935,* No. 14 University of Michigan Governmental Studies. Ann Arbor: University of Michigan Press.

Ranney, Austin. 1975. *Curing the Mischiefs of Faction, Party Reform in America.* Berkeley: University of California Press.

Remsen, Daniel S. 1895. *Primary Elections, A Study for Improving the Basis of Party Organization.* New York: G. P. Putnam's Sons.

Reynolds, John F. 2006. *The Demise of the American Convention System, 1880–1911.* Cambridge, U.K.: Cambridge University Press.

Reynolds, John F., and Richard L. McCormick. 1986. "'Outlawing Treachery': Split Tickets and Ballot Laws in New York and New Jersey, 1880–1914," *Journal of American History* 72 (3): 835–858.

Sarasohn, Stephen C. 1953. "The Regulation of Parties and Nominations in Michigan: The Politics of Election Reform." Unpublished Ph.D. dissertation, Columbia University.

Schattschneider, E. E. 1960. *The Semi-Sovereign People, A Realist's View of Democracy in America*. New York: Holt, Rinehart and Winston.

Silbey, Joel H. 1991. *The American Political Nation, 1838–1893*. Stanford, CA: Stanford University Press.

Sorauf, Frank. J. 1972. *Party Politics in America*. 2nd ed. Boston, MA: Little, Brown.

Struble, Robert. 1979. "House Turnover and the Principle of Rotation." *Political Science Quarterly* 94 (4): 649–667.

Ware, Alan. 2002. *The American Direct Primary, Party Institutionalization and Transformation in the North*. Cambridge, UK: Cambridge University Press.

Weeks, O. Douglas. 1948. "The White Primary: 1944–1948." *American Political Science Review* 42 (3): 500–510.

Wicker, Tom. 1992. "Let Some Smoke In." *New York Times Magazine*, June 14, p. 34.

Wolfe, Arthur Coffman. 1966. "The Direct Primary in American Politics." Unpublished Ph.D. dissertation, University of Michigan.

3

CANDIDATE EMERGENCE IN THE ERA OF DIRECT PRIMARIES

Jamie L. Carson and Ryan D. Williamson

Scholars of congressional elections typically focus most of their attention on the general election that occurs in November (see, e.g., Jacobson and Carson 2016). Nevertheless, congressional candidates that choose to run for elective office in the modern era have to get past two distinct hurdles – the primary and general election. Although primaries are the first stage in the winnowing process for candidates, they have only been around for about 100 years, depending on the state. Prior to the adoption of direct primaries in the early twentieth century, local and state parties were largely responsible for deciding which candidates would appear on the ballot in U.S. House races. This method of candidate selection eventually fell out of favor during the Progressive Era as a result of high levels of corruption and declining levels of electoral competition. In conjunction with a variety of electoral reforms such as the Australian ballot and voter registration that took place in the late nineteenth century, the implementation of direct primaries gave voters greater input in which candidates would run in the general election.

In this chapter, we analyze the effect that adoption of the direct primaries had on electoral competition in the *general* election via the emergence of experienced House candidates to better illustrate whether this reform legislation ultimately produced "better" candidates. We begin with a brief discussion outlining how congressional elections operated prior to the adoption of direct primary reform that was designed to increase citizen participation in the candidate selection process. We then discuss direct primaries in conjunction with the Progressive movement before systematically analyzing the consequences of changing the method for selecting candidates for office. Our findings indicate that this reform effort – though not solely responsible for the gradual decline in electoral competition or experienced candidate emergence in House general elections during this time – had the unintended effect of enabling weak candidates to represent their party. This, in turn, increased the probability of incumbent success, which served to further reduce overall levels of electoral competition. Finally, we conclude with a discussion of the implications our results have for the current state of primary elections as well as for future research on the topic.

Congressional Elections in the 1800s

Congressional elections held during the nineteenth century were very different affairs from what we are accustomed to in the modern era. As Kernell (1977, 672) describes, "Our image of congressional elections during this period is one of fiercely combative affairs which by modern standards produced intense voter interest, large turnout, and close elections." Politics in this era were extremely volatile as well. The populace was ever shifting, and elections were "characterized by high levels of partisanship and electoral competitiveness, and slight shifts in voting or turnout could turn whole elections" (Argersinger 1985, 671). Unlike the relatively lengthy and stable careers that most representatives have today, very few legislators during this period viewed service in the U.S. House as a long-term career. Following the norm or practice of "rotation" in office throughout the early part of the nineteenth century, most legislators would serve one or two terms in the House before exiting the chamber (Kernell 1977). As a result of norms like rotation and the greater competitiveness of elections, there was considerably more turnover in the lower chamber of Congress than we typically see today (Polsby 1968).

In light of this increased turnover in the U.S. House, candidate recruitment practices in the late nineteenth century were starkly different as well. Prior to the early 1890s, candidates were selected for inclusion on party ballots by "whatever practices party leaders thought appropriate" (Boatright 2013). As such, it would be appropriate to characterize this era as the height of power for political parties and party machines. One of the key means of influencing elections for party bosses was through candidate recruitment. Unlike modern era elections, which are often candidate centered, these elections were much more likely to be oriented around partisan goals. Here, state and local machines selected the candidates that would run for U.S. House seats. In order to receive the support of these bosses, one would have to demonstrate loyalty to the party. Bosses also sought to recruit candidates who could in turn recruit supporters for the party more broadly. This ultimately resulted in U.S. House members who were beholden to party bosses and the local machines instead of constituencies, however.[1]

Party machines were especially effective in recruiting candidates for office because they were also successful in funding candidates selected to run for House seats. Candidates in the modern era must assume certain risks – principally financial – when pursuing elective office. If they are not independently wealthy, they may be forced to take out a second mortgage on their home, drain their retirement account, or rely on the support of friends and family to fund their campaigns. However, political machines were able to largely negate these risks during this era by assuming the costs of campaigning, which they were willing to do in exchange for a loyal surrogate in Congress. If their preferred candidate was not as faithful as expected, the machine could simply offer its support to a more promising candidate during the next electoral season.

Candidates today must contend with another risk when pursuing a seat in the U.S. House of Representatives – opportunity costs in the form of losing whatever position they currently hold. A sitting member of the state legislature often must weigh the possibility of losing power and prestige against their probability of winning and therefore gaining a more prestigious position at the next level. However, during the nineteenth century, party bosses largely negated this cost as well. Candidates were essentially guaranteed some position in government regardless of how the election turned out. If they were successful in their bid for office, they received all of the benefits typically associated with being a member of Congress. However, if a candidate were to fail in his or her bid to win a seat, the party bosses could still offer that candidate a patronage position. Again, the party machines were willing to conduct their affairs in this manner because doing so provided them with a loyal surrogate within the U.S. House of Representatives (Carson and Roberts 2013).

The ability to not only underwrite congressional campaigns but also provide insurance to those who did not win the election provided parties with considerable power in recruiting candidates for office (Carson and Roberts 2013). This produced incredibly high levels of party support in Congress and led to significantly more competitive House elections. It simultaneously resulted in regular allegations of corruption and calls for a more democratic process, however, since party machines engaged in a variety of corrupt practices in an effort to win these more competitive races (Bensel 2004; Summers 2004; Ware 2002). Progressive Era reforms, including the adoption of the direct primary, were one of a series of proposals to remedy the situation by reducing the power of party bosses and making representatives more responsive and accountable to voters.

Progressive Era Reforms

The Progressive Era was born of a desire to reduce the power of party machines. Ideally, by reducing their power, government would become less corrupt and the electoral system would become more democratic. As has been detailed in previous works, the direct primary was one of numerous reforms witnessed by the United States during this era (on this point, see Ansolabehere et al. 2010; Boatright 2013; Merriam 1908; Merriam and Overacker 1928; Ware 2002) with one of the main goals of the movement – providing for a more democratic process of electing federal officials – in mind. By making voters directly responsible for selecting candidates, this reform would also serve to cripple the power of political parties, particularly party bosses, which would serve to reduce corruption in the selection process and the government more broadly.

Direct primaries were first adopted in Oregon and Minnesota in 1901. The last states to adopt the direct primary during the Progressive Era were West Virginia, Vermont, and Indiana in 1915. States such as Utah, New Mexico, Rhode Island, and Connecticut ultimately would not adopt this system until after the 1930s (Lawrence, Donovan, and Bowler 2011). This stands in stark contrast to two other Progressive Era reforms passed during this era. For example, the first state to adopt the Australian ballot was Massachusetts in 1888. But by the 1892 elections, the rest of the country had implemented the change as well. Similarly, the Eighteenth Amendment, which prohibited the manufacture and sale of alcohol and was widely considered as a progressive initiative at the time, took less than 18 months to ratify. The Senate Resolution passed the chamber on August 1, 1917, and Nebraska would ratify the amendment on January 16, 1919, finally eclipsing the necessary threshold for adoption.

The adoption of both the Australian ballot and Eighteenth Amendment also stood to curb the power of political parties and bosses. Without having voters cast a party ballot out in the open, as had previously been the case throughout the nineteenth century, political elites no longer had a means of enforcing existing norms by insuring compliance from citizens. Additionally, and since the early days of the republic, politicians had a long-standing tradition of wooing voters with free alcohol in exchange for their support on the day of the election. However, by making the consumption of alcohol illegal and placing a social stigma on it, candidates and the political machines that supported them lost a valuable tool they could employ while campaigning. Despite this, both measures were adopted quickly and easily by the individual states relative to the time it took to fully implement the direct primary.

This has spurred some debate over the ease of passage of the direct primary within states. Some would point to the relatively rapid adoption of the Australian ballot as anomalous, given how rare changes to electoral institutions can be (North 1990). Merriam and Overacker (1928) contend that the direct primary was a result of external pressures on those within the political parties. Reformists lobbied hard and managed to slowly push the change throughout the country, which has a certain intuitive appeal given the motivations behind the reform. Additionally, some of the first states to adopt the measure (between 1901 and 1905) were those where populist sentiments were the highest – Oregon, North and South Dakota, Montana – or where

Progressive politicians such as Robert La Follete were most prominent (Wisconsin in 1903 and Minnesota in 1905, for example). Conversely, New York – home of arguably the most infamous political machines in Tammany Hall – was one of the last states to implement this reform. Voters in New York would not get to participate in a direct primary until 1913.

Ware (2002) offers an alternative perspective, however, in his discussion of the American direct primary. He suggests that internal party pressures brought about electoral change, and that party leaders found a way to make the direct primary process work to their benefit. This account certainly has a specific appeal, given previous research demonstrating that institutional rules are more likely to undergo some sort of evolution if political elites are somehow advantaged by the change (see, e.g., Benoit 2004; Boix 1999; Grofman 1990; Rokkan 1970). Additionally, and as Key (1954) demonstrated, the direct primary could have allowed the majority party in a state to weaken the minority party and therefore perpetuate their one-party dominance. This is bolstered by the fact that primary laws would eventually be used by Democrats in southern states to disenfranchise African-Americans (Alilunas 1940; Overacker 1945).[2] Furthermore, as Ware (2002) points out, favorable public opinion alone is not a sufficient condition for implementing changes to existing political institutions, which is likely to be especially true for something as prominent as the candidate selection process.

More recently, Lawrence, Donovan, and Bowler (2011) have attempted to reconcile these differences in the development of primary elections and ultimately conclude that there is support for both arguments in the literature. Nevertheless, they continue by arguing that "the weight of our evidence supports the idea that rules changed in response to anti-party reform pressures" (Lawrence, Donovan, and Bowler 2011, 4). In addition to weighing in on the development of direct primaries, their work is also indicative of a growing body of research that focuses less on general elections in favor of explaining primary election outcomes. This budding area of research has resulted in conclusions that not only challenge conventional wisdom or popular narratives, but they also challenge each other at times – as demonstrated by competing narratives offered by Merriam and Overacker (1928) and Ware (2002).

Primaries in the Modern Era

Boatright (2013) was among the first to systematically analyze primary elections for both the U.S. House and Senate in a book-length treatment. He provides an in-depth look at several factors related to primary campaigns and demonstrates that primary challenges are quite rare, and successful ones even more so. This stands in stark contrast to the common narrative found in the media that an increasing number of candidates are "getting primaried" in contemporary House elections. Rather, Boatright argues that several high-profile cases of incumbents losing their primary has led the news media to focus more attention on these cases despite the fact that the number of incumbents defeated in primaries has remained relatively stable since World War II. Boatright also challenges the assertion, often perpetuated by the media, that congressional primaries are leading members of Congress to be more ideological, which then increases political polarization in Congress.

If we focus on the number of departures from the U.S. House as displayed in Table 3.1, we see that between 2000 and 2016 no more than 13 incumbents were defeated in any one year's primary elections. However, the election with the most defeated incumbents (2012) occurred immediately after a redistricting cycle, which resulted in eight incumbent defeats at the hands of other incumbents who had been drawn into the same district. General elections still provide consistently greater opportunities to unseat incumbents. Furthermore, and as the data in Table 3.1 clearly reveal, the most common means of incumbents leaving the House of Representatives is

Table 3.1 Number of U.S. House Incumbent Departures

Year	Primary Election Defeat	General Election Defeat	Retirement
2000	2	6	30
2002	6	8	36
2004	3	7	28
2006	2	22	27
2008	4	19	33
2010	4	54	37
2012	13	27	40
2014	4	13	38
2016	6	8	43

through retirement. Those most likely to face a serious challenger are incumbents who are vulnerable either through scandal or unfavorable national tides. But those same incumbents are generally politically savvy enough to recognize this, and therefore choose to pursue something else instead of taking the risk of losing an election. If they were forced to seek reelection, the numbers in the first two columns would likely be significantly greater.

Boatright (2013) was not the first scholar to explore candidate emergence in the context of congressional primary elections. In an earlier paper, Banks and Kiewiet (1989) examine the issue of why most incumbents are challenged in primary elections. As they note, experienced or high quality challengers are often deterred by the presence of incumbents and are more likely to run in open seat contests, but candidates that are considered "low" quality or political amateurs are not. In examining this unusual phenomenon, Banks and Kiewiet argue that low quality candidates often run against incumbents to maximize their chances of getting elected. Since high quality challengers are much more likely to win when there is no incumbent present, low quality candidates recognize that challenging an incumbent gives them the best probability, albeit small, of winning the election.

In terms of legislative behavior, Brady, Han, and Pope (2007) demonstrate that members of Congress face a dilemma when seeking reelection. They seek to better understand whether it is more advantageous to appeal to one's primary constituency, or whether incumbents should be more concerned with positioning themselves with general election voters in mind. They argue that members will more commonly align themselves closer to the former than the latter for two main reasons. First, the low turnout rates commonly seen in primary elections foster an environment in which a small number of ideologically extreme voters can sway the outcome in favor of the candidate closest to them. As such, they conclude, it is in the best interest of the incumbent to try to be that candidate whenever possible. Second, they also conclude that ideologically moderate incumbents are more likely to draw a primary challenger (*ibid.*, 98–99).[3]

However, Hall (2015) offers a different conclusion in the context of his study of primary elections. He contends that general election voters "punish the nomination of extreme candidates from contested primaries, on average" (*ibid.*, 32). In fact, the extent of the punishment is so severe that there is an observable ideological shift in the subsequent roll-call behavior in the opposition party's favor (i.e. "when a more extreme Democrat is nominated, the district's roll-call voting in the next Congress becomes more conservative, and vice versa when a more extreme Republican is nominated"; Hall 2015, 19).[4] This is due to the fact that voters seem to prefer *electable* candidates from within their own party to potentially more ideological ones. For example, having a more moderate Republican candidate in a highly competitive district is more important to Republican voters than having a more extreme Republican because the Election Day result is more likely to favor the Democratic candidate. Furthermore, given the incumbency advantage already enjoyed by U.S. House members, in addition to the prospect of losing the seat in the immediate election, losing that seat could have long term negative consequences in future elections as well.

In a more institution-centric analysis, McGhee et al. (2013) examine the openness of state legislative primaries and conclude that the degree of openness in primaries is not related to the ideology of candidates that are elected. In fact, their data suggest that increased openness produces the exact opposite of the intended effect – more open primaries actually lead to more extreme candidates emerging from party primaries in state legislatures. However, they offer the following cautionary tale regarding their findings: "we believe our findings generally fail to reject the null hypothesis of no effect from primary systems" (*ibid.*, 347). Based on this brief summary of much of the work on primaries, it appears that previous literature does not provide a definitive answer on what effect the existence of the primary can have on election outcomes.

The Effect of Direct Primaries

To evaluate the effect of direct primaries on congressional elections, we first consider descriptive trends before and after adoption by individual states at the beginning of the twentieth century. If the implementation of direct primaries was successful in seeking to reduce corruption, increase electoral competition, and overcome coordination problems, we should witness greater levels of qualified or "high" quality candidate emergence as well as more competitive elections in light of the fact that more formidable and experienced candidates are seeking elective office following the adoption of this reform. By integrating voters into the candidate selection process, candidates with greater name recognition, a record of accomplishments to point to, and who are more closely aligned ideologically with the congressional district should prevail more often in primary elections. Experienced or quality challengers commonly possess these characteristics and therefore should face an easier path to the general election following the implementation of direct primaries.

Figure 3.1 depicts the proportion of quality challengers that emerged in U.S. House elections between 1840 and 2014.[5] From this figure, we can see that this measure fluctuates greatly over time. During the first 30 years of this timespan, over 30 percent of all challengers previously held some elective office. There was a slight increase in this proportion over the remainder of the nineteenth century as over 35 percent of all challengers had previously been officeholders. By the turn of the century, the proportion of experienced candidates began to decline precipitously despite the fact that Progressive Era reforms – including the direct primary – spread rapidly during the first two decades of the twentieth century. By the end of the Progressive Era, all but four states had adopted the direct primary with the final adopters implementing a direct primary much later in the century. During this time, the proportion of quality challengers was halved with only 17 percent running in House races.

By the end of the Progressive Era in 1920, 44 of the 48 states had implemented a direct primary system, but only one-fifth of challengers were considered high quality. However, this upward trend was short-lived as only 15.5 percent of non-incumbent office-seekers had any previous elective experience between 1924 and 1944. During the next three decades, there was a substantial resurgence in the emergence of high quality candidates as nearly one in every four challengers served in an elective position prior to seeking a U.S. House seat. Since the mid-1970s, the proportion of quality challengers seeking a seat in the House of Representatives has fluctuated around 18.5 percent. More recently, the 2016 election tied with 1990 as the lowest

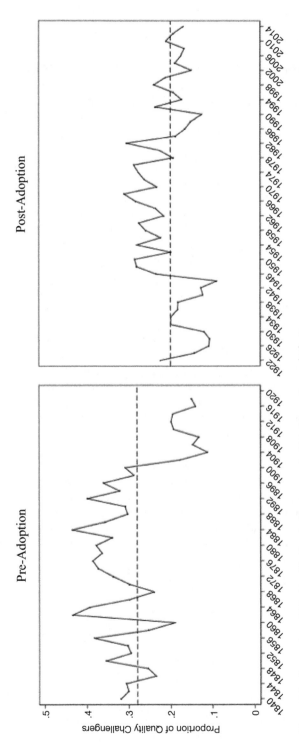

Figure 3.1 Proportion of Quality Challenger Emergence in U.S. House General Elections

percentage of quality challengers – 13 percent – running against incumbents in the post-World War II era.

Comparing levels of quality challenger participation before and after 1920 demonstrates that this reform did not encourage these candidates to run more often as many initially predicted. Prior to full implementation of direct primaries, over 27 percent of challengers previously held elective office. This number fell 7 points in the elections that have occurred since primaries began to be routinely used by the states.[6] Indeed, limiting the comparison to the 20 years before and after implementation does not offer any substantively different results. Again, there was a 2 percent decrease in the proportion of quality challengers in the era immediately following adoption of the direct primary.

Similarly, the adoption of direct primaries should produce more competitive elections, all else equal. The political parties – namely their local leaders – previously selected candidates they believed would best serve their electoral and policy interests, but that candidate may not have the broadest appeal to constituents. However, it stands to reason that whichever candidate survives a round of voting in a direct primary system will indeed have broader appeal. Therefore, even if high quality challengers are not emerging at increased levels after adoption of direct primaries as Figure 3.1 demonstrates, the candidates that do emerge could still possibly yield more competitive outcomes.

Building upon the previous results, Figure 3.2 depicts the proportion of competitive U.S. House general elections races between 1840 and 2014.[7] Earlier decades in this time span bore witness to historically high levels of electoral competition. Between 1840 and 1850, for instance, 43.4 percent of races were competitive, with over half of all elections classified as such in 1842. There was a brief downturn in the 1850s with 37.1 percent of races classified as competitive, but the trend increased quickly and enduringly with more than two out of every five elections generating a competitive outcome. The lone outlier during this period came in 1878 when almost three-quarters of elections were relatively one-sided. Though low for this period, it would still prove to be one of the more competitive election cycles in history. Between 1890 and 1920, 28.6 percent of races were classified as competitive with a new historic low of 16.5 percent in 1904.

An average of slightly more than one-third of House races were competitive prior to the 1922 election cycle. Though there was a modest decline in competitiveness over this same time span, the implementation of direct primaries did nothing to ultimately combat this trend. A mere 15.6 percent of House races have been competitive since the adoption of this reform – less than half of what was observed previously.[8] Moreover, with the exception of a few wave elections (e.g., 1994, 2006 and 2010), only about 10 percent of elections have been competitive during the past few decades.

Furthermore, in the 40 years immediately following the adoption of direct primaries by the states, 20.5 percent of U.S. House elections were competitive. This noticeable decline would continue between 1962 and 2014 as the average proportion of competitive races dipped to 11.6 percent. Over the entire history of congressional elections for which we have data, only 11 election cycles resulted in more than 90 percent of candidates winning by greater than 10 percentage points. Six of these 11 such instances have occurred between 1998 and 2014, which further illustrates the declining levels of electoral competitiveness in recent years.

Numerous factors have contributed to the decline in electoral competitiveness over time. Most notably are the advantages stemming from incumbency (see, e.g., Erikson 1971; Mayhew 1974; Ferejohn 1977; Cover 1977). More specific explanations range from institutional features such as legislative casework (Fiorina 1977), legislative activism (Johannes and McAdams 1981), advertising (Cover and Brumberg 1982), and redistricting (Erikson 1972; Cover 1977; Carson,

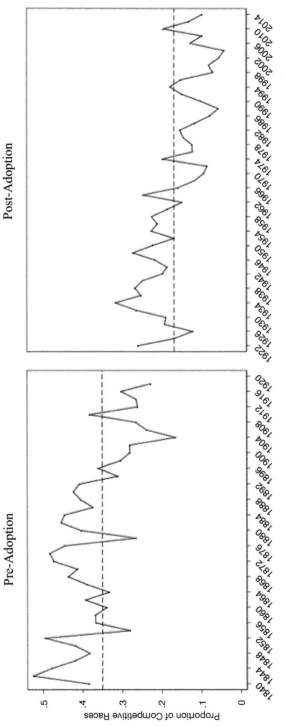

Figure 3.2 Proportion of Competitive U.S. House General Elections

Crespin, and Williamson 2014). Other scholars contend that the advantage can be explained by legislators' personal home styles in their congressional districts (Fenno 1978), rational entry and exit decisions by strategic candidates (Jacobson and Kernell 1981; Krasno 1994, Cox and Katz 1996), a growing "personal" vote (Cain, Ferejohn, and Fiorina 1987), and a greater emphasis on television appearances in a candidate-centered electoral era (Prior 2007). However, other works place a greater emphasis on the role of donations and money. Congressional campaigns have grown in cost over time (Abramowitz 1989, 1991) with a disproportionate amount of that money being raised and spent by incumbents (Jacobson and Kernell 1981; Herrnson 2012). Regardless, the evidence presented here illustrates that any effect direct primaries had on the vote distribution between competing candidates was minimal and short-lived.

Having focused on some descriptive trends in both challenger emergence and candidate competition across time, we now turn to a more sophisticated empirical analysis to evaluate additional factors that may be contributing to the patterns shown in Figures 3.1 and 3.2. As such, we estimate a logistic regression predicting the probability of a winning candidate for a U.S. House general election receiving 55 percent or less of the two-party vote for all elections between 1840 and 2014. Our main independent variable is an indicator variable denoting the end of the Progressive Era when 44 of the 48 states had adopted direct primaries. A negative and significant coefficient for this variable would reaffirm the conclusions drawn from the previous figures.

We also control for several factors known to contribute to the competitiveness of U.S. House elections. The first is whether a quality challenger decided to run in the election. Quality challengers are notably strategic in their decision to run and are experienced in winning elections, which generally results in races they participate in yielding closer outcomes. We also control for open seats. Given the relative ease with which incumbents are reelected to Congress, removing them from the contest produces two candidates who are at least theoretically more evenly matched. This then typically leads to more competitive elections. Next, we also include an exogenous measure of district preferences with the proportion of the two-party vote won by the Democratic presidential candidate within a district. This provides us with a measure of the homogeneity of a district. Increased homogeneity of voter preferences reduces the probability of a competitive election taking place as one candidate will lose votes for simply being a member of the "wrong" party.

Finally, we include three indicators denoting the partisanship of the winning candidate, whether a presidential election occurred at the same time, and whether a state was southern or not. The first is coded as 1 for Democratic winners and 0 for winners from another party. It allows us to capture any differences between the recruitment and campaign strategies employed by the parties. The second is coded 1 if a presidential election is occurring simultaneously and accounts for any effect increased turnout and presidential coattails might have on election outcomes. Consistent with prior literature, we treat southern states as unique in their political culture and environment. The 11 states that seceded from the Union during the Civil War are coded as southern while all other states are coded as non-southern. The results of this estimation are presented in Table 3.2 below.

As we expected, races featuring no incumbent, a quality challenger, weaker partisan preferences, and ones occurring outside of the South are consistently more competitive across time. Additionally, after controlling for these factors, elections occurring after implementation of direct primaries are significantly less likely to be competitive. Indeed, even limiting the analysis to the 30 years before and after adoption yields similar results. The predicted probabilities of competitiveness are depicted in Figure 3.3 to better illustrate the differences before and after the adoption of direct primaries by the states. Open seat races are more likely to be competitive

Table 3.2 Logistic Regression Estimates of Competitive Elections

	Coefficient (Rob. Std. Err.)
Post-Adoption	**−0.974**
	(0.044)
Quality Challenger Presence	**1.187**
	(0.041)
Open Seat	**0.832**
	(0.069)
Democratic Presidential Vote	**−0.084**
	(0.004)
Democratic Winners	0.038
	(0.049)
Midterm Elections	−0.045
	(0.030)
Southern States	**−0.746**
	(0.82)
Intercept	−0.006
	(0.065)
N	22160
Log-likelihood	−10259.65

Note: Bolded entries are significant at $p < 0.05$. Standard errors clustered by congressional district.

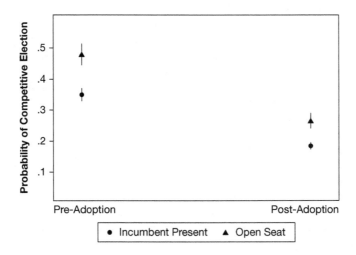

Figure 3.3 Predicted Probability of Competitive U.S. House Races

pre- and post-adoption. However, we also see that incumbent-contested elections prior to 1920 were more likely to be competitive than are open seat elections after 1920.

From these results, it appears that the direct primary resulted in the parties' nomination process leading to the emergence of candidates regarded as weaker by the party organization. This makes intuitive sense, as having stronger party machines allowed party elites to play a more centralized role in recruiting candidates for office. Amateur candidates had no proven record of support for the party's legislative agenda. Because of this, they were considerably less likely to be appealing to party bosses. The machine would therefore rely on those with a track record of voting the "right" way, which required some sort of voting record, and a voting record could only be accrued through elective experience. However, by placing the responsibility of selecting each party's candidate in the hands of voters, the disincentive for weaker candidates no longer existed. Indeed, the popular narrative of the time even created an incentive for candidates to tout their lack of any connection to party machines in order to win.

This reduction in the number of quality challengers running also resulted in the reduction in overall levels of competitiveness in House elections. Without challengers who had the experience of previously seeking office, name recognition, or a history of legislative accomplishments, incumbents faced fewer obstacles to winning reelection. Additionally, without parties to underwrite campaigns and offer job security to those who lost, candidates became much more risk averse with respect to seeking the party nomination. Therefore, candidates would only compete in races when their probability of winning was considerably high. This further allowed incumbents to retain their position when they otherwise may have been subject to a serious challenge as was common in the past.[9] Over time, these trends have only increased as campaigns have become more costly and fewer high quality candidates are willing to take the risk to run given the greater opportunity costs that are involved.

Conclusion

The results presented here are largely consistent with prior research examining candidate emergence following adoption of direct primaries. Among others, Ansolabehere et al. (2010, 190) conclude that, "primaries were never broadly competitive, even at the outset" and that "the competitiveness of federal and statewide primaries decreased sharply starting in the 1940s." However, we also see that adoption of the direct primary during the beginning of the twentieth century failed to elicit greater participation among quality challengers in general elections (and presumably in primary elections). As Maisel and Stone (2001) remind us, elections themselves are not sufficient for enhancing American democracy. *Competitive* elections are essential to a democratic system, and direct primaries did not offer much improvement in this way as those who pushed for their adoption originally believed they would.

To be clear, direct primaries are not solely responsible for the gradual decline in electoral competition or quality challenger emergence in House elections. However, taking control of the candidate recruitment process away from the party machines and granting that power to citizens did not help to reduce this decline either. In fact, it may have only hastened the decline that was already underway during the latter part of the nineteenth century as the party bosses were rapidly losing control of local factions of their party organizations. Despite these potentially worrisome trends, adoption of direct primaries has opened the door for other electoral reforms that could at least theoretically generate greater levels of competition and subsequently provide for enhanced representation between constituents and their elected representatives.

Because the Constitution allows individual states to determine the timing, place, and manner of elections, laws governing primaries vary considerably across the country. One of the more unique systems is the top-two, or jungle, primary utilized by California, Washington, and Louisiana. Under this system, all candidates for office – regardless of partisanship – appear on the ballot. After the votes are cast, the two candidates receiving the most support advance to the general election.[10] This enables congressional districts that are overwhelmingly favorable towards either the Democratic or Republican parties to select between candidates with the same partisan identification. This, in turn, can lead to more competitive outcomes as one candidate is no longer immediately dismissed by voters for being a member of the "wrong" party.

In the brief timespan that these types of elections have been in place – 2010 marked the first year that all three states successfully implemented this system – co-partisans competing for the same U.S.

House seat have become a relatively common phenomenon. For example, the 2016 California general election featured seven House races pitting two Democrats against each other. Similarly, two of Washington's ten congressional races featured co-partisans competing for a seat in the House. As such, if increased competition across the parties is the ultimate goal, then more states may want to follow the model of these states in future elections.

There are numerous other sources of variation in rules governing primary elections that could influence quality challenger emergence and competitiveness that have yet to be explored. For instance, 15 states currently impose some form of term limits on their state legislators. What effect, if any, does this legislation have on their willingness to then compete for a U.S. House seat? Building on Rohde's (1979) work on progressive ambition, if a member has reached his or her maximum number of years in the state House or Senate, it is fair to assume that he or she has interest in maintaining elective office. The seemingly natural progression would be a seat in the U.S. House. Therefore, once a member has been term-limited out of state office, he or she will then have to enter a congressional primary election. It is theoretically possible, then, that states that impose term limits on state legislators witness greater levels of quality challenger emergence and competition.[11]

More directly related to primary elections are the laws regulating the hurdles a candidate must clear in order to pursue office. These rules vary considerably across states with some being overtly cited as unduly strict. For example, an independent candidate in Georgia must obtain the signatures of five percent of registered voters in the district or jurisdiction the candidate seeks to represent – potentially thousands of signatures – in order to appear on the ballot for a U.S. House race. With such a high threshold, no independent candidate has successfully made it onto the ballot since 1964, and no minor party candidate has complied with the measure since it was first implemented in 1943 (Gray et al. 2012). In contrast, a candidate seeking a U.S. House seat in New Hampshire need only obtain 1,500 signatures to appear on the ballot. As these examples illustrate, implementing less burdensome ballot access laws could serve to noticeably alter who runs for, and ultimately wins, elections.

In conclusion, the direct primary – along with other Progressive Era reforms – aimed to reduce corruption, enhance citizen participation, and increase levels of competition in U.S. House elections. Control of the selection process by political parties was indeed reduced, but the adoption of direct primaries did not result in increased electoral competitiveness as originally conceived. Nonetheless, the candidate selection process still became more democratic, and without this important change other reforms would not be possible. Those seeking to further reform the electoral system should take heed of the lessons from history as they look for other institutional arrangements that might enhance electoral competition. The recent examples from California and Washington seem like a good place to start for other states looking to reform how their candidates are selected in direct primaries.

Notes

1 Summers (2004) offers a thoroughly engaging and descriptive account of party politics during this era of politics. See also Bensel (2004) for a rich history of voting in the nineteenth century.

2 Specifically, Texas passed legislation in 1923 banning participation of non-whites in primary elections. This legislation would be in place for more than 20 years, but was eventually ruled unconstitutional by the U.S. Supreme Court in *Smith v. Allwright* (321 U.S. 649, 1944).

3 See also Pyeatt (2015) for a discussion of how ideological or partisan extremity can influence a candidate's likelihood of being punished or rewarded in primary elections.

4 It is important to point out that this effect likely does not apply to "safe" districts in which voters will likely support one party's candidate regardless of his or her ideological leanings.

5 Quality challengers are defined as those who have previously held elective office. As noted at the outset of the chapter, our measure focuses on those quality challengers that made it past the primary and into the general election.

6 This difference is statistically significant as a difference-of-means test yields a *t*-value of 84.44.

7 A competitive race is defined as one in which the winning candidate received 55 percent or less of the two-party vote share.

8 This difference is statistically significant as a difference-of-means test yields a *t*-value of 226.48.

9 For more evidence on these and related points concerning the adoption of electoral reforms in the late nineteenth and early twentieth centuries, see Carson and Roberts (2013).

10 Louisiana does not have a primary election phase, per se. Instead, all candidates seeking a particular office appear on the general election ballot. If no candidate receives at least 50 percent plus one votes, the top two candidates proceed to a run-off in December of the election year.

11 At the same time, it is also possible that the number of quality challengers who emerge to run in U.S. House primaries may not be greater under these circumstances since they cannot strategically decide to emerge when conditions are ideal. Rather, they decide to run when they can no longer seek reelection in the state legislature. See Maestas, Fulton, Maisel, and Stone (2006) and Boatright (2013) for greater discussion of this phenomenon.

References

Abramowitz, Alan I. 1989. "Campaign Spending in U.S. Senate Elections." *Legislative Studies Quarterly* 14 (2): 487–507.

Abramowitz, Alan I. 1991. "Incumbency, Campaign Spending, and the Decline of Competition in U.S. House Elections." *Journal of Politics* 53 (1): 34–56.

Alilunas, Lee. 1940. "The Rise of the 'White Primary' Movement as a Means of Barring the Negro from the Polls." *Journal of Negro History* 25 (1): 161–172.

Ansolabehere, Stephen, John Mark Hansen, Shigeo Hirano, and James N. Snyder, Jr. 2010. "More Democracy: The Direct Primary and Competition in U.S. Elections." *Studies in American Political Development* 24 (1): 190–205.

Argersinger, Peter H. 1985. "New Perspectives on Election Fraud in the Gilded Age." *Political Science Quarterly* 100(4): 669–687.

Banks, Jeffrey S. and Roderick Kiewiet. 1989. "Explaining Patterns of Candidate Competition in Congressional Elections." *American Journal of Political Science* 33(4): 997–1015.

Benoit, Ken. 2004. "Models of Electoral System Change." *Electoral Studies* 23 (2): 363–389.

Bensel, Richard Franklin. 2004. *The American Ballot Box in the Mid-Nineteenth Century.* Cambridge, UK: Cambridge University Press.

Boatright, Robert. 2013. *Getting Primaried: The Changing Politics of Congressional Primary Challenges.* Ann Arbor: The University of Michigan Press.

Boix, Carles. 1999. "Setting the Rules of the Game: The Choice of Electoral Systems in Advanced Democracies." *American Political Science Review* 93(3): 609–624.

Brady, David W., Hahrie Han, and Jeremy C. Pope. 2007. "Primary Elections and Candidate Ideology: Out of Step with the Primary Electorate?" *Legislative Studies Quarterly* 3(1): 79–105.

Cain, Bruce, John Ferejohn, and Morris P. Fiorina. 1987. *The Personal Vote.* Cambridge, MA: Harvard University Press.

Carson, Jamie L. and Jason M. Roberts. 2013. *Ambition, Competition, and Electoral Reform: The Politics of Congressional Elections Across Time.* Ann Arbor: The University of Michigan Press.

Carson, Jamie, Michael H. Crespin, and Ryan D. Williamson. 2014. "Reevaluating the Effects of Redistricting on Electoral Competition, 1972–2012." *State Politics and Policy Quarterly* 14 (1): 162–174.

Cover, Albert D. 1977. "One Good Term Deserves Another: The Advantage of Incumbency in Congressional Elections." *American Journal of Political Science* 21 (3): 523–541.

Cover, Albert, and Bruce Brumberg. 1982. "Baby Books and Ballots: The Impact of Congressional Mail on Constituent Opinion." *American Political Science Review* 76 (2): 347–359.

Cox, Gary W. and Jonathan N. Katz. 1996. "Why Did the Incumbency Advantage in U.S. House Elections Grow?" *American Journal of Political Science* 40 (3): 478–497.

Erikson, Robert S. 1971. "The Advantage of Incumbency in Congressional Elections." *Polity* 3 (3): 395–405.

Erikson, Robert S. 1972. "Malapportionment, Gerrymandering, and Party Fortunes." *American Political Science Review* 66 (4): 1234–1245.

Fenno, Richard F. 1978. *Home Style: House Members in Their Districts.* London: Pearson Press.

Ferejohn, John. 1977. "On the Decline of Competition in Congressional Elections." *American Political Science Review* 71(1): 166–176.

Fiorina, Morris P. 1977. "The Case of the Vanishing Marginals: The Bureaucracy Did It." *American Political Science Review* 71 (1): 177–181.

Gray, Virginia, Russell L. Hanson, and Thad Kousser. 2012. *Politics in the American States: A Comparative Analysis.* 10th ed. Washington, D.C.: CQ Press.

Grofman, Bernard. 1990. *Political Gerrymandering and the Courts.* New York: Agathon Press.

Hall, Andrew B. 2015. "What Happens When Extremists Win Primaries?" *American Political Science Review* 109 (1): 18–42.

Herrnson, Paul S. 2012. *Congressional Elections: Campaigning at Home and in Washington.* Washington, DC: CQ Press.

Jacobson, Gary C. and Jamie L. Carson. 2016. *The Politics of Congressional Elections,* 9th ed. Lanham, MD: Rowman & Littlefield.

Jacobson, Gary C. and Samuel Kernell. 1981. *Strategy and Choice in Congressional Elections.* New Haven: Yale University Press.

Johannes, John R. and John C. McAdams. 1981. "The Congressional Incumbency Effect: Is It Casework, Policy Compatibility, or Something Else?" *American Journal of Political Science* 25 (3): 520–542.

Kernell, Samuel. 1977. "Toward Understanding 19th Century Congressional Careers: Ambition, Competition, and Rotation. *American Journal of Political Science* 21 (3): 669–693.

Key, V. O. 1954. "The Direct Primary and Party Structure: A Study of State Legislative Nominations." *American Political Science Review* 48(1): 1–26.

Krasno, Jonathan S. 1994. *Challengers, Competition, and Reelection: Comparing Senate and House Elections.* New Haven: Yale University Press.

Lawrence, Eric, Todd Donovan, and Shaun Bowler. 2011. "The Adoption of Direct Primaries in the United States." *Party Politics* 19(1): 3–18.

Maestas, Cherie D., Sarah Fulton, L. Sandy Maisel, and Walter J. Stone. 2006. "When to Risk It? Institutions, Ambitions, and the Decision to Run for the U.S. House." *American Political Science Review* 100(2): 195–208.

Maisel, L. Sandy, and Walter J. Stone. 2001. "Primary Elections as a Deterrence to Candidacy to the U.S. House of Representatives." In *Congressional Primaries and the Politics of Representation.* Ed. Peter F. Galderisi, Marni Ezra, and Michael Lyons. Lanham, MD: Rowman and Littlefield, 29–47.

Mayhew, David R. 1974. *Congress: The Electoral Connection.* New Haven: Yale University Press.

McGhee, Eric, Seth Masket, Boris Shor, Steven Rogers, and Nolan McCarty. 2013. "A Primary Cause of Partisanship? Nomination Systems and Legislator Ideology." *American Journal of Political Science* 58(2): 337–351.

Merriam, Charles E. 1908. *A Study of the History and Tendencies of Primary Election Legislation.* Chicago: University of Chicago Press.

Merriam, Charles E. and Louise Overacker. 1928. *Primary Elections.* Chicago: University of Chicago Press.

North, Douglass. 1990. *Institutions, Institutional Change and Economic Performance.* Cambridge, UK: Cambridge University Press.

Overacker, Louise. 1945. "The Negro's Struggle for Participation in Primary Elections." *Journal of Negro History* 30 (1): 54–61.

Polsby, Nelson. 1968. "The Institutionalization of the U.S. House of Representatives." *American Political Science Review* 62 (1): 144–168.

Prior, Markus. 2007. *Post-Broadcast Democracy: How Media Choice Increases Inequality in Political Involvement and Polarizes Elections.* New York: Cambridge University Press.

Pyeatt, Nicholas. 2015. "Party Unity, Ideology, and Polarization in Primary Elections for the U.S. House: 1956–2012." *Legislative Studies Quarterly* 40(4): 651–676.

Rohde, David. 1979. "Risk-Bearing and Progressive Ambition: The Case of Members of the United States House of Representatives." *American Journal of Political Science* 23 (1): 1–26.

Rokkan, Stein. 1970. *Citizens, Elections, Parties: Approaches to the Comparative Study of the Process of Development.* New York: McKay.

Summers, Mark Wahlgren. 2004. *Party Games: Getting, Keeping, and Using Power in Gilded Age Politics.* Chapel Hill: The University of North Carolina Press.

Ware, Alan. 2002. *The American Direct Primary: Party Institutionalization and Transformation in the North.* New York: Cambridge University Press.

4

SHOULD WE EXPECT PRIMARY ELECTIONS TO CREATE POLARIZATION?

A Robust Median Voter Theorem with Rational Parties

Gilles Serra

The introduction of primary elections is often presumed to carry important policy consequences. Every political party needs a procedure to nominate the person it will put forward for office at an upcoming election. Such a procedure is sometimes called a candidate-selection method (CSM), and primary elections are only one of many such methods. Historically, parties across the world have employed a diverse array of nomination processes such as delegate conventions and elite appointments, and only in recent times have primaries become more frequent.[1] In the United States, for example, the introduction of the direct primary is associated with the Progressive Era, roughly between 1890 and 1920. A number of legal reforms during this period were geared to disempowering party bosses. Primary elections were conceived as a way of transferring the responsibility to nominate candidates from a few hundred convention delegates to thousands of party members.[2] Among other goals, the reformers that advocate for primary elections in their countries are usually attempting to make parties more responsive to their rank-and-file members. Internal democracy is thus hailed as a major benefit of introducing primaries.[3]

Notwithstanding this valuable benefit, several observers have worried about the social costs they see in primary elections. One of the most-often mentioned costs of introducing primary elections is ideological polarization. Indeed, many scholars and pundits, especially in America, have conjectured that such CSM leads to the extremism of candidates' platforms. To be sure, some persuasive arguments can be made to expect such a polarizing effect, at least theoretically. A common claim is that primary voters have more extreme preferences than the general population, especially in closed primaries that only include registered adherents as compared to open primaries that include any citizen. This supposedly gives an advantage to extreme primary contenders, and forces moderate primary contenders to diverge from the ideological center. This popular claim remained speculative for many decades, until it started being tested by a series of increasingly sophisticated empirical articles in academic journals.

One of the pioneering papers testing this claim was that of Gerber and Morton (1998). The goal of their paper was to measure how different types of nomination procedure for congressional positions led to selecting candidates with different ideologies. They were particularly interested in whether the extremism of the selectorate led to the extremism of the nominees. They speculated that closed primaries have a polarizing effect:

> To the extent that members of the parties are ideologically distinct, we therefore expect the ideal point of the primary electorate median voter in closed primaries to reflect the ideological positions of the party's elite and to diverge substantially from the ideal point of the general electorate median voter. [. . .] The main hypothesis is that closed primaries will produce general election winners whose policy positions diverge substantially from their district's general election median voter.
>
> *Gerber and Morton 1998, 311–312*

Their statistical results supported this hypothesis by finding that representatives from closed primary systems were more extreme than representatives from other CSMs with more moderate selectorates (such as semi-closed, open, nonpartisan, and blanket primary systems). Other early studies seemed to confirm this finding which, in turn, encouraged theories to make this prediction. Indeed, given the traditional belief that primaries create polarization, along with a first wave of empirical papers that seemed to confirm this view, it is not surprising that a significant number of formal models have been developed to be consistent with such claims.[4]

While theoretically compelling, formal models predicting that primaries polarize candidates are at odds with the new empirical evidence. Indeed, some recent statistical studies have been casting doubt on this view, finding instead that closed primary elections have no effect, or a negligible one, on the extremism of candidates.[5] For example, McGhee, Masket, Shor, Rogers and McCarty (2014) use state-level data to gauge the effect of primary openness on the polarization of local legislatures. For each state, the authors measure the degree to which primary selectorates are inclusive rather than exclusive (meaning the degree to which primaries are open rather than closed), and they marry these data to estimations of the ideal points of state legislators. Surprisingly, they find their estimated effects to rarely be robust, meaning there is little effect of the type of CSM. In some of their specifications, there is a statistically significant effect but it goes in the opposite direction of the one expected: primaries that are more closed by virtue of having more exclusive selectorates (and which therefore should have more extreme voters) end up electing legislators that are more moderate.

These new statistical studies pose a challenge from the theoretical point of view. With several formal models of primaries predicting polarization, why are the newest empirical studies not finding it? One possible interpretation is that primaries have in fact a contingent effect, leading to polarization in some contexts but not in others. If so, is it possible to build a formal model where primaries do not lead to extremism? Such a model would allow us to compare its assumptions with the assumptions of models where primaries lead to extremism. In turn, this would help understand where extremism really comes from in those other theories, thus shedding light on this controversy.

Such is the goal of this chapter, where I develop a model to investigate the effect that we should expect from primary elections on policy polarization. The model is purposely simple: to the well-known linear model developed by Anthony Downs (1957), I only add a nomination stage with two political parties where candidates need to compete before being able to run for office. The model explicitly incorporates a number of features that are considered centrifugal, meaning that they create incentives for candidates to diverge from the center. First, I assume that the two parties have extreme ideologies on opposite sides of the median voter. Second, neither party cares about winning the election *per se*, but rather they care only about the policy implemented by the candidate who wins the election. Third, once a candidate promises a policy to her party in the primary, this promise becomes binding in the general election as well. Fourth, while candidates receive a payoff if they win the general election, I will assume that they also receive an independent payoff from winning the nomination in their parties. And fifth, I study the case where parties are risk-seekers, meaning that among two candidates yielding the same expected policy, parties prefer nominating a risky extremist to a riskless centrist. All these assumptions are stacking the deck in favor of obtaining extremism – and yet the model does not find any. In line with the most recent empirical literature, I find that closed primaries do not induce candidates to diverge from each other at all. One of the reasons is the rationality of primary voters: even if they have extreme ideal points, party members understand the importance of voting strategically by choosing a moderate candidate who can prevent the other party from winning. Hence my model underlines an understudied feature of primary elections that might have a profound effect on their outcomes: the rationality of party members whereby they vote strategically rather than sincerely.[6] It turns out that this assumption alone, at least in a bare-bones model, is enough to induce all primary candidates from both parties to converge completely to the median voter's ideal point.

In short, this chapter provides a median-voter theorem with competitive nominations. The result can be seen as "robust" in the sense that it generalizes a previous theory. In Serra (2015), I derived a median-voter theorem with nominations which included the first three of the conditions mentioned above: parties with extreme ideal points; parties that care about influencing policy rather than winning the election; and primary platforms that are binding in the general election. The model in this chapter extends the analysis by adding the last two conditions: candidates who value obtaining the nomination independently of winning the election; and parties who are risk loving. Given that the result remains unchanged, the theorem here can be considered a robustness check.

Structure of the Election

Timing

The election is modeled as a three-stage game between voters, parties and candidates. The three stages correspond to the platform announcements by candidates, the nominations by parties and the general election by voters, in this sequence. The goal of the election is to decide a policy to be implemented. Each policy platform is represented by a point x on the real line; hence the policy space is the set of real numbers. There are two parties, labeled L for the left-wing party and R for the right-wing party. Each party needs to nominate a candidate for office among those who are competing inside the party, often referred to as precandidates. There are four such precandidates, which are labeled l_1, l_2 for those in party L and r_1, r_2 for those in party R. The only distinguishable characteristic of each candidate is the policy platform she adopts. Hence, throughout the chapter I will make no distinction between a candidate and her platform, referring to l_1, l_2, r_1, r_2 when talking either about the candidates' platforms or the candidates themselves.

In the first stage, the four candidates announce their platforms simultaneously. A candidate's strategy consists of announcing a policy platform on the real line. We denote a profile of candidate strategies by S_c, with $S_c = (l_1, l_2, r_1, r_2)$. The platform that a candidate adopts during the nomination process represents a binding commitment: it will become her platform for the general election at the subsequent stage, and it will be the policy she implements if she is elected.[7]

In the second stage, for a given set of platform announcements S_c, party L must choose a candidate l_i and party R must choose a candidate r_j to compete against each other in the general election. So, after observing the profile (l_1, l_2, r_1, r_2), party L nominates either l_1 or l_2 while R

nominates either r_1 or r_2. Both parties nominate their candidates simultaneously.[8] We denote by S_L the strategy of L and by S_R the strategy of R. A party's strategy consists of a complete plan of action contingent on every possible situation in which it might be called upon to act. In the present context this implies specifying an action for each possible configuration of platforms that it may observe. Since every set of candidate platforms $S_c = (l_1, l_2, r_1, r_2)$ forms a subgame of this game, a strategy for a party specifies a nomination for each of those configurations. Lastly, in the third stage, voters elect a party to take office. We will assume that a median voter in the general electorate exists whose decision is pivotal. We call the median voter M.

The timing of the game is summarized as follows:

1 *Platform announcements*: All four candidates, r_1, r_2 in party R and l_1, l_2 in party L, announce their policy platforms simultaneously.
2 *Nominations*: Both parties, R and L, choose their nominees simultaneously.
3 *General election*: The median voter in the electorate, M, elects one of the two parties.

This being the basic structure of the election, here are details about the preferences of voters, parties and candidates.

Voters' Preferences

We will assume voters' preferences to be single-peaked and linear with ideal points on the real line. There exists a median voter, called M, whose preferences are decisive.[9] Her ideal point is known with certainty to everyone, and we normalize it to zero. M's utility function is thus given by

$$U_M(x) = -|x|$$

Given such preferences, the behavior of voters is trivial when they have to choose between the two parties: they will always vote for the one whose candidate has a platform closest to their ideal points, so the party whose candidate announced a platform closest to the median voter's ideal point will be elected. In other words, the party closest to zero will win. If the platforms of parties yield the same utility to M, then she will randomize her vote such that either party will win the election with equal probability. Hence if party R and party L were equidistant from zero, they would tie, having each a ½ probability of winning.

Risk-Averse, Risk-Seeking or Risk-Neutral Parties

Parties L and R care about the policy implemented by the elected official. In other words, they are policy-motivated meaning that they have ideal points over policy.[10] The only action taken by parties is to nominate their candidates for the general election. Each party holds a closed primary where all its members vote democratically to choose the nominee. Here I will eschew modeling explicitly the thousands, sometimes millions, of party sympathizers that attend a primary election. Instead I will assume that each party has a median member whose preferences will be decisive in the primary. In parallel research I have proved that, as long as all primary voters have single-peaked preferences, the platform preferred by the median party member is a Condorcet winner – and this will be true even when all party members are strategic rather than sincere (Serra 2017). An implication of this result is that a party can reasonably be treated as a unitary actor behaving strategically based on the ideal point of its median member.

Both parties are rational and forward looking, meaning they will try anticipating the other players' reactions. Using the jargon in political science, we would say that parties are *strategic* rather than *sincere*. As a consequence, a party will not blindly nominate the candidate closest to its ideal point. On the contrary, a party will often be willing to nominate a moderate candidate if she has a higher chance of winning the election. In essence, each party must find the candidate that best balances its desire for a partisan platform with its fear of letting the other party win. It will do so while taking into account the candidate that is expected to be nominated by the rival party, meaning that the simultaneous nominations made by parties L and R need to form a Nash Equilibrium.

I will assume the ideal points of both parties to be on opposite sides of the median voter, such that we genuinely have a left-wing party and a right-wing party. To simplify the presentation, we will assume that L's ideal point is -1 while R's ideal point is 1. For interpretation purposes, we should think of the locations -1 and 1 as being quite extreme on the left and the right of the political spectrum.[11] Parties have single-peaked preferences represented by the following utility functions:

$$U_R(x) = -|1-x|^a$$
$$U_L(x) = -|-1-x|^a$$

with $a > 0$

In the equations above, the parameter a represents each party's attitude toward risk as represented by the concavity or convexity of the utility functions. Indeed, different values of this parameter imply different levels of tolerance for risky lotteries between two outcomes. A value of $a > 1$ represents *risk-averse* parties (because it induces a concave utility function); a value of $a < 1$ represents *risk-seeking* parties (because it induces a convex utility function); and a value of $a = 1$ represents *risk-neutral* parties (because it induces a linear utility function).

It is interesting to study this parameter for several reasons. While most formal models assume that political actors are averse to risk, the opposite attitude of preferring to take on risk is also a valid assumption to make. In the real world, risk-seeking behavior often occurs in social, economic and political situations, so including it in our theories makes them more complete. Importantly, a love of risk can serve as a centrifugal force in this election, meaning that it provides some new incentives for platforms to diverge toward the extremes. To illustrate this point, consider the following scenario. We should start by recalling that this model does not exhibit any asymmetric information, as the preferences of all actors are common knowledge. This includes the location of the median voter and the median party members, which are known to everyone for sure. So when does risk play a role? Suppose one of the parties has the option between nominating an extreme candidate who would tie with the extreme candidate from the other party thus making the winner uncertain, or nominating a moderate candidate who would win the election for sure. A risk-seeking party might prefer nominating the extreme candidate that induces a lottery between the two parties, rather than the moderate candidate that ensures a centrist victory. In this sense, risk-seeking behavior incentivizes extremism. It is germane to explore whether this new centrifugal force would make the median-voter theorem collapse by inducing candidates to diverge from the center.[12]

As in many formal models, here we need to specify how indifferences are resolved. If a party knows that its two precandidates would lead to different outcomes in the election, it will always choose the one who ensures a policy closest to the party's ideal point – and it will do so with no regard to winning the election, which the party is not seeking to do. However, there are several hypothetical circumstances where a party would be indifferent between its two precandidates because they would both yield the same expected payoff. To break these indifferences, I will make the following three assumptions.

Indifference Assumptions: *Given the platform that the rival party is expected to adopt, if a party is indifferent between its two precandidates in terms of expected policy, it will choose according to the following assumptions.*

(IA1) *If both precandidates adopt the same platform making them indistinguishable, the party is forced to randomize equally between them.*

(IA2) *If both precandidates adopt different platforms, but both of them have the same probability of winning the election, the party can nominate either of them in equilibrium.*

(IA3) *If both precandidates adopt different platforms and they have different probabilities of winning the election, the party will choose the one that offers the highest probability.*

These assumptions imply that parties have a very mild preference for victory in the following sense: assumption IA3 represents a weak preference for winning the general election *per se*. It is akin to assuming that each party has a lexicographic benefit from being elected, which only plays a role when its options are indifferent in terms of policy.[13]

Candidates Who Value Being Nominated in Addition to Being Elected

Candidates are motivated by winning electoral contests. I assume they only value the perquisites from victorious elections, such as prestige, power and material benefits. Using the political science jargon we would say that they only care about their *ego-rents*. In particular, the candidates do not derive utility from the policy implemented. Not caring about policy gives candidates the freedom to announce any platform that best suits their goal of winning the nomination to later win the election.

In contrast to most existing models of primary elections, here I will assume that a candidate values obtaining her party's nomination *per se*, independently of winning the general election afterwards. In other words, I will assume that winning a primary election also grants some prestige, power, material benefits and other ego-rents.[14]

To be concrete, candidate *i* wishes to maximize the expected payoff from the primary process, labeled *P*, plus the expected payoff from the general election, labeled *G*. So she has the following utility function:

$$U_i\left(S_c, S_L, S_R\right) = P + G$$

where *P* is given by

$$P = \begin{cases} p \text{ if } i \text{ wins the primary election} \\ 0 \text{ otherwise} \end{cases}$$
with $p \le 0$

and *G* is given by

$$G = \begin{cases} g & \text{if } i \text{ wins the general election} \\ 0 & \text{otherwise} \end{cases}$$

with $g > 0$

So the values p and g correspond to the ego-rents received by the candidate from winning the primary and general elections, respectively.

Each candidate will choose her platform rationally, meaning she will take into account the reactions of other players. In particular, all candidates will try outguessing one another such that platform announcements form a Nash Equilibrium between the four of them. They are also forward looking, meaning that they will calculate the consequences of their announcements down the line, when it is the parties' turn to nominate a candidate, and then the voters' turn to elect a party. This structure implies that candidates will try balancing their need to please their parties who have extreme ideal points, with the subsequent need, if they are nominated, to appeal to the median voter who has a centrist ideal point. They must find this balance recalling that any platform they announce in the primary will remain their platform in the general election as well.

One immediate implication is that rational candidates would only consider adopting platforms in the following intervals. Candidates r_1 and r_2 in party R will restrict themselves to the interval $[0, 1]$ while candidates l_1 and l_2 in party L will restrict themselves to the interval $[-1, 0]$.

Equilibrium Concept

Our best prediction for the election result is an equilibrium of this game. We thus need to solve for all the equilibrium strategies of candidates, parties and voters. The game is solved by backward induction, and the type of equilibrium that we are looking for is *subgame perfect Nash equilibrium* (SPNE). A SPNE must induce a Nash Equilibrium (NE) in every subgame of the game, and therefore we need to find strategies S_c^*, S_L^* and S_R^* that induce a NE at every stage of the election. I will only consider pure strategies.[15]

Special focus will be placed on the location of the platforms that candidates will choose. We are particularly interested in exploring whether complete convergence or large divergences can be sustained in equilibrium. Will candidates adopt extreme platforms pandering to their parties, or will they announce centrist policies catering to the median voter? In turn, will parties nominate moderate candidates who can more easily win the election, or will they prefer partisans close to their ideal points? The following section provides answers in the context of this basic model.

The Null Effect of Primaries on Polarization

A Median Voter Theorem

We can now state a new theorem about the effect of primary elections on polarization. As it turns out, in this model, even with several centrifugal forces, there is no effect at all. Complete convergence is the only equilibrium, such that all candidates adopt completely moderate platforms before the nominations take place.

Theorem *The following will hold for any values of the parties' attitude toward risk, a, the candidates' payoffs from winning the primary election, p, and from winning the general election, g. In this election, there exists a unique outcome that can be sustained in equilibrium. In this outcome, all the candidates* converge to the median voter's ideal point such that $r_1 = r_2 = l_1 = l_2 = 0$. Party L randomizes between l_1 and l_2. Party R randomizes between r_1 and r_2. Voters randomize between party L and party R. And the policy implemented after the election is 0, the ideal point of the median voter.

This result is not trivial given the centrifugal forces that exist in the game. As I will illustrate below, there exist significant incentives for parties to request partisan platforms from their candidates. The theorem above shows that such centrifugal forces are more than compensated by centripetal forces incentivizing those same parties to converge to the center. In effect, this theorem is a generalization to primary elections of the classic median-voter theorem. The result makes the same predictions as the theorem in Serra (2015), but now with more general assumptions, so it can be considered a "robust" result.

The formal proof of this result comes in the appendix at the end of this chapter. It is fairly long, as it must study three separate cases corresponding to risk-averse, risk-seeking and risk-neutral parties. So, to gain insight into this type of elections, I give a shorter and more intuitive explanation in the following lines.

Election Dynamics

Insight can come from analyzing all the options that players in this game had, and understanding why none of these options was an equilibrium save for the ones described in the theorem. To this end, we need to analyze all the possible combinations of strategies to discard those not forming an equilibrium, namely those where at least one player could benefit from unilaterally changing her decision, keeping the decision of the other players fixed. In particular, we must analyze all the possible configurations of four platforms, two in the left-wing party and two in the right-wing party, to see whether rational candidates could conceivably announce them. The following six configurations are representative of the typical dynamics in this election.[16]

> **Example 1**: $0 \le r_1 < r_2 < -l_1 < -l_2 \le 1$
>
> - Profitable deviation: $r_1 \rightarrow r_2 + \varepsilon$
> - Is it an equilibrium? No

In this configuration, all candidates have announced platforms with different levels of extremism. Both left-wing candidates are more extreme than the right-wing candidates. If candidates were considering this configuration, there would be a strong centrifugal force in the election incentivizing some of the candidates to move even further away from the median voter. To see this, consider the incentives of candidate r_1. Should this become the actual configuration of platforms, party R would be sure to win the election with either of its candidates, r_1 or r_2. It could thus safely nominate the candidate closest to its ideal point, r_2, and still win the election. In this case, the centrifugal incentives would dominate inside party R such that the most moderate candidate r_1 would lose the nomination to the relatively more partisan candidate r_2. Being rational and forward looking, r_1 would want to avoid this outcome by moving toward its party's ideal point in order to steal the nomination from r_2. All things equal, r_1 would benefit from adopting a platform $r_2 + \varepsilon$ where ε is a small positive number, such that her platform is larger than r_2 to be more appealing to R, while still being more moderate than l_1 in order to win the election. Given that r_1 has this profitable unilateral deviation, this configuration cannot be an equilibrium.[17] Incidentally, it should be noted that party L has two different choices under this configuration, but both of them would lead to the same outcome, i.e., losing the election to R. According to the assumption IA2, then either l_1 or l_2 could be nominated by L.

Example 2: $0 = r_1 < r_2 = -l_1 = -l_2 \leq 1$

- Profitable deviation: If parties are risk-seeking, then $r_1 \rightarrow r_2$
- Is it an equilibrium? No

In this situation, the parties' attitude toward risk will play a crucial role. Let us assume throughout the example that $a < 1$ such that parties are risk-seeking. There is nothing to say about party L's decision, given that its two precandidates are indistinguishable, forcing it to randomize between l_1 and l_2 (as postulated by the assumption IA1 above.) Party R's decision is the interesting one as it presents a dilemma. On one hand, by nominating r_1 it would secure victory for sure with a policy of zero. On the other hand, by nominating r_2 it would induce a lottery where both parties would tie and hence each one would win the election with equal probability. Given that both parties would have platforms exactly on opposite sides of the median voter, the expected policy from this lottery would be zero. Here is where risk-seeking behavior will create a centrifugal force. If party R is a risk-seeker, it will prefer the lottery instead of the sure outcome, and hence it will nominate r_2 instead of r_1. Anticipating this outcome, it is clear that r_1 would not be satisfied with her choice because she would lose the nomination. She would prefer to deviate away from the center all the way to r_2's platform, in order to tie for the nomination and obtain a strictly positive probability winning the election. Given that at least one candidate wishes to change her location, this is not an equilibrium.[18]

Example 3: $0 < r_1 < -l_1 < r_2 < -l_2 \leq 1$

- Profitable deviation: $l_2 \rightarrow -r_1 + \varepsilon$
- Is it an equilibrium? No

This configuration would create centripetal forces in the election, meaning that candidates would have an incentive to become more moderate than they were planning. To see this, consider how nominations would play out in parties L and R. In principle, party L would find candidate l_2 most attractive as she is located closest to its ideal point. This is the candidate that party L would nominate if it was sincere instead of strategic. However, we postulated that both parties are rational, hence anticipating each other's strategies. If party L was planning to nominate l_2, R's best response would be to nominate r_2, but then L's best response would be to nominate l_1, in which case R's best response would be to nominate r_1. Hence both parties will "race toward the center." With rational parties, the two moderate precandidates will be nominated at the expense of the two partisan ones. What incentives does this create for candidate l_2? Given that she would lose the nomination under this configuration of announcements by the other candidates, she would prefer to adopt a drastically more moderate platform, such as $-r_1 + \varepsilon$ where ε is a small positive number. If she did so, competition with R would force L to nominate the new l_2 in order to win the election. This incentive for the most partisan candidate to become the most moderate one illustrates the strong centripetal force in this election, and discards this configuration as a possible equilibrium.[19]

Example 4: $0 < r_1 = r_2 = -l_1 = -l_2 = 1$

- Profitable deviation: $r_1 \rightarrow r_1 - \varepsilon$
- Is it an equilibrium? No

In this configuration, all candidates have adopted the ideal points of their respective parties, that is, they have located at $l_1 = l_2 = -1$ and $r_1 = r_2 = 1$, which we assumed to be the ideal points of the median party members in L and R. One possibility for this configuration is that candidates assumed – mistakenly – that their parties were sincere instead of strategic. In this case, parties would face identical precandidates such that L would not be able to distinguish between l_1 and l_2, and R would not be able to distinguish between r_1 and r_2. Parties would not really have a substantive choice, so they would simply randomize between their precandidates, giving them an equal chance of being nominated. Following the nominations, both parties will have candidates whose platforms are exactly equidistant from the median voter, hence tying in the election with an equal chance of winning. Candidates would have equal expected payoffs: if no candidate deviates from this agreement, each one can expect a probability of ½ of being nominated, and a probability of ½ of winning the election conditional on being nominated. However, the candidates cannot sustain this configuration in equilibrium, as each of them would benefit from deviating unilaterally to a slightly more moderate platform. For example, if r_1 moved infinitesimally toward the center, she would give party R the opportunity to nominate her to subsequently win the election for sure with a right-wing platform, instead of tying with L's left-wing platform. Hence this profile is not a NE.[20]

Example 5: $0 = r_1 = r_2 = l_1 < -l_2 \leq 1$

- Profitable deviation: $l_2 \to 0$
- Is it an equilibrium? No

Here every candidate has decided to converge completely to the center except for l_2 who has decided to remain more partisan. Irrespective of party L's nominee, party R will have to nominate a completely centrist candidate. So candidate l_2 is sure to lose the general election with her partisan platform, thus forgoing any chance of earning the payoff g. Can we imagine a justification for l_2 to adopt this non-centrist platform? Perhaps she hopes to win the nomination over l_1, thus receiving the payoff p for sure, even if she then loses the subsequent election. However, this calculation is misguided for the following reason. In this configuration, party L has the choice between two precandidates with different platforms. Yet the outcome would be the same irrespective of whom it nominates: the policy implemented will be zero either way. So L is indifferent in terms of policy between its two precandidates, and our indifference assumptions kick in. I had assumed in IA3 that in cases such as this one the party will choose the candidate that offers the highest chance of winning the election. This corresponds to l_1 who would have a probability of ½ of beating R's candidates, rather than l_2 whose probability is zero. Therefore, under this configuration, L will nominate l_1. Given that l_2 would currently receive a zero payoff, she would benefit from deviating all the way to the center of the spectrum to achieve strictly positive probabilities of being nominated and winning the election. Hence this is not an equilibrium.[21]

Example 6: $0 = r_1 = r_2 = l_1 = l_2$

- Profitable deviation: None
- Is it an equilibrium? Yes

In this configuration, all the candidates have converged fully to the median voter. Neither party has a choice for the nomination given that all precandidates are indistinguishable. Party L has no choice but to randomize between l_1 and l_2, while party R has no choice but to randomize between r_1 and r_2. Following the primaries, the median voter will face parties with identical platforms, and will hence randomize between the two. The policy implemented after the election will be 0, the ideal point of M. If no candidate deviates from this configuration, each candidate has a probability of ½ of being nominated, and a probability of ½ of winning the election conditional on being nominated. However, if any candidate, say l_2, deviated unilaterally to become slightly more extreme, parties would face the situation described in Example 5. We know from the analysis above that l_2 would not be nominated and hence would not win the election. Given that she would lose the chance of earning the payoff p and then the payoff g, this deviation is not profitable. Since this is true of all other candidates as well, none of them have a profitable unilateral deviation. So this represents an equilibrium – the only one in this election.[22]

These heuristic examples should convey intuitively why the theorem holds. (The complete formal proof comes in the appendix.) Now we are in a better position to discuss the implications of these results.

Discussion: Finding Out if Primaries Really Create Polarization

Adopting primary elections is thought to bring benefits to parties and to the party system as a whole, such as, notably, democratizing the selection of candidates which can otherwise be a quite undemocratic process. In spite of this benefit and others, there have been worries about some social costs that primary elections might carry. One such cost is alleged to be a larger polarization between the policies advocated by candidates from different parties.

In the American politics literature, it is often conjectured that CSMs with more exclusive selectorates will nominate candidates with more extreme platforms. For example, closed primaries, where only party members can vote, are presumed to elect more extreme nominees than open primaries, where non-registered citizens can vote. One alleged reason is that party members are typically composed of passionate activists rather than dispassionate moderates. A first set of statistical studies seemed to confirm this conjecture,[23] which spawned a theoretical literature claiming that primary elections cause candidates to diverge.[24]

However, the early empirical studies and the subsequent formal models are contradicted by the newer statistical research. A number of studies have been reporting a null finding in their correlations between closed primaries and candidate divergence.[25] How can we make sense of the contradictory empirical findings? One way is to use formal theory to try shedding light on this complex issue. My interpretation of the existing findings is that primary elections might have a contingent effect, causing polarization only under certain conditions. If so, it would be useful to have formal models predicting full convergence, meaning that primary candidates move to the center of the political spectrum. Theories of this kind could then be contrasted with theories making the opposite prediction to better understand the respective assumptions that led to contradictory predictions. This comparison would enable a better understanding of candidate selection, at least theoretically, which in turn could hopefully motivate further empirical studies.

This was the objective of my model in this chapter. In an attempt to be straightforward, I endeavored to add only essential features of primary elections to the well-established spatial voting model of Downs (1957). Before the standard election between two parties, I added a previous stage where each party holds a competitive nomination between two precandidates. The model included at least five features that can create centrifugal forces: (1) parties with ideal points on opposite sides of the median voter; (2) parties that are policy-motivated instead of office-motivated; (3) primary platforms that are sticky throughout the election; (4) an independent payoff to candidates from winning the primary; and (5) risk-seeking parties that prefer a lottery between two extreme candidates instead of winning the election with a moderate candidate.

Given these centrifugal forces, it is surprising that we did not find any polarization whatsoever. The result in this model is a median-voter theorem with primary elections, whereby all the candidates during the nomination process announce completely centrist platforms. What can account for this counter-intuitive result? It must be that some centripetal forces have more than compensated for the centrifugal ones. One of the most important forces illustrated by this model is the rationality of party members. A take-away point about primary elections is that strategic voting represents a powerful force driving parties toward the center. According to this view, it should not matter whether primary voters are super-extreme: if these primary voters are strategic, my model predicts that precandidates within the party will converge to the median voter. The same result was found in Serra (2015), namely that fully strategic parties should locate at the center in spite of holding primaries. While that previous research included the centrifugal forces (1), (2) and (3) mentioned above, this chapter is original in adding (4) and (5). Given that I find the same result, namely the complete convergence to the center of all candidates, the model in this chapter can be considered a robustness check.

These results, however, remain silent about boundedly-rational primary voters. If they voted sincerely, maybe some polarization would occur. In fact, I am finding theoretical support for this hypothesis in parallel research: in Serra (2017), I find that sincere voting in primary elections leads to more divergence than strategic voting. A final implication of this research can hopefully be conveyed: according to these findings, empirical research should pay more attention to a neglected variable, namely the degree of rationality of party members whereby they will vote strategically or sincerely in primaries. If this variable was contemplated more often in statistical studies of primaries, I believe we could make further progress in this debate.

Appendix: Proof of the Theorem

General Considerations

Without loss of generality, the configurations in Table 4.1, along with their symmetric counterparts, are an exhaustive list of all the possible configurations of platforms that candidates may adopt. All cases are mutually exclusive. We assume that l_1, $l_2 \in [-1, 0]$ and r_1, $r_2 \in [0, 1]$. With this list in mind, I proceed to prove the theorem in this chapter. The proof needs to be separated in three cases corresponding to risk-averse parties ($a > 1$), risk-seeking parties ($a < 1$), and risk-neutral parties ($a = 1$).

Proof with Risk-Averse Parties (a > 1)

The game must be solved by backward induction. The procedure will be the following: we start by solving the game at its last stage – the general election – and we find the median voter's strategy profile that forms a NE in every situation in which she might be called upon to act. Given this strategy by the median voter, we consider the reduced game at the second stage – the nominations by each party – and we find the strategies S_L^* and S_R^* that form a NE for the parties in every possible subgame in which they might be called upon to act. Finally, for each S_L^* and S_R^* we consider the reduced game at its first stage – the platform adoption – and we find all the strategies S_c^* that form a NE for the candidates. At this stage (the platform adoption), we know that a NE of the reduced game will be a SPNE of the game as a whole. This subsection will carry out this procedure for the case $a > 1$ while the following two sections will carry out the same procedure for the cases $a = 1$ and $a < 1$.

Table 4.1 All Possible Profiles of Strategies by Candidates

Configuration 1	$0 = r_1 = r_2 = -l_1 = -l_2$
Configuration 2	$0 < r_1 = r_2 = -l_1 = -l_2$
Configuration 3	$0 = r_1 = r_2 = -l_1 < -l_2$
Configuration 4	$0 < r_1 = r_2 = -l_1 < -l_2$
Configuration 5	$0 = r_1 = r_2 < -l_1 = -l_2$
Configuration 6	$0 < r_1 = r_2 < -l_1 = -l_2$
Configuration 7	$0 = r_1 < r_2 = -l_1 = -l_2$
Configuration 8	$0 < r_1 < r_2 = -l_1 = -l_2$
Configuration 9	$0 = r_1 = r_2 < -l_1 < -l_2$
Configuration 10	$0 < r_1 = r_2 < -l_1 < -l_2$
Configuration 11	$0 = r_1 < r_2 = -l_1 < -l_2$
Configuration 12	$0 < r_1 < r_2 = -l_1 < -l_2$
Configuration 13	$0 = r_1 < r_2 < -l_1 = -l_2$
Configuration 14	$0 < r_1 < r_2 < -l_1 = -l_2$
Configuration 15	$0 = r_1 < r_2 < -l_1 < -l_2$
Configuration 16	$0 < r_1 < r_2 < -l_1 < -l_2$
Configuration 17	$0 = r_1 = -l_1 < r_2 = -l_2$
Configuration 18	$0 < r_1 = -l_1 < r_2 = -l_2$
Configuration 19	$0 = r_1 = -l_1 < r_2 < -l_2$
Configuration 20	$0 < r_1 = -l_1 < r_2 < -l_2$
Configuration 21	$0 = r_1 < -l_1 < r_2 = -l_2$
Configuration 22	$0 < r_1 < -l_1 < r_2 = -l_2$
Configuration 23	$0 = r_1 < -l_1 < r_2 < -l_2$
Configuration 24	$0 < r_1 < -l_1 < r_2 < -l_2$
Configuration 25	$0 = r_1 < -l_1 = -l_2 < r_2$
Configuration 26	$0 < r_1 < -l_1 = -l_2 < r_2$
Configuration 27	$0 = r_1 < -l_1 < -l_2 < r_2$
Configuration 28	$0 < r_1 < -l_1 < -l_2 < r_2$

Third Stage

First we prove that sincere voting is a weakly dominant strategy for voters. When casting her ballot, a voter is either pivotal or not. If she is pivotal, then voting other than sincerely will make her worse off (or no better off if she is indifferent between both parties). If her vote is not pivotal then any strategy leads to the same outcome. Therefore, sincere voting is never worse and sometimes better than not voting sincerely, and hence it weakly dominates every other strategy for voters. If we assume that voters will never choose a weakly dominated strategy, they will vote sincerely. Given that the preferences of voters are symmetric and single-peaked, and that we assumed the existence of a median voter, the electorate will behave according to the preferences of this median voter. There are two possible subgames: either $r_i = -l_j$ or $r_i \neq -l_j$. In the latter case, the candidate closer to zero will win the election. In the former case, there is a tie between the candidates, and the median voter will decide by flipping a coin.

Second Stage

Without loss of generality, the configurations in Table 4.2, along with their symmetric counterparts, are an exhaustive list of all the possible subgames that parties may face, along with their corresponding Nash equilibria. I only list the equilibria in pure strategies. (Analyzing the possible

Table 4.2 Equilibria between Parties: Risk-Averse Case

		NE without IA3	NE with IA3
Subg. 1	$0 = r_1 = r_2 = -l_1 = -l_2$	(rand, rand)	(rand, rand)
Subg. 2	$0 < r_1 = r_2 = -l_1 = -l_2$	(rand, rand)	(rand, rand)
Subg. 3	$0 = r_1 = r_2 = -l_1 < -l_2$	(l_1, rand) and (l_2, rand)	(l_1, rand)
Subg. 4	$0 < r_1 = r_2 = -l_1 < -l_2$	(l_1, rand)	(l_1, rand)
Subg. 5	$0 = r_1 = r_2 < -l_1 = -l_2$	(rand, rand)	(rand, rand)
Subg. 6	$0 < r_1 = r_2 < -l_1 = -l_2$	(rand, rand)	(rand, rand)
Subg. 7	$0 = r_1 < r_2 = -l_1 = -l_2$	(rand, r_1)	(rand, r_1)
Subg. 8	$0 < r_1 < r_2 = -l_1 = -l_2$	(rand, r_1)	(rand, r_1)
Subg. 9	$0 = r_1 = r_2 < -l_1 < -l_2$	(l_1, rand) and (l_2, rand)	(l_1, rand) and (l_2, rand)
Subg. 10	$0 < r_1 = r_2 < -l_1 < -l_2$	(l_1, rand) and (l_2, rand)	(l_1, rand) and (l_2, rand)
Subg. 11	$0 = r_1 < r_2 = -l_1 < -l_2$	(l_1, r_1)	(l_1, r_1)
Subg. 12	$0 < r_1 < r_2 = -l_1 < -l_2$	(l_1, r_1)	(l_1, r_1)
Subg. 13	$0 = r_1 < r_2 < -l_1 = -l_2$	(rand, r_2)	(rand, r_2)
Subg. 14	$0 < r_1 < r_2 < -l_1 = -l_2$	(rand, r_2)	(rand, r_2)
Subg. 15	$0 = r_1 < r_2 < -l_1 < -l_2$	(l_1, r_2) and (l_2, r_2)	(l_1, r_2) and (l_2, r_2)
Subg. 16	$0 < r_1 < r_2 < -l_1 < -l_2$	(l_1, r_2) and (l_2, r_2)	(l_1, r_2) and (l_2, r_2)
Subg. 17	$0 = r_1 = -l_1 < r_2 = -l_2$	(l_2, r_1) and (l_1, r_2) and (l_1, r_1)	(l_1, r_1)
Subg. 18	$0 < r_1 = -l_1 < r_2 = -l_2$	(l_1, r_1)	(l_1, r_1)
Subg. 19	$0 = r_1 = -l_1 < r_2 < -l_2$	(l_1, r_1) and (l_1, r_2)	(l_1, r_1)
Subg. 20	$0 < r_1 = -l_1 < r_2 < -l_2$	(l_1, r_1)	(l_1, r_1)
Subg. 21	$0 = r_1 < -l_1 < r_2 = -l_2$	(l_1, r_1) and (l_2, r_1)	(l_1, r_1) and (l_2, r_1)
Subg. 22	$0 < r_1 < -l_1 < r_2 = -l_2$	(l_1, r_1) and (l_2, r_1)	(l_1, r_1) and (l_2, r_1)
Subg. 23	$0 = r_1 < -l_1 < r_2 < -l_2$	(l_1, r_1)	(l_1, r_1)
Subg. 24	$0 < r_1 < -l_1 < r_2 < -l_2$	(l_1, r_1)	(l_1, r_1)
Subg. 25	$0 = r_1 < -l_1 = -l_2 < r_2$	(rand, r_1)	(rand, r_1)
Subg. 26	$0 < r_1 < -l_1 = -l_2 < r_2$	(rand, r_1)	(rand, r_1)
Subg. 27	$0 = r_1 < -l_1 < -l_2 < r_2$	(l_1, r_1) and (l_2, r_1)	(l_1, r_1) and (l_2, r_1)
Subg. 28	$0 < r_1 < -l_1 < -l_2 < r_2$	(l_1, r_1) and (l_2, r_1)	(l_1, r_1) and (l_2, r_1)

mixed-strategy equilibria would not change the results, so I ignore them in this proof.) In this list, the pair of strategies (l_i, r_j) refers to the decision of party L to nominate l_i in conjunction with the decision of party R to nominate r_j. The strategy labeled "rand" is used when a party is forced to randomize equally between its two candidates because they are indistinguishable.

It will be important to keep in mind the indifference assumptions described in the text, which said the following. Given the platform that the rival party is expected to adopt, if a party is indifferent between its two precandidates in terms of expected policy, it will choose the one that offers the highest chance of winning the election (IA3). If both offer the same chance of winning the election and they both have distinct platforms, then either can be chosen in equilibrium (IA2). And if they both adopted the same platform making them indistinguishable, the party is forced to randomize between them (IA1). The third column lists all the NE in each subgame without applying the assumption IA3. The fourth column lists all the NE after eliminating those not conforming to IA3.

To be part of a SPNE, any strategy profile S_L^* and S_R^* must induce these NE in the corresponding subgames. Note that several subgames admit two equilibria in pure strategies. Out of those, subgames 3, 17 and 19 are reduced to having a unique equilibrium upon applying the indifference assumption IA3, and the rest remain with two NE even after applying this indifference assumption.

To illustrate how this table was derived, I will solve subgame 3. Party R does not have a real choice since both of its candidates have adopted indistinguishable platforms. According to assumption IA1, its unique available strategy is to randomize between r_1 and r_2. On the other hand, party L has a choice between $l_1 = 0$ and $l_2 > 0$. If L nominates l_1 it will tie with R and the policy implemented will be 0 for sure. If L nominates l_2 it will lose against R and the policy implemented will be 0 for sure as well. Hence, both nominations lead to the same policy outcome and give L the same utility. Therefore, in terms of policy, L is indifferent between l_1 and l_2, which leads to two possible Nash equilibria in pure strategies: (l_1, rand) and (l_2, rand). However, the second one will be eliminated by our indifference assumption IA3. According to this assumption, L has a lexicographic preference for victory that only plays a role when l_1 and l_2 would yield the same payoff in terms of policy. By nominating l_1 the party's probability of winning would be one-half, whereas by nominating l_2 it would be zero. Consequently, l_1 will be nominated instead of l_2, and the only NE that survives is (l_1, rand).

It is also illustrative to solve subgame 10. Party R does not have a choice because its two precandidates choose identical platforms. Party L can choose between two different candidates but they would both lead to the same outcome, namely, they would both lose against the candidate from the rival party. That is because either r_1 or r_2 are strictly closer to the median voter than both l_1 and l_2. According to assumption IA2, Party L can nominate either of its precandidates in equilibrium, which explains why this profile has two Nash equilibria in pure strategies: (l_1, rand) and (l_2, rand).

Analysis of the other 26 subgames follows similar steps.

First Stage

Without loss of generality, the profiles in Table 4.3, along with their symmetric counterparts, are an exhaustive list of all the possible profiles of platforms that candidates may adopt, along with a profitable deviation, if any. In this table, ε is a strictly positive number that is infinitesimally small.

I will prove why Profile 1 is an equilibrium for candidates and therefore a solution to this game. Suppose none of the candidates deviated from it. Then parties would face subgame 1, and we can see from Table 4.2 that each party randomizes between their candidates. So each candidate has a probability of ½ to be nominated and a probability of ½ to win the election conditional on being nominated. Their expected payoff is thus $(p/2) + (g/4)$. Suppose, on the other hand, that one of the candidates deviated unilaterally. Then parties would face subgame 3 or its symmetrical counterpart. The candidate that deviated might have been hoping to win the nomination for sure to receive a payoff p even if she later loses the election. However, this outcome would not materialize. As I analyzed above, the unique NE that survives our indifference assumptions in subgame 3 is the one where the centrist candidates are nominated to the detriment of the extreme candidate. Hence the candidate who deviated would lose the nomination and would obtain a zero payoff. Such a deviation is therefore not profitable, and the configuration is a NE.

Now I will prove that Profile 10 is not an equilibrium. In particular, I will show that a centrifugal force exists in this situation whereby candidate r_2 would prefer to become more extreme. As I analyzed above, if this profile is adopted then both candidates within party R would be tied to get the nomination, and whoever gets the nomination is sure to win the election. However, if r_2 moved to the right an infinitesimal amount, candidates would fall in Profile 16. According to Table 4.2 (and also Example 1 in the main text), in this profile, r_2 would secure the nomination

Table 4.3 Equilibria between Candidates: Risk–Averse Case

		Profitable Deviation	Is it a Nash Equilibrium?
Profile 1	$0 = r_1 = r_2 = -l_1 = -l_2$	None	Yes
Profile 2	$0 < r_1 = r_2 = -l_1 = -l_2$	$r_1 \rightarrow r_1 - \varepsilon$	No
Profile 3	$0 = r_1 = r_2 = -l_1 < -l_2$	$l_2 \rightarrow 0$	No
Profile 4	$0 < r_1 = r_2 = -l_1 < -l_2$	$l_2 \rightarrow l_1 + \varepsilon$	No
Profile 5	$0 = r_1 = r_2 < -l_1 = -l_2$	$r_2 \rightarrow r_2 + \varepsilon$	No
Profile 6	$0 < r_1 = r_2 < -l_1 = -l_2$	$r_2 \rightarrow r_2 + \varepsilon$	No
Profile 7	$0 = r_1 < r_2 = -l_1 = -l_2$	$r_2 \rightarrow r_2 - \varepsilon$	No
Profile 8	$0 < r_1 < r_2 = -l_1 = -l_2$	$r_2 \rightarrow r_2 - \varepsilon$	No
Profile 9	$0 = r_1 = r_2 < -l_1 < -l_2$	$r_2 \rightarrow r_2 + \varepsilon$	No
Profile 10	$0 < r_1 = r_2 < -l_1 < -l_2$	$r_2 \rightarrow r_2 + \varepsilon$	No
Profile 11	$0 = r_1 < r_2 = -l_1 < -l_2$	$r_2 \rightarrow r_2 - \varepsilon$	No
Profile 12	$0 < r_1 < r_2 = -l_1 < -l_2$	$r_2 \rightarrow r_2 - \varepsilon$	No
Profile 13	$0 = r_1 < r_2 < -l_1 = -l_2$	$r_1 \rightarrow r_2 + \varepsilon$	No
Profile 14	$0 < r_1 < r_2 < -l_1 = -l_2$	$r_1 \rightarrow r_2 + \varepsilon$	No
Profile 15	$0 = r_1 < r_2 < -l_1 < -l_2$	$r_1 \rightarrow r_2 + \varepsilon$	No
Profile 16	$0 < r_1 < r_2 < -l_1 < -l_2$	$r_1 \rightarrow r_2 + \varepsilon$	No
Profile 17	$0 = r_1 = -l_1 < r_2 = -l_2$	$r_2 \rightarrow 0$	No
Profile 18	$0 < r_1 = -l_1 < r_2 = -l_2$	$r_2 \rightarrow r_1 - \varepsilon$	No
Profile 19	$0 = r_1 = -l_1 < r_2 < -l_2$	$l_2 \rightarrow 0$	No
Profile 20	$0 < r_1 = -l_1 < r_2 < -l_2$	$r_2 \rightarrow r_1 - \varepsilon$	No
Profile 21	$0 = r_1 < -l_1 < r_2 = -l_2$	$r_2 \rightarrow r_1 + \varepsilon$	No
Profile 22	$0 < r_1 < -l_1 < r_2 = -l_2$	$r_2 \rightarrow r_1 + \varepsilon$	No
Profile 23	$0 = r_1 < -l_1 < r_2 < -l_2$	$r_2 \rightarrow r_1 + \varepsilon$	No
Profile 24	$0 < r_1 < -l_1 < r_2 < -l_2$	$r_2 \rightarrow r_1 + \varepsilon$	No
Profile 25	$0 = r_1 < -l_1 = -l_2 < r_2$	$r_2 \rightarrow r_1 + \varepsilon$	No
Profile 26	$0 < r_1 < -l_1 = -l_2 < r_2$	$r_2 \rightarrow r_1 + \varepsilon$	No
Profile 27	$0 = r_1 < -l_1 < -l_2 < r_2$	$r_2 \rightarrow r_1 + \varepsilon$	No
Profile 28	$0 < r_1 < -l_1 < -l_2 < r_2$	$r_2 \rightarrow r_1 + \varepsilon$	No

for sure and would then win the election. This is an improvement for the candidate, so Profile 10 cannot be a NE.

Analysis of the remaining subgames follows similar steps: it can be proved that none of them is a Nash Equilibrium (see the profitable deviations in each case). Thus Profile 1 is the unique NE of the reduced game, and it is the unique strategy profile of candidates that can be part of a SPNE. Therefore in any strategy profile S_c^*, S_L^* and S_R^* that forms a SPNE, the outcome will be the same: candidates adopt the platforms in Profile 1, which are $0 = r_1 = r_2 = -l_1 = -l_2$. This is exactly what the theorem says.

Proof with Risk-Seeking Parties (a < 1)

Once again, we solve the game by backward induction.

Third Stage

Sincere voting is still a weakly dominant strategy for the voters. The proof is the same as for risk-averse parties.

Second Stage

In Table 4.4, we list again all the possible subgames that parties may face, along with their corresponding NE. Note the use of the word "and" when several equilibria are possible, and the word "or" when only one out of two different equilibria is possible.

As we can see by comparing Table 4.4 for risk-seeking parties with Table 4.2 for risk-averse parties, all the subgames are solved the same way except for subgames 7, 8, 11, 12, 17, 18, 21 and 22.

As an illustration, I will derive the Nash equilibria in subgame 8. Party L does not have a real choice for nomination since both l_1 and l_2 have adopted indistinguishable platforms. Thus its only choice is to randomize between its two candidates. On the other hand, party R may nominate r_1 and win the election for sure, or nominate r_2 and tie with party L thus inducing a lottery between both parties. The preferred choice for R depends on the exact position of r_1. To be concrete, we need to think of a value called the *certainty equivalent*. This corresponds to the policy location that would give R the exact same payoff as a random draw between r_2 and $-r_2$. Since parties are risk-seekers, we know that the certainty equivalent for R is to the right of zero. If r_1 is to the left of that certainty equivalent, then R will prefer to take on risk by nominating r_2,

Table 4.4 Equilibria between Parties: Risk-Seeking Case

		NE without IA3	NE with IA3
Subg. 1	$0 = r_1 = r_2 = -l_1 = -l_2$	(rand, rand)	(rand, rand)
Subg. 2	$0 < r_1 = r_2 = -l_1 = -l_2$	(rand, rand)	(rand, rand)
Subg. 3	$0 = r_1 = r_2 = -l_1 < -l_2$	(l_1, rand) and (l_2, rand)	(l_1, rand)
Subg. 4	$0 < r_1 = r_2 = -l_1 < -l_2$	(l_1, rand)	(l_1, rand)
Subg. 5	$0 = r_1 = r_2 < -l_1 = -l_2$	(rand, rand)	(rand, rand)
Subg. 6	$0 < r_1 = r_2 < -l_1 = -l_2$	(rand, rand)	(rand, rand)
Subg. 7	$0 = r_1 < r_2 = -l_1 = -l_2$	(rand, r_2)	(rand, r_2)
Subg. 8	$0 < r_1 < r_2 = -l_1 = -l_2$	(rand, r_1) *or* (rand, r_2)	(rand, r_1) *or* (rand, r_2)
Subg. 9	$0 = r_1 = r_2 < -l_1 < -l_2$	(l_1, rand) and (l_2, rand)	(l_1, rand) and (l_2, rand)
Subg. 10	$0 < r_1 = r_2 < -l_1 < -l_2$	(l_1, rand) and (l_2, rand)	(l_1, rand) and (l_2, rand)
Subg. 11	$0 = r_1 < r_2 = -l_1 < -l_2$	(l_1, r_2)	(l_1, r_2)
Subg. 12	$0 < r_1 < r_2 = -l_1 < -l_2$	(l_1, r_1) *or* (l_1, r_2)	(l_1, r_1) *or* (l_1, r_2)
Subg. 13	$0 = r_1 < r_2 < -l_1 = -l_2$	(rand, r_2)	(rand, r_2)
Subg. 14	$0 < r_1 < r_2 < -l_1 = -l_2$	(rand, r_2)	(rand, r_2)
Subg. 15	$0 = r_1 < r_2 < -l_1 < -l_2$	(l_1, r_2) and (l_2, r_2)	(l_1, r_2) and (l_2, r_2)
Subg. 16	$0 < r_1 < r_2 < -l_1 < -l_2$	(l_1, r_2) and (l_2, r_2)	(l_1, r_2) and (l_2, r_2)
Subg. 17	$0 = r_1 = -l_1 < r_2 = -l_2$	(l_1, r_1) and (l_2, r_2)	(l_1, r_1) and (l_2, r_2)
Subg. 18	$0 < r_1 = -l_1 < r_2 = -l_2$	(l_1, r_1) and possibly (l_2, r_2)	(l_1, r_1) and possibly (l_2, r_2)
Subg. 19	$0 = r_1 = -l_1 < r_2 < -l_2$	(l_1, r_1) and (l_1, r_2)	(l_1, r_1)
Subg. 20	$0 < r_1 = -l_1 < r_2 < -l_2$	(l_1, r_1)	(l_1, r_1)
Subg. 21	$0 = r_1 < -l_1 < r_2 = -l_2$	(l_1, r_1) and possibly (l_2, r_2)	(l_1, r_1) and possibly (l_2, r_2)
Subg. 22	$0 < r_1 < -l_1 < r_2 = -l_2$	(l_1, r_1) and possibly (l_2, r_2)	(l_1, r_1) and possibly (l_2, r_2)
Subg. 23	$0 = r_1 < -l_1 < r_2 < -l_2$	(l_1, r_1)	(l_1, r_1)
Subg. 24	$0 < r_1 < -l_1 < r_2 < -l_2$	(l_1, r_1)	(l_1, r_1)
Subg. 25	$0 = r_1 < -l_1 = -l_2 < r_2$	(rand, r_1)	(rand, r_1)
Subg. 26	$0 < r_1 < -l_1 = -l_2 < r_2$	(rand, r_1)	(rand, r_1)
Subg. 27	$0 = r_1 < -l_1 < -l_2 < r_2$	(l_1, r_1) and (l_2, r_1)	(l_1, r_1) and (l_2, r_1)
Subg. 28	$0 < r_1 < -l_1 < -l_2 < r_2$	(l_1, r_1) and (l_2, r_1)	(l_1, r_1) and (l_2, r_1)

and the unique NE will be (rand, r_2). If r_1 is to the right of that certainty equivalent, then R will prefer to win for sure by nominating r_1, and the unique NE will be (rand, r_1). If r_1 is exactly at that certainty equivalent, then R will be indifferent between r_1 and r_2, and the assumption IA3 dictates that (rand, r_1) should be the NE.

Subgame 17 is also worth studying explicitly. Suppose L nominates l_2. Then if R nominates r_1 it will win the election for sure with a policy of zero for certain. But if it nominates r_2 it will tie with L thus inducing a lottery between two divergent policies with an average location of zero. Given that parties are risk-seeking, R prefers nominating the extreme but uncertain candidate r_2 instead of the centrist but riskless candidate r_1. The same logic applies to L so (l_2, r_2) is a NE. This result illustrates how a love of risk can act as a centrifugal force. However, this is not the only equilibrium. Suppose L nominates l_1. Then R is indifferent in terms of policy between its two precandidates, because they would both lead for sure to the same policy of zero. However, r_1 would have a ½ probability of winning the election whereas r_2 would have none; so the assumption IA3 dictates that r_1 should be chosen. The same logic applies to L so (l_1, r_1) is a NE. Which of the two equilibria would occur? In this context it is impossible to know, so both Nash equilibria are valid predictions.

The derivation of the equilibria in the remaining 26 subgames follows the same logic.

First Stage

In Table 4.5, we list again all the possible profiles of platforms that candidates may adopt, along with a profitable deviation, if any.

I will only prove explicitly that Profile 17 cannot be an equilibrium. We saw in the analysis above that such a profile by candidates could lead parties to adopt one of two Nash equilibria. We cannot know which one will be chosen by parties, but I will show that neither of them can be sustained as part of a SPNE. Candidates need to form a belief about the NE that will be adopted by parties. On one hand, if candidates believed that parties will choose (l_1, r_1), then precandidate r_2 would expect to lose the nomination; so she would prefer changing her location to zero, which would induce subgame 3. According to Table 4.4, this would give r_2 a strictly positive probability of being nominated and winning the election, which is an improvement. So Profile 17 could not be an equilibrium under this belief. On the other hand, if candidates believed that parties will choose (l_2, r_2), then precandidate l_1 would expect to lose the nomination; so she would prefer changing her location to l_2, which would induce subgame 7. According to Table 4.4 (and Example 2 in the main text), this would give l_1 a strictly positive probability of being nominated and winning the election, which is an improvement. So Profile 17 could not be an equilibrium under this belief. In sum, this profile cannot be sustained by candidates, whichever equilibrium is expected to be chosen by parties subsequently.

All other profiles are studied in a similar way. In particular, the proof that Profile 1 is a NE is the same as in the risk–averse case. From Table 4.5 we also conclude that Profile 1 is the only solution.

Proof with Risk-Neutral Parties (a = 1)

Once again, we solve the game by backward induction.

Third Stage

Sincere voting is a weakly dominant strategy for voters. The proof is the same as with risk-averse parties.

Table 4.5 Equilibria between Candidates: Risk-Seeking Case

		Profitable Deviation	Is it a Nash Equilibrium?
Profile 1	$0 = r_1 = r_2 = -l_1 = -l_2$	None	Yes
Profile 2	$0 < r_1 = r_2 = -l_1 = -l_2$	$r_1 \to r_1 - \varepsilon$	No
Profile 3	$0 = r_1 = r_2 = -l_1 < -l_2$	$l_2 \to 0$	No
Profile 4	$0 < r_1 = r_2 = -l_1 < -l_2$	$l_2 \to l_1 + \varepsilon$	No
Profile 5	$0 = r_1 = r_2 < -l_1 = -l_2$	$r_2 \to r_2 + \varepsilon$	No
Profile 6	$0 < r_1 = r_2 < -l_1 = -l_2$	$r_2 \to r_2 + \varepsilon$	No
Profile 7	$0 = r_1 < r_2 = -l_1 = -l_2$	$r_1 \to r_2$	No
Profile 8	$0 < r_1 < r_2 = -l_1 = -l_2$	$r_2 \to r_2 - \varepsilon$	No
Profile 9	$0 = r_1 = r_2 < -l_1 < -l_2$	$r_2 \to r_2 + \varepsilon$	No
Profile 10	$0 < r_1 = r_2 < -l_1 < -l_2$	$r_2 \to r_2 + \varepsilon$	No
Profile 11	$0 = r_1 < r_2 = -l_1 < -l_2$	$r_1 \to r_2$	No
Profile 12	$0 < r_1 < r_2 = -l_1 < -l_2$	$r_2 \to r_2 - \varepsilon$	No
Profile 13	$0 = r_1 < r_2 < -l_1 = -l_2$	$r_1 \to r_2 + \varepsilon$	No
Profile 14	$0 < r_1 < r_2 < -l_1 = -l_2$	$r_1 \to r_2 + \varepsilon$	No
Profile 15	$0 = r_1 < r_2 < -l_1 < -l_2$	$r_1 \to r_2 + \varepsilon$	No
Profile 16	$0 < r_1 < r_2 < -l_1 < -l_2$	$r_1 \to r_2 + \varepsilon$	No
Profile 17	$0 = r_1 = -l_1 < r_2 = -l_2$	If the NE is (l_1, r_1) then $r_2 \to 0$	No
		If the NE is (l_2, r_2) then $l_1 \to l_2$	
Profile 18	$0 < r_1 = -l_1 < r_2 = -l_2$	$r_2 \to r_1 - \varepsilon$	No
Profile 19	$0 = r_1 = -l_1 < r_2 < -l_2$	$l_2 \to 0$	No
Profile 20	$0 < r_1 = -l_1 < r_2 < -l_2$	$r_2 \to r_1 - \varepsilon$	No
Profile 21	$0 = r_1 < -l_1 < r_2 = -l_2$	$r_2 \to r_1 + \varepsilon$	No
Profile 22	$0 < r_1 < -l_1 < r_2 = -l_2$	$r_2 \to r_1 + \varepsilon$	No
Profile 23	$0 = r_1 < -l_1 < r_2 < -l_2$	$r_2 \to r_1 + \varepsilon$	No
Profile 24	$0 < r_1 < -l_1 < r_2 < -l_2$	$r_2 \to r_1 + \varepsilon$	No
Profile 25	$0 = r_1 < -l_1 = -l_2 < r_2$	$r_2 \to r_1 + \varepsilon$	No
Profile 26	$0 < r_1 < -l_1 = -l_2 < r_2$	$r_2 \to r_1 + \varepsilon$	No
Profile 27	$0 = r_1 < -l_1 < -l_2 < r_2$	$r_2 \to r_1 + \varepsilon$	No
Profile 28	$0 < r_1 < -l_1 < -l_2 < r_2$	$r_2 \to r_1 + \varepsilon$	No

Second Stage

In Table 4.6, we list again all the possible subgames that parties may face, along with their corresponding NE.

As we can see by comparing Table 4.6 for risk-neutral parties with Table 4.2 for risk-averse parties, all the subgames are solved the same way except for subgames 7, 11 and 17. Let us study subgame 7. Party L does not have a real choice since both of its candidates have adopted indistinguishable platforms. Its unique available strategy is to randomize between l_1 and l_2. On the other hand, party R has a choice between $r_1 = 0$ and $r_2 > 0$. If it nominates r_1 it will win the election over L and the policy implemented will be 0 for sure. If it nominates r_2 it will tie with L and the policy implemented will be a random draw between r_2 and $-r_2$, which represents a lottery with an average policy of zero. This presents a dilemma for R that it would not face if it was risk-averse instead of being risk-neutral. If R was risk-averse, we can see from Table 4.2 that it would prefer the riskless candidate r_1. However, now that R is risk-neutral, both candidates are

Table 4.6 Equilibria between Parties: Risk-Neutral Case

		NE without IA3	NE with IA3
Subg. 1	$0 = r_1 = r_2 = -l_1 = -l_2$	(rand, rand)	(rand, rand)
Subg. 2	$0 < r_1 = r_2 = -l_1 = -l_2$	(rand, rand)	(rand, rand)
Subg. 3	$0 = r_1 = r_2 = -l_1 < -l_2$	$(l_1,$ rand$)$ and $(l_2,$ rand$)$	$(l_1,$ rand$)$
Subg. 4	$0 < r_1 = r_2 = -l_1 < -l_2$	$(l_1,$ rand$)$	$(l_1,$ rand$)$
Subg. 5	$0 = r_1 = r_2 < -l_1 = -l_2$	(rand, rand)	(rand, rand)
Subg. 6	$0 < r_1 = r_2 < -l_1 = -l_2$	(rand, rand)	(rand, rand)
Subg. 7	$0 = r_1 < r_2 = -l_1 = -l_2$	(rand, r_1) and (rand, r_2)	(rand, r_1)
Subg. 8	$0 < r_1 < r_2 = -l_1 = -l_2$	(rand, r_1)	(rand, r_1)
Subg. 9	$0 = r_1 = r_2 < -l_1 < -l_2$	$(l_1,$ rand$)$ and $(l_2,$ rand$)$	$(l_1,$ rand$)$ and $(l_2,$rand$)$
Subg. 10	$0 < r_1 = r_2 < -l_1 < -l_2$	$(l_1,$ rand$)$ and $(l_2,$ rand$)$	$(l_1,$ rand$)$ and $(l_2,$rand$)$
Subg. 11	$0 = r_1 < r_2 = -l_1 < -l_2$	(l_1, r_1) and (l_1, r_2)	(l_1, r_1)
Subg. 12	$0 < r_1 < r_2 = -l_1 < -l_2$	(l_1, r_1)	(l_1, r_1)
Subg. 13	$0 = r_1 < r_2 < -l_1 = -l_2$	(rand, r_2)	(rand, r_2)
Subg. 14	$0 < r_1 < r_2 < -l_1 = -l_2$	(rand, r_2)	(rand, r_2)
Subg. 15	$0 = r_1 < r_2 < -l_1 < -l_2$	(l_1, r_2) and (l_2, r_2)	(l_1, r_2) and (l_2, r_2)
Subg. 16	$0 < r_1 < r_2 < -l_1 < -l_2$	(l_1, r_2) and (l_2, r_2)	(l_1, r_2) and (l_2, r_2)
Subg. 17	$0 = r_1 = -l_1 < r_2 = -l_2$	(l_1, r_1) and (l_1, r_2) and (l_2, r_1) and (l_2, r_2)	(l_1, r_1)
Subg. 18	$0 < r_1 = -l_1 < r_2 = -l_2$	(l_1, r_1)	(l_1, r_1)
Subg. 19	$0 = r_1 = -l_1 < r_2 < -l_2$	(l_1, r_1) and (l_1, r_2)	(l_1, r_1)
Subg. 20	$0 < r_1 = -l_1 < r_2 < -l_2$	(l_1, r_1)	(l_1, r_1)
Subg. 21	$0 = r_1 < -l_1 < r_2 = -l_2$	(l_1, r_1) and (l_2, r_1)	(l_1, r_1) and (l_2, r_1)
Subg. 22	$0 < r_1 < -l_1 < r_2 = -l_2$	(l_1, r_1) and (l_2, r_1)	(l_1, r_1) and (l_2, r_1)
Subg. 23	$0 = r_1 < -l_1 < r_2 < -l_2$	(l_1, r_1)	(l_1, r_1)
Subg. 24	$0 < r_1 < -l_1 < r_2 < -l_2$	(l_1, r_1)	(l_1, r_1)
Subg. 25	$0 = r_1 < -l_1 = -l_2 < r_2$	(rand, r_1)	(rand, r_1)
Subg. 26	$0 < r_1 < -l_1 = -l_2 < r_2$	(rand, r_1)	(rand, r_1)
Subg. 27	$0 = r_1 < -l_1 < -l_2 < r_2$	(l_1, r_1) and (l_2, r_1)	(l_1, r_1) and (l_2, r_1)
Subg. 28	$0 < r_1 < -l_1 < -l_2 < r_2$	(l_1, r_1) and (l_2, r_1)	(l_1, r_1) and (l_2, r_1)

equivalent because R is indifferent between obtaining the policy 0 for sure and facing a random draw with an expected policy of 0. Hence, in principle, this subgame has two Nash equilibria in pure strategies which are (rand, r_1) and (rand, r_2). However, only one can survive the assumption IA3, namely (rand, r_1), because r_1 allows L to win the election for sure whereas r_2 would only win with a probability of one half.

The study of subgames 11 and 17 follows similar steps.

First Stage

In Table 4.7, we list again all the possible profiles of platforms that candidates may adopt, along with a profitable deviation, if any.

Proving that Profile 1 is an equilibrium follows the same steps as before. And all the other profiles show the same profitable deviations as in Table 4.3 with risk-averse parties. So I omit any further analysis. In sum, the cases analyzed in Tables 4.2–4.7 prove the theorem in this chapter.

Table 4.7 Equilibria between Candidates: Risk-Neutral Case

		Profitable Deviation	Is it a Nash Equilibrium?
Profile 1	$0 = r_1 = r_2 = -l_1 = -l_2$	None	Yes
Profile 2	$0 < r_1 = r_2 = -l_1 = -l_2$	$r_1 \to r_1 - \varepsilon$	No
Profile 3	$0 = r_1 = r_2 = -l_1 < -l_2$	$l_2 \to 0$	No
Profile 4	$0 < r_1 = r_2 = -l_1 < -l_2$	$l_2 \to l_1 + \varepsilon$	No
Profile 5	$0 = r_1 = r_2 < -l_1 = -l_2$	$r_2 \to r_2 + \varepsilon$	No
Profile 6	$0 < r_1 = r_2 < -l_1 = -l_2$	$r_2 \to r_2 + \varepsilon$	No
Profile 7	$0 = r_1 < r_2 = -l_1 = -l_2$	$r_2 \to r_2 - \varepsilon$	No
Profile 8	$0 < r_1 < r_2 = -l_1 = -l_2$	$r_2 \to r_2 - \varepsilon$	No
Profile 9	$0 = r_1 = r_2 < -l_1 < -l_2$	$r_2 \to r_2 + \varepsilon$	No
Profile 10	$0 < r_1 = r_2 < -l_1 < -l_2$	$r_2 \to r_2 + \varepsilon$	No
Profile 11	$0 = r_1 < r_2 = -l_1 < -l_2$	$r_2 \to r_2 - \varepsilon$	No
Profile 12	$0 < r_1 < r_2 = -l_1 < -l_2$	$r_2 \to r_2 - \varepsilon$	No
Profile 13	$0 = r_1 < r_2 < -l_1 = -l_2$	$r_1 \to r_2 + \varepsilon$	No
Profile 14	$0 < r_1 < r_2 < -l_1 = -l_2$	$r_1 \to r_2 + \varepsilon$	No
Profile 15	$0 = r_1 < r_2 < -l_1 < -l_2$	$r_1 \to r_2 + \varepsilon$	No
Profile 16	$0 < r_1 < r_2 < -l_1 < -l_2$	$r_1 \to r_2 + \varepsilon$	No
Profile 17	$0 = r_1 = -l_1 < r_2 = -l_2$	$r_2 \to 0$	No
Profile 18	$0 < r_1 = -l_1 < r_2 = -l_2$	$r_2 \to r_1 - \varepsilon$	No
Profile 19	$0 = r_1 = -l_1 < r_2 < -l_2$	$l_2 \to 0$	No
Profile 20	$0 < r_1 = -l_1 < r_2 < -l_2$	$r_2 \to r_1 - \varepsilon$	No
Profile 21	$0 = r_1 < -l_1 < r_2 = -l_2$	$r_2 \to r_1 + \varepsilon$	No
Profile 22	$0 < r_1 < -l_1 < r_2 = -l_2$	$r_2 \to r_1 + \varepsilon$	No
Profile 23	$0 = r_1 < -l_1 < r_2 < -l_2$	$r_2 \to r_1 + \varepsilon$	No
Profile 24	$0 < r_1 < -l_1 < r_2 < -l_2$	$r_2 \to r_1 + \varepsilon$	No
Profile 25	$0 = r_1 < -l_1 = -l_2 < r_2$	$r_2 \to r_1 + \varepsilon$	No
Profile 26	$0 < r_1 < -l_1 = -l_2 < r_2$	$r_2 \to r_1 + \varepsilon$	No
Profile 27	$0 = r_1 < -l_1 < -l_2 < r_2$	$r_2 \to r_1 + \varepsilon$	No
Profile 28	$0 < r_1 < -l_1 < -l_2 < r_2$	$r_2 \to r_1 + \varepsilon$	No

Notes

1 For a recent survey of nomination procedures around the world, see Sandri and Seddone 2015.

2 A new account of the Progressive Era comes in Masket 2016.

3 A review of the positive and negative consequences of primaries that have been found in the literature, along with the causes for the introduction of primaries around the world, can be found in Serra 2018.

4 Models of primaries predicting divergence include, among others, Jackson, Mathevet and Mattes 2007; Adams and Merrill 2008; Serra 2011; Snyder and Ting 2011; Hummel 2013; Hortala-Vallve and Mueller 2015; Kselman 2015; Amorós, Puy and Martínez 2016; Grofman, Troumpounis and Xefteris 2016; and Serra 2017. Interestingly Kselman 2015 and Woon 2016 also find convergence in some circumstances.

5 Statistical studies claiming there is little to no effect of primaries on divergence include Hirano, Snyder, Ansolabehere and Hansen 2010; Peress 2013; and McGhee, Masket, Shor, Rogers and McCarty 2014.

6 It should be noted that several empirical studies of political behavior have found strategic voting in primary elections. See Hall and Snyder 2015 and the citations therein.

7 I am thus discarding the possibility of flip-flopping during the election season. One way to justify this assumption is that, in this election, flip-flopping would hurt the candidate's credibility so much that it would never be an optimal strategy. This should actually stack the deck in favor of divergence, given that any promise made to primary voters will be "sticky" throughout the election.

8 Table 4.1 in the appendix contains an exhaustive list of all the possible configurations of platforms that candidates may adopt.

9　All the results would hold for any symmetric and single-peaked utility function for voters. The linear one is used as an illustration.

10　This follows in the tradition of Wittman 1973 and Calvert 1985.

11　This adjustment to −1 and 1 is done for presentation purposes. It represents a slight loss of generality because it imposes that both parties have median members exactly at the same distance from the center; but we can readily prove that all the results would go through without this symmetry.

12　The theory in Serra 2015 found that primary elections did not induce any extremism; but it only considered strictly risk-averse parties. The present chapter extends the analysis to other attitudes toward risk.

13　The first two assumptions, IA1 and IA2, were also used in Serra 2015, but the third one, IA3, was not necessary in that previous model. This mild assumption became necessary now due to the candidates' payoff from winning the nomination independent of winning the election.

14　This represents an extension with respect to Serra (2015), which did not consider nominations to be valuable *per se*.

15　It can be proven that allowing players to use mixed strategies would not change the results, so I ignore them in the presentation.

16　This is not an exhaustive list of all the possible configurations. In this section, I only analyze the cases that build an interesting intuition. The proof in the appendix gives the exhaustive list of configurations and determines whether each of them is an equilibrium or not.

17　This example corresponds to Configurations 15 and 16 in Table 4.1.

18　This example corresponds to Configuration 7 in Table 4.1.

19　This example corresponds to Configuration 24 in Table 4.1.

20　This example corresponds to Configuration 2 in Table 4.1.

21　This example corresponds to Configuration 3 in Table 4.1.

22　This example corresponds to Configuration 1 in Table 4.1.

23　Such as Gerber and Morton 1998.

24　Such as those mentioned in Note 4. I present a more extensive literature review in Serra 2018.

25　Such as Hirano, Snyder, Ansolabehere, and Hansen 2010; Peress 2013; and McGhee, Masket, Shor, Rogers, and McCarty 2014.

References

Adams, James, and Samuel Merrill. 2008. "Candidate and Party Strategies in Two-Stage Elections Beginning with a Primary." *American Journal of Political Science* 52 (2): 344–359.

Amorós, Pablo, M. Socorro Puy, and Ricardo Martínez. 2016. "Closed Primaries versus Top-Two Primaries." *Public Choice* 167 (2): 21–35.

Calvert, Randall L. 1985. "Robustness of the Multidimensional Voting Model: Candidate Motivations, Uncertainty, and Convergence." *American Journal of Political Science* 29 (1): 69–95.

Downs, Anthony. 1957. *An Economic Theory of Democracy.* New York: HarperCollins.

Gerber, Elisabeth R., and Rebecca B. Morton. 1998. "Primary Election Systems and Representation." *Journal of Law, Economics, & Organization* 14 (2): 304–324.

Grofman, Bernard, Orestis Troumpounis, and Dimitrios Xefteris. 2016. "Electoral Competition with Primaries and Quality Asymmetries." Lancaster University Management School. Economics Working Paper series 2016/016.

Hall, Andrew B. and Snyder, James M. 2015. "Information and Wasted Votes: A Study of U.S. Primary Elections." *Quarterly Journal of Political Science* 10(4): 433–459.

Hirano, Shigeo, James M. Snyder Jr., Stephen D. Ansolabehere, and John Mark Hansen. 2010. "Primary Elections and Partisan Polarization." *Quarterly Journal of Political Science* 5 (2): 169–191.

Hortala-Vallve, Rafael, and Hannes Mueller. 2015. "Primaries: The Unifying Force." *Public Choice* 163 (3–4): 289–305.

Hummel, Patrick. 2013. "Candidate Strategies in Primaries and General Elections with Candidates of Heterogeneous Quality." *Games and Economic Behavior* 78 (1): 85–102.

Jackson, Matthew O., Laurent Mathevet, and Kyle Mattes. 2007. "Nomination Processes and Policy Outcomes." *Quarterly Journal of Political Science* 2 (1): 67–92.

Kselman, Daniel M. 2015. "A Median Activist Theorem for Two-Stage Spatial Models." In *The Political Economy of Governance: Institutions, Political Performance and Elections*, ed. Norman Schofield and Gonzalo Caballero. Switzerland: Springer, pp. 193–210.

Masket, Seth. 2016. *The Inevitable Party: Why Attempts to Kill the Party System Fail and How They Weaken Democracy*. New York: Oxford University Press.

McGhee, Eric, Seth Masket, Boris Shor, Steven Rogers, and Nolan McCarty. 2014. "A Primary Cause of Partisanship? Nomination Systems and Legislator Ideology." *American Journal of Political Science* 58 (2): 337–351.

Peress, Michael. 2013. "Candidate Positioning and Responsiveness to Constituent Opinion in the U.S. House of Representatives." *Public Choice* 156 (1): 77–94.

Sandri, Giulia, and Antonella Seddone. 2015. "Introduction: Primary Elections Across the World." In *Party Primaries in Comparative Perspective*, ed. Giulia Sandri, Antonella Seddone and Venturino Fulvio. Farnham: Ashgate, pp. 1–20.

Serra, Gilles. 2011. "Why Primaries? The Party's Tradeoff between Policy and Valence." *Journal of Theoretical Politics* 23 (1): 21–51.

Serra, Gilles. 2015. "No Polarization in Spite of Primaries: A Median Voter Theorem with Competitive Nominations." In *The Political Economy of Governance: Institutions, Political Performance and Elections*, ed. Norman Schofield and Gonzalo Caballero. Switzerland: Springer, pp. 211–229.

Serra, Gilles. 2017. "Contagious Sincerity: When Should We Expect Partisan Primaries in One Party to Induce Partisan Primaries in the Rival Party?" *CIDE Working Papers* DTEP–291 (June).

Serra, Gilles. 2018. "Primaries, Conventions, and Other Methods for Nominating Candidates: How Do They Matter?" In *The Oxford Handbook of Public Choice*, ed. Roger Congleton, Bernard Grofman, and Stefan Voigt. Oxford: Oxford University Press (forthcoming).

Snyder Jr., James M., and Michael M. Ting. 2011. "Electoral Selection with Parties and Primaries." *American Journal of Political Science* 55(4): 782–796.

Wittman, Donald. 1973. "Parties as Utility Maximizers." *American Political Science Review* 67 (3): 490–498.

Woon, Jonathan. 2016. "Primaries, Strategic Voting, and Candidate Polarization." Manuscript, University of Pittsburgh. On line http://recursos.march.es/web/ceacs/actividades/pdf/Woon.pdf.

PART II

Primary Voters and Primary Voting Laws

The chapters in this section consider the nature of the primary electorate and the ways in which changes in that electorate can influence election outcomes. One enduring question about primary elections has had to do with who should be eligible to vote in party primaries. As noted in the introduction to this book, much of the early research on primary elections explored the differences between closed primaries, in which only registered party members were eligible to cast ballots, and open primaries, which allow any voter to cast votes for whichever party he or she chooses. The chapters in this section make it clear that such questions have persisted. Moreover, the increased ideological sorting of the American parties has given these questions greater urgency. This is so despite the arguably intuitive conclusion that party members should have different views than members of the opposing party, or than voters who have chosen not to affiliate with either party, and evidence that primary voting laws actually make a difference has been scarce.

This section begins with an overview by Seth McKee of changes in the Democratic and Republican presidential electorates. McKee shows how it is possible to use exit poll data to analyze changes in the partisan competition of electorates by region. His piece shows the declining strength of the Democratic Party in the South. It also shows how the demographic characteristics of the two parties' primary electorates resemble each other and the general public.

Those who have advocated for closed primaries have historically argued that such laws limit the potential for mischief. Crossover voters – voters who have chosen to switch parties and vote in the primary of the party they have not affiliated with in the past – may do so for a variety of different reasons. They may have sincerely changed their political views. They may be excited about one candidate in the opposing party. Their preferred party may not have competitive primaries, so they may strategically want to aid the most acceptable candidate of the rival party. Or they may want to help the rival party choose a weak or unacceptable candidate, so as to aid their preferred party in the general election. Whatever the rationale for crossing over, there is the potential that crossover voting may change the composition of the electorate and the eventual nominees of the parties. In her contribution to this book, Barbara Norrander evaluates such claims using survey data; she finds little evidence that crossover voters act out of malice. This finding suggests that there is little reason for parties to try to limit such behavior.

Two chapters in this section consider the effect of primary type on voters and candidates. Matthew Geras and Michael Crespin consider the effects of closed and open primaries on voter turnout; they conclude that closed primaries tend to have lower turnout than open primaries.

Kristin Kanthak and Eric Loepp consider the consequences of primary type for candidate ideology. One might conclude from Geras and Crespin's chapter that closed primaries will also yield more ideologically extreme electorates, and thus favor more ideologically extreme candidates. Kanthak and Loepp show that closed primaries do tend to produce more ideologically divergent candidates. The effect, however, is very slight – certainly not enough to be responsible for the levels of polarization we see in American politics today. They argue, as well, that this may be a result of parties' beliefs about primary electorates, not of the composition of primary electorates themselves.

It should be noted that it has historically been very difficult to study primary election voters. We can study voter turnout, as the McKee chapter and the Geras and Crespin chapter do, but (as Norrander explains) surveys of primary voters have been scarce. It is easier to determine the effects of voting laws on outcomes, as is the case for the Kanthak and Loepp chapter. As Kanthak and Loepp point out, candidates may make assumptions about the primary electorate, and act on these assumptions even if they are ultimately unproven. This conclusion serves as a point of segue to the chapters in Part III. As we shall see there (particularly in Danielle Thomsen's chapter), there are many aspects of party and candidate strategy that are predicated on beliefs about the effects of primary rules. In many ways, considerations of the electorate and considerations of the candidates chosen by different types of electorates are two different ways of going about the same question.

5

SORTING DIXIE

The Changing Profile of Southern Presidential Primary Electorates

Seth C. McKee

This chapter takes a detailed look at changes in the demographic composition of voters partici-pating in Democratic and Republican presidential primaries in the American South[1] from 1988 to 2016. Over this span of eight presidential elections, the sorting of southerners into the major party primaries has constituted one of the most palpable and electorally consequential politi-cal transformations in American history. The well-known contemporary realignment of white southerners to the Grand Old Party (GOP) is perhaps most evident through an examination of the demography of presidential primary voters. Likewise, the changing nature of the coali-tion of Democratic primary voters provides a stark contrast since many of these electorates are now majority black. With the use of exit poll data, the major changes to the composition of Democratic and Republican primary electorates are demonstrated and analyzed. The passing of the old Democratic Solid South to the new Republican-dominant Dixie emerges in plain sight by chronicling the vast alterations in the makeup of southerners who participate in presidential primary contests.

The partisan transformation of the South from a one-party Democratic bastion (persist-ing from roughly the late 1800s to the 1950s) to a Republican-dominant region (commenc-ing around the 2000s; see Hayes and McKee 2008; McKee 2012) arguably has no parallel in American history (Bartels 2000; Black and Black 2002; Hood, Kidd, and Morris 2012). Curiously though, the bulk of scholarship chronicling and assessing this remarkable realignment is confined to general elections at various levels of officeholding (Black and Black 2002; Hood, Kidd, and Morris 2012; Lublin 2004; McKee 2010; Shafer and Johnston 2006; Valentino and Sears 2005). By comparison, studies of partisan change via primary contests are notably few (but see Clark 2014; Huffmon, Knotts, and McKee forthcoming; McKee and Hayes 2009, 2010; McKee 2017). This is surprising, since political transformations typically register first in primary elections (Stimson 2004). Indeed, it is perhaps fair to say that the best way to understand changes in the American electorate is to measure changes in the composition of the primary elector-ate. The American South has undergone the most pronounced changes in the composition of its primary electorate over the last several decades and this chapter makes it apparent that the transformation of the profiles of participants in Democratic and Republican contests is a telling case of why it is important to carefully study primary elections.

Since the start of the post-reform presidential primary era in 1972, when primaries became the main vehicle for nominating the major party presidential candidates, not until the 2000 election cycle did more southerners participate in Republican primaries than Democratic primaries (McKee and Hayes 2010). Figure 5.1 shows the percentage of Republican primary voters in southern states and South-wide for 1988, 2008, and 2016, the years examined throughout this chapter. Overall, in 1988, 35 percent of southern primary voters participated in the GOP contests. Except for South Carolina, where the Democratic Party held a caucus in 1988, in every southern state in this election cycle where both major parties held a presidential primary, more voters participated in the Democratic contest. Twenty years later in the 2008 election cycle, South-wide Republican participation was 40 percent of the two-party total. Primarily due to the greater excitement of the Democratic race between Hillary Clinton and Barack Obama and perhaps to a lesser extent because of the absence of a high profile southern Republican (apologies to Arkansas Governor Mike Huckabee), Democratic participation exceeded GOP primary voting in every state except Alabama and Florida. In 2016, however, the enthusiasm was clearly on the Republican side (see McKee 2017), and 61 percent of Dixie's primary voters cast Republican ballots. Only in Louisiana were more votes cast in the Democratic presidential contest.

The relative share of the southern electorate participating in the major party primaries is worth noting for any given election cycle because short-term conditions can alter participation patterns. Some groups of voters, like political independents, are especially susceptible to the vicissitudes of more pressing events. Nonetheless, there has been a general trend in favor of more Republican participation in southern primaries and this is to be expected since the GOP has attained a hegemonic position in elections from president down to state legislative races

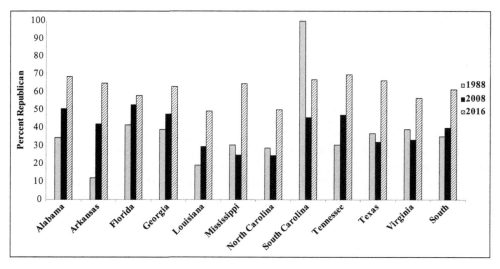

Figure 5.1   Republican Share of Southern Presidential Primary Votes: 1988, 2008, and 2016

Note: Data compiled by the author from Dave Leip's *Atlas of U.S. Presidential Elections* (http://uselec tionatlas.org/RESULTS/) for 2008 and 2016, and *CQ's Guide to U.S. Elections* (Kalb 2016) for 1988. Republican share of votes is out of the total cast for both major parties (Democratic plus Republican). In 1988 in South Carolina, only the Republican Party held a primary (South Carolina Democrats held a caucus) and that accounts for the 100 percent Republican vote share. The total major party presidential primary votes cast in 1988, 2008, and 2016 were 10,994,342; 18,448,528; and 19,993,729. The Republican share of the two-party presidential primary vote cast in the South in 1988, 2008, and 2016 was 35 percent, 40 percent, and 61 percent.

(McKee and Yoshinaka 2015). Of course, it also matters whether there is a sitting incumbent seeking reelection to the White House. When this is the case, primaries are rarely competitive or even held for the party of the president running for another term. The 1988, 2008, and 2016 elections are singled out because they are open contests and therefore both parties hold presidential primaries. Finally, unlike voting behavior – which is highly sensitive to the choice of candidates in a primary contest, which in turn invariably changes as the primary season advances – the composition of primary electorates is more durable. Put another way, South Carolina has been the first state to hold its primary contests in the South for decades now (especially for the GOP, see Huffmon, Knotts, and McKee forthcoming), but even though this means that other southern states go later in the calendar when some candidates have exited, the profile of voters participating in later contests does not appear to change that much.[2]

This chapter unfolds in the following manner. First, state-level changes in the composition of southern Democratic primary electorates are examined. Next, state-level alterations of southern Republican primary electorates are detailed. For both Democratic and Republican primary electorates, the data cover the 1988, 2008, and 2016 presidential elections. The analysis then turns to an accounting of region-wide changes between 1988 and 2008. The data are presented for all primary voters and then according to party primary, in order to show overall changes and then how they have played out within each major party primary. For consistency in longitudinal comparisons, these data are confined to the eight southern states that held presidential primaries for both major parties in 1988 and 2008.[3] The final analysis considers which factors condition the likelihood of being a Democratic primary voter as opposed to a Republican primary voter for 1988 and 2008. The chapter concludes with a brief summary statement of the significance of the substantial changes to southern presidential primary electorates. Primaries are a leading and durable indicator of tracking broader changes in American politics and the southern case is particularly notable for contributing to the contemporary state of political competition in a region now dominated by the Republican Party.

Democratic Primary Electorates in the South

In this section and the one that follows, four tables are shown and discussed in succession. All of the data are from state primary exit polls conducted in 1988, 2008, and 2016. The first two tables highlight state-level demographic changes; racial changes (percent white, black, and Latino) followed by alterations with respect to gender (percent female), age (percent over 44 years old), and education (percent with a college degree). The last two tables document changes in party identification (percent Democrat, independent, and Republican) and ideology (percent liberal, moderate, and conservative), respectively.

Table 5.1 displays the percentage of Democratic primary voters in southern states who were white, black, or Latino in 1988, 2008, and 2016. The most notable change over these three election cycles is the decline in white voters and the rise in African-American and Hispanic voters in southern Democratic primaries. Although the National Election Pool did not survey Louisiana voters in 2016, because the state has party registration and tracks registration according to race, it is possible to know the racial composition of Louisiana Democratic primary voters in 2016. In the 2016 Democratic primary in Louisiana, 61 percent of voters were black (McKee 2017). Hence, in every Deep South state in 1988 (South Carolina Democrats did not hold a primary) the Democratic primary electorate was majority white, whereas in 2016 all five of these states had majority black Democratic primary electorates, ranging from a low of 51 percent black in Georgia to a high of 71 percent African-American in Mississippi.

Table 5.1 Racial Composition of Democratic Primary Electorates: 1988, 2008, and 2016

Race	Year	AL	AR	FL	GA	LA	MS	NC	SC	TN	TX	VA
White	1988	55	86	80	64	62	54	71	–	72	66	64
	2008	44	80	66	43	47	–	62	43	67	46	61
	2016	40	67	48	38		24	62	35	63	43	63
	Difference	−15	−19	−32	−26	−15	−30	−9	−8	−9	−23	−1
Black	1988	45	13	17	35	37	45	29	–	27	23	34
	2008	51	17	20	51	48	–	34	55	29	19	30
	2016	54	27	27	51	–	71	32	61	32	19	26
	Difference	+9	+14	+10	+16	+11	+26	+3	+6	+5	−4	−8
Latino	1988	<1	1	1	<1	<1	1	<1	–	<1	10	<1
	2008	4	2	12	3	4	–	2	1	3	32	5
	2016	1	3	20	7	–	1	3	2	2	32	7
	Difference	<+1	+2	+19	+6	+3	0	+2	+1	+1	+22	+6

Note: Data compiled by the author. The 1988 (CBS News/*New York Times*) and 2008 (National Election Pool) raw exit poll data were made available through the Roper Center, and I thank Peter Enns, Rachel B. Schlass, and Brandon Cruz (all of the Roper Center) for helping me procure the data. The 2016 (National Election Pool) summary exit poll data were made available online via the following CNN website: http://www.cnn.com/election/primaries/polls. In 1988 the South Carolina Democratic Party held a caucus (hence no primary exit poll). In 2008 there was no National Election Pool exit poll for the Mississippi Democratic primary. In 2016 there was no National Election Pool exit poll for the Louisiana Democratic primary. In this table and all those after, the 1988 and 2008 data were weighted based on the weight variable in each exit poll.

Only in Virginia has the white share of the Democratic primary electorate remained essentially the same since 1988. Compared to 1988, in the other nine southern states the decline in the percentage of white voters goes from a low of 9 percentage points in North Carolina and Tennessee to a high of 32 percentage points in Florida. Florida and Texas have declining white Democratic primary electorates primarily because of the increase in Hispanic voters. In fact, only Texas and Virginia have a lower percentage of African-American voters in 2016 vis-à-vis 1988, and in both states, there has been substantial Latino growth (especially in Texas). The Deep South states remain overwhelmingly white and black in their composition of residents and thus the increase in Latino Democratic primary voters is relatively small, with the exception of Georgia, where Hispanic Democratic primary voters went from less than 1 percent in 1988 to 7 percent in 2016. The share of Latino Democratic primary voters has remained modest in 2016 in the Rim South states of Arkansas (3 percent), North Carolina (3 percent), and Tennessee (2 percent). In 1988, every southern Democratic primary electorate was majority white. In 2016, seven of the 11 southern states had majority–minority Democratic primary electorates.

Table 5.2 shows the percent female, percent older than 44 years, and the percent college graduates in Democratic primaries in the southern states for 1988, 2008, and 2016. Since 1988, there is a clear trend in more women participating in Democratic primaries in the South. To be sure, women constituted the majority sex in every Democratic primary in 1988, but their majority status has only solidified since then. In every Deep South state for which there is polling data in 2016 (excluding Louisiana), women voters comprise 60 percent or more of the Democratic primary electorate. The main reason why the female percent of voters is higher in

Table 5.2 Gender, Age, and Education of Democratic Primary Electorates: 1988, 2008, and 2016

Race	Year	AL	AR	FL	GA	LA	MS	NC	SC	TN	TX	VA
Female	1988	53	52	53	52	52	53	52	–	53	52	52
	2008	60	60	59	63	60	–	57	61	58	57	57
	2016	60	57	58	62	–	64	58	61	58	58	57
	Difference	+7	+5	+5	+10	+8	+11	+6	0	+5	+6	+5
> 44 Years	1988	53	57	63	49	52	55	56	–	52	49	52
	2008	61	67	72	53	68	–	65	61	61	56	59
	2016	61	65	65	64	–	60	61	65	64	58	59
	Difference	+8	+8	+2	+15	+16	+5	+5	+4	+12	+9	+7
College Grad	1988	27	20	33	35	30	23	34	–	33	32	42
	2008	35	39	46	53	34	–	44	37	35	43	57
	2016	51	44	48	54	–	43	58	40	56	51	64
	Difference	+24	+24	+15	+19	+4	+20	+24	+3	+23	+19	+22

Deep South Democratic primary electorates is tied directly to race. As mentioned, all of these electorates are now majority black, and it is also the case that black women far outnumber black men in their Democratic primary participation (see McKee 2017). In 2016, the share of female Democratic primary voters is 57 percent or higher in every southern state.

Minorities and women are two fundamental components of the vaunted Obama coalition that took shape in 2008. The increase in these Democratic primary subgroups is obvious in the southern states, but perhaps surprisingly, southern Democratic primary electorates have aged considerably since 1988. Compared to 1988, in 2016 the share of older voters (older than 44) has increased in every southern Democratic primary electorate. In 1988, only in the retirement mecca of Florida were more than 60 percent of Democratic primary voters over 44 years of age. In 2016, only the Texas and Virginia Democratic primary electorates contained a share of older voters that amounted to less than 60 percent of all voters. In short, there has been a notable graying of southern Democratic primary electorates.

One of the most impressive alterations in southern Democratic primary electorates is the increase in college graduates. In 1988, in no southern Democratic primary electorate were a majority of voters also college graduates. Virginia had the most with 42 percent, and Arkansas the least with 20 percent. Almost three decades later, six southern Democratic primary electorates were comprised of a majority of voters with a college degree. Virginia still led the way with 64 percent college graduates and South Carolina had the lowest number of college graduates (40 percent).

Table 5.3 presents data on the party identification of southern Democratic primary electorates in 1988, 2008, and 2016. Fortunately, the primary exit polls ask party identification. Just as party registration does not necessarily indicate party identification, nor should it be assumed that only Democrats (Republicans) participate in Democratic (Republican) primaries even if a primary is limited only to party registrants (e.g., Florida, Louisiana, and North Carolina administer closed primaries limited only to party registrants). In the late 1980s it should be expected that a lower share of Democratic identifiers participated in Democratic primaries if only because Republican participation in Republican primaries was so much lower. Nonetheless, in the southern states holding Democratic primaries in 1988, the share of Democratic identifiers was impressive.

Table 5.3 Party Identification of Democratic Primary Electorates: 1988, 2008, and 2016

Race	Year	AL	AR	FL	GA	LA	MS	NC	SC	TN	TX	VA
Democrat	1988	77	66	73	76	76	75	76	–	72	69	73
	2008	83	79	80	80	84	–	78	76	80	70	72
	2016	77	72	79	76	–	86	70	82	75	71	76
	Difference	0	+6	+6	0	+8	+11	–6	+6	+3	+2	+3
Independent	1988	18	27	22	19	15	15	18	–	21	26	21
	2008	11	17	15	16	11	–	17	20	16	21	20
	2016	20	24	18	20	–	13	28	16	23	26	22
	Difference	+2	–3	–4	+1	–4	–2	+10	–4	+2	0	+1
Republican	1988	5	7	5	5	10	10	6	–	7	6	6
	2008	6	4	4	4	5	–	5	4	3	9	8
	2016	3	4	3	4	–	2	3	3	2	3	3
	Difference	–2	–3	–2	–1	–5	–8	–3	–1	–5	–3	–3

At 66 percent, Arkansas had the lowest share of Democrats voting in a Democratic primary and Alabama had the highest at 77 percent. Compared to 1988, in 2016 the percentage of Democratic identifiers was the same or higher in every southern Democratic primary except for North Carolina. Driven by racially based partisan sorting, Mississippi now has the highest percentage of Democrats voting in its Democratic primary (86 percent) and North Carolina has the lowest (70 percent), due in part to a substantial increase in independent voters (+10 percentage points).

It makes more sense to compare the percentage of partisans than independents because the latter group exhibits the most variability in primary participation (e.g., in 2016 it appears that independents were drawn more to southern Republican primaries because of the candidacy of Donald Trump, see McKee 2017). With this in mind, between 1988 and 2016, there is a consistent drop in the percentage of Republican voters in southern Democratic primaries. Whereas in 1988 Louisiana and Mississippi each had 10 percent of their Democratic primary electorates comprised of Republican voters, in 2016 every southern Democratic primary electorate has a Republican share of identifiers below 5 percent.

Table 5.4 concludes this section with a look at the changing ideological composition of southern Democratic primary electorates. The compositional changes between 1988 and 2016 speak loudly to the remarkable ideological sorting occurring among Democratic primary voters. One should never lose sight of the fact that over an almost thirty-year period many older voters with more conservative views have exited the electorate and have been replaced by a more liberal generation of Democratic primary voters. In other words, over multiple decades, sorting of this nature is not just because the same voters have realigned their party identification with their ideological self-identity (Levendusky 2009), but also because of a voter replacement effect in which younger voters hold more politically congruent partisan and ideological identities (Abramowitz and Saunders 1998).

In 1988, in no southern Democratic primary electorate were even a third of voters liberal in their self-identification. At 32 percent, Virginia had the highest share of liberal Democratic primary voters and Arkansas had the least, at 16 percent. Interestingly, in 2016 Virginia still had the highest share of liberal Democratic primary voters (68 percent) and Arkansas still had the least (50 percent), but now at least half of every southern Democratic primary electorate was liberal – a remarkable transformation. Between 1988 and 2016, seven states underwent an

Table 5.4 Ideology of Democratic Primary Electorates: 1988, 2008, and 2016

Race	Year	AL	AR	FL	GA	LA	MS	NC	SC	TN	TX	VA
Liberal	1988	24	16	27	26	25	24	23	–	23	24	32
	2008	38	36	50	47	31	–	42	44	41	38	50
	2016	57	50	54	56	–	51	56	54	61	59	68
	Difference	+33	+34	+27	+30	+6	+27	+33	+10	+38	+35	+36
Moderate	1988	42	46	48	46	41	40	45	–	43	45	48
	2008	45	49	37	41	48	–	37	42	43	40	38
	2016	32	34	37	36	–	40	35	35	32	34	29
	Difference	−10	−12	−11	−10	+7	0	−10	−7	−11	−11	−19
Conservative	1988	34	39	25	27	33	36	32	–	34	31	20
	2008	17	15	13	12	22	–	21	15	17	22	12
	2016	11	16	9	9	–	10	9	11	7	7	3
	Difference	−23	−23	−16	−18	−11	−26	−23	−4	−27	−24	−17

increase in their share of liberal Democratic primary voters that was 30 percentage points or higher. Conversely, between 1988 and 2016 there has been an across-the-board drop in the share of conservative Democratic primary voters. In 1988 conservatives outnumbered liberals in every Democratic primary but Florida and Virginia. In 2016 conservatives are the smallest ideological category in every Democratic primary electorate and liberals are the most prominent. Simply put, between 1988 and 2016, southern Democratic primary electorates have undergone a dramatic ideological sorting. The surge in liberal identifiers has been offset by a concomitant decline in moderates and conservatives.

Republican Primary Electorates in the South

The contemporary southern Republican Party is distinguished by its overwhelmingly white constituency. Table 5.5 displays the racial composition of southern Republican primary electorates in 1988, 2008, and 2016. As the South has become more racially diverse, even the Republican primary electorate has become somewhat less white. In 1988, whites constituted over 90 percent of Republican primary voters in every southern state.[4] In 2016, four states had Republican primary electorates whose share of white voters was under 90 percent: Florida (78 percent), Georgia (88 percent), Texas (82 percent), and Virginia (86 percent).[5] Florida and Texas stand out because of the substantial increase in Latino voters, from 5 to 16 percent in the Sunshine State and from 3 to 10 percent in the Lone Star State. Interestingly and admittedly surprising, the reduction in the white share of voters in Georgia and Virginia is due primarily to an increase in black voters, from 2 to 7 percent in Georgia and from 2 to 9 percent in Virginia. Even accounting for the relatively larger decline in white voters in the aforementioned states, overall, in 2016, white voters still dominate southern Republican primary electorates.

Unlike the wholesale shift in greater female participation in Democratic primary electorates, there is no discernible pattern regarding the gender balance in Republican primary electorates (see Table 5.6). In 1988, half of the southern state Republican primary electorates were majority male and the other half majority female. In 2016, those states that had majority male Republican primary electorates in 1988 (Alabama, Florida, Georgia, Tennessee, and Texas) are

Table 5.5 Racial Composition of Republican Primary Electorates: 1988, 2008, and 2016

Race	Year	AL	AR	FL	GA	LA	MS	NC	SC	TN	TX	VA
White	1988	98	96	93	97	96	98	97	–	97	93	97
	2008	92	95	83	94	90	–	–	96	94	87	93
	2016	93	96	78	88	–	93	94	96	94	82	86
	Difference	−5	0	−15	−9	−6	−5	−3	0	−3	−11	−11
Black	1988	2	3	1	2	3	2	3	–	2	3	2
	2008	4	2	3	2	4	–	–	2	2	2	3
	2016	4	2	3	7	–	6	2	1	2	3	9
	Difference	+2	−1	+2	+5	+1	+4	−1	−1	0	0	+7
Latino	1988	<1	<1	5	<1	1	<1	<1	–	1	3	1
	2008	2	2	12	2	5	–	–	1	3	10	2
	2016	1	1	16	3	–	1	1	1	1	10	2
	Difference	<1	<1	+11	+2	+4	<1	<1	0	0	+7	+1

Note: In 1988 there was no CBS News/*New York Times* exit poll for the South Carolina Republican primary. In 2008 there was no National Election Pool exit poll for the Mississippi and North Carolina Republican primaries. In 2016 there was no National Election Pool exit poll for the Louisiana Republican primary.

now majority female. And some of the states that were majority female are now majority male (Arkansas, Virginia, and Louisiana in 2008 versus 1988). Overall, there is a fairly equal gender balance in Republican primary participation with just Arkansas and Virginia deviating more than a percentage point from a 50/50 split in the 2016 contests.

Like their Democratic primary counterparts, there has also been a clear graying of Republican primary participants since 1988. In 1988, only in Florida were more than 60 percent of Republican primary voters 45 or older (66 percent). By 2016, Alabama had the lowest share of voters over 44, at 66 percent; now five Republican primary electorates had a portion of over 44-year-old voters that exceeded 70 percent of the entire electorate (Arkansas, Florida, Mississippi, South Carolina, and Tennessee). Relative to Democratic primary voters, the aging of the GOP primary electorate is more notable. In nine of the Republican primary electorates the percentage increase in the older segment of voters between 1988 and 2016 is ten points or higher.

Lastly, Table 5.6 shows a consistent increase in the education of Republican primary electorates. In 1988, no Republican primary electorate had a majority of college graduates. In 2016, more than half of the voters in seven southern state Republican primary electorates were college graduates (less than half of the voters were college educated in Alabama, Arkansas, and Mississippi in 2016; and most likely Louisiana too, despite the absence of exit poll data). Obviously, the upward trends in age and education are not specific to one of the major party primary electorates in the South – this is a general trend among the entire southern presidential primary electorate.

Changes in the party identification of Republican primary voters are documented in Table 5.7. Even in 1988, the share of Democratic identifiers participating in GOP presidential primary contests was not substantial, except in the case of Georgia and Mississippi where Democrats accounted for 11 and 18 percent of these GOP primary participants, respectively (also the GOP primary in Arkansas in 2008 drew a significant share of Democrats, at 10 percent). By 2016, the Virginia Republican primary electorate contained the highest share of Democrats, at

Table 5.6 Gender, Age, and Education of Republican Primary Electorates: 1988, 2008, and 2016

Characteristic	Year	AL	AR	FL	GA	LA	MS	NC	SC	TN	TX	VA
Female	1988	47	55	49	49	51	53	50	–	48	48	51
	2008	47	49	44	48	49	–	–	49	47	49	47
	2016	51	48	51	51	–	50	50	49	50	50	47
	Difference	+4	–7	+2	+2	–2	–3	0	0	+2	+2	–4
> 44 Years	1988	56	56	66	47	46	57	52	–	56	47	51
	2008	67	65	75	61	68	–	–	67	60	64	63
	2016	66	74	74	69	–	71	67	73	75	68	68
	Difference	+10	+18	+8	+22	+22	+14	+15	+6	+19	+21	+17
College Grad	1988	41	38	35	41	39	27	32	–	38	41	48
	2008	42	42	50	51	43	–	–	51	44	49	57
	2016	44	45	53	53	–	44	51	54	51	53	60
	Difference	+3	+7	+18	+12	+4	+17	+19	+3	+13	+12	+12

a modest 6 percent – in every other GOP primary electorate Democratic affiliates comprised 5 percent or less of the total participants. The change in political independents reveals no crisp pattern between 1988 and 2016, and, as mentioned, this is partly due to a shift of independents in favor of GOP primaries in some states because of the allure of Donald Trump. By contrast, compared to 1988, in 2008 there is a consistent drop in the share of independent voters participating in Republican primaries. Despite the increase in independent voters after 2008 in several Republican primary contests, there is a general trend of more Republican identifiers since 1988. For instance, in 1988 three states had a portion of Republican affiliates under 60 percent (Arkansas, Georgia, and Mississippi). In 2016, every southern state Republican primary electorate was 60 percent Republican identifiers or higher, ranging from a low of 63 percent in

Table 5.7 Party Identification of Republican Primary Electorates: 1988, 2008, and 2016

Characteristic	Year	AL	AR	FL	GA	LA	MS	NC	SC	TN	TX	VA
Democrat	1988	6	4	3	11	7	18	2	–	6	4	5
	2008	4	10	3	5	2	–	–	2	4	2	3
	2016	4	5	3	5	–	5	2	2	4	3	6
	Difference	–2	+1	0	–6	–5	–13	0	0	–2	–1	+1
Independent	1988	36	34	18	31	18	24	20	–	24	27	25
	2008	16	19	16	14	9	–	–	17	19	18	18
	2016	27	32	22	25	–	20	30	22	33	27	29
	Difference	–9	–2	+4	–6	–9	–4	+10	+5	+9	0	+4
Republican	1988	58	62	79	59	75	58	78	–	70	69	70
	2008	81	71	81	81	88	–	–	81	77	81	79
	2016	69	63	75	70	–	76	69	76	63	70	65
	Difference	+11	+1	–4	+11	+13	+18	–9	–5	–7	+1	–5

Table 5.8 Ideology of Republican Primary Electorates: 1988, 2008, and 2016

Characteristic	Year	AL	AR	FL	GA	LA	MS	NC	SC	TN	TX	VA
Liberal	1988	5	5	9	5	8	10	6	–	8	6	4
	2008	7	7	11	9	9	–	–	7	7	8	8
	2016	2	2	3	3	–	1	2	1	2	2	3
	Difference	–3	–3	–6	–2	+1	–9	–4	–6	–6	–4	–1
Moderate	1988	31	38	39	32	30	29	30	–	30	33	35
	2008	21	26	29	25	20	–	–	24	20	20	27
	2016	20	17	27	18	–	15	19	17	16	17	25
	Difference	–11	–21	–12	–14	–10	–14	–11	–7	–14	–16	–10
Conservative	1988	64	56	52	63	62	61	63	–	61	61	60
	2008	72	67	61	66	71	–	–	69	73	72	65
	2016	78	82	70	79	–	84	79	81	82	82	72
	Difference	+14	+26	+18	+16	+9	+23	+16	+12	+21	+21	+12

Arkansas and Tennessee to a high of 76 percent Republicans in Mississippi and South Carolina. Short-term conditions will alter the share of independent voters and hence the portion of Republican identifiers, but this has little bearing on the portion of Democratic voters since now they comprise such a small share of GOP primary participants.

Like the previous section, the ideological sorting of Republican primary electorates is truly an eye-opener (see Table 5.8). Whereas southern Democratic primary electorates have taken on a pattern that is conceptualized primarily as "sorting" (see Levendusky 2009) since the vast increase in liberals comes mainly from the decline of conservatives, the ideological alteration of Republican primary electorates shows a higher degree of polarization. If the ideological sorting of voters is primarily driven by a reduction in the portion of moderates (as opposed to coming from a reduction in liberals/conservatives), then this is considered a polarized pattern. This is the case with respect to Republican primary electorates throughout the South. To be sure, since 1988 there has been a wholesale reduction in liberal voters participating in GOP primary contests, but this decline has been greatly surpassed by the larger decline in moderate voters. In other words, by 2016, the impressive increase in the share of conservative voters in GOP primary elections is due mainly to the reduction in moderate voters participating in these contests.

Although every Democratic primary electorate in the South in 2016 was at least 50 percent liberal in its voter composition, in only two states did liberals constitute more than 60 percent of the electorate (61 percent in Tennessee and 68 percent in Virginia, see Table 5.4). By contrast, in 2016, every Republican primary electorate was at least 70 percent conservative, and in at least five Republican primary electorates, conservatives were more than 80 percent of GOP primary participants (Arkansas, Mississippi, South Carolina, Tennessee, and Texas).[6] Southern voters in both major party primaries have aligned their ideological identity with the appropriate partisan contest, and this is especially true with respect to conservative identifiers voting in GOP presidential primaries.

Changes to the Southern Primary Electorate: 1988 versus 2008

Unfortunately, because of the recency of the 2016 exit polls the data are not accessible in raw form. In the previous two sections of the chapter, the 2016 data were made available in summary form compatible for presentation with the 1988 and 2008 data shown in Tables 5.1–5.8. In this section, summary data are shown for the entire South, but this means that the data consist only of the 1988 and 2008 election cycles. Since I have the raw exit poll data for 1988 and 2008, it is possible to pool all of the southern primary data together.[7] This said, there are some caveats that should be mentioned before proceeding. First, in some states exit polls were conducted in 1988 but not for 2008 (e.g., no Mississippi exit polls for both party primaries in 2008 and there was no North Carolina GOP primary exit poll in 2008). The common data source for 1988, the CBS News/*New York Times* exit polls, did not produce a poll for the South Carolina Republican primary (and recall there was no South Carolina Democratic primary for this year). Given these discrepancies that impact three southern states between 1988 and 2008, the pooled data for southern presidential primaries exclude all primary voters in Mississippi, North Carolina, and South Carolina. In other words, the pooled data are from the eight southern states that conducted exit polls for both major party primary voters in 1988 and 2008: Alabama, Arkansas, Florida, Georgia, Louisiana, Tennessee, Texas, and Virginia.

It is highly unlikely that the exclusion of primary voters in Mississippi, North Carolina, and South Carolina would significantly alter any conclusions regarding political behavior that is drawn from a very large sample of primary voters residing in the other eight southern states. Henceforth, southern primary electorates *in toto*, are confined to the above-mentioned eight states in which longitudinal comparisons are possible for both major party primary electorates surveyed in 1988 and 2008. It is useful to examine changes in southern primary electorates at the state-level, as was done in the last two sections. Likewise, there is value in assessing changes at the regional level, as will be the case in the two tables presented in this section. Further, because of the possibility of trends over time in the southern primary electorate, irrespective of party contest, it is prudent to show the data for all primary voters before showing the data with regard to voters participating in Democratic or Republican primary contests, respectively.

Table 5.9 presents data in 1988 and 2008 for all southern primary voters, Democratic primary voters, and then Republican primary voters for the same demographic characteristics highlighted in Tables 5.1–5.2 and 5.4–5.5 (race, gender, age, education for Democratic and Republican primary voters, respectively). In addition, there is one more characteristic highlighted because it is available for 1988 and 2008 (not currently available in the publicly released 2016 exit polls): the religion of primary voters. Although the religion question actually offers five response options (1. Protestant/Other Christian; 2. Catholic; 3. Jewish; 4. Something Else; and 5. None), for simplicity and given the prevalence of voters classified as such, only data from the "Protestant/Other" category are shown.

Starting with the racial characteristics of southern primary voters, overall, the share of whites has declined from 79 percent in 1988 to 71 percent twenty years later in 2008. Given the racial sorting among voters participating in Democratic and Republican primary contests, as expected, the portion of white voters has dropped considerably more among the more racially diverse southern Democratic primary electorate. White voters were 68 percent of Democratic primary voters in 1988 and they dropped to 56 percent in 2008. Interestingly, the increase in black voters in the southern Democratic primary electorate amounts to only 2 percentage points over the same period of time (from 29 to 31 percent).[8] The largest South-wide gain is found among Latino voters, who go from 2 percent of the southern Democratic primary electorate in 1988 to 10 percent in 2008. Although there is a six percentage-point drop in the share of white voters comprising the southern GOP electorate, this group remains 90 percent of all Republican primary participants. And between 1988 and 2008, the share of black voters in the southern Republican primary electorate inches up from 2 to 3 percent. The largest increase is again due to Latino voters, who go from 2 percent of the southern GOP primary electorate in 1988 to 5 percent twenty years later.

Table 5.9 Demographic Changes in Southern Primary Electorates: 1988 and 2008

Characteristic	1988	2008	Difference
All Voters			
White	79	71	−8
Black	18	19	+1
Latino	2	8	+6
Democratic Primary			
White	68	56	−12
Black	29	31	+2
Latino	2	10	+8
Republican Primary			
White	96	90	−6
Black	2	3	+1
Latino	2	5	+3
All Voters			
Female	51	54	+3
Democratic Primary			
Female	52	59	+7
Republican Primary			
Female	50	47	−3
All Voters			
> 44 Years	53	64	+11
Democratic Primary			
> 44 Years	53	62	+9
Republican Primary			
> 44 Years	53	66	+13
All Voters			
College Graduate	35	45	+10
Democratic Primary			
College Graduate	32	43	+11
Republican Primary			
College Graduate	40	47	+7
All Voters			
Protestant/Other	70	68	−2
Democratic Primary			
Protestant/Other	68	61	−7
Republican Primary			
Protestant/Other	74	77	+3

Note: The data presented in this table and Table 5.10 are confined to the eight southern states that conducted presidential primary exit polls for both major parties in 1988 and 2008: Alabama, Arkansas, Florida, Georgia, Louisiana, Tennessee, Texas, and Virginia.

Despite the common perception that gender is roughly a 50/50 proposition, women have become more participatory than men in contemporary American elections (Ansolabehere and Hersh 2012), and this has been the case specifically in the southern primary electorate. In 1988, women were slightly more prevalent than men (51 percent), but in 2008 female voters accounted for 54 percent of all southern primary voters. Women are now on the precipice of dominating the southern Democratic primary electorate, going from 52 percent of voters in 1988 to 59 percent twenty years hence. By contrast, there was an equal gender balance in the southern GOP primary electorate in 1988 but in 2008 women have become a slight minority of Republican primary voters (47 percent).

As evident from the state-level data already presented, the graying of the southern primary electorate is a major development. In 1988, 53 percent of the southern primary electorate was over 44 years old. In 2008, 64 percent of the southern primary electorate was over 44 years old. There is a 9 percentage-point increase in the older share of the southern Democratic primary electorate between 1988 and 2008 (from 53 percent over 44 in 1988 to 62 percent over 44 in 2008). The increase in the portion of older voters is even more pronounced among the southern Republican primary electorate, which was also 53 percent over 44 years old in 1988, but vaults to 66 percent over the age of 44 in 2008 (a 13 percentage-point increase).

Similar to an upward trend in older southern primary voters, there is a notable increase in the level of education possessed by southern primary participants. Overall, 35 percent of the southern primary electorate had a college degree in 1988. Twenty years later, 45 percent of the southern primary electorate had graduated from college. The increase in college graduates has been more notable among the southern Democratic primary electorate (going from 32 percent to 43 percent), but the percentage of college graduates remains higher among Republican primary voters (who go from 40 percent in 1988 to 47 percent in 2008).

Finally, changes in the portion of Protestant/Other Christian (POC) primary voters are insightful. Over this twenty-year span, the decline in POC southern primary voters is modest, going from 70 percent in 1988 to 68 percent in 2008. Nonetheless, there has been a partisan sort among POC voters (Green et al. 2014) and this is evident in Table 5.9. Within the southern Democratic primary electorate, the share of POC voters declines from 68 percent in 1988 to 61 percent in 2008. The so-called Religious Right in American politics (Wilcox and Robinson 2010) consists of a large share of Protestants of various Christian denominations and among the southern Republican primary electorate the portion of POC voters increases from 74 percent in 1988 to 77 percent in 2008.

Turning from demographic characteristics to more politically based features of the southern primary electorate, Table 5.10 presents data on party identification and ideology in 1988 and 2008. Starting with party identification, it is interesting to find that the share of Democratic identifiers has not changed, 45 percent of the southern primary electorate in 1988 and 2008. What has changed is the considerable 7 percentage-point reduction in the share of independents (from 23 to 16 percent) along with a commensurate 7 percentage-point increase in Republican affiliates (from 32 to 39 percent) between 1988 and 2008. To the extent that the southern primary electorate has moved from a dealigned pattern (a considerable portion of independents) to a realigned pattern (moving from political independence to a party affiliation), the southern GOP has clearly been the beneficiary. Nonetheless, in 2008 Democrats still outnumbered Republicans in the southern primary electorate.

With respect to partisan sorting into the appropriate party primary, there has clearly been more of this taking place within the southern Republican primary electorate. Whereas the portion of Democratic identifiers goes from 73 percent in 1988 to 78 percent in 2008 (+5 percentage points) within the southern Democratic primary electorate, on the Republican side, GOP affiliates were 69 percent in 1988 and increase to 80 percent of voters in the Republican primary electorate in 2008 (+11 percentage points). In 2008, there are hardly any mismatched partisans, meaning Democrats participating in the southern Republican primary (4 percent of the total) or Republicans voting in the southern Democratic primary (6 percent of the total). But the decline in independents in both major party primary electorates is significant, going from 21 percent in 1988 to 16 percent in 2008 in the southern Democratic primary and dropping from 26 percent independents in 1988 to 16 percent independents in 2008 in the southern GOP primary.

Table 5.10 Party Identification and Ideology of Southern Primary Electorates: 1988 and 2008

Characteristic	1988	2008	Difference
All Voters			
Democrat	45	45	0
Independent	23	16	−7
Republican	32	39	+7
Democratic Primary			
Democrat	73	78	+5
Independent	21	16	−5
Republican	6	6	0
Republican Primary			
Democrat	6	4	−2
Independent	26	16	−10
Republican	69	80	+11
All Voters			
Liberal	17	27	+10
Moderate	40	34	−6
Conservative	42	40	−2
Democratic Primary			
Liberal	25	41	+16
Moderate	45	42	−3
Conservative	30	16	−14
Republican Primary			
Liberal	6	8	+2
Moderate	34	23	−11
Conservative	60	68	+8

Finally, ideological sorting into the proper party primary is impressive between 1988 and 2008. Overall, the share of political moderates has declined from 40 percent in 1988 to 34 percent twenty years later. Even more substantial and a bit unexpected (since there has been no change in the ideological distribution of general election voters in the South over the same span of time, see McKee forthcoming), is the increase in liberal primary voters. Most of the decline in moderate voters is due to the 10 percentage-point increase in liberal primary voters who were 17 percent in 1988 and rise to 27 percent in 2008. The portion of conservative voters has changed only slightly between 1988 and 2008 – going from 42 percent to 40 percent over these two decades.

Of course, much more interesting is the alteration of the ideological distribution of voters participating in the major party primaries between 1988 and 2008. Among voters in the southern Democratic primary electorate, the sorting pattern jumps out. The share of moderates declines 3 percentage points over twenty years (from 45 to 42 percent). But the percentage of liberals goes from 25 percent in 1988 to 41 percent in 2008. Such a large increase in the portion of liberal voters is primarily due to the decline in conservatives, who go from 30 percent in 1988 (outnumbering liberals at this time) to a distinct minority of the southern Democratic primary electorate at 16 percent in 2008. In comparison, there were hardly any liberals participating in the southern Republican primary in 1988 (6 percent) or 2008 (8 percent). Rather, the sort comes primarily from a reduction in moderate voters (−11 percentage points) and an attendant increase in conservatives (+8 percentage points). Unlike the southern Democratic primary electorate, which enjoys a more equitable balance of moderate and liberal voters, the conservative dominance of the southern Republican primary electorate accounts for why the GOP occupies a far-right ideological position versus a center-left position in the case of the Democratic opposition.

Likelihood of Being a Democratic Primary Voter: 1988 and 2008

In this final section, multivariate analysis is employed to assess the likelihood that a southern primary exit poll respondent voted in the Democratic primary or the Republican primary for the eight southern states administering both major party primaries in 1988 and 2008. The dependent variable is coded 1 for a Democratic primary voter and 0 for a Republican primary voter. There are two pooled models, one for 1988 and another for 2008. The pooled models for these respective elections include data on the Democratic and Republican primary participants in the eight southern states. Given the existence of state-specific variation, in the pooled models there are state dummies included for seven of the eight states (Alabama is the omitted reference category, but the coefficients for the state dummies are not shown in the table) to serve as fixed effects. Also, all the models include robust standard errors and the data are weighted in accordance with the appropriate exit poll weight variable. Given the dichotomous coding of the dependent variable, probit regression is the method of choice. In addition to the pooled models for 1988 and 2008, separate regressions are run for each state primary electorate (e.g., Alabama primary voters in 1988). Thus, a total of 18 regressions have been estimated for the 1988 and 2008 presidential primary elections, the two pooled models for these respective years and then two models for each of the eight southern state primary electorates for 1988 and 2008.

The variables of interest consist of the same voter characteristics highlighted throughout the chapter: race, gender, age, education, religion, party identification, and ideology. All of these factors have been coded as dummy variables. Starting with race, the reference category is white and the models include dummies for black, Latino, and other. There is a clear expectation that compared to white respondents, black respondents are much more likely to be Democratic primary voters (as opposed to Republican primary voters). Gender is coded so that female equals 1 and male equals 0. It is expected that women are more likely to be Democratic primary voters in 2008, based on the descriptive data shown earlier. Next, with regard to age, respondents older than 44 are coded 1 and respondents younger than 45 are coded 0. Education is accounted for with a dummy for college graduates. In the case of religion, a dummy is coded 1 for Protestant/Other Christian and therefore anyone not identifying as such is coded 0.

For income, there is a dummy coded 1 for those making $50,000 or more and 0 if less than this amount. This is the first time an income variable makes an appearance since it does not make much sense to show over-time changes with a variable not adjusted for inflation. By contrast, even though this dollar amount is not nearly as substantial in 2008 versus 1988, the variable is included in order to see if higher income earners are more likely to be Republican primary voters. Turning to the more directly political variables, for party identification there are dummies included for Democrat and independent, with Republican the omitted comparison category. Similarly, for ideology, the dummies consist of liberal and moderate self-identifiers with conservative the omitted comparison category. With regard to party identification, it is clearly expected that Democrats and independents are more likely to be Democratic primary voters vis-à-vis Republicans. And likewise, compared to conservatives, liberal and moderate voters should be more likely to have participated in the Democratic primary.

Tables 5.11 and 5.12 show the results for all 18 models; the two pooled models followed by state-specific regressions for Alabama, Arkansas, Florida, and Georgia in Table 5.11 and the models for Louisiana, Tennessee, Texas, and Virginia in Table 5.12. The model results are

Table 5.11 Likelihood of Being a Democratic Primary Voter: 1988 and 2008

Variable	Pooled		Alabama		Arkansas		Florida		Georgia	
	1988	2008	1988	2008	1988	2008	1988	2008	1988	2008
Black	.99***	.86***	1.18***	1.07***	.66	.82*	.73***	.10	1.15***	1.62***
	(.08)	(.08)	(.21)	(.18)	(.41)	(.34)	(.20)	(.20)	(.15)	(.25)
Latino	.17	.23***	−.42	.41	1.47*	−.13	−.45*	.03	.07	.51#
	(.10)	(.07)	(.46)	(.40)	(.64)	(.29)	(.20)	(.11)	(.63)	(.27)
Other	.12	.08	1.15*	−.14	.30	−.39	1.09	.13	−.53	.30
	(.19)	(.12)	(.49)	(.18)	(.61)	(.40)	(.73)	(.20)	(.40)	(.38)
Female	−.07#	.19***	−.03	.09	−.24	.25*	−.16#	.13	−.02	.25*
	(.04)	(.04)	(.10)	(.12)	(.15)	(.10)	(.09)	(.09)	(.09)	(.11)
> 44 Years	−.10**	.07#	−.21*	.10	−.24	.06	.01	−.03	−.03	.04
	(.04)	(.04)	(.10)	(.12)	(.15)	(.10)	(.09)	(.09)	(.09)	(.12)
College Grad	.07#	.07#	−.11	.20	−.14	.26*	.00	−.18*	.11	.22#
	(.04)	(.04)	(.11)	(.13)	(.16)	(.10)	(.09)	(.09)	(.10)	(.11)
Prot./Other	−.05	−.18***	−.09	−.07	−.08	−.36**	−.13	.11	.26*	−.40**
	(.04)	(.04)	(.16)	(.16)	(.21)	(.12)	(.09)	(.09)	(.12)	(.13)
> $50K	−.09#	−.12**	−.06	−.14	−.28	−.32**	.16	−.15#	−.07	−.11
	(.05)	(.04)	(.12)	(.13)	(.22)	(.11)	(.12)	(.09)	(.11)	(.13)
Democrat	2.62***	2.71***	2.53***	2.61***	2.70***	2.44***	3.17***	3.15***	2.26***	2.46***
	(.05)	(.05)	(.15)	(.16)	(.19)	(.13)	(.13)	(.11)	(.11)	(.14)
Independent	1.26***	1.32***	1.03***	1.09***	1.19***	1.32***	1.60***	1.49***	1.11***	1.40***
	(.04)	(.04)	(.12)	(.13)	(.17)	(.13)	(.10)	(.11)	(.11)	(.13)
Liberal	.58***	.79***	.70**	1.10***	.29	.95***	.44***	.61***	.77***	1.08***
	(.06)	(.05)	(.25)	(.16)	(.22)	(.14)	(.13)	(.11)	(.15)	(.15)
Moderate	.25***	.59***	.26*	.97***	.03	.67***	.07	.30**	.57***	.58***
	(.04)	(.04)	(.10)	(.13)	(.19)	(.11)	(.10)	(.11)	(.10)	(.13)
Constant	−1.37***	−1.72***	−1.14***	−1.97***	−.52#	−1.63***	−1.44***	−1.70***	−1.82***	−1.89***
	(.08)	(.09)	(.20)	(.20)	(.28)	(.20)	(.14)	(.15)	(.16)	(.21)
Pseudo R²	.49	.62	.50	.67	.40	.54	.58	.63	.46	.69
Observations	13,752	15,320	1,692	1,485	1,105	1,572	2,314	2,532	1,891	1,674

Note: In this table and Table 5.12 the dependent variable is 1 = Democratic primary voter, 0 = Republican primary voter. Probit coefficients with robust standard errors in parentheses. The pooled models include state primary dummies with Alabama as the omitted category. Data were weighted. #$p \leq .10$, *$p \leq .05$, **$p \leq .01$, ***$p \leq .001$ (two-tailed).

presented in pairs for 1988 and then 2008 so that the reader can see what if any variation exists for any of the independent variables across these two election cycles. Most of the emphasis will be placed on the dynamics present within each of the pooled models since they provide a comprehensive picture of political behavior in the entire region as opposed to for a certain southern state. This said, the factors that consistently register an effect on whether a respondent was a Democratic primary voter are race, party identification, and ideology. These three voter characteristics are consistently statistically significant in 1988 and 2008 for the pooled models and most of the state-specific models.

Table 5.11 indicates that only in Arkansas in 1988 and Florida in 2008 is it the case that African-Americans are no more likely to be Democratic primary voters than are their white counterparts. In all of the remaining models, black voters are significantly more likely to be

Table 5.12 Likelihood of Being a Democratic Primary Voter: 1988 and 2008

Variable	Louisiana		Tennessee		Texas		Virginia	
	1988	2008	1988	2008	1988	2008	1988	2008
Black	1.46***	.76***	.77#	1.02***	.72***	.81***	1.01***	1.12***
	(.19)	(.21)	(.42)	(.24)	(.17)	(.15)	(.16)	(.18)
Latino	−.50	−.13	−.41	−.05	.59***	.45***	−.12	.51#
	(.56)	(.31)	(.74)	(.25)	(.18)	(.14)	(.46)	(.28)
Other	1.05**	−.05	−	−.15	−.44	.33	−.20	−.15
	(.35)	(.35)	−	(.28)	(.35)	(.21)	(.37)	(.29)
Female	−.14	.21	.19	.26*	.01	.16#	−.08	.11
	(.09)	(.13)	(.17)	(.10)	(.08)	(.09)	(.09)	(.10)
> 44 Years	.02	.22	−.37*	.11	−.11	.08	−.01	.09
	(.10)	(.14)	(.17)	(.11)	(.09)	(.09)	(.09)	(.10)
College Grad	.26**	−.03	.12	−.10	.13	.15	.03	.14
	(.10)	(.14)	(.21)	(.12)	(.10)	(.09)	(.09)	(.11)
Prot./Other	−.12	.02	−.29	−.17	.19#	−.22*	−.10	−.41***
	(.10)	(.13)	(.24)	(.14)	(.10)	(.10)	(.10)	(.11)
> $50K	−.03	.00	−.29	−.09	−.24*	−.05	−.08	.03
	(.12)	(.14)	(.22)	(.11)	(.11)	(.10)	(.10)	(.15)
Democrat	2.50***	3.36***	2.56***	2.76***	2.86***	2.68***	2.45***	2.58***
	(.12)	(.16)	(.24)	(.13)	(.12)	(.13)	(.12)	(.14)
Independent	1.19***	1.79***	1.16***	1.44***	1.43***	1.11***	1.13***	1.22***
	(.12)	(.15)	(.20)	(.13)	(.10)	(.10)	(.11)	(.12)
Liberal	.12	−.06	.26	1.16***	.90***	.65***	1.06***	.80***
	(.20)	(.19)	(.27)	(.13)	(.14)	(.13)	(.14)	(.15)
Moderate	.08	.27#	.30	.81***	.21*	.74***	.48***	.43***
	(.10)	(.14)	(.19)	(.12)	(.09)	(.10)	(.10)	(.12)
Constant	−1.11***	−1.76***	−1.10***	−2.04***	−1.55***	−1.42***	−1.39***	−1.26***
	(.12)	(.23)	(.28)	(.20)	(.13)	(.15)	(.14)	(.19)
Pseudo R²	.51	.71	.47	.66	.51	.57	.52	.58
Observations	1,813	1,598	623	2,007	2,420	2,884	1,893	1,568

Note: Probit coefficients with robust standard errors in parentheses. Data were weighted. #$p \leq .10$, *$p \leq .05$, **$p \leq .01$, ***$p \leq .001$ (two-tailed).

Democratic primary participants. Although in the pooled model for 2008 the Latino coefficient is highly significant, it is insignificant in the 1988 pooled model. In the separate state models, Hispanic voters are more likely to participate in the Democratic primaries of Arkansas in 1988, Georgia in 2008, Texas in 1988 and 2008, and Virginia in 2008. Most likely pointing to the significance of more Republican aligned Cuban-Americans in 1988, Latinos in Florida are significantly less likely to be Democratic primary voters.

Party identification displays its hefty effect in all of the regression estimates displayed in Tables 5.11 and 5.12. For the pooled models and those of every state and each year, Democrats and independents are much more likely to vote in the Democratic primary as compared to Republican identifiers. In the case of ideology, liberal and moderate voters are more likely than conservatives to participate in Democratic primaries except for the null findings in Arkansas and Louisiana for the 1988 election, and no significant differences in the case of liberal Louisiana voters in 2008, moderate voters in Florida in 1988, and liberal and moderate Tennessee voters in 2008. Outside of race, party identification, and ideology, there is considerable variation in the impact of the remaining independent variables for any given state and election cycle. Furthermore, as will be shown, these other demographic variables, even when they are statistically significant, register very small substantive effects on the likelihood of being a Democratic primary voter.

Turning specifically to the pooled models in 1988 and 2008, there is a lot of longitudinal continuity and in some cases notable changes in the factors affecting primary participation. Starting with effects that persist and register in the same direction for both election cycles, are the following variables: black, college graduate (though only marginally significant in 1988 and 2008; $p < .10$), income, party identification, and ideology. All of these voter characteristics operate in a manner that is expected. African-Americans, the highly educated, lower income, Democratic, independent, liberal, and moderate voters are more likely to participate in Democratic primary contests in 1988 and twenty years later this is still the case, in the 2008 election.

Now, turning to changes, as mentioned, Latinos were not any more likely to be Democratic voters in 1988 but they were more likely to participate in the 2008 Democratic primary contests. Whereas women were slightly less likely to vote in the 1988 Democratic primaries, they were significantly more likely to vote in the 2008 Democratic primaries. In 1988, older voters were more likely to be Republican primary voters, but in 2008 they were somewhat more inclined to participate in Democratic primaries. Finally, in line with the strong shift of religious conservatives to the southern GOP, in 1988 Protestant/Other Christians were not any more or less likely to be Democratic primary voters, but twenty years later these voters are much more likely to be Republican primary participants.

As is always the case with limited dependent variable models, the interpretation of effects warrants a discussion of predicted probabilities. Utilizing the observed-value approach (see Hanmer and Kalkan 2013), Table 5.13 displays the predicted probability that a voter participated in the Democratic primary contest in 1988 and 2008 based on those characteristics that registered statistical significance in the pooled models from Table 5.11. The first entered probability shows the likelihood of being a Democratic primary voter for the selected variable of interest and the second probability (on the same line) is the corresponding probability when the first variable does not take on its value (e.g., for 1988 in the first row is shown the likelihood of an African-American voter being a Democratic primary voter and the next probability is the likelihood of being a Democratic primary voter if the participant is not African-American). After displaying the probabilities for the specific variable of interest when it does and does not take on its value, the third (bracketed) entry in each row for 1988 and 2008 is the difference between the two probabilities. For instance, in 1988, black voters had a .75 probability of participating in the Democratic presidential primary as compared to a .56 probability for voters who were not African-American and this difference was 19 percentage points higher for black voters.

For variable categories with multiple entries because of more than one classification, like race, party identification, and ideology, it makes sense to examine the probabilities in descending order for each year. For example, in 2008 the likelihood of being a Democratic presidential primary voter was: .68 for blacks, .59 for Latinos, and .54 for whites. As mentioned above, outside of the race variable, the other demographic variables register very small (though statistically significant) effects on the probability of being a Democratic primary voter. In 1988, the differences in probabilities between women and men, older and younger voters, college graduates versus those with less than a college degree, and voters with incomes above and below $50,000 are never more than 2 percentage points. In 2008, for these same demographic characteristics, the probability difference exceeds 2 points only in the case of gender. Women in 2008 had a .57 probability of being Democratic primary voters, whereas the likelihood for their male counterparts was .54. The religion variable was significant in 2008, but in substantive terms, this meant

Table 5.13 Probability of a Democratic Primary Voter: Pooled Models 1988 and 2008

Characteristic	1988	2008
Race		
Black vs. non-Black	.75, .56 [+19]	.68, .54 [+14]
Latino vs. non-Latino	n.s.	.59, .55 [+4]
White vs. non-White	.56, .57 [−1]	.54, .56 [−2]
Gender		
Female vs. Male	.57, .58 [−1]	.57, .54 [+3]
Age		
> 44 Years vs. < 44 Years	.56, .58 [−2]	.56, .55 [+1]
Education		
College Grad vs. Not Graduate	.58, .57 [+1]	.56, .55 [+1]
Religion		
Prot./Other vs. Otherwise	n.s.	.55, .57 [−2]
Income		
> $50K vs. < $50K	.56, .58 [−2]	.55, .57 [−2]
Party ID		
Democrat vs. non-Democrat	.95, .27 [+68]	.93, .24 [+69]
Independent vs. non-Independent	.72, .48 [+24]	.71, .49 [+22]
Republican vs. non-Republican	.17, .57 [−40]	.18, .56 [−38]
Ideology		
Liberal vs. non-Liberal	.67, .56 [+11]	.66, .52 [+14]
Moderate vs. non-Moderate	.60, .55 [+5]	.61, .52 [+9]
Conservative vs. non-Conservative	.54, .57 [−3]	.49, .56 [−7]

Note: Predicted probabilities were generated from the results of the 1988 and 2008 pooled models shown in Table 5.11. The probabilities were computed based on the observed-value approach (see Hanmer and Kalkan 2013). "n.s." means the variable is not statistically significant at $p < .10$ (two-tailed) or less. Brackets show the percentage point difference for each set of probability entries.

that Protestant/Other Christian voters had a .55 likelihood of participating in the Democratic primary versus a .57 probability for voters not classified as Protestant/Other Christian.

Since the main drivers of voter sorting into presidential primaries are party identification and ideology, it follows that these variables register the greatest effects. In 1988, with respect to party identification, the likelihood of being a Democratic primary voter was .95 for Democrats, .72 for independents, and just .17 for Republicans. These probabilities are essentially the same for each party affiliation category twenty years later in 2008 (.93 for Democrats, .71 for independents, and .18 for Republicans). The probability differences for ideology categories are notable, although not nearly as large as the differences tied to party identification. In 1988, the likelihood of voting in the Democratic primary was .67 for liberals, .60 for moderates, and .54 for conservatives. In 2008, the only notable change in ideology probabilities is found among conservatives. At .49, conservative voters were now more likely to vote in the Republican presidential primary.

Conclusion

In contemporary southern politics, the last three decades have witnessed a tremendous alteration in the demographic and political profiles of voters who participate in Democratic and Republican presidential primary contests. The partisan transformation of the South from a one-party Democratic stronghold to a Republican bastion has been one of the main storylines of

American politics. Given the importance of this massive alteration to the party system in the nation's largest region, it remains perplexing that the vast literature examining this realignment concentrates primarily on general election contests. When parties shift course or positioning on major issues, the trigger point tends to be presidential contests (Carmines and Stimson 1989). But after an alteration in position-taking occurs (e.g., the GOP taking the conservative position on civil rights and the national Democratic Party moving to the liberal side on the same issue), the gradual sorting of the electorate in response to a change in party positioning is typically most palpable in the political behavior of primary voters. It is in these contests where voters receive the strongest signal from political elites of what the latest direction the party is taking on salient issues. With the party label held constant, many voters differentiate between their candidate choices on the basis of where these contenders position themselves on high profile, "easy" issues (Carmines and Stimson 1980). And those candidates who are not in line with the general direction of the party with regard to major issues (e.g., Rudy Giuliani was a pro-choice Republican whose candidacy never got off the ground in the 2008 GOP nomination contest), are essentially dead on arrival.

By dint of their preferences, primary voters can veto the positions of some candidates by voting for their opponents. Viewed in a different light, the preferred candidates are in a sense having their political agendas validated. But if the national Democratic and Republican parties chart a course that many primary voters oppose, then it is likely we will see substantial movement of certain groups in and out of the major party primary contests. The American South is ground zero for such a development. As the national parties have reversed themselves on salient issues like race/civil rights, and taken opposing stands with respect to moral issues, the general trend of a more liberal stance by Democrats and a more conservative position embraced by Republicans has spurred the sorting of southern presidential primary voters. The evidence of this transformation is patently obvious in the exit poll data examined in this study.

The Democratic Party has become much more racially diverse, and in every Deep South Democratic primary electorate African-American voters are now the majority group. Despite some increase in Latino participants (at least in Florida and Texas) and even African-Americans (in Georgia, Mississippi, and Virginia, see Table 5.5), in 2016 southern Republican primary voters remain an overwhelmingly white constituency. In addition to race, southern primary voters have sorted with respect to gender and religion. Women are on the brink of dominating southern Democratic primary electorates and in particular black women in Deep South Democratic primaries. Protestant and other Christian voters are drawn more to the Republican primary contests compared to voters of another faith or those who claim no religion. As the major parties have distinguished themselves on religious issues in a manner such that the GOP appears more devout and the Democratic Party more secular, this religious-based sorting makes sense.

Finally, because the Democratic and Republican parties have polarized in opposing ideological directions and this development has not escaped the notice of voters (Hetherington 2001), the most impressive transformation in the composition of southern presidential primary electorates is tied to ideological self-identification. In 1988, conservatives outnumbered liberals in most southern state Democratic primaries (see Table 5.4) and in every Democratic primary, moderates were the plurality group. By 2016, liberals comprise half of the Democratic primary electorate in every southern state, and their ascent has primarily come with a substantial decline in conservative participants. By comparison, even in 1988, only a small share of Republican primary voters identified as liberals. What has changed is the considerable decline in moderate voters in Republican presidential primaries. Now, every southern state Republican primary electorate is dominated by conservative voters (see Table 5.8). Contemporary southern Democratic primary electorates are racially diverse, majority female, more secular, and substantially more liberal than they were in the late 1980s. By contrast, southern Republican primary electorates are now markedly conservative, more Protestant/Christian, and remain overwhelmingly white in their racial composition.

Although both Democratic and Republican primary electorates have experienced a graying effect and an across-the-board increase in education, these characteristics hardly translate into strong political dispositions. The main dividing lines between most Democratic and Republican primary voters are firmly grounded in distinctions that resonate in the realm of politics. Gender, religion, and especially race and ideology, are characteristics that clearly drive political differences, and in the South, these deepening cleavages go a long way toward explaining the impressive sorting of its presidential primary electorates.

Notes

1 Throughout, the South is defined as the eleven former Confederate states: Alabama, Arkansas, Florida, Georgia, Louisiana, Mississippi, North Carolina, South Carolina, Tennessee, Texas, and Virginia. Further, in referring to southern subregions, the Deep South consists of Alabama, Georgia, Louisiana, Mississippi, and South Carolina and the Peripheral/Rim South includes Arkansas, Florida, North Carolina, Tennessee, Texas, and Virginia. The cardinal distinction between the Deep South and Peripheral South is the higher percentage of African-Americans in the former subregion and this primarily accounts for the greater racial polarization in political behavior among black and white voters residing in the Deep South (Black and Black 2012; McKee and Springer 2015).
2 Southern states typically go earlier in the primary calendar than non-southern states and, historically, this goes back to the creation of "Super Tuesday" in 1988, when southern Democratic elites (state lawmakers) conspired to place their state primary dates on the same day with the intention of shifting power in favor of the selection of a southern candidate (Stanley and Hadley 1987, 1989). In 1988, the South Carolina GOP held its primary on March 5 and all the remaining southern states held their major party presidential primaries on Super Tuesday March 8. In 2008, the southern states were much more spread out in conducting their primaries, with only four holding theirs on Super Tuesday February 5 (Alabama, Arkansas, Georgia, and Tennessee) and North Carolina was the last southern state to go on May 6. In 2016, the southern states were much more bunched together with six holding their primaries on Super Tuesday March 1 (Alabama, Arkansas, Georgia, Tennessee, Texas, and Virginia) and Florida and North Carolina the last southern states to go on March 15.
3 The states are Alabama, Arkansas, Florida, Georgia, Louisiana, Tennessee, Texas, and Virginia.
4 According to the 1988 ABC News exit poll of South Carolina Republican primary voters, over 97 percent were white and less than 2 percent were African-American (author's analysis of the data).
5 In Louisiana, 96 percent of the 2016 Republican presidential primary voters were white (author's examination of Louisiana Secretary of State's post-election statistical report).
6 I say at least five Republican primary electorates in 2016 because it is very likely that over 80 percent of Louisiana voters in the GOP primary self-identify as conservatives (a confident expectation in the absence of exit poll data).
7 Unfortunately, I do not have raw exit poll data for all state primaries held for these years (South and Non-South) and therefore I cannot make comparisons between the changes occurring in the South vis-à-vis those taking place in the rest of the nation.
8 Of course, in certain states the racial composition is considerably different, as all five Deep South-state Democratic primary electorates are now majority black (as mentioned in the discussion of Table 5.1).

References

Abramowitz, Alan I., and Kyle L. Saunders. 1998. "Ideological Realignment in the U.S. Electorate." *Journal of Politics* 60(3): 634–652.
Ansolabehere, Stephen, and Eitan Hersh. 2012. "Validation: What Big Data Reveal About Survey Misreporting and the Real Electorate." *Political Analysis* 20(4): 437–459.
Bartels, Larry M. 2000. "Partisanship and Voting Behavior, 1952–1996." *American Journal of Political Science* 44(1): 35–50.
Black, Earl, and Merle Black. 2002. *The Rise of Southern Republicans*. Cambridge: Harvard University Press.

Black, Merle, and Earl Black. 2012. "Deep South Politics: The Enduring Racial Division in National Elections," in *The Oxford Handbook of Southern Politics*, eds. Charles S. Bullock III and Mark J. Rozell. Oxford: Oxford University Press.

Carmines, Edward G., and James A. Stimson. 1980. "The Two Faces of Issue Voting." *American Political Science Review* 74(1): 78–91.

Carmines, Edward G., and James A. Stimson. 1989. *Issue Evolution: Race and the Transformation of American Politics*. Princeton: Princeton University Press.

Clark, John A. 2014. "The 2012 Presidential Nomination Process," in *Second Verse, Same as the First: The 2012 Presidential Election in the South*, eds. Scott E. Buchanan and Branwell DuBose Kapeluck. Fayetteville: University of Arkansas Press.

Green, John C., Lyman A. Kellstedt, Corwin E. Smidt, and James L. Guth. 2014. "The Soul of the South: Religion and Southern Politics in the New Millennium." In *The New Politics of the Old South*, eds. Charles S. Bullock III and Mark J. Rozell. Lanham, MD: Rowman & Littlefield.

Hanmer, Michael J., and Kerem Ozan Kalkan. 2013. "Behind the Curve: Clarifying the Best Approach to Calculating Predicted Probabilities and Marginal Effects from Limited Dependent Variable Models." *American Journal of Political Science* 57(1): 263–277.

Hayes, Danny, and Seth C. McKee. 2008. "Toward a One-Party South?" *American Politics Research* 36(1): 3–32.

Hetherington, Marc J. 2001. "Resurgent Mass Partisanship: The Role of Elite Polarization." *American Political Science Review* 95(3): 619–631.

Hood, M. V. III, Quentin Kidd, and Irwin L. Morris. 2012. *The Rational Southerner: Black Mobilization, Republican Growth, and the Partisan Transformation of the American South*. New York: Oxford University Press.

Huffmon, Scott H., H. Gibbs Knotts, and Seth C. McKee. Forthcoming. "First in the South: The Importance of South Carolina in Presidential Politics." *Journal of Political Science*.

Kalb, Deborah S. 2016. *Congressional Quarterly Guide to United States Elections*, 7th ed. Thousand Oaks, CA: Congressional Quarterly / Sage Publications.

Levendusky, Matthew. 2009. *The Partisan Sort: How Liberals Became Democrats and Conservatives Became Republicans*. Chicago: University of Chicago Press.

Lublin, David. 2004. *The Republican South: Democratization and Partisan Change*. Princeton: Princeton University Press.

McKee, Seth C. 2010. *Republican Ascendancy in Southern U.S. House Elections*. Boulder: Westview Press.

McKee, Seth C. 2012. "The Past, Present, and Future of Southern Politics." *Southern Cultures* 18(3): 95–117.

McKee, Seth C. 2017. "The 2016 Presidential Nomination Process." In *The Future Ain't What It Used to Be: The 2016 Presidential Election in the South*, eds. Scott E. Buchanan and Branwell DuBose Kapeluck. Fayetteville: University of Arkansas Press.

McKee, Seth C. Forthcoming. *The Dynamics of Southern Politics: Causes and Consequences*. Washington, D.C.: CQ Press.

McKee, Seth C., and Danny Hayes. 2009. "Dixie's Kingmakers: Stability and Change in Southern Presidential Primary Electorates." *Presidential Studies Quarterly* 39(2): 400–417.

McKee, Seth C., and Danny Hayes. 2010. "The Transformation of Southern Presidential Primaries." In *Presidential Elections in the South: Putting 2008 in Political Context*, eds. Branwell DuBose Kapeluck, Robert P. Steed, and Laurence W. Moreland. Boulder: Lynne Rienner Publishers.

McKee, Seth C., and Melanie J. Springer. 2015. "A Tale of 'Two Souths': White Voting Behavior in Contemporary Southern Elections." *Social Science Quarterly* 96(2): 588–607.

McKee, Seth C., and Antoine Yoshinaka. 2015. "Late to the Parade: Party Switchers in Contemporary US Southern Legislatures." *Party Politics* 21(6): 957–969.

Shafer, Byron E., and Richard Johnston. 2006. *The End of Southern Exceptionalism: Class, Race, and Partisan Change in the Postwar South*. Cambridge: Harvard University Press.

Stanley, Harold W., and Charles D. Hadley. 1987. "The Southern Presidential Primary: Regional Intentions with National Implications." *Publius* 17(3): 83–100.

Stanley, Harold W., and Charles D. Hadley. 1989. "Super Tuesday 1988: Regional Results and National Implications." *Publius* 19(3): 19–37.

Stimson, James A. 2004. *Tides of Consent: How Public Opinion Shapes American Politics*. Cambridge: Cambridge University Press.

Valentino, Nicholas A., and David O. Sears. 2005. "Old Times There Are Not Forgotten: Race and Partisan Realignment in the Contemporary South." *American Journal of Political Science* 49(3): 672–688.

Wilcox, Clyde, and Carin Robinson. 2010. *Onward Christian Soldiers? The Religious Right in American Politics*. Boulder: Westview Press.

6

THE NATURE OF CROSSOVER VOTERS

Barbara Norrander

Crossover voters are either the heroes or villains of primary electorates. To those concerned that partisan voters in primary electorates are too ideologically extreme, crossover voters are viewed as a moderating force. This assumption leads many primary reformers to seek out participation formats that downplay the importance of partisan voters and open up participation to more independents. On the other hand, to party officials crossover voters distort the will of the party's most loyal voters. Indeed, the Democratic Party in its late twentieth-century reform movement emphasized that participation in their presidential nominations should be open to all Democrats, rather than all voters. In the 1980s the Democratic Party even sued the state of Wisconsin to keep it from holding an open presidential primary, though the party subsequently relented and allowed states which traditionally used the format to continue to do so.[1] Arguments for and against the presence of crossover voters in partisan primaries are many and varied.

Positive views of crossover voters include normative concerns, such that all Americans should be able to participate in a primary without having to register as a partisan. The participation of independent voters in primary elections also may be beneficial to the party. The party's nominee eventually needs to win the general election, and the voice of crossover voters may help to choose a candidate who is more electable. Participation of crossover voters in a primary also may help recruit new voters to join the party's core supporters (Fowler, Spiliotes and Vavareck 2003; Norrander 1992).

Negative views of crossover voters depict them as less knowledgeable than partisan primary voters about candidates and issues, and as less likely to consider factors such as viability or electability (Fowler, Spiliotes and Vavareck 2003). Party leaders fear that crossover voters will engage in raiding behavior, supporting the weakest candidate to ensure the victory of their party's candidate in the fall election (Southwell 1988). Finally, various candidates have belied the role of crossover voters when they perceived that these voters gave additional support to an opposing candidate, such as Humphrey versus McGovern in the 1972 Wisconsin primary (Southwell 1988) and Romney versus Santorum in the 2012 Michigan primary.

Views of Crossover Voters by Social Scientists

The political science literature on crossover voters tackles two questions: (1) who should be considered a crossover voter, and (2) does the presence of crossover voters affect the primary outcome. Various answers have been given to the first question. Some political scientists count as crossover voters anyone who is not affiliated with the party holding the primary (Adamany 1976; Ranney 1972). However, other political scientists argue whether independent voters should be included as crossover voters. Some posit that all independents should be excluded from the ranks of crossover voters (Hedlund 1978). Others assert that independents leaning toward the party holding the primary should not be counted as crossover voters (Wekkin 1988). This latter position is often adopted because of the similarities in behavior between leaning independents and weak partisans (Petrocik 1974, 2009). Finally, while crossover voters are most frequently assumed to be a factor in open primaries, political scientists have found crossover voters across all formats, including both open and closed primaries (Alvarez and Nagler 1997; Norrander 2010; Norrander and Wendland 2016). Crossover voting can occur in closed primaries when a person's party identification does not match their party registration. While for most Americans their party identification matches their party registration (Finkel and Scarrow 1985), for some a discrepancy occurs. Thus, while they are a registered partisan, attitudinally, in terms of party identification, they think of themselves as an independent. Of course, this is not a complication in the 40 percent of states (e.g., open primary states) which do not ask for party preferences on their voter registration forms. Thus, while there are attitudinal partisans across all 50 states, registered partisans exist in only 60 percent of U.S. states.

Often overlooked in the debate on who is a crossover voter is that primary participation rules, and party registration, shape people's party identification (Burden and Greene 2000; Campbell et al. 1960; Finkel and Scarrow 1985; Gerber, Huber and Washington 2010; Norrander 1989; Thornburg 2014). In states where primary participation rules encourage people to register as a partisan, e.g. closed primary states, there are more partisans and fewer independents. In open primary states without party registration and without a need to have a partisan identity in order to participate in a primary election, there are more independents and fewer partisans. Semi-closed primary rules influence partisanship close to the pattern found in open primary states, as the independent identity is favored by participation rules that provide registered independents with more flexibility in primary participation. Semi-open primary rules, where individuals need to tell an election official which party's ballot they wish to use, function more like closed primaries. This format was actually the original format for a closed primary (Berdahl 1942). Semi-open primary states also have used a variety of techniques that cement more partisan identities, such as oaths of party loyalty, voter challenges and maintaining records of which party's primary a voter participated in (Holbrook and La Raja 2008). As the sizes of the partisan and independent groups vary across the states, so does their ideological orientation. In closed primary states the larger group of partisans are more moderate, while in open primary states the smaller group of partisans are more ideologically extreme (Norrander and Wendland 2016).

Another complication in the study of crossover voters, noted in the political science literature, is that voters may maintain multiple partisan identities. In the mid to late twentieth century the slow secular realignment in the South muddied the partisanship waters. Some Americans appeared to have dual partisanship (Jennings and Niemi 1966) or were "segmented-partisans" (Wekkin 1991), identifying as Republicans for national races and as Democrats for state and local politics. Dual partisanship may be less of an explanation today, after the slow secular realignment in the South solidified attachments of conservative voters to the Republican Party at all levels of government by the 1990s. Yet, some journalistic accounts of Donald Trump's supporters find a segment of voters who identify as Republican but are registered as Democrats (Cohn 2015). Other voters may maintain split partisan preferences across different issue areas, preferring one party on economic issues and the other on social issues. Depending on the central issues in a primary campaign, these voters may crossover to support a candidate supporting their preferred position on a specific issue (Ranney 1972; Wekkin 1991). The intertwining of partisanship and primary participation rules and some potential for lingering dual partisanship means that crossover voting can occur in all primary settings.

The second question tackles whether crossover voters influence the outcome of primary elections, with most social scientists downplaying this possibility. Fowler, Spiliotes and Vavreck (2003) in their New Hampshire study found no difference in candidate preferences for those registered as undeclared (i.e., independents) versus partisans. Studies of the open primary in Wisconsin likewise find few effects for the presence of independent voters in the electorate (Adamany 1976; Hedlund 1978; Ranney 1972), though Wekkin (1991) argues crossover voters helped Hart best Mondale in the 1984 Wisconsin primary. Other political scientists examining a wider variety of races also find some differences between the preferences of partisan and crossover voters but few instances where this significantly changed the outcome of the primary (Geer 1986; Hedlund, Watts and Hedge 1982; Lengle 1981; Southwell 1988, 1991). Thus, at best, social scientists report only a few isolated cases where crossover voters altered the outcome of a presidential primary.

Raiding behavior is especially discounted in the academic literature. Wekkin (1991) summarizing previous findings suggests that less than 5 percent of primary voters engage in activity meant to nominate a weaker candidate in the party opposite of their own (see for example, Adamany 1976; Hedlund 1978; Abramowitz, McGlennon and Rapoport 1981). This evidence of minimal raiding behavior is supported even in cases of orchestrated efforts, such as Rush Limbaugh's "operation chaos" encouragement of conservatives to vote for Hillary Clinton to prolong the 2008 Democratic primaries and make the nomination race more divisive (Stephenson 2011). Among reasons given for the dearth of raiding behavior is a lack of the political sophistication needed to cast a strategic vote. The uncertainty of the outcome of any primary battle would also dissuade individuals from crossing over to raid another party's primary or to know which candidate would be the strategically weakest candidate to support. Primary voters, if they cross over, appear to mostly want to hedge their bet and vote for a preferred candidate in the opposing party's primary (Abramowitz, McGlennon and Rapoport 1981; Southwell 1991; Wolf and Downs 2007). Thus, if their own party's candidate falters in the general election campaign, these voters still have a good second choice candidate.

How Large Is the Crossover Vote?

Perceptions of how many crossover voters exist are shaped by the existing data on primary voters. This endeavor is complicated by the lack of surveys of actual primary voters across a number of states and primary formats. For presidential primaries, the most typically available surveys are the media exit polls. These exit polls, however, contain only a three-category partisanship question. The independent category in the exit polls includes pure independents and independents that lean toward one party over the other. Independent leaners are distinctive from pure independents and often have more in common with partisan voters. Thus, some political scientists call them "hidden partisans" (Keith et al. 1992). With increasing partisan polarization, independent leaners have come even closer to the characteristics of partisans. Today, the ideology of independent leaners is closer to that of strong partisans than is the ideology of weak partisans to that of strong partisans (Abramowitz 2010: 58–59). Leaning independents are also as loyal as weak partisans in their vote choices (Abramowitz and Webster 2016). While prior researchers have adopted a wide variety of definitions for crossover voters, I support the position that independent leaners are not crossover voters. Leaning independents are participating in the primary of their most preferred party.

While the presidential primary exit polls do not separate primary voters' partisanship in the academic format of seven categories, the 2010 Cooperative Congressional Election Survey

(Ansolabehere 2012) contains the seven-category party identification scale and a validated vote for participation in these off-year state-level primaries. Tables 6.1a and 6.1b show the partisanship of those who participated in the Republican and Democratic primaries recoded to indicate whether their partisanship matched the party of the primary, the breakdown of the independent vote, and how many voted in the primary of the opposite party. Table 6.1a reveals that across all primary types, 51 percent of primary voters are strong partisans, 19 percent are weak partisans, and another 19 percent are independents who lean toward the party holding the primary. Table 6.1b collapses these three categories of primary voters into one and reveals that on average 89 percent of primary participants are not crossover voters. Instead, these voters are the core supporters of the party. The number of pure independents participating in the primaries is quite low, at 6 percent, and the proportion of true crossover voters (e.g., partisans from the opposite party and independents leaning toward the opposite party) is equally low, averaging 5 percent.

Table 6.1b also includes a breakdown of these figures for the different primary participation rules (see Appendix for states in each category). While crossover voters are frequently discussed in connection with open primaries, Table 6.1b reveals that the proportions of true crossover voters do not vary much by primary type (4 percent to 7 percent). Most of the voters across all primary types are core supporters composed of partisans and independents leaning toward the party. These core voters constitute between 85 percent (in open primaries) to 92 percent (in closed primaries) of primary voters. What differs across primary types is whether more of these core party voters designate themselves as partisans or whether they view themselves as independents who lean toward that party.

Table 6.1a Partisanship of Voters in 2010 Primaries (in Percentages)

	All Primaries	Closed Primaries	Semi-Closed Primaries	Semi-Open Primaries	Open Primaries
Own Party Strong Partisans	51	56	53	48	45
Own Party Weak Partisans	19	23	19	16	13
Own Party Leaners	19	14	18	24	26
Pure Independents	6	4	5	7	9
Opposite Party Leaners	3	2	3	3	3
Opposite Party Weak Partisans	1	1	1	1	2
Opposite Party Strong Partisans	1	1	1	1	2
Number of Cases	14,231	4,433	4,295	4,320	1,184

Table 6.1b Collapsing Partisanship into Three Categories (in Percentages)

	All Primaries	Closed Primaries	Semi-Closed Primaries	Semi-Open Primaries	Open Primaries
Own Party Partisans & Leaners	89	92	90	87	85
Pure Independents	6	4	5	7	9
Opposite Party Partisans & Leaners	5	4	5	5	7
Number of Cases	14,231	4,433	4,295	4,320	1,184

Source: 2010 Cooperative Congressional Election Survey.

That nearly 90 percent of primary voters are core supporters of the party greatly diminishes the importance of crossover voters in debates over the nature of primary electorates. It also brings up the question of why so few crossover voters exist even under a format, such as open primaries, that allows voters to move across party lines. Conditions for crossover voting are more scarce than often presumed. Even in open primary states, incentives or opportunities for crossover voting may be reduced by the structure of primary ballots. For state-level primary contests, multiple electoral offices appear on the primary ballot. A primary ballot may contain races for governor, senate, House of Representatives, state legislatures and local offices. This combination of races will tend to anchor partisans and independent leaners to their preferred party's primary. Further, the nationalization of partisan politics in recent decades ties a single partisan identity to races up and down the electoral ballot (Abramowitz and Webster 2016; Jacobson 2015).

Presidential primaries also present few opportunities for crossover voting. Crossover voting needs a circumstance where one's own party lacks a nomination contest or where the opposition party's primary contest is more exciting, such as being more closely fought. Such opportunities for crossover voting in presidential primaries occur in two settings. One is the lack of any primary contest in one's own party, such as when the party's sole candidate is an unchallenged incumbent president running for renomination (e.g. Republicans in 1984 and 2004, Democrats in 1996 and 2012). The second opportunity is late in the primary season when one's own party's nomination has been unofficially won by a leading candidate while the contest remains competitive for the opposing party (e.g. Republicans in 2008). However, circumstances for crossover voting in late presidential primaries are limited because presidential primaries held after mid-March are typically held jointly with the state's primaries for other offices. Nomination races in these state-level contests will likely keep most partisans from crossing over to the opposite party to participate in the presidential contest.

The Consequences of Primary Participation by Partisan and Crossover Voters

Reformers often argue that the presence of independent voters will ameliorate the ideological extremity of the partisan primary voters. Yet, here too, the ideological nature of partisan and independent primary voters, and especially the nature of the leaning independent primary voters, is not well understood. Independent leaners are typically better educated than weak partisans (Petrocik 1974), and education is one of the determinants of adopting an ideology. Further, in today's polarized political world, those with higher levels of education are more likely to perceive the positions of political parties and match their partisan identities, or partisan leanings, to these issues. Thus, even independents who lean toward a political party could be "ideologically extreme," such that adding them to the primary electorate does not greatly move the ideological orientation of primary voters in the moderate direction.

To investigate how partisanship influences the ideological composition of primary electorates, the 2010 CCES is once again used. This survey contains a validated vote for both the general and primary elections. The validated voter from the general election can be used to calculate the mean ideology of voters in each state. Subsequently, each individual primary voter's ideology can be compared to his or her state's general election "median voter" to calculate the ideological deviation of the primary voter from the typical voter in the state. This comparison is crucial, because the median voter across the 50 states does not have the same ideological orientation nor do they necessarily register as moderates. The typical red-state voter, on average, would be more conservative than the typical blue-state voter.

The CCES has a five-point ideology scale which was recoded to be centered on 0. Scores above zero reflect more conservative ideologies and scores below zero indicate more liberal identities. With the comparison of primary voters' ideologies to their states' general election median voter, positive coefficients indicate the primary voter is more conservative while negative values indicate the primary voter is more liberal. However, for ease of presentation in a bar chart, the absolute value of the ideological deviation from the states' median voter is used. A higher value indicates more ideological deviation, though this deviation is in the liberal direction for Democratic primary voters and in the conservative direction for Republican primary voters.

Figure 6.1 demonstrates the influence of different groups of partisan voters to the ideological nature of the Democratic Party's primary electorate. The first line in each set is the ideological orientation of the primary electorate if only strong Democrats participated. The second line adds in weak partisans, so this line is the ideology of the Democratic primary electorate if only Democrats (weak or strong) voted. The third line reflects the cumulative ideology of the primary electorate when independents leaning toward the Democratic Party are added. The pattern continues until the last line adds in the ideology of strong Republicans who crossed over and voted in the Democratic primary. With this addition, the final line also reflects the actual ideology of all voters in the 2010 primary. The influence of the addition of each group of voters is affected by both their ideology and the size of the group. Thus, while Republicans voting in Democratic primaries have more conservative orientations, their small numbers diminish how much influence they can have on the overall ideology of voters in Democratic primaries.

As Figure 6.1 reveals, the biggest change in the ideological orientation of Democratic primary electorates occurs with the change from only strong partisans to the inclusion of weak partisans. The subsequent addition of independents leaning toward the Democratic Party has

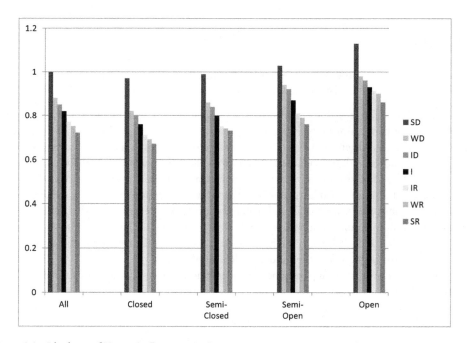

Figure 6.1 Ideology of Voters in Democratic Primaries, 2010

Source: 2010 Cooperative Congressional Election Survey.

Key: SD = strong Democrat, WD = weak Democrat, ID = independent leaning toward Democratic Democratic Party, I = pure independent, IR = independent leaning toward Republican Party, WR = weak Republican, SR = strong Republican.

little effect on the overall ideological orientation of the primary electorate. These three groups are the core voters in Democratic primaries, constituting almost 90 percent of voters. Both weak partisans and independent leaners ameliorate the more extreme ideology of strong partisans. Subsequent additions of other independents and crossover voters incrementally move primary electorates in the moderate direction, but none of these changes is as dramatic as the shift in ideology between strong and the weak partisans (and independent leaners).

Results in Figure 6.1 also illustrate patterns across primary types. Contrary to conventional wisdom, the most extreme electorate (represented by the position of the seventh line in each set) is found in open primary states. The extreme ideology of strong partisans in these states helps to move the overall ideological orientation of voters in open Democratic primaries to be more liberal than their states' general election voter. In contrast, strong partisans in closed primary states are the most moderate. One explanation for this pattern is that in closed primary states, voters' perceptions are influenced by party registration. The legal attachment shapes the attitudinal attachment and leads to more partisan adherents representing a greater diversity of issue positions and ideological identities. In open primary states, without a legal attachment, partisanship is influenced more by issues, and only those who strongly agree with a party's issue positions are likely to view themselves as strong partisans.

Figure 6.2 presents results for Republican primaries. Once again, the biggest change in ideological composition of primary electorates, in most cases, comes from the switch from an electorate composed of only strong partisans to one that includes weak partisans, as well. This is true for all primaries combined and for the closed and semi-closed primaries. However, for

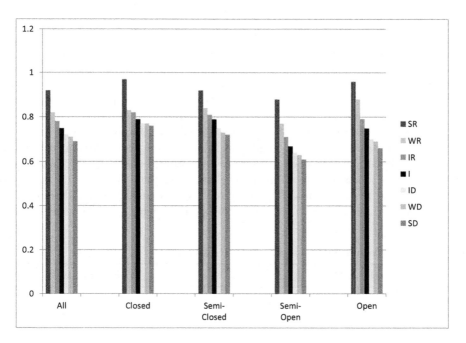

Figure 6.2 Ideology of Voters in Republican Primaries, 2010

Source: 2010 Cooperative Congressional Election Survey.

Key: SD = strong Democrat, WD = weak Democrat, ID = independent leaning toward Democratic Party, I = pure independent, IR = independent leaning toward Republican Party, WR = weak Republican, SR = strong Republican.

the semi-open and open primaries the addition of leaning independents also has a significant influence on the overall composition of the primary electorate. A partial explanation for the pattern for semi-open primary states is the predominance of southern states in this group. In these southern states, the dominance of Republican voters in the general election moves the state's median voter toward the preferences of the Republican Party. Thus, even strong partisans voting in southern Republican primaries are closer to their state's general election median voter.

Partisanship and Vote Choice in Presidential Primaries

A final consequence of any differences between crossover voters and partisan voters would occur if the two groups varied in their choice of candidates. Prior research on crossover voters in presidential primaries comes from the late twentieth century and generally finds little influence for crossover voters on primary outcomes (e.g., Southwell 1988, 1991). However, an update to contests at the beginning of the twenty-first century could change that view. Some recent candidates had greater appeal among independent voters. This would include John McCain and Ron Paul on the Republican side and Bernie Sanders in the Democratic contest. However, if presidential primaries are generally won by large margins, any differences in candidate preferences between partisan and crossover voters would have diminished influence on the outcome of primaries. This section of the chapter will first review the competitive levels of recent primary outcomes and second, measure the influence of crossover voters by using the media exit polls.

Table 6.2 investigates the competitive level of presidential primaries over the last three election cycles. Official vote percentages for winning and second-place candidates are compared. To maintain continuity with the next analysis of crossover voters, Table 6.2 only includes primaries and caucuses (Iowa and Nevada) where exit polls were conducted. However, the media cease to conduct exit polls after a race becomes uncompetitive, so primaries included in Table 6.2 are the most competitive ones. The typical margin of victory in presidential primaries is not narrow. The median margin of victory in presidential primaries ranges between 10 and 15 percentage points. Among the recent nomination races, the 2008 Republican contest was the most competitive (signified by the lower median margin of victory), and therefore presented more opportunities for switches in outcomes due to crossover voters. Of course, narrow victories do occur in any election cycle, and figures in Table 6.2 show the smallest margins between first- and second-place are 2 percentage points or less. On the other hand, the largest margins of victory are quite substantial. These largest margins of victory are often found in a candidate's home state, such as Bernie Sanders winning Vermont's primary by 72 percentage points, and Mitt Romney winning the 2008 Utah primary by 84 points and the 2012 Massachusetts primary

Table 6.2 Winning Margins in Presidential Primaries and Caucuses

	Median Margin	*Smallest Margin*	*Largest Margin*	*Number of Primaries with Exit Polls*
Democrats 2008	15.3	.8	43.8	37
Democrats 2016	15.6	.2	72.4	27
Republicans 2008	9.8	1.3	84.1	26
Republicans 2012	14.0	2.0	60.0	17
Republicans 2016	14.2	.2	35.1	26

Note: Table includes only primaries and caucuses for which exit polls are available. Entries based on official vote sources as compiled by the author (Norrander 2009, 2013, 2017).

Table 6.3 Changes in Presidential Primary and Caucus Outcomes if Only Partisans Voted

Event	Actual Winner	Winning Margin	Winner if Only Partisans Voted	Partisan Vote Margin
Democrats 2008				
Connecticut	Obama	4.0	Clinton	2
Missouri	Obama	1.4	Clinton	3
Democrats 2016				
Oklahoma	Sanders	10.4	Clinton	9
Michigan	Sanders	1.4	Clinton	18
Indiana	Sanders	4.9	Clinton	6
West Virginia	Sanders	15.6	Clinton	4
Wisconsin	Sanders	13.5	Clinton & Sanders tie	0
Republicans 2008				
New Hampshire	McCain	5.4	Romney	1
South Carolina	McCain	3.3	Huckabee	1
Florida	McCain	5	Romney & McCain tie	0
Alabama	Huckabee	4.2	McCain	2
Georgia	Huckabee	2.3	3-way tie: Huckabee, McCain & Romney	0
Missouri	McCain	1.5	Huckabee	5
Oklahoma	McCain	3.2	Huckabee & McCain tie	0
Republican 2016				
Missouri	Trump	.2	Cruz	3

Note: Winner if only partisans voted based on the candidate support by party identification in the exit polls as posted on CNN website. There was no change in winning candidates for the 2012 Republican contest.

by 60 points. Candidates also win by large margins when a state has a hefty number of their core supporters. For example, Clinton in 2016 won South Carolina's primary by 58.7 percentage points and Mississippi's primary by 66.2 percentage points due to the strong presence of African-American voters in southern Democratic primaries and their overwhelming support for Clinton.

To gauge the influence of crossover voters in presidential primaries, media exit polls are used to compare preferences of partisan voters to the actual outcome of the election. Media exit polls only ask a three-part party identification question: whether a voter is a Democrat, independent or Republican. Thus, while independents leaning toward the party holding the primary should be considered as core supporters of the party, media exit polls do not allow for this refinement. The media exit polls are used to measure which candidate won the highest support among partisan voters. The difference between the support for a candidate solely among partisans and the actual primary outcome is one indicator of the influence of crossover voters. When the winning candidate among partisan voters is different from the winning candidate in the actual primary vote, crossover voters changed the outcome of that primary.

Table 6.3 lists those presidential primaries in which a change in winner would occur if only partisans had voted. The table lists the actual winner of the primary and the margin of that win, followed by the "winner" if only partisans had voted and the margin of that victory. The 2012 Republican contest is missing from this table because none of the primary winners would have differed if only Republicans voted. This might be unexpected, since without any Democratic contest in that year, voters would have had more incentives to crossover to the Republican primaries. Perhaps the extent of partisan polarization today hinders the desires of voters to cross over and vote in the primary of their lesser preferred party.

Two other nomination races had minimal influence from crossover voters. In the 2016 Republican contest, only one primary outcome would have changed if only Republicans had voted. This was the essentially tied Missouri primary where it took five weeks for Donald Trump to be declared the official winner (Associated Press 2016). If only Republicans had voted, Ted Cruz would have won over Trump by 3 percentage points. The 2008 Democratic contest between Barack Obama and Hillary Clinton also would be essentially unchanged due to switches in first-place finishes. In only two primaries did crossover voters favor Obama to the extent that Clinton would have won if only Democrats voted. A switch in a second-place finish, however, may have changed the timbre of the media coverage of the Iowa caucuses. While Obama clearly won the Iowa caucuses, John Edwards garnered less than a half of a percentage point more support than did Clinton. Thus, Edwards was declared the second-place finisher while Clinton's third-place finish became fodder for media questions on the validity of Clinton's frontrunner status (Reuters 2008). If only Democrats had participated in the Iowa caucuses, Clinton would have garnered second-place by 8 percentage points over Edwards.

In 2016, Clinton also was disadvantaged by the presence of crossover voters in five states. If only partisans voted, Clinton would have won in four of these states and tied with Sanders in Wisconsin. Thus, crossover voting in the 2016 Democratic primaries made it a bit more difficult for Clinton to win the nomination. Nevertheless, across all primaries, Clinton won the most votes and the most pledged delegates. Even if all the presidential primaries had been open primaries, Sanders still would not have won the Democratic nomination (Enten and Silver, May 26, 2016). This is true in part because across all primary formats, partisans outnumber independent voters.

The presidential nomination contest most affected by crossover voters was the 2008 Republican contest. In five primaries, John McCain was the actual winner while if only Republicans voted another candidate would have won. However, which candidate would have won varied by the primary and, in some cases, the difference would have been McCain sharing first place with another candidate. Additionally, in two primaries, it was Huckabee who benefited from the support of crossover voters, and McCain was among the disadvantaged candidates. Perhaps Romney in 2008 was the most disadvantaged by the presence of crossover voters. Without them, Romney would have won in New Hampshire and tied with McCain in Florida. Romney dropped out of the contest after the Super Tuesday primaries, having won only three primaries: his "home states" of Michigan, Massachusetts and Utah. Without crossover voters, Romney would have added two more early victories to his column. Romney also was the rare candidate disadvantaged by the delegate distribution rules used in Republican primaries. With the actual rules, which varied across the primaries, McCain led Romney 680 to 270 delegates at the close of Super Tuesday. If all of the primaries used statewide proportional representation rules, Romney would have led McCain by 425 to 422 delegates (Norrander 2010, 85). Romney in 2008, more than any other recent candidate, had the right to complain that the rules were stacked against him.

Conclusions

Much ado is made of the role of crossover voters in primary elections. Some view crossover voters as an asset, bringing a more moderate voice to the primary electorate and helping to choose a more electable candidate. Others worry that crossover voters distort the preferences of the party's core supporters and create opportunities for the mischief created when opposing partisans raid a primary. Most social science research, however, tends to downplay the significance of crossover voters.

This chapter contributes to that theme. While the nuances of the partisanship of presidential primary voters are difficult to uncover due to a lack of survey data, data from off-year primary elections demonstrated that nearly 90 percent of primary voters are partisans or independents who lean toward the party holding the primary. Thus, the primary electorate is composed of those with a loyalty to the party, especially today in a world of polarized parties and the nationalization of elections at all levels of government. Examining different primary formats (open, closed and in between) reveals few differences in the general partisan composition of primary electorates. Open primaries have more independents than closed primaries, but again these are overwhelmingly independents leaning toward the party. Moreover, under all formats, partisans comprise the majority of primary voters.

The ideological orientation of primary voters is influenced by the presence of crossover voters, but the biggest change comes between strong partisans (who are the most ideologically extreme) and weak partisans and leaning independents (who are somewhat less extreme). The influence of crossover voters' ideology (other independents and opposite party partisans) is diminished by their small numbers. Patterns are similar across the different participation formats (e.g., open versus closed) and mostly the same across the two parties. However, the overall ideology of primary electorates does not conform to the conventional wisdom that open primary electorates are more moderate than those found in closed primary states. On the Democratic side, open primaries had the most ideologically extreme electorate, because they have the most ideologically extreme strong partisans. For Republican primaries, closed and semi-closed primaries do have more ideologically extreme electorates. The semi-open Republican primaries have the most moderate electorates, but this is explained by the predominance of this format in the southern states where Republican voters have moved the general election median voter further to the conservative side.

In some, but not all, presidential nomination contests, candidate choice is slightly influenced by the presence of independents and opposite party partisans participating in a party's primaries. The existence of crossover voters had no effect on the 2012 Republican contest and altered the outcome of only one or two primaries in the 2008 Democratic and 2016 Republican nomination races. Clinton in 2016 was disadvantaged in five primaries that Sanders won with the support of crossover voters, and Romney lost two crucial early contests (New Hampshire and Florida) in 2008 that he would have won if only Republicans had voted. Still, these cases of a switch in the winning candidate comprise only 11 percent of the primaries in which this change could be measured.

Several reasons explain why crossover voters have minor effects on the outcome of presidential primaries. One reason is that the average primary is won by a margin of more than 10 percentage points. Narrow victories are generally required for a change in a portion of the vote to alter the outcome. A second explanation is that across participation formats (open, closed and in between) the majority of primary voters are partisans and not independents or other crossover voters. Third, the candidate advantaged by the presence of crossover voters is not always consistent across nomination contests, such as the 2008 Republican contest where in some cases Huckabee rather than McCain was the advantaged candidate. Finally, even if a number of primary outcomes may have changed, there is little reason to suspect that this would have altered the overall outcome of the nomination. In the end, crossover voters are neither the bugaboo feared by their critics nor the savior of the primaries as proposed by their supporters.

Appendix

A.1 Classification of Primary Type by States and Parties, 2010

Closed	Semi-Closed	Semi-Open	Open
Connecticut	Alaska – Rep.	Alabama	Alaska – Dem.
Delaware	Arizona	Arkansas	Hawaii
Florida	California	Georgia	Idaho
Kentucky	Colorado	Illinois	Michigan
Maryland	Iowa	Indiana	Minnesota
Nevada	Kansas	Mississippi	Montana
New Mexico	Maine	Missouri	North Dakota
New York	Massachusetts	Ohio	Utah – Dem.
Oklahoma	Nebraska	South Carolina	Vermont
Oregon	New Hampshire	Tennessee	Wisconsin
Pennsylvania	New Jersey	Texas	
South Dakota – Rep.	North Carolina		
Utah – Rep.	Rhode Island		
	South Dakota – Dem.		
	West Virginia		
	Wyoming		

Source: Holbrook and La Raja (2008).

Note: For the 2010 analyses, Louisiana and Washington State are excluded because of their nonpartisan primaries. Virginia is excluded because of no validated votes in CCES. The Alaska Democratic Party shared a blanket primary with the Alaskan Independence Party and Libertarian Party. Since Alaska Democratic Party's candidates received the bulk of the primary votes, we have classified it as an open primary. In 2010, the South Dakota Democratic Party allowed independents to vote in its primary (Springer 2012). Utah law allows the political parties to choose the format for their primaries (FairVote 2012). Some states use a different primary format for presidential primaries. For example, Arizona holds semi-closed congressional primaries and closed presidential primaries.

Note

1 The U.S. Supreme Court in *Democratic Party of the United States v. Wisconsin ex rel. LaFollette*, 450 US 107 (1981), supported the national party's efforts to ban open primaries.

References

Abramowitz, Alan I. 2010. The *Disappearing Center*. New Haven, CT: Yale University Press.

Abramowitz, Alan I., and Steven Webster. 2016. "The Rise of Negative Partisanship and the Nationalization of U.S. Elections in the 21st Century." *Electoral Studies* 41 (1): 12–22.

Abramowitz, Alan I., John McGlennon, and Ronald Rapoport. 1981. "A Note on Strategic Voting in a Primary Election." *Journal of Politics* 43 (4): 899–904.

Adamany, David. 1976. "Communications: Cross-over Voting and the Democratic Party's Reform Rules." *American Political Science Review* 70 (3): 536–541.

Alvarez, R. Michael, and Jonathan Nagler. 1997. "Analysis of Crossover and Strategic Voting." Pasadena: California Instititute of Technology Social Science Working Paper Number 1019.

Ansolabehere, Stephen. 2012. Cooperative Congressional Election Study, 2010: Common Content. [Computer File] Release 2: August 10, 2012. Cambridge, MA: Harvard University, http://cces.gov. harvard.edu.

Associated Press. April 19, 2016. "Cruz Won't Seek Recount of Missouri Primary Loss to Trump." *Fox News*, http://www.foxnews.com/politics/2016/04/19/cruz-wont-seek-recount-missouri-primary-loss-to-trump.html

Berdahl, Clarence A. 1942. "Party Membership in the United States, I." *American Political Science Review* 36 (1): 16–50.

Burden, Barry C., and Steven Greene. 2000. "Party Attachments and State Election Laws." *Political Research Quarterly* 53 (1): 63–76.

Campbell, Angus, Philip E. Converse, Warren E. Miller, and Donald E. Stokes. 1960. *The American Voter*. New York: John Wiley & Sons.

Cohn, Nate. 2015. "Donald Trump's Strongest Supporters: A Certain Kind of Democrat." *New York Times*, December 31, http://www.nytimes.com/2015/12/31/upshot/donald-trumps-strongest-supporters-a-certain-kind-of-democrat.html (accessed January 4, 2016).

Enten, Harry, and Nate Silver. May 26, 2016. "The System Isn't 'Rigged' Against Sanders." *FiveThirtyEight* http://fivethirtyeight.com/features/the-system-isnt-rigged-against-sanders/

FairVote. 2012. "Congressional and Presidential Primaries: Open, Closed, Semi-Closed, and 'Top Two'." May, 2012. http://www.fairvote.org/research-and-analysis/presidential-elections/congressional-and-presidential-primaries-open-closed-semi-closed-and-top-two/, accessed May 5, 2014.

Finkel, Steven E., and Howard A. Scarrow. 1985. "Party Identification and Party Enrollment: The Difference and the Consequence." *Journal of Politics* 47 (3): 620–642.

Fowler, Linda L., Constantine J. Spiliotes, and Lynn Vavreck. 2003. "Sheep in Wolves' Clothing: Undeclared Voters in New Hampshire's Open Primary." *PS: Political Science & Politics* 36 (1): 159–163.

Geer, John G. 1986. "Rules Governing Presidential Primaries." *Journal of Politics* 48 (4): 1006–1025.

Gerber, Alan S., Gregory A. Huber, and Ebonya Washington. 2010. "Party Affiliation, Partisanship, and Political Beliefs." *American Political Science Review* 104 (3): 720–744.

Hedlund, Ronald D. 1978. "Crossover Voting in a 1976 Open Primary." *Public Opinion Quarterly* 41 (3): 498–514.

Hedlund, Ronald D., Meredith W. Watts, and David M. Hedge. 1982. "Voting in an Open Primary." *American Politics Quarterly* 14 (1): 55–73.

Holbrook, Thomas M. and Raymond J. La Raja. 2008. "Parties and Elections." In *Politics in the American States: A Comparative Analysis*, 9th edition, ed., Virginia Gray and Russell L. Hanson. Washington, D.C.: CQ Press, pp. 61–97.

Jacobson, Gary C. 2015. "Obama and Nationalized Electoral Politics in the 2014 Midterm." *Political Science Quarterly* 130 (1): 1–25.

Jennings, M. Kent, and Richard G. Niemi. 1966. "Party Identification at Multiple Levels of Government." *American Journal of Sociology* 72 (1): 86–101.

Keith, Bruce E., David B. Magleby, Candice J. Nelson, Elizabeth Orr, Mark C. Westlye, and Raymond E. Wolfinger. 1992. *The Myth of the Independent Voter*. Berkeley, CA: University of California Press.

Lengle, James I. 1981. *Representation and Presidential Primaries: The Democratic Party in the Post Reform Era*. Westport, CT: Greenwood Press.

Norrander, Barbara. 1989. "Explaining Cross-State Variation in Independent Identification." *American Journal of Political Science* 33 (3): 516–536.

Norrander, Barbara. 1992. *Super Tuesday: Regional Politics and Presidential Primaries*. Lexington: University Press of Kentucky.

Norrander, Barbara. 2009. "Democratic Marathon, Republican Sprint: The 2008 Presidential Nominations." In *The American Elections of 2008*, ed., Janet M. Box-Steffensmeier and Steven E. Schier. Lanham, MD: Rowman and Littlefield, pp. 33–54.

Norrander, Barbara. 2010. *The Imperfect Primary: Oddities, Biases, and Strengths of U.S. Presidential Nomination Politics*. New York: Routledge.

Norrander, Barbara. 2013. "Fighting Off Challengers: The 2012 Nomination of Mitt Romney." In *The American Elections of 2012*, ed. Janet M. Box-Steffensmeier and Steven E. Schier. New York: Routledge, pp. 48–72.

Norrander, Barbara. 2017. "The Conventional Versus the Unconventional: Presidential Nominations in 2016." In *Winning the Presidency 2016*, ed. William J. Crotty. New York: Routledge.

Norrander, Barbara and Jay Wendland. 2016. "Open Versus Closed Primaries and the Ideological Composition of Presidential Primary Electorates." *Electoral Studies* 42 (2): 229–236.

Petrocik, John R. 1974. "An Analysis of the Intransitives in the Index of Party Identification." *Political Methodology* 1 (1): 31–47.

Petrocik, John R. 2009. "Measuring Party Support: Leaners Are Not Independents." *Electoral Studies* 28 (3): 562–572.

Ranney, Austin. 1972. "Turnout and Representation in Presidential Primary Elections." *American Political Science Review* 66 (1): 21–37.

Reuters. January 3, 2008. "Hillary Clinton Places Third in Iowa Setback: CNN." January 3, http://www.reuters.com/article/us-usa-politics-clinton-idUSN0214716420080104

Southwell, Priscilla. 1988. "Open Versus Closed Primaries and Candidate Fortunes, 1972–1984." *American Politics Quarterly* 16 (2): 280–295.

Southwell, Priscilla. 1991. "Open Versus Closed Primaries: The Effect on Strategic Voting and Candidate Fortunes." *Social Science Quarterly* 44 (3): 789–796.

Springer, Jennifer. 2012. "South Dakota Voter Registration Down." *Ballotpedia*, August 14, 2012. http://ballotpedia.org/South_Dakota_voter_registration_down, accessed May 5, 2014.

Stephenson, E. Frank. 2011. "Strategic Voting in Open Primaries: Evidence from Rush Limbaugh's 'Operation Chaos'." *Public Choice* 148 (3): 445–573.

Thornburg, Matthew P. 2014. "Party Registration and Party Self-Identification: Exploring the Role of Electoral Institutions in Attitudes and Behaviors." *Electoral Studies* 36(1): 137–148

Wekkin, Gary D. 1988. "The Conceptualization and Measurement of Crossover Voting." *Western Political Quarterly* 41 (1) : 105–114.

Wekkin, Gary D. 1991. "Why Crossover Voters are Not 'Mischievous Voters': The Segmented Partisanship Hypothesis." *American Politics Quarterly* 19 (1): 229–247.

Wolf, Michael R., and Andrew Downs. 2007. "The Missing 3,847 Voters: Strategic Voting in a Congressional Primary." *Indiana Journal of Political Science* 10: 10–22.

7

THE EFFECT OF OPEN AND CLOSED PRIMARIES ON VOTER TURNOUT

Matthew J. Geras and Michael H. Crespin

In late June 2016, the voters in New York's 19th congressional district went to the polls to pick candidates to stand on the party lines for the general election. Since Rep. Chris Gibson (R–NY) was retiring, there were strong candidates in both the Democratic and Republican races seeking to run in a competitive district that Barack Obama won by six points in 2012. Nevertheless, there were only 17,007 voters on the Democratic side and 13,714 votes cast for the Republican candidates for an overall turnout of under 13 percent (Hamilton 2016). In contrast, statewide turnout in Georgia's primary was just over 20 percent.[1] One major difference between the two states that might explain the difference in turnout is who is allowed to vote in the primary elections. In New York, only registered party members are allowed to vote in party primaries. This is not true in Georgia where there is no party registration and voters may pick either ballot on primary day. Since many potential voters are excluded, it is not surprising that turnout was lower in the closed primary state compared to the open one. In this chapter, we provide a systematic test of the hypothesis that primary type will influence turnout rates in over 2,000 contested House primaries across nine election years from 2000 to 2016. In short, our results show us the New York–Georgia differences are not an anomaly and that closed primaries are associated with lower levels of voter turnout.

Below, we first discuss some of the previous work that has examined turnout in U.S. Elections. We then briefly outline our theoretical expectations followed by descriptive measures of turnout by primary type. Finally, we present a more thorough test of our hypotheses to show that primary type influences turnout in congressional elections.

Turnout in Primary Elections

The literature on turnout in U.S. elections is ample, so we will only focus on the highlights here. Political participation scholars are concerned with why citizens vote (Wolfinger and Rosenstone 1980), potential changes in turnout over time (McDonald and Popkin 2001; Burnham 1965), and why voters bother to cast a vote at all as they weigh costs and benefits (Aldrich 1993; Riker and Ordeshook 1968). In general, there are a few larger scale factors that consistently influence turnout – voter demographics, race-specific characteristics, and state institutional laws and rules. Most of the research examines turnout in the general election, although a few scholars do pay attention to primaries. Throughout, researchers study the question using both surveys and actual turnout data for all levels of elections – presidential, congressional, and state races. More recently, scholars have started to use experiments to probe specific ways campaigns can increase turnout by contacting voters (Green and Gerber 2015).

Wolfinger and Rosenstone's (1980) *Who Votes?* is the seminal work that explains how individual voter demographics can influence decisions to vote. The authors argue that education is the key predictor of the decision to vote where more education predicts higher turnout. Other individual factors that matter are income, occupation, age, marital status, and race of the voter (Rosenstone and Hansen 1993; Leighley and Nagler 1992a; Teixeira 1987; Verba and Nie 1987; Wolfinger and Rosenstone 1980). Political attitudes such as efficacy and party identification may also influence turnout choice (Abramson and Aldrich 1982; Teixeira 1987). Although there is a debate regarding stability in the size of the effects of individual variables over time, more educated and higher SES citizens are still more likely to vote (Shields and Goidel 1997; Leighley and Nagler 1992a, 1992b; Burnham 1987).

In terms of race-specific factors, several interrelated variables matter, including spending, competitiveness, and district political characteristics (Patterson and Caldeira 1983; Caldeira and Patterson 1982). Citizens might turn out at higher rates because they think their vote "matters" more (Aldrich 1993) or as a result of get-out-to-vote campaigns by candidates, parties, and other interested actors (Cox and Munger 1989). Of course, it takes money to generate excitement, so higher spending tends to correlate with increased turnout (Caldeira and Patterson 1982). Methodologically it is difficult to sort out which of the district variables are most informative because they tend to move together, but it is theoretically clear how they can make a difference.

Legal features at the state level can also drive turnout decisions by making it more or less difficult to vote (Rosenstone and Wolfinger 1978). These variables include issues related to polling hours, mail in ballots, ease of absentee voting, and variations in registration laws such as motor-voter or Election Day registration (Southwell and Burchett 2000; Knack 1995; Fenster 1994; Caldeira, Patterson, and Markko 1985). Some rules such as Election Day registration increase turnout, but other reforms such as early voting did not pan out as predicted (Burden et al. 2014; Hershey 2009). More recently voter ID laws have been implemented in several states. Since they increase the cost to voting, the expectation is they will work to reduce turnout; however, the results have been mixed (Grimmer et al. 2017; Hajnal, Lajevardi, and Nielson 2017; Alvarez, Bailey, and Katz 2008; Mycoff, Wagner, and Wilson 2007) depending on other laws in place and the unit of analysis. Researchers have found though that different subgroups do shoulder legal costs in different ways (Highton 2004).

Although most of the turnout research is centered on the general election, some does examine primary races. For the most part, the same general factors that influence turnout in November matter for primary elections (Kenney and Rice 1985), although there are some variables that are unique to primaries, such as only allowing registered party members to vote (Norrander 1991; Moran and Fenster 1982). In primaries, there is an expectation that moving from closed to open rules will increase the levels of participation (Jewitt 2014). While this is not always the case for presidential primaries (Norrander 1991), evidence suggests an increase in turnout for gubernatorial primaries (Kenney 1983), and under some circumstances for Senate races as well (Kenney 1986). Although we would expect to find more ideologically extreme voters or candidates in closed races compared to open primaries (Gerber and Morton 1998), this does not always hold (Norrander and Wendland 2016) and is contingent on other factors (Kaufmann, Gimpel and Hoffman 2003; Kanthak and Morton 2001). While there is a fear of "raiding" in open primary systems, Southwell (1991) suggests this does not happen all that often.

Compared to literature on presidential primaries, fewer scholars study congressional races and most focus on the Senate, largely due to the difficulty in acquiring data at the district level.

Turnout for congressional primaries hovers at around 25–35 percent, although this is also contextual. Voter participation in primaries has declined since the 1930s and 40s (Boatright 2014, 77–79). Just like other types of contests, turnout for Senate primaries is higher when races are close, or when there is a contested presidential primary on the same day (Kenney 1986). Further, when the Democratic Party dominated the South, turnout was often higher in the primary than in the general election.

Primary Type and Turnout: Expectations

Overall, the existing literature finds several factors that influence levels of voter turnout in American elections. In this chapter, however, we are most interested in examining the effects of primary laws on voter turnout in congressional primaries. Specifically, we build off of Jewitt's (2014) existing theoretical framework that predicts that voter turnout in primary elections will increase as the electoral process becomes more open.

In the United States, there are four major types of primary elections: open, closed, hybrid, and top-two.[2] Parties that utilize open primaries allow all voters the opportunity to vote, regardless of their party affiliation, as long as they meet the qualifications to vote in the general election. On the other end of the spectrum, parties that use closed primaries only allow affiliated partisan voters to participate. Hybrid primaries fall between these two extremes, in that they require registered partisans to vote in the primary for the party to which they are registered, but they allow unaffiliated voters to vote in either the Republican or Democratic primary.[3] Finally, in recent years, California and Washington have begun using top-two primaries at the congressional level. During a top-two primary, all candidates for office, regardless of their party affiliation, appear on the same ballot. The two candidates who receive the most votes, again regardless of party affiliation, advance to the general election. Our main hypothesis then is relatively straightforward as we expect that as restrictions increase, turnout should decline, because subsets of voters are not allowed to participate. This means turnout in open primary states should be higher compared to closed elections. Although there is nothing stopping a citizen from registering with a party so they can vote in a primary, not everyone wants to do so. Some are truly independent and do not want to affiliate with a party while others might not want to spend the time and effort to pick one party.[4] Hybrid and top-two allow all registered voters to participate, so we also expect turnout to be higher in these states compared to closed races. Below we discuss our data and present our results.

Measuring Voter Turnout in Primary Elections

In order to examine the effect of primary laws on voter turnout and to test our hypotheses, it is necessary to examine primary elections across the country over a significant period of time. As a result, we examine voter turnout in all congressional primary elections from 2000 to 2016 where there were at least two candidates on the ballot. [5] While examining such a lengthy time period allows us to exploit considerable variation in regard to both primary voter turnout and primary format, it also requires a significant amount of data collection. Pettigrew, Owen, and Wanless (2014) have greatly contributed to the political science community by compiling U.S. House of Representatives primary election results from 1956 to 2010. Moreover, they collect biographical information on primary candidates as well as election-specific data such as the type of primary and the number of candidates running for office. The analysis presented in this chapter both relies on this data, aggregating it to the election level when necessary, and extends the data in some key aspects to include the 2012, 2014, and 2016 election cycles.

The key dependent variable for our analysis is voter turnout at both the congressional district-level and the individual primary election level. Unfortunately, measuring voter turnout in primary elections is not as straightforward as one might think and makes studying House elections more difficult (Boatright 2014, 85). Determining the numerator is easy and is the number of votes casts in a particular election. The Federal Election Commission compiles that number in each primary. Determining the denominator, the population of eligible primary voters, is more complicated. While we acknowledge that there are several ways to measure primary voter turnout (see Burden and Ezra 1999 and Geys 2006), we measure turnout as the total number of votes cast in each primary divided by the voting age population of each congressional district. The voting age population of each congressional district was obtained from the U.S. Census Bureau through either the official census, which is conducted every ten years, or through the annual American Community Survey.[6]

This measure of voter turnout is conservative and if anything underestimates voter turnout since it relies on the voting age population instead of the voting eligible population (McDonald and Popkin 2001). That being said, we argue that the voting age population is a reasonable denominator to use in the context of primary elections, since neither estimates of the voting eligible population (McDonald and Popkin 2001) at the congressional district level, nor estimates of partisan registration rates at the state or congressional district level are available for all states. The latter point is especially valid in open primary states without party registration. While the exact level of turnout is debatable, our methods allow us to collect a consistent variable over our timeframe and every state. Further, since we are most interested in testing *differences* between types and not the overall percentage of turnout, our measure is sufficient.

Factors that Influence Levels of Voter Turnout

Since the goal of this chapter it to estimate the effect of several different primary laws on rates of voter turnout, our main independent variables are dichotomous variables that indicate the type of primary being contested by each party within each state. While each state party may enforce unique primary rules that create nuanced differences across parties and states, we classify primary elections into four major categories and create a dichotomous variable for each category. Starting with the classification system laid out by Pettigrew, Owen, and Wanless (2014), we use several sources including the National Conference of State Legislatures, Fair Vote, and Ballotpedia to determine who is eligible to vote in both the Democratic and Republican primaries in each state. Specifically, we classify each primary as either an open primary, a closed primary, a hybrid primary, or a top-two primary.

In order to ensure we are making accurate estimates as to the effects of each type of primary on voter turnout, it is necessary to control for several factors that have been previously found to influence levels of voter turnout. First, we control for several election-specific factors such as whether or not each congressional district has an incumbent seeking reelection. Specifically, since we are analyzing individual primaries, we distinguish between open seats, a Republican incumbent seeking reelection, and a Democratic incumbent seeking reelection. Next, we control for both the total number of candidates running in each primary election as well as the total number of quality candidates seeking each nomination.[7] In order to incorporate the ideological leanings of each congressional district and acknowledge that some districts advantage either Republican or Democratic candidates, we control for the proportion of the two-party vote each party received in the last general election. When we are analyzing Republican primaries, we use the Republican vote share, and when we are analyzing Democratic primaries, we include the Democratic vote share. Finally, we control for the total amount of funds raised between all primary candidates according to the most recent FEC reporting deadline prior to each primary. Taken together, these variables help to control for the competitiveness of a particular district.

In addition to the election-specific control variables, we also control for numerous state-level variables that may influence voter turnout. First, we control for the number of weeks that each primary is held prior to the general election as an acknowledgement that interest in a congressional race may fluctuate throughout the course of an election cycle. Due to the recent debate over voter identification requirements, we use a dichotomous control variable for whether or not a strict voter identification law is in effect in each state during each election cycle. We use Hajnal, Lajevardi, and Nielson (2017) to identify strict voter identification laws. We also control for whether or not a Senate election is taking place during each election cycle because additional elections are likely to increase interest in political campaigns. While the state-level variables just outlined control for state-specific factors that may vary from one election cycle to the next, there are many other potential factors that can influence turnout, such as demographics, education levels, and political culture that change at much slower rates. Since we are largely interested in testing for differences across primary types, we decided to simply add fixed effects for both states and election years rather than create measures for each possible covariate. This way, we control for other factors, but do not estimate separate coefficients. Because our dependent variable, turnout, is a proportion we estimate generalized linear models with a logit link.

Descriptive Analysis

Figure 7.1 displays the total number of contested congressional primaries that occurred from 2000 to 2016, broken down by primary type. We call a primary contested if there is more than

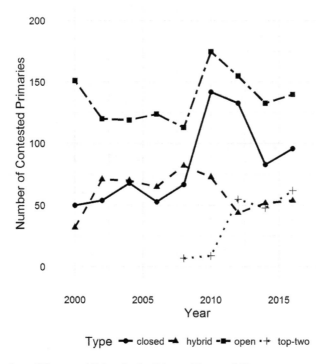

Figure 7.1 Number of Contested Primaries by Primary Type and Year

one candidate in either of the Democratic or Republican contests. Across the entire time period, open primaries were most common with at least 100 open primaries being contested in each election cycle. The second most common type of primary across this time period was closed primaries. From 2000 to 2008, the number of contested closed primaries fluctuated between 50 and 75, but 2010 and 2012 saw a spike in the number of contested closed primaries and since this time, there have been at least 80 contested closed primaries in each election cycle. Out of each type of primary, the frequency of contested hybrid primaries has remained the most stable across this time period with there never being any fewer than 32 contested elections (2000) and never being any more than 82 contested elections (2008). Finally, Washington became the first state to hold top-two primaries at the congressional level in 2008. California also began holding top-two primaries in 2010. Considering only two out of 50 states use top-two primaries, a surprising number of these primaries are contested. Since 2010, there have been at least 48 contested top-two primaries each election cycle and in 2012 and 2016, there were more top-two primaries contested than there were hybrid primaries. Overall, we can expect this trend to continue if more states choose to adopt similar electoral reforms at the congressional level.

While the number of contested primaries has fluctuated since 2000, congressional primary voter turnout has remained mostly stable and relatively consistent across each type of primary. Figure 7.2 displays the mean congressional district-level voter turnout by primary type across the last nine election cycles. At least from this initial descriptive perspective, there seems to be little relationship between the openness of a primary and levels of voter turnout. From 2000 to 2006, voter turnout hovered between 16 percent and 20 percent, regardless of primary type. Since 2008, there has been greater variation in primary voter turnout with a slight tendency for higher levels of participation in open primaries compared to hybrid or closed primaries, particularly in

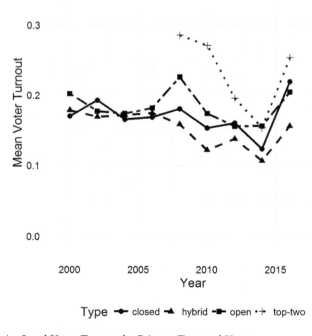

Figure 7.2 District-Level Voter Turnout by Primary Type and Year

2008 and 2014. Additionally, since their inception, top-two primaries experienced higher levels of primary voter turnout than traditionally expected. In three of the last five election cycles, mean voter turnout in top-two primaries has been greater than 25 percent. Moreover, mean voter turnout in top-two primaries has been never been lower than the average turnout rates in the other three types of primaries. However, in 2014 turnout hovered around 15.5 percent in both top-two and open primaries.

Systematic Results

On the whole, while descriptive results are informative and useful in examining overarching trends, in order to truly analyze the relationship between primary laws and voter turnout, more systematic analysis is necessary. Table 7.1 displays the results of three generalized linear models estimating the effect of each of our independent and control variables on voter turnout across three different scenarios. The first model estimates the effect of each state-level variable on district-level, both Republican and Democratic, and voter turnout in states where Republicans and Democrats follow the same primary guidelines. The other two models incorporate all of our campaign- or election-specific variables in order to analyze their effect on voter turnout at the individual partisan primary level. Specifically, model 2 analyzes voter turnout in Republican primaries and model 3 analyzes voter turnout in Democratic primaries. In all cases, open primaries are the excluded reference category so the primary type variables should be interpreted compared to open races. Since top-two primaries contain candidates from both parties, we exclude these races from the partisan models.

District-Level Voter Turnout

At the congressional district level, it is important to note that some of the 2,070 total observations are based upon one contested primary, meaning only one of the two primaries was contested in a given year, while the other observations are based upon two contested primaries. In order to control for this, we include a binary variable to indicate when an observation was based on two contested elections. Therefore, it is not surprising that there is a significant positive relationship between two contested primaries and district-level voter turnout. The other three state-level control variables – weeks until the general election, the presence of a strict voter identification law, and Senate election – all also have a positive and statistically significant relationship on district-level voter turnout. Theoretically, this means that district-level voter turnout increases as the amount of time between the primary election and general election increases. Similarly, and somewhat surprisingly, states that enforce strict voter identification laws appear to have higher levels of district-level voter turnout than states that do not enforce such laws.[8] Finally, as expected, district-level voter turnout increases when a Senate primary election takes place at the same time as the House primaries.

Ultimately, the district-level voter turnout model only provides limited support for our expectations. While we find that there is a statistically significant negative relationship between district-level voter turnout and hybrid primaries in comparison to open primaries, there is no significant differences in voter turnout between open, closed, and top-two primaries. Although it may seem odd that voter turnout decreases when going from an open primary to a hybrid primary, but not when going from an open primary to a closed, one potential explanation is that perhaps hybrid primaries create confusion as to which voters are eligible to participate. While closed primaries are ultimately more restrictive in terms of voter participation, they at least provide a clear guideline in that only registered partisans are allowed to vote if they choose to do so.

Table 7.1 GLM Estimating Voter Turnout in Primary Elections

Variables	District-Level Primaries	Republican Primaries	Democratic Primaries
Closed	−0.0511	−0.2153 *	−0.1926 *
	(0.0824)	(0.0787)	(0.0851)
Hybrid	−0.3008 *	−0.2998 *	−0.4550 *
	(0.0770)	(0.0752)	0.0786
Top-Two	0.0107		
	(0.0784)		
Democratic Incumbent		−0.3794 *	
		(0.0392)	
Republican Incumbent			−0.4024 *
			(0.0487)
Open Seat		−0.1445 *	−0.2294 *
		(0.0380)	(0.0512)
Number of Quality Candidates		0.1238 *	0.0933 *
		(0.0174)	(0.0201)
Number of Candidates		0.0161	0.0363 *
		(0.0084)	(0.0116)
Party's Previous Vote Share		0.7520 *	0.4072 *
		(0.0718)	(0.0822)
Fundraising ($10,000s)		0.0004 *	0.0006 *
		(0.0001)	(0.0002)
Weeks Till General Election	0.0104 *	0.0127 *	0.0073 *
	(0.0028)	(0.0031)	(0.0029)
Strict Voter ID Law	0.1232 *	0.0995 *	0.0166
	(0.0504)	(0.0456)	(0.0640)
Senate Election	0.1183 *	0.0430 *	0.0999 *
	(0.0257)	(0.0253)	(0.0323)
Both Contested	0.7278 *		
	(0.0254)		
(Constant)	−2.0948 *	−2.8591 *	−2.4249 *
	(0.1280)	(0.1329)	(0.1874)
Log-Likelihood	−272.9	−121.8	−112.2
AIC	669.8	375.6	354.3
BIC	1019.1	719.3	682.5
N	2,070	1,350	1,151

Robust Standard Errors in Parenthesis *p <0.05

Note: The effect of each predictor on voter turnout is displayed. The reference category for the primary variables is an open primary, and for the models estimating voter turnout by party, the reference category for the incumbency status of each race is an incumbent from the party being analyzed. Though they are not shown, each model is estimated with both state and year fixed effects.

In this case, maybe the lower rates of district-level voter turnout in hybrid primaries compared to open primaries have less to do with openness and more to do with confusion.

Since the magnitudes of individual coefficients are difficult to interpret when dealing with generalized linear models, we also compute the predicted district-level voter turnout for each individual state based upon the 2016 election cycle. Figure 7.3 displays these predictions along with their corresponding 95 percent confidence interval. Not surprisingly, based on the results in Table 7.1, there is not a consistent trend in terms of which states have higher levels of turnout

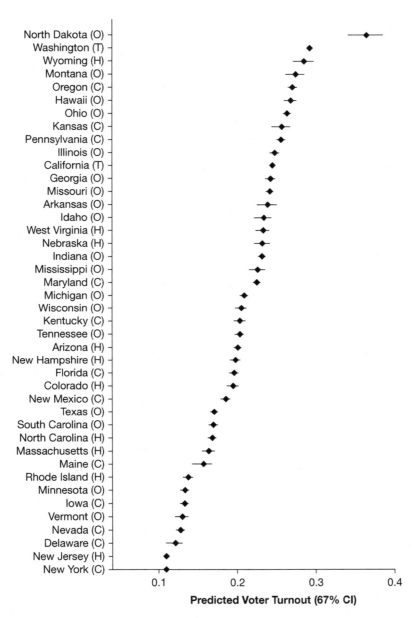

Figure 7.3 Predicted District-Level Voter Turnout by State

Note: Displayed is the predicted district-level voter turnout along with its 67 percent confidence interval for each state in which Democrats and Republican hold the same style of primary. Each predictor variable is set to match the 2016 political climate in each state. O stands for open primary, T stands for top-two primary, C stands for closed primary, and H stands for hybrid primary.

compared to their primary type. In fact, the three states with the highest predicted district-level turnout each have a different primary type. North Dakota, an open primary state in 2016, has the highest predicted turnout by quite a bit. This is probably due to the fact that it is the only state that does not require voter registration. Second on the list is Washington, which, as previously mentioned, conducted top-two primaries in 2016, and third is Wyoming, which held hybrid primaries. There are also several states near the top of the list who held closed primaries, including Oregon, Kansas, and Pennsylvania. One potential explanation for this trend is that beyond primary type, these states may have a political culture which places greater emphasis on political participation. While individual state features such as political culture are controlled for with state fixed effects, these controls do not necessarily explain the impact that these factors may have on voter turnout during primary elections. That being said, there does not appear to be a geographic trend in levels of voter turnout.

On the whole, our analysis of district-level voter turnout aligns with the descriptive results we presented earlier as well as past research. Boatright (2014) finds turnout for congressional primaries hovers around 25–35 percent and Figure 7.3 reveals that 21 states are projected to have district-level voter turnout greater than 20 percent. Ultimately, the key limitation of our analysis thus far is that we have not yet considered the influence of campaign and election-specific factors on voter turnout. This is what we turn to next by analyzing voter turnout at the partisan primary level.

Partisan Primary-Level Turnout

The second and third models from Table 7.1 display the results of our analysis of Republican and Democratic primaries. The dependent variable here measures the total votes cast in each primary, divided by the voting age population in the district. This means we are underreporting turnout, albeit in a consistent fashion across types. As discussed earlier, this allows us to test our hypotheses regarding differences in turnout levels, but will not always accurately reflect turnout rates.

Both models highlight the importance of campaigns when examining voter turnout. For both parties, as the number of quality candidates, the party's previous vote share, and the total amount of fundraising throughout the primary increase, so does voter turnout. Similarly, partisan primary level voter turnout appears to be much higher when a party's incumbent is seeking reelection. This is probably due to incumbents' increased name recognition, as well as to the sorts of campaign tactics that are used in races where the incumbent is facing a challenger. In addition to the number of quality candidates, there is a statistically significant positive relationship between the total number of candidates running for office and voter turnout in Democratic primaries.

In terms of state-level effects on partisan primary level turnout, the results are similar to those for the district-level turnout. Senate elections increase turnout, as does an increase in the number of weeks between the primary election and the general election. Here, the presence of strict voter identification laws appears to increase turnout in only Republican primaries.

While there appeared to be little relationship between primary laws and voter turnout at the congressional district level, primary laws seem to have quite a bit of impact on voter turnout at the partisan primary level. Moreover, the relationship between turnout and primary format largely fall in line with our expectation that as primary laws become more open, political participation increases. Changing from an open Republican primary to either a closed or hybrid Republican primary decreases voter turnout. That being said, there is no difference in Republican primary voter turnout when comparing hybrid primaries to closed primaries. In Democratic primaries, voter turnout decreases when switching from an open primary to either a hybrid or a closed primary and also when switching from a closed primary to a hybrid primary. As was the case when examining district-level turnout, hybrid primaries seem to result in the lowest levels of voter turnout, especially for Democrats.

The magnitudes of these differences can be seen graphically in Figure 7.4, which displays predicted voter turnout for each type of primary by political party for the 2016 election cycle.

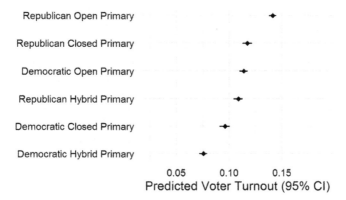

Figure 7.4 Predicted Primary-Level Voter Turnout

Note: Displayed is the predicted voter turnout and corresponding 95 percent confidence interval by political party and primary type. Each of the district and state-level variables is set to either the median or mode for each political party. The state fixed effect is set to Michigan because Michigan was found to have the median voter turnout in Figure 7.3 and the year fixed effect is set to 2016.

While voter turnout in 2016 appears to be higher in Republican primaries than in Democratic primaries, this might be an artifact of creating the figure since each of the state and district-level variables are set to either the median or mode isolated by political party. During the time period under analysis, Republicans were advantaged over Democrats in terms of fundraising and incumbency, which likely explains the higher levels of turnout. However, it is also important to note that had we examined voter turnout during a different election cycle or based on aggregate estimates without year fixed effects, it is likely that voter turnout would have been higher in Democratic primaries or at least equivalent to levels of turnout in Republican primaries.

What is of more theoretical interest is the change in voter turnout in relation to the openness of each state's primary laws. For both the Republicans and the Democrats, voter turnout was highest during open primaries and lowest during hybrid primaries. The predicted difference in turnout between these two types of primaries appears to amount to about 2 to 3 percent. As a result, our expectations hold up in regard to open primaries allowing for the highest level of political participation, although it appears more research needs to be conducted in order to better understand the differences in voter turnout between hybrid and closed primaries. While theory would lead us to believe that turnout would be higher during hybrid primaries than closed primaries, this does not appear to be the case. As stated previously, potential explanations for this odd finding are that hybrid primaries cause confusion as to who is allowed to vote in each party's primary or that the states that use hybrid primaries have political cultures that do not place a higher importance on political participation.

Conclusion

Due to the measurement issues discussed at the beginning of the chapter, calculating voter turnout for congressional primary elections is a difficult task. However, the analysis presented in this chapter shows that even an imperfect measure of voter turnout can help to shed new light on the forces that drive political participation during congressional primaries. Overall, we find that in the context of congressional primaries, campaigns matter to a great extent in determining how many people vote. This is, of course, consistent with previous research. Additionally, several state-specific factors, such as the Senate's electoral calendar and the timing of primaries more generally, can affect levels of voter turnout. During both Democratic and Republican primaries, voter turnout was higher in states where there was a Senate election taking place and in states that held their primary elections several weeks or even months before the general election.

Finally, in what is of most interest to this chapter, primary registration laws appear to affect levels of primary voter turnout at the margins. We find that at both the district level and the partisan primary level, voter turnout in open primaries is higher than voter turnout in hybrid primaries. Similarly, at the partisan primary level, we find that voter turnout in closed primaries is lower than voter turnout in open primaries. On the whole we find some degree of support for the theory that primary voter turnout increases as the primary process becomes more open. Ultimately, while scholars, activists, and practitioners all have found that there is no "silver bullet" to drastically increase levels of political participation in the United States, implementing more open primaries, or potentially even top-two primaries, may be a way to modestly increase voter turnout during congressional primary elections.

Notes

1 "State says primary turnout was around 20 percent in Georgia," 27 May 2016, retrieved from http://www.wctv.tv/content/news/State-says-primary-turnout-was-around-20-percent-in-Georgia-381121711.htm

2 Some states, such as Utah, largely rely on caucuses to pick party candidates. Owing to the uniqueness of these systems, we do not include them in our analysis here.

3 Sometimes hybrid primaries are broken down further into sub-classifications, mainly based on whether or not unaffiliated voters need to register with a party to vote (see "State Primary Election Types," 2016, retrieved from www.nscl.org/research/elections-and-campaigns/primary-types.aspx). Since these differences are subtle, and sometimes difficult to tease out, we chose to stick with the broader hybrid primary category.

4 We only really tackle major party primaries here. In some states such as New York, several minor parties do appear on the General Election ballot.

5 Based on this definition, primaries in which a single candidate sought the nomination were eliminated from our analysis, as were any nomination contests that took the form of a party convention. Finally, we excluded all observations from Louisiana except for primaries taking place in 2008 and 2010 when they held closed partisan primaries.

6 Since the American Community Survey only began in 2005, the voter age population at the congressional district level was not available for the years 2002 and 2004. However, the Census Bureau did provide annual state population estimates for these years. Beginning with these estimates, we were able to approximate the district-level voting age population for 2002 and 2004. We first divided the state population estimates by the number of congressional districts in each state and then multiplied the estimated district populations by the percentage of voters who were over the age of 18 in 2000 and 2005.

7 We use Jacobson's (2013) dichotomous measure of whether or not a candidate has prior political experience to measure candidate quality.

8 Since our voter ID measure is just acting as a control variable, we offer a note of caution in drawing inferences from our analysis in terms of this law influencing turnout. If we wanted to determine the effect of voter ID laws on turnout we would likely use a different research design.

References

Abramson, Paul R., and John H. Aldrich. 1982. "The Decline of Electoral Participation in America." *American Political Science Review* 76(3): 502–521.

Aldrich, John H. 1993. "Rational Choice and Turnout." *American Journal of Political Science* 37(1): 246–278.

Alvarez, R. Michael, Delia Bailey, and Jonathan N. Katz. 2008. "The Effect of Voter Identification Laws on Turnout." *Social Science* Working Paper 1267R, California Institute of Technology.

Boatright, Robert G. 2014. *Congressional Primary Elections*. New York: Routledge.

Burden, Barry C., and Marni Ezra. 1999. "Calculating Voter Turnout in US House Primary Elections." *Electoral Studies* 18(1): 89–99.

Burden, Barry C., David T. Canon, Kenneth R. Mayer, and Donald P. Moynihan. 2014. "Election Laws, Mobilization, and Turnout: The Unanticipated Consequences of Election Reform." *American Journal of Political Science* 58(1): 95–109.

Burnham, Walter Dean. 1965. "The Changing Shape of the American Political Universe." *American Political Science Review* 59(1): 7–28.

Burnham, Walter Dean. 1987. "The Turnout Problem." In *Elections American Style*, ed. A James Reichley. Washington: Brookings, pp. 109–110.

Caldeira, Gregory A., and Samuel C. Patterson. 1982. "Contextual Influences on Participation in US State Legislative Elections." *Legislative Studies Quarterly* 7(3): 359–381.

Caldeira, Gregory A., Samuel C. Patterson, and Gregory A. Markus. 1985. "The Mobilization of Voters in Congressional Elections." *The Journal of Politics* 47(2): 490–509.

Cox, Gary W., and Michael C. Munger. 1989. "Closeness, Expenditures, and Turnout in the 1982 US House elections." *American Political Science Review* 83(1): 217–231.

Fenster, Mark J. 1994. "The Impact of Allowing Day of Registration Voting on Turnout in US Elections from 1960 to 1992: A Research Note." *American Politics Quarterly* 22(1): 74–87.

Gerber, Elisabeth R., and Rebecca B. Morton. 1998. "Primary Election Systems and Representation." *Journal of Law, Economics, & Organization* 14(2): 304–324.

Geys, Benny. 2006. "Explaining Voter Turnout: A Review of Aggregate-Level Research." *Electoral Studies* 25(4): 637–663.

Green, Donald P., and Alan S. Gerber. 2015. *Get Out the Vote: How to Increase Voter Turnout*. Washington, DC: Brookings Institution Press.

Grimmer, Justin, E. Hersh, M. Meredith, J. Mummolo, C. Nall. 2017. Comment on "Voter Identification Laws and the Suppression of Minority Votes." Working paper produced for Stanford University.

Hajnal, Zoltan, Nazita Lajevardi, and Lindsay Nielson. 2017. "Voter Identification Laws and the Suppression of Minority Votes." *The Journal of Politics* 79(2): 363–379.

Hamilton, Matthew. 2016. "Congressional Primary Turnout was Average – and Underwhelming." *Albany Times Union*. June 29. http://blog.timesunion.com/capitol/archives/264809/congressional-primary-turnout-was-average-and-underwhelming/ [Last accessed 4/1/2016]

Hershey, Marjorie Randon. 2009. "What We Know About Voter-ID Laws, Registration, and Turnout." *Political Science & Politics* 42(1): 87–91.

Highton, Benjamin. 2004. "Voter Registration and Turnout in the United States." *Perspectives on Politics* 2(3): 507–515.

Jacobson, Gary. 2013. *The Politics of Congressional Elections*. 8th ed. New York: Pearson.

Jewitt, Caitlin E. 2014. "Packed Primaries and Empty Caucuses: Voter Turnout in Presidential Nominations." *Public Choice* 160(3–4): 295–312.

Kanthak, Kristin, and Rebecca Morton. 2001. "The Effects of Electoral Rules on Congressional Primaries." In *Congressional Primaries and the Politics of Representation*, ed. Peter Galderisi, Marni Ezra, Michael Lyons. Lanham, MD: Rowman and Littlefield, pp. 116–131.

Kaufmann, Karen M., James G. Gimpel, and Adam H. Hoffman. 2003. "A Promise Fulfilled? Open Primaries and Representation." *Journal of Politics* 65(2): 457–476.

Kenney, Patrick J. 1983. "Explaining Turnout in Gubernatorial Primaries." *American Politics Quarterly* 11(3): 315–326.

Kenney, Patrick J. 1986. "Explaining Primary Turnout: The Senatorial Case." *Legislative Studies Quarterly* 11(1): 65–73.

Kenney, Patrick J., and Tom W. Rice. 1985. "Voter Turnout in Presidential Primaries: A Cross-Sectional Examination." *Political Behavior* 7(1): 101–112.

Knack, Stephen. 1995. "Does 'Motor Voter' Work? Evidence from State-Level Data." *The Journal of Politics* 57(3): 796–811.

Leighley, Jan E., and Jonathan Nagler. 1992a. "Individual and Systemic Influences on Turnout: Who Votes? 1984." *The Journal of Politics* 54(3): 718–740.

Leighley, Jan E., and Jonathan Nagler. 1992b. "Socioeconomic Class Bias in Turnout, 1964–1988: The Voters Remain the Same." *American Political Science Review* 86(3): 725–736.

McDonald, Michael P., and Samuel L. Popkin. 2001. "The Myth of the Vanishing Voter." *American Political Science Review* 95(4): 963–974.

Moran, Jack, and Mark Fenster. 1982. "Voter Turnout In Presidential Primaries: A Diachronic Analysis." *American Politics Quarterly* 10(4): 453–447.

Mycoff Jason D., Michael W. Wagner, and David C. Wilson. 2007. "The Effect of Voter Identification Laws on Aggregate and Individual Level Turnout." Presented at American Political Science Association Annual Meeting, Chicago.

Norrander, Barbara. 1991. "Explaining Individual Participation in Presidential Primaries." *Western Political Quarterly* 44(3): 640–655.

Norrander, Barbara, and Jay Wendland. 2016. "Open Versus Closed Primaries and the Ideological Composition of Presidential Primary Electorates." *Electoral Studies* 42 (1): 229–236.

Patterson, Samuel C., and Gregory A. Caldeira. 1983. "Getting out the Vote: Participation in Gubernatorial Elections." *American Political Science Review* 77(3): 675–689.

Pettigrew, Stephen, Karen Owen, and Emily O. Wanless. 2014. "U.S. House Primary Election Results (1956–2010)." doi: 10.7910/DVN/26448, Harvard Dataverse, V4, UNF: 6: CO5mjgzxwopCZB2/gc AepQ==.

Riker, William H., and Peter C. Ordeshook. 1968. "A Theory of the Calculus of Voting." *American Political Science Review* 62(1): 25–42.

Rosenstone, Steven, and John M. Hansen. 1993. *Mobilization, Participation and Democracy in America*. New York: Macmillan Publishing.

Rosenstone, Steven J., and Raymond E. Wolfinger. 1978. "The Effect of Registration Laws on Voter Turnout." *American Political Science Review* 72(1): 22–45.

Shields, Todd G., and Robert K. Goidel. 1997. "Participation Rates, Socioeconomic Class Biases, and Congressional Elections: A Cross Validation." *American Journal of Political Science* 41(2): 683–691.

Southwell, Priscilla L. 1991. "Open Versus Closed Primaries: The Effect on Strategic Voting and Candidate Fortunes." *Social Science Quarterly* 72(4): 789–796.

Southwell, Priscilla L., and Justin I. Burchett. 2000. "The Effect of All-Mail Elections on Voter Turnout." *American Politics Quarterly* 28(1): 72–79.

Teixeira, Ruy A. 1987. *Why Americans Don't Vote: Turnout Decline in the United States, 1960–1984*. Westport, CT: Greenwood Publishing Group.

Verba, Sidney, and Norman H. Nie. 1987. *Participation in America: Political Democracy and Social Equality*. Chicago: University of Chicago Press.

Wolfinger, Raymond E., and Steven J. Rosenstone. 1980. *Who Votes?* New Haven, CT: Yale University Press.

8

STRATEGIC CANDIDATE ENTRY

Primary Type and Candidate Divergence

Kristin Kanthak and Eric Loepp

A central debate in our understanding of primaries is simple: does primary type matter? Most of the discussion around this debate has centered on the question of whether or not different primary types lead to different kinds of candidates, with some evidence that there is a correlation between primary type and the kinds of representatives that emerge (Gerber and Morton 1998; Kanthak and Morton 2001) but a good deal more suggesting that primary type matters little in the subsequent behavior of legislators (Bullock and Clinton 2011; Hirano, Snyder, Ansolabere and Hansen 2010; McCarty, Poole and Rosenthal 2006; McGhee 2010; McGhee, Masket, Shor, Rogers and McCarty 2014; Pearson and Lawless 2008; Rogowski and Langella 2015).[1] Yet this creates something of a puzzle, because the evidence is clear that primary voters are more extreme than general election voters (Brady, Han, and Pope 2007; Carey and Polga-Hecimovich 2006; Jacobson 2012; Kaufmann, Gimpel and Hoffman 2003; Sinclair 2006).[2] Why don't more ideologically extreme voters nominate similarly extreme candidates in a manner consistent with the Downsian (Downs 1957) spatial logic that undergirds much of the literature on legislative behavior? We attempt to answer that question by taking a step back in the electoral process to before the election, at the stage of candidate emergence. Voters obviously can select only from those candidates who have chosen to run. In order, for example, for open primaries to result in more moderate legislators, open primaries must attract more moderate candidates. Otherwise, these relatively more moderate voters have no relatively more moderate candidate to select. In the current project, then, we explore the question of how ambitious candidates respond to primary type to determine whether or not those candidate emergence patterns are compatible with the patterns we would need to see for primary type to have an effect on candidate selection and subsequent legislative behavior.

The question of whether or not primary type has an effect on candidate emergence is important. This is a particularly pressing issue today, as recent work finds that increasingly polarized legislatures are discouraging ideological moderates from running for office (Thomsen 2014). This is especially true when the state party is more proximate to the legislator than is the congressional party (Aldrich and Thomsen 2016). Furthermore, the types of candidates that emerge (either in the primary or the general election) can affect who a legislator chooses to work with in the legislature (Alvarez and Sinclair 2012; Olivella, Kanthak and Crisp 2017) and primary type can have an effect on a legislator's level of particularism once elected to office (Bagashka and Clark 2016). But at the same time, we also know that potential candidates respond to the world around them when they are making decisions about running (Fox and Lawless 2011; Maisel and Stone 1997; Rohde 1979), taking into account realities of the primary electoral environment (Hassell 2016). Most important, we know that state-level institutions can affect the decision calculus of potential candidates when they decide whether or not to enter a particular race (Maestas, Fultton, Maisel and Stone 2006). As an electoral institution, then, primary type may affect which types of candidates emerge.

According to the theory laid out by Gerber and Morton (1998), more open primaries translate to more moderate primary electorates, as those voters who are more moderate and less partisan can participate. For example, a moderate Republican or independent may choose to vote in the Democratic primary if she has a preferred candidate running in that primary. Because closed primaries allow only party regulars to vote, the theory explains, resultant general election candidates will reflect the more partisan nature of these primary electorates. And indeed, these different electorates will select different candidates: Changing the primary type, the theory goes, will change the electorate and thereby the types of candidates who end up winning the election and representing the district in the legislature. But because voters can select only the candidates who have chosen to run, the theory can operate as expected only when the ideological composition of candidates running in a primary aligns with the ideological makeup of the voters participating in it. Yet we know little about how *candidates* respond to different primary types. This question of candidate emergence is our focus here. We offer a direct measure of the distance between the two general election candidates to determine whether or not primary type affects polarization within a particular legislature. If closed primaries, for example, yield more polarized candidates, the best way to measure this is to take account directly of the level of polarization between the two candidates, and this is exactly what we do.

We find that candidates do, indeed, respond differentially to different primary types. In open and nonpartisan primaries, candidates tend to be more moderate, meaning that these theoretically more moderate electorates have moderate candidates from which to choose. Despite this, semi-open primaries actually produce more *extreme* candidates, which is the opposite of what we would expect, given our theoretical expectations. Further exploration reveals that these results are based largely on the strategies of Republican candidates: Democratic candidates do not respond differently to nonpartisan and open primaries, and respond contrary to expectation in semi-open primaries. Despite these statistically significant results, the effects are substantively small, accounting for only very tiny differences in the amount of polarization of the candidates. We argue that the fact that these differences are so tiny explains the effect of primary type on the ideology of the resultant winning candidates: primary type matters in terms of polarization of emerging candidates, but not very much. We outline our theoretical expectations in more detail in the section below.

Theoretical Expectations

In the extant literature, the theory of polarization via primary type is largely a story about voters: more ideological voters produce more ideological general election candidates. But this is possible only if potential candidates are responding appropriately to the expected effects of primary type. Do more ideologically polarized candidates anticipate that they will do well in closed primary elections, and thereby choose to run? Do more moderate candidates know they will have an advantage in open primary systems, and thereby enter the race? Choosing whether or not to run, however, is complicated, and primary type is only one of many considerations. How might that consideration affect the types of candidates that emerge from each type of primary?

In this section, we outline the candidate selection process in more detail, highlighting the effect of strategic candidates' entry decisions on the theory itself.

We can think of the process from primary type to general election winners as divided into three stages. If primary type is to affect general election winners as the theory anticipates, all three stages must align to make that happen. First, voters must not only be different based on primary type, but that difference must be large enough to result in a difference in the candidates that result from different types of primaries.[3] Second, and largely ignored in the literature,[4] different primary types must attract different types of candidates. More open primaries should attract more moderate candidates and more closed primaries must attract more polarized candidates. Without a sufficient supply of (non)polarized candidates, (non)polarized voters cannot vote for them, even if they prefer to do so. And third, primary outcomes must have a strong effect on general election outcomes. Hall (2015), for instance, demonstrates that more extreme primary winners are in fact less likely to win general elections. If more closed primaries tend to result in more extreme candidates for one party than they do for another, for example, these extreme candidates would lose general elections and we would see little effect of primary voting as we would expect from the theory. In other words, being able to detect an effect of primary type on legislator ideology requires a number of specific criteria to be met. This means that slight differences caused by primary type may easily be washed out by other factors, making evidence of them difficult to find. Yet even these slight, easily hidden differences might matter, however. If the effect of a different pool of primary voters is being washed out by decisions potential candidates are making, we may not be able to discern the actual effect of primary type, one that more strategic candidates might be able to exploit.

Because of this, understanding how primary type affects candidate emergence – and candidate polarization – can tell us much about how policy is made even if the effect is not so dramatic as changing the actual ideology of the winning candidates. If these candidates emerge but do not win, they may determine legislative behavior in ways that may be difficult to assess. We know, for example, that the identity of the challenger can often affect winners' subsequent legislative behavior as winners seek to emulate those who have recently challenged them (Sulkin 2005) and can affect how legislators think about how they will win the next election (Olivella, Kanthak and Crisp 2017).

Note that we do not mean to imply that potential candidates think strategically about which states to run in based on the state's primary type. Although some candidates surely think about relocating to run for office,[5] we expect that this is the exception rather than the rule. We intend to argue, rather, that primary type *plays a role* in the decision calculus that faces potential candidates as they choose whether or not to run. If the theory operates as expected, for example, we might expect moderate candidates to be more willing to run when open primary rules mean the candidate can appeal to non-party regulars. In this sense, the primary type renders the proposition of running more attractive to particular types of candidates. This makes running somewhat more likely to yield greater expected utility than whichever other options that potential candidate can pursue if she decides to forego running. In turn, this effect on the decision calculus makes those candidates the primary rules favor somewhat more likely to run. When we take all these individual personal decisions together, then, we can observe an effect of the primary type on the types of candidates who choose to run. And indeed, the question of who runs is intricately linked to questions of policy throughout the legislative process. Primary voters can select only from among those candidates who have chosen to run, and general election voters can select only from among those candidates who have both chosen to run and have won their primaries. If voting is the key to representation, then, voting rules are the key to the nature of that representation. In the next section, we turn to the question of how to assess the types of candidates that emerge from different primary types.

The Data

Scholars have made considerable progress in quantifying the ideologies of elected politicians in recent decades. The most well-known scaling method – the Poole and Rosenthal (1985) NOMINATE system – estimates the ideal points of legislators from roll-call voting records. While the method is well accepted, it is unsuitable for our purposes because our principle theoretical interest lies in analyzing *candidates* rather than elected officials. Ideological mapping systems that rely on voting records cannot capture the ideology of individuals who campaign for office but do not win. Yet non-winning candidates must make the same strategic decisions about when and where to run. Indeed, to the extent that primary systems affect candidates' calculations about whether or not to run, they should affect incumbents and challengers in similar ways, since both groups of politicians target the same (potential) voters. Thus we need a standardized measure of ideology that includes both winners and losers.

Until recently, such measures were not available. However, Bonica (2014) presents an alternative method to NOMINATE that chronicles the ideological space not only of political candidates at various levels of government, but of interest groups and individual donors. The method relies on campaign contributions, which, because they are extensively documented and publicly available, serve as "vast repositories of observational data on revealed preferences" (Bonica 2014, 367). Common-space campaign finance scores (or CFscores) assume that donors will make contributions to candidates that are ideologically proximate to themselves (i.e., candidates that share donors' political views) but will be less likely to give to candidates who are more ideologically distant.[6] Bonica uses these contribution records to estimate the ideological preferences of over 50,000 state and federal candidates during the period 1979–2012. These map extremely well onto the same liberal-conservative space as other methods used to estimate politicians' preferences (e.g., DW-NOMINATE scores). Like NOMINATE, negative CFscores reflect a more liberal ideology and positive values indicate a more conservative ideology.

In order to conduct our analysis, we first integrate into the Bonica dataset indicators for the five basic types of primary systems in each state in each year; they represent our key independent variables. *Closed* primary systems are the most restrictive for voters – only registered partisans within a party can participate in the party's primary. No crossover voting is allowed, nor are independent voters allowed to participate. *Semi-closed* systems are somewhat less restrictive; they allow independent voters to participate but not members of other political parties. *Semi-open* systems allow voters to vote in whatever primary they wish but they must do so publicly. Pure *open* systems allow registered voters to participate privately in any primary they wish. In *nonpartisan* primaries all voters can vote for all candidates and the top two candidates in the primary election – regardless of partisan status – advance to a run-off general election. Table 8.1 replicates a table summarizing these differences from McGhee et al. (2014).

Our analysis addresses two related but distinct questions. First, is candidate polarization (that is, the ideological distance between candidates) more pronounced in more closed primary

Table 8.1 Primary Types

	Crossover Allowed?	Independents Only?	Public Decision?	Registration?	Choose Parties?
Pure Closed	No	N/A	N/A	N/A	N/A
Semi-closed	Yes	Yes	Yes	Sometimes	Yes
Semi-open	Yes	No	Yes	Sometimes	Yes
Pure Open	Yes	No	No	No	Yes
Nonpartisan	Yes	No	No	No	No

systems? Second, do different primary systems attract ideologically distinct candidates in general? Data for the latter question are straightforward – we simply use the estimated CFscore in the Bonica dataset as our dependent variable. However, the first question requires some manipulation of the data. Since here we are concerned with general elections, we eliminate all candidates in the dataset who did not succeed in their primary election bids – that is, candidates that were active in the primaries but were not active in the general election. We also eliminated all third-party general election candidates. We thus ensured that for every congressional race featuring multiple candidates there were exactly two candidates in the general election.[7] In some nonpartisan elections these two candidates were members of the same party, but in nearly all instances races featured one Republican and one Democrat. For example, the 2010 House race for the Alaska at-large congressional seat includes six candidates in the Bonica dataset. Only the two that ran in the general election – incumbent Don Young (R) and challenger Harry Crawford (D) were retained for this initial analysis. To create our dependent variable, we calculated the absolute value of the difference in CFscore[8] between the two principal general election candidates within congressional districts in particular states in each year of the analysis. Following the example above, in 2010 the polarization factor in the Alaska at-large race was 1.359, or the difference between Young's CFscore of 0.361 and Crawford's CFscore of −0.998. Note that races featuring an unchallenged incumbent are not included in our first analysis, as no measure of candidate polarization is possible without two candidates. Table 8.2 presents summary information on our polarization measure more generally.

The ideological distance (polarization) between general election candidates, our dependent variable, is regressed on the primary typology discussed above, with closed primaries serving as the reference (omitted) category. Primary type coefficients, then, represent differences in polarization relative to closed primaries, and we therefore expect all primary indicators to be negative. In keeping with previous work on the subject (McGhee 2010; Rogowski and Langella 2015), we also include fixed effects for states and election cycles to capture variance between states and over time. Since primary types are established at the state-level, we cluster errors on states. Finally, we include as a control variable a measure of political preferences at the Congressional district-level, measured as the percentage of the two-party vote share won by the Democratic presidential nominee in the most recent presidential election. We collect data on all primary elections from 2000 to 2010.

In this way, we have a direct measure of polarization of the general election candidates for each district in our dataset. This provides a better measure of the effect of primaries for a number of reasons. First, we need not rely solely on winners. Rather, we can assess directly the effect of the primary itself by directly comparing both parties' candidates. If closed primaries cause the selection of more extreme candidates, but differentially for both parties, it may be the case that the general election selects the more moderate candidate, thus mitigating the effect of primary type. Second, we have a measure of polarization that is specific to each district. If primary type is affecting polarization, it will do so vis-à-vis the median voter of that particular district, not

Table 8.2 Summary Statistics of Polarization Data

	CFscore (Republicans)	CFscore (Democrats)	CFscore (Overall)	Polarization Measure
Lowest Value	−2.83	−4.82	−4.82	0.02
Highest Value	4.36	1.28	4.36	5.79
Mean Value	0.93	−0.89	0.00093	1.88
Standard Deviation	0.39	0.47	1.01	−0.58

vis-à-vis the legislature writ large. In other words, a primary may select candidates that are polarized *for that district*, but that effect would not be clear if the district itself is polarized with respect to the rest of the legislature. Third, we have a measure of ideological polarization that is based not on partisan activities (like floor voting) within the legislature, but rather on outside forces, thus mitigating the effect of partisan agenda control on polarization.

In the next section, we draw on these data to assess the types of candidates who run in each type of primary.

Results

We call on the data described in the previous section to assess the types of candidates who enter different types of primary elections. In order, as the theory states, for open primary voters to select more moderate candidates, more moderate candidates must run when primaries are more open. In that sense, we would expect to see less polarization as primary type becomes more open.

To assess the effect of primary type on district-level candidate polarization, we regress the polarization of the general election candidates within a district (i.e. the difference between the Democratic candidate's CFscore and the Republican candidate's CFscore in each district). The regressions include state-level fixed effects and election cycle dummies, the coefficients of which we omit here for space. We omit from the model "closed primaries," which therefore serve as the reference category. Thus all coefficients indicate the marginal difference in candidate polarization relative to closed primary elections. Since we expect more open primaries to generate more moderate candidates, we anticipate negative coefficients on all primary types in the model. We present these results in Table 8.3.

As is clear from these results, primary type *does* have an effect on the kinds of candidates that emerge from primary elections. More specifically, candidates that emerge from nonpartisan and open primaries are significantly *less* polarized than candidates that come from closed primary elections. Notably, and contrary to the expectation of the theory, semi-open primaries have significantly *more* polarized general election candidates than do closed primaries. This is an unexpected outlier result similar to one found in previous work on the subject (Kanthak and Morton 2001). Remember that semi-open primaries allow voters unaffiliated with the party

Table 8.3 Ideological Difference Between General Election Candidates

	Polarization
Semi-closed	−0.2878 (−1.46)
Semi-open	0.563* (2.52)
Open	−0.493* (−2.20)
Nonpartisan	−0.483* (−2.30)
District Ideology	−0.617*** (−5.27)
Dummies omitted for space	**
Constant	1.703*** (7.30)
Observations	1864

Note: *t* statistics in parentheses; *p < 0.05, **p < 0.01, ***p < 0.001.

to participate, but they must do so publicly. Potentially, this structure of primary may attract candidates who are attempting to re-make the party by making it more extreme. Perhaps they enter because they are expecting to attract new voters to the party who will publicly declare their allegiance and thereby change the party's ideal point, thus explaining why ideologically extreme candidates appear to be more attracted to semi-open contests. This is a question for potential future research.

If primaries are producing significantly different levels of polarization, that means that parties must be producing different types of candidates under different primary types. Notably, however, that effect need not be symmetric. The decisions of one party are enough to drive the polarization effect. This is because if one party ignores primary type, but the other is sensitive to it, the sensitive party's movements can change polarization by themselves.

For this reason, we now consider the effects of primary type on the ideology of primary candidates. To do this, we regress CFscores directly on primary types (with the same control variables included) to assess the impact of primary type on individual candidate ideology across parties. These results are presented in Table 8.4.

These analyses, then, indicate that primary type has a statistically significant effect on both the types of candidates who *win* primaries and the types of candidates who *enter* primaries. Both open and nonpartisan primaries produce less polarized candidates than do closed primaries, as one would expect given the theory. Furthermore, the effect is driven almost entirely by the Republican Party, a result that is paralleled in Nielson and Visalvanich (2017). Republicans tend to run significantly more moderate candidates in these types of primaries than they do in closed primaries. Democrats tend to show a similar pattern, although it does not even approach statistical significance.

Notably, however, semi-open primaries produce candidates that are *more* polarized than in closed primaries. This is counter to expectation, and is also based on differences in both parties. Specifically, Democrats produce more liberal candidates under semi-open primaries than they do under closed primaries, whereas Republicans produce significantly more conservative candidates under the same circumstances. Indeed, semi-open primaries represent the only primary type in which Democrats produce candidates that are ideologically different from those they produce in closed primary elections.

Table 8.4 Effects of Primary Type on Candidate Ideology

	Democrats	*Republicans*
Semi-closed	−0.0169 (−0.14)	−0.267* (−2.50)
Semi-open	−0.478** (−3.25)	0.230* (1.99)
Nonpartisan	0.0354 (0.26)	−0.330** (−2.66)
Open	0.154 (0.95)	−0.266* (−1.98)
District Ideology	1.014*** (15.20)	0.561*** (7.37)
Dummies omitted for space	**	**
Constant	−0.816*** (−5.43)	0.708*** (5.75)
Observations	2280	2175
R2	0.292	0.276

Note: *t* statistics in parentheses; *p < 0.05, **p < 0.01, ***p < 0.001.

Exactly how much polarization is correlated with primary type? Figure 8.1 attempts to shed light on that question. In order to assess the substantive effects we have uncovered, we need to dig a bit deeper into the nature of our district-level candidate polarization measure. The polarization variable cannot take on values lower than 0 or higher than 8, because the Bonica ideology scores are bounded at -4 and 4. In reality, however, the greatest ideological distance in the data set is 5.8. As is clear from Figure 8.1, the effect of primary type on the amount of polarization in a particular district is rather muted. Indeed, for any particular Congressional district, changing from one primary type to another constitutes a change of, at most, a few tenths of a point on an 8-point scale. These differences, although statistically significant, are not large enough to drive a dramatic effect on partisan polarization, nor would we expect that even knowledgeable primary voters would draw substantially different conclusions about candidates who differ by such small margins. For context, the difference between the extremism we would expect from the least-polarizing system (nonpartisan) to the most polarizing (open) is about the same as the difference in CFscores between Nancy Pelosi and Charles Rangel, both known as relatively liberal legislators, ideologically indistinguishable from one another on most issues.

In other words, slight differences in polarization of candidates are not great enough to create large differences in the level of polarization within general election candidates in a particular district, as measured by CFscores. Although the result is statistically significant in some cases, the substantive effect is washed out by the many, many other factors that go into determining which candidates choose to run in primaries and ultimately end up winning those primaries to go on to compete in the general election.

This result highlights the complexity of the relationship between political institutions and the actors they can affect. Our model indicates that primary type does, in fact, affect the choices candidates make. Candidates seem to consider their own ideology and the primary type they face when they are making the decision of whether or not to run. But this is only one of several considerations candidates must take into account. They are looking for the right time to run, the right personal situation, their own level of political ambition, and more when they are making

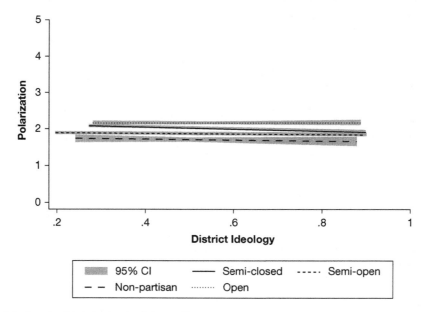

Figure 8.1 Level of Polarization by Primary Type

the complex decision of whether or not to run. Our results indicate that primary type plays a role in that decision calculus, but it is not dramatically central to the decision. Furthermore, without a strong effect on the supply of candidates, primary type has a difficult time explaining the results of those elections. The types of choices voters need to behave in the way the theory expects do not appear to be available to them.

Concluding Thoughts

The question of whether or not primary type affects the kind of representation voters can expect to receive is an important one. Furthermore, the theory explaining how primary type affects election outcomes is attractive, parsimonious, and sound: affecting the pool of eligible voters affects the ideology of that pool, which then affects the kinds of candidates which are chosen. But more often than not, the evidence fails to support that theory. Why?

We argue in the current chapter that the reason this theory achieves support only part of the time is because the theory assumes that voters have the choices available to them in the form of candidates for the primary election. If this is not true, then voters cannot make the kinds of choices the theory relies on them to make. Because of this, the theory does not appear to have its expected effect on legislator ideology, results that are consistent with those of McGhee et al. (2014) and others.

This finding plays up the difficulty in pinpointing the effects of political institutions on the choices political actors make. Do potential candidates consider primary type when deciding whether or not to run? Yes, but not very much. Having this information allows us to ask a more nuanced question about why primary type affects legislator ideology only sometimes, and even then, not very much, because candidates are likely prioritizing other considerations. The reason for this is that elections are complex processes, made up of a series of actors making a series of complex decisions. For institutions to matter, they may need to matter in several key places and for several different actors. Additional work is necessary to tease out more precisely how these institutions interact with actors to shape voters' choice sets and, ultimately, legislative behavior in office. For now, we contribute additional empirical evidence that primary types do not appear to singularly affect the likelihood that different types of candidates choose to run for office. Nor do ideological disparities between general election candidates appear to result from the primary system a state chooses for its nomination contests. While many popular accounts of legislative polarization blame primaries for encouraging the emergence of extreme candidates, the evidence does not bear this out.

Notes

1 But see Norrander and Wendland (2016) and Hill (2015).
2 But they may not have sufficient information to bring their ideological extremity to bear when choosing a candidate (Hirano, Lenz, Pinkovskiy and Snyder 2015).
3 Although this assumption itself may be flawed. See Ahler, Citrin and Lenz (2016).
4 But see Rogowski and Langella (2015) for an exception.
5 Hillary Clinton, for example, reportedly selected New York as her home after she left the White House, based at least partly on the electoral climate there, which she deemed favorable to her efforts.
6 The assumption that donors are more likely to contribute to like-minded politicians is well-supported (see, e.g., Ensley, Tofias and De Marchi 2009; McCarty, Poole and Rosenthal 2006).
7 A handful of miscoded cases resulted in the inclusion of some third-party candidates in the general election. These cases were discarded. In some nonpartisan races, the two general election candidates were members of the same political party.
8 Here, we diverge from Rogowski and Langella (2015), which uses only the raw CFscores.

References

Ahler, Douglas J., Jack Citrin, and Gabriel S. Lenz. 2016. "Do Open Primaries Improve Representation? An Experimental Test of California's 2012 Top-Two Primary." *Legislative Studies Quarterly* 41(2): 237–268.

Aldrich, John A. and, Danielle M. Thomsen. 2016. "Party, Policy, and the Ambition to Run for Higher Office." *Legislative Studies Quarterly* 42(2): 321–343.

Alvarez, R. Michael and Betsy Sinclair. 2012. "Electoral Institutions and Legislative Behavior." *Political Research Quarterly* 65(3): 544–557.

Bagashka, Tanya, and Jennifer H. Clark. 2016. "Electoral Rules and Legislative Particularism: Evidence from U.S. State Legislatures." *The American Political Science Review* 110(3): 441–456.

Bonica, Adam. 2014. "Mapping the Ideological Marketplace." *American Journal of Political Science* 58 (2): 367–386.

Brady, David W., Hahrie Han, and Jeremy C. Pope. 2007. "Primary Elections and Candidate Ideology: Out of Step with the Primary Electorate?" *Legislative Studies Quarterly* 32(1): 79–105.

Bullock, Will, and Joshua D. Clinton. 2011. "More a Molehill than a Mountain: The Effects of the Blanket Primary on Elected Officials Behavior from California." *Journal of Politics* 73 (3): 915–30.

Carey, John M., and John Polga-Hecimovick. 2006. "Primary Elections and Candidate Strength in Latin America." *Journal of Politics* 68(3): 530–543.

Downs, Anthony. 1957. *An Economic Theory of Democracy*. New York: Harper.

Ensley, Michael J., Michael W. Tofias, and Scott De Marchi. 2009. "District Complexity as an Advantage in Congressional Elections." *American Journal of Political Science* 53(4): 990–1005.

Fox, Richard L., and Jennifer L. Lawless. 2011. "Gaining and Losing Interest in Running for Office: The Concept of Dynamic Political Ambition." *The Journal of Politics* 73(2): 443–462.

Gerber, Elisabeth, and Rebecca B. Morton. 1998. "Primary Election Systems and Representation." *Journal of Law, Economics, and Organization* 14(2): 304–324.

Hall, Andrew B. 2015. "What Happens When Extremists Win Primaries?" *American Political Science Review* 109(1): 18–42.

Hassell, Hans J. G. 2016. "Party Control of Party Primaries: Party Influence in Nominations for the US Senate." *The Journal of Politics* 78(1): 75–87.

Hill, Seth J. 2015. "Institution of Nomination and the Policy Ideology of Primary Electorates." *Quarterly Journal of Political Science* 10(4): 461–487.

Hirano, Shigeo, Gabriel S. Lenz, Maksim Pinkovskiy, and James M. Snyder. 2015. "Voter Learning in State Primary Elections." *American Journal of Political Science* 59(1): 91–108.

Hirano, Shigeo, James M. Snyder, Stephen Ansolabehere, and John Mark Hansen. 2010. "Primary Elections and Partisan Polarization in the U.S. Congress." *Quarterly Journal of Political Science* 5 (2): 169–191.

Jacobson, Gary C. 2012. *Politics of Congressional Elections*. 8th ed. New York: Pearson.

Kanthak, Kristin, and Rebecca B. Morton. 2001. "The Effects of Electoral Rules on Congressional Primaries." In *Congressional Primaries and the Politics of Representation*, ed. Peter F. Galderisi, Marni Ezra, and Michael Lyons. Lanham, MD: Rowman and Littlefield pp. 116–31.

Kaufmann, Karen M., James G. Gimpel, and Adam H. Hoffman. 2003. "A Promise Fulfilled? Open Primaries and Representation." *The Journal of Politics* 65(2): 457–476.

Maestas, Cherie D., Sarah Fultton, L. Sandy Maisel, and Walter J. Stone. 2006. "When to Risk It? Institutions, Ambitions, and the Decision to Run for the U.S. House." *American Political Science Review* 100(2): 195–208.

Maisel, L. Sandy, and Walter J. Stone. 1997. "Determinants of Candidate Emergence in U.S. House Elections: An Exploratory Analysis." *Legislative Studies Quarterly* 22(1): 79–96.

McCarty, Nolan, Keith T. Poole, and Howard Rosenthal. 2006. *Polarized America: The Dance of Ideology and Unequal Riches*. Cambridge, MA: MIT Press.

McGhee, Eric. 2010. *Open Primaries*. San Francisco: Public Policy Institute of California.

McGhee, Eric, Seth Masket, Boris Shor, Steven Rogers, and Nolan McCarty. 2014. "A Primary Cause of Partisanship? Nomination Systems and Legislator Ideology." *American Journal of Political Science* 58(2): 337–351.

Nielson, Lindsay, and Neil Visalvanich. 2017. "Primaries and Candidates: Examining the Influence of Primary Electorates on Candidate Ideology." *Political Science Research and Methods* 5(2): 397–408.

Norrander, Barbara, and Jay Wendland. 2016. "Open versus Closed Primaries and the Ideological Composition of Presidential Primary Electorates." *Electoral Studies* 42: 229–236.

Olivella, Santiago, Kristin Kanthak, and Brian F. Crisp. 2017. "And Keep Your Enemies Closer: Building Reputations for Facing Electoral Challenges." *Electoral Studies* 46 (1): 75–86.

Pearson, Kathryn, and Jennifer L. Lawless. 2008. "Primary Competition and Polarization in the U.S. House of Representatives. Unpublished manuscript.

Poole, Keith T., and Howard Rosenthal. 1985. "A Spatial Model for Legislative Roll Call Analysis." *American Journal of Political Science* 29(2): 357–384.

Rogowski, Jon C., and Stephanie Langella. 2015. "Primary Systems and Candidate Ideology: Evidence from Federal and State Legislative Elections." *American Politics Research* 43(5): 846–871.

Rohde, David W. 1979. "Risk-Bearing and Progressive Ambition: The Case of Members of the United States House of Representatives." *American Journal of Political Science* 23(1): 1–26.

Sinclair, Barbara. 2006. *Party Wars: Polarization and the Politics of National Policy Making.* Norman: University of Oklahoma Press.

Sulkin, Tracy. 2005. *Issue Politics in Congress.* New York: Cambridge University Press.

Thomsen, Danielle M. 2014. "Ideological Moderates Won't Run: How Party Fit Matters for Partisan Polarization in Congress." *The Journal of Politics* 76(3): 786–797.

PART III

Candidates and Parties in Primary Elections

While the chapters in the previous section all addressed some aspect of voting behavior in primary elections, the chapters in Part III all concern the behavior of candidates. As long as primary elections have existed, there have been questions raised about the types of candidates who would benefit from them. During the early years of the twentieth century, some people speculated that candidates with no firm ties to the party would be advantaged. The successes of some wealthy individuals or media barons reinforced these arguments. In studies of southern primaries, it was often argued that demagoguery was rewarded in the primary system. Yet such claims are difficult to measure. In more recent years, analyses of congressional polarization have argued that ideologically extreme candidates often have an advantage in primaries. Many studies of primary competition have also asked whether the sorts of candidates who are advantaged in primary elections are necessarily the strongest general election nominees. If candidates must stray from the ideological center, or make appeals to a small minority of voters, what are the consequences for their parties, and indeed for the health of democratic politics?

The six chapters in this section present three different ways of considering this topic. The section begins with three considerations of the relationship between primary election outcomes and general election outcomes. Shigeo Hirano and James Snyder consider statewide election data across the entire history of the U.S. direct primary; they show that areas of the state that provide candidates' strongest primary support tend also to provide them with their strongest general election support. This suggests that the strategies candidates use in their primary campaigns do tend to spill over into the general election. Jeffrey Lazarus explores the hypothesis that divisive primaries harm candidates in the general election, arguing that primary divisiveness is a consequence of weak candidates – it is correlated with general election divisiveness, but it does not cause it. And Robert Boatright and Vincent Moscardelli explore the relationship between party surges in the general election, contending that large partisan swings in the general election are often preceded by greater-than-usual turmoil in the primaries.

A second theme in this section is the relationship between primary elections and candidate extremism or moderation. Caitlin Jewitt and Sarah Treul consider the effects of primary challenges to congressional incumbents, distinguishing between competitive primary challenges and ideological primary challenges. They conclude that these challenges tend to push candidates away from the positions of the majority party in Congress, whether they are of that party or of the minority party. Danielle Thomsen considers the fate of moderate candidates in primaries, exploring the conditions under which moderates might be advantaged in primaries.

Third, Casey Dominguez explores the relationship between political parties and primary election candidates. Given the effects of primaries on party success and party coherence, it makes senses that political party organizations and interest groups would seek to shape the outcomes of primaries to their advantage. Dominguez discusses how this occurs and notes differences between Democratic and Republican candidates in the composition of their primary election campaign contributions.

The chapters all address, in one way or another, the question of what we believe should be the purpose of primaries. Is primary competition healthy for our political system? It is easy to argue that competitive elections yield better politicians, but as these chapters show, this is not always the case. Competition can harm the ability of parties to choose strong candidates, and primary competition can prevent us from being given meaningful choices in general elections. As we shall see in other sections of the book, democratic candidate selection processes do not always yield democratic outcomes.

9

THE DIRECT PRIMARY AND VOTING BEHAVIOR IN U.S. GENERAL ELECTIONS[1]

Shigeo Hirano and James M. Snyder, Jr.

Conventional wisdom in the political science literature is that U.S. elections became much less party-centered around the 1960s. Aldrich and Niemi (1990) refer to the post-1960s era as the "sixth party system."[2] In summarizing the studies on this transformation in voting behavior, Aldrich (1995, 253) writes:

> Together these studies show that there was an important shift in elections to all national offices in or about 1960, demonstrating that voters respond to candidates far more than previously. Voting became candidate-centered, and so parties as mechanisms for understanding candidates, campaigns, and elections became less relevant.

Understanding why U.S. electoral politics became less party-centered during this period continues to be an active area of research.

The existing literature examining the changes in U.S. voting behavior tends to focus on the changes in the U.S. political environment in the 1960s that potentially increased the salience of individual politicians' attributes and weakened traditional party organizations – e.g., changes in campaign advertising technologies such as the rise of television, the replacement of patronage with civil service employment, and an increase in the personal resources available to elected officials for constituency service. These factors led voters to see parties as less relevant, and party attachments weakened. Campbell (2007, 68) describes the process as follows:

> Since the 1960s the role of the political parties in American politics has fundamentally changed. A series of technological, institutional, legal, and cultural shifts diminished their once central function as the organizers and inclusive mobilizers of American elections. They ceded control over nominations and were pushed aside by new candidate-centered campaigns. Technological advances allowed candidates to speak directly to the people, and the parties lost their monopoly.

The introduction of direct primary elections largely occurred several decades prior to this period of candidate-centered politics, and consequently the literature does not commonly connect primaries with the increasing salience of candidate attributes in U.S. elections.[3]

161

While the literature on primary elections, with a few exceptions, does not explicitly link primaries to changes in voting behavior, this relationship is often implied in the way primaries are connected to the weakening of political party organizations.[4] The traditional view is that primaries provided incentives for candidates to cultivate their personal reputations in the electorate in order to win their party's nomination (e.g., Key 1964; Herrnson 1988).[5] For example, Jacobson (2004, 15–16) writes:

> A fundamental factor [in the decline of parties] is clearly institutional: the rise and spread of primary elections as the method for choosing party nominees for the general election . . . Primary elections have largely deprived parties of their most important source of influence over elected officials. Parties no longer control access to the ballot and, therefore, to political office. They cannot determine who runs under their label and so cannot control what the label represents . . . parties typically have few sanctions and little influence [on nominations].

If political party organizations were significantly weakened by primaries, then they might not have been able to cultivate the party's reputation within the electorate, or directly influence voting, as strongly as when they controlled the nomination process.

With the party organizations weakened, candidates had stronger incentives to cultivate a personal vote. In addition, the efforts of candidates to cultivate personal reputations to secure their party's nomination and the attachments voters make with the nominee during the primaries could conceivably spill over into the general election. This spillover would dampen partisan voting and strengthen the correlation in the electoral outcomes between the primary and general elections.

Other factors might also reduce the amount of purely partisan voting under primaries. For example, under the convention system, party leaders often tried to balance their statewide tickets geographically or ethnically. Well-balanced tickets supposedly helped the party attract votes from all regions of the state. This became more difficult under primaries because of the difficulty in coordinating the choices of many thousands of voters. Thus, for example, the share of Democratic nominees for statewide offices in Massachusetts who came from the Boston area increased sharply after the introduction of primaries. This happened because a large share of the Democratic voters in Massachusetts lived in the Boston area, and these voters evidently preferred candidates from their home city and region to those from other areas. These candidates were also likely to be more attractive to independent voters from the Boston area, and possibly even some Boston-area Republicans – e.g., they would probably be perceived at a minimum as being more sympathetic to the problems facing Boston and Bostonians, and also maybe more willing to fight for policies and programs and spending that favored Boston. This "pro-Boston-area attribute" would then result in a correlation between votes in the primary and general elections.

In some elections, particular issues or bundles of issues – prohibition, Progressivism, the New Deal – arise, which, at least in some states or regions, cut across the usual party divisions at least to some degree. Candidates with strong positions on these issues – wets or dries, progressives or stalwarts, pro- or anti-New Dealers – might attract voters both in the primary and the general election on the basis of their positions, again producing a correlation between votes in the primary and general elections. In other work we find clear evidence that this occurs in the primary elections.

While the traditional literature suggests that primaries could weaken party-centered politics, more recent work argues that parties were becoming weaker even earlier. Reynolds (2006) argues that the emergence of "hustling" candidates who often had high political ambitions and campaigned for their party nominations was part of a move towards candidate-centered politics in the early decades of the twentieth century, and contributed to the adoption of direct primaries. Thus, the introduction of direct primaries may have been a response to the rising candidate-centered focus of U.S. politics rather than the cause of candidate-centered politics.[6] The potential endogeneity of the adoption of primary elections makes it difficult to disentangle the causal effect of primaries on declining partisan voting. However, both this line of reasoning and the traditional literature would predict a decline in partisan voting to coincide with the adoption of primaries.

While these literatures might predict the change in partisan voting, the extent to which general election outcomes are linked to voting behavior in primaries remains an open question. An empirical literature that examines the effect of divisive primaries on general election outcomes for non-presidential elections finds mixed results.[7] The studies in this literature focus on the relationship between candidates' overall support in the primary and general elections. If candidates appeal to certain segments of the electorate, then this would not necessarily be captured by aggregating votes at the district or state level. Moreover, these studies also tend to focus on the second half of the twentieth century, so they provide little insight into candidate-centered voting prior to the sixth party system.

In this chapter, we begin by asking a simple question: Did the introduction of direct primary elections coincide with a decline in partisan voting in general elections? Such a relationship would suggest that candidate-centered politics became an increasing part of U.S. elections almost a half-century prior to the sixth party system in the 1960s.

To answer the first question, we employ a strategy that exploits the variation in the introduction of direct primaries across states to examine whether there is an association between personal voting and the use of primary elections. We employ a dataset on aggregate voting returns across all statewide elected officials from 1880 to 2006 to measure personal voting by the amount of "split ticket" voting across these offices within a particular state election. Using a differences-in-differences design, we separate the effect of direct primaries from variables that may affect personal voting within states and may also be trending over time. We also add a variable to capture the changes in ballot form that occurred before and around the time primaries were being introduced and were also perceived to influence split ticket voting.

With this first research design we find evidence that the introduction of primaries is associated with an increase in split ticket voting. More specifically we find evidence of a "transition period" in the first half of the twentieth century – from about 1890 to 1920 – during which the degree of split ticket voting rose sharply in those states that adopted a comprehensive, mandatory primary. The estimated rise in split ticket voting associated with the introduction of the direct primary is at least as large as the rise following the introduction of the straight party lever/circle.

We then turn to questions regarding the connection between voting behavior in the primary and general election. More specifically we ask: Do the candidate attributes that appeal to primary voters also affect general election voting behavior? Does this relationship exist even in the early decades of the twentieth century?

To address these questions we exploit a newly constructed dataset of county level primary and general election returns from 1906 to 2006. These data allow us to investigate whether the areas where candidates receive electoral support in the primary are also the areas where their general election vote shares are above what would be expected given the election-specific factors and the partisan normal vote in the areas. Such an association would suggest that the candidate attributes salient in the primary are also salient in the general elections. If this association exists even in the period prior to 1960, then this would provide further evidence of candidate-centered electoral politics earlier than is commonly discussed in the political science literature.

We find evidence that counties where a nominee does well in the primary election are also the counties where the nominee does well in the general election even in the early decades of the twentieth century. Thus, personal voting on the basis of candidate attributes appears to have existed in the general elections even prior to the rise in the sixth party system in the 1960s. However, the coefficient estimates are relatively modest. This suggests – not surprisingly – that the variation in general election outcomes across counties largely reflects other factors, such as partisanship or candidates' general election appeals.

We also include a brief discussion regarding whether the appeal of candidate attributes may spill over across offices. In particular, we might expect personal voting for top-of-the-ticket offices to spill over to down-ballot offices. We find that the counties that support the top-of-the-ticket nominees in the primaries are also the counties where the down-ballot nominees from the same party receive higher than expected general election vote shares, even after the primary vote shares of the down-ballot nominees are taken into account. This apparent spillover effect is only significant in the early decades of the twentieth century.

Primaries and Split Ticket Voting

One indicator of candidate-centered voting is the degree to which the electorate engages in "split ticket" voting. In party-centered systems we would expect voters to vote for all of the candidates from the same party across offices within an election. A crude measure of split ticket voting is the variation in the two-party vote across offices in a given election.[8] This is obviously a lower bound on the total amount of split ticket voting, since individual voters may split their tickets in different ways that cancel one another. However, the correlation between split ticket voting measured at the individual level and the aggregate-level proxies is quite high.[9]

We augmented the data in Ansolabehere and Snyder (2002), Ansolabehere et al. (2006), and Ansolabehere et al. (2010), to create a nearly complete dataset of election returns for all state-wide races in all states for the period 1880–2006.[10] For each state-year in which there are three or more statewide races, we construct the variable *Standard Deviation* as follows:

$$Standard\ Deviation_{kt} = \frac{1}{N_{kt}-1}\left[\sum_{i=1}^{N}\left(V_{jkt}-\bar{V}_{kt}\right)^2\right]^{1/2}$$

where N_{kt} is the number of statewide races in state k in year t, V_{jkt} is the Democratic share of the two-party vote in race j in state k in year t, and $\bar{V}_{kt}$ is the average of the Democratic percentage of the two-party vote across all races in state k in year t. We only include races contested by both major parties, and we drop races in which a third-party candidate received more than 15 percent of the total vote.[11]

Figure 9.1 shows a graph of the average value of *Standard Deviation* in each year. The black circles are for the set of states that adopted a comprehensive, mandatory primary election law during the period 1900–1915 and did not subsequently repeal the law, while the gray triangles are for the states that did not.[12]

The two curves are similar overall, showing a small but clear increase in *Standard Deviation* starting around 1900, and a larger increase between 1960 and 1980. One obvious difference between the curves is that the early increase is noticeably larger for the states that adopted a comprehensive mandatory primary, and that a large gap opens between these states and states without primaries starting around 1918. This is intriguing because, as noted above, the period 1900–1915 was the era in which most states adopted their primary laws.

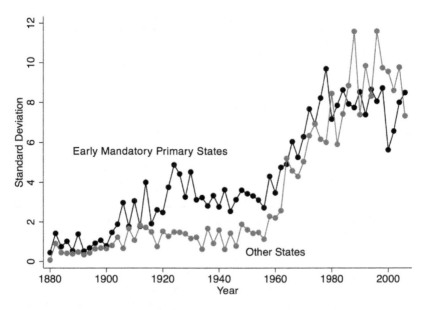

Figure 9.1 Standard Deviation of the Statewide Office Vote Shares for States that Introduced Mandatory Direct Primaries between 1900 and 1915 (in black) and States that Introduced Mandatory Direct Primaries after 1915 (in grey)

For the states adopting a comprehensive mandatory primary, there are three "plateaus," one from about 1880 to 1900, another from about 1922 to 1958, and a third from about 1972 to 2006. The average value of *Standard Deviation* during the first plateau is 0.9, the average value in the second plateau is 3.5, and the average value in the third plateau is 7.9. Thus, for these states the shift from the first period to the middle period was about 37 percent of the total change between the first period and the third, clearly a non-trivial change.[13]

Regression analyses show that the difference in split ticket voting between those states that adopted primaries early on and those that did not is statistically significant and substantively important. In these analyses we can also compare the relative importance of primary elections and other institutional factors, such as ballot form, which scholars argue should also have influenced split ticket voting during the period prior to the 1960s. Several existing studies find some changes in split ticket voting associated with ballot form (e.g., Rusk 1970; Campbell and Miller 1957).[14] Thus, the specification we use includes the following independent variables: *Direct Primary*$_{st}$ = 1 if state *s* employed primary elections in year *t*; *Straight Ticket*$_{st}$ = 1 if state *s* had a straight party lever/circle on the ballot in year *t*; *Office Block*$_{st}$ = 1 if state *s* used the office block ballot form in year *t*; *Party List*$_{st}$ = 1 if state *s* used the party list ballot form in year *t*.[15] Note that the coefficients on the two ballot form variables, i.e., *Office Block* and *Party List*, are relative to the excluded category, which is the pre-Australian ballot "party ballot." For this analysis we focus on the period 1880 to 1960.

The results are shown in Table 9.1. In the first two columns we only include year fixed effects. In the middle two columns we include year and state fixed effects. In the last two columns we include year effects, state effects and state-year trends. In columns 2, 4 and 6 we include indicators for differences in ballot form, such as whether there is an easy option to vote a straight party ticket or whether candidates are grouped by office or party, that are often argued to affect split ticket voting.

Table 9.1 Primaries and Split Ticket Voting in Statewide Elections, 1880–1960

	Dependent Variable = Standard Deviation					
Direct Primary	1.87	1.52	1.01	0.87	0.59	0.53
	(0.29)	(0.26)	(0.19)	(0.18)	(0.26)	(0.25)
Straight Ticket		−1.30		−0.58		−0.45
		(0.33)		(0.36)		(0.32)
Office Block		1.27		0.27		0.25
		(0.63)		(0.36)		(0.35)
Party List		1.10		−0.02		0.06
		(0.70)		(0.53)		(0.53)
State FE	No	No	Yes	Yes	Yes	Yes
State–Year Trends	No	No	No	No	Yes	Yes

Note: Year fixed effects included in all specifications. Standard errors are in parentheses. Standard errors are clustered by state in all specifications. The number of observations is 1128 in all specifications.

When fixed effects and time trends are not included, the direct primary is found to have a similar effect on split ticket voting as whether a straight party ticket option is included on the ballot.[16] The coefficients on all of the variables are noticeably smaller in magnitude as state fixed effects and state-year trends are included. When state fixed effects and state trends are included in the regression, only the introduction of primary elections appears to be associated with a statistically significant change in split ticket voting.

This analysis does not necessarily identify the causal effect of adopting a mandatory primary law on *Standard Deviation*. For example, as noted above, trends in the power of party organizations might be the real cause of the increase in split ticket voting. Strong party organizations might have prevented the adoption of primary laws in their states and might also have reduced the amount of split ticket voting. Of course, because the analysis includes state and year fixed effects, it must be that party organizational strength *changed* within states over time and in different states at different times (i.e., not as the result of a nationwide shock such as a transformative presidential election or federal patronage laws). In addition, the analysis including state-year trends suggests that the rise in split ticket voting following the introduction of primaries was significantly larger than the linear trends in split ticket voting occurring within states during this period.

At a minimum, the analysis above clearly identifies two patterns in split ticket voting: (1) there was a significant increase in split ticket voting much earlier than the conventional wisdom in the political science literature would suggest; and (2) this increase was especially noticeable in states that adopted a comprehensive mandatory primary between 1900 and 1915.

Candidate Attributes in Primary and General Elections

In this section we examine the link between the electoral appeal of candidates in the primary and the support nominees receive in the general election. As we noted above, the existing literature provides mixed evidence that such a connection exists. We use a new dataset of county level primary election returns from 1906 to 2006 to provide evidence that the candidate attributes that affect primary election outcomes also affect general election outcomes. With this new dataset we can exploit the multiple county level primary and general election returns for party nominees within races and multiple primary and general election returns for the same county across races. This allows us to examine whether the areas where general election candidates had higher than expected vote shares are also the areas where these candidates had relatively high vote shares in the primary election.

Data and Methods

We have assembled a new dataset of county level primary election returns for the period 1906 to 2006. We collected most of the historical data on official state primary electoral returns from official state reports, state yearbooks and statistical registers, and state legislative manuals. We also incorporated information for senatorial and gubernatorial elections in southern states between 1920 and 1972 from two ICPSR datasets (I00072 and I00071). Although the dataset does not cover every primary election for every state during the period under investigation, it includes most of the elections from 47 states.[17] We merge this primary data with county level general election data. We have almost all county level senate and gubernatorial general election data for the period until 2006 from an updated version of ICPSR I0001.[18] We have been able to collect most county level primary elections data for this same period.

We also gathered county level primary and general election returns for down-ballot state-wide offices for the 43 states that had down-ballot elections.[19] This dataset includes election returns for lieutenant governor, secretary of state, treasurer, auditor, comptroller, and attorney general. Part of these data comes from ICPSR 7861. For the period 1990 to 2006 we used the county level general election data for down-ballot offices from Meredith (2013). We gathered the remaining data from official state reports, state yearbooks and statistical registers, and state legislative manuals. This dataset is not as comprehensive as the dataset for governors and senators as we are still missing the county level primary or general election results for a number of the down-ballot elections.

Following the literature we assume that the county level election outcomes are determined by factors specific to local areas (e.g., partisanship), candidate attributes that appeal to constituents across counties (e.g., quality and incumbency), candidate attributes that appeal to voters in certain counties (e.g., specific policy positions) and contest-specific factors.[20] These candidate attributes and county- or race-specific factors are often difficult to measure. We exploit the structure of the data to help us identify the relationship between the electoral support of particular candidate attributes in the primaries and the general elections. For example, if we assume that county partisanship does not vary significantly across elections within decades, then we can account for this, as well as other county-specific features, with county fixed effects that vary by decade. Similarly, if we assume that candidate quality has the same appeal across counties within races, then we can account for candidate quality, as well as other race-specific factors, with race-specific fixed effects.

Although we cannot directly observe the candidate attributes that appeal to primary and general election voters, we can observe the variation in areas where the candidates received support in the primary election. Since primary voters presumably make decisions based upon candidate attributes separate from their partisan affiliation, we would expect a candidate's county level primary vote shares to be a proxy for the local support for the attributes of that candidate.

Thus, the basic specification we estimate is as follows:

$$V_{ij} = \alpha_i + \gamma_j + \theta P_{ij} + \varepsilon_{ij}$$

where the dependent variable, V_{ij}, is the general election vote share of the Democratic Party candidate in county i and race j.[21] The term α_i denotes a fixed effect for county i, which captures characteristics of county i such as partisanship. We allow α_i to vary by decade, which allows for characteristics such as county partisanship to change over time. The term γ_j is a fixed effect for contest j, which captures contest-specific factors such as the quality of the candidates running in contest j. The term P_{ij} is the difference between D_{ij} and R_{ij}, where D_{ij} (R_{ij}) is the Democratic (Republican) nominee's share of the top two candidates' vote in the Democratic (Republican) primary election preceding general election contest j.[22] That is, for simplicity, we are assuming that primary vote shares of the Democratic nominee will have the same relationship with general election support as the primary vote share of the Republican nominee.[23]

If candidate attributes that affect primary election outcomes are also salient in the general election, then we would expect θ to be positive. We examine whether this relationship exists for both top-of-the-ticket offices, i.e., governor and senator, as well as down-ballot offices. We might expect the relationship to be stronger for top-of-the-ticket races since the candidates in these races tend to receive more resources and media attention to cultivate their personal vote.

We allow θ to vary over time to examine whether the relationship between the candidate attributes salient in the primary and general election outcomes is mainly in the post-1960 era of candidate-centered politics. If candidate attributes are salient in elections in the pre-1960 period, then we would expect the coefficient on the primary vote share to be positive and statistically significant when we focus on races during the early period. A positive coefficient would provide further evidence that the political science literature focusing on the rise in candidate-centered politics in the post-1960 period may be understating the relevance of candidate attributes earlier in the century.

We should note that this research design does not identify the causal effect of primary competition on the general election voting. We do not know whether the attributes of the party nominees would have generated the same pattern of county level general election support even if the primary had not occurred. However, a positive estimate of θ would indicate that certain candidate attributes are salient in both the primary and general election.

Results

The results in Table 9.2 show that the candidate attributes which affect primary election outcomes also appear to influence general election outcomes. The top panel of Table 9.2 includes all offices. The results in column 1 in this panel, which includes all years, finds that on average, the areas where candidates do well in primary elections are also areas where the candidates do better than expected in the general election. If a party nominee's primary vote share is 40 percentage points higher in county A as compared to county B, then, on average, the nominee's general election vote share is about 2.8 percentage points higher in county A compared to B.[24]

We also estimate θ separately for top-of-the-ticket and down-ballot offices. The results for the top-of-the-ticket (down-ballot) offices are in the second (third) panel of Table 9.2. The association between the county level primary and general election returns is stronger for governors and senators relative to down-ballot offices. If a party's senatorial or gubernatorial nominee's primary vote share is 40 percentage points higher in county A as compared to county B, then, on average, the nominee's general election vote share is about 3.6 percentage points higher in county A compared to B. For down-ballot office nominees this difference in primary election vote shares is associated with a 1.6 percentage point higher vote share in the general election.

While the larger estimates of θ for the top-of-the-ticket as compared to down-ballot offices may be determined by a number of alternative factors, one likely explanation for the difference is that voters have more exposure to information about candidates for top-of-the-ticket offices either through the media or the election campaigns. We know, at least in the recent period, that

Table 9.2 Primary Electoral Support and General Election Outcomes

	All Years	Pre-1960	Post-1960
All Offices			
Primary Support	0.07	0.06	0.09
	(0.01)	(0.01)	(0.01)
Observations	224145	114739	109406
Governor and Senator			
Primary Support	0.09	0.08	0.10
	(0.01)	(0.01)	(0.01)
Observations	127050	61498	65552
Down–ballot Offices			
Primary Support	0.04	0.03	0.07
	(0.01)	(0.01)	(0.01)
Observations	97095	53241	43854

Note: The dependent variable is the county level general election Democratic vote share of the Democratic and Republican vote. Primary support is the Democratic nominee's vote share minus the Republican nominee's vote share. State-county fixed effects that vary by decade and race fixed effects are included in all regressions. Standard errors clustered by state are in parentheses.

top-of-the-ticket primary candidates have significantly more newspaper mentions in the months prior to the primary election as compared to down-ballot candidates.[25]

Did these candidate attributes affect primary and general election outcomes even in the pre-1960 period? Column 2 of Table 9.2 includes all elections prior to 1960. Column 3 includes all elections after and including 1960. The results in these two columns suggest that the candidate attributes salient in the primary elections were related to general election outcomes even prior to the 1960s. If a party nominee's primary vote share is 40 percentage points higher in county A as compared to county B, then, on average, the nominee's general election vote share is about 2.4 percentage points higher in county A compared to B in the period prior to 1960. This difference is 3.2 percentage points for senate and gubernatorial nominees and 1.2 percentage points for down-ballot nominees. Thus, even in this early period before the rise of the sixth party system, candidate attributes were affecting both primary and general elections.

As the existing literature and the analysis from the second section would suggest, the relationship between primary and general election vote shares is larger in the post-1960 period. Again, if a party nominee's primary vote share is 40 percentage points higher in county A as compared to county B, then, on average, the nominee's general election vote share is about 3.6 percentage points higher in county A compared to B in the period after 1960. This difference is 4.0 percentage points for top-of-the-ticket nominees and 2.8 percentage points for down-ballot nominees.

While these coefficient estimates suggest that candidate attributes affect both primary and general election outcomes, the effects are relatively modest. Even in the candidate-centered period between 1960 and 2006, a one percentage point difference in county level primary vote share for a top-of-the-ticket office is associated with only a tenth of a percentage point difference in county level general election vote share. This is perhaps not surprising. Partisanship is still the most important determinant of voting behavior. Moreover, candidates may adjust their appeals in their general elections by highlighting different attributes.

Spillover Effects

While the above evidence suggests that a candidate's attributes may affect their support in both the primary and general election, we do not know whether a candidate's attributes will have a spillover effect on other concurrent races. Coattail effects have long been discussed in the literature.[26] Meredith (2013) finds that in the recent period, a percentage increase in the governor's personal vote increases the secretary of state or attorney general's vote share by 0.1 to 0.2 percentage points. In this section we investigate whether the candidate attributes salient in the primary races for top-of-the-ticket statewide offices affect the general election support for nominees from the same party in races for down-ballot statewide offices. One potential mechanism by which this could occur is if the top-of-the-ticket nominees mobilize voters in particular areas to turn out and these voters also support the down-ballot candidates with the same partisan affiliations. We also examine whether the reverse relationship exists – i.e., areas where the down-ballot candidate does well in the primaries are also the areas where the top-of-the-ticket candidates do well in the general elections.

To estimate this spillover effect we employ a similar specification as the one used in the previous section. For the analysis of general election support in down-ballot races we include the primary vote share of the top-of-the-ticket nominees from the same party in addition to the down-ballot primary vote share, county fixed effects and race fixed effects. The top-of-the-ticket vote share is the higher of the party's gubernatorial or senatorial nominees' primary vote shares in that county and year. Similarly, for the analysis of general election support in top-of-the-ticket races, we include the highest primary vote share among the down-ballot offices in that county and year.

When we pool across all years, we find that the primary support for the top-of-the-ticket nominees is correlated with down-ballot general election outcomes. When we divide the results between races before and after 1960, we find that the spillover effect is strongest during the early part of the century. There is little evidence that the spillover effect from top-of-the-ticket to down-ballot races is present in the post-1960 period.

Consistent with other studies of reverse coattail effects in the U.S., we find no significant evidence that down-ballot primary support is correlated with the top-of-the-ticket general election outcomes. The coefficient estimates are not only small in magnitude and not statistically significant, but also of the opposite sign in some analyses. This result suggests that there is little reverse spillover of the personal attributes of down-ballot candidates on the top-of-the-ticket general elections. This result is not very surprising because, as we mentioned above, down-ballot candidates are often given less media attention and have access to fewer campaign resources.

Conclusion

The results above indicate that there are clear linkages between primary and general elections. First, although scholars often discuss the rise of candidate-centered politics in the 1960s, our state level analyses indicate that there was a rise in split ticket voting much earlier in the century, particularly in states that introduced mandatory direct primaries between 1900 and 1915. Second, our county level analyses suggest that candidate attributes salient in the primaries are also salient in the general elections, and this was true even in the decades prior to the 1960s. Finally, the electoral appeal of top-of-the-ticket candidates appears to have a modest effect on voting for down-ballot candidates, at least in the early part of the twentieth century.

The findings above establish a clear association, but do not identify the specific mechanisms. One possibility is that there are issues or attributes unique to the electoral circumstances that influence voters in both the primaries and general elections in similar ways – e.g., one candidate has a pro-gun position, which both primary and general election voters use to guide their decisions. Another possibility is that the primary campaign "spills over" into the general election – e.g., issues or attributes emphasized by the primary election candidates become salient also in the general election. Hirano et al. (2015) use survey data from primary elections to show that primary voters can learn about the ideological positions of the candidates over the course of the primary campaign.

In our prior work we show that the introduction of primary elections appeared to weaken party loyalty among mid-western and western Republican congressmen (Ansolabehere et al. 2007). In subsequent work we show this holds especially for issues featured on the Progressive agenda. This might be an example of what we find here, both in the aggregate and the county level results. In the aggregate, split ticket voting might increase because some Republican candidates on the ballot are progressives and others are stalwarts, and voters distinguish between them. In addition, this attribute – "how much of a progressive or stalwart is candidate A or B?" – might affect voting in both the primary and the general election at the county level, depending on how much the voters in various counties support progressive policies and politicians.

If primaries do in fact affect general election voting behavior, then candidates must think strategically about the spillovers across the races. Primaries can provide information to nominees about how the candidates appeal to certain types of voters. Thus, primaries could potentially affect policy agendas and outcomes. For example, do primaries lead campaigns, even in the general election, to raise new issues? Do primaries raise the salience of particular candidate attributes, which would have otherwise been ignored? In addition, candidates' strategies in the primary elections should incorporate expectations about how the primary campaign might affect the general election.[27] Further theoretical and empirical research is clearly necessary to fully assess the relationship between primary and general elections.

Notes

1 This chapter incorporates material from an earlier manuscript titled "The Direct Primary and Candidate Centered Voting in U.S. Elections." We thank the numerous research assistants at Columbia, Yale and MIT who have helped assemble the county level primary election returns. We also thank Marc Meredith for the county level down-ballot general election data for 1990 to 2006. We gratefully acknowledge support from the National Science Foundation under grants SES-0617556 and SES-0959200. The opinions, findings, and conclusions or recommendations expressed in this article do not necessarily reflect the views of the National Science Foundation.

2 Aldrich cites numerous articles and books, including Nie, Verba and Petrocik (1979), Alford and Brady (1989), Wattenberg (1990, 1991), Jacobson (1992), and Shively (1992). Some recent literature argues that personal voting, based on incumbency and quality, may have had a role in elections even in the strong party era prior to the 1890s (e.g., Carson et al. 2007; Reynolds, 2006).

3 Candidate attributes refer to attributes other than partisan affiliation – e.g., regional connections, ethnicity, factional affiliations, specific policy positions, etc.

4 Two notable exceptions are Harvey and Mukherjee (2006) and Ansolabehere et al. (2007). They find some evidence that partisan voting may have declined after the introduction of primaries.

5 Key (1964, p. 342), as cited in Miller, Jewell and Sigelman (1988, p. 4596), writes that "the adoption of the direct primary opened the road for disruptive forces that gradually fractionalized the party organization. [T]he primary system . . . facilitated the construction of factions and cliques attached to ambitions of individual leaders." Herrnson (1988, p. 26) writes: "The introduction of the direct primary encouraged candidates to develop their own campaign organizations, or pseudo-parties, for contesting primary elections." In the Carey and Shugart (1993) ranking of electoral systems in terms of their incentives to cultivate personal votes, the use of primaries is an important factor in identifying the United States as a relatively candidate-centered system.

6 Reynolds (2006, p. 102) cites several historical works that describe an "increasingly candidate-centered orientation of electoral campaigns" around the turn of the twentieth century.

7 For example, Born (1981), Kenney and Rice (1984), and Romero (2003) find some evidence that divisive primaries affect general election outcomes. Hacker (1965) and Kenney (1986) find little evidence that divisive primaries have an effect on general election voting. Ware (1979) discusses why primaries may not necessarily have a negative effect on candidates' general election prospects.

8 Harvey and Mukherjee (2006) and Ansolabehere et al. (2007) also examine the relationship between split ticket voting and the introduction of primaries. However, unlike our study that examines the split ticket voting across races for multiple offices, they only focus on the relationship between gubernatorial and U.S. House votes. Also our study allows for within-state trending in split ticket voting that could reflect within-state changes in the strength of party organizations.

9 Using data from exit polls and the CCES we know that split ticket voting tends to be higher at the individual level than the aggregate level differences would suggest. However the measures of split ticket voting using state level data are highly correlated with measures using individual level data. Consider, for example, split ticket voting for senate and governor for the period 1982–2006. For each state-year with both a Senate and Governor race, let s_{ikt} be a dummy variable equal to 1 if respondent i in the exit poll voted for candidates from different parties in the Senate and Governor races (including third-party and independent candidates), and 0 otherwise; let N_{kt} be the number of respondents in the exit poll; and let $S_{kt}^I = \left(1/N_{kt}\right)\sum_{i=1}^{N_{kt}} s_{ikt}$ be the overall amount of split ticket voting at the individual level. Let D_{kt}^G (D_{kt}^S) be the aggregate Democratic share of the two-party vote in the Governor (Senate) race; and let $S_{kt}^A = \left|D_{kt}^G - D_{kt}^S\right|$ be the aggregate measure of split ticket voting. The correlation between is S^I and S^A is .72 ($N = 157$).

10 Statewide races include offices such as U.S. senator, governor, lieutenant governor, attorney general, secretary of state, treasurer, auditor/comptroller/controller, superintendent of education, commissioner of agriculture, public utility commissioner, corporation commissioner, and lands commissioner. We also include races for various statewide offices specific to certain states. See Ansolabehere and Snyder (2002), Ansolabehere et al. (2006), and Ansolabehere et al. (2010) for a complete list of sources and offices used in this analysis.

11 We dropped Alaska, Hawaii, Georgia, Louisiana, Maine, Mississippi, New Hampshire, New Jersey, and South Carolina. Alaska and Hawaii had not received statehood in the early decades of the 20th century. The other states had too few years with 3 or more contested general elections.

12 Each state is weighted equally in each year. We group the odd-numbered years together with the previous even-numbered year – e.g., 1881 with 1880, etc.

13 Calculated as follows: 100(3.5 − .9)/(7.9 − .9) = 37.1 See Table 9.1

14 Rusk (1970) finds that the split ticket voting increased in states that adopted the Australian ballot, and the increase was especially large in states with office-bloc ballots and no party lever. Burnham (1965) also finds an increase in split ticket voting around this period but does not link the changes to any specific electoral institutions. Campbell and Miller (1957) also find that ballot form influences split ticket voting using survey data. As Campbell et al. (1960, p. 275) state in *The American Voter*, "Any attempt to explain why the voter marks a straight or split ballot must take account of the physical characteristics of the election ballot."

15 We also ran specifications including a measure of party competition. This variable was never statistically significant and did not substantively change the coefficient estimates on our main variables of interest.

16 We find no statistically significant evidence that the introduction of the Australian ballot is associated with an increase in split ticket voting. The estimated coefficients on the ballot form variables are particularly sensitive to choice of time period and specification.

17 Alaska, Hawaii and Connecticut are not included in this analysis. Louisiana post-1975 is also dropped from the analysis since the state moved to a top-two primary.

18 Data for the 2002, 2004 and 2006 Senate election data were purchased from http://uselectionatlas.org.

19 Maine, New Hampshire, New Jersey and Tennessee do not have primary elections for the down-ballot offices included in this study.

20 The vote share in county i of electoral contest j can be written as follows: $V_{ij} = N_i + Q_j^D + Q_j^R + \theta_1 A_{ij}^D + \theta_2 A_{ij}^R + Z_j + \varepsilon_{ij}$, where N^i is the partisanship of county i. The terms Q_j^D and Q_j^R are characteristics of candidates that affect their vote share evenly throughout the district. We might think of this as the overall quality of candidates or the incumbency advantage. The A_{ij}^D and A_{ij}^R terms denote non-partisan attributes of the Democratic and Republican candidates that affect their support in county i in the primary leading up to general election contest j. The Z_j term captures partisan tides, or other factors such as specific issues, that have the same effect across all counties in race j.

21 We excluded uncompetitive general election races – i.e., races where the Democratic or Republican candidate received more than 95 percent of the vote. The main results do not substantively change when these races are included.

22 In primaries with runoffs, we use the first round vote share of the nominee.

23 The specification we estimate captures the different variables in the equation described in note 18. In particular, α_i captures N_i, and γ_j captures Q_j^D, Q_j^R and Z_j. In the specification we estimate we constrain θ_1 to be equal to $-\theta_2$. Because we use the Democratic and Republican primary vote as proxies of A_{ij}^D and A_{ij}^R, P^{ij} is simply the primary vote share of the Democratic candidate minus the primary vote share of the Republican candidate. When we estimate separate θ_1 and θ_2 coefficients on the Democratic and Republican primary vote shares, the coefficient magnitudes are similar overall with minor differences within each time period. In particular, $|\theta_2|$ is slightly larger than $|\theta_1|$ in the early period and the reverse is true in the later period. This difference may reflect the factional divisions that existed in the Republican Party in the early period and the divisions within the Democratic Party in the later period.

24 The difference of 40 percentage points represents about two standard deviations.

25 We examined the number of times primary candidates were mentioned relative to the word "election" during the months prior to a primary election in the newspapers included in newslibrary.com during the period 1998 to 2006. The top-of-the-ticket candidates received significantly more newspaper mentions relative to the down-ballot candidates.

26 See Meredith (2013) for a review of this literature.

27 Existing literature discusses this point in terms of ideological competition – adopting extreme positions in the primaries may hurt candidates in the general election. Our findings suggest that such considerations hold more broadly.

References

Aldrich, John H. 1995. *Why Parties? The Origin and Transformation of Political Parties in America*. Chicago: The University of Chicago Press.

Aldrich, John H., and Richard G. Niemi. 1990. "The Sixth American Party System: The 1960s Realignment and the Candidate-Centered Parties." Unpublished manuscript. Duke University Program in Political Economy.

Alford, John R., and David W. Brady. 1989. "Personal and Partisan Advantage in U.S. Congressional Elections, 1846–1986." In *Congress Reconsidered*, ed. Lawrence C. Dodd and Bruce I. Oppenheimer. 4th ed. Washington, D.C.: CQ Press, pp. 156–169.

Ansolabehere, Stephen, and James M. Snyder. 2002. "The Incumbency Advantage in U.S. Elections: An Analysis of State and Federal Offices, 1942–2000." *Election Law Journal: Rules, Politics, and Policy*. 1(3): 315–338.

Ansolabehere, Stephen, J. Mark Hansen, Shigeo Hirano, and James M. Snyder. 2006. "The Decline of Competition in U.S. Primary Elections, 1908–2004." In *The Marketplace of Democracy*, ed. Michael McDonald and John Samples. Washington, DC: Brookings Institution Press, Ch. 4, pages 74–101.

Ansolabehere, Stephen, J. Mark Hansen, Shigeo Hirano, and James M. Snyder. 2010. "More Democracy: The Direct Primary and Competition in U.S. Elections." *Studies in American Political Development*. 24 (1): 190–205.

Ansolabehere, Stephen, Shigeo Hirano, and James M. Snyder. 2007. "What Did the Direct Primary Do to Party Loyalty in Congress?" In *Process, Party and Policy Making: Further New Perspectives on the History of Congress*, Volume 2, ed. David Brady and Mathew D. McCubbins. Stanford, CA: Stanford University Press, Ch. 2, pages 21–36.

Born, R. 1981. "The Influence of House Primary Election Divisiveness on General Election Margins, 1962–1976." *The Journal of Politics*. 42 (3): 640–61.

Burnham, Walter Dean. 1965. "The Changing Shape of the American Political Universe." *The American Political Science Review* 59 (1): 7–28.

Campbell, Andrea L. 2007. "Parties, Electoral Participation, and Shifting Voting Blocs." In *The Transformation of American Politics: Activist Government and the Rise of Conservatism*, ed. Paul Pierson and Theda Skocpol. Princeton, NJ: Princeton University Press, pp. 68–102.

Campbell, Angus, and Warren Miller. 1957. "The Motivational Basis of Straight and Split Ticket Voting." *The American Political Science Review* 51 (2): 293–312.

Campbell, Angus, Philip E. Converse, Warren E. Miller, and Donald E. Stokes. 1960. *The American Voter*. New York: Wiley.

Campbell, Angus, Philip E. Converse, Warren E. Miller, and Donald E. Stokes. 1957. *The American Voter*. Chicago: University of Chicago Press.

Carey, John M., and Matthew S. Shugart. 1993. "Incentives to Cultivate a Personal Vote: A Rank Ordering of Electoral Formulas." *Electoral Studies* 14 (2): 417–439.

Carson, Jamie L., Erik J. Engstrom, and Jason M. Roberts. 2007. "Candidate Quality, the Personal Vote, and the Incumbency Advantage in Congress." *The American Political Science Review* 101 (2): 289–301.

Hacker, A. 1965. "Does a Divisive Primary Harm a Candidate's Election Changes?" *The American Political Science Review* 59 (1): 105–110.

Harvey, Anna, and Bumba Mukherjee. 2006. "The Evolution of Partisan Conventions, 1880–1940." *American Politics Research* 34(3): 368–398.

Herrnson, Paul S. 1988. *Party Campaigning in the 1980s*. Cambridge: Harvard University Press.

Hirano, Shigeo, Gabriel S. Lenz, Maksim Pinkovsky, and James M. Snyder, Jr. 2015. "Voter Learning in State Primary Elections." *American Journal of Political Science* 59 (1): 91–108.

Jacobson, Gary C. 1992. *The Politics of Congressional Elections*, 3rd ed. New York: HarperCollins.

Jacobson, Gary C. 2004. *The Politics of Congressional Elections*. 6th ed. New York: Harper Collins.

Kenney, Patrick J. 1986. "Explaining Primary Turnout: The Senatorial Case." *Legislative Studies Quarterly* 11(1): 65–73.

Kenney, Patrick J., and T.W. Rice. 1984. "The Effect of Primary Divisiveness in Gubernatorial and Senatorial Elections." *The Journal of Politics* 46 (4): 904–915.

Key, V.O. Jr. 1964. *Politics, Parties and Pressure Groups*. New York: Crowell.

Meredith, Marc. 2013. "Exploiting Friends-and-Neighbors to Estimate Coattail Effects." *American Political Science Review* 107 (4): 743–765.

Miller, Penny M., Malcolm E. Jewell, and Lee Sigelman. 1988. "Divisive Primaries and Party Activists: Kentucky, 1979 and 1983." *The Journal of Politics* 50 (2): 459–470.

Nie, Norman H., Sidney Verba, and John R. Petrocik. 1979. *The Changing American Voter*. Cambridge: Harvard University Press.

Reynolds, John F. 2006. *The Demise of the American Convention System, 1880–1911*. New York: Cambridge University Press.

Romero, David W. 2003. "Divisive Primaries and Incumbent General Election Performance: Prospects and Costs in U.S. House Races." *American Politics Research* 38 (4): 931–955.

Rusk, Jerrold G. 1970. "The Effect of the Australian Ballot Reform on Split Ticket Voting: 1876–1908." *The American Political Science Review* 64 (4): 1220–1238.

Shively, W. Phillips. 1992. "From Differential Abstention to Conversion: A Change in Electoral Change, 1864–1988." *American Journal of Political Science* 36 (2): 309–330.

Ware, A. 1979. "Divisive Primaries: The Important Questions." *British Journal of Political Science* 9: 381–384.

Wattenberg, Martin P. 1990. *The Decline of American Political Parties: 1952–1988*. Cambridge: Harvard University Press.

Wattenberg, Martin P. 1991. *The Rise of Candidate-Centered Politics: Presidential Elections of the 1980s*. Cambridge: Harvard University Press.

10

DIVISIVE PRIMARIES

When Do They Hurt in the General Election?

Jeffrey Lazarus

The divisive primary hypothesis predicts that when a primary election contest is hard-fought, or the eventual winner of the primary wins by a close margin, the party will do poorly in the general election. This relationship between primary and general election outcomes was first posited by Key (1953) and tested by Hacker (1965), and has been a venerable part of the elections literature ever since. However, despite the divisive primary hypothesis' very compelling theoretical underpinnings, it has a tepid empirical track record. For every study which finds that divisive primaries harm party nominees, there's another one which says they don't.

These studies reveal that which office a candidate is running for appears to determine whether divisive primaries are harmful. They clearly hurt party nominees in presidential elections (e.g., Gurian et al. 2016) and Senate elections (e.g., Kenney and Rice 1984). However, there is less evidence that they hurt candidates running for governor (e.g., Kenney and Rice 1984), and none whatsoever for the House of Representatives (e.g., Lazarus 2005) or state legislatures (Hogan 2003). Despite this checkered empirical record, though, the idea of the harmful divisive primary remains a popular one. It's essentially common wisdom – everybody "knows" that a closely fought primary election hurts you in the general election. Newspapers run stories with titles like "Wisconsin Republicans Worried about Crowded Senate Primary" (Bauer 2017), and which posit that "it's an open question whether [Kansas] Democrats could recover from a divisive [gubernatorial] primary battle in time for the general election" (Shorman and Lowry 2017). Such concerns are ubiquitous.

One reason for these concerns is that even though divisive primaries don't *cause* nominees to do poorly in down-ballot elections, there is nonetheless a strong correlation between primary and general election outcomes. This correlation is spurious, however (Lazarus 2005; Kenney 1988; Born 1981). Vulnerable incumbents draw strong challengers into primary elections, which creates divisive primaries in the same districts where the vulnerable incumbents do poorly in the general election. In other words, in House elections both primary and general election outcomes are endogenous to incumbent vulnerability, and this creates an apparent divisive primary effect where one does not actually exist. There's also some evidence of this pattern in gubernatorial (Partin 2002) and state legislative (Hogan 2003) races as well. Observers of politics who note this correlation may not be aware of its spurious nature, and attribute causality where it doesn't exist.

In this chapter, I first go over the logic underpinning the divisive primary hypothesis, discussing its causal mechanisms and providing an example for each. Next, I review the literature which has investigated the divisive primary effect at each electoral level. Third, I present an empirical test of the divisive primary effect in Senate and gubernatorial elections which controls for the type of endogeneity observed in House elections. Even with the controls I find strong evidence of a divisiveness effect in Senate elections; in gubernatorial elections the evidence is much weaker. Finally, in the conclusion I posit that the primary difference between races where divisive primaries hurt and the ones where they don't is voter attention. If voters aren't paying enough attention during the primary to know what happened during that stage of the election, it's not possible for them to factor primary election results into their general election decision-making.

The Logic of the Divisive Primary

As I just mentioned, one reason the idea of the harmful divisive primary remains firmly entrenched is because of how ubiquitous it appears to be. A second reason is because the logic underpinning the concept is simple and intuitive. There are three main reasons to think a divisive primary would hurt a party's nominee in the general election; it's also easy to find examples which illustrate all three.

First, divisive primaries can alienate supporters of the losing candidates in the primary election; these supporters might refuse to vote for the nominee in the subsequent general election. A closely fought primary produces a relatively large number of voters whose first-choice candidate does not appear on the general election ballot. Even though these voters share a party identification with someone on the November ballot, they may not want to vote for that candidate. This refusal might stem from policy differences. If the primary election candidates represent moderate and ideologically extreme factions of the party, voters for the losing candidate may find the winner simply too far from their ideological preferences to vote for. Additionally, more fundamental in-group/out-group dynamics are also at work here: voters, having chosen a candidate to support and identify with, may simply refuse to give up that identification to vote for a different candidate (Kenney and Rice 1987). For either reason, voters who supported a losing primary candidate may not vote for the party's nominee in the general election.

Both of these factors likely played a role among Democrats in the 2016 presidential election. In the primary election that year, liberal Bernie Sanders gave the relatively centrist Hillary Clinton a surprisingly tough primary election fight. Even though Clinton ultimately prevailed, a small but significant fraction of Sanders supporters refused to fall in line behind Hillary Clinton after the primary elections concluded. Many of them either did not vote for president at all, or rallied behind liberal third-party candidate Jill Stein. In a poll conducted in August of that year, 31 percent of Sanders voters reported that they would not be voting for Clinton in the general election (Walker 2016).

Second, divisive primaries may provide a party nominee's general election opponent with damaging ammunition. The loser of a closely contested primary election, even though he lost, must have found some campaign tactic which was effective against the eventual nominee – if he hadn't the primary would not have been close. It might be a scandal in the party nominee's past, a policy position the nominee holds which is not congruent with the electorate, a type of debate question the nominee doesn't answer well, or anything that represents an electoral weakness. This weakness would also serve a general election opponent well, even though that general election opponent might not have discovered it had the primary election not been fought so closely.

That was the case for the prison furlough issue which George Bush used against Michael Dukakis in the 1988 presidential election. In 1986, Willie Horton was a convicted murderer in Massachusetts who was temporarily released from prison for a weekend furlough. He was supposed to return to prison at the end of the weekend, but instead escaped. A short time later he assaulted a couple and raped the woman. Dukakis was governor of Massachusetts at the time, and had strongly supported the furlough program Horton used to escape prison. During the presidential election two years later, Democratic candidate Al Gore brought up the furlough program during a primary election debate (although he did not mention Horton by name). Dukakis went on to win the nomination, but in the general election the Bush campaign focused relentlessly on Horton, turning him into a central issue in the campaign in order to make Dukakis appear soft on crime. The issue played a significant role in Dukakis' defeat that year, and it may not have happened if Gore hadn't mentioned the furloughs – Bush's campaign chief Lee Atwater claimed to have learned about Horton from watching the Democratic primary election debate (Simon 1990).

The third reason a divisive primary election might hamper a nominee in the general election is that a hard-fought primary election is simply expensive. A bruising contest during the primary election can leave the winning campaign strapped for resources by the end. When the general election rolls around, the nominee has to start from scratch. This happened to Tommy Thompson, the Republican nominee in Wisconsin's 2012 Senate election. The Republican primary was a tight four-way battle between Thompson, a relative centrist, and three more conservative candidates. Thompson only won 34 percent of the vote, beating second-place finisher Eric Hovde by 3.2 percent. One of the reasons it was so close was that Hovde, a self-funded candidate, spent almost $6 million of his own money in his attempt to win the primary, forcing Thompson to match him. Thompson did, and won the primary, but his campaign entered the general election essentially broke. His Democratic opponent in the general election, Tammy Baldwin, had no competition in the primary, and was able to focus her entire $15 million war-chest on the general election. Baldwin won the general election by six points, in no small part because she was able to outspend Thompson almost five-to-one (Sullivan and Blake 2012).

These three factors – alienating the voters of the losing candidates, providing ammunition to the other party's nominee, and costing a lot of money – combine to make a divisive primary election a scary proposition for a candidate or party organization. In the next section, I discuss what the evidence says about when candidates should be scared and when they probably don't need to worry.

Do Divisive Primaries Hurt? Well, That Depends . . .

The logic underpinning the divisive primary hypothesis appears to be iron-clad, but appearances can be deceiving. Observers of American elections have been debating whether the hypothesis holds true since Key (1953) first proposed it, and at first glance the literature doesn't appear to offer a clear answer. Some studies provide strong evidence that divisive primaries hurt party nominees in the general election, and others clearly fail to provide such evidence. For this reason, a quick glance at the literature can be confusing. However, sorting the studies by political office reveals that whether divisive primaries hurt candidates depends in large part on what type of election you're looking at.

Before diving in I will note that I'm skipping over several methodological debates that have taken place within the literature; the most involved of these is over how scholars should measure divisiveness. Regardless of the details, however, every author in this literature measures divisiveness by observing in some way how close the results of a primary election are. Throughout this section, a "divisive" primary is one in which the winner won a relatively small amount of the vote in that election.

In presidential elections, study after study confirms that party nominees are indeed hamstrung in the general election when the primary election was divisive. These studies have looked at the issue from a variety of methodological perspectives, and they all reach the same conclusion. First and foremost, candidates coming out of divisive primaries receive fewer votes in the general election, just like the hypothesis predicts (Atkeson 1998; Gurian et al. 2016; Kenney and Rice 1987; Lengle et al. 1995).[1] In addition to this, scholars have also investigated the individual-level underpinnings of these vote totals. Surveys indicate that candidates coming out of divisive primaries receive lower levels of approval from survey respondents (Kenney and Rice 1987; Southwell 1986, 2010; Stone 1986). As well, party activists and volunteers are less likely to do work for these candidates in the general election (Stone 1984, 1986; Stone et al. 1992; Buell 1986). All told, candidates coming out of divisive primaries are at a significant disadvantage relative to candidates coming from easy primary contests.

Gurian et al. (2016) propose that the divisive primary effect is so strong at the presidential level because divisiveness can influence voters at both the state and the national level. At the state level, when one state's primary election is close, this causes the party's nominee to do relatively poorly *in that state* in the subsequent general election. But there's also a national-level effect: when a party's primary election is closely fought nationally – both in the aggregated state primaries and in the national media – this can hurt the party's presidential candidate in the general election in *all* states. Gurian et al. (*ibid.*) estimate the effect of divisiveness on general election outcomes in all post-WWII presidential elections; they conclude that divisiveness cost a general election candidate at least one state in most of these contests, and in some years the count exceeded 10 states.

The only other office for which there is consistent empirical support for a divisive primary effect is the Senate. In fact, the empirical investigation into divisive primaries began with Senate elections, when Hacker (1965) found no evidence that a divisive primary influenced whether a Senate candidate won or lost. Later, Bernstein (1977) corrected a number of methodological flaws in Hacker's original work, and found that divisive primaries do hurt Senate candidates – even when examining Hacker's original cases. Subsequent literature consistently shows that Senate candidates coming out of divisive primaries get a lower vote in the general election (Abramowitz 1988; Kenney and Rice 1984; Segura and Nicholson 1995). Only Kenney's (1988) findings are ambiguous; we shall return to this study shortly.

Contrary to the findings for Presidential and Senate races, there's very little substantial evidence of an effect in any other type of election. Four studies investigate gubernatorial races. Two find no effect whatsoever (Hacker 1965; Pierson and Smith 1975). Kenney and Rice (1984) find that divisive primaries do depress general election vote shares in gubernatorial elections, but the effect is much smaller than the corresponding effect in Senate elections, and not as robust. Partin (2002), however, finds something unusual. He analyzed challenger vote totals, and finds that an incumbent party challenge is associated with challengers doing better in the general election, consistent with the hypothesis. But he also finds that when the challenger's primary is contested there's a small but significant *increase* in the challengers' vote share – the opposite of what the divisive primary hypothesis predicts. What explains this unexpected result?

I believe the answer can be found in divisive primary studies on House races. Here, studies reveal a correlation between how close a primary election is and how well the candidate does in a general election, but the relationship isn't causal (Born 1981; Kenney 1988; Lazarus 2005). The confounding factor is how electorally vulnerable the incumbent is. Because people deciding to run for election are strategic, more of them run against weak incumbents, when the chance for a challenger to win is the highest. And the strongest challengers – the ones with the connections, expertise, and skill to win elections – are the most strategic. As a result, when an incumbent is weak, both more challengers run against them, and stronger challengers run against them (Black 1972; Jacobson and Kernell 1981; Lazarus 2008). All of these challengers, by running against each other and the incumbent at the same time, create divisive primaries.

From there, what happens depends on whether the divisive primary is the incumbent's party or the challenger's party. In the incumbent's party, the party nominee is almost always the incumbent, even if he's weak. Only about one percent of House incumbents ever lose primary elections. But when the incumbent is weak he is going to do relatively poorly in the general election, at least compared to other incumbents. The fact that this happens after the incumbent survived a close primary creates the appearance of a divisive primary effect: incumbents who get a lower vote share in the primary also get a lower vote share in the general. But the poor primary election result doesn't *cause* the poor general election result. Rather, each is a consequence of the fact that the incumbent is weak.

Something different happens on the challenger's side, though, and this is where we can explain Partin's (2002) unusual result. When the challenger's party primary is close, it's once again usually because a weak incumbent draws several candidates into the race. These candidates split the vote, making the primary a "divisive" one, and the winner goes on to the general election. But here, the party nominee doesn't do worse than usual in the general election; she does *better* – because she's running against a weak incumbent. This flips the divisive primary hypothesis on its head: challengers coming out of a divisive primary tend to do better in the general election than challengers coming out of an easy primary.

This pattern of findings – that divisive primaries appear to "hurt" incumbents and "help" challengers – has been found for every office other than the Senate and President, including gubernatorial elections (Partin 2002), U.S. House elections (Herrnson 2000), and state legislative elections (Hogan 2003). Some scholars observing this pattern erroneously conclude that a divisive primary somehow helps challengers prepare for the general elections, perhaps by honing campaign skills or by providing connections to donors. However, more methodologically sophisticated studies show that both relationships – the negative relationship between primary divisiveness and general election outcomes on incumbents' side, and the positive one on challengers' side – are indeed endogenous to incumbent vulnerability. Born (1981) demonstrates this using two-staged least squares regression to account for the endogeneity, and Lazarus (2005) and Kenney (1988) estimate general election vote shares while controlling for incumbent vulnerability. All four studies find that once the endogeneity is accounted for, both divisive primary effects go.

Kenney (1988) investigates whether incumbent vulnerability is responsible for the divisive primary effect in Senate elections, and indeed he finds that they are. However, Kenny's measure of incumbent vulnerability is non-standard in today's literature. Looking at CQ weekly report accounts of Senate elections, he codes for factors which would seem to make an incumbent vulnerable (scandal, poor polling, and the like), and created a "vulnerable" dummy variable based on these findings. However, Kenny did no robustness checks on his coding, and subsequent literature has revealed more nuanced and reliable measures of vulnerability as well. Indeed, Lazarus (2005) uses these measures to demonstrate endogeneity in House elections. In the following section, I present a test similar to that performed by Lazarus (*ibid.*), but applied to Senate and gubernatorial races.

Divisive Primaries in Senate and Gubernatorial Elections

In this section I test whether incumbent vulnerability is responsible for any observed correlation between primary election divisiveness and general election outcomes in Senate and gubernatorial elections. To do this, I collected data on elections to both offices between 1998 and 2014. I use OLS regression to estimate the share of the two-party vote the incumbent party candidate received in each type of election. Focusing on the two-party vote (to the exclusion of third-party candidates) ensures that the general election vote totals are zero-sum – if the incumbent's vote share goes up, the challenger's necessarily goes down. This way, the single dependent variable can estimate the effect divisiveness has on both incumbents' and challengers' general election vote share.

The key independent variables measure primary election divisiveness. I operationalize divisiveness by taking the share of the primary vote going to that election's winning candidate – that is, the party's nominee in the general election.[2] Each model has two divisiveness variables: *inc-party vote* is the share of the incumbent party primary vote won by that party's party nominee, and *out-party vote* is the corresponding value for the challenger's party. The main empirical prediction of the divisive primary hypothesis is that a nominee's general election vote share is high when his or her primary election vote share is high, and vice versa. Once again, the dependent variable measures the incumbent party nominee's vote share. Formally, then, the hypothesis predicts that the coefficient on *inc-party vote* is positive and significant, and the coefficient on *out-party vote* is negative and significant.

I measure incumbent vulnerability in two ways. First, I include the standard measure of vulnerability: *lagged vote* is the incumbent party's share of the two-party vote in his or her most recent election. In those cases where the incumbent is running for reelection, *lagged vote* represents a direct measure of the incumbent's electoral strength and likelihood of winning. In the cases where the incumbent has retired or otherwise moved on and the seat is open, it is a more indirect measure of the partisan legacy the incumbent leaves behind in the state. Second, I include variables which indicate the number of candidates running in each primary election. *Inc-party candidates* captures the number running in the incumbent party primary, and *out-party candidates* captures the number running in the challenger party primary. In using these variables, I follow Lazarus (2005), who used similar variables to capture the endogeneity of incumbent vulnerability in House elections, and found that when estimations of general election vote share controlled for incumbent vulnerability in this way, the independent effect of primary election vote share disappeared. If the divisive primary effect is endogenous to incumbent vulnerability in the present study as it is in House elections, then when the *candidate* variables are included in the model, the *inc-party vote* and *out-party vote* will not be significant.

The models also include a set of control variables which account for other factors which influence general election results. Foremost among these is *incumbent running*, a dummy variable coded 1 if the incumbent is seeking reelection and 0 if the incumbent is not. *Incumbent running* should be positive and significant in all models, reflecting the advantages incumbents enjoy when seeking reelection. *Presidential vote* is the share of the two-party popular vote won by the presidential candidate of the incumbent's party in the state, and is included to capture the general partisan leaning of the state. *Presidential vote* should be positive and significant in the models, reflecting the fact that Republican candidates do better in Republican-leaning states, and Democrats do better in Democratic-leaning states. Next, I include *incumbent party spending* and *challenger party spending*, both operationalized as the logged number of dollars the respective candidate spent on the election. In gubernatorial elections, Partin (2002) finds that the relationship between spending and general election outcomes is straightforward: candidates get more votes when they spend more money. But Jacobson (1987) shows that this is not the case in congressional elections. Here, incumbents predominantly spend money to win reelection only if they are forced to by facing a strong challenger. This results in a couple of counterintuitive empirical results: that incumbents' vote shares correlate more strongly with challenger spending levels than with incumbent spending levels, and that incumbents' vote shares are negatively correlated with how much the incumbent spends on reelection. Finally, *Democratic incumbent* is a dummy variable coded 1 if the incumbent is a Democrat, and 0 otherwise.[3]

Empirical Results: Senate

Results for the Senate are presented in Table 10.1. Model 1 contains just the divisiveness variables, without the controls for the number of candidates in the primary election. In this model, *inc-party vote* is positive and significant, as predicted by the divisive primary hypothesis. According to the model, every additional percentage point of the vote the incumbent party nominee receives in the primary is associated with an additional .06 percentage point received in the general election. Thus, a nominee who wins a primary election with 65 percent of the vote receives, on average, 0.6 percent more of the vote in the general election than one who wins a primary with 55 percent. The standard deviation on *inc-party vote* is 19.1. We can use this to compare an incumbent party nominee who is one standard deviation above the mean in their primary vote share to a nominee who is one standard deviation below the mean. The nominee coming out of the less divisive primary wins, on average, 2.3 percentage points higher vote share in the general election than the nominee coming out of the more divisive primary. Measured this way, the effect is small but potentially enough to affect a close election. It is about on par with the size of the effect of divisiveness found in previous studies of Senate elections.

By contrast, *out-party vote* is not significant. According to this model, then, challenger party divisiveness does not appear to influence general election results. Nonetheless, it is worth noting

Table 10.1 Effect of Divisive Primary Elections in Senate Races

	Model 1	Model 2
Inc-party vote	.061*	.114***
	(.306)	(.037)
Inc-party candidates	—	.980**
		(.362)
Out-party vote	−.050	−.098***
	(.023)	(.031)
Out-party candidates	—	−.878**
		(.338)
Lagged vote	.092*	.100*
	(.047)	(.047)
Democratic incumbent	−.616	.118
	(1.09)	(1.11)
Incumbent running	4.74***	5.19***
	(1.41)	(1.40)
Presidential vote	.092	.064
	(.301)	(.296)
Incumbent party spending	.185	.161
(logged)	(.427)	(.422)
Challenger party spending	−1.81***	−1.74***
(logged)	(.180)	(.179)
Constant	66.0***	65.2***
	(17.5)	(17.6)
N	270	270
Adjusted *R*-squared	.398	.416

Note: $^*p < .05$; $^{**}p < .01$; $^{***}p < .001$, one-tailed tests.

that this model does include one control for incumbent vulnerability in *lagged vote* and still the initial results indicate that divisiveness has at least some effect on Senate elections.

Model 2 includes the controls for the number of candidates running in the primary election. Once again, these variables account for how attractive the incumbent (if running) is to run against. If the divisiveness effect is endogenous, then these variables will be significantly related to incumbents' general election vote share, while *inc-party vote* and *out-party vote* will not be. However, results indicate that this is not the case – here, all four variables related to the primary election are significant. First, both *inc-party candidates* and *out-party candidates* are significantly related to the dependent variable. Second, not only is *inc-party vote* significant as in Model 1, but its coefficient has almost doubled in size. Finally, the coefficient on *out-party vote* has also doubled in size, and this variable is now significant as well. Thus it appears that in Senate elections, controlling for the number of candidates in the primary election reveals an even stronger divisiveness effect than is indicated by not controlling for them.

In Model 2 the coefficient on *inc-party vote* indicates that, controlling for the number of primary candidates, every additional point of vote the incumbent party nominee wins in the primary is associated with .114 percentage points in the general election. Here, the same two hypothetical incumbent party nominees discussed above – one a standard deviation below and the other a standard deviation above the mean on *inc-party vote* – are now separated by 4.4 percentage points in their general election vote share. Additionally, the coefficient on *out-party vote* is negative, as the divisive primary hypothesis predicts: the incumbent party nominee should do worse – and correspondingly, the challenger party nominee do better – in the general election, as the challenger party nominee gets more votes in the primary. The coefficient reveals that for every additional point the challenger party nominee gets in the primary, the incumbent party nominee gets .098 points less in the general. The standard deviation on *out-party vote share* is 23.1. Now we take our two hypothetical incumbent party nominees from above and this time vary *out-party vote* – in other words, vary how divisive the challenger party primary is – by one standard deviation above and below the mean on *challenger vote share*. Now our two hypothetical nominees are separated by 4.5 percentage points in the general election.

Note that the effects of *inc-party vote* and *out-party vote* are not mutually exclusive – the divisiveness of the two parties' primary election contests vary independently of one another. Taken together, the two effects can be quite sizeable. Once again let's envision two hypothetical incumbent party nominees. One – we'll call her Lucky – won a primary with a vote share one standard deviation above the mean for her party, and is also facing a challenger who won a primary with a vote share one standard deviation below the mean for the challenger's party. In other words, Lucky's primary was not divisive, but her general election opponent's was. The second incumbent party nominee – Unlucky – has the opposite circumstance. Unlucky won a primary with a vote share one standard deviation below the mean, and is facing a challenger party nominee who won a primary with a vote share one standard deviation above the mean. So Unlucky's primary was divisive, while her opponent's was not. To calculate the effect of primary divisiveness on Lucky's and Unlucky's general election performance, we simply add the two effects – 4.4 percentage points for *inc-party vote* and 4.5 points for *out-party vote*. Thus Lucky will do 8.9 percentage points better in the general election, on average, than Unlucky, just as a result of divisive primary elections. That is a very large effect, larger even than estimations of the effect of incumbency (including the crude one estimated here – the coefficient on *incumbent running* in Model 2 indicates that incumbents only outperform same-party non-incumbents by 5.19 percentage points). The effect of primary election divisiveness, then, has the potential to be huge.

With these results as our guide, we can point to a number of elections where a divisive primary played a key role in preventing a party nominee from winning a Senate race. For example, in 1998 an open Kentucky Senate seat was being contested by House members Scotty Baesler and Jim Bunning. Baesler, the Democrat, ran in a bruising primary election contested by six candidates. He won 34 percent of the vote, only five points better than the second-place finisher. By contrast, Bunning sailed through his primary – he had just one opponent, and easily won by a count of 74 to 26. The general election was a tight contest throughout, but Bunning ultimately prevailed, winning 50.3 percent to Baesler's 49.7 percent. Like Tommy Thompson's Wisconsin Senate bid discussed above, Baesler's primary contest left him with virtually no funds to contest the general election; this cost him momentum heading into the contest and likely votes in November (Foerstel 1998). A similar story can be told about Senator Slade Gorton's (R-WA) 2000 unseating by Maria Cantwell. Gorton barely survived an eight-way primary, while Cantwell easily dispatched her two primary opponents. Gorton lost the contest by only 2,200 votes, or 0.09 percent. Mark Kirk (R-IL) at least in part owed his narrow 2010 win to the fact that his Democratic opponent, Alexi Giannoulias, had run in a five-way primary on which he spent $2.2 million and still only won by five percentage points; Kirk won his primary by 37 points. Just in 2010, divisive primaries on the Democratic side likely helped Republicans win Senate seats in Indiana, Massachusetts, and Pennsylvania.

Turning to the candidate variables themselves, both are significant but in the opposite direction from what we might expect. The coefficient on *inc-party candidates* is positive, meaning that for each additional candidate running in the incumbent party primary election the incumbent party nominee receives .98 percentage points *more* in the general election. Correspondingly, the coefficient on *out-party candidates* is negative, meaning that for each additional candidate running on the challenger side the incumbent loses .878 percent of the vote. This cuts against the effect of the vote share variables somewhat, as the number of candidates running in a primary is, itself, a measure of the level of competition in the primary. But here the effect is opposite to what the divisive primary thesis predicts: measured this way, competition in the primary election is associated with a party nominee doing better in the general election, not worse.

The apparent contradiction between the two sets of variables is likely explained by how they interact with one another in real-life scenarios. Once again, consider two hypothetical incumbent party nominees, both of whom won 52 percent of the vote in their primary elections. But this time, imagine that one of them had just a single primary opponent, and the other had six. A 52 percent vote share in an election against a single opponent is a weaker showing, and is a symptom of much greater overall electoral vulnerability, than a 52 percent showing in an election with six opponents. This is likely why *inc-party candidates* is negative: the more opponents you have in an election the more impressive a given vote share is. And this electoral strength likely carries over into the general election. A similar, corresponding effect may also be going on among challenger party candidates to create the negative coefficient on *out-party candidates*.[4] However, there might also be a second, distinct causal mechanism at work here. It might be that, as per the discussion in the literature review above, weak incumbents draw more challenger party candidates into the race, and subsequently, the weak incumbent does poorly in the general election.[5]

Empirical Results: Governor

Results for gubernatorial races are presented in Table 10.2. Consistent with prior analyses of divisive primary effects in gubernatorial races, the evidence points to a much weaker effect here than in Senate races. Models 1 and 2 in this analysis correspond to the same models in the Senate analysis. For governors, Model 1 provides no evidence that primary election vote share on either side influences the general election vote share: neither *inc-party vote* nor *out-party vote* is significantly related to the dependent variable.

Table 10.2 Effect of Divisive Primary Elections in Gubernatorial Races

	Model 1	*Model 2*
Inc-party vote	.015	072*
	(.028)	(.037)
Inc-party candidates		1.07**
	—	(.439)
Out-party vote	.028	.003
	(.023)	(.034)
Out-party candidates		−.422
	—	(.421)
Lagged vote	−.008	−.0002
	(.055)	(.055)
Democratic Incumbent	−2.08*	−1.80
	(1.15)	(1.15)
Incumbent Running	7.48***	7.56***
	(1.30)	(1.29)
Presidential Vote	−.207	−.218
	(.297)	(.294)
Incumbent spending (logged)	.922***	.892***
	(.280)	(.278)
Challenger spending (logged)	−1.28***	−1.23***
	(.250)	(.248)
Constant	63.4***	58.95***
	(15.5)	(15.8)
N	227	227
Adjusted *R*-squared	.323	.336

Note: $^*p < .05$; $^{**}p < .01$; $^{***}p < .001$, one-tailed tests.

Model 2, which controls for the number of candidates running in each primary election, tells a somewhat different story. Here, *inc-party vote* is positive and significant as predicted by the divisive primary hypothesis. However, *out-party vote* is still not significant. Even after controlling for the number of candidates in the primary election, then, only incumbent party divisiveness appears to be significantly related to general election vote outcomes. The coefficient is smaller here – .072, compared to .114 in Model 2 for Senate races – indicating that the size of the effect is smaller as well. For each additional percent of the vote the incumbent party nominee wins in the primary election, his or her vote share goes up by .072 percentage points. Hypothetical gubernatorial incumbent party nominees who won primary elections with vote shares one standard deviation above and below the mean, respectively, should be separated by 3.1 percentage points in the general election. This is not a trivial amount, but it falls far short of the 8.9 percentage points in general election vote share that divisiveness is potentially responsible for in Senate elections.

Model 2 also reveals that *inc-party candidates* is positive and significant in much the same way as it is in Model 2 looking at the Senate above: each additional candidate the incumbent party nominee defeats in the primary election is associated with just over a percentage point of share in the general. Once again this indicates that, holding primary election vote share constant, a victory over a large number of primary election candidates reveals a stronger electoral position than a victory over a small number of candidates. *Out-party candidates* is not significantly related to the dependent variable.[6]

Conclusion

This chapter's primary empirical contribution is to confirm that the divisive primary effect in Senate, and to a lesser extent gubernatorial, elections is not endogenous. Prior studies establish that the effect is endogenous in U.S. House races. In elections to that office, observed correlations between primary and general election outcomes are not causal, but are themselves both a result of how electorally strong or weak the incumbent is (Born 1981; Kenney 1988; Lazarus 2005). Indirect evidence also suggests that the same phenomenon exists in gubernatorial (Partin 2002) and state legislative (Hogan 2003) elections. To assess whether this is the case, I followed Kenney (1988) and especially Lazarus (2005) in directly controlling for incumbent vulnerability, and also the number of candidates running in the primary election (as an on-the-ground measure of how vulnerable the incumbent is), when testing for a divisive primary effect. In both Senate and gubernatorial races, the divisive primary effect is robust to those controls. Indeed, controlling for the number of candidates in each race increases the effect in both cases. Thus for both offices the evidence indicates that primary election divisiveness is not endogenous.

The empirical analysis presented here also confirms some prior findings regarding divisive primary elections. As with previous studies, I find that divisive primaries have a substantively larger effect on general election outcomes in Senate races than in gubernatorial races. However, the size of the effect found here is substantively larger than that found by Abramowitz (1988) and Kenney and Rice (1984). It is possible that, the prior studies being 30 years old as of this writing, the divisive primary effect has grown over time. Or, it is possible that controlling for the number of candidates in the primary election reveals that divisiveness is more harmful than was previously appreciated. Either way the results presented here suggest that in Senate elections, divisiveness has a consistent and potentially very large negative effect on vote shares for party nominees. A second and related difference between the two offices is that in Senate elections, both incumbent party and challenger party divisiveness influence general election outcomes, whereas only incumbent party divisiveness influences gubernatorial general elections.

One issue that future studies should address is the state of primary election divisiveness in gubernatorial elections. With conflicting findings from a number of different studies it is difficult to state conclusively whether or not divisive primaries hurt gubernatorial candidates. Perhaps they do so only under some as-yet-unspecified condition, which is represented in some studies' data more than it is in others. This is one area where there is still a gap in our knowledge.

Another pressing question raised by this study and the literature as a whole, is why there is such a stark difference between offices. In other words, why does primary election divisiveness have such a strong influence on Presidential and Senate elections, a small and inconsistent one on gubernatorial elections, and none at all on House and state legislative elections? One possible explanation is the extreme difference in salience between the different types of elections. Presidential elections capture the attention and interests of voters much more consistently and thoroughly than any other type of election, and the next-most salient types of elections after that are Senate and gubernatorial elections. It could be that voters' attention during primary elections is a necessary condition for the primary to influence general election outcomes. This makes some sense on the surface: in down-ballot races, a majority of general election voters simply don't pay attention to who is running in the primary election, and may not even know when it took place or that it took place at all. When this is the case, there's no reason to expect the primary election to influence voters' general election vote choices. More work is needed to establish the cause of the variation in when primary election divisiveness is harmful, whether it's this cause or something different.

Notes

1 Wichowsky and Niebler (2010) find that in the 2008 general elections Obama actually did better in areas where Clinton was most competitive in the previous primary election, contrary to the predictions of the divisive primary hypothesis. However, this study measures divisiveness in a non-standard fashion – by measuring Obama's and Clinton's ad-buys in various media markets.

2 Empirical results are virtually identical if I operationalize divisiveness by observing the margin by which the party nominee won the primary election. Indeed, the two variables – primary election vote share and primary election vote margin – correlate at .97 on the incumbent's side, and .96 on the challenger's side.

3 The results presented in this section are robust to a number of alternative specifications and modeling choices. Limiting the analysis to only races in which the incumbent ran does not substantively alter results, nor does including the interaction of *incumbent running* and *lagged vote.*

4 In fact, when I re-run model 2 without the primary vote variables, neither candidate variable is significant.

5 I also ran a model similar to Model 2, but one which included *logged inc-party candidates* and *logged out-party candidates*. Both variables have severe skews, with a disproportionate number of races having a low number of candidates but a small number having 10 or more. Logging the skewed variable gives it a more normal distribution, and ensures that a small number of outlying observations are not responsible for the observed relationship. However, the results of this lin-log model are substantively similar to those of Model 2. In fact, the effects of primary election divisiveness appear to be stronger in this analysis: the coefficient on *inc-primary vote* and *chal-primary vote* are both larger in the lin-log model than in Model 2.

6 I ran the same lin-log model for governors as I did for Senators. In this case though, there is one significant difference between Model 2 and the lin-log model: *out-party candidates* is significant. Thus accounting for the variable's skewed distribution reveals a relationship with the dependent variable. The coefficient on *out-party candidates* is negative, indicating that the more challenger party candidates there are in the primary, the worse the incumbent does in the general election. Once again, this controls for *out-party vote*, so this may demonstrate that if a challenger party nominee defeats a large number of challengers in a primary, this demonstrates electoral strength. Or it might be that, as per the discussion in the literature review above, weak incumbents draw more challenger-party candidates into the race, and subsequently, the weak incumbent does poorly in the general election.

References

Abramowitz, Alan I. 1988. "Explaining Senate Election Outcomes." *The American Political Science Review* 82(2): 385–403.

Atkeson, Lonna Rae. 1998. "Divisive Primaries and General Election Outcomes: Another Look at Presidential Campaigns." *American Journal of Political Science* 42(2): 256–271.

Bauer, Scott. 2017. "Wisconsin Republicans Worry about Crowded Senate Primary." *Madison Times.* May 9. https://www.realclearpolitics.com/articles/2017/05/08/wisconsin_republicans_worry_about_crowded_senate_primary_133817.html

Bernstein, Robert A. 1977. "Divisive Primaries Do Hurt: U.S. Senate Races, 1956–1972." *The American Political Science Review* 71(3): 540–545.

Black, Gordon S. 1972. "A Theory of Political Ambition: Career Choices and the Role of Structural Incentives." *American Political Science Review* 66(1): 144–155.

Born, Richard. 1981. "The Influence of House Primary Election Divisiveness on General Election Margins, 1962–76." *Journal of Politics* 43(3): 641–661.

Buell, Emmet H. 1086. "Divisive Primaries and Participation in Fall Presidential Campaigns: A Study of 1984 New Hampshire Primary Activists." *American Politics Quarterly* 14(2): 376–390.

Foerstel, Karen. 1998. "Senate Hopefuls' Trial By Fire." *CNN All Politics*, July 11. http://www.cnn.com/ALLPOLITICS/1998/07/14/cq/senate.html.

Gurian, Paul-Henri, Nathan Burroughs, Lonna Rae Atkeson, Damon Cann, and Audrey A. Haynes. 2016. "National Party Division and Divisive State Primaries in U.S. Presidential Elections, 1948–2012." *Political Behavior* 38(3): 689–711.

Hacker, Andrew. 1965. "Does A 'Divisive' Primary Harm a Candidate's Election Chances?" *The American Political Science Review* 59(1): 105–110.

Herrnson, Paul. 2000. *Congressional Elections*, Third Edition. Washington, D.C.: Congressional Quarterly Press.

Hogan, Robert E. 2003. "The Effects of Primary Divisiveness on General Election Outcomes in State Legislative Elections." *American Politics Research* 31(1): 27–47.

Jacobson, Gary C. 1987. "Running Scared: Elections and Congressional Politics in the 1980's." In *Congress: Structure and Policy*, eds. Mathew McCubbins and Terry Sullivan. New York: Cambridge University Press, pp. 39–90.

Jacobson, Gary C. and Samuel Kernell. 1981. *Strategy and Choice in Congressional Elections*. New Haven: Yale University Press

Kenney, Patrick J. 1988. "Sorting Out the Effects of Primary Divisiveness in Congressional and Senatorial Elections." *Western Political Quarterly* 40(3): 765–777.

Kenney, Patrick J. and Tom W. Rice. 1984. "The Effect of Primary Divisiveness in Gubernatorial and Senatorial Elections." *Journal of Politics* 46(4): 904–915.

Kenney, Patrick J. and Tom W. Rice. 1987. "The Relationship Between Divisive Primaries and General Election Outcomes." *American Journal of Political Science* 31(1): 31–44

Key, V.O. 1953. *Politics, Parties and Pressure Groups*. New York: Thomas Y. Crowell.

Lazarus, Jeffrey. 2005. "Unintended Consequences: Anticipation of General Election Outcomes and Primary Election Divisiveness." *Legislative Studies Quarterly* 30(2): 435–461.

Lazarus, Jeffrey. 2008. "Buying in: Testing the Rational Model of Candidate Entry." *Journal of Politics* 70(4): 837–850.

Lengle, James I., Diana Owen, and Molly W. Sonner 1995. "Divisive Nominating Mechanisms and Democratic Party Electoral Prospects." *Journal of Politics* 57(2): 370–383.

Partin, Randall W. 2002. "Assessing the Impact of Campaign Spending in Governors' Races." *Political Research Quarterly* 55(2): 215–233.

Pierson, James E., and Terry B. Smith. 1975. "Primary Divisiveness and General Election Success: A Re-examination." *Journal of Politics* 37(3): 555–562.

Segura, Gary M., and Stephen P. Nicholson. 1995. "Sequential Choices and Partisan Transitions in U.S. Senate Delegations: 1972–1988." *Journal of Politics* 57(1): 86–100.

Shorman, Jonathan, and Bryan Lowry. 2017. "Democratic Primary Battle for Governor More Likely as Ward Opens Door to Run." *Wichita Eagle*. http://www.kansas.com/news/politics-government/article146024544.html

Simon, Roger. 1990. "How a Murderer and Rapist Became the Bush Campaign's Most Valuable Player." *The Baltimore Sun*. November 11. http://articles.baltimoresun.com/1990-11-11/features/1990315149_1_willie-horton-fournier-michael-dukakis

Southwell, Priscilla L. 1986. "The Politics of Disgruntlement: Nonvoting and Defection among Supporters of Nomination Losers, 1968–1984." *Political Behavior* 8(1): 81–95.

Southwell, Priscilla L. 2010. "The Effect of Nomination Divisiveness on the 2008 Presidential Election. *PS: Political Science and Politics* 43(2): 255–258.

Squire, Peverill. 1989. "Challengers in U.S. Senate Elections." *Legislative Studies Quarterly* 14: 531–545.

Stone, Walter J. 1984. "Prenomination Candidate Choice and General Election Behavior: Iowa Presidential Activists in 1980." *American Journal of Political Science* 32(2): 361–378.

Stone, Walter J. 1986. "The Carryover Effect in Presidential Elections." *The American Political Science Review* 80(2): 271–280.

Stone, Walter J., Lonna Rae Atkeson, and Ronald B. Rappaport. 1992. "Turning on or Turning Off? Mobilization and Demobilization Effects of Participation in Presidential Nomination Campaigns." *American Journal of Political Science* 36(3): 665–691.

Sullivan, Sean, and Aaron Blake. 2012. "Tommy Thompson wins Wisconsin's Republican Senate Primary." *Washington Post*. August 15. https://www.washingtonpost.com/politics/2012/08/14/3edf9322-e680-11e1-936a-b801f1abab19_story.html?utm_term=.8a0f87649436

Walker, Jesse. 2016. "CNN Poll: 13% of Sanders Supporters are Backing Jill Stein, 10% Want Gary Johnson." *Reason.com*. August 2. http://reason.com/blog/2016/08/02/cnn-poll-13-of-sanders-supporters-are-ba.

Wichowsky, Amber, and Sarah E. Niebler. 2010. "Narrow Victories and Hard Games: Revisiting the Primary Divisiveness Hypothesis." *American Politics Research* 38(4): 1052–1071.

11

IS THERE A LINK BETWEEN PRIMARY COMPETITION AND GENERAL ELECTION RESULTS?

Robert G. Boatright and Vincent G. Moscardelli

In recent years, discussion of primary elections, and in particular congressional primary elections, has frequently focused upon the potential for ideologically extreme factions within the parties to influence the selection of nominees. In particular, analyses of the 2010, 2012, and 2014 elections have alleged that the Republican backlash against President Obama's agenda was felt both in general election opposition to Democrats and in efforts to "primary" Republicans who had supported various aspects of this agenda. There is, then, the possibility that general election surges might be accompanied by increased unrest in the primaries as well, but there is no established theory of patterns in congressional primary election competition over time. Our understanding of congressional general election competition has for decades been shaped by theories regarding partisan seat swing. Indeed, one could argue that the decisions of candidates and party leaders themselves rest on a small set of regular patterns – presidential coattails, midterm backlashes against the incumbent president, "waves" of party support, and so forth. In this chapter we explore the relationship between such general election voting patterns and competition in congressional primaries.

At first glance, it would seem that congressional primary competition should be immune to such patterns. After all, there are no partisan cues within primary elections, and there is little evidence that attitudes about the president or about party performance in Congress should have an obvious influence on primaries. Literature on congressional primaries has thus emphasized factors such as regional differences between the parties, voter eligibility rules for primaries, or other factors that may change over time but have no obvious relationship to individual election years. Some studies have focused upon the role of primary voting or ballot access rules in structuring outcomes (for citations see below), while others have explored changes in the organizational strength of political parties across regions and over time.

Boatright (2013, 89–91), however, has documented the declining differences between regions of the country and party organizational strength in one type of primary – intraparty challenges to incumbents. Boatright contends that if ever parties had the ability to structure primary competition, they have lost that ability over the past forty years. He notes, however, that challenges to incumbents appear to be more common in years where there is a partisan surge. That is, Democratic incumbents were more likely to face challenges from the left in good Democratic years such as 1974 and 2006, and Republican incumbents were more likely to face challenges from the right in good Republican years such as 1994 and 2010. We can add to this observation the common sense expectation, drawn from literature on candidate emergence, that challenger primaries (that is, primaries whose nominee expects to face a sitting incumbent in the general election) and open seat primaries should be more crowded in a party that expects to pick up seats in a given election year. There may be some cases where parties recruit strong candidates and/or take steps to stave off primary competition, but such efforts still seem unlikely to deter all interested candidates.[1] In short, we can develop an argument about partisan tides that speaks to competition in all different types of primaries.

We thus know more about the relationship between primaries and partisan tides than might seem apparent at first. In this chapter we seek to systematize these findings to develop a theory of patterns in primary competition across time. We conclude that challenger primary competition is highly sensitive to the expected competitiveness of the general election; open seat primary competition is somewhat less so, on account of the idiosyncratic nature of which seats are open in which years; and incumbent primaries are more competitive within the party that expects to gain seats. While some of these results are intuitive, the incumbent primary results are not at first glance intuitive. When put together, this set of observations provides a clear linkage between primary and general election competition that has thus far been lacking in the literature on congressional elections.

The Insulation of Primaries from National Trends

It has been slightly over a century since the introduction of primary elections in the United States. Not all states have consistently required parties to use primary elections to choose nominees over this time, and in the states which have used primaries the rules governing candidate and voter eligibility in the primaries have varied substantially. These variations make comparing primary elections across time difficult; it is not always clear that individual variables applied to one primary are necessarily comparable to what might appear to be similar variables for another primary. Political scientists have solved this problem in three different ways.

The Decline of Competitiveness: First, Ansolabehere, Hansen, Hirano, and Snyder (2006, 2007, 2010; hereafter Ansolabehere et al.) have sought to explain the decline in competition in primary elections from the 1930s to the 1970s. These articles show that competition in congressional elections was quite common in the 1920s but declined steadily thereafter, reaching a stable and low level by the 1980s. Variations in state primary rules are endogenous to the Ansolabehere et al. studies – if states change their primary laws in order to reduce competition, the precise nature of the rules is less consequential for their argument than is the outcome of the rule changes. In addition, the lengthy time period under consideration in these articles takes precedence over short-term variation. If primary competition is more common, for instance, in a high turnover year such as 1992, this increase may look impressive in relationship to competition levels in 1988 or 1990, but relatively insignificant in comparison to the level of competition in the 1930s. Overall, however, the explanation Ansolabehere et al. provide for declining competitiveness suggests that this decline had little to do with overall changes in *general* election competitiveness. General elections, too, became less competitive over this period, but at a different rate and for different reasons. The Ansolabehere et al. findings also suggest that any analysis of a connection between primary and general election competition must either account for an overall decline in competition or be limited to the past three to four decades.

Primary Rules: A major area of inquiry which precedes Ansolabehere et al.'s work is the study of the effects of different types of primary rules. Primary elections have generally been classified into types based on citizens' eligibility for voting. In a closed primary, only previously registered members of a party are eligible to vote. In an open primary, a voter can choose to vote in either party's primary upon arriving at the polls. More "open" variants, such as the blanket, jungle, or top-two primaries allow voters to choose candidates of either party on the same ballot (though not for the same office). Variations on open and closed primaries also exist. Most studies of primary rules (Burden 2001; Gerber and Morton 1998; Kanthak and Morton 2001; Telford 1965) have sought to assess the degree of moderation of eventual nominees; evidence is mixed as to whether primary rules have any effect at all. One important factor that interacts with primary type, however, is the date of the primary: if candidates adopt positions in order to win the primary, they may shift their positions once they have won the nomination, but their ability to do so will be affected by how much time they have between the primary and the general election (Galderisi and Ezra 2001).

The adoption of a particular primary type, or a change in primary type, may be driven by partisan considerations and may be aimed at insulating the dominant party from partisan waves (see Boatright 2014a). It is thus not entirely exogenous to the state of national politics. Because primary rules are "sticky," however, it is arguably possible to separate open and closed primary states for analysis and to avoid here a detailed consideration of the timing of the adoption of primary voting rule changes.

Primary Divisiveness: A third approach to sorting out the relationship between primary and general election competition is to look at whether competitive primaries help or hurt nominees. Studies of the divisiveness of congressional primaries have had mixed results – Hacker (1965) argued that they have no effect on general election outcomes; in a study of Senate primaries, Bernstein (1977) argued that they hurt the stronger party but not the weaker party; and in their study of Senate and gubernatorial races, Kenney and Rice (1984) found that the impact of divisiveness varies by party and office, and that these differential effects are conditioned by the degree of primary divisiveness experienced by the other party in that same election (see also Kenney and Rice 1987). A 1975 study of House races by Piereson and Smith found that divisive primaries hurt in competitive districts but not in uncompetitive ones.[2] Alvarez, Canon, and Sellers (1995) find that general election challengers benefit from competitive primaries while incumbents' general election fortunes are harmed by competitive primaries; these effects are magnified when primary dates are close to the general election. Ware (1979), finally, questions the methodology behind such studies, arguing that close races are not ipso facto more competitive than lopsided ones. More recent studies of divisiveness have also criticized the methodology of these earlier studies. Jeffrey Lazarus (2005) summarizes the preponderant theme of the early literature – divisive primaries help challengers and hurt incumbents (or help "outsider candidates" and harm "insider candidates") in the general election – and then argues that this literature has matters backwards. Lazarus argues that more candidates will get into a race when their chance of winning the seat is higher, so the appropriate thing to look at is the number of candidates running, not necessarily the closeness of the race. The more candidates there are in a primary, and the more money is spent in the primary, the better the party does in the general election – not because multiple candidates have run or spent money, but because the emergence of multiple candidates and the high level of spending are a consequence of the likelihood that the primary nominee will win the general election. The effects here are stronger for the out party, or nonincumbent party, than for the incumbent party. Another recent study, by Johnson, Petersheim, and Wasson (2010) generally corroborates Lazarus's results but measures the effects of the primary date on general election outcomes; the authors contend that competitive late primaries yield better general election results for out parties. The excitement generated by nonincumbent primaries, in this accounting, dissipates quickly but can have an effect on general elections if the primary and general elections are close enough.

The literature on the link between primary and general election competition has proceeded largely on the individual level, whereas this chapter explores competition at the national level, or at least at the level of aggregations of races rather than at the individual level. Yet the literature reviewed here suggests first of all that there is a plausible reason for there to be a relationship, and second, that parties or candidates might act to encourage or discourage competition based on their expectations of what will happen in the general election. Individual-level analyses, however, tend to posit a relationship in a forward-looking manner, exploring the effects of primary divisiveness on candidates' and parties' fortunes come November.

In the case of the Ansolabehere et al. work, primary competitiveness is observed but explained in a long-term, institutional manner – why did primaries become less competitive across decades? In the other two types of literature, primaries serve as independent variables – what sorts of nominees are produced by different primary types, or what sorts of general election results are the consequences of a particular level of primary competition? As Lazarus (2005) has pointed out, primary competition may well be a function of the expected outcome rather than the cause of the actual outcome, and hence we should look at the factors that create competition. We diverge from Lazarus here, however, in seeking to analyze the effects of the larger political environment rather than the individual general election race, and we diverge from Ansolabehere et al.'s approach in looking more directly at the context of particular elections rather than seeking to identify secular trends that stand above such elections. All of these studies suggest that there are reasons that candidates or parties might have taken steps to insulate primaries from national fluctuations in partisan support, but that such a relationship might still be expected to exist absent deliberate efforts to counteract it.

The Connection between Primaries and Partisan Waves

From the inception of primary elections, political elites have had many expectations about how primaries might change American electoral politics. One of the early objections to primary elections was that they stripped political parties of their traditional balancing function. Such balancing was generally seen as a matter of ensuring that different geographic constituencies had representation, or that officers alternated among different constituency groups (Hormell 1923). There is nothing inherently democratic about ticket balancing, and, as Ware (2002) suggests, this may have been an activity that often brought grief to party leaders. For some progressives, balancing was a means of satisfying ethnic blocs at the expense of quality candidates – while in today's politics (in the United States and elsewhere) balancing a ticket to ensure representation by women or by minority racial groups is often a goal for liberals (Reynolds 2006, 187). There is also, however, a diminution of ideological conflict entailed in balancing. Primary elections can be sensitive to ideological unrest among voters – even in instances where the candidates do not win, the presence of candidates with a particular viewpoint may be a sign of turmoil in the electorate. Absent the ability to placate such groups, parties have no choice but to watch such conflict play out in the electorate.

In addition, many Progressive reformers worried that, given a potentially uninformed electorate, newspapers would play a dominant role in determining the winners of primary elections (Norris 1923; Boots 1922; Fanning 1905, 53; West 1923). The main concern here was that the media would have different priorities from political parties – most notably that newspapers, and, later, other media, would seek to emphasize differences among candidates, or to amplify critiques of governmental policy. While it is by no means clear that the media have done this consistently, this concern did presage the media-driven, candidate-centered campaigns that were to come.

These sorts of concerns indicated that from the beginning some saw the potential for primary elections to be influenced by national events. The party system, however, was not sufficiently nationalized for this to be the case. That is, most of the more systematic primary challenges (by which we mean, primary challenges that were not based solely on characteristics of individual candidates or officeholders) were decidedly regional in nature, as shown by unusual primary laws or results in states such as California, Minnesota, and North Dakota. In such instances, qualitative researchers have drawn a clear link between economic disarray and primary competition (see e.g. Morlan 1955). In each of these cases, however, the dominant party in the state (in these examples, the Republicans) was diverse enough that an intraparty challenge made more sense than a challenge from the opposition (Democratic) Party. By the late twentieth century, however, more states had competition between the two parties and the two major parties had become more ideologically consistent. Primary competition was not necessarily a substitute for general election competition; instead, primary competition could be linked to expectations about the general election in ways that it could not in the earlier years of the twentieth century. And yet, as we have seen most recently with the Tea Party, ideological factions that see themselves in opposition to the parties themselves still appear. Is there a way to discuss the appearance of these sorts of factions, not in terms of their consequences for the general election, but, following Lazarus, as consequences themselves of the dynamics of general election competition?

To assess the relevance of national levels of competition to primary competition, we turn to a consideration of the salient features of the literature on party surge and decline. Alan Abramowitz points out that

> a House election is more than a collection of 435 local contests. . . . No matter how personally popular an incumbent may be, his or her fate depends in part on which way and how strongly the national political tide is running in a given election year.
>
> *1991, 38*

Each election has its own partisan dynamic, and political scientists have developed several theories – some competing, some complementary – to understand these partisan rhythms.

Campbell (1997) identified an enduring presidential "pulse" to congressional elections, in which the party of the winning presidential nominee picks up seats in the House in presidential election years and then loses seats in the subsequent midterm election. In fact, just twice in the past 40 years and just three times since the turn of the twentieth century has the president's party picked up seats in the midterm election.[3] The earliest efforts to understand this relationship emphasized the concept of presidential coattails (Bean 1948), although analysts quickly expanded on this explanation by incorporating variation in turnout between presidential and midterm election years into their theories (see, e.g., Campbell 1960). Implicit in these arguments was the idea that the larger the margin by which a president is elected, the larger the number of fellow partisans swept into Congress, some representing districts that had historically been represented by members of the other party. As such, presidential year successes left the president's party overexposed in subsequent midterm elections, in which they were forced to defend seats that would be held by the opposing party under more "normal" circumstances (Oppenheimer, Stimson, and Waterman 1986). The "exposure thesis" builds on this explanation and sits at the nexus of explanations of party surge and decline that hinge on structural forces and those that treat midterms as referenda on the president's performance. In this account, the president's party's performance in the midterm is driven not only by the extent to which it is exposed in districts in which it has historically struggled, but also the extent to which it is exposed in districts in which vulnerable incumbents have chosen to retire (Gaddie 1997).

Kernell (1977) proposes an alternative causal process in which voters motivated and mobilized by disappointment in the president's performance explain much of the loss of seats experienced by the president's party in midterm elections. Often, this disappointment is operationalized in terms of economic growth and unemployment (Tufte 1975). More recently, Fiorina (1996) has argued that midterm voters who perceive the president's party as having moved too far to the right (in the case of Republicans) or left (in the case of Democrats) use midterm elections as an opportunity to "balance" or offset the presidential advantage by enlarging the ranks of his opponents in Congress. This work builds on Erikson's (1988) argument that the president's party is punished in midterm simply for holding the White House, what he dubbed the "presidential penalty" explanation of electoral decline in midterm elections.

Forecasting models represent another approach to understanding party fortunes in congressional elections. Economic voting models abound (see, e.g., Lewis-Beck and Stegmaier 2000; Campbell 2014). However, while the best models yield predictions of aggregate vote and seat changes that correlate very highly with actual vote and seat changes, the number of missed predictions in any given year is actually quite high, with the number of missed predictions often approaching or surpassing the total number of seats that changed hands in a given election, especially in what might be labeled as "party wave" elections after the fact (Brady, Fiorina, and Wilkins 2011). That said, the most accurate forecasting models regularly explain more than ninety percent of the variance in House election outcomes.

As we discuss below, forecasting models and other theories about partisan surges are less relevant here for their content than for the fact that they suggest the political class has reasonably accurate means of predicting what will happen, and that these beliefs could plausibly shape candidate entry and competitiveness in primaries.

Expectations

In this chapter, we consider the relationship between congressional primary competition, on the one hand, and general election competition between the parties on the other. We are not looking at the effect of the individual primary election on the nominee's general election performance; rather, we are concerned with the relationship between expectations about party advantage in an election year and the appearance of candidates of each party in primary elections. We know from literature on candidate emergence that serious congressional candidates will seek to run in years when they perceive the general election climate to be favorable – that is, when (assuming they win the primary) they will, to take two examples, appear on the same ballot as a popular presidential candidate of their party, or in a midterm year in which the opposition party's president is unpopular. Furthermore, we know from the literature on partisan surges that there are predictable regularities in congressional voting. When a president wins election or reelection, more often than not his party gains seats in Congress. Although there are some exceptions, the greater a presidential candidate's margin of victory, the larger the seat gain for that candidate's party in Congress. Similarly, with only two exceptions over the past forty years, the president's party can expect to lose seats in a midterm election year. Large party swings in midterm election years, such as 1974, 1994, 2006, and 2010, were somewhat predictable well in advance of the general election. Expectations about general election voting can influence candidates' decisions to run for office, thus increasing primary election competition.

Candidate expectations can be difficult to quantify. First, there is certainly variation in the expected degree of turnover in a particular election cycle – we cannot, for instance, simply assume that all midterm elections will be similarly disastrous for the incumbent president's party. Second, a candidate must file for the primary as early as ten months before the general election in some states

(Ansolabehere and Gerber 1996), and candidates who are capable of raising significant amounts of money must often begin preparing for the election much earlier than that. Expectations are, therefore, fallible, subjective, and difficult to quantify. We can, however, use estimates of competitiveness in the general election (at the national level, again to at least proxy for expectations). It may be too much to assume that candidates have perfect foresight about how elections will play at the national level, but it seems safe to say that candidates at least have a sense of which way the wind is blowing.

There are different ways to think about national patterns in elections, however. If we are keeping matters at the national level – that is, considering how prospective primary candidates are thinking about the election's broader context than about the characteristics of the district or the incumbent – we can think about partisanship or generally about the public's dissatisfaction with Congress. Some elections may be characterized by a hostility toward one party, as arguably was the case in 2010, while others may be characterized by a hostility toward incumbents and politicians more broadly, as may have been the case in 1992. It makes sense to look at partisan swing (the seat gain for one party) as well as overall turnover, as measured by the number of defeated incumbents of both parties. The national political context can also be assessed using other ex post measures, such as the number of seats which were decided by less than a ten-point margin.

It is also important to consider the consequences for different kinds of primaries. In this chapter we consider the effects of primary rules (for instance, open or closed primaries, or primaries with or without a pre-primary endorsement by the party), region of the country, party, and district partisanship. What is most consequential in our effort to describe different types of primaries, however, is the differences between open seat primaries, primaries for the nomination to challenge an incumbent (which we shall describe simply as challenger primaries), and primaries featuring an incumbent. The relationship between these races and the national partisan context should differ, and it is based on these differences that we develop our hypotheses here.

Open Seat Primaries occur for a variety of reasons, some of which are directly related to the departing incumbent's assessment of his or her chances in the general election (and, in rare instances, the primary). The number of incumbents who retire increases in election years expected to be difficult for the departing incumbent's party (Hibbing 1982a, b, c), but departures also occur because incumbents wish to seek higher office or simply because incumbents wish to leave politics. The number of open seats is somewhat correlated ($r = .38$) with partisan swing in the next general election – that is, there tend to be more retirements in the party that would go on to lose seats in the general election, although the differences are not as striking as one might expect at first glance. From 1970 to 2010, an average of 21 (20.9) members of the party that went on to lose seats in the general election retired per cycle. The comparable number for members of the party that eventually picked up seats in November was 17 (16.8). But that said, retirements, and the resulting open seats, have been shown to be a major factor in aggregate seat changes in the House (Gaddie 1997). In light of this, we hypothesize here that

- Because at least some retiring incumbents will have done so out of concern about the impending general election, open seat primaries will, on average, be less competitive within the party harmed by the national partisan swing than within the party advantaged by the swing; furthermore,
- Competition in open seat primaries will be higher in years marked by a higher overall level of turnover, irrespective of party.

Challenger primaries are perhaps the clearest case of primary elections whose competitiveness is dependent on the general election context. The more vulnerable incumbents of one party are, the more likely it is that candidates of the other party will line up to challenge them. Hence,

– Challenger primaries in the party expected to gain seats will be more competitive than primaries in the party expected to lose seats.

It is more difficult than in the open seat case to predict the effects of general election turnover without reference to partisanship, however. Since 1970, there have only been five elections (1976, 1988, 1990, 2000, and 2002) out of twenty-three where one party did not win more than seventy percent of the races where incumbents were defeated. These were all election years in which a very small number of seats changed hands at all. There are, then, no election years in recent memory where the defeat of a large number of incumbents was not a rebuke of one party. Hence, we expect that

– Heightened competition in challenger primaries in high turnover years will be limited to the party expected to gain seats in that year.

Finally, we have what might appear at first to be counterintuitive expectations about *incumbent primaries*. We expect competition in incumbent primaries to follow a different logic according to party. For one thing, it is relatively rare for incumbents to face primary opposition at all. Some incumbents certainly face primary opponents for reasons unrelated to the incumbent's partisanship or ideological stance – that is, a percentage of primary challenges will simply be waged by ambitious challengers or by challengers unhappy about nonpolicy matters such as ethical wrongdoing by the incumbent. We have no reason to expect such challenges to cluster in one party or to be more prevalent in particular types of election years.[4]

However, at least some primary challenges to incumbents will be ideological in nature, as signified by Tea Party challenges to sitting Republican incumbents in recent elections. How can we understand the relationship of such races to partisanship? Consider two different scenarios:

First, primary challenges may be indicative of a party's difficulty in holding together a diverse coalition. Following the logic of theoretical models such as Riker's (1982) "minimum winning coalition" model and Alfred Hirschman's (1970) distinction between "exit and voice," some primary challenges may be a product of the same intraparty disagreements that may cause some other party members to flee the party altogether. Hence, incumbent primary challenges may be more common in a party that expects to lose seats in the upcoming election.

Second, however, partisan surges are often related to an overall increase in enthusiasm among those who hold strong ideological views. In 2010, for instance, some Tea Party activists channeled their dissatisfaction into supporting challenges to sitting Democrats, while others channeled their dissatisfaction into supporting challenges to Republicans they deemed insufficiently hostile toward the Democratic Party's agenda. The same might be said about Democratic activists in 1974. Incumbent primary challenges may, according to this logic, be more common in parties expecting to gain seats than in parties expecting to lose seats.

As we shall see below, the two parties differ in the relationship between challenges to incumbents and overall partisan trends. The Democratic Party – arguably the party with the broader and more unwieldy coalition during much of the time period considered here (see Freeman 1986 for a discussion) – follows the first logic more closely, while Republicans follow the second. While our aim here is not necessarily to revise established theories of differences in party culture (as has been done in recent work on party networks), party differences do comprise part of the story.

Merely to find that there is a systematic relationship between primary and general election competition is, we would contend, an overdue contribution to the literature. However, we would argue that it is just as important to argue that there logically *should* be a connection – that if one believes voters' views on the performance of the party in power has anything to do with general election turmoil, one should be sensitive to the effects that those same views have on voters' choices in primaries.

Data and Methodology

In the analyses that follow, we consider all major party elections for the House of Representatives from 1970 through 2012, excluding special election primaries and primaries in which two incumbents faced each other. We have separated open seat primaries, challenger primaries, and incumbent primaries. We begin our analysis in 1970 for two reasons: first, for convenience – as we discuss below, this is the first election for which we have coding for incumbent primaries that distinguishes between ideological and nonideological challenges – and second, because as of 1970 congressional districts were required to be equal in size and primary elections had begun to adopt standardized rules in response to the McGovern Commission's mandates regarding presidential convention delegates.[5]

For all of these races we consider competitiveness in relationship to the eventual general election outcomes – again, not as a determinant of general election outcomes but as a consequence of reasonably correct expectations about the national political context as it would be reflected in the general election results. While the partisan surge and decline literature suggests that there are a variety of complicated predictive variables we might use, for our purposes here we simply assume that the dimensions of the general election results are somewhat known in advance, and that for the sake of simplicity we can simply use the eventual results to reflect elite expectations about party fortunes in any given election. We thus use two general election measures here: the total partisan swing, measured both as a raw number (the absolute value of the change in party representation) and as a positive or negative number for each party; and the total number of defeated incumbents, again in the aggregate and for each party. These two measures capture both the effects of partisan swings and the overall unrest in the electorate.

We measure competitiveness, our dependent variable, differently for the three election types. In the case of open seat and challenger primaries, we follow several recent studies (Canon 1978; Herrnson and Gimpel 1995; Hogan 2003; Brogan and Mendilow 2012) in employing a fractionalization index which is operationalized as

$$ F = 1 - \Sigma \left[\left(C_1\right)^2 + \left(C_2\right)^2 + \left(C_3\right)^2 + \left(C_4\right)^2 \dots \right] $$

where F is the fractionalization index, C_1 is the percentage of the total vote received by the first candidate, C_2 is the percentage of the total vote received by the second candidate, and so on. This yields an index where a one-candidate race has a fractionalization index of zero and a race where two candidates split the vote would have a fractionalization index of 0.5 (or $1 - (0.5^2 + 0.5^2)$). The larger the number of similarly competitive candidates, the closer the index is to 1 – that is, a race with ten candidates who received ten percent of the vote each would have an index of $1 - [(.1)^2 \times 10]$, or 0.9. The intuition behind these indices, in other words, is that an election where one candidate gets most of the votes is not very fractionalized, even if there are multiple candidates; races with two candidates with similar vote share are split, and those with more than two equally competitive candidates are even more divided.

The fractionalization index is adept at capturing differences in competition in races where competition between multiple candidates is the norm. For incumbent primaries, however, we would contend that fractionalization is not necessarily the best indicator of competition. As noted above, the vast majority of incumbents run without serious primary opposition. Thus, following Boatright (2013) we distinguish here between incumbents who run without a serious opponent and incumbents who were held to 75 percent or less of the primary vote. We thus have a binary measure – either incumbents faced a credible challenge or they did not. Because challenges to incumbents are so few, it is also easy to categorize primary challenges as being related to ideology or not. Again, open seat and challenger primary competition is always about the partisanship of the incumbent or departing incumbent – in the challenger party case, all challengers disagree with that incumbent's political views, while in open seat races the candidate of the party that does not hold the seat also disagrees. It is possible and, we would argue, necessary, to separate primary challenges to incumbents that have an ideological or policy component from those that do not.[6] Boatright (2013, 65–72) uses descriptions in the *Almanac of American Politics* and *Politics in America* to identify such races, and we use his measurements here.

We thus have a set of main independent variables having to do with the partisan context of the election, and a set of main dependent variables, having to do with competition in the primary. We supplement this with a number of district-based measures, used to draw finer distinctions in competitiveness. At times we distinguish between districts according to primary rules (open, closed, and so forth), using data drawn from Kanthak and Morton (2001), McGhee, Masket, Shor, and McCarty (2010), and Boatright (2014a). We also discuss partisanship of the districts (as opposed to the partisanship of the candidates) using current or most recent party presidential vote share in the district. Finally, we take into account the distinctive history of Democratic Party primaries in the one-party South and the changes in Democratic Party strength in the South since the 1960s, and we discuss differences by region, distinguishing southern[7] from nonsouthern states. While these various factors do not appear in our hypotheses themselves, their inclusion accounts for a variety of potential alternate accounts of changes in primary election competition over the period studied here.

Results

We begin here with a broad look at the relationship between primary competition and general election competition for our three different types of races. Table 11.1 shows bivariate correlations between, on the one hand, various indicators of primary competition, and on the other, two indicators of general election competitiveness, the number of incumbents defeated in the general election (columns 1–3) and the seat swing (columns 4–6). The table shows these correlation coefficients in the aggregate and by party. Coefficients that our hypotheses predict to be significant are shown in bold; for all, the predicted correlation should be positive.

Five of the six aggregate correlation coefficients (presented in columns 1 and 4) are significant, and all are positive. Correlations between challenger primary competition and general election turnover are the highest ($r = .814$), but open seat correlations are all still significant as well. Our hypotheses regarding incumbent primaries were somewhat more cautious, and perhaps justifiably so; incumbent primary challenges are highly and positively correlated with the number of incumbent defeats in the general election ($r = .662$), but the correlation with seat swing is small ($r = .248$) and not significant.

Correlations within both parties between challenger primary competition and general election turnover are also highly significant, but none of the predicted open seat or incumbent primary coefficients is significant. For Republicans, open seat competition is related to the total

Table 11.1 Correlations between Level of Primary Competition and General Election Results

	Incumbents defeated in general (Total)	Dem Incumbents defeated in general	Rep Incumbents defeated in general	Seat Swing (Total)	Seat Swing (D to R)	Seat Swing (R to D)
Open seat Fractionalization	**.431***			**.567****		
Dem Open seat Fractionalization		.300	**.137**		.299	**.106**
Rep Open seat Fractionalization		**.347**	−.178		**.509***	−.238
Challenger Fractionalization	**.814****			**.632****		
Dem Challenger Fractionalization		.008	**.509***		−.148	**.479***
Rep Challenger Fractionalization		**.731****	−.243		**.783***	−.316
Incumbents challenged in primary	**.662****			.248		
Dem Incumbents challenged in primary		.526*	**.051**		.320	**−.015**
Rep Incumbents challenged in primary		**.336**	.147		**.313**	.127

Note: Coefficients in bold are those predicted to be significant in hypotheses. All cases except fractionalization index are sums for each category in individual election years. Fractionalization is as defined in paper text. **$p < .01$; *$p <.05$.

number of seats changing from Democratic to Republican hands ($r = .509$) but not with the number of incumbent defeats − something that may say more about the nature of the open seats in play than about partisan competition. Competition in Republican incumbent primaries is positively correlated with both measures of Republican gain in the general election, but the correlations are not significant. As we note below, however, correlations for the period from 1970 through 2010 *are* significant, indicating, perhaps, that the nature of Republican primary challenges has changed in recent election cycles. And oddly, Democratic incumbent primary challenges are positively correlated with the number of *Democratic incumbents* defeated in the general election but not with the number of incumbent Republicans defeated in the general election, a result that clearly merits further investigation.

These correlations show that most of our expectations are borne out in the full-time series, but they highlight neither unusual elections nor changes in the relationship between primary and general election competition over time. To explore this, we turn to a series of visual depictions of the trends from 1970 through 2012.

Open Seat Primaries

Open seat primaries might appear to be the races that would most clearly show the influence of national trends, but as Table 11.1 showed, the results are decidedly mixed. Open seat primaries are more competitive in years when large numbers of incumbents lose and seat swings are high, but when we disaggregate by party, we find that only one of our hypotheses − that Republican open seat primaries will be more competitive in years when Republicans pick up seats − is supported in the bivariate analysis. A visual inspection of the time trend for the two parties, however, suggests that open seat competition is at least somewhat sensitive to substantial surges even if the overall correlation matrix shows that it is not sensitive in the aggregate to smaller changes. Figure 11.1 shows fractionalization in Democratic and Republican open seat primaries, with lines inserted, for viewing convenience, in years generally considered to be surge years for one party.[8] The time series here suggests three things: first, that three of the surges in the time series, 1974, 1994, and 2010, are associated with unusually high fractionalization within the party that benefitted from the surge; second, that in two of these surge years *both* parties exhibited unusually high levels of fractionalization; and third, that the Democratic Party generally had higher fractionalization than the Republican Party before 1992 but had uniformly lower fractionalization afterwards. The 1992 election, which was, as we shall see in other parts of this chapter, particularly tumultuous, does not exhibit an unusually high level of fractionalization in its open seat primaries.

Figure 11.2 shows variations in open seat competition over time according to the competitiveness of the general election, the region of the country, and whether the seat is newly created. As one might expect, there is more competition in races where the nominee stands a better chance of winning the general election, but there is no obvious pattern across time. With the exception of 1974, the surge years show heightened competition for open seat races regardless of the prospective nominees' general election prospects. These figures also show that the Democratic decline in fractionalization is somewhat driven by the party's decline in the South;

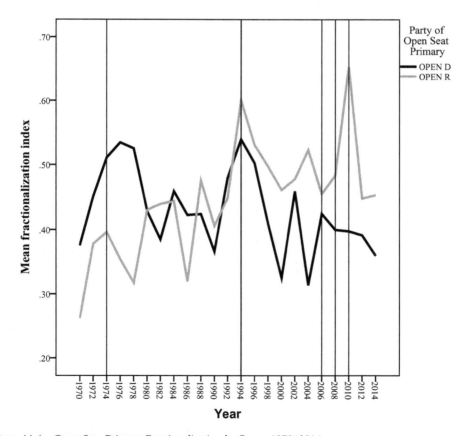

Figure 11.1 Open Seat Primary Fractionalization by Party, 1970–2014

southern primaries are more competitive than other Democratic races before 1992 but less so afterwards. Our ability to make inferences based on region, however, is limited because the number of open seat races in the South is quite small in many years in this time series. Finally, newly created seats are not noticeably more competitive than other open seats. Separate time series broken out by primary type (not shown) show no clear differences.

The time series here show that in most high turnover years, there is heightened primary competition. The low correlations overall between open seat primary fractionalization and seat swing suggest that the small number of open seat races, the trend toward greater competition in Republican primaries, and the changing role of the South in the Democratic coalition all interact to make this relationship more complicated than it might be in other types of races.

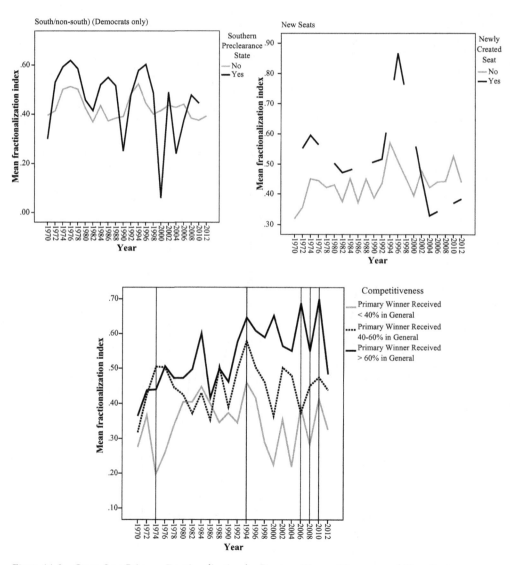

Figure 11.2 Open Seat Primary Fractionalization by Region, Competitiveness, and New Seats

Challenger Primaries

The relationship between primary and general election competition is much more straightforward for challenger primaries. There are more of them, so idiosyncrasies cause less variation when we look at patterns over time. As we saw in Table 11.1, the correlation coefficients are all significant and signed in the correct direction. Challenger primaries are most competitive when the party holding the primary expects to do well in the general election. Figure 11.3 shows this relationship across time, with lines again to mark surge years. Here, not only is there greater competition in surge years within the party that benefits from the surge, but there is also reduced competition within the party that is harmed by the surge. There are still some anomalies here, however; most notably, Democratic challenger primaries were unusually competitive in 1984 despite the party's lackluster showing in that year's general election. In contrast to the pattern for open seats, both parties saw heightened competition in challenger primaries in 1992, the lone high turnover year for both parties in this period.

Figure 11.4 shows two alternate breakdowns of the challenger primary time series. Most of the heightened competition in challenger primaries takes place within districts where the nominee goes on to receive at least 40 percent of the general election vote. That is, primary competition is clearly driven by the expectation that the nominee will have a chance of victory in November. Fractionalization in primaries for the challenger nomination in less competitive

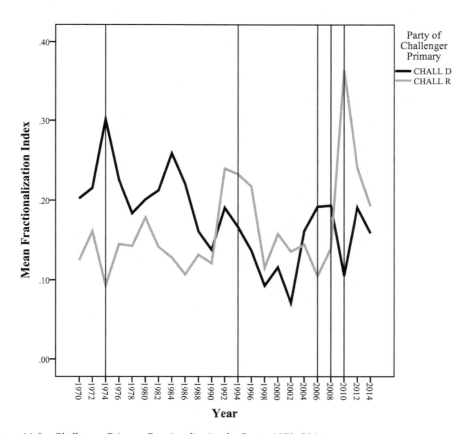

Figure 11.3   Challenger Primary Fractionalization by Party, 1970–2014

seats is relatively consistent through 2008 but grows noticeably in 2010 and 2012. This growth took place exclusively on the Republican side – perhaps a reflection of the growing role of the Tea Party even in safe Democratic districts. The growth in competitiveness in Republican primaries is also driven in part by the party's growing support in the South; southern challenger primaries, which tended to take place in the Republican Party during the 1970s and 1980s, were less competitive than primaries in other parts of the country during this time but the regional difference disappeared after 1992. As is the case for open seats, there is no discernible pattern to the competitiveness of challenger primaries that relates to rules governing voter eligibility in primaries.

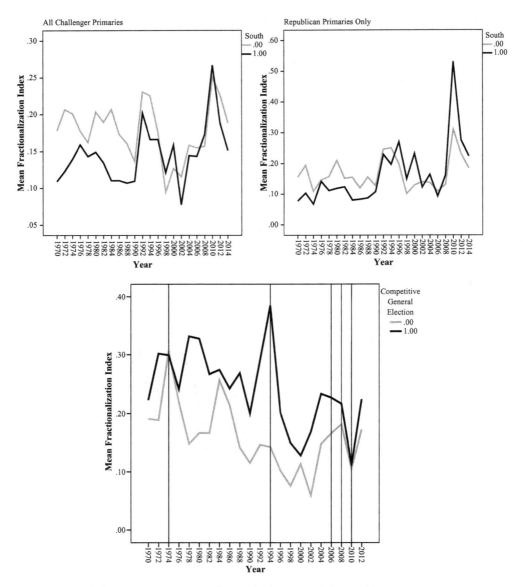

Figure 11.4 Challenger Primary Fractionalization by Region and Competitiveness

Both of the hypotheses regarding challenger primaries are clearly borne out; while party differences do shape the time series here somewhat, they do not obscure the fact that nominations worth having inspire greater competition.

Incumbent Primaries

As noted above, competition in incumbent primaries is not the norm; therefore, we use a different measurement of competitiveness in looking at primary challenges to incumbents. Figure 11.5 shows the relationship between general election defeats of incumbents and primary challenges in which the incumbent was held to less than 75 percent of the vote. For almost all years shown here, these numbers move in tandem. There are only two two-election periods in which this is not the case: 1976 and 1978, when the number of primary challenges stayed constant while the number of defeated incumbents fell; and 2012, when the number of primary challenges was also high despite low general election turnover. It is notable that these two periods each followed a surge election (1974 and 2010), perhaps indicating that a sort of lag effect was taking place.

Figure 11.6 shows breakdowns of this relationship by party. As we expected, the party benefitting from surges tends to see more primary challenges. As Table 11.1 showed, Republican primary challenges are more closely related to Republican support in the general election than is the case for Democrats. This relationship holds even when we separate challenges in the South, both in the aggregate and within the Democratic Party (Figure 11.7). This relationship is also not affected by voter eligibility rules (not shown) or by the competitiveness of the district in the general election, as measured by Democratic Party district presidential vote (Figure 11.8).

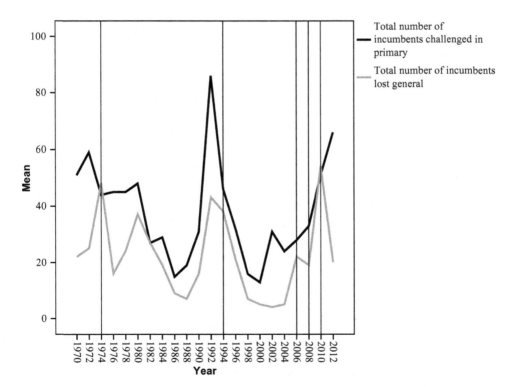

Figure 11.5 Primary Challenges to Incumbents and General Election Turnover, 1970–2012

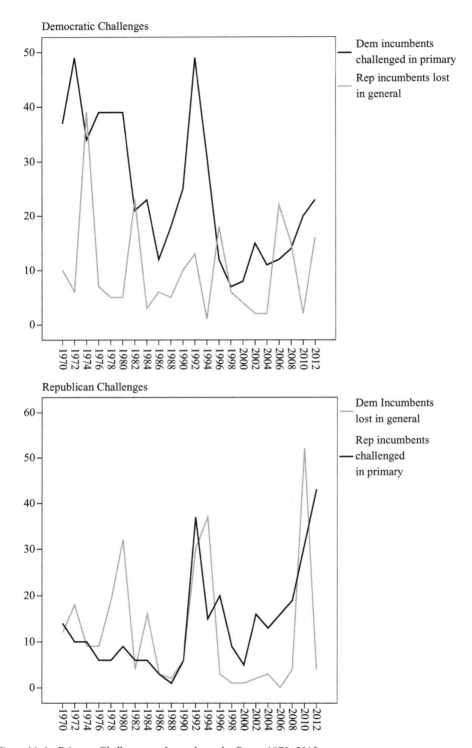

Figure 11.6 Primary Challenges to Incumbents by Party, 1970–2012

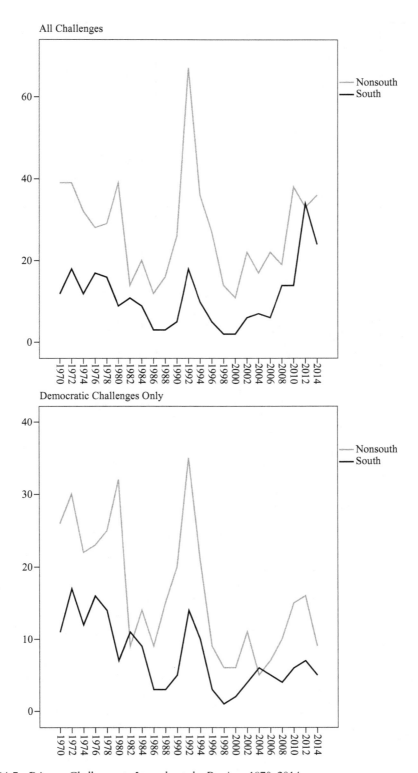

Figure 11.7   Primary Challenges to Incumbents by Region, 1970–2014

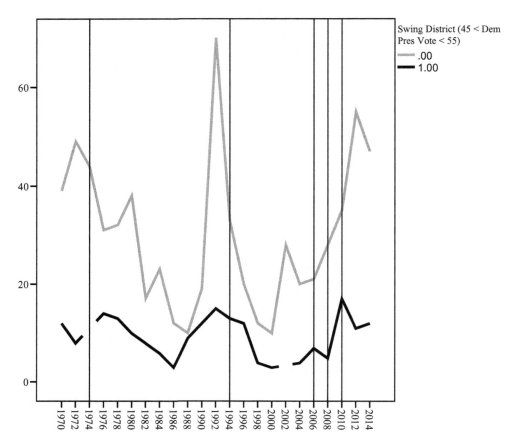

Figure 11.8 Primary Challenges to Incumbents by District Competitiveness, 1970–2014

Note: District Democratic Vote Percentages not calculated for all districts in 1974 and 2002 because of redistricting.

We have coded primary challenges to incumbents in order to isolate instances where incumbents were challenged by a candidate running farther from the political center – that is, Democratic incumbents facing primary opponents running from the left or Republican incumbents facing opponents running to their right. Figure 11.9 shows the incidence of such challenges; the upper panel shows the relationship from 1970 through 2014, and, given the anomalous surge in challenges beginning in 2010, the lower panel shows only ideological challenges before 2010. The lower panel shows that there is an increase in ideological primary challenges within the Democratic Party around the time of that party's most successful general elections; similarly, ideological challenges in the Republican Party increase around 1994.

These patterns clearly show that primary challenges to incumbents are more common when a party expects to gain seats in the upcoming election. This is arguably a function of unrest among strong ideologues within the electorate, particularly on the Republican side. There are a few eras that do not quite accord with this logic: the period in the late 1970s, discussed above; 1992,

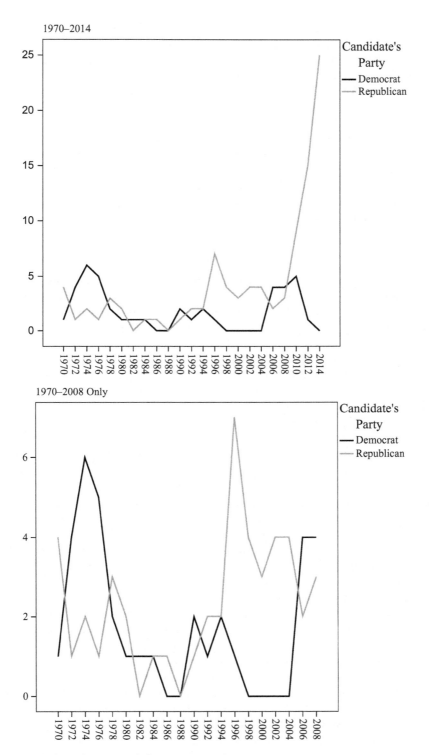

Figure 11.9 Ideological Primary Challenges to Incumbents

when there was high general election turnover in both parties and a substantial amount of unrest in both parties' primaries; and the most recent two elections, where primary challenges (and in particular ideological primary challenges) have climbed within the Republican Party despite relatively uneventful general elections.

Finally, to return to the particular circumstances of the Republican Party primary challenges. When we began this chapter, using data from 1970 through 2012, we were struck by the reasonably strong ($r = .521$, p < .05) correlation between Republican primary challenges to incumbents and general election defeats of Democratic incumbents. Given the circumstances of that election, we speculated that such challenges were a function of the enthusiasm of party ideologues, and that they correlated with partisan surges. Although there are definite "surges" in primary challenges – particularly ideological primary challenges – the 2010 election, an anomalous election in so many ways, appears to have been almost singlehandedly responsible for this apparent connection.

Conclusions

Our exploration of congressional primary competition here corroborates our assertion that reasonable expectations about general election results shape primaries. This in itself is unsurprising; as we noted above, this has been demonstrated in analyses of individual campaigns so it should be expected in the aggregate. What studies of competition in the aggregate provide, however, is an indication that what matters is not just the subjective calculations of individual candidates – that is, answers to the question of whether a primary victory is likely to yield a seat in Congress – but ideological unrest within the electorate that can inspire campaigns even in a losing cause. We suspect that this is what drives the relationship between incumbent primary competition and general election turnover, a relationship that is perhaps our least intuitive finding.

It is also striking that when there are party surges during this time period, competition takes an election cycle or two to decline to its prior levels. A stylized account of this phenomenon might take into account both ideological unrest and subjective expectations on the part of candidates. One can imagine, for instance, a conservative activist viewing 1994 as a promising time to run, whether he or she resides in a district represented by a Democrat or a Republican (or one that is open in 1994). Similarly, one can imagine a conservative activist looking at the results of the 1994 campaign, lamenting that he or she did not run in that year, and laying the groundwork for a 1996 campaign. Perhaps such considerations explain the sustained high level of competition in the Republican Party following the 2010 election, or Democratic primary challenges to incumbents in 2010 (an election year that, despite the blow it dealt to Democrats, followed on the heels of two good Democratic years).

Although differences between primary election rules and between regions of the country are often presented as explanations for competition in primaries, we find little evidence that either of these provides an explanation of changes in primary competition across time. There is likely some relationship between primary rules and voter turnout, and politicians have long assumed that primary rules can make a difference in individual close races (see Boatright 2014b). Similarly, Democratic primary elections were indisputably more competitive in the one-party South for much of the twentieth century. What the time series here show, however, is that both of these factors are swamped by aggregate trends in general election partisan competition. To the extent that there is a story to tell here about what determines primary competition, it is likely one about party and party culture. Competition in Republican primaries is both more sensitive to general election competition and more common than it once was. These two factors merit explanation, but they are also potentially in conflict with each other; the 2012 and 2014 elections have had unusually high levels of competition in Republican primaries of all types despite relatively low general election turnover in both years and modest overall performance in one of them.

This chapter relies largely on aggregate data. We experimented with a number of individual-level estimates of competitiveness and of district composition. There is certainly much room for more nuanced explorations of these data, particularly with regard to the types of districts where competition is more or less related to partisan trends. We have confined ourselves here to looking at region, rules, general election competition, and presidential vote share. Such factors could likely be combined into a multivariate model. We would hold, however, that breaking down districts too finely would miss the important point here: the national "mood," as reflected by partisan competition, determines the nature of intraparty competition. There is a "pulse" to primaries just as there is a pulse to general elections, although this primary pulse may beat a little more erratically than its general election counterpart.

Finally, it is entirely possible that the partisan general election patterns might simply be a reflection of some other underlying variable. Many forecasting models take into account public support for Congress. Changes in public attitudes toward Congress, or toward the party that controls Congress, may drive both primary and general election results. In an election year marked by particularly low public approval of Congress, perhaps primary competition might be determined by a bipartisan desire to replace members of both parties. But then again, such a theory would assume that a public dissatisfied with Congress would still contain many people who find the prospect of serving in that body appealing.

Notes

1 In fact, in post-mortems of the 2014 midterms, several journalists have linked Republican successes to efforts by the Republican establishment – including party leaders in both chambers as well as outside groups like the U.S. Chamber of Commerce – to "avoid the kinds of disastrous candidates . . . whose extreme positions and outré comments hampered the GOP up and down the ballot in 2012 and 2010" (Altman 2014; see also Peters and Hulse 2014, and Jaffe and Kamisar 2014).

2 For other studies of divisiveness, see Berry and Canon 1993; Born 1981; Johnson and Gibson 1974; Kenney 1988; Kenney and Rice 1987; and Miller, Jewell, and Sigelman 1988.

3 These are the elections of 1926, 1998, and 2002, all of which were held under unusual circumstances. The 1926 election is unique in that the president's party lost seats (as expected) but actually improved its share of the two-party vote over the previous election due to La Follette's strong showing (16.6 percent) in the 1924 presidential election. The 1998 and 2002 elections took place on the heels of, respectively, the impeachment of President Clinton and the September 2001 attacks.

4 Or perhaps more accurately, we have no reason to expect such challenges to change across time, absent unusual external stimuli. Studies of the 1992 election have attributed the extremely high number of competitive primaries, of retirements, and of competitive general election races to a combination of partisan factors, changes in redistricting practices, the presence of a major scandal that affected many incumbents, and a change in House rules that affected the ability of retiring incumbents to convert their campaign treasuries to personal use (Groseclose and Krehbiel 1994). This is, to say the least, an unusual set of circumstances.

5 The McGovern Commission rules pertained to delegate selection in Democratic presidential primaries and encouraged states to use primaries for the selection of delegates. In adopting these rules, many states also increased their use of primaries for the selection of nominees for other offices. For discussion, see Boatright 2014a, 62–64.

6 While we begin with the assumption that ideological/policy-based challenges and challenges on other grounds (e.g., scandals or allegations of incompetence) are driven by independent and distinct considerations, we acknowledge that one might condition the other in some cases. For example, a moderate incumbent who is embroiled in a scandal might draw a more ideologically extreme challenger who perceived the incumbent to be unbeatable, absent revelations or allegations of wrongdoing.

7 Alabama, Arkansas, Florida, Georgia, Kentucky, Louisiana, Mississippi, North Carolina, South Carolina, Tennessee, Texas, and Virginia.

8 We are not particularly scientific in marking these; while 1974, 1994, and 2010 clearly constitute surges in terms of the change in party support, there is little consensus about what an appropriate threshold should be. We mark 2006 and 2008 here, but we note that these elections actually had lower turnover than other unmarked elections, including 1992 and 1980. The lines we use to mark these should thus be taken more as a way of helping the reader note patterns than as an integral part of our argument.

References

Abramowitz, Alan I. 1991. "Incumbency, Campaign Spending, and the Decline of Competition in U.S. House Elections." *Journal of Politics* 53(1): 34–56.

Altman, Alex. 2014. "How the Republican Establishment Got its Groove Back." *Time*. 5 November. Online: http://wp.me/p5HMd-eVGw.

Alvarez, R. Michael, David T. Canon, and Patrick Sellers. 1995. "The Impact of Primaries on General Election Outcomes in the U.S. House and Senate." Unpublished ms., California Institute of Technology.

Ansolabehere, Stephen, and Alan Gerber. 1996. "The Effects of Filing Fees and Petition Requirements on U.S. House Elections." *Legislative Studies Quarterly* 21(2): 249–64.

Ansolabehere, Stephen, John Mark Hansen, Shigeo Hirano, and James M. Snyder, Jr. 2006. "The Decline of Competition in US Primary Elections, 1908–2004." In *The Marketplace of Democracy: Electoral Competition and American Politics*, ed. Michael P. McDonald and John Samples. Washington, DC: Brookings Institution and Cato Institute, pp. 74–101.

Ansolabehere, Stephen, John Mark Hansen, Shigeo Hirano, and James M. Snyder, Jr. 2007. "Incumbency Advantages in U. S. Primary Elections." *Electoral Studies* 26(3): 660–668.

Ansolabehere, Stephen, John Mark Hansen, Shigeo Hirano, and James M. Snyder, Jr. 2010. "More Democracy: The Direct Primary and Competition in U.S. House Elections." *Studies in American Political Development* 24(2): 190–205.

Bean, Louis. 1948. *How to Predict Elections*. New York: Knopf.

Bernstein, Robert A. 1977. "Divisive Primaries Do Hurt: US Senate Races, 1956–1972." *American Political Science Review* 71(2): 540–545.

Berry, William D., and Bradley C. Canon. 1993. "Explaining the Competitiveness of Gubernatorial Primaries." *Journal of Politics* 55(2): 454–471.

Boatright, Robert G. 2013. *Getting Primaried: The Changing Politics of Congressional Primary Challenges*. Ann Arbor: University of Michigan Press.

Boatright, Robert G. 2014a. *Congressional Primary Elections*. New York: Routledge.

Boatright, Robert G. 2014b. "Retrenchment or Reform? Changes in Primary Election Laws, 1928–1970." Paper presented at the Annual Meeting of the New England Political Science Association, Woodstock, VT.

Boots, Ralph S. 1922. "The Trend of the Direct Primary." *American Political Science Review* 16(3): 412–431.

Born, Richard. 1981. "The Influence of House Primary Election Divisiveness on General Election Margins, 1962–1976." *Journal of Politics* 43(3): 640–661.

Brady, David W., Morris P. Fiorina, and Arjun S. Wilkins. 2011. "The 2010 Elections: Why Did Political Science Forecasts Go Awry?" *PS: Political Science and Politics* 44(2): 247–250.

Brogan, Michael J., and Jonathan Mendilow. 2012. "Public Party Funding and Intraparty Competition: Clean Elections in Maine and Arizona." *International Journal of Humanities and Social Science* 2(6): 120–132.

Burden, Barry C. 2001. "The Polarizing Effects of Congressional Primaries." In *Congressional Primaries and the Politics of Representation*, ed. Peter F. Galderisi, Marni Ezra, and Michael Lyons. Lanham, MD: Rowman and Littlefield, pp. 95–115.

Campbell, Angus E. 1960. "Surge and Decline: A Study of Electoral Change." *Public Opinion Quarterly* 24(2): 397–418.

Campbell, James E. 1997. "The Presidential Pulse and the 1994 Midterm Congressional Election." *Journal of Politics* 59(3): 830–857.

Campbell, James E. 2014. "The 2014 Midterm Election Forecasts." *PS: Political Science* 47(4): 769–771.

Canon, Bradley. 1978. "Factionalism in the South: A Test of Theory and a Revisitation of V. O. Key." *American Journal of Political Science* 22(3): 833–848.

Erikson, Robert S. 1988. "The Puzzle of Midterm Loss." *Journal of Politics* 50(4): 1011–1029.

Fanning, C. E. 1905. *Selected Articles on Direct Primaries*. Minneapolis, MN: H. W. Wilson.

Fiorina, Morris P. 1996. *Divided Government*. Boston, MA: Allyn and Bacon.

Freeman, Jo. 1986. "The Political Culture of the Democratic and Republican Parties." *Political Science Quarterly* 101(3): 327–356.

Gaddie, Ronald Keith. 1997. "Congressional Seat Swings: Revisiting Exposure in House Elections." *Political Research Quarterly* 50(3): 699–710.

Galderisi, Peter F., and Marni Ezra. 2001. "Congressional Primaries in Historical and Theoretical Context." In *Congressional Primaries and the Politics of Representation*, ed. Peter F. Galderisi, Marni Ezra, and Michael Lyons. Lanham, MD: Rowman and Littlefield, pp. 11–28.

Gerber, Elizabeth R., and Rebecca B. Morton. 1998. "Primary Election Systems and Representation." *Journal of Law, Economics, and Organization* 14(2): 304–324.

Groseclose, Timothy, and Keith Krehbiel. 1994. "Golden Parachutes, Rubber Checks, and Strategic Retirements from the 102nd Congress." *American Journal of Political Science* 38(1): 75–99.

Hacker, Andrew. 1965. "Does a 'Divisive' Primary Harm a Candidate's Chances?" *American Political Science Review* 59(1): 105–110.

Herrnson, Paul S., and James G. Gimpel. 1995. "District Conditions and Primary Divisiveness in Elections." *Political Research Quarterly* 48(1): 101–116.

Hibbing, John R. 1982a. "Voluntary Retirements from the House in the Twentieth Century." *Journal of Politics* 44(4): 1020–1034.

Hibbing, John R. 1982b. "Voluntary Retirement from the U.S. House: The Costs of Congressional Service." *Legislative Studies Quarterly* 7(1): 57–74.

Hibbing, John R. 1982c. "Voluntary Retirement from the U.S. House of Representatives: Who Quits?" *American Journal of Political Science* 26(3): 467–484.

Hirano, Shigeo, and James M. Snyder. 2011. "The Direct Primary and Candidate-Centered Voting in U.S. Elections." Unpublished ms., Columbia University.

Hirschman, Albert O. 1970. *Exit, Voice, and Loyalty*. Cambridge, MA: Harvard University Press.

Hogan, Robert E. 2003. "Competition in State Legislative Primary Elections." *Legislative Studies Quarterly* 28(1): 103–126.

Hormell, Orren Chalmer. 1923. "The Direct Primary Law in Maine and How it Worked." *Annals of the American Academy of Political and Social Science* 106: 128–141.

Jaffe, Alexandra, and Ben Kamisar. 2014. "Has the Tea Party Been Tamed?" *The Hill*. Online: http://thehill.com/blogs/ballot-box/223278-after-victories-tea-party-wont-back-down

Johnson, Donald Bruce, and James R. Gibson. 1974. "The Divisive Primary Revisited: Party Activists in Iowa." *American Political Science Review* 68(1): 67–77.

Johnson, Gregg B., Meredith-Joy Petersheim, and Jesse T. Wasson. 2010. "Divisive Primaries and Incumbent General Election Performance: Prospects and Costs in U.S. House Races." *American Politics Research* 38(5): 931–955.

Kanthak, Kristin, and Rebecca Morton. 2001. "The Effects of Electoral Rules on Congressional Primaries." In *Congressional Primaries and the Politics of Representation*, ed. Peter F. Galderisi, Marni Ezra, and Michael Lyons. Lanham, MD: Rowman and Littlefield, pp. 116–131.

Kenney, Patrick. 1988. "Sorting Out the Effects of Primary Divisiveness in Congressional and Senatorial Elections." *Western Political Quarterly* 41(4): 765–777.

Kenney, Patrick J., and Tom W. Rice. 1984. "The Effect of Primary Divisiveness in Gubernatorial and Senatorial Elections." *Journal of Politics* 46(3): 904–915.

Kenney, Patrick J., and Tom W. Rice. 1987. "The Relationship Between Divisive Primaries and General Election Outcomes." *American Journal of Political Science* 31(1): 31–44.

Kernell, Samuel. 1977. "Presidential Popularity and Negative Voting: An Alternative Explanation of the Midterm Congressional Decline of the President's Party." *American Political Science Review* 71(1): 44–66.

Lazarus, Jeffrey. 2005. "Unintended Consequences: Anticipation of General Election Outcomes and Primary Election Divisiveness." *Legislative Studies Quarterly* 30(3): 435–461.

Lewis-Beck, Michael S., and Mary Stegmaier. 2000. "Economic Determinants of Election Outcomes." *Annual Review of Political Science* 3: 183–219.

McGhee, Eric, Seth Masket, Boris Shor, and Nolan McCarty. 2010. "A Primary Cause of Partisanship? Nomination Systems and Legislator Ideology." Paper presented at the Annual Meeting of the American Political Science Association, Washington, DC.

Miller, Penny M., Malcolm F. Jewell, and Lee Sigelman. 1988. "Divisive Primaries and Party Activists: Kentucky, 1979 and 1983." *Journal of Politics* 50(2): 459–470.

Morlan, Robert L. 1955. *Political Prairie Fire: The Nonpartisan League, 1915–1922.* Minneapolis: University of Minnesota Press.

Norris, George. 1923. "Why I Believe in the Direct Primary." *Annals of the American Academy of Political and Social Sciences* 106: 22–30.

Oppenheimer, Bruce I, James A. Stimson, and Richard W. Waterman 1986. "Interpreting U.S. Congressional Elections: The Exposure Thesis." *Legislative Studies Quarterly* 20(2): 227–248.

Peters, Jeremy W., and Carl Hulse. 2014. "Republicans' First Step Was to Handle Extremists in Party." *New York Times,* 5 November. Online: http://nyti.ms/1wwm0mR.

Piereson, James E., and Terry B. Smith. 1975. "Primary Divisiveness and General Election Success: A Re-Examination." *Journal of Politics* 37(2): 555–562.

Reynolds, John F. 2006. *The Demise of the American Convention System, 1880–1911.* New York: Cambridge University Press.

Riker, William. 1982. *Liberalism Against Populism.* Prospect Heights, IL: Waveland Press.

Telford, Ira Ralph. 1965. "Types of Primary and Party Responsibility." *American Political Science Review* 59(1): 117–118.

Tufte, Edward R. 1975. "Determinants of the Outcomes of Midterm Congressional Elections." *American Political Science Review* 69(3): 812–826.

Ware, Alan. 1979. "'Divisive' Primaries: The Important Questions." *British Journal of Political Science* 9(3): 381–384.

Ware, Alan. 2002. *The American Direct Primary.* New York: Oxford University Press.

West, Victor J. 1923. "The California Direct Primary." *Annals of the American Academy of Political and Social Sciences* 106: 116–127.

12

IDEOLOGICAL PRIMARIES AND THEIR INFLUENCE IN CONGRESS

Caitlin E. Jewitt and Sarah A. Treul

Fred Upton, a moderate Republican, was first elected in 1986 to represent the people of Michigan's fourth congressional district.[1] Perhaps due in part to the district's location on the shores of Lake Michigan,[2] one of Upton's most prominent issues early in his congressional career was environmental regulation. As recently as 2007 Upton worked across the aisle with Democrats to pass the Energy and Independence and Security Act, which, among other things, promoted the production of clean renewable fuels, offered incentives for the development of plug-in hybrids, and banned the manufacturing of incandescent light bulbs. In 2009 Upton even spoke about the importance of reducing emissions and, while attending the Copenhagen Climate Change Conference, stated that lowering emissions would be good for the world (Sheppard 2011). In fact, Upton's climate change positions were so out of line with mainstream conservative thinking of the time that in 2010 when Upton's name began circulating among Republicans as a potential chairman for the House Committee on Energy and Commerce, many conservatives came out against Upton, calling him a RINO (Republican In Name Only). During the battle for the committee chairmanship, the Tea Party organization FreedomWorks launched a campaign against Upton, portraying him as pro-environment and pro-regulation. Despite the opposition, Upton went on to become the chairman of the Energy and Commerce committee in the 112th Congress (2011–2012), a position he served in until the 115th Congress.

While the above portrait of Upton paints him as fairly moderate on the environment, the environmental and regulation record of Upton shifted dramatically post-2009 with his environmental issue positions becoming increasingly conservative. What led Upton to reevaluate his moderate stances on the environment? Since any legislator's primary goal is reelection (Mayhew 2004), we suggest the best answer to this question might be found by looking at his campaigns for reelection. More specifically, we turn to the effect his primary campaigns had on his legislative behavior, given that competition for many members of Congress has shifted from the general election to the primary stage. In 2010 Upton faced a primary challenge from the Tea Party in his bid for reelection – his first serious challenge since winning office in 1986 and his first primary challenge since 2002. The 2010 Republican primary pitted Upton against former Michigan state representative Jack Hoogendyk. Hoogendyk ran to Upton's right with the backing of the Tea Party, Club for Growth, and Right to Life Michigan. He ran his campaign on an ideological platform, frequently suggesting that Upton was too moderate to represent the residents of Michigan's sixth district. Although Upton managed to defeat Hoogendyk in the primary, he did so by less than twenty percent of the vote. Upton's close primary contest is a trend in primary campaigns. Primary challengers from the extreme of the party are increasingly targeting incumbents, hoping to capitalize on a primary electorate that tends to be more ideological in its preferences.

Despite Upton's victory, the real story here might be the long-lasting effects the Hoogendyk campaign had on Upton's record in Congress. Hoogendyk's competitive, ideological primary challenge signaled to Upton that a significant portion of his reelection constituency (Fenno 1978) was not supportive of his more moderate positions. After the 2010 election, Upton's issue positions and legislative behavior clearly shifted. This shift was perhaps most evident on environmental issues. On December 28, 2010, after defeating Hoogendyk and wining the general election, Upton penned an op-ed in the *Wall Street Journal*, co-authored with Tim Phillips, President of Americans for Prosperity, titled "How Congress Can Stop the EPA's Power Grab." In making the case for Congress to step in and delay the Environmental Protection Agency's (EPA) regulation of carbon dioxide emissions and other greenhouse gases, Upton and Phillips wrote, "[T]he principal argument for a two-year-delay is that it will allow Congress time to create its own plan for regulating carbon. This presumes that carbon is a problem in need of regulation. We are not convinced." After facing an ideological primary challenge Upton clearly shifted his stance on carbon regulation, becoming less environmentally friendly. In one way, Upton's issue position shift on the environment can be seen as a victory for the Hoogendyk campaign platform. Even though Hoogendyk himself was not victorious, his more extreme policy agenda position prevailed.

Upton's behavior shift may have paid off electorally as well; Hoogendyk once again challenged Upton in the 2012 primary, but this time Hoogendyk lost by over 30 percent. Primary voters rewarded Upton for shifting his issue agenda to the right. Although anecdotal, we believe Fred Upton's ideological primary challenge and the subsequent shift in his legislative behavior and policy positions is indicative of a larger trend. We expect that with competitive, ideological primaries becoming increasingly common, those incumbents fortunate enough to win reelection are responding to these challenges by shifting their legislative behavior to signal to the electorate (particularly primary voters) and potential primary challengers that they are not only responsive, but also are more ideologically extreme than previously thought.

Changing Primary Challenges

As Boatright (2014) demonstrates, the number of primary challenges and competitiveness of those challenges has waxed and waned over the years. The 1970s, for instance, saw a rather steady level of primary competition, but this fell off in the 1980s. Perhaps in part due to redistricting (e.g. Hetherington et al. 2003; Carson et al. 2006), 1992 then saw a massive increase in the number of competitive primaries. From here, the number of competitive primaries once again steadily declined throughout the remainder of the 1990s and then began to increase again post-2004. Looking at a more recent period of time, Figure 12.1 shows the number of competitive primary challenges from 2002 to 2012. For the purposes of this figure, a competitive primary is operationalized as one where the incumbent received less than 75 percent of the vote.

Though there is variation in the number of competitive primaries over time, the reason behind the competitive primaries has also evolved. The competitive primary challenges in the 1970s occurred as interest groups backed progressive primary challengers on particular issues (Brady et al. 2007), whereas today, the central reason for the increased level of primary competition is ideological. That is, primary challengers are throwing their name in the ring to challenge incumbents precisely because they do not see the incumbent as ideologically extreme enough. For example, Hoogendyk challenged Upton in the 2010 Republican primary because he believed Upton to be too moderate on issues including abortion, the environment, and taxes.

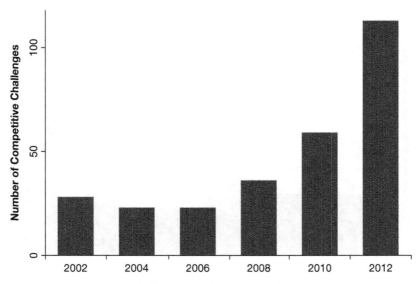

Figure 12.1 Competitive Primary Challenges 2002–2012

Recent congressional primaries more frequently pit a new type of challenger – an ideological challenger – against incumbents. These candidates are distinct in that they frequently target the incumbent from the party's more extreme ideological flank. In other words, incumbent Democrats are challenged by candidates more liberal than they are and incumbent Republicans are challenged by more conservative candidates. Even if they do not win, these ideological primary challengers tend to perform well, as primary voters often exhibit a strong preference for more ideologically extreme candidates (Brady et al. 2007).

Previous research indicates that the primary electorate is often more ideologically extreme than the general electorate (Brady et al. 2007; Burden 2004; Jacobson 2004). Given the ideological extremity of the primary electorate compared to the general election electorate, is it not surprising that recent ideological candidates have found primaries to be fertile ground to launch congressional campaigns. In the wake of *Citizens United v. FEC* (2010), which lifted restrictions on campaign donations from outside funding sources, it is now possible for an ideological challenger to be well-funded without having to self-finance or rely on party support. While Boatright (2014) finds no evidence for the level of primary competition being different today than it was in the past, he finds that the financing of these challenges has changed over the course of the past decade. Primary challengers today, particularly ideological primary challengers, are raising more money and much of this money is coming from donors (individual and otherwise) who reside outside of the district. The willingness of financial contributors to support candidates advocating for more extreme positions enables these types of candidates to emerge. Additionally, many of these ideological challengers rely on small donations from around the country. These contributions, coupled with the involvement of interest groups such as the Club for Growth and MoveOn.org, provide circumstantial evidence for the nationalization of primary challenges and that there are donors (individual and otherwise) who want to unseat incumbents or, at the very least, send these incumbents a strong message about their ideological positions and policy preferences.

The amount of financial support behind ideological primary challengers, coupled with the primary electorate's dissatisfaction with the status quo and moderate policies, likely contributed to

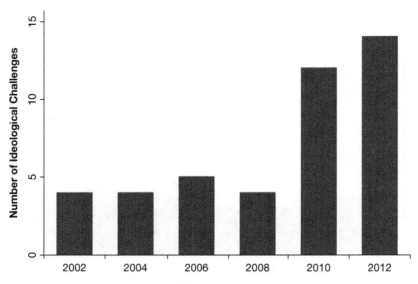

Figure 12.2 Ideological Primary Challenges 2002–2012

the large increase in ideological primary challenges. Figure 12.2 demonstrates the rise in ideological primary challenges from 2002 to 2012. In this figure, and elsewhere in this analysis, ideological challenges are measured as those that focused on the incumbent's positions perceived to be too moderate mounted from the left for Democrats and from the right for Republicans; these are based on the categorization and data presented in Boatright (2014).

What is particularly interesting about these ideological challenges is that, for the most part, they are a subset of competitive primaries. In other words, most of the ideological primaries that occur are competitive, which is concerning for incumbents seeking to return to Congress. For many incumbents, the fear of losing an election has shifted away from the general election and to the primary election, particularly as they observe these increasingly frequent ideological challenges. This is especially the case in districts that lean reliably to one party, as there is often no true competition in the general election. The data bear out an incumbent's fear of a primary challenge, as Tables 12.1 and 12.2 show that primary challenges that come from the ideological extreme tend to be competitive as well.

Table 12.1 Ideological and Competitive Primaries, 2002–2012

	Non-competitive	*Competitive*	*Total*
Unknown challenge	2	60	62
Non-ideological challenge	455	180	635
Ideological challenge	1	42	43
Total	458	282	740

Notes: This table examines cases where the incumbent faced a primary challenge and won. A competitive primary is one where the winning candidate received less than 75 percent of the vote. An ideological challenge is one where the primary challenge was ideologically positioned to the right for Republican candidates and to the left for Democratic candidates. An unknown challenge is one where there was a primary challenge, but no clear, compelling reason (e.g. ideological, scandal, age) for the challenge.

Table 12.2 Ideological and Competitive Primaries, 2010–2012

	2010		2012		
	Non-competitive	Competitive	Non-competitive	Competitive	Total
Unknown challenge	1	22	0	13	36
Non-ideological challenge	100	26	90	86	302
Ideological challenge	1	11	0	14	26
Total	102	59	90	113	364

Notes: This table examines cases where the incumbent faced a primary challenge and won. A competitive primary is one where the winning candidate received less than 75 percent of the vote. An ideological challenge is one where the primary challenge was ideologically positioned to the right for Republican candidates and to the left for Democratic candidates. An unknown challenge is one where there was a primary challenge, but no clear, compelling reason (e.g. ideological, scandal, age) for the challenge.

Table 12.3 Ideological Challenges and Quality Candidates, 2002–2012

	Non-quality Candidate	*Quality Candidate*	*Total*
Unknown challenge	46	16	62
Non-ideological challenge	543	92	635
Ideological challenge	29	14	43
Total	618	122	740

Notes: This table examines cases where the incumbent faced a primary challenge and won. An ideological challenge is one where the primary challenge was ideologically positioned to the right for Republican candidates and to the left for Democratic candidates. An unknown challenge is one where there was a primary challenge, but no clear, compelling reason (e.g. ideological, scandal, age) for the challenge.

That is, ideological extreme primary challengers tend to receive a substantial share of the vote. From 2010 to 2012, twenty-five of the twenty-six primaries that were classified as ideological were also competitive. From 2002 to 2012, forty-two out of forty-three ideological challenges were competitive, with the incumbent receiving less than 75 percent of the vote. If an incumbent is challenged ideologically in the primary that challenge is likely to also result in a competitive, or close, primary.

That ideological challenges tend to also be competitive is likely the result of the monetary support these candidates have and, perhaps most importantly, the fact that many of these ideological challengers are quality candidates, who have previously held elected office. Between 2002 and 2012, fourteen of the forty-three ideological challengers were quality candidates.

Effects of Increasingly Competitive and Ideological Primaries

Although it is interesting to note the fluctuations in competitive primaries and the rise in ideological primaries, we are focused on moving beyond these descriptives and exploring their consequences. Past research offers conflicting findings as to whether primary competition hurts the eventual nominee in the general election (e.g. Bernstein 1977; Kenney and Rice 1984) or helps (e.g. Born 1981; Kenney 1988). The work of Jewitt and Treul (2014) sheds some light on this by taking advantage of the Tea Party's presence in the 2010 Republican primaries. Using the Tea Party as a measure of divisiveness – separate from competitiveness – the authors find that competitive Republican primaries and competitive Democratic primaries increased turnout in the general election. They also conclude that divisive Republican primaries, where there was a Tea Party candidate in the race, increased the party's vote share in the general election.[3] We build on the framework of Jewitt and Treul (2014), and maintain that there is an important distinction between a competitive primary, which indicates that the election was close, and a divisive primary, which signifies a division or fissure within the party. Here, instead of utilizing the presence of the Tea Party as an indication that the primary was divisive, we expand the measure of divisiveness to include ideological primary challenges.[4] We contend that an ideological challenge, as opposed to a primary challenge based on age, scandal, or local issues, signifies a serious divide within the party, qualifying it as a divisive contest. In sum, we believe it is essential to examine the effects of both ideological (divisive) and competitive primaries.

Additionally, we are less concerned with the influence of a competitive or divisive primary on electoral outcomes and more interested in the effects on legislative behavior. We aim to assess the role a divisive, ideological primary has on the congressional behavior of members of Congress who are fortunate enough, like Representative Fred Upton, to return to Congress after an ideological challenge. We posit that, like Upton, these returning incumbents might be susceptible to behavior shifts due to stiff primary competition coming from the ideological extreme of the party.

Given the increase in and recent prevalence of competitive and ideological primaries, we ask whether these new types of challenges are having an effect on the behavior of incumbents once reelected. We explore the impact of these ideological challenges above and beyond the effect of a competitive, but non-ideological, primary challenge. Similarly to what we observed in the case of Fred Upton, we suspect that incumbents who defeat ideological challengers in the primary and go on to win the general election might change their legislative behavior in order to fend off a future ideological challenge. Their goal is to alter their behavior in Congress and be more ideological so that they are less likely to have an ideological challenge in a subsequent primary.

As ideological challenges become increasingly common and incumbents fear these challenges, perhaps more than a general election challenge, members of Congress may have to reconsider where to position themselves on an array of issues. As Boatright (2014, 101) notes, "[the party] establishment has become less able to protect its members from its conservative flank and [. . .] so called cross-pressured legislators must increasingly worry about protecting both their right and left flanks." Since many of the most competitive primary challenges today are coming at incumbents from the ideological extreme flank of the party, members are rightfully concerned about this type of challenge. Given this, it is worth exploring how ideological primary competition influences the behavior of the incumbents lucky enough to be reelected to Congress.

Expectations

As noted above, past literature on the consequences of primary competition typically examines the effect of the primary challenges on general election success, rather than on behavior in Congress. Much of the previous literature suggests that competitive primaries tend to hurt the eventual nominee in the general election (e.g. Bernstein 1977; Kenney and Rice 1984). The eventual nominee may be wounded in the general election from a competitive primary because voters are unwilling to shift their support from their preferred candidate to the eventual nominee. Theoretical explanations as to why voters may be hesitant to support the party nominee include that voters may be turned off by the intra-party conflict, may experience a "sore loser" type of effect, may possess feelings of disgruntlement, indifference, or alienation toward the nominee, or they may have ideological concerns about how closely their personal views align with the ideological positions of the nominee (Kenney and Rice 1987; Southwell 1986; Sullivan 1977; Blake and Mouton 1961; Stone 1986; Zipp 1985).

While the majority of previous scholarship on the effects of competitive primaries centers on the general election, there is some more recent work examining the consequences of primaries on congressional behavior (e.g. Boatright 2014; Hirano et al. 2010). Hirano et al. (2010) utilize NOMINATE scores to test changes in roll call behavior and uncover little evidence that primary election outcomes contribute to extreme roll call voting records. The authors suggest that their findings indicate that the increase in extreme ideological primary challenges, or the threat thereof in the case of Hirano et al. (2010), is not what is driving polarization in Congress. That is, the more extreme voting we see in Congress today cannot be the result of these ideological challenges pushing members of Congress to the extreme in their voting behavior. In his comprehensive work on congressional primaries, Boatright (2014) also examines whether primary challenges affect the congressional behavior of winning incumbents in the next Congress. He examines the consequences of several types of primary challenges on congressional behavior using changes in NOMINATE scores. Regardless of the type of primary challenge, even for extreme ideological challenges, he also finds little meaningful change in a member's NOMINATE score (Boatright 2014). Each of the aforementioned authors expects primaries to pull members of Congress away from the political center, but these various empirical investigations mentioned above all fail to find this effect on congressional behavior.

We diverge from previous literature on the effect of ideological primaries, which finds that members who faced such challenges do not become more ideologically extreme in their voting, by proposing that the effect of ideological primary challenges is conditioned on whether the member belongs to the majority or the minority party. That is, members of the minority party who face an ideological challenge do not have the option of voting against their own party to illustrate that they are more extreme. Thus, for a minority member returning to Congress after an ideological challenge the only option is to continue to vote with her party. For members of the minority, facing an ideological primary challenge should not affect their observable party behavior in Congress. However, a member of the majority party who faced an ideological challenge is in a more tenuous position. The member can, of course, continue to vote with her party, but this allows for little signaling to ideological primary voters and potential future challengers that the member is now more ideologically extreme. Therefore, we expect that a member of the majority who is returning to Congress after an ideological primary will actually be increasingly likely to vote with the minority party. For majority members, especially in today's polarized Congress, fear of being pegged as a puppet of the party, and continuing to vote the party line might, once again, encourage an extreme ideological challenge. These members find it beneficial to vote *against* the majority party, as a way to signal their maverick behavior. Voting against the majority party allows them to claim ideological extremism and independent behavior – hopefully warding off a future extreme, ideological challenge.

In addition to asserting a conditional relationship that influences congressional voting behavior, we also are able to leverage our data that parses out primaries by more than just their level of competition. Prior to this investigation, only Boatright (2014) has broken out primary competition and its behavioral consequences by more than just a measure of competition. We employ a measure of divisiveness, which we operationalize below as an ideological primary challenge. We believe that these ideological primaries indicate a split in the party and signal that at least some members of the party do not believe the incumbent is extreme enough. We capitalize on our ability to focus on the effects of divisiveness while controlling for the competitiveness of the primary challenge.

As previously mentioned, Boatright (2014) also includes a measure for type of primary (ideological or not) and a measure of competitiveness (whether the incumbent was held to less than 60 percent of the vote) in his model assessing the consequences of primary challenges on congressional behavior. However, Boatright fails to find an effect and we believe this is the direct result of not taking into account the conditional relationship about majority party status. We do not expect all members to change their behavior uniformly when challenged by an ideological extremist in the primary. Rather, we expect members in the majority party will vote *less often* with their party following an ideological (divisive) primary challenge than they did before the primary challenge. For members of the minority party, we expect to see no differences in voting behavior following an ideological primary challenge.

Theory and Hypotheses

Competitive Primaries

Given the mixed findings regarding the role competitive primaries play in general election outcomes, we have no a priori expectation regarding the effect a competitive primary challenge plays on changing a member's legislative behavior once reelected to Congress. Research on competitive primaries has found that some of these primaries hurt the winning candidate in the general election, but other studies find this effect to be overstated. We expect, therefore, that it is not primary competition so much as the *type* of primary competition that influences the incumbent's behavior when returning to Congress. This leads us to generate one hypothesis regarding primary competition:

> **Hypothesis 1:** A competitive primary will not affect a member's voting behavior upon returning to Congress, holding all else equal.

Ideological Primaries

Given prior literature that shows different effects for competitive primaries and ideological primaries on general election outcomes, we expect to find similar results when examining congressional behavior in the following Congress as well. Therefore, unlike with competitive primaries where we do not expect to observe legislative behavior changes, we do expect the presence of an ideological challenger to influence congressional behavior. It is first important to note that we do not believe an ideological primary challenge is enough to warrant a change in a member's legislative behavior. The member must also know that her changes in voting behavior are observed by constituents, potential challengers, and potential campaign contributors.[5]

Given the importance of observational behavior change to the member we do not think members of the minority party will change their legislative behavior (in any observable way). Minority party members have no real method by which to demonstrate behavioral change (based on votes) after an ideological primary challenge.[6] That is, for a member of the minority party who faced an ideological primary and would now like to demonstrate a behavior change, she cannot show, using votes alone, a more extreme ideological position as, at the end of the day, the vote will still appear as cast with the minority party and against the majority party. There is no clear way for a minority party member to demonstrate via a vote that she is more ideologically extreme than she was in the previous Congress.

On the other hand, a member of the majority party, who faced an ideological primary challenge, does have the opportunity to change her roll call behavior. In this case, the member has a choice with regard to her voting behavior after returning to Congress. The member can continue to vote with the majority party *or* the member can change her voting behavior and vote *against* her party more frequently. If the majority party member continues to vote with the majority party it signals no behavior change to the electorate, future ideological challengers, or donors.

However, if the member occasionally votes *against* the majority party these votes can be used by the member to signal to key principals that she is not simply a pawn of the party leadership, but rather an independent (perhaps more ideological) member. Unlike a member of the minority party, a member of the majority party has the option of disobeying the party leadership. She can cast a vote against the party as a way to signal publicly that the party is not extreme enough.[7] Of course, these votes against the majority party will appear as if the member is supporting the minority party, but, in reality, the incumbent is simply signaling ideological independence from the majority party. The goal for the majority party member who behaves in this way is to ward off the emergence of future ideological challengers in the next primary election. Based on this, we expect ideological primary challenges to affect returning members of Congress differently depending on their party status. This leads us to generate two hypotheses:

> **Hypothesis 2:** Among minority party members who face an ideological primary challenge, we will not observe a difference in their propensity to vote with their party when compared to members of their party who face a non-ideological primary challenge.

> **Hypothesis 3:** Among majority party members who face an ideological primary challenge, we will observe more votes cast against their party than before the primary challenge when compared to fellow party members who face a non-ideological primary challenge.

Data and Methods

We develop and test our theory by analyzing primary challenges in the U.S. House of Representatives from 2002 to 2012 and corresponding voting changes in the following Congress. Given our research question, the unit of analysis is House incumbents who face a primary challenge (any type), win their primary, and win the subsequent general election and return to Congress. We compare House members' voting behavior in the Congress prior to and immediately after the primary challenge.

Since our expectation is that the relationship between ideological primaries and voting is conditioned on whether a member of Congress is a member of the majority party, we are interested in the extent to which a member of Congress votes with or against his party upon returning to Washington. Therefore, rather than examine NOMINATE scores, we are more concerned with the extent to which a majority party member displays ideological independence, especially on important (easily observable) issues. We capture whether a member of the majority party is exhibiting ideological independence from his party by the percent of the time that the member votes against his party. We operationalize this as the percent of time that the member votes with the Minority Party Leader on key votes. We choose to use key votes as these are thought to be votes that are the most salient. According to *Congressional Quarterly*, key votes are selected based on the extent to which they meet one or more of the following criteria: a matter of major controversy, a test of presidential or political power, or have potential ramifications for the nation and the lives of Americans. Given these criteria, key votes are often likely to be more partisan. Additionally, given their selection criteria, these are the votes the general public is likely to be more aware of, as they are more likely to generate media attention or be the focus of members, parties, or future challengers. Therefore, a member of the majority party who faced an extreme ideological primary challenge may be more likely to vote against her party on these votes to prove that she is truly independent in her voting behavior.[8]

To reiterate our expectations, we do not expect the presence of a competitive primary alone to influence a member's propensity to vote with its party on key votes. However, we do expect the presence of an ideological primary to have an effect on the member's frequency of voting with the party depending on whether the member is a part of the minority or the majority party.

Table 12.4 The Impact of Ideological Primary Challenges on Key Votes in the House

	β *(Robust Std. Error)*
Ideological Challenge	7.57*
	(2.05)
Competitive Primary	1.05
	(1.84)
Majority Party	−1.56
	(1.36)
Majority Party*	−2.13
Ideological Challenge	(2.59)
Closed Primary	−0.36
	(1.35)
Semi-open Primary	−1.51
	(1.37)
District Ideology	0.04
	(0.023)
Vote Share in	−2.84
General Election	(4.09)
In-party Spending	0.42
	(0.92)
Constant	80.87*
	(13.46)
Number of Cases	410
R-squared	0.038
	$F_{(10,399)}$
	11.23

Notes: These cases include U.S. House races between 2002 and 2012 where an incumbent defeated a primary challenger and returned to Congress. The dependent variable is the change in the percent of the time the member voted with the Minority Leader on key votes. Cell entries are unstandardized OLS regression coefficients with robust standard errors. $* \leq .05$.

The model presented in Table 12.4 displays the effect of ideological and competitive primaries on the change in the percent of the time the member voted with the Minority Leader on key votes. With regard to our first hypothesis, the model shows that the competitiveness of the primary does not impact voting behavior. The presence of a competitive primary decreases the propensity to vote with the Minority Leader on key votes, but it is not significant.

Turning to our second and third hypotheses, when we assess the role of an ideological primary on the member's rate of voting with the Minority Leader on key votes, we see the conditional effect we expected for members of the majority party. First of all, the coefficient on *ideological challenge* tells us that a member of the minority party who faced an ideological primary challenge votes with the Minority Leader on key votes 7.57 percent of the time more often than she did before the ideological primary challenge ($p < .001$).

To examine the effect an ideological primary has on members of the majority party, we calculate the appropriate linear combination by adding together the coefficients on *ideological challenge* and *majority party × ideological challenge* (see Table 12.5). From this we find that a member of the majority party who faced an ideological primary challenge *also increased* the percent of the time she voted with the Minority Leader on key votes compared to a member of the majority party

Table 12.5 Comparing the Impact of Ideological Primary Challenges and Majority Party Status on Support for the Minority Party Leader on Key Votes in the House

β
(Robust Std. Error)
H2: Ideological Minority Compared to Non-ideological Minority
7.57*
(2.05)
H3: Ideological Majority Compared to Non-ideological Majority
6.02*
(2.61)

Notes: These comparisons are based on the model in Table 12.4. The dependent variable for this model is the change in the percent of the time the member votes with the Minority Leader on key votes from the Congress before a primary challenge to the one following it. The two comparisons depict the difference in voting with the Minority Leader when comparing one group to another group and are based on House races between 2002 and 2012 where an incumbent defeated a primary challenge. Ideological indicates that the incumbent faced an ideological primary challenge while non-ideological means that the incumbent faced a primary challenge that was not ideological in nature. Majority means that the incumbent returned to the House as a member of the majority party, while minority represents incumbents who returned to the House as a member of the minority party. *$p < .05$.

who faced a non-ideological primary challenge. More specifically, a majority party member who faced an ideological primary challenge votes with the Minority Leader 6.02 percent more often than she did in the Congress prior to the ideological primary challenge ($p = .022$).

Conclusion

The findings presented here suggest that it is ideological primary challenges, not competitive challenges, that cause a member of Congress to change her legislative behavior upon returning to Congress. Yet, this change in voting behavior is conditioned on whether or not the return-ing incumbent member is a part of the majority or minority party. Members of the majority party who face an ideological primary challenge become significantly more likely to vote with the Minority Party Leader on key votes in the next Congress, whereas members returning to Congress as a part of the minority party continue to vote with the Minority Party Leader on key votes and, in fact, are found to do so at a higher rate than they were before the ideological primary challenge.

With ideological primaries becoming increasingly common – from 2008 to 2012 ideological challenges were the most common reason for a primary challenge – these findings have impli-cations for representation and responsiveness in Congress. Even though most incumbents suc-cessfully defeat these types of primary challenges, the findings presented here demonstrate that even an unsuccessful ideological primary challenge is affecting legislative behavior in Congress. These types of challenges lead to reelected members altering their support for their party in order to demonstrate legislative independence, likely to ward off future primary challenges.

Future work in this area remains to be done. First of all, it would be worth linking the votes of the majority party members who, upon return, cast more votes with the Minority Leader with their comments on the votes. Our theory relies on the assumption that these votes are cast to prove that the majority party member is not a pawn of the party, but rather an independent-minded ideologue who will withhold party support in an observable way by voting with the minority when he or she does not think the majority is being ideological enough. While the intuition behind this makes sense, it would be ideal to match these votes up with the member's talking points. We expect that speeches around these votes would express the member's dissatisfaction with the moderate position of the majority party.

Second, the theory presented here has potential repercussions for the behavior of parties in the U.S. Congress. With ideological primary challenges becoming increasingly common, the findings here show that parties (particularly the majority party) may need to rely on gaining moderate members of a minority party to pass legislation if enough members of the majority party defect. In some ways, this notion is already playing out in Congress. Former Speaker John Boehner frequently struggled to get the majority party membership to coalesce around the party's position, often relying on Democrats in the minority to pass major legislation such as Hurricane Sandy relief, the so-called Fiscal Cliff, and a clean CR for Homeland Security funding. Current Speaker Paul Ryan faces similar challenges in his negotiations with and reliance on the conservative Freedom Caucus within his party. As more members of the majority become reluctant to support moderate or, at least, median positions in Congress, does the majority party frequently have to turn to the minority party to claim legislative victories? Studying this question is somewhat confounded by the majority party's ability to keep divisive legislation off the agenda, but even just for legislation that must pass, the question is vital. This question, and the frequency with which this occurs, has important implications for theories of parties in the U.S. Congress.

Lastly, there is a natural follow-up to this study that explores the likelihood of a primary challenge after a member undergoes changes in her legislative behavior. Do members who become more ideological in their voting behavior, conditioned on which party they are a member of, succeed in fending off future ideological primary challenges?

This chapter demonstrates that members who face ideological primary challenges are certainly responsive to these signals from their constituents when they return to Congress. This suggests that the presence of an ideological primary challenge, even if not competitive or successful, can reap behavioral consequences in Congress. The more ideological extreme primary electorate is influencing the legislative battle in Congress and, as ideological primaries become increasingly common, this victory is only going to grow more pronounced. Ideological primaries have consequences and these types of primaries, above and beyond the typical competitive versus non-competitive dichotomy, need to be taken seriously by the parties, incumbents, and voters.

Notes

1 Due to redistricting following the 1990 census, Upton became the representative of Michigan's sixth congressional district beginning in 1993.
2 Upton's district is the southwestern-most district in Michigan. It stretches from the Indiana border in the south to the southern border of Ottawa and Kent counties in the north. It includes numerous communities located along the shoreline of Lake Michigan.
3 Because the authors operationalize a divisive primary as one where a Tea Party candidate ran against an incumbent Republican, the finding that a divisive primary increased vote share in the general election only applies to the Republican Party.
4 Given the authors' measure of divisiveness, we are confident that the 2010 primaries they coded as divisive (those with a Tea Party candidate challenging an incumbent) are a subset of those coded as ideological above. This will be discussed in further detail below.
5 This underlying assumption will influence the selection of our dependent variable to be discussed in greater detail below and the conditional relationship we are proposing.
6 Although changes in voting behavior will not be evident for a minority party member there are other ways for these members to demonstrate a behavior change. These include, but are not limited to, bill sponsorship, bill co-sponsorship, talking points, speeches, etc. While these are certainly interesting ways to assess the legislative consequences of ideological challenges they fall beyond the scope of this chapter.

The goal of this chapter is to show how the conditional relationship posited here is essential to uncovering findings regarding the effect of ideological primary challenges on legislative behavior.

7 It is important to note that voting against the party on more votes in the Congress following the ideological challenge does not necessarily imply anything about the member's ideology. In fact, a fairly moderate member of the majority party might be a prime target for an ideological primary challenge. And for this member, even casting a few votes against the majority party in the post-challenge Congress may be enough to signal ideological independence.

8 If there were key votes *Congressional Quarterly* classified as such, but that were votes on which the majority party was rolled on final passage, we do not include these in the calculation of the dependent variable. In these cases, a vote with the minority party would actually be suggestive of a moderate position and therefore they are excluded.

References

Bernstein, Robert A. 1977. "Divisive Primaries Do Hurt: U.S. Senate Races, 1956–1972." *American Political Science Review* 71 (1): 540–545.

Blake, Robert R., and Jane Sygley Mouton. 1961. "Reaction to Intergroup Competition Under Win-Lose Conditions." *Management Science* 7 (2): 420–435.

Boatright, Robert G. 2014. *Getting Primaried: The Changing Politics of Congressional Primary Challenges.* Ann Arbor: The University of Michigan Press.

Born, Richard. 1981. "The Influence of House Primary Election Divisiveness on General Election Margins." *The Journal of Politics* 43 (3): 640–661.

Brady, David W., Hahrie Han, and Jeremy C. Pope. 2007. "Primary Elections and Candidate Ideology: Out of Step with the Primary Electorate?" *Legislative Studies Quarterly* 32 (1): 79–105.

Burden, Barry C. 2004. "Candidate Positioning in US Congressional Elections." *British Journal of Political Science* 34 (1): 211–227.

Carson, Jamie L., Erik J. Engstrom, and Jason M. Roberts. 2006. "Redistricting, Candidate Entry, and the Politics of Nineteenth Century U.S. House Elections." *American Journal of Political Science* 50 (2): 283–293.

Fenno, Richard F. 1978. *Home Style: House Members in Their Districts.* Boston: Little, Brown, and Company.

Hetherington, Marc J., Bruce A. Larson, and Suzanne Globetti. 2003. "The Redistricting Cycle and Strategic Candidate Decision in U.S. House Races." *The Journal of Politics* 65 (4): 1221–1235.

Hirano, Shigeo, James M. Snyder Jr., Stephen Ansolabehere, and John Mark Hansen. 2010. "Primary Elections and Partisan Polarization in the U.S. Congress." *Quarterly Journal of Political Science* 5 (1): 169–191.

Jacobson, Gary. 2004. *The Politics of Congressional Elections*, 6th edition. New York: Pearson.

Jewitt, Caitlin E., and Sarah A. Treul. 2014. "Competitive Primaries and Party Division in Congressional Elections," *Electoral Studies* 35 (1): 140–149.

Kenney, Patrick J. 1988. "Sorting Out the Effects of Primary Divisiveness in Congressional and Senatorial Elections," *Political Research Quarterly* 41 (4): 765–777.

Kenney, Patrick J., and Tom W. Rice. 1984. "The Effect of Primary Divisiveness in Gubernatorial and Senatorial Elections." *The Journal of Politics* 46 (4): 904–915.

Kenney, Patrick J., and Tom W. Rice. 1987. "The Relationship Between Divisive Primaries and General Election Outcomes," *American Journal of Political Science* 31 (1): 31–44.

Mayhew, David. 2004. *Congress: The Electoral Connection*, 2nd edition. New Haven: Yale University Press.

Sheppard, Kate. 2011. "Fred Upton's Climate Changeup" January 4. Mother Jones. http://www.mother jones.com/blue-marble/2011/01/fred-upton-global-warming

Southwell, Priscilla L. 1986. "The Politics of Disgruntlement: Nonvoting and Defection Among Supporters of Nomination Losers, 1968–1984." *Political Behavior* 8 (1): 81–95.

Stone, Walter J. 1986. "The Carryover Effect in Presidential Elections." *American Political Science Review* 80 (2): 271–279.

Sullivan, Denis G. 1977. "Party Unity: Appearance and Reality," *Political Science Quarterly* 92: 635–645.

Upton, Fred, and Tim Phillips. 2010. "How Congress Can Stop the EPA's Power Grab" December 28. *The Wall Street Journal.* https://www.wsj.com/articles/SB10001424052748703929404576022070069905318

Zipp, John F. 1985. "Perceived Representativeness and Voting: An Assessment of the Impact of 'Choice' vs. 'Echoes'." *American Political Science Review* 79 (1): 50–61.

13

WHEN MIGHT MODERATES WIN THE PRIMARY?

Danielle M. Thomsen

The sharp rise in partisan polarization in Congress has been one of the most prominent topics of academic debate for the past decade. In the 115th Congress, there is no ideological overlap between the two parties, and the distance between the Republican and Democratic parties is at a record high (McCarty, Poole, and Rosenthal 2006). One of the most commonly cited explanations for polarization is the primary election system. Senator Charles Schumer summarized this view in an editorial in the *New York Times*: "The partisan primary system, which favors ideologically pure candidates, has contributed to the election of more extreme officeholders and increased political polarization. It has become a menace to governing." As Schumer and many others have suggested, primary voters are believed to pull candidates away from the center and warp the national balance of the electoral system. This argument has been so powerful that almost all who seek congressional reform advocate for changes to the primary system (i.e., Fiorina, Abrams, and Pope 2006; Mann and Ornstein 2012).

Despite the logical appeal of the party primary argument, the relationship between primary elections and congressional polarization is far from clear. On the one hand, a large body of research shows that party activists have become increasingly extreme over the past few decades (e.g., Fiorina et al. 2006; Layman and Carsey 2002; Layman et al. 2010; Theriault 2008). Abramowitz (2010) provides one of the most comprehensive accounts of how the politically engaged subset of Americans is deeply divided along ideological lines. And of course, it is these individuals who are the most likely to participate in primary elections. Indeed, the Pew Research Center (2014) released a comprehensive report on mass polarization showing that Americans with more consistently conservative and liberal views are much more likely to vote in the primary than those with a mix of conservative and liberal views.

At the same time, political scientists have struggled to find linkages between partisan primaries and polarization. For one, the evidence that ideologues fare better in primaries is mixed (Brady, Han, and Pope 2007; Hall and Snyder 2015; Hirano et al. 2010), and across studies, the magnitude of the effect of candidate ideology on primary outcomes is small (Hall and Snyder 2015). Furthermore, Hirano et al. (2010) show that the introduction of primary elections, the level of primary turnout, and the threat of primary competition are not associated with partisan polarization in roll call voting. Differences in primary rules also seem to provide few answers. Closed primaries, or those in which only party members can vote, do not produce more extreme candidates than open primaries (McGhee et al. 2014; Rogowski and Langella

2015; but see Gerber and Morton 1998). Sides and Vavreck (2013) attribute these collective dead ends to the fact that primary voters look similar on many measures to other voters within their party (see also Geer 1988; Norrander 1989). They conclude, "Polarization does not seem to emanate from voters at any stage of the electoral process" (Sides and Vavreck 2013, 11).

Additional evidence on the limited impact of primaries comes from recent reforms. Most notably, the implementation of the top-two primary in 2012 in California was predicted to increase turnout and thereby diminish the effect of extreme voters on candidate selection. The top-two primary was widely expected to help moderate candidates, although subsequent studies suggest that this goal was perhaps too optimistic. Moderate candidates fared no better under the top-two primary than they would have in closed primaries (Ahler, Citrin, and Lenz 2016), and if anything, California lawmakers took more extreme positions after the adoption of the top-two primary (Kousser, Phillips, and Shor, forthcoming). Ahler et al. (2016) attribute the failure of the reform to the fact that voters are largely unaware of the ideological orientation of candidates. Hirano et al. (2015) show that voters do learn about candidate ideology in gubernatorial and senate races, but there is little indication that they do so in races with limited media coverage and resources.

It is difficult to examine how much primary voters favor extremists over moderates because moderates are much less likely to run for Congress than those at the extremes (Thomsen 2014, 2017). We can nevertheless look at the various conditions under which moderates are more likely to win. This chapter draws on primary election results to explore the relationship between candidate ideology and primary election outcomes from 1980 to 2010. Like previous scholars, I find that moderates are less likely to win the primary and receive a lower percentage of the primary vote than those at the extremes. Yet I also show that the effect of Republican liberalism and Democratic conservatism diminishes as the number of primary candidates increases, particularly in open seats. I do not sort through the various mechanisms here, but it is possible that the ideological signal is too muddled or the information is too costly to obtain in these cases. Thus, although primary voters may prefer extremists to moderates, moderate candidates may have more hope in some primary elections than in others.

When Might Moderates Win?

With respect to how central ideology is to candidate evaluations and vote choice, the conventional wisdom is certainly that primary voters today prefer ideological extremists over moderates and that they are a propelling force behind the increase in partisan polarization. And indeed, scholars have shown that party activists and the most politically engaged public have become more ideologically extreme over time (Abramowitz 2010; Fiorina et al. 2006; Layman and Carsey 2002; Layman et al. 2010; Theriault 2008). In addition, a greater proportion of consistently conservative Republicans and consistently liberal Democrats participate in party primaries than those who hold a mix of liberal and conservative positions (Pew Research Center 2014). Studies of election results also suggest that moderates are less likely to win the primary than conservative Republicans and liberal Democrats, although the size of the effect of ideology on election outcomes is surprisingly small across studies (Hall and Snyder 2015).

Yet the relationship between candidate ideology and primary election outcomes is not likely to be the same across contexts, and the fact that primary voters have a hard time distinguishing between same-party candidates makes it difficult to see how they can always reward or punish based on ideology (Ahler et al. 2016). We can think of a variety of scenarios in which moderate candidates, or at least relatively moderate candidates, could gain support from primary voters. In particular, it may be an especially tall order to reward ideological extremity in a primary when there are more candidates on the ballot. Voters have to invest different amounts of energy into learning about candidate ideology depending on the configuration of candidates, and additional candidates on the ballot will require more effort from voters to learn about their various positions. Thus, it is possible that Republican liberalism and Democratic conservatism has a diminishing effect on primary outcomes as the number of candidates in the race increases. Even if primary voters prefer ideologues to moderates, the effect of being a moderate may diminish when there are more candidates on the ballot. In these cases, the ideological signal may be too muddled or the information may be too costly to obtain.

It is also the case that primary victories are dramatically unequal in how much they contribute to party change in Congress. Incumbents rarely face primary challenges, and even when they do, members of Congress do not alter their behavior much as a result (Boatright 2013; see also Poole 1998). Increases in partisan polarization are thus mainly occurring through member replacement processes (Theriault 2006). In short, it is the election of the new guard not the reelection of the old guard that is spurring party change in Congress. Furthermore, as Gaddie and Bullock (2000, 1) write, "Open seats, not the defeat of incumbents, are the portal through which most legislators enter Congress." Compared to the relatively few candidates who defeat incumbents, open seat winners have the largest influence on the party's ideological course. As a share of incoming replacements, open seat victors are a key factor in whether and how much the gulf between the parties widens or diminishes.

The goal here is not to identify the specific mechanism for why liberal Republicans and conservative Democrats are more or less likely to gain support from primary voters, but rather to learn more about the conditions under which moderates are more likely to win the primary than we would otherwise expect. The main contribution of this chapter is thus largely empirical, but the broader theoretical point is that candidates are not chosen in isolation. They are embedded among many others, and it is the array of choices that matters for electoral outcomes and the persistence of polarization in Congress. To be sure, it is often the case that candidates, particularly incumbents, are unopposed in a primary, but it is rarely the case that open seat races do not attract an ample field of primary candidates. And it is primarily through replacement processes that the ideological gulf between the two parties has continued to widen. In sum, the composition of candidates has an important impact on which individuals are ultimately elected, but research on polarization has for the most part overlooked how the makeup of choices affects the electoral fortunes of congressional candidates.

Primary Elections Data

The main concern here is how the relationship between moderate ideology and primary election outcomes changes as the number of primary candidates increases. The analyses are based on primary election results for the U.S. House of Representatives from 1980 to 2012. Primary election results were obtained from the Federal Election Commission (2008–2012) and the *America Votes* series (Scammon, McGillivray, and Cook 1980–2006). These data were merged with Bonica's (2014) ideology estimates of candidates who ran for congressional office during this time (CFscores). Bonica (2014) uses campaign finance data to place the vast majority of congressional candidates on a common ideological scale.[1] The CFscores are calculated based on the mix of donations that candidates receive, and they range from approximately −1.5 to 1.5, with positive values indicating more conservative candidates while negative values denote more liberal candidates. What is particularly advantageous about these data is that they allow us to make comparisons among candidates who won as well as lost the primary. The dataset includes a total of 24,153 Republican and Democratic primary candidates; of the more than 24,000 candidates who appeared on the primary ballot, 17,656 (73 percent) have ideology scores.[2]

There is no precise way to define "ideological moderates." Two American politicians during this time period who were widely considered to be moderates, however, were Senator Olympia Snowe (R-ME) and Representative Bart Gordon (D-TN). Snowe was a veteran moderate Republican from Maine who served for more than three decades in both the U.S. House and Senate, and she deviated from her party on many occasions and on the most controversial issues, including abortion, gay rights, and health care. Gordon was a Blue Dog Democrat who represented Tennessee for more than 25 years, and he voted against the Democrats on various issues during his tenure in office as well. By way of illustration, I use the positions of these two politicians to provide one estimate of moderation. As Figure 13.1 shows, the percentage of Republican and Democratic primary winners who were as moderate, or more so, than Snowe or Gordon has declined over time. In 1980, nearly 19 percent of Republican and Democratic primary winners were at least as liberal as Snowe and at least as conservative as Gordon, respectively, but this figure dropped to just 4 percent by 2012.

However, we can also see that candidates who are not quite as moderate as Snowe and Gordon but nevertheless more moderate than the party mean in Congress still make up a sizeable proportion of primary winners. Furthermore, these numbers have remained relatively stable over time, with candidates on the moderate side of the party in Congress constituting 32 percent of primary winners in 1980 and 36 percent of winners in 2012. The higher values in part reflect the victories of incumbents who are on the moderate side of the party mean, but we can also see similar rates among non-incumbent candidates in open seat races. To be sure, the

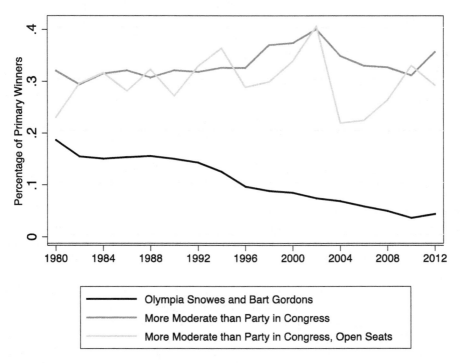

Figure 13.1   Ideological Moderates as a Proportion of Primary Winners, 1980–2012

Source: America Votes; Federal Election Commission; Bonica (2014).

party mean has changed in important ways over time – with both parties moving away from the center and toward the extremes – but it does not seem to be the case that candidates who are on the moderate side of the party in Congress comprised a much larger share of non-incumbent winners 30 years ago than they do today.

Thus, while ideological moderates have consistently made up a minority of primary winners, these data provide us with ample opportunity for an analysis of electoral outcomes across relatively moderate U.S. House candidates. Of the 12,927 candidates who won their primary from 1980 to 2012, 4,280, or 33 percent, were on the moderate side of the party in Congress. Only 1,335 primary winners (10 percent) were as moderate as Snowe and Gordon during this time period, but this is still a sizeable number of candidates. Lastly, there were 1,528 non-incumbent candidates who won in open seats during this time period, and 455 (30 percent) were more moderate than the party in Congress.

I use a series of regressions to analyze the relationship between candidate ideology and primary election outcomes. The dependent variables are primary election victory and primary vote share.[3] The main independent variable is the candidate's CFscore, coded as Republican liberalism and Democratic conservatism.[4] We are interested in the relationship between moderate ideology and primary outcomes, but we are particularly interested in the conditions under which that relationship differs. I include an interaction between moderate ideology and the total number of candidates in the primary, as the effect of Republican liberalism and Democratic conservatism is expected to diminish as the number of candidates increases. Primary voters may have a harder time distinguishing among candidates, or the information may be too costly to obtain in these cases, but again, I do not sort through the various mechanisms here.

Several control variables are included in the models as well. First, sitting members of Congress generally sail to primary election victory, and I include a dummy variable for incumbents. House candidates who raise more money are also expected to be more successful at the ballot box, and contributions are obtained from Bonica's (2014) dataset and measured as logged values of total campaign receipts. In addition, the number of primary candidates is expected to be negatively associated with primary vote share and primary victory. I account for candidates' own party presidential vote share in the congressional district, as candidates are expected to be less likely to win the primary in more favorable partisan districts (Stone and Maisel 2003). Lastly, I include a dummy variable for Republican candidates. All of the models include state and year fixed effects.

Candidate Configurations and Primary Election Outcomes

This section analyzes the conditions under which moderate candidates are more likely to attract support from primary voters. The results are presented in Tables 13.1 and 13.2 below. The dependent variable in Table 13.1 is primary election victory, and the dependent variable in Table 13.2 is primary vote share. The full model is provided in Column 1. In terms of the main variables of interest, liberal Republicans and conservative Democrats are less likely to win the primary and receive a smaller percentage of the primary vote than conservative Republicans and liberal Democrats, which is consistent with the conventional wisdom that moderates have a harder time in the primary than ideologues. However, the magnitude of the effect of ideology is small (see also Hall and Snyder 2015). A one-unit increase in Republican liberalism or Democratic conservatism, which is comparable to a shift from Michele Bachmann to Olympia Snowe on the Republican side or a shift from Keith Ellison to Bart Gordon on the Democratic side, results in a 6.4 percentage point decrease in the likelihood of primary victory (from 44.3 to 37.9 percent) and a 2.0 percentage point decrease in primary vote share (from 37.3 to 35.3 percent).[5]

Table 13.1 The Relationship Between Moderate Ideology and Primary Victory, 1980–2012

	(1) All	(2) Interaction	(3) Open Seats
Moderate Ideology (Republican liberalism; Democratic conservatism)	−0.06** (0.01)	−0.07** (0.01)	−0.15** (0.03)
Number of Primary Candidates	−0.04** (0.00)	−0.04** (0.00)	−0.02** (0.00)
Moderate Ideology x Number of Primary Candidates	——	0.00 (0.00)	0.01* (0.00)
Incumbent	0.37** (0.01)	0.37** (0.01)	——
Log of Mean Receipts Raised	0.08** (0.00)	0.08** (0.00)	0.15** (0.00)
Own Party Presidential Vote Share	−0.01** (0.00)	−0.01** (0.00)	−0.01** (0.00)
Republican	−0.03** (0.01)	−0.03** (0.01)	−0.05** (0.01)
Constant	−0.12 (0.08)	−0.13 (0.08)	−1.29** (0.15)
Number of Observations	9,994	9,994	3,269
R^2	0.35	0.35	0.32

Note: Entries are OLS regression coefficients with standard errors in parentheses. All models include state and year fixed effects. **$p < 0.01$, *$p < 0.05$.

Table 13.2 The Relationship Between Moderate Ideology and Primary Vote Share, 1980–2012

	(1) All	(2) Interaction	(3) Open Seats
Moderate Ideology (Republican liberalism; Democratic conservatism)	−0.02** (0.00)	−0.03** (0.01)	−0.05** (0.01)
Number of Primary Candidates	−0.04** (0.00)	−0.04** (0.00)	−0.03** (0.00)
Moderate Ideology x Number of Primary Candidates	——	0.00* (0.00)	0.01** (0.00)
Incumbent	0.28** (0.00)	0.28** (0.00)	——
Log of Mean Receipts Raised	0.03** (0.00)	0.03** (0.00)	0.06** (0.00)
Own Party Presidential Vote Share	−0.00** (0.00)	−0.00** (0.00)	−0.00** (0.00)
Republican	−0.01** (0.00)	−0.01** (0.00)	−0.01** (0.01)
Constant	0.24** (0.03)	0.23** (0.03)	−0.17** (0.05)
Number of Observations	9,994	9,994	3,269
R^2	0.63	0.63	0.55

Note: Entries are OLS regression coefficients with standard errors in parentheses. All models include state and year fixed effects. **$p < 0.01$, *$p < 0.05$.

Our additional concern here is whether the relationship between ideology and election outcomes changes as the number of primary candidates increases. Column 2 presents the results with the interaction between moderate ideology and the number of primary candidates. The interaction is positive and significant in Table 13.2, indicating that moderates receive a larger percentage of the primary vote as the number of primary candidates increases, but the size of the effect is small. The relationship is positive in Column 2 of Table 13.1 but does not reach conventional levels of statistical significance.

Yet as noted above, all primary victories do not contribute equally to party polarization in Congress, and open seat victors are a key factor in whether and how much the ideological gulf between the parties widens or diminishes. Thus, I also restrict the analyses to open seats to examine the relationship between candidate ideology and primary outcomes in these electoral contexts as well. The rest of the section focuses on the results in Column 3 in Tables 1 and 2 given the disproportionate impact of open seat victors on party change in Congress. The relationship between moderate ideology and primary election victory and primary vote share is again negative, but the positive and significant interaction term in both models is of greater concern here.

The left and right panels of Figure 13.2 present the marginal effect of moderate ideology on primary election victory and primary vote share as the number of primary candidates increases. Again, these values are for open congressional seats. Moderates are less likely to win the primary than those at the extremes, but as the number of candidates increases, the negative effect of Republican liberalism and Democratic conservatism diminishes. When there are four and eight primary candidates, the same one-unit increase as above in Republican liberalism and Democratic conservatism decreases the likelihood of winning by 10.9 and 6.6 percentage points, respectively, and reduces the primary vote share by 3.2 and 1.2 percentage points, respectively. In fact, candidate ideology does not matter much at all for primary vote share when there are a large number of candidates in the primary, though this is certainly a minority of races in terms of frequency. (There are 584 non-incumbent candidates who ran in open seat races with at least 8 candidates, or 18 percent of the total.) However, the main point is that although Republican liberalism and Democratic conservatism is for the most part a barrier – albeit a relatively small one – to electoral success in contemporary party primaries, it appears to be less of a barrier as the number of primary competitors increases.

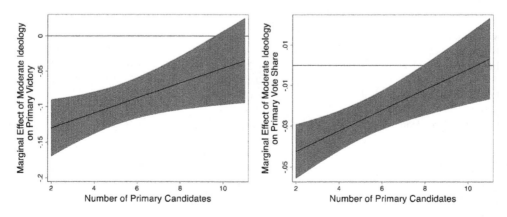

Figure 13.2 Marginal Effect of Moderate Ideology on Primary Victory and Vote Share Across Number of Primary Candidates, 1980–2012

Note: Values are estimated from the model in Column 3 in Tables 13.1 and 13.2.

With respect to the control variables, the results are largely consistent with expectations. Incumbency has a huge effect on primary election outcomes, as it is very rare for incumbents to lose in the primary. The primary vote share for incumbents is 28 percentage points higher than it is for non-incumbents, and the effect of incumbency dwarfs that of all the other variables. As the number of primary candidates increases and as the district becomes more favorable to a candidate's party, her likelihood of primary victory and her percentage of the primary vote is expected to decrease. In addition, candidates who raise more money are expected to be more successful in the primary.

In sum, the findings suggest that it is more difficult for liberal Republicans and conservative Democrats to attract support in primary elections than those at the extremes, but the magnitude of the effect of candidate ideology on primary vote share is not as large as the conventional wisdom would suggest. And more importantly here, the relationship between ideological moderate and primary outcomes also depends on the particular configuration of candidates on the ballot, and the negative effect of Republican liberalism and Democratic conservatism diminishes as the number of candidates increases. I do not sort through the various mechanisms here for why this is the case, but perhaps it is too costly for primary voters to obtain information on the various competitors or the ideological signal is too muddled. Indeed, previous research has shown that voters have a difficult time distinguishing between same-party candidates (Ahler et al. 2016), particularly in races with limited media coverage and resources (Hirano et al. 2015).

Conclusion

The data conform to the conventional wisdom that primary voters are more likely to favor ideologues over moderates. Indeed, very liberal Republicans and very conservative Democrats are unlikely to prevail in the current polarized environment, and the findings support the general narrative about the attitudes and beliefs of primary voters. Nevertheless, we can leverage newly available ideology data to examine the conditions under which candidate ideology may matter more or less for electoral outcomes and gain insight into when moderates might be more likely to win than they would otherwise. This chapter is a first step toward that goal.

The broader message is that although primary voters may prefer ideologues to moderates, conservative Republicans and liberal Democrats may not always have the upper hand in primary contests. Candidate ideology does not outweigh all other variables, and again, the magnitude of the relationship between moderate ideology and primary vote share is surprisingly small (see also Hall and Snyder 2015). Moreover, candidates are not chosen in isolation, and the collective arrangement of candidates matters for who is ultimately elected to office. Polarization scholars have paid less attention to the configuration of choices that voters face and the implications of these various configurations for the electoral fortunes of moderate candidates. For those who bemoan the rise of polarization in Congress, these findings should be seen as good news. Primary voters may be more likely to select moderates or ideologues depending on the choices that are presented to them. Perhaps instead of focusing on changing primary laws, the first step for reformers who wish to diminish the ideological gulf between the two parties should be to encourage more moderates to run for office. Regardless of the configuration of choices on the ballot, in order for a moderate candidate to get elected, there must be a moderate for voters to choose.

Notes

1 See Bonica (2014) for a full description of the data and validation.
2 The Bonica dataset includes candidates who filed with the Federal Election Commission. Candidates who do not exceed the $5,000 threshold of campaign fundraising are not required to file. Those who are excluded are thus more likely to be long-shot candidates, but it is not clear that they are more likely

to be extremists. Even so, these excluded candidates comprised only 8 percent of primary winners and 0.04 percent of general election winners, so they have virtually no effect on polarization in Congress. Furthermore, the Bonica data provide the best publicly available measures of the ideological positions of primary winners and losers over time.

3 Like most studies of primary election outcomes, I exclude primary candidates who are unopposed (e.g., Lawless and Pearson 2008). Of the 17,656 primary candidates with CFscores, 8,420 (43 percent) were unopposed.

4 Ideological centrism can be measured in a variety of ways. I use the left-right positions of candidates (e.g., Rogowski and Langella 2015) on the CFscore scale, but the findings are the same if ideology is measured as the distance from the most extreme candidate in the primary (e.g., Hall and Snyder 2015).

5 Olympia Snowe and Bart Gordon are the moderates referenced above. Michele Bachmann retired from Congress in 2014, but she was at the conservative end of the GOP during her time in office and she was an outspoken leader of the Tea Party movement. Keith Ellison is one of the most liberal members in Congress, and he was co-founder of the Congressional Progressive Caucus. All other variables are set at their mean or mode so these values are for non-incumbents. The values of course vary significantly by candidate type.

References

Abramowitz, Alan I. 2010. *The Disappearing Center: Engaged Citizens, Polarization, and American Democracy*. New Haven, CT: Yale University Press.

Ahler, Douglas J., Jack Citrin, and Gabriel S. Lenz. 2016. "Do Open Primaries Improve Representation? An Experimental Test of California's 2012 Top-Two Primary." *Legislative Studies Quarterly* 41(2): 237–68.

Boatright, Robert. 2013. *Getting Primaried: The Changing Politics of Congressional Primary Elections*. Ann Arbor: University of Michigan Press.

Bonica, Adam. 2014. "Mapping the Ideological Marketplace." *American Journal of Political Science* 58(2): 367–387.

Brady, David W., Hahrie Han, and Jeremy C. Pope. 2007. "Primary Elections and Candidate Ideology: Out of Step with the Primary Electorate?" *Legislative Studies Quarterly* 32(1): 79–105.

Fiorina, Morris P., Samuel J. Abrams, and Jeremy C. Pope. 2006. *Culture War? The Myth of a Polarized America*. New York: Pearson/Longman.

Gaddie, Ronald Keith, and Charles S. Bullock III. 2000. *Elections to Open Seats in the U.S. House: Where the Action Is*. Lanham, MD: Rowman & Littlefield.

Geer, John. 1988. "Assessing the Representativeness of Electorates in Presidential Primaries." *American Journal of Political Science* 32(4): 929–945.

Gerber, Elisabeth R., and Rebecca B. Morton. 1998. "Primary Election Systems and Representation." *Journal of Law, Economics, and Organization* 14(2): 304–324.

Hall, Andrew B., and James Snyder. 2015. "Candidate Ideology and Electoral Success." Working Paper, Harvard University.

Hirano, Shigeo, Gabriel S. Lenz, Maksim Pinkovskiy, and James M. Snyder, Jr. 2015. "Voter Learning in State Primary Elections." *American Journal of Political Science* 59(1): 91–108.

Hirano, Shigeo, James M. Snyder, Jr., Stephen Ansolabehere, and John Mark Hansen. 2010. "Primary Elections and Partisan Polarization in Congress." *Quarterly Journal of Political Science* 5: 169–191.

Kousser, Thad, Justin Phillips, and Boris Shor. Forthcoming. "Reform and Representation: A New Method Applied to Recent Electoral Changes." *Political Science Research and Methods*.

Lawless, Jennifer L. and Kathryn Pearson. 2008. "The Primary Reason for Women's Underrepresentation? Reevaluating the Conventional Wisdom." *Journal of Politics* 70(1): 67–82.

Layman, Geoffrey C. and Thomas M. Carsey. 2002. "Party Polarization and 'Conflict Extension' in the American Electorate." *American Journal of Political Science* 46(4): 786–802.

Layman, Geoffrey C., Thomas M. Carsey, John C. Green, Richard Herrera, and Rosalyn Cooperman. 2010. "Activists and Conflict Extension in American Party Politics." *American Political Science Review* 104(2): 324–346.

Mann, Thomas E., and Norman J. Ornstein. 2012. *It's Even Worse Than It Looks: How the American Constitutional System Collided with the New Politics of Extremism*. New York: Basic Books.

McCarty, Nolan, Keith T. Poole, and Howard Rosenthal. 2006. *Polarized America: The Dance of Ideology and Unequal Riches*. Cambridge: Massachusetts Institute of Technology Press.

McGhee, Eric, Seth Masket, Boris Shor, Steve Rogers, and Nolan McCarty. 2014. "A Primary Cause of Partisanship? Nomination Systems and Legislator Ideology." *American Journal of Political Science* 58(2): 337–351.

Norrander, Barbara. 1989. "Ideological Representativeness of Presidential Primary Voters." *American Journal of Political Science* 33: 570–587.

Pew Research Center. 2014. "Political Polarization in the American Public." Washington, DC: Pew Research Center.

Poole, Keith T. 1998. "Changing Minds? Not in Congress!" GSIA Working Paper 1997–22. Carnegie-Mellon University.

Rogowski, Jon C. and Stephanie Langella. 2015. "Primary Systems and Candidate Ideology: Evidence from Federal and State Legislative Elections." *American Politics Research* 43(4): 846–871.

Scammon, Richard M., Alice V. McGillivray, and Rhodes Cook. 1980–2006. *America Votes 14–27: A Handbook of Contemporary American Election Statistics.* Washington, DC: CQ Press.

Schumer, Charles. 2014. "End Partisan Primaries, Save America." *New York Times*, July 21, p. A21.

Sides, John, and Lynn Vavreck. 2013. "On the Representativeness of Primary Electorates." Paper presented at the conference Political Representation: Fifty Years after Miller and Stokes, Vanderbilt University, March 2013.

Stone, Walter J., and L. Sandy Maisel. 2003. "The Not-So-Simple Calculus of Winning: Potential U.S. House Candidates' Nomination and General Election Chances." *Journal of Politics* 65(4): 951–977.

Theriault, Sean M. 2006. "Party Polarization in the U.S. Congress: Member Replacement and Member Adaptation." *Party Politics* 12(4): 483–503.

Theriault, Sean M. 2008. *Party Polarization in Congress.* New York: Cambridge University Press.

Thomsen, Danielle M. 2014. "Ideological Moderates Won't Run: How Party Fit Matters for Partisan Polarization in Congress." *Journal of Politics* 76(3): 786–797.

Thomsen, Danielle M. 2017. *Opting Out of Congress: Partisan Polarization and the Decline of Moderate Candidates.* New York: Cambridge University Press.

14

PRIMARY ELECTIONS AND GROUP DYNAMICS

Examining the Makeup of the Party Coalitions

Casey B. K. Dominguez

Political parties are usually defined as coalitions that run candidates for office in order to control government and achieve policy outcomes (Downs 1957; Schlesinger 1985; Sorauf 1984). Because American parties choose candidates in primary elections, rather than the more controlled internal processes used by parties in other countries, there is always some question about whether American party nominees are really loyal to the party itself, or whether they are independent agents who will make promises to anyone (inside the party or not) in order to get elected (Herrnson 1988, 2001; Jacobson 2001; Silbey 1990). Lacking enforceable party platforms, there are also real questions about whether there really is "a party" to whom we might ask candidates to be loyal. But the fact of the matter is that partisan elected officials do control government policy. The substantive priorities of the parties do differ by party. And some (if not all) important policy positions are the subject of widespread, if not universal, agreement among the party's representatives in office. Since officeholders are not bound by platforms, or handpicked by party leaders, where does that policy agreement come from?

Primary elections help us answer some of those questions about party composition, policy positions, and identity. When a party nominates a candidate, it makes a statement about what the party itself cares about. In primary elections, groups and individuals in a party coalition fight with each other over which candidate embodies the best set of values and who articulates the best set of issue positions. The groups and individuals who are involved in a party's primary contests are those that have the first (and potentially among the greatest) effects on the issue positions the candidate takes. Research suggests that incumbents pay the most attention to their primary election constituency (Brady, Han and Pope 2007). Presumably they also pay attention to the interest and issue groups that shaped the promises the incumbent made to that primary constituency. If some groups are habitually in the business of participating in a party's primaries, across space and time, it is reasonable to bet that their preferences will be reflected by many of that party's nominees and eventual officeholders. Therefore, if we want to understand how parties adopt core issue positions, and how they evolve over time, it is important to understand how the party coalitions manifest themselves in primary elections.

Because participation in primary elections is mostly limited to partisans, examining those partisan actors who engage in primary campaigns helps us to define the "base" of the political parties. Although the press mostly considers the "base" of the party to be a bounded group of ordinary voters, research on voting behavior strongly suggests that voters' positions on issues are malleable and subject to elite guidance (Achen and Bartels 2016). In keeping with a recently developed but prominent strain of research that considers party coalitions to be *primarily* inter-est group coalitions (Bawn et al. 2012) rather than voter coalitions, this chapter will examine the elite, group-centered coalitions that emerge in primary elections. This chapter delves into federal primary elections for the House, Senate, and President, not by examining particular candidates, but by focusing on the groups that compose the party coalitions that are active in primaries. The goal is to use primary elections as a way of understanding the makeup of the party coalitions themselves.

This chapter will make three main points. First, it will argue that some primary elections are more systematically interesting and important for understanding party coalitions than others. Second, it will show that (obviously) the Democratic and Republican primary coalitions are quite distinct, and that their differences are made evident by examining campaign contributions to primary election candidates in each party. Finally, it will use data gathered from primary elec-tions to show how the party coalitions themselves have changed over time, and how changes in those coalitions are consistent with the partisan polarization so widely observed in the last two decades.

What Do We Know about Primary Elections and the Composition of Party Coalitions?

Most research on sub-national primary elections has focused not on the party's involvement in candidate selection, but on the emergence of candidates themselves. One reason for that focus is that for many years, the dominant mode of thinking about congressional elections has put can-didates in the drivers' seat, and so when scholars conceptualized the nature of primary elections, they focused on the "emergence" of candidates and the candidate-specific determinants of their success. This research taught us that incumbency, the distribution of partisanship in the district and the quality of the nominee have the biggest effects on which party wins any given congres-sional election (Bond, Covington and Fleisher 1985; Jacobson 2001; Stone and Maisel 1999).

The research on candidate emergence has shown us that primary election environments are fundamentally shaped by the competitiveness of the general election. More candidates want to run in races they think they can win, and so few run to challenge strong incumbents, and more (and better) candidates run in open seat primary contests (Banks and Kiewiet 1989; Bianco 1984; Hogan 2003; Lazarus 2005).

Another focus in the study of legislative primary elections has been the relative prevalence and consequences of divisiveness and negative campaigning. Some studies have shown that highly divisive primaries have no effect on the party's general election fortunes (Geer and Shere 1992) while others suggest that divisive primaries hurt the party (Kenney and Rice 1987) or hurt Democrats more than Republicans (Kenney and Rice 1984; Lengle, Owen and Sonner 1995). Some evidence suggests that intense primary battles can cause the activists who aligned themselves with the losing candidates to refuse to participate in the general election or support the eventual nominee (McCann, Partin, Rapoport and Stone 1996; Miller, Jewell and Sigelman 1988; Stone, Atkeson and Rapoport 1992). Parties can also take actions to reduce this divisive-ness (Dominguez 2005; Herrnson and Gimpel 1995; Kazee 1983).

This literature mostly assumes that factionalism and divisiveness is driven by candidate loy-alty and candidate characteristics, and so the makeup of factions themselves is not a particular focus of study. Recent work on political parties, however, suggests that the party coalitions may have other important actors besides candidates – including activists, donors, and affiliated interest groups (Bawn et al. 2012; Bernstein 1999; Cohen et al. 2008; Masket 2004; Monroe

2001; Schwartz 1990; Skinner 2007). These actors share information, strategy, and resources with each other, but not with the other side (Heaney et al. 2012; Koger et al. 2009; Skinner 2007; Skinner, Masket and Dulio 2012). If we consider the parties to be coalitions of these many actors, we are able to ask new and different questions about primary elections.

In the party coalition paradigm, members of the coalition drive primary election dynamics through intergroup competition and coordination. Whether they concentrate their support or divide it among many candidates measurably affects the course of the primary race itself (Cohen et al. 2008; Dominguez 2011). Winning primary candidates, in this model, are simply the product of those machinations. From this perspective, primary elections become one of our only windows into describing and modeling party coalition management because they are one of the only moments when party coalition members engage with each other in the public eye.

Research about primary elections does not tell us very much about variation in coalition deliberation because the scholarly literature has traditionally treated all groups (outside of the formal party committees) as nonpartisan. That definition discourages observers from considering activist groups as members of a coalition who could be airing and adjudicating explicitly intrapartisan disagreements in primary elections. Recently, however, interest group and party scholars have now opened up the possibility that some groups should be considered explicit members of party coalitions. That opens the door to asking *who the partisan groups are*, and *how these partisan groups behave* in primary elections. To assess a group's partisanship, this chapter relies on campaign contributions to each of the two major parties' candidates for federal office.

The data presented here suggests that it is useful to define boundaries around the groups in the party's coalition, because watching changes over time in those groups' involvement in primary elections sheds important light on the nature of the party itself.

Contribution Data

The Federal Election Commission (FEC) collects and makes public all contributions made by groups and individuals to candidates for federal office. They also collect and make public the data on independent expenditures made on behalf of those candidates. The analysis that follows will make use of group contributions to Democratic and Republican candidates in different types of primary elections in order to describe the party coalitions over a 32-year period, from 1984 to 2016.[1]

Looking at donor political committees in this period, our first observation is that there is *very wide* variance in how much total money the committees give to federal candidates in this 32-year period. Some groups gave as little as $10, total, while others gave more than $500,000,000. Figure 14.1 shows the number of groups that gave in each category. The modal group gave a total of about $100,000. Over three decades, with allowable contributions of $5,000 per candidate, that modal group, and most others, could give money in as few as 20 races. Such groups probably don't have the kind of widespread or sustained influence over elections or candidates to figure into a story about national party composition and change.

A total of 10,830 Political Action Committees gave contributions to Democratic or Republican candidates in this time period. However, most of the money was actually given by a tiny fraction of the committees. The top 1,083 (10%) of PACs gave 87 percent of all of the organizational money contributed to or spent on behalf of federal candidates. Therefore, most of the analysis in this chapter focuses on that top 10 percent of PACs.

Most of these groups would probably claim to be nonpartisan, but there are reasons to be skeptical of such suggestions. Like voters who claim to be "independent," but are reasonably consistent partisans, some subsets of groups are probably disguised partisans. And like voters, there is probably some spectrum of partisan attachment from the strong, long-term partisans, to more

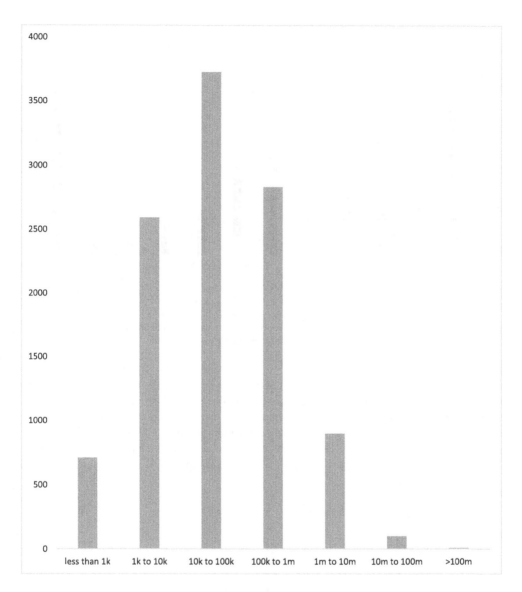

Figure 14.1 Number of PAC Committees, by Total Contributions (Primaries and General Elections), 1984–2016 (U.S. Dollars)

fair-weather partisan supporters. A group that gives more than 80 percent of its contributions to Republicans may be able to make a weak claim to independence, but it does not survive any reasonable amount of scrutiny. That threshold could be set at 75 percent, or at 90 percent, but here we will use the 80 percent cutoff to define "partisan" groups. Groups that give between 21 percent and 79 percent of their contributions to each party will be considered loosely "nonpartisan."[2]

It is straightforward to assess the partisan lean of each group by adding up all of the group's contributions to Democratic candidates and to Republican candidates, and calculating what percent of the group's total contributions went to one party. Figure 14.2 uses the Democrats as a reference point. It shows the number of groups that gave a particular percentage of their contributions to

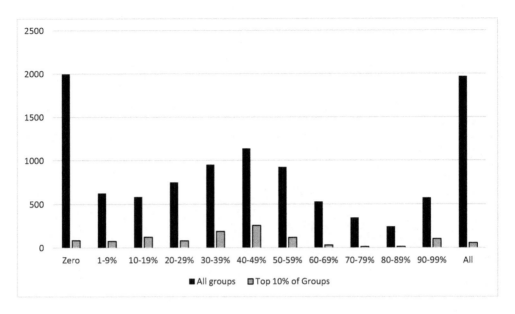

Figure 14.2   Number of All Groups and Top Groups by Percentage of Expenditures to Democratic
Candidates (Primaries and General Elections), 1984–2016

Democrats. Among all groups, the distribution appears roughly bimodal – there appear to be a large
number of groups that only give money to candidates in one party. However, most of these groups
are relatively poor and don't give that much money or to that many candidates. Figure 14.3 zooms
in and restricts the partisan analysis to cumulative donations by the top 10 percent of PACs. This
reveals that there are about 400 very loyal groups – clustered at the two ends of the distribution –
that predominantly support candidates in only one of the two parties. It also shows that there is a

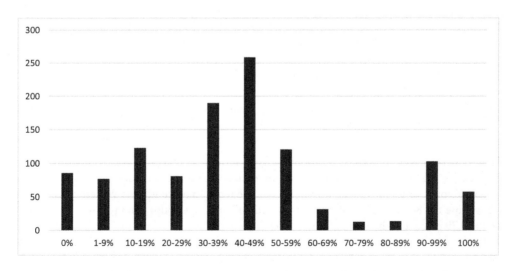

Figure 14.3   Number of Top 10 percent of PACs, by Percent of Total Expenditures Going to
Democratic Candidates (Primaries and General Elections), 1984–2016

sizeable number of "leaning," or perhaps "access-buying" groups that give to both parties, but in this period these access-buying groups tended to give more to Republicans than to Democrats. The overwhelming majority of the access-buying groups are corporate PACs and Trade Associations.

The Democrats are more heavily reliant on their most loyal groups than Republicans are. The 178 most loyal Democratic PACs (>80% to Dems) play an enormous role in getting Democratic candidates elected. Though they make up a little over 1 percent of all PACs, they supplied 61 percent of all money raised by or spent on behalf of all federal Democratic candidates in this time period. Republicans have more diverse sources of money. The 206 most loyal Republican groups (>80% to Reps) only contributed 46 percent of all of the money contributed to or spent on behalf of all Republican federal candidates in the time period. Clearly, the few hundred most loyal groups are critical parts of each party's infrastructure.

The Party Coalitions

Any reasonable political observer can make some smart guesses about the types of groups in the Democratic coalition, the Republican coalition, and the nonpartisan/access-buying pool. Figure 14.4 probably confirms many of these suspicions, while also revealing some less intuitive insights.

It is probably unsurprising to see that more than a quarter of Republican-loyal committees are either corporations or trade associations. Corporations and trade associations also dominate the nonpartisan groups that divide their support more evenly among the two parties' candidates. It is also unsurprising, though perhaps not widely recognized, that about a third of the groups

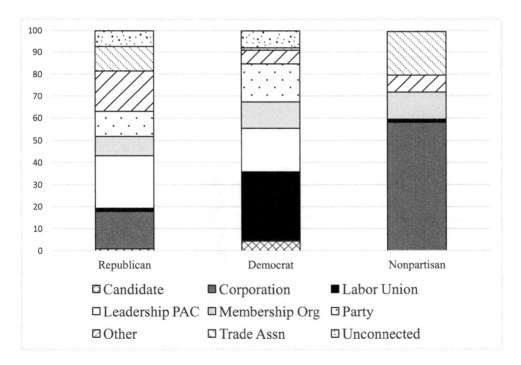

Figure 14.4 Percentage of the Total Number of Elite Groups That Give At Least 80 Percent to Republicans, 80 Percent to Democrats, or Are Nonpartisan, (in Primaries and General Elections) by PAC Classification Type

that were most loyal to Democrats, and contributed the greatest amount of money to them over this time period, were labor unions. Explicitly partisan groups like state and federal party committees are important to each party, as are Leadership PACs (which are formed by members of Congress to raise money for each other's races). Though the number of Leadership PACs is small in the overall PAC universe, they make up about a third of the most loyal and most important fundraisers for both parties' candidates. We will note later that the relative importance of formal party committees and Leadership PACs has changed significantly over time.

Not All Primary Elections Are the Same: Different Environments Have Different Group Dynamics

So far, we have just been looking at overall total contributions, in both general elections and primary elections. But of course, primary elections are our special concern. Of all money contributed to candidates or spent on their behalf by the top 10 percent of committees ($6.9 billion over 32 years, including both partisan and nonpartisan committees), 30 percent ($2.1 billion) was spent in primary elections.

Contributions to candidates in general elections should be expected to be heavily weighted toward access-buying groups. Those groups have a well-known inclination to support incumbents and sure-bets. They are not interested in wading into factional fights or wasting money on candidates who won't be in a position to affect policymaking in Washington.

The groups that make up the party coalitions, however, have compelling motivations to be involved in primary elections. A group with a strong position on abortion, for example, wants to make sure that every candidate in its affiliated party shares that group's position on abortion. Selecting true-believer candidates means the groups don't have to spend as much time lobbying on policy later, and helps to ensure that the groups have access to the party's agenda. Groups that want to affect the policy positions of everyone in a party, writ large, have good reasons to be involved in many different primary elections. So if we want to understand how party positions develop in the first place and change over time, it might prove useful to zoom in on certain kinds of primary elections, and the groups that become involved in them. The distribution of groups in Figure 14.5 helps to justify this strategy.

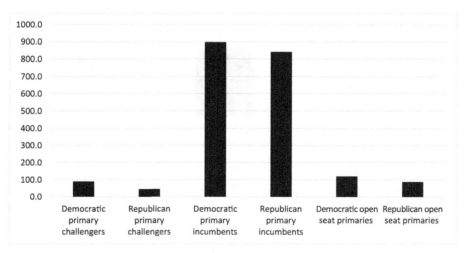

Figure 14.5 Total Primary Contributions, in Millions of U.S. Dollars, All Groups in All Years, by Type of Primary Election

The vast majority of the money (82%) contributed in federal primaries is contributed to candidates in incumbent renomination primaries. Those primaries are overwhelmingly likely to be uncontested by serious challengers, and to feature either no competition or only token opposition. Why, then, do these incumbents raise so much money in their primary races? The answer is that they do not necessarily *spend* the money, they just raise it. PAC committees are legally allowed to contribute one $5000 check to a candidate in the general election, *and one in the primary*. So by giving to an incumbent in both races, even if the primary election is obviously uncontested, groups can effectively double their campaign contribution to a sitting member of Congress. It would be reasonable to expect that access-buying, relatively nonpartisan groups (who don't give more than 80 percent of their total contributions to one party's candidates) would take special advantage of this rule. That is what we are seeing in Figure 14.5. Neutral groups give two-thirds of all of the money contributed in incumbent primaries, and those neutral groups devote 85 percent of their overall primary resources to those incumbent primaries.

The other two types of primaries, those to nominate candidates to run in open seats, and those to run as challengers to incumbents, are far less attractive to access-buying groups, because it is far less certain that any particular challenger or open seat primary candidate will actually be elected to Congress. For groups trying to influence the makeup of the party's elected membership, however, these primaries are the most important ones. Open seat primaries are the main way that new members get elected to Congress for the first time. So we should expect to see most of the money in those primaries being contributed by the more partisan groups. Figure 14.6 confirms this hypothesis.

Primaries to nominate new candidates, either as challengers to incumbents, or as nominees in open seat races, draw the attention of the more partisan groups. The most loyal Democratic groups spend the vast majority of money in Democratic primary contests to nominate challengers to incumbents and nominees in open seats.

Loyal Republican groups are major participants in primaries to nominate challengers to incumbents, but in open seat primaries, neutral groups outspend loyal Republican groups. That seems somewhat puzzling, except that on the Republican side there may be less difference between the 70 percent loyal Republican groups and the 80 percent loyal Republican groups. Most of the PACs that give between 70 percent and 80 percent of their money to Republicans are corporations and trade associations with similar profiles to the 80 percent to 90 percent loyal Republican PACs.

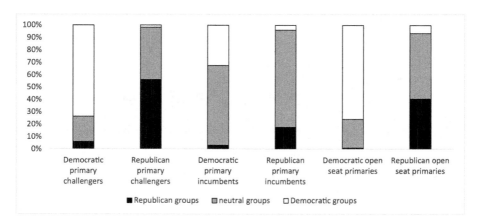

Figure 14.6 Percentage of Money Spent by Top Groups in Each Type of Primary Election, by Partisanship of the Group

In both parties, the nonpartisan groups spend most of the money to nominate or fill the campaign coffers of incumbents, regardless of whether they face primary opposition. These nonpartisan groups participate far less in challenger primaries and somewhat less in open seat primaries, as noted above. This pattern has persisted throughout the 1984–2016 period.

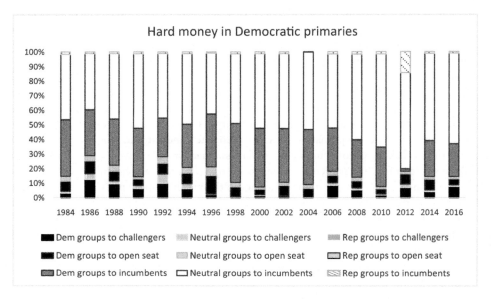

Figure 14.7a Hard Money Contributed in Democratic Primaries, by Race Type and Group Type

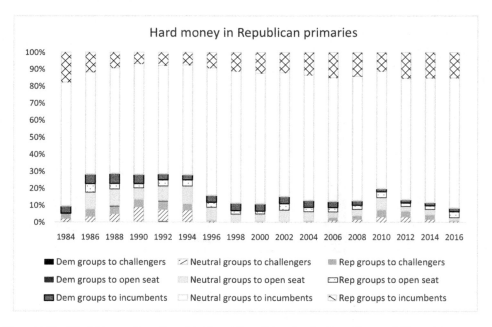

Figure 14.7b Hard Money Contributed in Republican Primaries, by Race Type and Group Type

Figures 14.7a and 14.7b shows that the overwhelming majority of money contributed in primary elections has always been contributed to incumbents. Figure 14.7a shows that neutral and democratic-leaning groups giving to incumbents has always (since 1984) dominated Democratic primary hard money donations. Figure 14.7b shows that at least 60 percent of all Republican primary hard money contributions have always been neutral groups giving to Republican incumbents. Because neutral groups giving in incumbent primaries so dominate the overall primary election hard money pool, it is necessary to look at the other types of groups and the other types of primaries to see the party network in action selecting nominees. The next two sections will focus on each party's coalition in turn.

The Democratic Coalition

In both open seat and challenger primaries, and in both hard money contributions and independent expenditures, Democratic candidates get the most contributions from blue collar labor unions. Figure 14.8 shows the cumulative dollar totals for each type of group for the whole period.

Across the whole 32 years, including both hard and soft money, the biggest contributor to non-incumbent Democratic primary candidates was the Service Employees International Union (SEIU). The SEIU was joined by the American Federation of State, County, and Municipal Employees (AFSCME), the Association of Trial Lawyers, the Teamsters, the International Brotherhood of Electrical Workers (IBEW), two teachers' unions (the National Education Association and the American Federation of Teachers), the Machinists' Union, and the UAW. Figure 14.8 shows that several dozen blue collar unions dominate contributions to Democrats. Membership organizations like the Human Rights Campaign (an LGBT rights group) fall far behind organized labor in overall contributions to Democrats. Ideological groups in the "other" category, like Americans for Democratic Action or Moveon.org, also fall way down

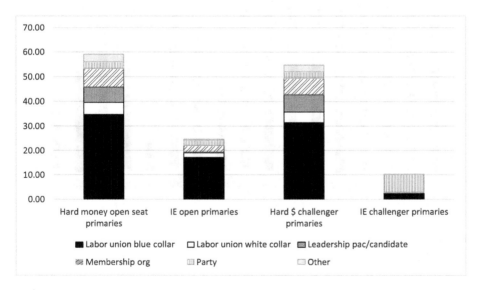

Figure 14.8 Contributions and Independent Expenditures by Elite Democratic-Leaning Groups in Non-Incumbent Democratic Primaries, 1984–2016 Totals, in Millions of U.S. Dollars

on the list. Official party committees outspend labor groups in primaries to nominate challengers to incumbents, but otherwise party committees and Leadership PACs are far outspent by labor as well.

When we examine the composition of the Democrats' nominating coalition over time, we see the overall dominance of blue collar labor unions is maintained, although some other patterns emerge as well. Figure 14.9 focuses on primary contributions to Democrats in open seats in each election cycle.

As seen in Figure 14.9, in open seat primaries, blue collar labor groups dominate both direct candidate contributions and independent expenditures. The leading hard money blue collar contributors in open seats are the International Brotherhood of Electrical Workers, the Teamsters, and the Food and Commercial Workers unions. Teachers groups and AFSCME (American Federation of State, County, and Municipal Employees) top the list of white collar unions. However, in recent years, Leadership PACs, membership groups, and "other" (including issue-based and ideological) groups have played an increasingly large role in nomination contests in both presidential and midterm years. Leadership PACs may receive a larger proportion of their money from access-buying (and corporate-dominated) groups, as would be expected for incumbents. The membership and "other" groups that have also contributed more over time include the Human Rights Campaign, NARAL (National Abortion

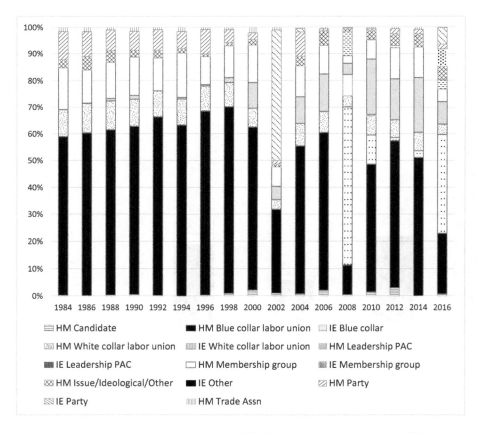

Figure 14.9 Top Democratic Groups' Proportion of Total Hard Money Contributions (HM) and Independent Expenditures (IE) in Open Seat Democratic Primaries

Rights Action League), EMILY's List (focusing on electing pro-choice women), the National Committee to Preserve Social Security, the Sierra Club, League of Conservation Voters and MoveOn.org. The proportion of all Democratic group contributions in Democratic primaries contributed by blue collar labor groups peaked in 1998, when those groups contributed more than two-thirds of the money contributed by the top Democratic groups to Democratic primary candidates. In 2016, blue collar groups composed only about half of the hard money contributions received by Democrats.

Democratic groups rarely use independent expenditures in open seat primaries. Only a few groups have done so (including the United Food and Commercial Workers, affiliates of the Service Employees International Union, EMILY's List, the League of Conservation Voters, MoveOn.org, and the Human Rights Campaign) but those independent expenditures are also dominated by the blue collar groups, which in presidential years supplant blue collar hard money contributions for the largest overall category of coalition primary spending.

In primaries to nominate challengers to incumbents, hard money contributions have been similarly dominated by Electrical workers, Teamsters, Teachers, AFSCME, and the UAW, while soft money primary expenditures has been led by the Service Employees International Union and affiliates, as well as the party committees. Despite labor giving more money than other groups in nearly every year, contributions to challenger primary candidates has been increasingly led by Leadership PACs in the last decade.

What does this analysis tell us about the Democratic party as a whole? It certainly says that new federal candidates need to jostle for support from a fairly predictable list of groups. Blue collar labor unions have dominated the Democratic coalition for a generation, and continue to do so. (Given that labor unions also provide the foot-soldiers in most Democratic campaigns it is almost surprising that we do not call it the Labor party.) The Democrats' dependence on and loyalty to organized labor is surely not lost on Republicans, who have undertaken prominent efforts to undermine unions, especially public employee unions, in recent years. This picture helps us to understand why the Democratic party puts the interests of working people prominently in their party platforms, and why Democrats favor increases in the minimum wage. It poses as a puzzle, however, why the Democrats turned toward free trade and against the core interests of organized labor in a certain amount of wage protectionism. The time series also shows us that in the long term, the Democratic party may be beginning a trend toward relying on social issue groups and ideological groups for a greater share of its primary campaign resources.

In their general elections, and once they have won election and become incumbents, Democrats also raise money from a large number of access-buying corporate groups and trade associations. In incumbent re-nomination primaries, Democrats also receive a great deal of money from realtors, beer wholesalers, car dealers, home builders, bankers, and doctors, among many others. Whether and to what degree their initial support from organized working people is diluted by wealthier interests is an important empirical and political question that is made more specific by examining the data in this way.

The Republican Coalition

Let us now examine primary contributions to Republican candidates from the most loyal (>80%) Republican leaning groups.

Republican primary candidates receive the most money in direct contributions from a recognizable coalition of groups and corporations. The top donors to Republican primary candidates in all races are a mixture of nonpartisan groups and highly partisan ones, but the leading party-loyal contributors are groups in the building industry (Associated Builders and Contractors), the energy sector (Exxon Corporation, Koch Industries), other business groups like the National Federation of Independent Business, Raytheon Corporation, and the National Restaurant Association, and issue groups like the National Rifle Association.

Figure 14.10 shows the distribution of primary contributions over time in open seat races. In Republican open seat primary races, three stories stand out: first, there is noticeable stability in the proportions of hard money contributed by membership, ideological, and corporate groups over time. There was a jump in the amounts spent by all groups around 2002, but a lot of stability before and after that. Second, the biggest trend in the data is the replacement of formal party contributions in open seat primaries by Leadership PAC contributions. That replacement happened about the time that the Republican party took over the House for the first time in 40 years, in 1994.

Finally, it is worth noting that in some years, including 2016, corporations in the energy sector actually contribute a greater proportion of the total given to open seat Republican candidates than all other loyal Republican corporations and trade associations combined. Driving that finding is the fact that total contributions from most groups stayed flat on average since 2002, while Leadership PAC contributions quintupled and energy sector corporate contributions tripled in the last decade.

As we saw with the Democrats, primaries do not draw as many independent expenditures as general elections do. However, even though open seat primaries did not draw much attention in independent expenditures, we can see a growth in issue-based (abortion, guns) and ideological PAC expenditures since 2008. In 2012 and 2014, ideological group independent

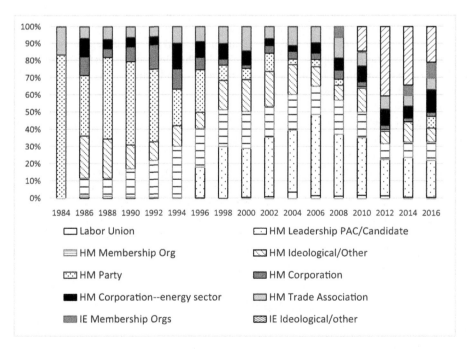

Figure 14.10 Republican Groups' Proportion of Hard Money Primary Contributions and Independent Expenditures in Open Seats

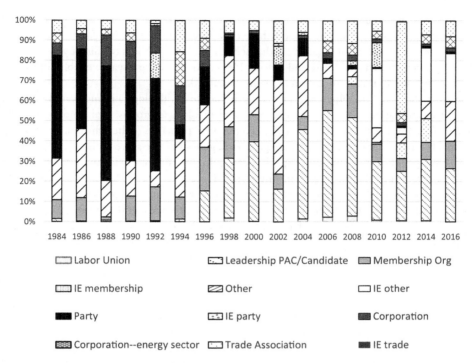

Figure 14.11   Republican Groups' Proportion of Hard Money Primary Contributions and Independent Expenditures in Primaries to Nominate Challengers to Incumbents

expenditures were double those of primary contributions from any other sector. Leading independent spenders were from groups like Citizens United, TeaPartyExpress, and Republican Majority Campaign.

In primaries to nominate challengers to incumbents, we see a similar story about Leadership PACs replacing formal party committees as the main contributor to Republican primary candidates. Figure 14.11 shows the totals spent in primaries to nominate challengers to incumbents including both hard money contributions and independent expenditures. Business groups make up a fairly small proportion of the total contributions from the most loyal groups. Corporations and trade associations maxed out their proportion of contributions to challenger primaries in 1994. The "other" category, which includes many ideological groups, are major contributors to challenger primary candidates after 1994. A wide variety of ideological groups outspend corporate groups in these races, and in addition, conservative groups also spend considerable amounts in independent expenditures in challenger primaries. Independent spenders include conservative groups like Eagle Forum, the National Right to Life PAC, the NRA, Citizens United, and Tea Party Express. If you combine independent expenditures and hard money, in 2014 and 2016, groups in the issue/ideological category spent more than 40 percent of the money in Republican challenger primaries.

What does this analysis tell us about the Republican Party? Broadly, it tells us that Republicans are the more pro-business, pro-corporate party. It also highlights the really significant degree to which companies in the energy sector are loyal to the Republican party and participate in its internal deliberations. The animosity that Republican officeholders, especially those elected in recent years, have for environmental regulations and climate change science seems very consistent with the early and consistent support these candidates get from oil and gas companies. This may be fairly obvious, but it is not clear that scholars and the public have directly tied primary election participation to candidate and officeholder positions. More research establishing a more causal relationship between those forces seems warranted.

Second, these data highlight the increasing influence of ideologically motivated groups in Republican primaries in the last decade. Issue and ideological groups spend most of the "80 percent party loyal" money spent to decide Republican primaries (although recall from Figure 14.6 that business-dominated nonpartisan groups do give a sizeable share of the overall open seat primary contributions). Business groups, however, do not compete with independent expenditures spent by ideological groups in primaries.[3] These data may help us to understand the war between older, more Main Street or Wall Street Republicans, and the more ideological members elected in recent years. The primary elections in which new Republican candidates are chosen, especially in safe seats, have in recent years been heavily influenced by ideological groups, not business groups. If newly elected Republican officeholders are ideological rather than pro-business conservatives, that may be one reason why.

Discussion

Contemporary events show us that it is important to understand how parties are composed, but researchers are just beginning to explore how to measure party composition and how to track changes in it over time. This chapter suggests that in primary elections, especially open seat and challenger primaries, it is possible to see the activity of the party's core groups. The groups that get involved in open seat and challenger primaries are quite distinct, and look like what close observers would expect the current party coalitions to look like. Republicans have more business and trade groups, and more purely ideological groups in their inner circle. Democrats have labor and issue groups but very few ideological groups per se in their inner circles. In both parties, new candidates vying for their first election to the House, the Senate, or the presidency have to contend with the active involvement of these groups in their primary elections.

Examining the involvement of these highly partisan groups in primary elections over time reveals important patterns. The Democrats have been, and remain, a party heavily constructed by blue collar labor unions, although recent election cycles suggest that there may be a relative increase in the influence of other issue groups like gay rights organizations and women's groups. The Republicans have been, and remain, a party of business, but the increase in ideological groups' involvement in primaries may help to explain the extreme ideological polarization of the Republican party in recent years. Scholars struggle to explain how the party has become so radically conservative while their voters' issue positions have not. The relative importance of ideological groups in the emergence of Republican party nominees may help to explain that development.

Notes

1 The data for this analysis are compiled from the "FEC PAC Summary" and "Contributions to Candidates (and other Expenditures) From Committees" files, available at www.fec.gov for years 1984 through 2016. Political Action Committees, which are the most longstanding form of campaign committee, are allowed to make one $5000 contribution to a candidate in the Primary, and one $5000 contribution to a candidate in the General election. Those contributions are labeled as "P" or "G" in the FEC databases. Candidates' reporting committees are also labeled by party and by whether they are running as an Incumbent, a Challenger to an incumbent, or as a new candidate in an Open Seat. I developed

a simple computer code (in Matlab) that searches each year's file for each PAC's identifying number and sums its contributions to Democratic and Republican candidates, then computes a proportion of the total that goes to the Democratic and Republican parties. The raw data (downloadable at http://www.fec.gov/finance/disclosure/ftpdet.shtml) are first sorted by candidate committees, self-identified as "DEM" and "REP," for each year. All contributions to those candidate committees that are defined as "24A (Independent expenditure opposing election of candidate), 24C (Coordinated party expenditure), 24E (Independent expenditure advocating election of a candidate), 24F (Communication cost for a candidate), 24H (Honorarium to candidate), 24K (Contribution made to nonaffiliated committee), 24N (Communication cost against candidate), 24P (Contribution made to possible federal candidate including in-kind contributions), 24R (Election Recount disbursement)" are combined into total amounts given to each party's candidates on those lists by every PAC in every year.

2 Replicating the analysis with a 70% cutoff makes very little difference to the results.

3 Business groups do not appear to do any primary election independent spending through the PACs in this dataset, though they may participate through 501c3 groups or others that are not analyzed here.

References

Achen, Christopher, and Larry M. Bartels. 2016. *Democracy for Realists: Why Elections Do Not Produce Responsive Government.* Princeton, NJ: Princeton University Press.

Banks, Jeffrey S., and D. Roderick Kiewiet. 1989. "Explaining Patterns of Candidate Competition in Congressional Elections." *American Journal of Political Science* 33(4): 997–1015.

Bawn, Kathleen, Martin Cohen, David Karol, Seth Masket, Hans Noel, and John Zaller. 2012. "A Theory of Political Parties: Groups, Policy Demands and Nominations in American Politics." *Perspectives on Politics* 10(3): 571–597.

Bernstein, Jonathan. 1999. "The Expanded Party in American Politics." Ph.D. diss., University of California, Berkeley.

Bianco, William T. 1984. "Strategic Decisions on Candidacy in U.S. Congressional Districts." *Legislative Studies Quarterly* 9(2): 351–364.

Bond, Jon R., Cary Covington, and Richard Fleisher. 1985. "Explaining Challenger Quality in Congressional Elections." *Journal of Politics* 47(2): 510–529.

Brady, David W., Hahrie Han, and Jeremy C. Pope. 2007. "Primary Elections and Candidate Ideology: Out of Step with the Primary Electorate?" *Legislative Studies Quarterly* 32(1): 79–105.

Cohen, Marty, David Karol, Hans Noel, and John R. Zaller. 2008. *The Party Decides: Presidential Nominations Before and After Reform.* Chicago: University of Chicago Press.

Dominguez, Casey B. K. 2005. "Before the Primary: Party Participation in Congressional Nominating Processes." Ph.D. diss., University of California, Berkeley.

Dominguez, Casey B. K. 2011. "Does the Party Matter? Endorsements in Congressional Primaries." *Political Research Quarterly* 64(3): 534–544.

Downs, Anthony. 1957. *An Economic Theory of Democracy.* New York: HarperCollins.

Geer, John G., and Mark E. Shere. 1992. "Party Competition and the Prisoner's Dilemma: An Argument for the Direct Primary." *Journal of Politics* 54(3): 741–761.

Heaney, Michael T., Seth Masket, Joanne Miller, and Dara Strolovich. 2012. "Polarized Networks: The Organizational Affiliations of Party Convention Delegates." *American Behavioral Scientist* 56(12): 1654–1676.

Herrnson, Paul S. 1988. *Party Campaigning in the 1980s.* Cambridge, MA: Harvard University Press.

Herrnson, Paul S. 2001. *Playing Hardball: Campaigning for the U.S. Congress.* Upper Saddle River, NJ: Prentice Hall.

Herrnson, Paul S., and James G. Gimpel. 1995. "District Conditions and Primary Divisiveness in Congressional Elections." *Political Research Quarterly* 48(1): 117–134.

Hogan, Robert E. 2003. "Sources of Competition in State Legislative Primary Elections." *Legislative Studies Quarterly* 28(1): 103–126.

Jacobson, Gary. 2001. *The Politics of Congressional Elections*, 5th ed. New York: Longman.

Kazee, Thomas A. 1983. "The Deterrent Effect of Incumbency on Recruiting Challengers in U.S. House Elections." *Legislative Studies Quarterly* 8(2): 469–480.

Kenney, Patrick J., and Tom W. Rice. 1984. "The Effect of Primary Divisiveness on Gubernatorial and Senatorial Elections." *The Journal of Politics* 46(4): 904–915.

Kenney, Patrick J., and Tom W. Rice. 1987. "The Relationship between Divisive Primaries and General Election Outcomes." *American Journal of Political Science* 31(1): 31–44.

Koger, Gregory, Seth Masket, and Hans Noel. 2009. "Partisan Webs: Information Exchange and Party Networks." *British Journal of Political Science* 39(3): 633–653.

Lazarus, Jeffrey. 2005. "Unintended Consequences: Anticipation of General Election Outcomes and Primary Election Divisiveness." *Legislative Studies Quarterly* 30(3): 435–461.

Lengle, James I., Diana Owen, and Molly W. Sonner. 1995. "Divisive Nominating Mechanisms and Democratic Party Electoral Prospects." *Journal of Politics* 57(2): 370–383.

Masket, Seth. 2004. "A Party by Other Means: The Rise of Informal Party Organizations in California." Ph.D. diss. University of California, Los Angeles.

McCann, James A., Randall W. Partin, Ronald B. Rapoport, and Walter J. Stone. 1996. "Presidential Nomination Campaigns and Party Mobilization: An Assessment of Spillover Effects." *American Journal of Political Science* 40(3): 756–767.

Miller, Penny M., Malcolm E. Jewell, and Lee Sigelman. 1988. "Divisive Primaries and Party Activists: Kentucky 1979 and 1983." *The Journal of Politics* 50(2): 459–470.

Monroe, J.P. 2001. *The Political Party Matrix*. Albany: State University of New York Press.

Schlesinger, Joseph A. 1985. "The New American Party System." *American Political Science Review* 79(4): 1152–1169.

Schwartz, Mildred A. 1990. *The Party Network: The Robust Organization of Illinois Republicans*. Madison: The University of Wisconsin Press.

Silbey, Joel H. 1990. "The Rise and Fall of American Political Parties 1790–1990." In *The Parties Respond: Changes in the American Party System*, ed. L. Sandy Maisel. Boulder, CO: Westview Press, pp. 3–20.

Skinner, Richard. 2007. *More than Money: Interest Group Action in Congressional Elections*. Lanham: Rowman and Littlefield.

Skinner, Richard, Seth Masket, and Dave Dulio. 2012. "527 Committees and the Political Party Network." *American Politics Research* 40(1): 60–84.

Sorauf, Frank. 1984. *Party Politics in America*. New York: Little Brown.

Stone, Walter J., and L. Sandy Maisel. 1999. "The Not-So-Simple Calculus of Winning: Potential U.S. House Candidates' Nomination and General Election Chances." Paper presented at the Annual Meeting of the American Political Science Association.

Stone, Walter J., Lonna Rae Atkeson, and Ronald B. Rapoport. 1992. "Turning on or turning off? Mobilization and Demobilization Effects of Participation in Presidential Nomination Campaigns." *American Journal of Political Science* 36(3): 665–691.

PART IV

U.S. Presidential Primaries

The chapters in this section consider U.S. presidential primaries. Presidential primaries are quite different from direct primaries because presidential primaries are held for the purpose of selecting convention delegates. It was not until the 1960s that presidential candidates actually began to campaign in primaries, and it was not until the 1970s that the parties required delegates be bound on the first ballot to the candidate they were pledged to. Furthermore, since the 1970s the two major parties have tinkered with rules regarding when primaries may be held and how delegate allocation must work. Because of these changes and because of the relatively short life, so far, of the presidential primary system, there is not a great deal of certainty about how primaries should work. It is evident, however, that since the 1970s presidential primaries have served as venues in which parties seek to shape the process in order to produce the best possible nominee.

All of the chapters in this section reflect on the challenges the 2016 election has posed to our understanding of how presidential primaries should work. Marty Cohen's chapter visits one of the most influential books of the past decade on primaries, Cohen, Karol, Noel, and Zaller's *The Party Decides*. The main argument of this book was that American political parties generally decide on a candidate before the primaries actually begin, and party elites work to confer the nomination with as little conflict as possible. This clearly was not the case in 2016. Cohen's chapter alleges that the theory of that book is alive and well; it explains the Democratic nomination contest well, and the Republican contest played out the way it did because the Republican Party never did decide upon a candidate. In the subsequent chapter, Wayne Steger questions the logic of *The Party Decides* and provides an alternate account of the primary process.

One of the challenges in studying presidential primaries is deciphering the logic of their sequential nature. Candidates are able to gain (or lose) momentum on account of the states that vote at particular times and on account of choices of other candidates regarding where to spend money. Even if the parties do tend to get the nominees they want, the process can often take longer than expected, and, especially in early primaries where there may be a dozen or more candidates, prospective nominees must think about how to respond to what other candidates are doing and how to address issues that matter to some states but may not resonate in others. While in direct primaries, candidate characteristics such as prior political experience or the ability to raise money may be decisive, the results of individual presidential primaries can be far less predictable.

The final two chapters in this section illustrate some of these unpredictable features. Dante Scala discusses the role of ideology in presidential primaries, discussing how Donald Trump, a candidate seemingly out of step with the Republican Party on many issues, was able to win the nomination in 2016. And David Hopkins describes the evolution of presidential primary debates. These debates, Hopkins notes, have often ruined the campaigns of experienced and highly qualified candidates while briefly advantaging much less experienced candidates who had the good fortune to perform well on television. Both Hopkins and Scala show some of the peculiarities of multi-candidate, multi-state primary competitions. Given all of the quirks that all four of the chapters in this section illustrate, it is in many ways a surprise that most American presidential primaries have had predictable outcomes.

There is a voluminous literature on other aspects of presidential primary elections. The bibliographies of these chapters list some of the foundational works on U.S. presidential primaries. Larry Bartels' *Presidential Primaries and the Dynamics of Public Choice* (Princeton University Press, 1988) discusses the phenomenon of momentum in presidential primaries. William Mayer and Andrew Busch's *The Frontloading Problem in Presidential Nominations* (Brookings Institution, 2003) is, as the title suggests, a consideration of how "frontloading" of different states' primaries has influenced the primary process. Mayer and Busch also consider the role the media plays in "winnowing" the primary field. There are several studies of the politics of the states that vote earliest in the primary season and the ways these states can distort primary outcomes; two such books are David Redlawsk, Caroline Tolbert, and Todd Donovan, *Why Iowa?* (University of Chicago Press, 2010) and Dante Scala, *Stormy Weather: The New Hampshire Primary and Presidential Politics* (Palgrave Macmillan, 2003). And retrospectives on spending in various elections, including the Brookings Institution series edited by David Magleby, and the *Making of the Presidential Candidates* series edited by William Mayer, often include chapters on the financing of presidential primaries and on campaign advertising in primaries.

Given, however, the substantial changes in presidential primaries over the past three election cycles, the goal in this section has been to provide the reader with an understanding of some of the best research that is focused upon U.S. presidential primaries as they are conducted in 2016.

15

2016

One Party Decided

Marty Cohen

The presidential election of 2016 might have made a good sequel to the harrowing film *Sophie's Choice*, since both Hillary Clinton and Donald Trump had higher unfavorable ratings than any candidate since the beginning of polling on the subject. For the first half of the year, Secretary Clinton was being investigated by the Justice Department and the FBI for setting up her own email server during her tenure as head of the State Department. Donald Trump combined racist and ethnocentric rhetoric with a habit of not telling the truth and absolutely no governing experience. Yet both of these candidates were able to win their party's nomination despite all of their flaws and misfortunes.

Both Clinton and Trump received a majority of convention delegates, but their paths to that ultimate victory could not have been more different. Clinton, the Democratic nominee, was from the beginning the almost unanimous choice of party elites and began the race in such a position of strength that her main competition was a septuagenarian, self-avowed Democratic Socialist who for most of his political career had not even been registered as a Democrat. Trump, the Republican nominee, on the other hand, had virtually no elite support during the invisible primary period but benefited from a field of 17 in which nobody came close to marshalling the lion's share of establishment support. In the battle for control of presidential nominations between party elites and voters, between forces of unity and factional tendency, the Democratic and Republican races of 2016 produced two wildly different outcomes. In 2016, one party clearly decided and the other party clearly did not. Why was the Republican establishment bulldozed by Trump and his movement? Why were they and their preferred candidates impotent in the face of Trump's boasts and taunts? In attempting to answer these questions, I will present an argument which seeks to explain how two nomination campaigns can turn out so differently regarding how well the party was able to control things.

In 2008, three of my colleagues and I wrote *The Party Decides*, a study of the "invisible primary," the process by which party elites agree upon a nominee before the presidential primaries have concluded. In a recent publication (Cohen et al. 2016), we revisited presidential nominations after a series of relatively wild contests that were not included in the featured analysis of the original work. The unorthodox triumph of Donald Trump, which was a broadside against the book's fundamental theoretical premises, was the precipitating cause of this second look, but in reality something had been going on since 2000 when party insiders George W. Bush and Al Gore cruised to their party's nominations. When looked at in hindsight, presidential nominations since the McGovern-Fraser reforms have sometimes been captured by factional outsiders and other times by unifying, establishment favorites. More specifically, the early period (1972–1976) and the later period (2004–2016) were notable for the successes and near-misses of the former while the middle period (1980–2000) was characterized almost exclusively by fairly easy wins by the latter. We have attributed the loss of control in the early phase to a learning period in which the party had not yet mastered the post-reform system. Their ability to utilize the invisible primary to coordinate around a broadly acceptable choice and then marshal resources to help them win the nomination created the middle period mentioned above. What remains to be discussed here is how factions reasserted themselves and kept the party from deciding as easily as it had in the past. We argue that major trends over the past two decades – the rise of new political media, the flood of early money into presidential nominations, and the conflict among party factions – have made it easier for factional candidates and outsiders to challenge elite control of nominations (Cohen et al. 2016, 701).

The explosion of political communication in recent cycles has all but eliminated the invisibility of the "invisible primary." This invisibility was important because it gave a relatively small group of party officials and group leaders a near monopoly over the early politics of presidential nominations, a monopoly they exercised for the benefit of party unity. Now we see cable news, blogs, and digital mainstream websites provide potential voters with a bonanza of "inside baseball" political news. Editors will give more coverage to the candidates who get the most clicks and page-views enabling ordinary citizens to become real-time players in nominee selection through their influence over who gets covered. In addition to the increase in coverage from traditional news media and the emergence of new media sources, there has been a significant increase in the number of debates between the candidates. Again, the public is treated to a public battle among the candidates that simply was not visible years earlier. The result has been the death of the invisible primary, and with it, the freedom of party elites to converse among themselves without the country-at-large having an influence (Cohen et al. 2016, 703–704). This development was right in Donald Trump's wheelhouse as he made the most of the increased coverage to create what appeared to be a mass movement without the normal trappings of a presidential nominating campaign.

The increased availability of early money has also impacted the nominating process in such a way as to hinder the ability of party elites to control the process. While having lots of money during the invisible primary is no guarantee of success, it is necessary to build an operation capable of sustaining a candidate throughout the pre-Iowa period, not to mention through the grueling series of primaries and caucuses that allocate convention delegates. The loosening of campaign finance laws has enabled more candidates to find that small cadre of big donors to keep their candidacies afloat without the support of traditional party leaders. And even those without access to big donors can exploit internet fundraising opportunities to compete in the money primary as well. In the past, elite endorsements would often come with important resources, not least of which was money. In this way, party leaders acted as gatekeepers, keeping the field manageable and freezing out unwanted candidates. Those days seem to be gone as evidenced by the bloated 2016 Republican field – bloated in terms of the number of candidates, and in terms of the amounts of cash they raised (Cohen et al. 2016, 704–705). The large field worked in Trump's favor as the establishment "lane" was crowded, and those candidates vying for elite support split that support throughout the invisible primary and even after the voters started going to the polls.

The state of factional harmony within parties also varies over time, and certainly within the Republican Party it appears to have deteriorated greatly in recent cycles. When a party is divided by strong factions, it follows that it will be more difficult for elites to settle on a unity candidate early on in the process. The rise of social conservatives in the 1990s and the Tea Party after Barack Obama's election in 2008 have roiled the GOP and resulted in a civil war that has claimed many congressional incumbents and former Speaker of the House John Boehner in recent years (Cohen et al. 2016, 703). Trump's outsider status was a boon to his chances and people seemed to like and support him precisely because he had no experience and precious few ties to the Republican establishment. The Democrats have their own factional strife, as evidenced most clearly by Bernie Sanders' insurgent candidacy, but the current minority party appears to be more unified in opposition to President Trump than the majority GOP.

Donald Trump's nomination in 2016 was a shock to pundits, political scientists, and the American public. Very few individuals in any of the above categories thought it possible that he would end up victorious and go on to represent the GOP in the general election. I have laid out three systemic reasons why Trump was able to succeed when so many predicted he would fail. Before analyzing both the Democratic and Republican races in depth, I will chronicle the history of presidential nominations with an emphasis on the post McGovern-Fraser period highlighted in our book *The Party Decides*.

A History of Presidential Nominations

Every year toward the end of October, millions of Americans shop for Halloween costumes. In the rubber mask aisle, there are the usual ghouls and goblins, Elvises and Frankensteins, witches and wizards. Every fourth year, in addition to those potential disguises, the major party nominees have their masks on the same shelves, considering Election Day is less than a week after Halloween. Al Gore and George W. Bush, the contenders for the presidency in 2000, were especially popular choices. However, you could get a Gore or Bush mask in October of *1999*, a full year before the eve of the general election and months before a single vote had been cast for either party's potential nominees. Yet there they were: Bush and Gore, as if they had already clinched their party's nomination and were pitted against each other to become the 43rd president of the United States.

This was a strange phenomenon, and it was one that flew in the face of the conventional wisdom regarding presidential nominations. After all, since the reforms of the late 1960s and early 1970s it was widely understood that to win nomination, candidates had to compete and succeed in a series of state-by-state primaries and caucuses that would allocate convention delegates. But sure enough, there were those masks well before Iowa and New Hampshire had commenced, let alone before the rest of the nation's primary and caucus voters had had their say.

Bush and Gore were the prohibitive favorites because they had dominated the invisible primary, leading by large margins on important measures of support such as endorsements, poll standing, money, and media coverage. Vice-President Gore was pushed in New Hampshire by Senator Bill Bradley, but Gore ended up winning every single primary and caucus that cycle. And Senator John McCain did defeat President George W. Bush in New Hampshire. But once Bush won in South Carolina, the nomination was thereafter never really in doubt. So something had changed by 2000, but what exactly?

The historical arc of presidential nominations has bent toward greater democratization. In the early decades of the Republic, congressional caucuses were convened to nominate presidential candidates. Members of Congress alone decided who would represent the parties on the general election ballot. In 1831, the Anti-Masonic Party held the first presidential nominating convention and the Democratic Party followed suit a year later. This was an opportunity to expand the universe of individuals who would decide on the party's standard-bearer. Conventions brought together political leaders and at least some rank-and-file voters so they all could come to an agreement regarding who might best unite the party and win the White House. For almost a century and a half, this was how things worked. Presidential primaries became a part of the process starting in 1912 but they were mere "eyewash" as Harry Truman put it decades later. They were tests of a candidate's strength in the electorate that might help the elites discern the contenders' vote-getting ability, but no more than that. In 1968, Vice-President Hubert Humphrey could gain the Democratic nomination for president without actively competing in any of the primaries held that spring. Of course, the calamity that was the 1968 Democratic National Convention shone a bright and harsh light on the elitist nature of presidential nominations. Actual voters were given very little say in who would be on the November ballot and the time had come once again for wider participation in the process. Subsequently, the Democratic Party created the McGovern-Fraser Commission, which sought to give rank-and-file party voters more of a say in the nomination process. The end result of the commission's recommendations was that both parties in most states adopted "binding" primaries forcing candidates to compete for convention delegates that would be allocated on the basis of the primary results.

Taking the ultimate decision-making power out of the hands of party elites and empowering ordinary voters drastically changed the dynamic of presidential nominating politics throwing the old order out of the window. George McGovern and Jimmy Carter both came out of nowhere to get the Democratic nomination in the first two open contests under the new regime.[1] These two Democrats capitalized on the novel dynamic and mobilized a plurality of voters turning them into a majority of delegates. This new volatility was noted by the discipline and a conventional wisdom began to take hold that was a mixture of Nelson Polsby and Larry Bartels. The former (Polsby 1983) argued that factional candidates only need appeal to and mobilize a plurality of partisans in the various state primaries and caucuses to be victorious. The latter (Bartels 1988) zeroed in on riding media-driven momentum gained from surprising early victories in either Iowa or New Hampshire to the nomination. Polsby published in 1983, Bartels in 1988 and both were understandably influenced by the wild and wooly contests of the 1970s and early 1980s.[2] But in October of 1999, one looked back and saw a much more orderly process in hindsight. And one noticed in particular that those who pulled off surprise victories early on in the season (George H. W. Bush in 1980, Gary Hart in 1984, Paul Tsongas in 1992, and Pat Buchanan in 1996) ultimately were defeated by candidates who seemed to have much broader support within the party. So, what had happened in the years since "Jimmy Who?" shocked the political world by riding 27 percent in Iowa, and 28 percent in New Hampshire to the top of the pack and all the way to the White House?

This is the question that motivated *The Party Decides* (Cohen et al. 2008). We argue in the book that parties had temporarily lost control over their nominating process, and that the results in 1972 and 1976 were two candidates on the Democratic side that would never have gotten the party elites behind them under the old convention system. In some ways, the voters made inferior choices, as McGovern was trounced by Nixon and Carter had enormous difficulty governing because he did not possess the party connections many of his Oval Office predecessors did. So it was clear as the 1980s began that parties could not control their nominations as they had done in the pre-McGovern-Fraser era. But when one starts to observe the nominations of the 1980s, then the 1990s, and 2000, a pattern emerges and the nomination cycles during that period in fact look relatively orderly. In each contest from 1980 to 2000, a clear frontrunner emerged early on in the process. In fact, if one studies the invisible primary, the year before voting begins (which we think is essential to understanding what happens *after* the voting begins), one can make the argument that party elites were trying to coordinate behind a broadly acceptable candidate much as they used to do during the convention. Through the use of public endorsements, party leaders were attempting to have that conversation among themselves about who would be the best representative of the party and who would be the best choice to take on the opposing party in the fall. This coordination process or conversation could not happen at the convention in the smoke-filled rooms anymore. It had to happen earlier and crucially before the voters had their say because the voters had proved to be unpredictable and less than savvy in their few chances picking nominees post-McGovern-Fraser. Moreover, party leaders came to realize they could actually make it easier for their chosen candidate to be successful in the delegate chasing process. Endorsements could be quite valuable for candidates vying to be their party's nominee. Endorsements, we believe, are not only a show of public support, but a promise of private support that can take the form of money and other campaign resources that help a candidate collect votes. Endorsements also can be a cue to voters about who is acceptable and an imprimatur of respectability and gravitas depending on who is doing the endorsing. Of course, not all endorsements are created equal. Colin Powell's endorsement of Barack Obama in 2008 is on one end of the spectrum, and perhaps Britney Spears' endorsement (and then apparent retraction of said endorsement) of Hillary Clinton in 2016 would be on the other end in terms of helpfulness.[3]

We began to study the invisible primary in a systematic fashion. We believed endorsements were the best measure of party support and went about searching for and collecting them – who endorsed whom, when did they endorse, how much might different endorsements be worth. We found that from 1980 to 2000, the pre-Iowa leader in endorsements became the eventual nominee every time. And with one exception (the 1988 Democratic primary), there was a clear endorsement leader. There could, of course, be a spurious relationship between endorsements and electoral success, and there are other potential predictors that might be correlated with both our chosen independent variable (endorsements) and our dependent variable (delegates won). Money, poll standing, and media coverage are also potential predictors of success. When all four are included in a multiple regression, endorsements show the most robust effects. Even more noteworthy, early endorsements are a predictor itself of later poll standing, money raised, and media coverage rather than the other way around. So, it is not just party leaders bandwagoning to who the donors, voters, or reporters think is the best candidate. The money, public support and media coverage seem to follow the choice of party elites measured in the form of endorsements.

We believe that the period from 1980 to 2000 was very orderly, and we believe that we have captured that dynamic fairly well. But after 2000, things got a little trickier. The 2004 Democratic contest was not as methodical. The eventual nominee, John Kerry, had only the third-most endorsements pre-Iowa, and just as importantly only three Democratic governors had endorsed someone during the invisible primary, with two of those being favorite son endorsements for Richard Gephardt from the Governor of Missouri and for John Edwards from the Governor of North Carolina. In 2008, neither the Democratic or Republican contest appeared to conform to the pattern so dominant from 1980 to 2000. Barack Obama was a distant third in endorsements, and Senator John McCain was locked in a three-way duel for endorsement leader with former Massachusetts Governor Mitt Romney and former New York City Mayor Rudy Giuliani. We did uncover a story regarding some leaders holding back their support on the Democratic side, wanting to support Obama but afraid to do so prematurely and inviting backlash from the Clintons. Nonetheless, Clinton was the establishment favorite – not to the extent that she was in 2016, but still the favorite – and she lost. McCain benefited from a fractured field to his right and won the nomination, but the party really did not decide for him pre-Iowa. So in retrospect, 2008 was also not so good for the theory. But then in 2012 Romney, the clear establishment choice, fought off a series of challengers who benefited from intense media coverage and rose in the polls to each briefly take the lead away from the former governor of Massachusetts. At various times Michele Bachmann, Herman Cain, Rick Perry, Newt Gingrich, and Rick Santorum led in the polls. But one by one, Romney parried their charges and ultimately prevailed. He may not have been the best candidate, but establishment support buttressed his campaign and he got the nomination in the end. An optimistic reading of the four contests from 2004 to 2012 would give our theory credit for one, and only partial credit for the other three.

That brings us to 2016. This would be one of those cycles, like 2008, 2000, and 1988 before it when both parties would hold open nomination contests for the presidency of the United States. The remainder of this chapter will focus on the Democratic and Republican races in light of, and with an eye toward, *The Party Decides*.

The Democrats: Hillary's to Lose

When beginning to analyze the 2016 Democratic nomination contest one should go back almost eight years, to June 7, 2008. On that date, Hillary Rodham Clinton eloquently and poignantly recognized the 18 million cracks in the glass ceiling that resulted from her strong but ultimately unsuccessful bid for the presidency. That powerful imagery, combined with her full-throated endorsement of Barack Obama, kept herself in the good graces of party elites yearning for unity after a tough primary battle. It also assured that if she wanted to try again, they would be there for her to make a different kind of history in the future. And so it was on April 12th, 2015 when Clinton officially declared her candidacy, she immediately became the overwhelming favorite to win the Democratic nomination and be the first woman to head a major party's presidential ticket.

Why was Clinton such a prohibitive favorite right from the start of her campaign? First of all, she was the runaway leader in the polls. In a CNN poll taken the week after her announcement she garnered 69 percent, which was miles ahead of her closest challenger, Vice-President Joe Biden (11 percent), a man who had not given the slightest inkling at the time that he was interested in the top job. Bernie Sanders, who would go on to be Clinton's strongest challenger was polling third with five percent. This polling dominance reflects a second factor leading to Clinton's frontrunner status and that is the lack of high-profile competition. In addition to Sanders, a Democratic Socialist Senator from Vermont, there was only the former Maryland Governor Martin O'Malley, former one-term Virginia Senator Jim Webb, and former *Republican* Senator Lincoln Chafee. In terms of prestige and star power, the field running against Hillary was pretty thin.[4] And finally, not only did Hillary Clinton have the support of rank-and-file Democrats early on in the race, but she had already demonstrated strong support from political elites within the party. In fact, before she entered the race on April 12, she had received more weighted endorsements than anyone else would get *over the course of the entire contest*. Charles Schumer, the senior senator from New York, endorsed Clinton as early as November of 2013 and many of Schumer's fellow members of Congress followed suit in the months prior to her official campaign kick-off.

In *The Party Decides* we identify four invisible primary fundamentals that have the ability to predict how well a candidate will do in the actual primaries and caucuses that determine who gets the nomination. These fundamentals are polls, money, media coverage, and endorsements. As stated earlier, we believe endorsements are the strongest predictor both in terms of overall final delegate shares but also as the driving force behind changes in some of the other fundamentals throughout the invisible primary season. In the next section, I will analyze the 2016 Democratic race in terms of these four fundamentals.

Clinton's commanding lead in the polls when she declared her candidacy was bound to shrink as the campaign began in earnest. With Biden remaining on the sidelines her main competitor in the polls became Vermont Senator Bernie Sanders. Sanders began to tap into the anti-Clinton feeling within the party, especially among young voters. He captivated them with his call for more government services to reduce income and wealth inequality. He also got to Clinton's left on trade and other economic issues. The only issue where he ceded the more progressive stance was on gun control due to his longtime representation of a rural, gun-friendly state. Figure 15.1 shows the polling trend, based on monthly CNN polls from April 2015 until January 2016. Clinton's lead over Sanders at the beginning of her campaign was a whopping 64 points. In each of the next five months, that lead would shrink with the September poll showing only a 10-point lead for the seemingly unbeatable frontrunner. That difference would balloon to 28 points in December but on the eve of the Iowa caucuses it was Clinton over Sanders by only 52–38. There were several reasons why Sanders was able to close so much ground on Clinton during the invisible primary. First, Clinton's return to the campaign trail shone new light on some old controversies, like her use of a private server while Secretary of State, the terrorist attack in Benghazi that also occurred during her tenure at the State Department, and the lucrative speeches she gave on Wall Street. Second, Sanders benefited from being the only legitimate challenger to Clinton in the race. Therefore, he sopped up virtually all of the anti-Clinton people that existed in the party. Another look at Figure 15.1 shows the anemic numbers of O'Malley, Webb, and Chafee. Finally, Sanders was able to create a strong grassroots movement that was powered mostly by young newcomers to the political process. He also appealed to the progressive wing of the party who had always been somewhat skeptical of Hillary Clinton dating back to her vote for the Iraq War in 2002 and the centrist policies she was linked to by means of being the first lady during Bill Clinton's presidency. And crucial to Sanders' surge in the polls was his ability to raise a great deal of money in small increments

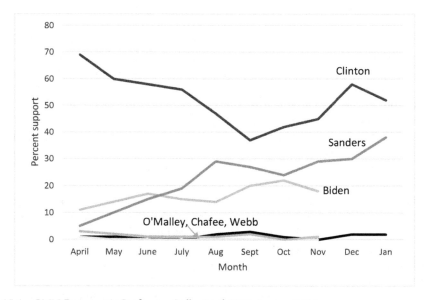

Figure 15.1   CNN Democratic Preference Polls, April 2015–January 2016

Note: Data gathered by the author from http://www.realclearpolitics.com/epolls/2016/president/us/2016_democratic_presidential_nomination-3824.html#polls.

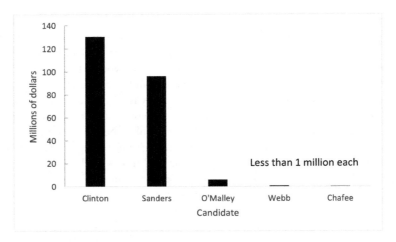

Figure 15.2   Democratic Fundraising pre-Iowa

Note: Data gathered by the author from www.fec.gov.

adding to the perception that he was fighting for the little guy and Clinton was in the pocket of various moneyed interests.

Clinton's fundraising prowess was certainly well documented throughout the 2016 presidential campaign. And indeed, right out of the gate she raised an incredible 47.55 million dollars during the second quarter of 2015. This haul was over three times the amount that Senator Sanders raised during that time. But in the remaining months leading up to the Iowa caucuses on February 1, Sanders achieved close to parity with Clinton as Figure 15.2 displays. As Sanders gained in the polls he was able to raise more money. This covariance is not surprising as it is easy to imagine a virtuous cycle working in Sanders' favor as the invisible primary wore on.

Not only did Sanders gain in the polls and the money chase, he also garnered more media coverage as Iowa approached. However, he never equaled Clinton on this fundamental measure. Every month of the invisible primary saw Hillary Clinton mentioned more often in front page stories in *The New York Times*. Over the entire invisible primary period, defined here as January 1, 2015 to January 31, 2016, Clinton was mentioned in 246 stories to Sanders' 76.[5] That is a ratio of just over three to one. However, not all publicity is good publicity in American politics and these figures do not address the split of positive and negative coverage. In fact, Figure 15.3 shows that Clinton's coverage was decidedly more negative than Sanders' during 2015. The daily beating that Clinton was taking in the press surely took its toll on her favorability ratings and made the nominating contest closer than maybe it should have been.[6]

The final fundamental that is worth studying in detail is elite endorsements. In fact, we believe elite endorsements are one of the keys to determining the outcome of presidential nominations. They have proven to be a strong predictor of final delegate share and early endorsements do a better job of predicting the other three fundamentals than polls, money, and media do. Endorsements are an area in which it was simply no contest between Clinton and Sanders. To reiterate, Hillary Clinton received more weighted endorsements before she declared her candidacy than anyone else got throughout the entire process, pre- and post-Iowa! Big-name endorsements came early and often for Secretary Clinton as she nabbed all 13 governors who endorsed pre-Iowa, 36 of 39 U.S. Senators, and 148 of 157 U.S. House members.

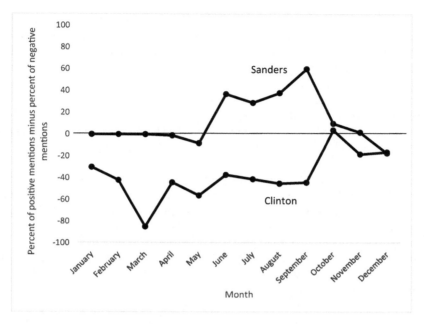

Figure 15.3 Tone of 2015 Democratic Media Coverage

Note: Data gathered by the author from http://scholar.harvard.edu/thomaspatterson/home.

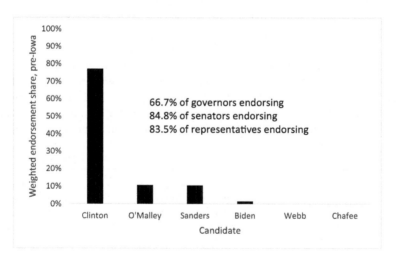

Figure 15.4 Weighted Democratic Endorsement Share pre-Iowa

Note: Data gathered by *The Party Decides* team.

Figure 15.4 shows each candidate's share of all weighted endorsements during the invisible primary. Clinton garnered 77.2 percent while O'Malley and Sanders were far behind at 10.8 percent and 10.5 percent respectively. If elite endorsements are evidence of who the party supports then it was crystal clear that the candidate of choice in the Democratic Party was Hillary Clinton. Not only did she gain a huge majority of endorsements but an unusually large proportion of

Democratic officials elected to federal office were willing to publicly signal their support for the former first lady. Table 15.1 situates 2016 within the rest of the post-McGovern-Fraser system and it is clear how much of an establishment choice Clinton was in historical terms. The only two Democratic candidates who came close to equaling Clinton were the incumbent president in 1980, Jimmy Carter, and the incumbent Vice-President in 2000, Al Gore.

Hillary Clinton's dominance in the endorsement derby was not the only support for the notion that the party decided she should be the nominee. The Democratic National Committee, led by vocal Clinton supporter Debbie Wasserman Schultz, called for only five sanctioned debates before the Iowa caucus, and scheduled three of the five on weekend nights in what was widely seen as a way to minimize viewership, and in turn, the potential of negative exposure for the front-running candidate with the most to lose. As it was later revealed thanks to the infamous Russian hack of DNC emails, debate scheduling was just the tip of the iceberg in terms of what lengths party leaders were willing to go to smooth Clinton's path to the nomination. But it was something that *did not* happen that may make the strongest case for our theory regarding the ability of party elites, when united, to pave the way for their preferred candidate to become the nominee.

According to those close to him, Vice-President Biden privately stewed throughout the early stages of the nominating campaign as he got an up close and personal view of Hillary Clinton positioning herself as the rightful heir to President Obama and his two terms in office. Biden believed that he was better positioned to carry on Obama's legacy and cement it with another Democratic victory in November of 2016. He also could not understand the missteps Clinton made regarding the setting up of the private email server while she led the State Department, and her inability to handle the criticism and scrutiny that inevitably came her way from Republicans and the press. But Biden was never encouraged by Democratic elites to make the race; his boss, for instance, praised Biden in public but privately kept his cards close to his chest when it came to who he favored to be his potential successor. When Biden's son Beau passed away in May of 2015, some confidants hinted to the public that Beau's dying wish was to have his father make one more run for the White House. What happened next is not new to presidential nominating politics. Potential candidates put out feelers and test the waters before making the leap into a campaign. All accounts suggest Biden did just that and got nothing in return. He could not dislodge supporters of Hillary despite all of her weaknesses as a candidate. With Clinton still in a strong position, with most of the Democratic establishment firmly behind her, there was

Table 15.1 Pace and Character of Endorsements in Democratic Nominating Contests

Year	Nominee	% of Governors Endorsing Nominee Pre-Iowa	% of Senators Endorsing Nominee Pre-Iowa
1976	Carter	0.0%	0.0%
1980	Carter	65.6%	15.5%
1984	Mondale	29.4%	15.2%
1988	Dukakis	3.8%	3.6%
1992	Clinton	41.4%	10.7%
2000	Gore	52.9%	57.8%
2004	Kerry*	0.0%	4.2%
2008	Obama*	10.7%	0.0%
2016	**Clinton**	**72.2%**	**78.3%**

* Not the pre-Iowa endorsement leader

Note: Data gathered by *The Party Decides* team.

nothing for Biden to do but remain on the sidelines. And this left only Bernie Sanders standing in the way of Clinton's coronation as the first woman to be nominated for president by a major political party in the United States.

At least it was supposed to be a coronation. While Hillary Clinton's tight grip on the nomination was ever only slightly loosened, it was far from a cakewalk. The challenge was fierce right from the beginning as the two leading candidates fought to a virtual tie in Iowa. Clinton declared victory on caucus night before the networks were willing to call it. She ended up winning by 0.2 percent of the vote, and she took heart in that narrow victory considering the embarrassment handed to her eight years ago by Iowa caucus goers when she finished third to Barack Obama and John Edwards. The next contest was in New Hampshire, and Sanders from neighboring Vermont was heavily favored to win the Granite State. He did, but Clinton bounced back later in February to win Nevada by five points and South Carolina by almost fifty. Among African-Americans in South Carolina, Clinton did even better than Obama eight years earlier, winning 90 percent of the black vote. African-Americans and Latinos were seen early on as Clinton's "firewall" against the insurgent candidacy of Bernie Sanders who was failing miserably to make inroads among these minority communities. As the nominating campaign went on it became clear that Sanders was doing better in states with lower minority populations and it followed that unless he could somehow do better among African-Americans and Latinos he simply could not overtake Clinton in the delegate chase.

March 1st was Super Tuesday, and Clinton held serve, winning eight of 12 contests. A week later, Clinton was expected to take Mississippi and Michigan rather easily and while the former state voted as predicted, Michigan stunned everyone by giving Sanders a narrow victory. The surprise upset in Michigan appeared to give Sanders some much-needed momentum and, in fact, that victory dominated news coverage in the following days. But the Senator from Vermont could not capitalize on that win in other delegate-rich Midwestern states such as Ohio, Illinois and Missouri that voted the following Tuesday. In the weeks and months that followed, the two candidates traversed the nation campaigning for votes and delegates. Sanders and Clinton traded rhetorical punches in a series of debates, and both candidates saw successes with voters. Sanders did well out west in late March and early April while Clinton did very well in the Northeast and Mid-Atlantic states in mid and late April. May saw each candidate claim important victories but throughout the back-and-forth Clinton never really came close to relinquishing her delegate lead, whether one counted the controversial superdelegates or not. As the nominating campaign came to an end on June 7, Sanders needed a substantial victory in California to have any chance of supplanting Clinton as the presumptive nominee. Clinton responded with a seven-point win in the delegate-rich Golden State and also won New Jersey, New Mexico, and South Dakota, leading her to declare victory that evening as she had finally won a majority of the pledged delegates.

When delving into some of the exit polls, another aspect of our theory was borne out. Clinton won self-identified Democrats by a large margin and actually lost independents who voted in Democratic primaries and caucuses (Noel 2016). And interestingly considering the media narrative, it was not only nonwhite Democrats who went for Clinton. Party identifiers of all races and ethnicities took the cue of their leaders, as *The Party Decides* would suggest, and they helped deliver her the nomination over Sanders.

The Republicans: The Unthinkable Happens

While much of the Democratic establishment was "ready for Hillary" when she formally declared her candidacy for the presidency of the United States in April of 2015, virtually nobody in the Republican establishment was ready for the wrecking ball that would ultimately obliterate them in the 2016 campaign. When Donald J. Trump entered the race on June 16th, 2015 by descending on an escalator in Trump Tower and then delivering a tirade against Mexican immigrants the country was aghast but also bemused. This real estate developer and reality television star had no political experience, no establishment support, and therefore was not taken seriously as a candidate. Despite the fact that Trump led in the polls soon after his controversial announcement, virtually nobody thought this man could become the Republican standard-bearer. However, in retrospect the Republican Party was ripe for a hostile takeover. There were rifts in the party that went back at least as far as the emergence of the Tea Party in 2009. More recently, the ouster of House Speaker John Boehner and the subsequent difficulty of finding his replacement highlighted the internal dissention within the GOP. An anti-establishment feeling was already in place among grass-roots conservatives and they flocked to Trump and his ostentatiously outsider status. He was favored precisely *because* he had no experience and no establishment support. Trump's astounding victory in the 2016 Republican primaries and caucuses completely contradicts the theory we put forth in *The Party Decides*. The party did not come close to deciding—at least not before the Iowa caucus. And when they did decide rather publicly that Trump was unacceptable, it was manifestly a case of too little, too late.

The Republican nominating season was notable and unprecedented for the sheer number of candidates making the race. Seventeen hopefuls threw their hats into the ring, necessitating a series of tiered debates in which national polling determined who would be on the main stage in prime time and who would be relegated to an earlier face-off with fewer viewers. This upended the usual dynamic present in both parties since the McGovern-Fraser reforms of focusing on the early voting states, most notably Iowa and New Hampshire. Since national polling determined debate placement, candidates were compelled to broadcast their messages over the national airwaves and spent considerably less time and effort on retail politicking in Iowa and New Hampshire than candidates in previous cycles. The large, fractured field and the emphasis on national media attention were huge benefits to the candidacy of Trump. His was not a typical campaign and it was clear very early on that this was not a typical campaign season.

When examining the four invisible primary fundamentals we identify as being significant predictors of candidate success, Donald Trump fared well in the polls and with the media. However, his fundraising lagged behind his rivals and he secured a paltry number of elite endorsements compared with the other top contenders. Table 15.2 shows that in the four months prior to Trump's entry into the race, three different candidates held the top spot, with none of them getting more than 17 percent. The large field and the lack of a true frontrunner left the door open for Donald Trump to catch fire, and only weeks after declaring his candidacy, move straight to the top of the polls. From July to January, according to CNN's polling, Trump led the Republican field every month, increasing his lead from four percentage points in the dead of summer to 22 percentage points in the middle of winter. In that last CNN poll before the Iowa caucuses, only Trump and Senator Ted Cruz managed to poll in double-digits.

Despite Trump's strong showing in the polls throughout the portion of the invisible primary in which he was active, pundits discounted his chances of winning the nomination. They cited past poll leaders at similar points in their races as evidence that Trump would not translate poll numbers into actual votes and delegates. They pointed to Rudy Giuliani in 2008 and a series of poor performers in 2012, such as Michele Bachmann, Rick Perry, and Herman Cain, who nonetheless led the national polls at some juncture. We were also extremely skeptical of Trump's chances during the invisible primary for similar reasons. Early polls have often been mostly reflective of name recognition, and Trump arguably was better known than any other candidates, including Jeb Bush, the brother and son of a U.S. President.

Table 15.2 Poll Leaders in the 2016 Republican Nomination Campaign

Month	Leader	Runner-up	Third place
February 2015	Huckabee	Bush	Paul, Walker
	17%	12%	11%
March 2015	Bush	Walker	Paul
	16%	13%	12%
April 2015	Bush	Walker	Paul, Rubio
	17%	12%	11%
May 2015	Rubio	Bush	Huckabee, Walker
	14%	13%	10%
June 2015	Bush	Trump	Huckabee
	19%	12%	8%
July 2015	Trump	Bush	Walker
	19%	15%	10%
August 2015	Trump	Bush	Carson
	24%	13%	8%
September 2015	Trump	Fiorina	Carson
	24%	15%	14%
October 2015	Trump	Carson	Bush, Rubio
	27%	22%	8%
November 2015	Trump	Cruz	Carson
	36%	16%	14%
December 2015	Trump	Cruz	Carson, Rubio
	39%	18%	10%
January 2016	Trump	Cruz	Rubio
	41%	19%	8%

Note: Data gathered by the author from http://www.realclearpolitics.com/epolls/2016/president/us/2016_republican_presidential_nomination-3823.html.

One area where Trump was outperformed by Bush, and by several other candidates, was fundraising. The top five candidates in pre-Iowa fundraising were, in order: Ben Carson, Cruz, Marco Rubio, Bush, and Trump.[7] But Trump put a positive spin on this list, saying that he was largely financing his own campaign and therefore "could not be bought" by big-dollar donors. In addition, Trump was lapping the field in terms of free media, due to the wall-to-wall coverage of his every tweet, speech, and rally. From the day he announced his candidacy to the end of 2015, Trump garnered 34 percent of the news coverage of GOP hopefuls. Bush was second with 18 percent and Rubio and Carson tied for third with 14 percent. And it was largely positive coverage that Trump was getting despite his constant carping at the media during and after he received the Republican presidential nomination. Of the eight news organizations monitored by Media Tenor, the percentage of positive or neutral coverage ranged from a high of 74 percent from *USA Today* to a "low" of 63 percent of what *The New York Times* relayed to its readers. Therefore, none of these major newspapers and television networks gave Trump more than 37 percent negative coverage during the invisible primary period.[8]

Despite all of that free, positive news coverage and despite the robust poll numbers, Donald Trump was not able to secure much support from Republican elites in the form of publicly reported endorsements. Using the weighted system from *The Party Decides*, Trump gained only 3.6 percent of the endorsements pre-Iowa. The spread of endorsements can be seen in Figure 15.5. Trump's total was only good for ninth out of 17 candidates. This was the main reason

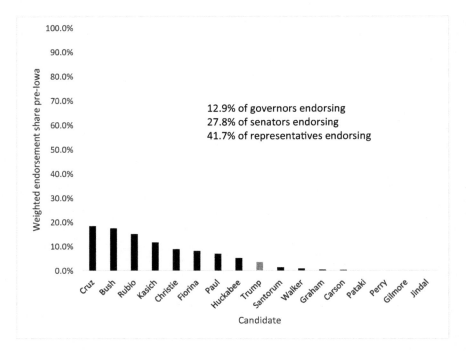

12.9% of governors endorsing
27.8% of senators endorsing
41.7% of representatives endorsing

Figure 15.5 Weighted Republican Endorsement Share pre-Iowa

Note: Data gathered by *The Party Decides* team.

many in the discipline and the media gave Trump such little chance of winning the nomination. As we argue in *The Party Decides*, early endorsements have been very predictive of success in collecting the delegates necessary to secure the nomination. Trump's ultimate victory despite lacking any major endorsements was a significant blow to our theory and its predictive ability.

However, it was not as if the party chose someone and Trump beat him or her. For many reasons that I will discuss in the next section, the Republican Party did not decide in 2016. Less than 15 percent of governors endorsed, less than 30 percent of senators endorsed, and less than 45 percent of representatives endorsed pre-Iowa during the most recent cycle. Those numbers are significantly lower than in past Republican contests. Figure 15.6 shows the trend in gubernatorial endorsements in the post McGovern-Fraser era. Gubernatorial endorsements were at their lowest in 2016, and Donald Trump became the first Republican nominee not to grab a single one pre-Iowa.

Even after the field narrowed post-Iowa to a four-horse race, Trump did not fare well among Republican elites. Rubio garnered 37 percent of the post-Iowa endorsements to lead the way. Cruz had 27 percent and Trump and Kasich were further behind with 17 percent each. So, the party certainly did not bandwagon to Trump even as he began clearly demonstrating the ability to translate his gaudy poll numbers into votes and thereby delegates. But what the party clearly could not do is stop Trump at this point in the process. High-profile endorsements meant to deny Trump the nomination were seemingly useless. Governor Nikki Haley endorsed Marco Rubio days before a South Carolina primary that Trump won easily. And months later, Governor Mike Pence endorsed Ted Cruz before the Indiana primary with similarly futile results. The tardiness of these endorsements was suboptimal as they did not give the endorsing governors enough time to transfer their campaign infrastructure to their preferred candidates.

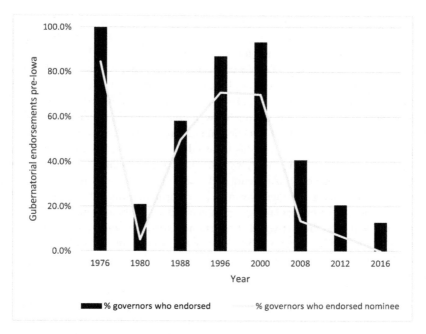

Figure 15.6 Republican Gubernatorial Endorsements pre-Iowa

Note: Data gathered by *The Party Decides* team.

Early endorsements allow for this and therefore seem to be more useful in winning primaries and caucuses. Eleventh-hour endorsements do not seem to be as potent.

Whereas the Democrats had a clear frontrunner and a relatively small field of candidates as the 2016 invisible primary got under way, the Republican nomination chase had the look of a free-for-all from the beginning. While Jeb Bush led the potential field in terms of name recognition and fundraising ability, and appeared to be the favorite before anybody had officially announced, the Bush surname was clearly not as intimidating as it used to be and in fact many argued it would be an albatross around the candidate's neck thanks to his older brother's rocky eight years in the White House. Bush fatigue was a real thing among the general public and even among committed Republicans.

The first candidate to officially announce was Ted Cruz on March 23, 2015. Then came fellow U.S. Senators Rand Paul and Marco Rubio in April, and a glut of candidates followed in May and June. Bush's official announcement took place on June 15, but as would become commonplace during the campaign, the former governor of Florida was one-upped a day later when Donald Trump began his quest with a fiery opening speech in which he insulted an entire ethnic group from the podium at Trump Tower in New York. When former Virginia governor Jim Gilmore announced on July 30, he became the seventeenth and final candidate to be the 2016 Republican nominee for president.

As mentioned briefly earlier, because of the sheer size of the field the dynamic was dramatically different than in past GOP nominating campaigns. In order to get in the prime time debates candidates had to finish in the top tier in *national* polling. So there was considerably less retail campaigning in Iowa and New Hampshire and more of an emphasis on increasing the national profile of the candidates. This played right into the hands of Donald Trump, who did not have much of a ground game but had terrific name recognition and the ability to command intense press coverage throughout the invisible primary. Trump led the polls so he always faced off in the "main event" debate and his performances were noteworthy. His schoolyard taunts were surprisingly effective and they took their toll on his main opponents. Jeb Bush was "low energy." Marco Rubio was "Little Marco." Ted Cruz became "Lyin' Ted." And even when he took on Carly Fiorina's appearance or offered a crude reason why Megyn Kelly was asking him tough questions it did not seem to hurt his popularity among those already predisposed to supporting him. Maybe more importantly, his opponents were very reluctant to directly criticize Trump in return. The reasoning seemed valid at the time but in retrospect it backfired – "big league," as Trump would say. Most of the pundits believed Trump was far from 100 percent serious about running for president. One theory was that he was just trying to negotiate a better deal from NBC for his show Celebrity Apprentice. Another theory was that he was hoping to build his general brand and increase the net worth of his company. A third theory was that he never wanted to be president and he was taking a giant ego trip across the nation. Finally, even if none of those theories was valid the fact was that he had no experience and very little in the way of a traditional campaign and his quest was bound to fizzle or flame out. His opponents, therefore, did not want to be on the record as criticizing Trump, in turn alienating or even insulting his supporters. Each of them wanted to be eligible to receive that considerable support when Trump dropped out. Certainly there was no coordinated effort to bring down Trump and individually there was not much in the way of negative campaigning coming his way. The other contenders were busy attacking each other hoping to be the reasonable, establishment alternative to Trump if it came down to that. So, Bush and Rubio spent millions attacking each other. Cruz played nice with Trump while hammering Rubio. And the rest of the hopefuls were trying to get what little coverage was left when the networks and cable news shows took a break from lavishing attention on Mr. Trump.

As the winnowing intensified in the weeks leading up to the Iowa caucuses, most experts still felt as though Trump's strong showing in the polls would not translate to victories in the primaries and caucuses. And indeed Trump could only manage a second place finish in Iowa gaining 24 percent of the vote. Ted Cruz was victorious with 28 percent and Rubio closely trailed Trump with 23 percent. Trump's whole persona was predicated on success and victory, and he clearly lost the first time the voters had their say. Maybe Trump would indeed prove to be a paper tiger and the party would dodge a bullet despite their inability to coordinate around anyone pre-Iowa. But eight days later, Trump responded with a resounding win in New Hampshire and it became clear many party elites simply did not get it. Republican leaders were still endorsing long shots like Chris Christie in the days leading up to New Hampshire. Christie was polling in the single digits and was not the threat to Trump that Rubio, Cruz, or even Kasich might have been. This lack of foresight was really astonishing and the party's inability or unwillingness to at least try to stop Trump through some coordination around a viable alternative allowed Trump to build a delegate lead through the first month of contests. A plurality of Palmetto State voters ignored their popular governor's endorsement of Marco Rubio and gave Trump a major victory. Trump took South Carolina and all 50 delegates which was particularly notable, considering the role the state has played in recent Republican presidential nominating history. Prior to 2012, it had consistently been seen as a firewall for the establishment candidate. It saved George H. W. Bush in 1988 against Bob Dole and it turned around and saved Dole eight years later against Pat Buchanan. In 2000, George W. Bush scored a big win over insurgent John McCain, and eight years after that it chose the new establishment favorite McCain over Romney and Mike Huckabee.

After Trump's win in the Nevada caucuses, he was the clear leader in delegates and the prohibitive favorite to win his party's nomination. The viable alternatives had dwindled to three:

Ted Cruz, Marco Rubio, and John Kasich. Yet with the exception of a half-baked plan to have Rubio supporters in Ohio vote for Kasich over Trump and Kasich supporters in Florida vote for Rubio over Trump on March 15, the three challengers were still doing a heck of a job splitting the anti-Trump vote. The vote-swap may have helped Kasich, as he won his home state, but it did not help Rubio, as he was crushed in his home state leading to his withdrawal from the race.

As the calendar moved into April, it was a three-man race and Trump was heading into some potentially friendly states in his home region. Going into the so-called "Acela Primary," named for the Amtrak line that runs through the northeast corridor, Donald Trump had built a big delegate lead without winning a majority of voters in any state. On April 26, he managed the feat five times. In New York, Maryland, Connecticut, Delaware, and Pennsylvania, the Republican frontrunner dominated Cruz and Kasich, winning 57 percent of the cumulative vote and 111 out of 124 delegates. Trump was on the verge of an astounding victory and talk of a brokered convention was becoming more and more of a pipe dream for the Never Trumpers. Indiana came next and Governor Mike Pence's endorsement of Ted Cruz was not enough to thwart Trump, who won the Hoosier State easily despite being outspent four-to-one. Cruz dropped out that night and Kasich followed him out the door the following day. On May 4, 2016, Donald Trump became the Republican Party's presumptive nominee for president.

It was a stunning achievement for someone with absolutely no political experience. It was also a tremendous disaster for the Republican Party as they failed miserably to coordinate behind a candidate who was broadly acceptable to the major policy demanders in the party. Donald Trump was a loose cannon who held some seriously problematic issue positions for major swaths of the party's base. Trump also had extremely high unfavorable ratings and went into the general election as a clear underdog to Secretary Clinton. It is important to note that the fact Trump was able to win the presidential election does not undermine this point. The general election results revealed the incredible weakness of the Democratic nominee. Clearly, a more broadly acceptable Republican without Trump's personal and political baggage could have, and likely would have, won a bigger victory in the general election. The problems that the Republican Party is currently facing despite holding the White House and both chambers of Congress are directly attributable to the man in the Oval Office. Trump's missteps and the intense opposition he is receiving from the courts, the media, and the American public are, at the time of this writing, threatening to render the electoral triumph achieved by the GOP meaningless in terms of policy.

What Next?

Political parties are notoriously adaptive and have historically fought through both intentional reforms designed to weaken them and circumstantial developments that have threatened their power. Presidential nominations are one of the most important functions that a party undertakes. They are too important to allow reforms and circumstances to get in the way of elite control for too long. I would expect the parties to adjust to the most recent changes in the political landscape and regain control of their nominations. In 2016, the Democratic Party, despite vitriolic criticism of its tactics, did decide early in favor of a candidate and helped her beat back a serious challenge from outside the establishment. Secretary Clinton thoroughly dominated the endorsement derby and led wire-to-wire, despite some important primary victories achieved by Senator Sanders. There will certainly be calls to open up the process in the aftermath of his insurgent campaign. However, unless Sanders' supporters dive deeply into the arcane world of internal Democratic Party politics, I would not expect many changes in how the process works. With Donald Trump in the White House, progressives of all stripes seem to have much more pressing concerns than how nominations work. As for the Republicans, they clearly did not decide in 2016 and are currently paying the price for their inability to nominate a highly qualified, unifying candidate to take on an extremely vulnerable opponent. They allowed Trump to skate through the invisible primary without facing too much scrutiny or attacks on his personal or public life. The result was a strong outsider campaign that came out swinging in Iowa and New Hampshire and took an early delegate lead despite only being able to secure pluralities during the first few months of primaries and caucuses. Trump effectively clinched the nomination with a dominant performance in the Acela Primary, reducing the rest of the field to rubble. In their defense, the Republicans may be forgiven for not having it in the front of their mind what can happen to a party when they allow the voters to decide. It had been 40 years since Jimmy Carter stormed to the nomination and the presidency without building the close relationships within his party necessary to govern effectively. And it had been 44 years since the Democratic Party had changed the rules and forfeited control over the process almost entirely to the electorate. The result of that nomination campaign was George McGovern who was trounced by President Nixon, a man who would not survive his second term due to the scandal of Watergate. For the Republicans going into their next contested nomination campaign, whether that is in 2020 or 2024, the old saying "Fool me once, shame on you. Fool me twice, shame on me," might be quite pertinent. As to whether you will ever again be able to purchase presidential Halloween masks a year in advance, that remains to be seen. But I would not bet against the two parties expending a great deal of energy and innovation to revert to the golden era of orderly, unifying nominations.

Notes

1 By open, I mean there is no incumbent president in the mix.
2 Senator Gary Hart almost replicated McGovern and Carter's feat in 1984 against the establishment favorite, former Vice-President Walter Mondale.
3 This is why every endorsement we collected was weighted on a scale from 0 to 1 with higher numbers representing a more valued endorsement. For example, celebrities are given the lowest weight of .1 while governors are given one of the highest weights of .8.
4 Joe Biden would dip his toe much deeper into the water after the tragic death of his son Beau. But he ultimately decided against making the race and I discuss that in the context of our theory later in this section.
5 This newspaper data was gathered by *The Party Decides* team.
6 Her negative coverage continued into the general election campaign and can also be contrasted with her Republican opponent's generally positive coverage.
7 This ordering does not include Super PAC spending and independent expenditures. Not only would those figures change the rankings but they would also likely increase the gap between Trump and his closest competitors for the nomination.
8 These outlets were *USA Today*, Fox News Channel, *Los Angeles Times, Wall Street Journal*, CBS, NBC, *Washington Post*, and the *New York Times*. All media data in this paragraph gathered by the author from http://scholar.harvard.edu/thomaspatterson/home.

References

Bartels, Larry. 1988. *Presidential Primaries and the Politics of Public Choice*. Princeton, NJ: Princeton University Press.

Cohen, Marty, David Karol, Hans Noel, and John Zaller. 2008. *The Party Decides*. Chicago: University of Chicago.

Cohen, Marty, David Karol, Hans Noel, and John Zaller. 2016. "Party versus Faction in the Reformed Presidential Nominating System." *PS* 49 (3): 701–708.

Noel, Hans. 2016. "Sanders needs open primaries because he's not winning Democrats." April 25th, http://www.vox.com/mischiefs-of-faction/2016/4/25/11501542/sanders-open-primaries-not-winning-democrats

Polsby, Nelson. 1983. *Consequences of Party Reform*. Berkeley, CA: Institute of Governmental Studies Press.

16

CITIZEN CHOICE IN PRESIDENTIAL PRIMARIES

Wayne Steger

The ability to put candidates on the ballot makes political parties the arbiters of representative democracy (Schattschneider 1960, 140–41). As arbiters, the parties have the capacity to choose candidates that serve partisan interests, potentially at the expense of the broader public (Bawn et al. 2012). That makes nominations a critical concern for the parties and for the citizenry. Historically, presidential nominations were the domain of party leaders negotiating in proverbial smoke-filled rooms, with little input by party members around the country. The McGovern-Fraser Committee reforms sought to give greater legitimacy to the party's presidential nominee by making the process more open and participatory (Ceaser 1979; Crotty 1977; Ranney 1975). Voters in reformed caucuses and primaries gained a voice in the selection of the nominee (Polsby 1983; Shafer 1983). The introduction of greater participation in binding primaries and caucuses, however, may or may not have achieved the purpose of handing the control over the nomination to citizens who identify with the major political parties. The campaign occurring before the voting begins can influence the outcome of voting. In particular, *The Party Decides* thesis holds that party insiders may still hold considerable influence over the selection of presidential nominees if they work together before the caucuses and primaries begin (Cohen, Karol, Noel, and Zaller 2008; Steger 2000).

Party insiders can collude to advantage their preferred candidate by coalescing behind one candidate and signaling to party groups, activists, donors and the media which candidate is preferred (Cohen, Karol, Noel, and Zaller 2008). While numerous candidates may appear on the ballot, some of them may not be viable in the sense of having a realistic chance of winning. Party leaders have been able to coalesce to a substantial degree in about three-fifths of the open presidential nominations since the 1970s (Steger 2015, 2016). Party insiders' influence, however, is conditional on the extent of their participation in trying to influence the race, the timing of their involvement, and the degree of convergence among party insiders (Steger 2013, 2016). When party insiders fail to coalesce behind a frontrunner during the invisible primary – the phase of the campaign occurring before the onset of the caucuses and primaries – then more candidates remain viable options for voters (Steger 2015, ch. 7). Voters are relatively empowered in this scenario because they gain choice among more candidates.

Voters' options also may be influenced by the decisions of candidates. Every presidential nomination cycle invites a great deal of speculation about who will seek the presidential nomination. Indeed, this speculation game usually begins at one party convention and continues

273

until the nomination campaign is in full swing three to four years later. Party voters will have more, and more meaningful options when multiple quality candidates enter the race. Their choices will be limited if some of these candidates act strategically and decide not to run. A large number of politicians want to be president, but most ultimately decide that the conditions are not optimal for an attempt in a given year (Burden 2002; Peabody, Ornstein, and Rohde 1976; Steger 2006). Thus some nomination races have a large number of candidates, like the 2016 Republican nomination, while other races feature only one or two major candidates, like the 2016 Democratic nomination race. The entry into the race by a heavyweight candidate – one who polls over 50 percent in national surveys three and four years before the nomination – tends to deter many of the potential candidates so that the race is between a single, strong frontrunner and other candidates who may or may not be viable (Adkins, Dowdle, Petrow, and Steger 2015; Brown 2011). Races without an early, strong frontrunner tend to attract more entrants and the competition for the nomination is more intense (Butler 2004; Steger 2015, ch. 9). Candidate decisions to withdraw from the race also affect voter choice in the primaries, particularly those occurring later in the sequential primary season. Traditional candidates with governing experience tend to withdraw from the race earlier than non-traditional, issue-advocacy candidates who may remain in the race as a symbolic option (Norrander 2006).

The critical thing for evaluating party voters' control over the nomination is how meaningful their options are when they cast ballots in the primaries. Decisions by prospective candidates and/or party insiders can create an imbalanced race with one strong candidate and a number of lesser candidates who do not have a reasonable chance of winning. In this scenario, voters can choose, but their vote is more or less an up or down plebiscitary option to accept or reject the frontrunner. This came close to happening in 1984 when the pre-primary favorite, former Vice President Walter Mondale, came close to losing to an unexpectedly strong rival, Senator Gary Hart. The 2016 Democratic nomination also followed this pattern when early favorite Hillary Clinton faced an unexpectedly strong challenge by Senator Bernie Sanders. However, even in these cases – when many primary voters rejected the party favorite – the frontrunner ultimately prevailed. In other races with a strong, early frontrunner, the frontrunner went on to prevail, as happened in 1980 (Ronald Reagan), 1988 (George H. W. Bush), and 2000 (Al Gore on the Democratic Side and George W. Bush on the Republican side).

Nomination campaigns have been more competitive in races where there was no particularly strong frontrunner in early national polls and/or party insiders failed to engage in the process and unify strongly behind a frontrunner. This scenario played out in 1972 (George McGovern), 1976 (Jimmy Carter), 1988 (Michael Dukakis), 1992 (Bill Clinton), 2004 (John Kerry), and 2016 (Donald Trump). In races like these, the outcome of the race was in doubt and primary voters decided which of the candidates on the ballot would win the nomination. In between these two types of nominations are a number of races in which there was a moderately strong frontrunner (judging by early polls and party insider endorsements). In these races, the frontrunner has an advantage but there remained some doubt about whether the frontrunner would prevail, as in 1996 (Bob Dole), 2008 (Hillary Clinton), 2012 (Mitt Romney). When multiple candidates on the ballot have a reasonable chance of winning, then voters are relatively more empowered because their choices rather than those of prospective candidates or party insiders will determine which of the relatively competitive candidates will get the delegates needed to win the presidential nomination at the convention.

Beyond subjective judgements about how a race is going to play out, there is a systematic way to measure the competitiveness of a nomination race and to measure the extent to which primary voters have meaningful choices. Specifically, this chapter will use a measure of competition and a measure of "competitively equivalent" candidates to assess in a systematic way, how much choice voters really have in the primaries. The empowerment of voters – a central component of all theories of democracy – requires that voters have some choice of candidates beyond a plebiscitary vote of confidence in the candidate mediated by actors and processes before the elections (Held 1987, 154–166). If some or most of the candidates cannot realistically win the nomination, then these candidates exist as symbolic options for voters who do not prefer the frontrunner. Symbolic statements have meaning, but the option remains symbolic rather than a choice that decides the leadership of the political party.

The number of viable candidates on the ballot has been measured with the normalized Herfindal-Hirschman Index (HHI). Economists and financial analysts have long used this index as a metric for assessing the number of competitively equivalent firms in a market.[1] Political scientists have used the measure to analyze multi-party and multi-candidate elections (Hickman 1992; Steger, Hickman, and Yohn 2002; Taagepera and Laakso 1989). I explain the calculation of the measure below. For now, it is sufficient to note that this measure has been adapted to measure the number of competitively equivalent – or viable – options that voters can select among, which makes it useful for assessing the extent to which the invisible primary narrows the choices of primary voters before they get the chance to cast ballots (Steger 2015, ch. 7).

The measure also can be used to evaluate differences in voter choice across presidential primaries. Voters in early states typically have more, and different, options available than do voters in states holding a caucus or primary later in the primary season (Norrander 2000). The results of the early elections affect the choices available to voters in subsequent caucuses and primaries. Candidates who do better than expected in the earliest elections gain momentum going into subsequent caucuses and primaries (Aldrich 1980; Bartels 1988). These candidates typically receive more and more favorable media coverage, increased fundraising, and greater ability to compete in the ensuing caucuses and primaries – thus staying in the race as viable options for voters. Voters in later states, however, typically have fewer choices because the sequential process winnows candidates (Norrander 2006). Winnowing reduces voter choice in primaries occurring later because they typically select among fewer candidates (Atkeson and Maestas 2009; Mayer and Busch 2004). Analyzing patterns of competition and attrition thus enables us to draw inferences about the choices exercised by voters across states.

The next section discusses the importance of voter empowerment in democracy, particularly in an era of polarized political parties. After that, the chapter will analyze patterns of competition within and across presidential nomination cycles. Focusing on competition within each nomination campaign will enable us to gauge differences in voter choice across states. The chapter will finish with a more detailed analysis of the differences between the 2016 Democratic and Republican presidential primaries.

Electoral Competition and the Implications of Political Polarization

Electoral competition plays a central role in representative democracy, helping to ensure responsiveness and accountability to citizens (McDonald and Samples 2006, ch. 1). Voters are empowered to hold government officials accountable, to the extent that they have meaningful choices between candidates (Schumpeter 1942, 81–83). Competition among political organizations and leaders provides voters with the opportunity to make meaningful choices (Schattschneider 1960). Electoral competition is critical, if only because elected officials act to avoid risks of defeat (Fiorina 1977; Mayhew 1974). In this view, successful representation by elected officials should result in less competitive elections, so low levels of competition do not necessarily imply a less responsive government. This argument, however, assumes that voters with only one option on the ballot are satisfied with the choice that they have. A candidate who runs unopposed does so because other candidates decide not to run. In this case, the decisions of candidates rather than voters determine who is elected. The empowerment of voters – a central component of all theories of democracy, requires that voters have some choice of candidates beyond a plebiscitary vote of confidence in the candidate mediated by actors and processes before the elections (Held 1987). The power to choose reduces as competition declines and the number of candidates with a realistic chance of winning, approaches one. At that point, any other option on the ballot is symbolic.

If party insiders and group leaders collude to support one candidate over other candidates before the election occurs, then party insiders can give their preferred candidate tremendous advantages in attracting the votes of citizens (Butler 2004; Cohen, Karol, Noel, and Zaller 2008). In practice, this means tilting the playing field before the voters cast ballots, so that voters effectively select among a limited set of candidates who are acceptable to party insiders. Partisan voters tend to follow the cues of party elites when party elites unify behind a candidate early in a presidential nomination campaign (Steger 2015, ch. 6–9). The less competitive a nominating election is, the more likely that factors other than voters' choices determine the outcome.[2]

Beyond accountability, responsiveness, and empowerment of citizens, electoral competition produces a number of other benefits to democratic process and society. Close elections provide a strong incentive for the candidates and parties to organize and mobilize the electorate (McDonald and Samples 2006, ch. 1). Empirical studies generally support the relationship between competition and voter turnout (Patterson and Caldeira 1984; Wolfinger and Rosenstone 1980). Electoral competition also increases the information available to voters as political parties promote their candidate and because the news media give greater coverage to campaigns that are competitive (McDonald and Samples 2006, 7). Electoral competition also facilitates the watchdog function of the media. There is no assurance that commercial media will engage in investigative journalism, which is costly to perform and has only some probability of success. Electoral competition facilitates discovery of "abuses of power" and communication of that information to voters, because competing parties watch each other for reasons of self-interest, each trying to expose the wrongdoings of the other for their own benefit.[3] This matters, because the costs of monitoring government must be absorbed by someone other than voters, who are busy with their own lives and lack the time or access to do so. Even people who do pay attention to politics must rely on the media and political parties to monitor and expose problems with candidates or parties.

Note that electoral competition might also cause problems for democratic nations. Competitive nominating elections help ensure responsiveness of party nominees to core constituencies of party activists and identifiers, whose votes are needed to win intra- and inter-party elections (Issacharoff and Pildes 1998). This may be good or bad for the country as a whole. A problem arises when the preferences of party activists come at the expense of the interests of the broader public, as noted earlier. Another problem is that responsiveness to ideologically oriented constituents constrains elected officials' ability to operate as trustees of the public good (McDonald and Samples 2006, 8–11). Elected officials need discretion to negotiate and bargain after elections, which competitive elections might constrain (Pitkin 1972). The problems of activist constraint have been exacerbated in the past decade by increasingly frenzied ideological commentators on Fox and MSNBC cable news, talk radio, and a multitude of digital media. Conservative digital media (e.g., Breitbart.com, The Blaze, The Daily Caller, Chicks on the Right, RedState, and Infowars) and liberal digital media (e.g., Addictinginfo, Bipartisan Report, Crooks and Liars, Daily Kos, Forward Progressives, MoveOn, and Talking Points Memo) provide a constant stream of information that enflame party activist passions. These passions constrain the ability of elected officials to compromise while in office.

These issues for representation and governance arise when the parties are polarized. In a polarized political environment, parties and candidates pursue the "politics of the base." They respond to the passions of policy-demanding party constituencies in order to mobilize their partisan supporters to win elections (Abramowitz 2010; Barrileaux, Holbrook, and Langer 2002). Political polarization increases the pressure to produce policies that satisfy the more ideologically extreme preferences of their party base. As a result, both parties try to direct a disproportionate share of government benefits to their constituencies while imposing a disproportionate share of the costs on the other side's constituencies. For example, Democrats are willing to raise taxes on Republican constituencies to pay for programs that disproportionately benefit Democratic constituencies, while Republicans are willing to cut spending in programs that disproportionately benefit Democratic constituencies in order to get tax cuts and other programs for their own constituents.

Political polarization thus increases the stakes involved in winning *institutional* control of Congress and the White House. Institutional control is critical because it confers the capacity to exercise control over the agenda and the content of policy, which is necessary for satisfying constituent demands (Cox and McCubbins 1993). Institutional control is a system level consideration because the legislative process contains multiple pivot points in which legislation can be defeated (Krehbiel 1998). Winning the presidency is especially important to a political party's policy goals because the president has the greatest capacity to set the policy agenda and the president occupies the most critical pivot point in the legislative process. The president's capacity to veto legislation greatly changes the power equation in the legislative process. If a party controls Congress but not the White House, the majority party in Congress needs to overcome presidential vetoes with two-thirds majorities in both chambers, which places a very high political hurdle to overcome to deliver benefits to party constituencies. For the minority party in Congress, winning the White House is tantamount to blocking the congressional majority. The presidency thus is the most critical position for delivering benefits to party constituencies.

While the parties are polarized, they remain national coalitions of groups and ideological factions. Presidential nominations are consequential because the presidential nominee of a party plays an outsized role in shaping public perceptions of what a party stands for and setting expectations about what it will do if it wins the election. Thus, nominations are contested by ambitious candidates who want the office *and* by groups and activists who want their causes and preferences represented by the party's nominee. Who exerts influence in the nomination process affects who becomes the nominee and what policies will be pursued if the party wins.

Measuring Competition in Presidential Nominations in the Modern Era

Historically, party leaders selected presidential nominees in proverbial smoke-filled rooms at the national conventions, with little input by citizens (David, Goldman, and Bain 1960; Reiter 1985). Reforms of the nomination process in the 1970s enabled more candidates, particularly those outside a party's mainstream, to compete for the presidential nomination (Asher 1984, 199–201; Polsby 1983). The proliferation of primary elections and reforms of party caucuses also enabled larger numbers of citizens to participate in the selection of the party nominee (Polsby 1983). While democratizing the nomination process, citizens voting in presidential caucuses and primaries may not have as much choice as it appears. As explained earlier, decisions by prospective candidates and by party insiders may result in a ballot with candidates who have very different chances of winning (Cohen, Karol, Noel, and Zaller 2008). Citizens are empowered to select their leaders when they have several viable candidates to choose among in an election. Assessing the competitiveness of elections and the degree of voter choice among candidates with a realistic chance of winning, provides insights into which scenario plays out in a given election year.

There also will be variation in voter choice across the primary season as candidates are winnowed from the race. Running for a presidential nomination is costly, especially once the primaries begin because of the need for organization, travel and advertising. Candidates begin the primary season with variable amounts of name recognition, public support, campaign funds, organization, and media exposure. Candidates who fail to attract much support in the early caucuses and primaries find their fundraising diminished, their campaign organizations cut back, and they lack the resources to advertise (Norrander 2006). Further, their ability to campaign through the news media – which is free (but earned) – is difficult because they get less coverage and what coverage they do get is more critical (Bartels 1988; Haynes, Gurian, Crespin, and Zorn 2004; Patterson 1980, 43–48). For example, in the 2016 Republican nomination, candidates like Chris Christie and Rick Santorum received few votes in the Iowa Caucus and New Hampshire primary and could not realistically continue their campaigns. Candidates with plenty of funds raised and held in reserve, like Jeb Bush in 2016, can continue in the race for a while but they too will face diminished capacity to campaign. At some point, the strategic calculus changes and the odds of winning grow thin as they fall further behind in the delegate count (Norrander 2006). At some point before the end of the caucuses, some candidates may stop campaigning because they realize they cannot win, as Marco Rubio did after losing his home state primary in Florida. As a result, there tend to be fewer viable candidates and less competition in later primaries than in those occurring at the beginning of the primary season.

The number of viable candidates that voters select among have been measured in various ways, but the Herfindahl-Hirschman Index has been shown to be a particularly useful measure in competitive markets with multiple contestants (Steger 2015, ch. 6). The HHI, for example, is used to measure the competitiveness of professional sports leagues, economic markets, and elections with more than two parties or candidates (Bardhan and Yang 2004; Owen, Ryan, and Weatherston 2008; Steger, Hickman, and Yohn 2002; Taagepera and Laakso 1989). The index is calculated in two stages. The first step involves summing the square of the candidates' vote shares, $H = \Sigma c_i^2$, where c_i = each candidate's share of the vote. The inverse of H provides a measure of the number of competitively equivalent options available to voters. This measure is to estimate the number of effective political parties and candidates in multi- party/candidate electoral systems like presidential nominations. I will use the 2016 New Hampshire primary results to illustrate the measure. On the Republican side, 11 candidates divided the vote, with the top five candidates getting 35.72 percent, 15.93 percent, 11.79 percent, 11.11 percent, and 10.66 percent. The next six candidates gained 14.79 percent of the vote.[4] For this distribution of votes for 11 candidates, H is calculated to be 5.04 competitively equivalent candidates. This number can be interpreted as a voter having a choice among five viable candidates and some symbolic options. On the Democratic side, Sanders received 61.3 percent of the vote, Clinton received 38.4 percent and Martin O'Malley received 0.03 percent of the vote. This distribution of the vote yields an H of 1.91 percent of the vote – indicating that voters chose among approximately two viable candidates. The measure improves on just counting the number of candidates on the ballot because some candidates do not have a realistic chance of winning and thus are not as meaningful an option for voters. For the first part of the analysis in Figure 16.1, the votes across all primaries are combined for calculating H, excluding votes as noted above as well as any candidate gaining less than 0.1 percent of the aggregate primary vote. For the analyses of the 2016 nomination in Figure 16.3, H is calculated separately for each caucus and primary.

The second step in the analysis involves calculating a normalized index, HHI = $(H - 1/N)$ / $(1 - 1/N)$, where N is the total number of candidates in the race. The normalized HHI statistic measures the competitive balance of the election using the distribution of the vote while controlling for the number of candidates in the race. This feature allows us to compare the competitiveness of elections with different numbers of candidates. For ease of presentation, I inverted the normalized HHI, so that high scores indicate more competition (no candidate dominates) while low scores indicate less competition. The resulting measure is bounded at one in the case of a perfectly competitive and a score of zero indicates no competition. The New Hampshire race described above has an inverted HHI of .8817, indicating a highly competitive race. The Anti-Trust division of U.S. Department of Justice (DOJ) uses the normalized HHI to determine whether a merger of corporations would excessively restrict market competition. Given the inversion of the normalized HHI statistic, the DOJ criterion establishes .75 as the threshold above which races would be considered competitive and scores below that mark indicate little competition.[5]

These measures work well for comparing the choices available to voters across campaigns with different numbers of candidates appearing on the ballot as well as comparing the competitiveness of nominations across caucuses and primaries. A low number of competitively equivalent or viable candidates and a low normalized HHI score indicate that there is little competition and voters have less meaningful choice about which candidate to nominate.

Competition across and within Presidential Nomination Campaigns

We begin with the number of candidates competing in presidential nominations from 1972 through 2016 (see Figure 16.1). Figure 16.1 shows the average number of viable or competitively equivalent candidates that represent the choices available to voters across the primaries taken together. Although there are few cases on which to base inferences, the patterns suggest the two political parties may be trending in different directions over time. Democratic primary voters chose among a larger number of competitive candidates in the 1970s, but fewer in recent decades. Republicans had fewer competitive candidates until the last three nominations. In part, the differences reflect the in- versus out-of-power party. Nominations with incumbent presidents have little competition (usually) and Republicans had an incumbent president seeking renomination in five elections between 1972 and 2004, while the Democrats had an incumbent president in three elections. Incumbency, however, does not account for all of the differences. The different trends also correspond to changing factionalism in the Democratic and Republican Parties that has been occurring as the parties realign at the elite and mass levels.

Voters in Democratic primaries had choices over a greater number of viable candidates in the 1970s, in part because the Democratic Party was more factionalized in the 1970s and 1980s than it has been since the 1990s. Between the 1930s and 1990s, the Democratic Party was a large national coalition of relatively conservative southern Democrats and more liberal non-southern Democrats. Multiple candidates sought presidential nominations by competing to be the preferred candidate of the various factions in the party (Brams 1978). The Democratic Party coalition slowly became more homogeneous and liberal as conservative southern white elites and party identifiers gravitated from the Democrats to the Republican Party through intergenerational replacement or simply by switching party allegiances (Paulson 2007). Southern white Democratic politicians and party identifiers began leaving the party in 1964 and that pattern continued through the 1990s. By the late 1990s, most Democrats in the southern states were African-American or living in large urban areas. There remain divisions among Democrats, but the differences along ideological and cultural dimensions are less than they used to be. The differences between progressives like Elizabeth Warren and centrists like Hillary Clinton are not as great as the differences of the 1960s and 1970s when Democrats had leaders like George

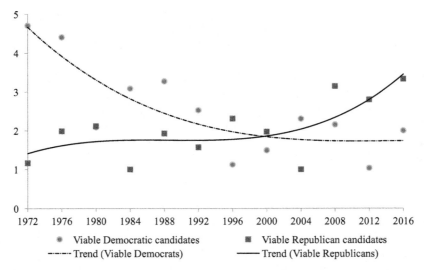

Figure 16.1 Number of Viable or Competitively Equivalent Candidates in Presidential Primaries, 1972–2016

Source: The number of competitively equivalent candidates in a nomination campaign is defined by $H = 1/\sum c_i^2$, where C = candidate share of the aggregate primary vote.

McGovern on the left and George C. Wallace on the right. Since the 1990s, Democratic nominations typically have involved candidates vying to become the leading candidate of left-of-center "mainstream" Democrats and progressive Democrats.

The Republican Party has long had divisions between moderates and conservatives, but these divisions were not nearly as great as those of the Democratic Party. Between 1964 and the 1990s, however, conservative southern white Evangelicals increasingly joined the Republican Party, particularly during and after the Reagan years. Moderate Republicans in northeastern states and the West Coast have been slowly gravitating to the Democratic Party, but that movement is not as complete as the movement of southern whites to the Republican Party. The regional and ideological divisions within the Republican Party have increased. Across presidential nominations, the proportion of very conservative voters has been increasing, while the size of the moderate faction has been declining – though it has not disappeared (Olson and Scala 2015). The resulting Republican coalition is larger but more internally divided than that of the 1960s. Such divisions correspond to a larger number of viable candidates contesting Republican presidential primaries.

In addition to ideological factionalism, the Republican Party has experienced a substantial divide between an establishment, business-oriented party faction and a more ideological, anti-establishment coalition. After the 2008 bailout of big banks and the election of Barack Obama, Tea Party Republicans organized to challenge "establishment" Republicans who held moderate positions or who compromised with Barack Obama (Skocpol and Williamson 2013). Although the Tea Party movement had faded as an organized political force by 2016, the underlying sentiments remained in the form of strong anti-establishment attitudes. Exit polls from the 2016 Republican caucuses and primaries show that supporters and detractors of Donald Trump fell mainly along the lines of wanting an "outsider" candidate versus a candidate with more experience (more on this below). A consequence of these multiple, crosscutting cleavages in the

Republican Party has been an increase in the number of candidates competing to be the leader of different factions (Steger 2017).

Figure 16.2 shows the competitiveness of the presidential primaries, using the normalized HHI as an indicator of the competitive balance across the nominations of elections from 1972 to 2016. The figure includes the names of the eventual nominee for each party in each election. It is important to note that Figure 16.2 represents the competitiveness across all of the primaries taken together. Nominations are more competitive when there are two or more candidates competing across the entire range of primaries. Nominations are less competitive when there is a dominant candidate with little or no opposition. This usually happens when there is an overwhelming favorite in the race – as when an incumbent president is running for renomination for a second term. Nominations are also less competitive if there are viable candidates contesting the nomination, but the frontrunner quickly gains momentum and rival candidates drop out of the race, in which case mid- and late-season primaries are less competitive. This point is discussed in the analysis of the 2016 primaries below.

Regarding the first point, five of the eight presidents who sought a second term in the post-reform era (1972 to the present) were basically unchallenged when they sought renomination. Ronald Reagan and George W. Bush faced no opponents. Although largely unreported, several minor candidates challenged the renominations of Richard Nixon in 1972, Bill Clinton in 1996, and Barack Obama in 2012. These candidates had only a very small impact on the primary vote and did not significantly affect the competitiveness of the primaries. Three presidents, however, faced challengers who were more significant. In general, presidents face a challenge to their renomination when there are major factional divisions in the party and the president is unpopular with the public. Defeating an incumbent president is exceptionally difficult and most potential rivals do not attempt it. The three presidents who faced challengers (Gerald Ford in 1976, Jimmy Carter in 1980, and George H. W. Bush in 1992) fit this pattern. These renomination challenges are not the main concern of this chapter and interested readers can find a more detailed discussion elsewhere (Steger 2015, ch. 6). What is worth noting is that a president who is unpopular within his or her party is likely to face a challenge and the challenger will stand

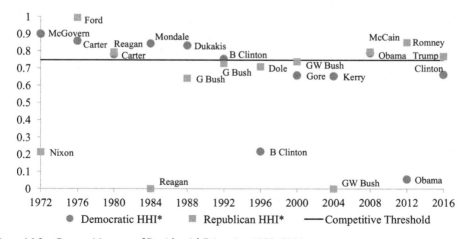

Figure 16.2 Competitiveness of Presidential Primaries, 1972–2016

Note: Normalized Herfindahl-Hirschman Index of the aggregate primary vote. Scores above the threshold indicate a competitive race across the primaries taken together.

at least as a symbolic option on the ballot for disaffected partisans. All three of the incumbent presidents who faced such a challenge were defeated in the general election.

Excluding the races involving an incumbent president, most presidential nominations have been just above or just below the threshold indicating competitive nomination races. Since 1972, ten of the 16 open races – those without an incumbent president – have been in the range indicating a competitive presidential nomination. Seven of these ten races were Democratic nominations and three were Republican nominations.

In all of these competitive races, the majority of party elites did not publicly back a candidate before the caucuses and primaries. In some of these races, there was a party favorite in the sense that a majority of party elites did endorse a preferred candidate, as Cohen, Karol, Noel and Zaller (2008) have found in *The Party Decides*. However, an equally critical factor is how many elites – of those who could endorse a candidate – actually do so during the invisible primary (Steger 2016). In all of the competitive nomination races, the leading candidates received endorsements from fewer than half of the party elites that could have endorsed them during the invisible primary. In each case, two or more candidates were viable competitors and the primaries were more competitive. To put some flesh on the bones provided by the figures, it is worth looking at these races in some descriptive detail.

Although data on presidential endorsements is scant for the presidential nominations of the 1970s, there is little indication that George McGovern (1972) or Jimmy Carter (1976) was the preferred candidate of Democratic Party insiders in those years. Indeed, McGovern and Carter were widely described as outsider candidates during their campaigns. Both won their nomination campaigns by gaining momentum during the caucuses and primaries (Aldrich 1980). Walter Mondale had more party insider support than any of his rivals in 1984, but many Democratic elites refrained from endorsing him or any other candidate before the primaries began. Mondale had only about a quarter of the possible endorsements that he could have had. He faced a strong challenge from Colorado Senator Gary Hart who did much better than expected in the early caucuses and primaries (Bartels 1988). Mondale narrowly won the 1984 primaries and he gained a majority of convention delegates with the help of Democratic super-delegates. Democratic insiders divided their support among multiple candidates in 1988, and the eventual nominee, Michael Dukakis was endorsed by fewer than ten percent of all the Democratic Party insiders. Democratic Party insiders mostly stayed on the sidelines in the invisible primary before the 1992 Democratic primaries, waiting for New York's Mario Cuomo to enter the race. Cuomo ultimately decided not to run, leaving the race relatively wide open. The candidate with the most endorsements was Bill Clinton, but he also was endorsed by fewer than ten percent of all Democratic Party elites. Democratic Party elites also stayed on the sidelines during the invisible primary for the 2004 Democratic nomination, jumping on John Kerry's bandwagon only after he won critical victories in the Iowa Caucus and New Hampshire primary. Hillary Clinton had more party insider support in 2008, but she did not have the support of a majority of Democratic Party elites before the primaries. Of all the open Democratic presidential nominations since 1972, the majority of Democratic Party elites publicly backed a candidate during the invisible primary only in 2000 with Vice President Al Gore and with Hillary Clinton in 2016. In both years, the primaries were not in the range considered to be competitive, though the score for the 2016 primaries is right at the margin identifying a competitive race (I discuss this race below, noting for now that it is distinctive from other nomination campaigns).

The Republican races that were competitive fit a similar pattern, in that the three candidates with competitive primaries lacked the support of a majority of Republican elites during the invisible primaries. McCain and Romney received less than a quarter of the party elite endorsements that could have been made in 2008 and 2012, respectively. Donald Trump had no endorsements from elite Republican Party officials before the primaries began. Those that jumped on his bandwagon did so only as he demonstrated support in the caucuses and primaries. Indeed, Trump won despite opposition from party insiders. Trump will be discussed below.

The six open nominations that had less competitive primaries (see Figure 16.2) all had a stronger frontrunner who had more substantial support from party insiders during the invisible primary. Ronald Reagan was a clear frontrunner going into the 1980 Republican nomination, though it is worth noting that moderate Republican insiders opposed Reagan's nomination but divided their support between George H. W. Bush, Bob Dole, and John Anderson. Reagan's support among grass roots Republicans, however, was strong and he quickly winnowed the field in the 1980 primaries. George W. Bush was Reagan's Vice President and he received the support of about forty percent of elite Republican Party insiders before the primaries; others either refrained from backing a candidate or supported Senate Minority leader Bob Dole. Bush gained substantial momentum beginning with the New Hampshire primary and most of his opponents were winnowed quickly. Over forty percent of elite Republican insiders supported Dole's third campaign for the Republican nomination and his opponents were substantially less competitive in the 1996 Republican Primaries. Then Texas Governor George W. Bush had the most support from party insiders of any Republican to seek the nomination in the post-reform era. He faced little opposition in the primaries and quickly secured the nomination in 2000.

On the Democratic side, the two open nominations races that were not competitive (by the .25 threshold) were that of Al Gore in 2000 and Hillary Clinton in 2016. Gore and Clinton both had overwhelming support from party insiders during the invisible primary. Gore faced only one rival who had little chance of winning after Gore won strong victories in the Iowa Caucus and the New Hampshire primary. Clinton ultimately prevailed, but the media made the race look more competitive than it actually was. Although Sanders attracted energetic support from progressive Democrats, especially younger voters, Clinton won with almost 56 percent of the caucus and primary vote. There is a caveat to this observation, however, in that many of the primaries were not competitive even though the race was relatively competitive across the caucuses and primaries. Of all the nominations since 1972, the Clinton–Sanders race has a distinctive pattern across the primary season (see below).

Overall, open presidential nominations of the post-reform era have given voters meaningful choices of candidates, at least through the early caucuses and primaries. As Figure 16.1 shows, in most of these races and in three races involving an incumbent president seeking renomination, there have been competitive candidates on the ballot. Caucus and primary voters have at least symbolic options even in cases where the frontrunner is likely to win. In races in which party elites refrained from backing a candidate during the invisible primary, the primaries and caucuses are competitive. In races in which the majority of elites engaged in the process by backing a candidate, and unified around a frontrunner, the result is a less competitive race across all of the primaries taken together. This pattern suggests that party insiders may have helped tilt the playing field in favor of a preferred candidate, but this pattern holds only when party insiders actively engage in the process and unify behind a candidate before the primaries (Steger 2016).

A Closer Look at the 2016 Presidential Nomination Races: Momentum and Winnowing

The 2016 Democratic and Republican presidential nomination races exhibited substantially different dynamics. On the Democratic side, Hillary Clinton was the overwhelming favorite of party insiders. She netted almost 97 percent of the possible endorsements by elite elected Democratic officials. She also had an extensive fundraising network already in place among big

Democratic donors owing to her previous campaign in 2008. In very early polls during 2013 and 2014, Clinton consistently polled over fifty percent among self-identified Democrats and Democratic leaners. None of the politicians rumored to be considering a nomination campaign, like Vice President Joe Biden and Senator Elizabeth Warren, entered the race. This helped clear the path to victory for Hillary Clinton who was expected to face minimal resistance to her nomination. Senator Bernie Sanders, a self-described Democratic Socialist, challenged Clinton. Sanders began the race with little money, name recognition, and campaign organization. Sanders gained momentum in the latter half of 2015 through Twitter and word-of-mouth as progressive Democratic activists and young Democrats embraced his progressive, populist messages. Further, liberal digital media supported Sanders' left-wing populist campaign. Sanders' followers and the audiences of digital media outlets shared stories on social media, expanding the reach of his insurgent campaign. By the time the caucuses and primaries began, Sanders had become a serious rival to Clinton for the nomination.

Figure 16.3 indicates that Sanders and Clinton were both viable, competitively equivalent candidates from the Iowa Caucuses on February 2 until the last caucuses and primaries in June. Democratic voters in most states had a choice between both candidates. Note that there were several states in early March in which Democratic voters did not have two competitively equivalent candidates. Sanders ran notably weaker in some states, particularly in large southern states in which African-American voters comprised a large proportion of the Democratic voting population. Clinton, however, ran poorly in a few other states in the high plains and Pacific Northwest, where Sanders ran well. This is unusual, in that one candidate or the other won states by large margins with closely contested primaries scattered in between. Overall, however, the trendline (dotted line) indicates a relatively balanced and competitive campaign between two candidates throughout the caucuses and primaries. There were, however, enough primaries that generated lopsided results that the overall competitiveness score, shown in Figure 16.2,

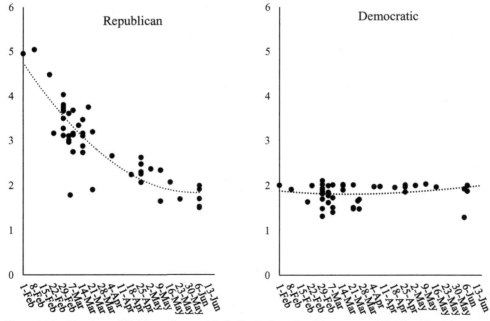

Figure 16.3 Number of Viable or Competitively Equivalent Candidates across 2016 Presidential Caucuses and Primaries

is not considered competitive across the caucuses and primaries. Despite hype surrounding Sanders' campaign, Clinton was highly likely to win the nomination after the southern states held their primaries (and in which Sanders was not competitive).

The 2016 Republican campaign shaped up differently. First, there was no clear frontrunner in national polls in 2013 and 2014 when candidates are usually calculating their chances against other potential candidates. Ultimately, there were 16 nationally recognized Republican candidates, but none drew more than 20 percent in national polls through the June of 2015. Indeed, the race was highly fluid and nine candidates led in various national polls from 2013 through the end of 2015.[6] Republican Party elites virtually stayed out of the race during the invisible primary with only about a third making any endorsement, and those that did publicly support a candidate divided their support among several candidates. As such, none of the Republicans in the race could claim to have been a strong frontrunner or a party favorite when the primaries began. Trump led in national polls by the end of the invisible primary, but his support was far below levels at which the frontrunner was able to win the nomination in the caucuses and primaries.

Despite the large field of candidates, many did not get much traction in the race when the caucuses and primaries began. Figure 16.3 shows that the Republican race began with five competitively equivalent candidates in the Iowa and New Hampshire primaries – the most since the Democratic race of 1976. Many of the candidates, however, were winnowed from the field after they failed to place near the top in the Iowa Caucuses and the New Hampshire primary. The winnowing pattern exhibited in the Republican race in Figure 16.3 is typical of presidential nomination campaigns of the post-reform era. The race begins with a number of candidates, but those that fail to attract support in the earliest nominating elections usually drop out of the race.

One major implication in a race like this is that voters in states holding a caucus or primary on a later date have fewer options on the ballot. After Iowa and New Hampshire, the race essentially narrowed to three major candidates – Donald Trump, Ted Cruz, and Marco Rubio with Ben Carson and John Kasich continuing in the race with less support. The race continued to narrow with Trump slowly gaining momentum to become the frontrunner. Still, Republican voters continued to have choices among at least two competitively equivalent candidates throughout the caucus and primary season. This has been the pattern in the last three Republican nominations.

Figure 16.4 shows the competitive balance of the Republican and Democratic presidential caucuses and primaries. On the Republican side, the race began as a highly competitive race in Iowa and New Hampshire, but the competitiveness of the race declined as Donald Trump gained momentum and as most of his rivals were winnowed from the field of candidates. Although voters had choices by the end of the race, the competitive balance had shifted decidedly in favor of Donald Trump. Together, the two figures for the Republican race reflect a classic case of "campaign momentum" of the type that propelled Jimmy Carter to the Democratic nomination in 1976. It is clear that Republican caucus and primary voters rather than mediation by party insiders determined that Trump would win the nomination.

The competitiveness of the 2016 Democratic race, shown in the right panel of Figure 16.4, looks very different. The race began in the Iowa caucuses as a perfectly competitive race – the HHI score indicates a perfect tie. There were a few near perfectly competitive races from the beginning to the end of the primary season as Clinton and Sanders ran almost evenly in Iowa, Massachusetts, Missouri, Illinois, Connecticut, Kentucky, New Mexico, South Dakota, and the District of Columbia. In between, however, there were a number of states in which either Clinton (southern states) or Sanders (Pacific Northwestern states) had decided advantages. These states often had little competition between the two candidates. Both, however, won enough states to make it a two-person race throughout the entire caucus and primary season.

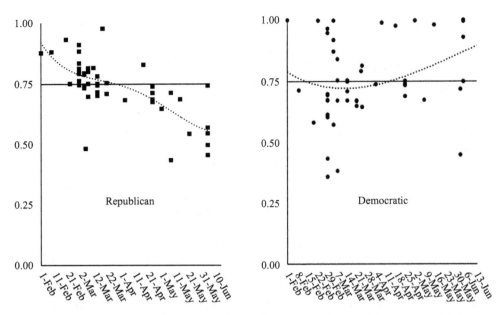

Figure 16.4 Competitiveness of 2016 Republican and Democratic Presidential Caucuses and Primaries

The difference was that Clinton won more of the big states with larger numbers of delegates to the national convention. The competitiveness of the race indicates that caucus and primary voters determined the outcome. Despite Clinton's overwhelming support by party insiders, there is little evidence that party elites were able to mediate the nomination by rallying to Clinton's banner during the invisible primary phase of the campaign. While their support undoubtedly helped Clinton, the patterns of competition and voter choice do not indicate a successful collusive effect to minimize competition and deny voters the opportunity to exercise a free choice in the caucuses and primaries.

Conclusions

The reforms of the early 1970s were intended to democratize the presidential process, enabling rank-and-file party activists and identifiers to have a voice in the selection of the party's presidential nominees. The evidence provided here indicates that the reforms have had that effect. In almost all of the open nominations, primary voters have had meaningful choices among two or more competitively equivalent candidates who had a realistic chance of winning. In addition, in three of the seven nominations with an incumbent seeking reelection, voters have had meaningful choices or at least a symbolic option with which they could express disapproval of the incumbent. There can be little question that the post-reform era is relatively democratic in this sense. Primary voters generally have meaningful choices in all but a few nomination races (particularly those with an incumbent president and a few others in which party elites overwhelmingly backed a candidate that early polls showed having a sizeable lead).

Competition in elections provides voters with meaningful choices, helping ensure responsiveness, accountability and citizen empowerment over the political system, or at least over the political class of each party. In nominating elections, such empowerment serves to make party candidates responsive and accountable to party constituencies, which comes with advantages and disadvantages for the country. While voters have meaningful choices, there have been quite a few nominations in which the playing field has tilted in favor of an early favorite who enters the race, secures substantial party insider support, and goes on to win the nomination with the support of a majority of caucus and primary voters. When most party insiders engage in the process by publicly backing a candidate *and* unify behind a frontrunner during the invisible primary, the primaries have not been as competitive. In every case where party insiders refrained from jumping into the race behind a frontrunner, the result has been a more competitive race during the caucuses and primaries. These races in particular are highly competitive through at least the early caucuses and primaries. Voters in later states often have fewer choices than do voters in states holding primaries earlier in the calendar. In this respect, voters in these later occurring primaries have less power and influence over the nomination.

Notes

1 The Federal Reserve uses the index to measure market competition and market share (see Rhoads 1993, 188). The Justice Department has long used the measure to evaluate corporate mergers (Calkins 1983).
2 There are numerous possibilities including party insider collusion, the distribution of voter preferences, geographic or ideological sorting, and so on.
3 That is, unless both major parties have moved into a mutually advantageous electoral collusion, with each side accepting corruption on the part of the other in exchange for ignoring corruption on their own part.
4 The vote shares of candidates who received at least one-tenth of one percent of the total number of votes cast in a primary to ensure that the measure is as inclusive and as close to the total number of votes cast as possible. The measure uses the summed vote shares of candidates meeting this criterion, rather than the total number of votes cast in a primary. Votes for unidentified "others" and "scattered write-ins" are excluded since vote shares are not identifiable for individual candidates. Similarly, "uncommitted" votes are excluded since these votes do not reflect the success of individual candidates.
5 See http://www.justice.gov/atr/public/guidelines/hhi.html.
6 See http://www.realclearpolitics.com/epolls/2016/president/us/2016_republican_presidential_nomination-3823.html.

References

Abramowitz, Alan. 2010. *The Disappearing Center*. New Haven, CT: Yale University Press.
Adkins, Randall E., Andrew J. Dowdle, Greg Petrow, and Wayne Steger. 2015. "Progressive Ambition, Opportunism, and the Presidency, 1972–2012." Paper presented at the annual meeting of the Midwest Political Science Association, Chicago, IL.
Aldrich, John. 1980. *Before the Convention: Strategies and Choices in Presidential Nominations*. Chicago, IL: University of Chicago Press.
Asher, Herbert B. 1984. *Presidential Elections and American Politics*, 3rd ed. Homewood, IL: Dorsey Press.
Atkeson, Lonna Rae, and Cherie D. Maestas. 2009. "Meaningful Participation and Evolution of the Reformed Presidential Nominating System." *PS: Political Science & Politics* 42(1): 59–64.
Bardhan, Pranab, and Tsung-Tao Yang. 2004. "Political Competition in Economic Perspective." Department of Economics Working Paper E04-341. University of California, Berkeley: Institute of Business and Economic Research.
Barrilleaux, Charles, Thomas Holbrook, and Laura Langer. 2002. "Electoral Competition, Legislative Balance, and American State Welfare Policy." *American Journal of Political Science* 46(2): 415–427.
Bartels, Larry M. 1988. *Presidential Primaries and the Dynamics of Public Choice*. Princeton, NJ: Princeton University Press.
Bawn, Kathleen, Martin Cohen, David Karol, Seth Masket, Hans Noel, and John Zaller. 2012. "A Theory of Parties: Groups, Policy Demanders and Nominations in American Politics." *Perspectives on Politics* 10(3): 571–597.
Brams, Steven J. 1978. *The Presidential Election Game*. New Haven, CT: Yale University Press.
Brown, Lara. 2011. *Jockeying for the American Presidency: The Political Opportunism of Aspirants*. Amherst, NY: Cambria Press.

Burden, Barry C. 2002. "United States Senators as Presidential Candidates." *Political Science Quarterly* 117(1): 81–102.

Butler, Richard L. 2004. *Claiming the Mantle: How Presidential Nominations are Won and Lost Before the Votes are Cast.* Boulder, CO: Westview Press.

Calkins, Stephen. 1983. "The New Merger Guidelines and the Herfindahl-Hirschman Index." *California Law Review* 71: 402–429.

Ceaser, James W. 1979. *Presidential Selection.* Princeton, NJ: Princeton University Press.

Cohen, Marty, David Karol, Hans Noel, and John Zaller. 2008. *The Party Decides: Presidential Nominations Before and After Reform.* Chicago: University of Chicago Press.

Cox, Gary W., and Matthew D. McCubbins. 1993. *Legislative Leviathan: Party Government in the House.* New York: Cambridge University Press.

Crotty, William. 1977. *Political Reform and the American Experiment.* New York: Crowell.

David, Paul T., Ralph M. Goldman, and Richard C. Bain. 1960. *The Politics of National Party Conventions.* Washington, DC: Brookings Institution.

Fiorina, Morris P. 1977. *Congress: Keystone of the Washington Establishment.* New Haven, CT: Yale University Press.

Haynes, Audrey A., Paul-Henri Gurian, Michael H. Crespin, and Christopher Zorn. 2004. "The Calculus of Concession: Media Coverage and the Dynamics of Winnowing in Presidential Nominations." *American Politics Review* 32: 310–337.

Held, David. 1987. *Models of Democracy.* Stanford, CA: Stanford University Press.

Hickman, John. 1992. "The Effect of Open Seats on Challenger Strength in Japanese Lower House Elections." *Legislative Studies Quarterly* 17(3): 573–584.

Issacharoff, Samuel, and Richard H. Pildes. 1998. "Politics as Markets: Partisan Lockups of the Democratic Process." *Stanford Law Review* 50: 643–717.

Krehbiel, Keith. 1998. *Pivotal Politics: A Theory of US Lawmaking.* Chicago, IL: University of Chicago Press.

Mayer, William G., and Andrew E. Busch. 2004. *The Frontloading Problem in Presidential Nominations.* Washington DC: Brookings Institution.

Mayhew, David R. 1974. *Congress: The Electoral Connection.* New Haven, CT: Yale University Press.

McDonald, Michael P., and John Samples, eds. 2006. *The Marketplace of Democracy: Electoral Competition and American Democracy.* Washington DC: Cato Institute & Brookings Institution.

Norrander, Barbara. 2000. "The End Game in Post-Reform Presidential Nominations." *Journal of Politics* 62(4): 999–1013.

Norrander, Barbara. 2006. "The Attrition Game: Initial Resources, Initial Contests and the Exit of Candidates During the US Presidential Primary Season." *British Journal of Political Science* 36(3): 487–507.

Olson, Henry, and Dante Scala. 2015. *The Four Faces of the Republican Party and the Fight for the 2016 Presidential Nomination.* New York: Palgrave Macmillan.

Owen, P. Dorian, Michael Ryan, and Clayton R. Weatherston. 2008. "Measuring Competitive Balance in Professional Team Sports Using the Hirschman-Herfindahl Index." *Review of Industrial Organization* 31(2): 289–302.

Patterson, Samuel C., and Gregory A. Caldeira. 1984. "The Etiology of Party Competition." *American Political Science Review* 78(3): 691–707.

Patterson, Thomas E. 1980. *The Mass Media Election.* New York: Praeger.

Paulson, Arthur. 2007. *Electoral Realignment and the Outlook for American Democracy.* Boston, MA: Northeastern University Press.

Peabody, Robert L., Norman J. Ornstein, and David W. Rohde. 1976. "The United States Senate as a Presidential Incubator: Many are Called but Few are Chosen." *Political Science Quarterly* 91(2): 237–258.

Pitkin, Hannah. 1972. *Representation and Democracy.* Berkeley: University of California Press.

Polsby, Nelson W. 1983. *Consequences of Party Reform,* New York: Oxford University Press.

Ranney, Austin. 1975. *Curing the Mischiefs of Faction: Party Reform in America.* Berkeley: University of California Press.

Reiter, Howard L. 1985. *Selecting the President: The Nominating Process in Transition.* Philadelphia: University of Pennsylvania Press.

Rhoads, Stephen A. 1993. "The Herfindahl-Hirschman Index." *Federal Reserve Bulletin* 79: 188–189.

Schattschneider, E. E. 1960. *The Semi-Sovereign People.* New York: Harcourt Brace.

Schumpeter, Joseph. 1942. *Capitalism, Socialism, and Democracy.* London: Allen and Unwin.

Shafer, Byron E. 1983. *Quiet Revolution: Reform Politics in the Democratic Party, 1968–1972.* New York: Russell Sage.

Skocpol, Theda, and Vanessa Williamson. 2013. *The Tea Party and the Remaking of Republican Conservatism.* New York: Oxford University Press.

Steger, Wayne P. 2000. "Do Primary Voters Draw from a Stacked Deck? Presidential Nominations in an Era of Candidate-Centered Campaigns." *Presidential Studies Quarterly* 30(3): 727–753.

Steger, Wayne P. 2006. "Stepping Stone to the White House or Tombstone on Presidential Ambition? Why Senators Usually Fail When They Run for the White House." *American Review of Politics* 27(1): 45–70.

Steger, Wayne P. 2013. "Two Paradigms of Presidential Nominations." *Presidential Studies Quarterly* 43(2): 377–387.

Steger, Wayne P. 2015. *A Citizen's Guide to Presidential Nominations: The Competition for Leadership.* New York: Routledge.

Steger, Wayne P. 2016. "Conditional Arbiters: The Limits of Political Party Influence in Presidential Nominations." *PS: Political Science & Politics* 49(4): 709–715.

Steger, Wayne P. 2017. "The Republican Primaries." In *Campaigning for President 2016*, ed. Dennis Johnson and Lara Brown. New York: Routledge.

Steger, Wayne P., John Hickman, and Ken Yohn. 2002. "Candidate Competition and Attrition in Presidential Primaries, 1912–2000." *American Politics Research* 30(3): 528–554.

Taagepera, Rein, and Markku S. Laakso. 1989. *Seats and Votes: The Effects and Determinants of Electoral Systems.* New Haven, CT: Yale University Press.

Wolfinger, Raymond E., and Steven J. Rosenstone. 1980. *Who Votes?* New Haven, CT: Yale University Press.

17

THE FUZZY FRONTRUNNER

Donald Trump and the Role of Ideology in Presidential Nomination Politics

Dante J. Scala

Throughout the "exhibition season" of the 2016 Republican presidential nomination contest, pundits opined that Donald J. Trump's lack of ideological consistency ultimately would doom his campaign, once the novelty of the mogul's campaign dissipated. As with so many predictions regarding Trump, this was entirely mistaken. After losing the Iowa caucuses, Trump rebounded with wins in New Hampshire and South Carolina, and carried the great majority of primaries on his way to the nomination. Trump's triumph raises an alarming number of questions about our understanding of the nomination process, including: Does ideology matter? Do primary and caucus participants have the interest and capability to use ideology as a means to choose a candidate from a crowded field?

To determine the importance of candidate ideology to Republican primary and caucus voters in 2016, I examine two sources of survey data. Using the Cooperative Congressional Election Study (CCES),[1] I consider whether voters of different ideologies actually take differing positions on policy issues. In addition, I study whether primary and caucus participants were able to place Republican presidential candidates consistently on an ideological spectrum ranging from liberal and moderate to very conservative. Exit polls from various caucus and primary states allowed me to track whether voters of varying ideologies identified particular candidates as their ideological "champions" and attached their support accordingly. Finally, using CCES data, I consider the strength of voter ideology as a predictor of vote choice, as compared to a host of other factors, including socioeconomic status and partisanship.

All told, survey data undercut the notion that the 2016 Republican nomination contest signaled the end of ideology as a significant factor to primary and caucus participants. Ideological differences among candidates in a crowded field were not unintelligible to Republican voters – but they were, to borrow a term, somewhat "fuzzy" around the edges. One of Trump's preternatural political gifts was his ability to present himself as appealing (or at least acceptable) to Republican voters of various ideological stripes. As a result, the mogul was able to win the lion's share of support from an historically crucial bloc of Republican primary voters – self-described "somewhat conservatives" (Olsen and Scala 2016). Trump's success among these mainstream conservatives was enhanced after several other center-right candidates were knocked out in the early rounds. In contrast, Trump's chief competitors in the latter stages of the nomination contest, Texas Senator Ted Cruz and Ohio Governor John Kasich, staked out early claims to groups on the ideological extremes of the party. Then, to their dismay, they found themselves marooned there, unable to build bridges to other factions of the party and form majority coalitions. Trump's triumph tells us that primary and caucus participants do not use ideology as a diamond-cutter, making fine distinctions between one candidate and another. But voters do use it as a rough-and-ready cue for making nomination decisions. As a result, ideological considerations once again were a key part of nomination dynamics.

The Fuzzy Frontrunner

As Trump was settling in as the GOP frontrunner in summer 2015, journalist and commentator Josh Barro contended that beneath the bombast, "a surprising fact emerges: Mr. Trump is a moderate Republican." Barro noted that Trump had not taken a no-tax pledge; he was not unequivocally against a single-payer system for health care; his concept of tax reform resembled the stance of former Florida Governor Jeb Bush; he favored allowing abortions under certain circumstances; he advocated higher tariffs, not more free trade; and he supported the status quo on entitlements such as Social Security. Only on immigration did the mogul clearly adopt a very conservative position (Barro 2015).

A more systematic attempt to place Trump on the ideological spectrum concurred with Barro's conclusion. Crowdpac, which uses campaign finance data, voting records, and issue statements in order to score candidates, pegged Trump at 4.9 on a 10-point conservative scale. This score placed Trump left of center among the Republican candidates for the nomination. He was more conservative than New Jersey Governor Chris Christie, Ohio Governor John Kasich, and former Pennsylvania Senator Rick Santorum, but to the left of Bush and Florida Senator Marco Rubio, and far left of Ben Carson, Texas Senator Ted Cruz and Kentucky Senator Rand Paul. Political scientist Seth Masket (2016) contended that Crowdpac's score was "plausible," but "highly unreliable." After all, Trump had no voting record to use as a basis for calculations. In addition, just weeks before Iowa and New Hampshire were to vote, Trump's campaign had issued very few specific public policy proposals, "with the exception of his ideologically extreme positions on immigration and refugees." The candidate had an inventory of comments on various issues, but these also were problematic:

> His past statements suggest he is supportive of current funding levels for Social Security and Medicare and supportive of same-sex marriage, and that his pro-choice positions have recently evolved to "pro-life with exceptions." But he's been so vague on these issues – all he's really focused on is building a border wall and bombing ISIS – that it's difficult to know where he actually stands. *The Trump ideal point in the chart above should really look like a very diffuse probability cloud.*
>
> Masket 2016, italics mine

In other words, intentionally or not (but certainly loudly), Trump was fuzzy. And as one of the first authoritative studies of the modern nomination process argued, fuzziness is potentially a high-reward strategy in a crowded nomination contest.

Going Fuzzy

Steven Brams, one of the first political scientists to study the modern nomination process, argued that primary and caucus participants seriously considered candidates' positions on public policy issues in making their voting decisions (1978). But he noted that candidates could pursue tactics that would enable them to appeal to voters of different ideological stripes simultaneously, and thus build coalitions of voters that spanned traditional dividing lines.

Brams began his analysis with the traditional assumptions of spatial theory. Candidates' positions on a given issue, as well as those of primary and caucus voters, can be placed on a continuum. Voters will look for a candidate whose position on important issues most closely matches their preferred position. Candidates respond to voters by adopting issue positions that are closest to most voters on the policy spectrum. Candidates may be forthright in their response, or they may choose to be "fuzzy" or ambiguous.

Both types of responses have risks and rewards. A candidate's clear and stark position statement will attract like-minded voters who praise him for his principles, but may repel others who find the candidate's position too distant from their own. Candidates might instead pursue a "fuzzy" strategy: by making ambiguous statements, their positions on issues may plausibly cover a range of possible ideologies and thus appeal to a wide spectrum of voters. Going "fuzzy" may backfire. A candidate might be branded as a flip-flopper. Or more subtly, voters might perceive a candidate's position to be further away from their own than the candidate intends. A candidate may be willing to take these risks, especially if he is a centrist attempting both to retain more moderate voters while reaching out to more ideological ones. This is a crucial task, given the sequential nature of the presidential nomination process, and the rapidly fluctuating political environment that candidates may face.

Candidates for the presidential nomination must accumulate delegates in a series of primaries and caucuses over a period of months. They win the prize not so much by gathering much-vaunted "momentum," as by avoiding attrition (Norrander 2006). In the early stages, for example, candidates must first contend with challengers who compete for votes from the same segment of the party electorate, whether it be moderates or religious conservatives (Brams 1978; for a case study of how primary voters made strategic choices in the 1988 primaries, see Cain et al. 1989).

This war of attrition was especially challenging in 2016, when seventeen Republicans vied for the nomination. Multicandidate primaries tend toward instability. When only two candidates contest a primary, both will seek the median position on issues in order to win a majority. When more than two candidates enter the fray, however, the median no longer is optimal. Rivals may win a plurality by lining up to the right or left of the center, leaving a centrist candidate with a relatively narrow base of voters. In a multicandidate primary, each candidate has to take into account the strategies of others: "Winning depends on the choices that all players make" (Brams 1978). The complexity of the task only intensifies if campaigns are fought over multiple issues of significance to voters (see Aldrich 1980 and Norrander 1986; for later work on spatial voting models in nomination contests, see Kenny and Lotfinia 2005).

Given the vulnerability of the center position in a multicandidate primary, centrist candidates would be wiser to line up to the right of center and forgo the moderate voter in the early rounds of the nomination process. A right-of-center candidate will be able to pick up more moderate voters in the latter stages, once other centrists drop out because they lack sufficient support. The survivors of the early rounds of a nomination contest will have more space on the ideological spectrum, and thus be in a position to start to build coalitions that cross ideological lines. Voters in later contests will have easier decisions to make with far fewer candidates, but they also may have to choose between "second-best" candidates after their most-preferred choice is eliminated.

Does Ideology Matter?

After Brams, other political scientists challenged the notion that most participants in the presidential nomination process are able to make meaningful ideological distinctions among candidates from the same party, especially in a crowded field. Ordinary voters often appear ideologically inconsistent, if not altogether ignorant, compared to political activists who are capable of employing concepts such as "liberal" or "conservative" correctly in their internal belief structures, and externally in debates with others (Herrera 1992). In the twentieth century, activists led the conservative Right against pragmatic party members more interested in winning and retaining political office (Clarke et al. 1991; Costain 1980; also see McCann 1995). Although activists think more readily in ideological terms, they do not always place ideology first in their list of priorities when choosing a candidate. Delegates to the 1980 Republican convention tended to hold electability in higher importance than ideology, though many George H. W. Bush delegates remained loyal to their fellow moderates despite seeing Ronald Reagan as the candidate more likely to win the general election (Stone and Abramowitz 1983).

Compared to party activists, primary and caucus voters' grasp of ideological concepts appears weak. A study of national survey data demonstrated that although Republican primary voters were more likely to use ideological terms in political discussions than their general-election counterparts, they were not more consistent in their beliefs. Nor did primary voters use ideological identification as a means to choose the candidate most suitable for them (Norrander 1989). Even the most politically engaged members of the general public offer ideological answers that are flawed, with "misunderstandings, top of the head responses, order effects, poor retention, and various satisficing strategies" (Jennings 1992). All told, primary voters' ability to identify "the candidate who represents their own values and concerns" appears lacking (Lau 2013). Even setting aside these cognitive difficulties, voters simply might not be very concerned about a candidate's ideology, compared to other factors in their decisions (Mayer 2008; Sides and Vavreck 2013).

Other scholars have affirmed the importance of ideology to primary and caucus voter decisions. Another study of the 1980 Republican primary, for example, found that when voters viewed Reagan as more conservative than his competitors, they were more likely to draw connections between their ideology and their vote choice (Wattier 1983). Ideology also might aid voters in drawing conclusions about candidates' qualities (Kenney and Rice 1992). Ideology also might serve as a "short cut" for voters who do not know the specifics about where candidates stand on issues. Less knowledgeable voters might still be able to compare ideologies of candidates – moderates versus conservatives, for example – and choose one who seems to be the best match. Admittedly, voters can use ideological cues only if candidates are interested in drawing stark contrasts between themselves and their competitors. Voters' ideology also may be quite malleable. They may view a candidate as ideologically compatible because they simply prefer that candidate. A popular candidate might persuade voters to adopt his ideology as their own (Downs 1957; Kenney 1993; Popkin 1994; Wattier 1983).

If primary and caucus voters cannot distinguish ideological differences, it may be that those contrasts are in fact too weak to discern. Interparty polarization has created intraparty "homogenization" within fields of presidential primary candidates, argues Paulson (2009). The 2008 Republican nominee, Arizona Senator John McCain, was often depicted as the alternative for moderate and liberal GOP primary voters, but he was in fact squarely in the conservative mainstream on many issues. His so-called "moderation" paled in comparison to that of Nelson Rockefeller a generation earlier, during an age in which there were clear differences between "Rockefeller Republicans" and Barry Goldwater conservatives. The major political parties – and their contenders for nominations – no longer possess the internal diversity that once prompted floor fights at national conventions.

Despite the increasing ideological homogeneity of their political parties, candidates for the nomination appear to make some campaign decisions for ideological reasons. For example, conservative candidates in Republican primaries more aggressively attack moderate and liberal primary opponents with negative advertising than fellow conservatives (Ridout and Holland 2010; for contrasting conclusion, see Haynes and Rhine 1998). In addition, forecasting models indicate that more ideological candidates achieve greater vote shares over the course of the nomination season, even after taking into account factors such as pre-Iowa national polls and elite endorsements (Steger 2008).

The Four Faces of the Republican Party

A comprehensive examination of exit-poll data from 2000 to 2012 identified four factions in the Republican Party electorate, based on ideology and religious affiliation: liberals and moderates, somewhat conservative voters, very conservative evangelicals, and very conservative seculars (Olsen 2014; Olsen and Scala 2016).

In a conservative party, liberals and moderates retain influence in the Republican nomination electorate. Prior to 2016, their favored candidate won two of the last three nominations. These voters are distinctive for their ambivalence toward the GOP. Many prefer to identify themselves as independents rather than Republicans. They are more secular than other Republicans, and are more likely to be pro-choice on abortion. These voters tend to unite early in the nomination season. They championed McCain in 2000 and again in 2008, and backed Mitt Romney in 2012.

As Table 17.1 shows, the percentages of moderates participating in 2016 Republican primaries and caucuses ranged from 15 percent to 38 percent, according to exit polls taken in 26 states.[2] They were most prominent in the Northeast, including the first-in-the-nation primary state of New Hampshire. Their presence was least significant in the southern states, as well as the first-in-the-nation Iowa caucus and the Nevada caucus.

"Somewhat conservative" voters are the most numerous portion of the Republican nomination electorate, typically representing 35 to 40 percent.[3] To become the nominee, a candidate must win their support. Prior to 2016, somewhat conservative voters backed Bob Dole in 1996, George W. Bush in 2000, McCain in 2008, and Romney in 2012. These voters' preferences can be inferred from the characteristics of their favored candidates. They are conservative in both ideology and temperament, rejecting candidates who advocate for transformative change. They are neither populist nor libertarian.

> They are perfectly satisfied to pay taxes for things they value and that seem to work for them, such as old age entitlements, decent public schools and universities, good roads, and public safety. They do, however, want to be "left alone" inasmuch as they do not think bureaucrats or other elites have their best interests at heart when they try to tax, regulate, or dominate them in the name of "public interest."
>
> *Olsen and Scala 2016: 61*

As in previous election cycles, somewhat conservative voters were a significant portion of every caucus and primary electorate, regardless of region. In almost every primary and caucus in 2016, somewhat conservative voters were a plurality, according to exit polls. (The only exceptions to this were in a few Deep South states, and the border state of Missouri.)

The "very conservative" faction of the Republican Party may be divided into two parts, evangelicals and seculars. Evangelical voters are most prominent in the southern and border states, where they may represent one of four primary and caucus-goers, if not more. They also have a very strong presence in caucus states, including Iowa, the first event on the nomination calendar.

Table 17.1 Ideological Composition of Republican Electorates, by State (Percentages)

State	Date	Region	Moderate or Liberal	Somewhat Conservative	Very Conservative
Iowa*	Feb. 1	Midwest	15	45	40
New Hampshire	Feb. 9	Northeast	29	45	26
South Carolina	Feb. 20	South	18	43	38
Nevada*	Feb. 23	West	16	45	40
Alabama	March 1	South	22	40	38
Arkansas	March 1	South	18	41	41
Georgia	March 1	South	21	42	38
Massachusetts	March 1	Northeast	38	44	18
Oklahoma	March 1	South	19	38	43
Tennessee	March 1	South	18	40	41
Texas	March 1	South	19	43	39
Vermont	March 1	Northeast	33	43	24
Virginia	March 1	South	28	40	32
Michigan	March 8	Midwest	25	47	28
Mississippi	March 8	South	16	37	47
Florida	March 15	South	30	39	31
Illinois	March 15	Midwest	28	46	26
Missouri	March 15	Midwest	21	39	40
North Carolina	March 15	South	19	42	37
Ohio	March 15	Midwest	28	42	31
Wisconsin	April 5	Midwest	27	43	31
New York	April 19	Northeast	29	47	24
Connecticut	April 26	Northeast	30	46	24
Maryland	April 26	South	25	47	28
Pennsylvania	April 26	Northeast	27	43	30
Indiana	May 3	Midwest	23	44	33

Source: Various exit polls

Note: * = Caucus.

These voters backed George W. Bush in 2000, Arkansas Governor Mike Huckabee in 2008, and former Pennsylvania Senator Rick Santorum in 2012. In 2016, two-thirds of very conservative participants in primaries and caucuses described themselves as "born again," according to CCES data.

Very conservative seculars are prominent inside the Beltway where many national political and media elites reside, but nationwide only represent a small proportion of the Republican nomination electorate. In 2016, 23 percent of very conservative participants in the GOP nomination process said that religion was no more than "somewhat important," if that. Not coincidentally, this bloc of voters typically settles for second-best choices for the nominee. None of their champions (Jack Kemp and Pete DuPont in 1988; Steve Forbes or Phil Gramm in 1996 and 2000; Fred Thompson or Mitt Romney in 2008; Herman Cain, Rick Perry, or Newt Gingrich in 2012) prospered in the later stages of the nomination process. Other factions tend to be repelled by these candidates, either because their economic policies are too radical, or because their interest in moral issues is too shallow. Altogether, voters who identified as "very conservative" typically made up one-third of Republican primary and caucus electorates, according to exit polls. Their numbers were smallest in the Northeast, and largest in the South. In both caucuses surveyed in Iowa and Nevada, very conservative voters were plentiful.

Voter Ideology and Issue Positions

One test of whether voter ideology matters, especially in party primaries and caucuses, is if it serves as a reliable predictor of a voter's positions on various issues. The CCES asked primary and caucus voters a variety of questions across various issue categories, including the use of military force, gun control, immigration, abortion, the environment, crime, gay marriage, and budget priorities.

Generally speaking, ideological groupings of voters took positions on issues that were consistent with their self-described position on the ideological continuum (Table 17.2). Liberal and moderate voters set themselves apart from more conservative voters most distinctively. They were more likely to be pro-choice on abortion; to be more lenient with illegal immigrants; to favor gun control and environmental regulation; to support the elimination of mandatory minimum sentencing for non-violent drug offenders; and to be more reluctant to employ U.S. military force except in cases of helping the United Nations uphold international law. Conservative voters occupied a middle ground in the Republican nomination electorate, though they tended to stand closer to very conservative

Table 17.2 Issue Positions of Republican Primary and Caucus Voters, by Ideology (Percentages)

Issue	Liberals and moderates	Conservatives	Very conservative voters
Abortion			
Pro–choice	54	26	12
Only abortion in case of rape, incest, health of woman at stake	50	66	54
Prohibit all abortions after 20 weeks of pregnancy	69	85	86
Immigration			
Grant legal status to illegal immigrants	43	30	19
Identify and deport illegal immigrants	56	70	81
Gun control			
Background checks	87	78	67
Ban assault rifles	55	35	25
Environment			
Raise fuel efficiency	60	42	36
Require minimum amount of renewable fuels	53	31	22
Gay marriage			
Favor	63	31	12
Crime			
Increase police on the street	63	72	72
Eliminate mandatory minimums for non–violent drug offenses	63	49	41
Approve use of U.S. military force			
To help the U.N. uphold international law	43	29	22
To ensure the supply of oil	25	29	31
To destroy a terrorist camp	75	86	84
To intervene in case of genocide or civil war	38	39	40
To protect American allies	75	84	82

Source: Cooperative Congressional Election Study.

voters than liberal and moderate ones. The differences between conservative and very conservative voters were minimal on questions concerning crime prevention and the use of military force.

The Nomination Season Unfolds

The first events of the nomination season, the Iowa caucuses and the New Hampshire primary, demonstrated that Trump had established himself as an attractive candidate – not just to the working-class voters so often described as Trump's base, but to the "somewhat conservative" voters at the very center of the GOP. These early events also hinted that his remaining competitors for the nomination were too weak or too factional to build the coalitions necessary to win a majority of convention delegates.

Texas Senator Ted Cruz, who assiduously courted Iowa's evangelicals for months, was rewarded with a victory on caucus night. Cruz carried 34 percent of evangelicals (who comprised 64 percent of caucus-goers) and 44 percent of very conservative voters (40 percent of caucus-goers), according to exit polls. By winning Iowa, Cruz relegated his main competitors for the conservative evangelical vote – physician Ben Carson, former Arkansas Governor Mike Huckabee, and former Pennsylvania Senator Rick Santorum – to also-ran status. But among Iowa's somewhat conservative voters, as Tables 17.3, 17.4 and 17.5 show, Cruz finished third, behind Florida Senator Marco Rubio and Donald Trump.

Table 17.3 Candidate Performance in Primaries and Caucuses, among Moderate Voters (Percentages)

State	Date	Trump	Kasich	Cruz	Rubio
Iowa*	2/1/2016	34	7	9	28
New Hampshire	2/9/2016	32	27	4	8
South Carolina	2/20/2016	34	21	7	23
Nevada*	2/23/2016	55	6	7	27
Alabama	3/1/2016	40	9	13	27
Arkansas	3/1/2016	36	11	16	29
Georgia	3/1/2016	44	11	9	30
Massachusetts	3/1/2016	48	29	3	15
Oklahoma	3/1/2016	35	11	17	30
Tennessee	3/1/2016	45	11	12	20
Texas	3/1/2016	34	9	26	24
Vermont	3/1/2016	34	40	5	15
Virginia	3/1/2016	23	20	7	40
Michigan	3/8/2016	37	36	12	8
Mississippi	3/8/2016	52	17	22	7
Florida	3/15/2016	42	13	12	25
Illinois	3/15/2016	41	32	15	10
Missouri	3/15/2016	43	21	23	9
North Carolina	3/15/2016	40	28	20	9
Ohio	3/15/2016	31	59	4	4
Wisconsin	4/5/2016	40	28	29	*
New York	4/19/2016	46	42	13	*
Connecticut	4/26/2016	46	48	4	*
Maryland	4/26/2016	50	35	10	*
Pennsylvania	4/26/2016	57	28	12	*
Indiana	5/3/2016	61	14	22	*

Source: Exit polls

Note: *Rubio dropped out of the nomination contest March 15. Cruz left the race May 3. Kasich withdrew May 4.

** = Caucus.

Table 17.4 Candidate Performance in Primaries and Caucuses, among Somewhat Conservative Voters

State	Date	Trump	Kasich	Cruz	Rubio
Iowa**	2/1/2016	24	2	19	29
New Hampshire	2/9/2016	38	14	9	11
South Carolina	2/20/2016	35	6	17	25
Nevada**	2/23/2016	50	4	16	26
Alabama	3/1/2016	46	5	17	20
Arkansas	3/1/2016	36	3	24	29
Georgia	3/1/2016	42	6	17	29
Massachusetts	3/1/2016	51	13	8	22
Oklahoma	3/1/2016	25	3	31	33
Tennessee	3/1/2016	43	6	16	26
Texas	3/1/2016	30	4	37	23
Vermont	3/1/2016	35	27	8	23
Virginia	3/1/2016	39	7	11	34
Michigan	3/8/2016	37	24	23	11
Mississippi	3/8/2016	53	10	27	7
Florida	3/15/2016	48	6	15	31
Illinois	3/15/2016	40	17	29	11
Missouri	3/15/2016	43	11	38	6
North Carolina	3/15/2016	46	12	32	8
Ohio	3/15/2016	38	48	10	2
Wisconsin	4/5/2016	36	15	47	*
New York	4/19/2016	67	23	10	*
Connecticut	4/26/2016	67	23	9	*
Maryland	4/26/2016	56	25	15	*
Pennsylvania	4/26/2016	62	21	15	*
Indiana	5/3/2016	55	8	34	*

Source: Exit polls

Note: *Rubio dropped out of the nomination contest March 15. Cruz left the race May 3. Kasich withdrew May 4.
** = Caucus.

Table 17.5 Candidate Performance in Primaries and Caucuses, among Very Conservative Voters (Percentages)

State	Date	Trump	Kasich	Cruz	Rubio
Iowa**	2/1/2016	21	0	44	15
New Hampshire	2/9/2016	36	6	23	13
South Carolina	2/20/2016	29	3	35	19
Nevada**	2/23/2016	38	1	34	22
Alabama	3/1/2016	41	2	29	15
Arkansas	3/1/2016	26	1	43	20
Georgia	3/1/2016	35	3	37	17
Massachusetts	3/1/2016	47	4	26	16
Oklahoma	3/1/2016	29	1	43	19
Tennessee	3/1/2016	34	3	39	17
Texas	3/1/2016	23	3	57	11
Vermont	3/1/2016	27	22	19	21
Virginia	3/1/2016	36	3	31	23

Michigan	3/8/2016	35	14	38	11
Mississippi	3/8/2016	41	4	51	3
Florida	3/15/2016	48	2	26	23
Illinois	3/15/2016	36	9	49	5
Missouri	3/15/2016	36	3	55	4
North Carolina	3/15/2016	33	6	54	5
Ohio	3/15/2016	36	33	26	2
Wisconsin	4/5/2016	28	5	65	*
New York	4/19/2016	62	11	27	*
Connecticut	4/26/2016	55	15	28	*
Maryland	4/26/2016	54	11	34	*
Pennsylvania	4/26/2016	48	10	41	*
Indiana	5/3/2016	45	3	50	*

Source: Exit polls.

Note: *Rubio dropped out of the nomination contest March 15. Cruz left the race May 3. Kasich withdrew May 4.

** = Caucus.

Rubio's third-place finish in Iowa, fueled by a late surge, appeared to be proof that he was finally making good on his much-vaunted potential as a national candidate. Part of that potential was the Florida senator's supposed capability to reach out to various factions of the party and build a coalition. But in New Hampshire, it was Trump who proved to be the unifying candidate, cruising to a 20-point victory. (After a spurt of momentum post-Iowa, Rubio faded badly in the run-up to New Hampshire after a poor debate performance the weekend before the primary. He finished fifth.) Trump's margin was even larger among the Granite State's somewhat conservative voters. The mogul's victory in the Granite State did not only bolster his campaign heading into South Carolina; it also effectively finished the campaigns of several potential center-right challengers for the "somewhat conservative" voter, such as former Florida Governor Jeb Bush, New Jersey Governor Chris Christie, and businesswoman Carly Fiorina.

One center-right candidate that gained from New Hampshire was Ohio Governor John Kasich. His second-place finish, however modest (he only won 16 percent of the vote), was a positive surprise for a candidate who had struggled for months in the shadow of better-financed competitors. Kasich relied heavily on independents and moderate Republican voters in New Hampshire, much like former Utah Governor Jon Huntsman had in his 2012 presidential bid. Kasich also finished in second place among New Hampshire's "somewhat conservatives," though far behind Trump.

The next state on the calendar eleven days later, South Carolina, cemented the pattern for the remainder of the nomination season. Trump and Rubio demonstrated ability to reach across ideological lines and build coalitions, though Trump's voter base typically dwarfed the Florida senator's. Cruz and Kasich displayed support predominantly from one ideological faction, but were unable to cross ideological lines and appeal to other types of Republican voters.

Through the months of March, Trump won primaries in New England (Massachusetts and Vermont), the Midwest (Illinois, Michigan, and Missouri), and across the heartland of the party in the South (Alabama, Arkansas, Georgia, Mississippi, North Carolina, Tennessee, and Virginia). Cruz carried primaries in his home state of Texas, as well as neighboring Oklahoma, as well as a few caucuses. Rubio failed to capitalize on an opportunity to defeat Trump in Virginia, then was trounced in his home state and left the race. Kasich did win his home state's primary, but was unable to extend his success elsewhere.

Table 17.6 Candidate Performance by Voter Ideology (Percentages)

	Liberals and moderates	*Conservatives*	*Very conservative voters*
Kasich	19	8	3
Trump	49	53	44
Cruz	10	23	41
Rubio	10	10	5

Source: Cooperative Congressional Election Study.

In the late stages of the nomination season, Cruz made one successful stand in the Wisconsin primary, where he (not coincidentally) won a plurality of somewhat conservative voters. Trump then shrugged off this defeat, capturing the remainder of the primaries on the calendar.

Exit-poll data from various primaries and caucuses were confirmed by nationwide CCES data on respondents who reported participating in nomination events (Table 17.6). Of the four final survivors of the 2016 nomination contest, only Trump pulled roughly equally well from all ideological segments of the electorate, from liberals and moderates to very conservative voters. Rubio was the only one of Trump's top competitors able to put together a coalition of voters that achieved some degree of ideological balance, albeit a much smaller one than the eventual nominee's.

The last two competitors standing at the end of the nomination season, Cruz and Kasich, possessed voter bases that were factions, not coalitions. Cruz's performance among very conservative voters nearly matched Trump's, but fell off by nearly one-half among conservative voters – a group one might have expected to be ideal coalition partners for the Texas senator. Cruz repelled voters who were the farthest away ideologically from his position: fewer than one of ten self-described moderates and liberals supported him. Kasich's voter base was the mirror image of Cruz's support. His voters came predominantly from the moderate-liberal wing of the party. His support among the adjoining ideological bloc of conservative voters dropped steeply to less than 10 percent. His very conservative supporters were a minuscule group.

Trump's Ideological Rating

During the nomination campaign, commentators often took note of Trump's heterodox (if not outright contradictory) positions on numerous issues of importance to the Republican electorate. Based on the remarks of the commentariat, one might surmise that Republican voters would come to various and contradictory conclusions as to where Trump stood on the ideological spectrum. But this was not the case, according to CCES data.[4] On the whole, Republican primary and caucus voters of various ideological stripes were quite consistent in their placement of Trump on an ideological spectrum.

Pluralities of each type of voter – self-identified liberals and moderates; conservatives; and very conservative voters – identified the eventual nominee as "somewhat conservative," i.e. in the mainstream of the GOP electorate. Far fewer voters placed him on the extremes of the party, either as a liberal or as someone who was very conservative (Table 17.7).

Supporters of Trump's last two remaining opponents, Cruz and Kasich, differed significantly in their ideological composition. Cruz was most popular among very conservative voters, while Kasich attracted moderates. However, both Cruz adherents and Kasich supporters possessed a common assessment of Trump's ideology. Large numbers of both groups placed Trump on the left side of the ideological spectrum, rating him as either a liberal or a "middle of the road" politician.

Table 17.7 Trump's Ideological Rating by Different Groups of Voters (Percentages)

Trump's rating	Liberal	Middle of the road	Somewhat conservative	Conservative	Very conservative
All caucus and primary voters	12	22	30	21	8
Trump voters	6	20	31	29	10
Cruz voters	20	26	32	14	4
Kasich voters	13	23	23	14	9
Liberals and moderates	15	23	24	14	9
Conservatives	9	23	33	24	6
Very conservative voters	13	17	31	25	12

Source: Cooperative Congressional Election Study.

Cruz adherents, who most often identified themselves as very conservative or conservative, were the most likely to brand Trump as a liberal. Almost half of Cruz supporters did not consider Trump even to be "somewhat" conservative, instead placing him to the left of that category. Far fewer Cruz partisans were willing to place Trump on the right end of the ideological spectrum. Given Cruz's efforts to depict himself as the one true conservative in the race, his supporters' rating of Trump might be regarded as a manifestation of personal loyalty to the Texas senator. But Kasich voters, who often identified themselves as moderates, largely agreed with the assessment of Cruz supporters: they also were much more likely to identify Trump with the left wing of the Republican Party.

Trump voters themselves placed their favored candidate squarely in the ideological mainstream of their party, albeit right of center. More than half described him as either somewhat conservative or conservative. A significant minority pegged Trump as a "middle of the road" candidate, to the left of "somewhat conservative." Few voters placed him on the extremes of the party, either on the far left or the far right.

Six out of every ten primary and caucus voters identified themselves as Republicans. These participants rated Trump in a fashion similar to how Trump voters themselves saw him – that is, as a candidate in the mainstream of their party. A plurality pegged him in the "somewhat conservative" category, and more than three-quarters placed him in the three middle categories, from "middle of the road" to "conservative." Only one of five Republicans placed Trump on the extremes – about half of these described him as a liberal, the other half as very conservative.

Three of ten primary and caucus voters identified themselves as independent of party affiliation. These voters, who identified themselves more often as liberal or moderate than Republican voters, were also more likely to place Trump on the left side of the ideological spectrum. Only one in five independents described Trump as either conservative or very conservative.

Issue Positions of Trump, Cruz, and Kasich Voters

An examination of the issue positions of Trump, Cruz, and Kasich voters indicates that Trump voters often occupied an intermediate position on the spectrum (Table 17.8), between the more liberal supporters of the Ohio governor and the more conservative backers of the Texas senator. This was the case in both social issues (abortion and gay marriage) and government regulation (environmental policy and gun control). But on Trump's hallmark issue, immigration, Trump

Table 17.8 Issue Positions of Republican Voters, by Candidate Choice (Percentages)

Issue	Kasich	Trump	Cruz
Abortion			
Pro-choice	43	36	16
Only abortion in case of rape, incest, health of woman at stake	50	63	61
Prohibit all abortions after 20 weeks of pregnancy	71	79	88
Immigration			
Grant legal status to illegal immigrants	54	27	26
Identify and deport illegal immigrants	42	77	71
Gun control			
Background checks	91	80	69
Ban assault rifles	61	38	25
Environment			
Raise fuel efficiency	59	49	33
Require minimum amount of renewable fuels	54	37	22
Gay marriage			
Favor	61	36	23
Crime			
Increase police	57	75	67
Eliminate mandatory minimums for non–violent drug offenses	69	49	49
Race			
White people have advantages because of skin color	48	17	15
Racial problems are rare	25	38	45
Approve use of U.S. military force			
To help the U.N. uphold international law	50	31	23
To ensure the supply of oil	19	31	30
To destroy a terrorist camp	81	83	86
To intervene in case of genocide or civil war	46	37	38
To protect American allies	84	78	86

Source: Cooperative Congressional Election Study.

voters were as willing as Cruz supporters to deny illegal immigrants legal status, and more willing to deport them. Trump voters also were quite similar to Cruz backers on crime policy, and the use of military force. Finally, Trump and Cruz supporters held similar views on matters of race. They were similarly likely to assert that white people did not enjoy advantages over members of other races, and that racial problems were rare in America.

The Significance of Ideology

To determine whether voters' ideology remained a significant factor in determining their vote, even after controlling for a host of other variables, the author performed a logistic regression on the data from self-declared primary and caucus participants in the CCES (Table 17.9). The dependent variable was the respondent's vote choice. The following variables were included: gender; age (divided into four categories: 18–29-year-olds, 30–44, 45–60, and older than 60); level of education (specifically, whether the respondent possessed a college degree); marital status;

Table 17.9 Logistic Regression of Trump, Kasich, and Cruz Vote

	Trump	Kasich	Cruz
Age	0.17***	−0.06	−0.08**
	(7.02)	(−1.35)	(−2.88)
Female	−0.09*	0.17*	−0.12*
	(−2.13)	(2.44)	(−2.29)
College degree	−0.70***	0.84***	0.29***
	(−15.65)	(11.44)	(5.42)
Married	−0.06	−0.11	0.15*
	(−1.12)	(−1.49)	(2.37)
Income $100,000	−0.14*	0.30***	−0.09
	(−2.52)	(3.66)	(−1.41)
Evangelical	−0.23***	−0.53***	0.46***
	(−4.97)	(−6.84)	(8.51)
Republican	0.44***	−0.16*	−0.26***
	(9.03)	(−2.13)	(−4.47)
Conservatism	−0.13***	−0.60***	0.84***
	(−4.15)	(−13.24)	(21.06)
Constant	0.15	0.06	−4.48***
	(1.06)	(0.32)	(−24.34)
N	16,311	16,311	16,311

Source: Cooperative Congressional Election Study.

Note: t statistics in parentheses; $^*p < 0.05$, $^{**}p < 0.01$, $^{***}p < 0.001$.

income (whether the respondent's annual income was $100,000 or greater); and whether a respondent identified as a "born again" Christian.

After controlling for all of these variables, a voter's ideology remained a significant factor in determining vote choice. The more conservative the voter, the less likely that voter was to support Trump. In addition, males were more likely to vote for Trump than females. Older voters were more likely to support Trump than younger voters. Those with lower levels of socioeconomic status – i.e. those with lower incomes, or lacking a college degree – were more likely to vote for Trump. Born-again voters were less likely to do so. Finally, self-identified Republicans were more likely to support Trump than independents.

Cruz voters presented a far different profile. The more conservative the voter, the more likely that voter was to support Cruz. In addition, unlike Trump voters, those with a college degree were more likely to back the Texas senator. Self-identified born-again voters were more likely to be Cruz voters. Unlike Trump, a voter's self-identification as a Republican was not a positive factor for Cruz, suggesting that ideology was a more powerful component than party identification.

Kasich voters also represented a distinctive niche in the Republican primary electorate. The less conservative the respondent, the more likely the respondent was to support the Ohio governor. Unlike Trump and Cruz, Kasich drew more support from women than from men. College-educated voters and those with higher incomes were more likely to support Kasich. Born-again voters were less willing to do so. Republicans also were less likely to back the Ohio governor, suggesting that independents were a source of strength for him.

Conclusions

As outlandish as a Trump nomination appeared when the mogul entered the fray in June 2015, his path to become the Republican standard bearer was a well-worn trail. Just like George W. Bush, John McCain and Mitt Romney, Donald Trump became the champion of "somewhat conservative" voters in the party's mainstream. He did so in part by establishing his ideology in a "fuzzy" manner, not a purist one, with a mixture of moderate and conservative positions. Voters correctly pegged Trump as a center-right candidate overall, but some of his positions (particularly on crime and immigration) were appealing to the far right of the GOP.

One might explain Trump's victory as a classic momentum play. The candidate won early contests in New Hampshire and South Carolina, gained even greater media attention, and won the support of voters in later contests who leaped onto the bandwagon. But this may give the oft-cited phenomenon of momentum too much credit for the outcome, and not enough to the power of attrition. As Norrander (2000, 2006) explains, the nomination contest is more a matter of remaining alive than gaining momentum, which often fades after a brief burst. Attrition, in contrast, has a long-term effect because the departure of candidates from a race is almost always permanent. Such was the case in 2016. After Iowa and New Hampshire, a slew of center-right competitors to Trump left the field. Marco Rubio stood as the only other candidate who had displayed potential to build coalitions across ideological lines. Once Rubio was gone, Trump had the center of the party to himself.

Ted Cruz was yet another candidate from the far-right wing of his party who found himself trapped on an ideological island in the presidential nomination process. During the early primaries and caucuses, the Texas senator was able to establish himself as the champion of very conservative voters, consolidating their support. In later contests, however, he proved unable (except in the Wisconsin primary) to build bridges to other factions of the Republican Party. Cruz was unable to forge coalitions despite the fact that his main opponent had shallow allegiances to the Republican Party and held heterodox positions on a number of issues supposedly important to Republican voters. In the midst of Cruz's last-ditch effort to stop Trump, former Speaker of the House John Boehner – the prototypical mainstream, "somewhat conservative" leader (Olsen and Scala 2016) – described him as "Lucifer in the flesh," and declared he would not vote for him against Hillary Clinton if he were the GOP nominee (Graham 2016).

John Kasich faced little of the enmity that Ted Cruz suffered from his fellow Republicans, yet he too found himself marooned after the first primaries and caucuses. Unlike Cruz, Kasich was no one's idea of a radical Republican. In fact, a popular governor of a large swing state seemed a tailor-made candidate for GOP voters seeking a flight to safety from the volatile, unpredictable Trump. Although the Ohio governor's upbeat, bipartisan message proved attractive to moderates, it repelled voters from other factions of the party just as readily as Cruz's more abrasive personality and ideologically extreme positions. Just like Jon Huntsman four years earlier, Kasich's outreach to moderates and independents paid modest dividends in the first-in-the-nation primary, but the road out of New Hampshire turned out to be a cul-de-sac. Kasich could not take advantage of his surprise finish in New Hampshire because, regardless of momentum, mainstream Republican voters did not find his candidacy attractive.

This survey of the 2016 Republican nomination process reminds us that for all the discussion of Trump's disruptive populism, many conventional, mainstream Republicans found themselves comfortable with his candidacy – at least compared to the alternatives. Does this mean that ideology has lost meaning for current-day Republican voters? Foundational studies of the nomination process suggest a more subtle phenomenon in play. Primary and caucus voters do not possess an exact measure of a candidate's ideology, but they are able to use ideology as a rough-and-ready cue in order to estimate a candidate's position on a spectrum. Because voters are only estimating, candidates can be intentionally "fuzzy," blurring their ideological position in order to appeal to a wide variety of voters. Fuzzy candidates run the danger of being portrayed as wishy-washy. Trump's bombastic, populist tone may have helped to prevent this depiction, as well as his harsh positions on crime, terrorism, and illegal immigration. And once Iowa and New Hampshire demolished most of his competition, Trump occupied the high ground in the center of the Republican nomination electorate – not a squishy moderate, not too conservative, but just conservative enough in the minds of mainstream Republican voters.

Notes

1 The Cooperative Congressional Election Study (CCES) is a national stratified sample survey which asks a battery of questions about demographic characteristics and political attitudes (Ansolabehere and Schaffner, 2017). The survey sample contacted 16,695 voters who said they participated in the Republican nomination process. Measures of candidates' performance in specific primaries and caucuses were gathered from exit-poll data available online, as well as an online election atlas (Leip n.d.).
2 CCES data from the 2016 survey confirm that the so-called conservative party still contains a significant percentage of moderates, and even a small percentage of liberals. Approximately three out of ten Republican primary and caucus voters identified themselves as either liberal (3 percent) or moderate (26 percent). The percentage of moderates and liberals was almost double the portion of self-described "very conservative" voters in the Republican nomination electorate. Self-described independent voters – 30 percent of this electorate – were far more likely to describe their ideology as moderate or liberal than self-described Republicans.
3 The CCES did not offer "somewhat conservative" as an option to respondents in identifying their ideology. Instead, CCES offered the options of "conservative," as opposed to "liberal," "moderate," or "very conservative." Slightly more than half described themselves as conservative.
4 The CCES asked voters to place candidates along an ideological spectrum by classifying them in one of the following categories: "liberal," "middle of the road," "somewhat conservative," "conservative" and "very conservative." They also were asked to rate themselves ideologically, albeit with slightly different categories ("liberal," "moderate," conservative," and "very conservative").

References

Aldrich, John H. 1980. *Before the Convention: Strategies and Choices in Presidential Nominating Campaigns.* Chicago: University of Chicago Press.
Ansolabehere, Stephen, and Brian F. Schaffner. 2017. "CCES Common Content, 2016." doi:10.7910/DVN/GDF6Z0, *Harvard Dataverse*, V1, UNF: 6: XRWBSCTbPDuGIDvAN1TOzQ==
Barro, Josh. 2015. "Donald Trump, Moderate Republican." *The New York Times*, August 14. https://www.nytimes.com/2015/08/18/upshot/donald-trump-moderate-republican.html?_r= 0
Brams, Steven J. 1978. *The Presidential Election Game.* New Haven, CT: Yale University Press.
Cain, Bruce E., I. A. Lewis, and Douglas Rivers. 1989. "Strategy and Choice in the 1988 Presidential Primaries." *Electoral Studies* 8 (1): 23–48.
Clarke, H. D., E. Elliot, and T. H. Roback. 1991. "Domestic Issue Ideology and Activist Style: A Note on 1980 Republican Convention Delegates." *Journal of Politics* 53 (2): 519–534.
Costain, Anne N. 1980. "Changes in the Role of Ideology in American National Nominating Conventions and Among Party Identifiers." *Western Political Quarterly* 33 (1): 73–86.
Crowdpac. 2017. https://www.crowdpac.com/about.
Downs, Anthony. 1957. *An Economic Theory of Democracy.* New York: Harper.
Graham, David A. 2016. "John Boehner on Ted Cruz: 'Lucifer in the Flesh'." *The Atlantic*, April 28. https://www.theatlantic.com/politics/archive/2016/04/john-boehner-ted-cruz-lucifer/480315/
Haynes, Audrey A., and Staci L. Rhine. 1998. "Attack Politics in Presidential Nomination Campaigns: An Examination of the Frequency and Determinants of Intermediated Negative Messages against Opponents." *Political Research Quarterly* 51 (3): 691–721.
Herrera, Richard. 1992. "The Understanding of Ideological Labels by Political Elites: A Research Note." *Western Political Quarterly* 45 (4): 1021–1035.
Jennings, M. Kent. 1992. "Ideological Thinking among Mass Publics and Political Elites." *Public Opinion Quarterly* 56 (2): 419–441.

Kenney, Patrick J. 1993. "An Examination of How Voters Form Impressions of Candidates' Issue Positions During the Nomination Campaign." *Political Behavior* 15 (2): 265–288.

Kenney, Patrick J., and Tom W. Rice. 1992. "A Model of Nomination Preferences." *American Politics Quarterly* 20 (2): 267–286.

Kenny, Lawrence, and Babak Lotfinia. 2005. "Evidence on the Importance of Spatial Voting Models in Presidential Nominations and Elections." *Public Choice* 123 (3): 439–462.

Lau, Richard R. 2013. "Correct Voting in the 2008 U.S. Presidential Nominating Elections." *Political Behavior* 35 (2): 331–355.

Leip, Dave. n.d. Atlas of U.S. Presidential Elections. http://uselectionatlas.org/

Masket, Seth. 2016. "Good Luck Distinguishing the Extremists from the Moderates." *Vox.* http://www.vox.com/mischiefs-of-faction/2016/1/21/10800990/cant-distinguish-extremists-from-moderates.

Mayer, William G. 2008. "Voting in Presidential Primaries: What We Can Learn from Three Decades of Exit Polling." In *The Making of the Presidential Candidates 2008*, ed. William G. Mayer. Lanham, MD: Rowman & Littlefield, pp. 169–203.

McCann, James A. 1995. "Nomination Politics and Ideological Polarization: Assessing the Attitudinal Effects of Campaign Involvement." *Journal of Politics* 57 (1): 101–120.

Norrander, Barbara. 1986. "Correlates of Vote Choice in the 1980 Presidential Primaries." *Journal of Politics* 48 (1): 156–167.

Norrander, Barbara. 1989. "Ideological Representativeness of Presidential Primary Voters." *American Journal of Political Science* 33 (3): 570–587.

Norrander, Barbara. 2000. "The End Game in Post-Reform Presidential Nominations." *Journal of Politics* 62 (4): 999–1013.

Norrander, Barbara. 2006. "The Attrition Game: Initial Resources, Initial Contests and the Exit of Candidates During the US Presidential Primary Season." *British Journal of Political Science* 36 (2): 487–507.

Olsen, Henry. 2014. "The Four Faces of the Republican Party," *The National Interest* (March–April).

Olsen, Henry, and Dante J. Scala. 2016. *The Four Faces of the Republican Party.* New York: Palgrave Macmillan.

Paulson, Arthur. 2009. "Party Change and the Shifting Dynamics in Presidential Nominations: The Lessons of 2008." *Polity* 41(3): 312–330.

Popkin, Samuel L. 1994. *The Reasoning Voter: Communication and Persuasion in Presidential Campaigns.* Chicago: University of Chicago Press.

Ridout, Travis N., and Jenny L. Holland. 2010. "Candidate Strategies in the Presidential Nomination Campaign." *Presidential Studies Quarterly* 40 (3): 611–630.

Sides, John, and Lynn Vavreck. 2013. *The Gamble: Choice and Chance in the 2012 Presidential Election.* Princeton: Princeton University Press.

Steger, Wayne P. 2008. "Forecasting the Presidential Primary Vote: Viability, Ideology and Momentum." *International Journal of Forecasting* 24 (2): 193–208.

Stone, Walter J., and Alan I. Abramowitz. 1983. "Winning May Not Be Everything, But It's More than We Thought: Presidential Party Activists in 1980." *American Political Science Review* 77 (4), 945–956.

Wattier, Mark J. 1983. "Ideological Voting in 1980 Republican Presidential Primaries." *Journal of Politics* 45 (4): 1016–1026.

18

TELEVISED DEBATES IN PRESIDENTIAL PRIMARIES

David A. Hopkins

Introduction: Oops Goes a Candidate

When Texas Governor Rick Perry announced his candidacy for president of the United States in August 2011, many political experts predicted that he would immediately establish himself as a serious contender for the 2012 Republican nomination. Perry was then the longest-serving governor in America, having been elected three times to lead the second-largest state in the nation as the culmination of a long political career in which he had never suffered defeat. He boasted the capacity to raise significant funds from an extensive donor network of wealthy Texas Republicans, as well as a more consistently conservative record in office than the party's initial frontrunner, former Massachusetts governor Mitt Romney. Perry appeared to have the characteristics of a formidable candidate, and Romney advisors worried that he might well represent the biggest obstacle to the success of their own campaign (Institute of Politics 2013, 20). But Perry's presidential candidacy ultimately turned out to be an utter flop. He placed a distant fifth in the first-in-the-nation Iowa caucus on January 3, 2012, winning just 10 percent of the vote, and withdrew from the race two weeks later after receiving less than 1 percent in the New Hampshire primary.

In retrospect, Perry's advisors blamed their candidate's failure on a number of tactical mistakes – including a late entry into the race, insufficient organization, and the absence of a compelling campaign message (Institute of Politics 2013, 66–69). But no single factor doomed Perry's 2012 presidential bid more than the self-inflicted damage suffered by the governor in the series of debates held among the Republican contenders on national television in the months prior to the onset of the primary season itself. Perry had entered the debates as a leading aspirant in the Republican field; at their conclusion, he had not only turned himself into an also-ran but had even become a national punchline.

Perry's first stumble occurred in a September 22, 2011 event aired on Fox News Channel. Asked by moderator Chris Wallace to explain his relatively moderate record on immigration – a departure from his otherwise conservative policy platform – Perry defended his support of a law that allowed students who had entered the United States illegally to qualify for the reduced tuition rates offered to state residents by the Texas public university system. "There is nobody on this stage who has spent more time working on border security than I have," Perry told Wallace. "But if you say that we should not educate children who have come into our state for no other reason than they've been brought there by no fault of their own, I don't think you have a heart" (American Presidency Project 2011). Perry's rivals and conservative media figures immediately attacked him for implying that opposing the provision of public benefits to illegal immigrants amounted to cruelty, and his standing in national surveys of potential Republican primary voters quickly began to erode. Perry had been leading Romney by a 28 percent to 21 percent margin on the day of the debate, as measured by the Real Clear Politics poll aggregator; by mid-October, Perry had slipped to third place, trailing both Romney and businessman Herman Cain (Real Clear Politics 2012).

In a subsequent debate held in Rochester, Michigan on November 9 and televised by the financial news channel CNBC, Perry, though desperately in need of a strong performance, instead suffered even more self-inflicted damage. While touting his plans to cut the size of the federal government, Perry could only name two of the three cabinet departments that his own campaign had proposed to eliminate, mentioning Commerce and Education before frantically searching his mind for the identity of the third. The moment was sufficiently awkward that several of Perry's rival candidates even tried, unsuccessfully, to help him jog his memory before he gave up, conceding, "the third one . . . I can't [remember]. Sorry. Oops!" (Later in the evening, Perry finally recalled that he also supported eliminating the Department of Energy, which earned him a relieved ovation from the audience in the hall.)

Perry's "Oops" moment not only became fodder for critical post-debate analyses by political commentators but also immediately earned him relentless mockery in the larger pop-culture universe. YouTube reported that a clip of the gaffe was the single most-watched internet video in the United States the following day (YouTube Trends 2011). Late-night comedians repeatedly lampooned Perry's forgetfulness, with *Saturday Night Live* portraying the governor as a dim-witted good-ol'-boy who flailed around helplessly on stage to the excruciating embarrassment of the other candidates before admitting that "I can't say stuff good, the words don't talk right." Journalists began to report that Perry's fundraising had fallen well below expectations (Dunham 2011), and his standing in public opinion polls suffered an irreversible decline. Perry's disastrous debate performances were sufficiently memorable that they continued to damage his political reputation when he mounted a second presidential bid four years later, which only lasted three months before Perry concluded that the baggage of his previous mistakes prevented him from attracting the necessary support to run a competitive 2016 campaign.

The rapid fall of Rick Perry illustrates the significant, and potentially pivotal, role that televised debates now play in presidential nomination politics. Debates among the candidates of each party prior to and during the presidential primary season have proliferated over the past two decades, as measured by the number of events held per election and the size of the national audience. Perry was one of several recent candidates whose presidential chances were strongly affected by their performance in these increasingly crucial events. Recognizing the growing power of debates to determine the identity and policy platform of the presidential nominees, both parties' national committees have acted to assert procedural control over their number, timing, and sponsorship. Like candidates, strategists, and media analysts, Democratic and Republican party leaders have concluded from experience that televised debates have become a central component of the presidential nomination process.

How Pre-Nomination Debates Differ from General Election Debates

Traditionally, both academic scholarship and popular media accounts have devoted much more attention to the series of debates held between the major-party nominees in the weeks prior to the November general election than to the earlier events of the primary season. The fall debates have attracted consistently large viewing audiences and produced a number of memorable campaign moments ever since they were famously inaugurated in 1960 by John F. Kennedy and Richard M. Nixon. According to American political lore, Kennedy's superior debate performance – especially his personal skill in using the medium of television to cultivate a positive impression among the voting public – gave him an ultimately decisive advantage in what turned out to be a very close election. Ever since, many popular commentators have habitually treated the fall debates as a major milestone in presidential campaigns that hold the power to determine the occupant of the White House for the succeeding four years. Systematic studies of public opinion, however, indicate that these events usually exert only modest and temporary effects on the distribution of candidate support in the electorate – suggesting that media hype tends to exaggerate the importance of the general election debates in deciding the presidency (Benoit, Hansen and Verser 2003).

There are several reasons why debates held during the nomination phase of the campaign, though they do not receive the same degree of publicity or viewership as the fall events, are actually more likely to exert significant influence over voters' perceptions and predispositions. First, the presence of strong partisan ties in the electorate sharply limits the proportion of voters who remain open to persuasion by both candidates in general elections, while the debates themselves occur amid a whirlwind fall campaign that bombards attentive citizens with a barrage of other information about the policies and personalities of the two main contenders. Even a particularly strong – or weak – performance by a nominee in a general election debate is unlikely to shake the vast majority of voters from their existing loyalties, and the measurable shifts that sometimes do occur in the candidate horse race in favor of the debate "winner" usually dissipate well before the election itself.

During the nomination period, in contrast, voters' preferences are much more weakly held and are thus susceptible to significant influence by campaign events. At this preliminary stage, citizens are weighing support among candidates within their own party rather than across party lines, removing the most powerful determinant of vote choice in general elections. Voters often must choose from among a field of more – and sometimes many more – than two candidates, and they usually possess limited existing knowledge of the various contenders (especially those presidential aspirants who have not previously sought national office and are not otherwise familiar to the public). In the absence of strongly held voter predispositions or other sources of information, a debate can supply a burst of positive or negative publicity that can easily exert a significant and lasting effect on the relative standing of a particular candidate (Best and Hubbard 1999; McKinney and Warner 2013).

In addition, debate participation is a more important element of candidates' communication, publicity, and campaign-building strategies during the pre-nomination phase than in the general election. Primary debates provide candidates with low-cost access to a national audience of politically attentive party activists, donors, and elected officials as well as ordinary voters. Candidates seek to impress these influential figures and attract their active support – or, at the least, dissuade them from backing a rival – at a point when they are still forming a campaign organization and amassing a financial war chest.

Finally, the long series of debates held prior to and during the sequence of presidential primaries and caucuses may play a role in shaping the policy positions and priorities of the eventual nominee – and thus the national party itself. The contestation of internal party differences during the nomination phase can result in the formation of a broadly held agreement among party politicians about the contemporary preferences and demands of the party membership. As the various contenders within each party's field of candidates jockey for position, they test out policy proposals and themes in front of primary voters, responding to, and sometimes co-opting, the campaign platforms of their opponents. Even candidates who ultimately fail to win the nomination themselves can leave a residue of influence on the party, and thus on the trajectory of national politics, by advancing views and ideas during the debates that are adopted by the party's eventual standard-bearer.

While debates during the presidential primary period are neither as venerable a tradition nor as well-studied a campaign phenomenon as the debates held between the general election contenders in the weeks before the November election, they have recently come to serve as critical elements of the nomination process and thus important milestones on the road to the White House. Debates among presidential nomination seekers have been held for decades – in fact, they even predate the landmark Kennedy–Nixon general election debates of 1960 – but they have achieved a newfound prominence over the past several presidential elections, due to significant changes in the American media and technology universe. As more citizens tune in to watch, candidates face an increasing pressure to hone their debating skills and avoid making mistakes that could permanently derail their presidential ambitions.

The History of Presidential Primary Debates

The first face-to-face debate between candidates for the presidential nomination of a major party took place in 1948 between New York governor Thomas E. Dewey and former Minnesota governor Harold Stassen. Dewey, the Republican presidential nominee in 1944, had started the 1948 campaign as the apparent frontrunner for the nomination, though Stassen's victories in the Wisconsin and Nebraska primaries had established him as a serious rival by the time of the debate. On the eve of the May 18 Oregon primary election, Dewey and Stassen met in Portland to face off before a national radio audience estimated at 40 million listeners (Elving 2015). The two candidates were engaged to debate a single question – "Should the Communist Party of the United States be outlawed?" – with Stassen taking the affirmative position and Dewey the negative, although they referred to other issues as well during their hour-long exchange (Benoit et al. 2002, 18–21). History has judged Dewey the winner of the debate, in part because he defeated Stassen in the following day's vote and went on to capture the Republican nomination for a second time, losing narrowly in the general election to incumbent president Harry S. Truman.

The first nationally televised pre-nomination debate occurred in 1952, at the dawn of the television age; unusually, it was a bipartisan event sponsored by the League of Women Voters and *Life* magazine. Three Democratic presidential candidates and three Republicans debated two questions determined by a survey of female voters conducted by the League (Dwight Eisenhower, the eventual Republican nominee, did not attend but was permitted to send a representative, Ford Foundation president Paul G. Hoffman, in his place). The event was televised by ABC and was also broadcast nationally on the radio (Kendall 2000, 67–68). Four years later, Democratic presidential candidates Adlai Stevenson and Estes Kefauver participated in the first intra-party debate before a national television audience, held on May 21, 1956 in advance of the Florida primary. Press accounts (e.g. Baker 1956) emphasized the limited policy disagreement between the candidates; Stevenson's subsequent narrow victory in the Florida vote aided his ultimately successful bid for the Democratic nomination that year.

Over the next two decades, debates occurred rarely and sporadically during the nomination season. But after the process of presidential nominations was fundamentally reformed in the 1970s, requiring the vast majority of delegates to both parties' national conventions to be selected directly by voters and pledged to support specific candidates, debates evolved into a familiar component of the post-reform system. With state primaries and caucuses becoming both more plentiful in number and more crucial to the outcome, candidates began to view

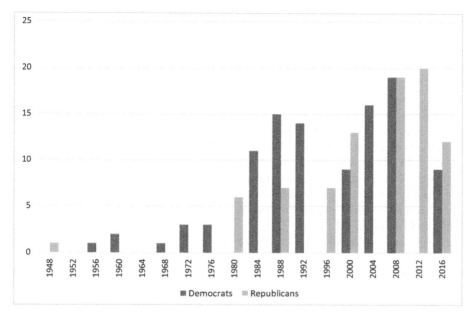

Figure 18.1   The Growth of Presidential Primary Debates, 1948–2016

Source: 1948–2012 data from Kondik and Skelley (2015); 2016 data from American Presidency Project, "Presidential Debates."

repeated participation in debates as an important means of winning voter support – while the rise in popular interest encouraged media outlets to sponsor a growing number of events. As Figure 18.1 demonstrates, Republicans held a then-record six debates during the 1980 primaries, which was quickly surpassed by the Democrats' 11 events in 1984 and 15 in 1988. Primary debates continued to increase thereafter, reaching a peak in 2008 and 2012 before intervention by the national party committees reduced their number in the 2016 election.

Cases in which an incumbent president is running for a second term represent an exception to this trend. Even when incumbents face an active challenger for renomination from within their party (as Richard Nixon did in 1972, Gerald Ford in 1976, Jimmy Carter in 1980, and George H. W. Bush in 1992), no sitting president has yet agreed to meet an opponent in a primary debate. It is likely that incumbents have viewed such events as offering much more political risk than reward, giving challengers a unique opportunity to match – and perhaps even best – the current occupant of the White House on a national stage.

The Rising Influence of Debates

Before the 1990s, pre-nomination debates usually lacked a wide real-time viewership. Some debates were not televised outside the state in which they were held, or were carried only on the radio. One well-known 1980 debate prior to the New Hampshire primary was restricted to the two leading Republican contenders, Ronald Reagan and George H. W. Bush, though Reagan maneuvered to put Bush in an awkward position by demanding the inclusion of other candidates in attendance immediately before the event began – thundering at a moderator who attempted to cut the power to his microphone that "I paid for this microphone" (referring to the fact that the Reagan campaign had footed the bill for the debate). Though the moment is remembered as a turning point marking Reagan's comeback in New Hampshire after losing to Bush in the Iowa caucus, there was no live television coverage of the event at all. Instead, film of Reagan's dramatic declaration was frequently replayed later on newscasts, giving him positive publicity and overshadowing the later exchanges between the candidates on substantive issues (Shirley 2009).

The major broadcast networks presumably viewed most primary debates as holding a finite appeal for a national viewing audience, and perhaps chafed at the limited opportunities that the format provides for the airing of lucrative paid advertisements. But debates held considerably more promise for the niche markets of cable television channels. Beginning in the 1980s, the non-profit C-SPAN network began providing national simulcasts of primary debates produced by local broadcast stations (such as New Hampshire's WMUR); by the 2000 election, nearly all debates in which most or all of the leading presidential candidates participated were broadcast either on a major network or on at least one of the national cable news channels such as CNN, MSNBC, and Fox News Channel.

The proportion of the American public with access to cable television also increased substantially during this period, from 20 percent of households in 1980 to 56 percent in 1990 and 68 percent in 2000 (U.S. Census Bureau 2002, 699). Soon thereafter, the growth of high-speed internet access facilitated the widespread online transmission of broadcast-quality video clips and streaming, providing another highly accessible technological avenue by which citizens could view debates. By the 2008 election, the video-hosting site YouTube had become one of the most-visited addresses on the Web – a status that it has retained over the succeeding decade. The emergence of 24-hour cable news and internet video has further amplified the importance of debates by allowing Americans who may not have viewed the events in real time to be exposed later to any noteworthy segments; unusual debate occurrences such as Rick Perry's "oops" moment are routinely replayed dozens of times on cable news and spread virally online to thousands of social media consumers.

Pre-nomination debates are not only increasingly plentiful in number but have generated growing voter interest over time. In the 2008 campaign, Democratic debates attracted an average of 4.7 million viewers per event, with the top-rated debate attracting 9 million viewers; the 2008 Republican debates averaged 3.1 million viewers with a peak of 7 million. In 2012, Republican debates averaged 5.1 million viewers with a peak of 8 million (there were no Democratic debates in 2012). In 2016, Democrats averaged 8 million viewers per debate with a high point of 16 million; while Republican debates drew an average audience of 15.5 million with a top mark of 24 million – reflecting the unusual popular fascination with the presidential candidacy of Donald Trump (O'Connell 2016; Rosenberg and Murphy 2016).

The rise of cable news and the internet has affected both the number and timing of pre-nomination debates. Previously, debates were often organized by state parties or local television stations and were usually held immediately prior to, or during, the primary season itself. In 1984, for example, the first Democratic debate was held on January 15, nine days before the first-in-the-nation Iowa caucus, while the final event did not occur until June 3, two days before the final set of primaries in California and five other states. In recent years, however, many events have been scheduled well in advance of the primary calendar, beginning in the spring or summer of the year before the election. The first debate of the 2008 Republican nomination race occurred on May 3, 2007, the first debate of the 2012 race occurred on May 5, 2011 (with 13 of the election's 20 debates held prior to January 1, 2012), and the first debate of the 2016 contest was held on August 6, 2015.

These early events occur at a stage when many candidates are still building their campaign organizations, attracting financial donors, and introducing themselves to the party electorate outside their home state. For this reason, a debate performance widely judged as substandard can prove damaging, or even fatal, to their presidential ambitions well before the voting even begins. Minnesota governor Tim Pawlenty learned this lesson during his short-lived bid for the 2012 Republican nomination. In a June 2011 television interview, Pawlenty had attacked his rival Mitt Romney for implementing a health care reform plan in Massachusetts that resembled that of Democratic president Barack Obama, quipping that the 2010 Affordable Care Act should be dubbed "Obamneycare." But when given the opportunity to repeat the charge in Romney's presence two days later at a debate in New Hampshire, Pawlenty dodged the question, disappointing conservative media figures who hoped that he would attack Romney on the issue. Pawlenty's widely noted failure to impress party activists by criticizing Romney in person prevented him from gaining popular or financial support in the succeeding weeks, and he dropped out of the race by the end of the summer (Weigel 2011).

Wisconsin governor Scott Walker similarly began the 2016 presidential campaign as one of the leading candidates for the Republican nomination by media consensus. Walker had earned national attention due to a conflict with public employee unions that had led Democrats to force a recall election of the governor in 2012, which Walker had survived with help from a number of conservative interest groups. A typical poll taken in Iowa one week after his official entry into the race in July 2015 found Walker in first place, attracting support from 22 percent of likely Republican caucus attendees. But Walker turned out to be an unsteady campaigner on the national stage, and he found particular difficulty in standing out among a large field of debate participants. His surprisingly forgettable showing in the first debate of the season – *Politico* referred to Walker as "sleepy," while ABC News characterized his performance as "lackluster" – quickly damaged the campaign's fundraising efforts (Gass 2015; Phelps 2015). When he demonstrated little improvement in the second event one month later, Walker's funding dried up entirely, forcing him out of the race only two months after he had jumped in. "Scott, for whatever reason, didn't connect on TV," lamented a major financial backer of Walker's. "And if you can't make it on television today in national politics, you're dead" (Healy and Burns 2015).

The first few debates of the campaign may thus prove to be the most politically consequential, even though they occur months before the sequence of primaries and caucuses begin and up to a full year before the final state events on the nomination calendar. A study of the 2012 Republican debates conducted by Schiffer (2017) concluded that the earliest debates exerted the greatest influence on voter preferences (as measured by Facebook "likes"), which became less open to change as the sequence of events progressed. Early debates may hold a sense of novelty that attracts a unique level of interest among citizens. The estimated 24 million viewers who watched the first Republican debate of the 2016 campaign – reflecting the unparalleled national interest generated by Donald Trump's entry into the presidential race – represented the largest audience for a non-sports cable broadcast in American history (Koblin 2016). The twelfth and final Republican debate, held the following March, attracted only 12 million viewers by comparison (O'Connell 2016).

While erstwhile leading contenders can suffer significant and even fatal damage to their campaigns by making a poor impression among debate-watchers, other candidates have viewed debate participation as a unique opportunity to attract personal publicity that they might not otherwise receive. Since the 1990s, an increasing number of unconventional candidates – such as business executives Morry Taylor (1996), Herman Cain (2012), and Carly Fiorina (2016); former ambassador Alan Keyes (1996, 2000, and 2008); religious conservative interest group leader Gary Bauer (2000); and retired heart surgeon Ben Carson (2016) – who lack the usual political experience or campaign infrastructure associated with serious aspirants to the nomination of a major party have nonetheless sought to benefit from the substantial nationwide exposure provided by debates and other public events. Cain's effective promotion of his tax reform plan during several debates in the fall of 2011 even helped to propel him briefly to the front of the Republican field in national public opinion surveys before allegations of personal misconduct surfaced that drove him from the race.

With candidate fields often swollen by the presence of large numbers of individuals with varying claims to legitimate competitiveness, debate organizers have been forced to impose qualifying criteria to determine which contenders should be permitted to participate. Most commonly, eligibility for a particular event is based on candidates' standing in recent public opinion surveys of party voters or, if the debate is being held after the start of the primary season, on the candidates' order of finish in previous primaries and caucuses. The 2016 election in particular attracted such a large number of Republican candidates – seventeen in all, though some ultimately dropped out before the voting began – that several networks imposed a tiered format, reserving the regularly scheduled prime-time debate for the top candidates and holding a second event, dubbed the "undercard" or "kiddie table" debate by some pundits, for the rest of the field. Even so, the crowded debate stage proved unwieldy, limiting the amount of camera time that some candidates received – to their later vocal dissatisfaction.

It is clear that candidates now view debate participation as an essential component of an effective presidential campaign, even if they are running more to promote themselves or raise issues than to realistically vie for the nomination. Harvard law professor Lawrence Lessig announced his candidacy for the 2016 Democratic presidential nomination in September 2015, dedicating his campaign to the cause of pressuring federal officeholders to enact wide-ranging campaign finance reform. But Lessig failed to register measurable support in the opinion polls employed to determine debate eligibility, preventing him from appearing alongside his better-known opponents and prompting him to exit the race two months later. In his withdrawal announcement, Lessig lamented his exclusion, observing that "it was clear that getting into the Democratic debates was *the* essential step in this campaign" and claiming that the Democratic Party, by imposing participation requirements, "won't let me be a candidate" (Weigel 2015; Frizell 2015). For Lessig, and undoubtedly for other candidates as well, running for president was simply not worth the effort without the opportunity to gain the public attention provided by televised debates.

The Institutionalization of Primary Debates

Lessig's complaint that the Democratic Party had effectively excluded him from the presidential race by enforcing rules restricting access to the debate stage raises an important set of broader questions about how and why party organizations have recently acted to seize influence over the pre-nomination debate schedule. Before 2016, primary debates were essentially unregulated by the national parties. Debate sponsors would independently arrange dates, venues, and formats, extending invitations to whichever candidates they wished to participate. After 2012, the leaders of both parties acted on their growing frustration with the pre-nomination debate process, bringing primary debates under greater control of the national committees. These leaders viewed debates with suspicion as representing a potentially serious threat to the central interest of the party: that the nomination process produce a well-qualified nominee who could unite the party's own supporters and compete effectively against the opposition in the general election.

Party officials often express concern that the repeated thrusts and parries of debate rhetoric will result in a divided party or politically wounded nominee. In particular, they worry that candidates will use debates as a platform to play to the ideological activists of the party, promoting extreme policy positions that turn out to be liabilities in a general election (Martin 2014).

In 2012, for example, frontrunner Mitt Romney adopted a hardline stance on immigration during the Republican primaries, in part to ease concerns from conservative purists that he was too moderate to lead the party. During a January debate in Florida, Romney proposed resolving the problem of illegal immigration via what he termed "self-deportation" – a statement that was later viewed by many Republican leaders as fatally damaging their chances of attracting significant Latino support in the general election race against Barack Obama. After Obama defeated Romney in November, Republican National Committee chair Reince Priebus referred to Romney's remark as a "horrific comment to make [that] obviously . . . hurts us" as a party (Blake 2013).

Party leaders also view the live debate setting as allowing candidates who are quick at repartee or gifted at reciting memorable sound bites to benefit at the expense of rivals with superior experience, knowledge, strategic acumen, campaign organization, or appeal outside the party base, imposing a systematic disadvantage on the contenders who possess the political assets held to be most valuable in general elections. In the Republican nomination race of 2012, for example, former House Speaker Newt Gingrich gained considerable positive publicity for his debate performances – especially his penchant for directing rhetorical fury at questions from moderators that he characterized as demonstrating anti-conservative bias or as otherwise unfair – that buoyed his candidacy for months despite a relative lack of financial resources or support from party elites. Because Gingrich was widely regarded by Republican leaders as a weak potential nominee, his success in using televised debates to attract popular support was, to them, a decidedly unwelcome development (Azari and Masket 2016).

Even if outsider or insurgent candidates do not actually best their more conventional opponents on the debate stage, the events may still work to their net advantage. Barack Obama did not consistently outdebate Hillary Clinton during their competitive and hard-fought battle for the Democratic presidential nomination in 2008, but Obama, only partway through his first term in the U.S. Senate at the time, still appeared to benefit from the events merely by demonstrating that he could hold his own against a better-known and more experienced opponent – which undercut Clinton's chief line of attack against Obama as an upstart who was insufficiently prepared to assume the presidency. Similarly, Donald Trump was not often judged the most fluid or articulate debater during the 2016 Republican nomination race, but Trump managed to avoid committing damaging gaffes while aiming memorably belittling comments at his opponents – such as his mocking characterization of Jeb Bush as "low-energy" and his dismissive swipe at Marco Rubio as "Little Marco" – that proved disorienting to his targets and rendered them unable to respond effectively. For national Democratic and Republican officials who tend to be sympathetic to the veteran politicians within their party, debates increasingly represent less a valuable opportunity for internal deliberation and decision-making than a serious potential threat to be contained as much as possible.

Motivated by these concerns, both national party committees acted in the wake of the 2012 election to assert greater control over pre-nomination presidential debates. The Republican National Committee passed a resolution allowing party leaders to formally recognize, and help to organize, a limited series of debates. Any candidate who participated in a debate that was not endorsed by the national party would risk being excluded from the official events – thus compelling the candidates to follow the RNC's organizational lead. Democrats enacted a similar provision as well.

By these measures, the parties acted to gain control over the number, timing, moderators, and broadcast outlets of the debates. Priebus and other Republican leaders had concluded from experience that there had been too many debates in recent elections, giving excessive publicity to secondary candidates and repeatedly exposing front-runners to damaging attacks. In addition, some previous debates had been sponsored by media sources deemed hostile to the party (especially MSNBC for Republicans and Fox News Channel for Democrats) or had been moderated by figures viewed as aligned with the opposition (such as ABC's George Stephanopoulos, a former top aide to Bill Clinton, who controversially moderated a Republican debate in late 2011). Control by the national party could therefore allow leaders to prevent unfriendly questioners or networks from exerting influence over the nomination process.

So far, only the 2016 campaign exists as a test of the effects of these newfound party-initiated regulations. In a formal sense, the parties' attempts to gain influence over the debate system was an immediate and unmitigated success. The number of debates was reduced substantially on both sides: Republicans held 12 debates during the 2016 campaign and Democrats only nine – as compared to a record 20 Republican debates in 2012 and 19 debates for each party in 2008. No candidate risked exclusion from the officially designated debates by participating in any unsanctioned events, while MSNBC and Fox News Channel were denied the opportunity to host debates for Republicans and Democrats, respectively.

More generally, however, it is difficult to view the parties as having accomplished the larger goals that the institutionalization of debates was designed to achieve. If Republican national leaders anticipated that gaining official control of the debate process would tilt the field of competition toward a conventionally experienced and elite-backed nominee, their hopes were dashed by the ultimately successful candidacy of Donald Trump. Even the newfound power of the national party to exert a right of approval over debate moderators did not prevent charges of favoritism from arising once again in 2016. Trump accused conservative Megyn Kelly, then the host of a prime-time program on Fox News Channel, of peppering him with hostile questions during the first debate of the campaign in August 2015; he retaliated for this perceived unfairness by boycotting a later Fox-televised debate also co-moderated by Kelly.

On the other side of the partisan aisle, the Democratic National Committee's role in determining the number and timing of pre-nomination debates in 2015–2016 provoked substantial criticism from supporters of Bernie Sanders, who viewed DNC chair Debbie Wasserman Schultz as using her organizational authority to structure the mechanics of the nomination process to the advantage of frontrunner Hillary Clinton. The DNC approved only nine debates – less than half of the number held during the party's previous multi-candidate nomination contest in 2008 and matching the lowest number of debates in a Democratic race without an incumbent president in 40 years – prompting unheeded calls from the Sanders campaign, several prominent DNC members, and even House Minority Leader Nancy Pelosi to add more events to the calendar (Schleifer 2015). In addition, some critics accused the party of intentionally scheduling debates to limit the size of the television audience and therefore their capacity to upend Clinton's march to the nomination. One debate was held on the Saturday before Christmas in 2015, while another occurred over the Martin Luther King Jr. holiday weekend in January 2016. The debate schedule fueled some Sanders backers' perceptions that their candidate was the victim of procedural unfairness, especially when combined with other elements of the nomination process that disadvantaged Sanders, such as the existence of closed primaries and unpledged superdelegates (see DeMoro 2016). Regardless of their objective validity, these frustrations ultimately impeded the efforts of Democratic leaders to unify the party faithful around Clinton's candidacy once the primary season ended in June 2016.

Like the timing of state primaries and the formulas governing the allocation of convention delegates, candidate debates are now subject to regulation by the national party committees. As with these other components of the presidential nomination system, however, there is no guarantee that the enactment of party rules will produce the results intended by their proponents. The events of 2016 serve as a powerful lesson that the power of party leaders to influence the outcomes of nomination contests via the exercise of procedural prerogatives remains limited and highly contingent. Yet it is unlikely that the national parties will quickly or easily relinquish the formal authority that they have recently asserted over the organization and timing of televised debates, and the future may well bring an even more extensive set of applicable restrictions imposed by officials who continue to view the conduct of these events as critical to the interests of the parties they serve.

Conclusion: Debates in a Changing Nomination System

In a sense, primary debates have become a synecdoche for the contemporary presidential nomination system of which they are an increasingly fundamental component. The reforms to the process that were introduced in the 1970s, and that have been subject to almost continuous mechanical tinkering ever since, were intended to democratize party nominations by transferring control of nominations from party "bosses" to rank-and-file citizens, thus bestowing the outcome with an indisputable representative legitimacy. Yet the benefits of these reforms have been much more mixed in practice than in theory. Some scholars contend that party leaders have managed to recapture control over nominations via other means, thus "beating reform" (Cohen et al. 2008); others have concluded that changes to the system have merely empowered alternative sets of actors – such as the news media – and favored different types of candidates (Polsby 1983). The parties themselves are in a constant state of dissatisfaction, fiddling with various attributes of the process – the existence and proportion of superdelegates, the extent of front-loading in the primary calendar, the prevalence of winner-take-all delegate allocation, the degree of temporal primacy afforded Iowa and New Hampshire – with the objective of improving its outcomes while simultaneously protecting its validity in the eyes of the public.

Public debates among candidates for office, like primary elections themselves, ostensibly comport to an ideal of democracy in action. They appear to provide citizens with the unique opportunity to judge the various contenders for themselves without elite intermediation, based on whatever criteria they wish, and to make a fair and informed choice of standard-bearer to lead the party into electoral battle with the opposition. Yet the capacity of a momentary triumph – or, more commonly, blunder – in the midst of a single exchange on live television to exert a lasting effect on the electoral fate of a candidate raises serious questions about whether the increasing influence of debates on presidential nominations is indeed a welcome development. Do debates really further the goal of providing the American people with a choice of attractive, competent, and well-suited nominees for the presidency?

Consider the plight of Senator Marco Rubio of Florida, widely considered a talented and formidable politician when he entered the race for the 2016 Republican presidential nomination. Rubio's third-place showing in the first-in-the-nation Iowa caucus raised expectations that he would successfully unite Republican voters dissatisfied with the top two finishers, Ted Cruz and Donald Trump, behind his own candidacy. Rubio appeared to receive a significant boost from his Iowa performance and subsequent favorable media coverage; according to the FiveThirtyEight poll aggregator, his support in the New Hampshire primary rose from 10 percent to 16 percent in just five days, pushing him from fourth to second place in the state (FiveThirtyEight 2016).

Unfortunately for Rubio, he suffered an inopportune setback due to a damaging performance in a debate televised nationally by ABC three days before the New Hampshire primary. Under rhetorical attack from New Jersey governor Chris Christie for lacking the necessary experience to be president, Rubio oddly repeated the same response – referring to "the fiction that Barack Obama doesn't know what he's doing" – four separate times, appearing only to confirm Christie's accusations that Rubio could only offer voters a "memorized 25-second speech" rather than a set of real-world accomplishments. Media analysts seized on the moment after the debate was over, endlessly replaying the Rubio "malfunction" on television and the internet while burying the candidate in a blizzard of bad publicity. As a result, his campaign lost its momentum, finishing a disappointing fifth in the New Hampshire vote and folding five weeks later after winning just one of 29 state primaries and caucuses – leaving Trump in commanding position to win the Republican nomination.

It is hardly surprising that party leaders might conclude from such examples as the Rubio gaffe that debates not only hold the potential to play a pivotal role in determining presidential nominations, but also cannot be counted upon to benefit candidates who are best-positioned to unify the party, defeat the opposition, and govern successfully once elected. But any action by the party organizations to scale back the number of debates or otherwise attempt to limit their influence risks a backlash from critics who charge that they are violating a norm of internal party democracy by unjustly "rigging the system" in favor of "insiders" and squelching the voice of the people (Azari and Masket 2016). As long as primary voters continue to use debates to help them make up their minds, party elites will face serious constraints on their ability to steer the presidential nomination process in their own preferred direction.

References

American Presidency Project. n.d. "Presidential Debates." http://www.presidency.ucsb.edu/debates.php

American Presidency Project. 2011. "Republican Candidates Debate in Orlando, Florida" (transcript). September 22. http://www.presidency.ucsb.edu/ws/index.php?pid=96795

Azari, Julia, and Seth Masket. 2016. "Presidential Primary Debates and Internal Party Democracy." Paper delivered at the Annual Meetings of the American Political Science Association, Philadelphia, PA, September 3.

Baker, Russell. 1956. "Stevenson, Kefauver Find Agreement in TV Debate." *New York Times*, May 22, p. 1.

Benoit, William L., Glenn J. Hansen, and Rebecca M. Verser. 2003. "A Meta-Analysis of the Effects of Viewing U.S. Presidential Debates." *Communication Monographs* 70: 335–350.

Benoit, William L., P. M. Pier, LeAnn M. Brazeal, John P. McHale, Andrew Klyukovski, and David Airne. 2002. *The Primary Decision: A Functional Analysis of Debates in Presidential Primaries*. Westport, CT: Praeger.

Best, Samuel J., and Clark Hubbard. 1999. "Maximizing 'Minimal Effects': The Impact of Early Primary Season Debates on Voter Preferences." *American Politics Research* 27 (2): 450–467.

Blake, Aaron. 2013. "Priebus: Romney's Self-Deportation Comment Was 'Horrific.'" *Washington Post*, August 16. https://www.washingtonpost.com/news/post-politics/wp/2013/08/16/priebus-romneys-self-deportation-comment-was-horrific/

Cohen, Marty, David Karol, Hans Noel, and John Zaller. 2008. *The Party Decides: Presidential Nominations Before and After Reform*. Chicago: University of Chicago Press.

DeMoro, Roseann. 2016. "10 Ways the Democratic Primary Has Been Rigged From the Start." *Salon*, March 30, http://www.salon.com/2016/03/30/10_ways_the_democratic_primary_has_been_rigged_from_the_start_partner/

Dunham, Richard S. 2011. "Rick Perry Fundraising Hit After Debates Gaffes." *San Francisco Chronicle*, November 17. http://www.sfgate.com/politics/article/Rick-Perry-fundraising-hit-after-debate-gaffes-2289214.php

Elving, Ron. 2015. "Before Bright Lights and Rapid Fire, There Was 1948 and One Question." *National Public Radio*, November 10. http://www.npr.org/2015/11/10/455399441/before-bright-lights-and-rapid-fire-there-was-1948-and-one-question>

FiveThirtyEight. 2016. "2016 Primary Forecasts: N.H. Republican Primary." https://projects.fivethirtyeight.com/election-2016/primary-forecast/new-hampshire-republican/

Frizell, Sam. 2015. "Lawrence Lessig Would Not Have Qualified For CBS Debate." *Time*, November 5. http://time.com/4102049/democratic-debate-cbs-lawrence-lessig/

Gass, Nick. 2015. "Poll: Walker Leads in Iowa, Followed by Trump." *Politico*, July 20. http://www.politico.com/story/2015/07/poll-iowa-gop-scott-walker-leads-donald-trump-second-120352

Healy, Patrick, and Alexander Burns. 2015. "Scott Walker Ends His 2016 Presidential Run." *New York Times* FirstDraft blog, September 21. https://www.nytimes.com/politics/first-draft/2015/09/21/scott-walker-quits-2016-presidential-race/

Institute of Politics. 2013. *Campaign for President: The Managers Look at 2012.* John F. Kennedy School of Government, Harvard University. Lanham, MD: Rowman & Littlefield.

Kendall, Kathleen E. 2000. *Communication in the Presidential Primaries: Candidates and the Media, 1912–2000.* Westport, CT: Praeger.

Koblin, John. 2016. "Even Without You-Know-Who, Debate Still Drew 12.5 Million Viewers." *New York Times*, January 30, p. A13.

Kondik, Kyle, and Geoffrey Skelley. 2015. "Eight Decades of Debate." *Sabato's Crystal Ball, University of Virginia*, July 30. http://www.centerforpolitics.org/crystalball/articles/eight-decades-of-debate/

Martin, Jonathan. 2014. "Republicans Tighten Grip on Debates in 2016 Race." *New York Times*, May 10, p. A12.

McKinney, Mitchell S., and Benjamin R. Warner. 2013. "Do Presidential Debates Matter? Examining a Decade of Campaign Debate Effects," *Argumentation and Advocacy* 49 (1): 238–258.

O'Connell, Michael. 2016. "TV Ratings: 12th GOP Debate Drops to 11.9 Million Viewers on CNN." *Hollywood Reporter*, March 11. http://www.hollywoodreporter.com/news/tv-ratings-12th-gop-debate-874461

Phelps, Jordyn. 2015. "4 Things That Took Scott Walker from Frontrunner to Longshot Candidate." *ABC News*, September 14. http://abcnews.go.com/Politics/things-scott-walker-frontrunner-longshot-candidate/story?id=33685097

Polsby, Nelson W. 1983. *Consequences of Party Reform.* New York: Oxford University Press.

Real Clear Politics. 2012. "2012 Republican Presidential Nomination." http://www.realclearpolitics.com/epolls/2012/president/us/republican_presidential_nomination-1452.html

Rosenberg, Simon, and Chris Murphy. 2016. "2016 Presidential Primary Debate Audience—Final Tally." *New Democrat Network*, May 25. http://ndn.org/sites/default/files/blog_files/President%20Primary%20Debate%20Audiences%20for%202008%202016%20-%20Final.pdf

Schiffer, Adam J. 2017. "Debates and Partisan Enthusiasm Before the 2012 Republican Primaries." *Presidential Studies Quarterly* 47 (2): 293–310.

Schleifer, Theodore. 2015. "Pelosi Joins Call to Add More Democratic Primary Debates." *CNN*, September 18. http://www.cnn.com/2015/09/18/politics/nancy-pelosi-democrats-debates-2016/

Shirley, Craig. 2009. *Rendezvous with Destiny: Ronald Reagan and the Campaign That Changed America.* Wilmington, DE: Intercollegiate Studies Institute.

U.S. Census Bureau. 2002. *Statistical Abstract of the United States, 2002.* Washington, DC: U.S. Government Printing Office.

Weigel, David. 2011. "Pawlenty Explains His Campaign-Ending 'Obamneycare' Whiff." *Slate*, December 1. http://www.slate.com/blogs/weigel/2011/12/01/pawlenty_explains_his_campaign_ending_obamneycare_whiff.html

Weigel, David. 2015. "Larry Lessig Ends Presidential Campaign, Citing Unfair Debate Rules." *Washington Post*, November 2. https://www.washingtonpost.com/news/post-politics/wp/2015/11/02/larry-lessig-ends-presidential-campaign-citing-unfair-debate-rules/

YouTube Trends. 2011. "Rick Perry's 'Oops': The Morning After on YouTube." November 10. http://youtube-trends.blogspot.com/2011/11/rick-perrys-oops-morning-after-on.html

PART V

Primaries Outside of the United States

Primary elections have become a major area of study outside of the United States over the past decade. As noted in the introduction, the landmark study on this subject has been Reuven Hazan and Gideon Rahat's 2010 book *Democracy Within Parties: Candidate Selection Methods and Their Political Consequences*. There, Hazan and Rahat detail many of the different methods of candidate selection in democracies and discuss the consequences of these methods for governance. Because many of the democracies that have established primaries (or things that look like them) are party-centered parliamentary systems, it is not at all clear how relevant the experience of a candidate-centered first-past-the-post system like the United States will be for these nations. Some of the appealing features of primaries – from the strategic party goals discussed in Part I of this book to the excitement generated by charismatic candidates – transcend national boundaries. But this raises many questions about how candidates who must run in primary elections will behave as legislators. These questions have been central to studies such as Giulia Sandri, Antonella Seddone, and Fulvio Venturino's 2015 book *Party Primaries in Comparative Perspective*, an edited volume that brought together research in primaries conducted over several years as part of a project of the European Consortium for Political Research. They have also (as Alan Ware noted in Chapter 1 of this volume) raised the question of what primaries actually are. It is not in fact clear that the sorts of candidate selection methods used within political parties truly count as "primaries" in the American sense if they do not include the mass electorate.

The cases in this Part do not necessarily provide a comprehensive account of all of the different primary systems worldwide, but they were chosen to provide a sampling of how primaries have been adapted to fit the circumstances of different regions and different types of political traditions. The first two chapters in this section consider the legislative consequences of primary elections. Reuven Hazan and Reut Itzkovich-Malka provide an overview of candidate selection methods today in Europe. The authors here show that candidate selection methods can influence legislative behavior across all different types of party systems. The introduction of primaries, or inclusive candidate selection methods that resemble them, tend to weaken the power of political parties over their members. It is unclear where this will lead European parties in the long run.

Indriði H. Indriðason and Gunnar Helgi Kristinsson address one interesting aspect of measuring the consequences of primaries. In weak party systems, advances have been made in measuring parties' coherence within legislators. Yet in systems where legislators are expected to support their parties at all times, it is harder to assess the effects of elections on candidates. Using the case of Iceland, a nation that has used primaries for longer than most other parliamentary systems, Indriðason and Kristinsson provide other measurements of the effects of primaries, including legislators' speeches and bill introductions. They show that primary competition increases the level of activity among legislators.

The next two chapters in this section consider the decision to hold primaries. Kathleen Bruhn's study of Latin American primary elections shows that primaries can be used in many of these countries when political parties have strategic reasons to hand the task of candidate selection to voters, and they can be avoided when involving the public will be detrimental to party goals. Likewise, Nahomi Ichino and Noah Nathan explore the use of primaries in African democracies, with particular emphasis on Ghana. This study, which draws upon several prior works by the authors on African elections, shows the importance of primary elections in combatting corruption and vote-buying in new democracies. However, it also shows the difficulty of using them in systems where the parties often are not organized along ideological lines. Both of these chapters demonstrate the importance of democratizing candidate selection in nations where democracy is not well-established.

In Chapter 23, Scott Pruysers and Anthony Sayers consider the use of primary elections in Canada. As is the case in Latin America, Canadian primaries are held at the discretion of the parties, and the parties have tended to adopt different types of decision rules and voting rules that suit their immediate aims. Unlike the Latin American case, however, Canadian primary elections have become sufficiently institutionalized that parties rarely choose simply not to use them at all. They are now expected by most voters. The Canadian parties have also, like many European parties, expanded their use of primaries for party leadership positions over the past two decades.

Finally, in Chapter 24 Marino De Luca explores the use of primary elections in Italy since the early 1990s. Italy has now used primary elections more extensively than any nation other than the United States. De Luca shows that Italy has developed a primary election system that distinctively embodies the nation's political character. Parties and individual candidates initially adapted primaries to suit their own political needs, but enthusiasm about primaries in the media and among the general public has led to their widespread adoption at most levels of government. Although the specific rules of primaries vary across parties, their use is now routine. It is certainly possible, perhaps even likely, that the development of primaries in Italy will be followed by greater experimentation with them in other democracies in the years to come.

19

MIND THE GAP

The Effects of Intra- and Inter-Party Competition on Party Unity in Parliamentary Democracies

Reuven Y. Hazan and Reut Itzkovitch-Malka

General elections and candidate selection methods are two of the most central institutions in any democratic regime. Their centrality is, first and foremost, due to the fact that these institutions determine the distribution of political power and the identity of political elites. The literature clearly postulates that the choice of an electoral system will have consequences for, among other factors, voting and legislative behavior (see, for example: Carey and Shugart 1995; Katz 1997; Rae 1967; Taagepera and Shugart 1989). Candidate selection methods, which have only recently received growing scholarly attention, also have ramifications for legislative behavior and party unity (Gallagher and Marsh 1988; Hazan and Rahat 2010; Narud, Pedersen and Valen 2002; Ranney 1981; Schattschneider 1942).

Almost any prospective or incumbent politician in any country must pass two barriers, not one, in order to become a legislative representative – they must first be chosen by a party selectorate and only subsequently elected by the voters. Each of these two barriers can vary in relevance, and also in nature – each can be either more personal or more under party control – but both are present, both have consequences, and both must be taken into account if we want to understand legislative behavior. Yet, when it comes to legislative behavior the vast majority of the ongoing research continues to focus on the electoral system and its effects. In other words, most scholars attribute legislative behavior to the way legislators are *elected* by the general public, and not to the way they are *selected* by their parties.

We seek to address both barriers in a more comprehensive way, and present a better explanation of legislative behavior. However, we face some difficulty in our attempt to examine the influence of these two independent variables on our dependent variable – party unity. Legislators' voting behavior is heavily constrained in parliamentary systems where we see very little variance in party unity (Carey 2009; Depauw and Martin 2009; Heidar 2006; Sieberer 2006) – but their attitudes and norms of behavior regarding party unity are far less constrained and present much more variance. In order to overcome the no-variance problem we are faced with, we can investigate party unity, both as it is perceived by the legislators and how it exhibits itself in the legislature, by conceptualizing it as a sequential decision-making process. To gain insight into the intra-party dynamics surrounding party unity we use attitudinal data, as this is the best way to understand the different stages legislators undergo when deciding how to behave. Hence, while this research does not address legislators' actual voting behavior, it provides an understanding of the inner processes legislators and parties undergo before a legislator's vote is cast in the plenum.

This chapter analyzes the effects of candidate selection methods, electoral systems and the interplay between them on party unity. Our main argument is that one must take into account the effects of both intra-party (candidate selection) and inter-party (electoral systems) competition, and the interaction between them, in order to better explain legislators' attitudes and behavior. When it comes to party competition, the literature on the determinants of legislative behavior remains largely unidimensional, focusing only on electoral systems. We suggest that by expanding this focus to include the candidate selection dimension we can improve our understanding of how our elected representatives behave. Using attitudinal data from the PARTIREP[1] project combined with data collected on candidate selection methods in 34 European parties in 10 countries (for a full list of the countries and parties included in this research see the Appendix), we are able to show that the candidate selection method – the first of two barriers legislators must pass in order to be reelected – conditions the influence of the electoral system on legislative behavior. That is, the interaction between the intra- and the inter-party dimensions offers a better interpretation than the traditional unidimensional explanation for party unity.

Intra- and Inter-Party Competition

Candidate selection methods are defined as "the predominantly *extralegal* process by which a political party decides which of the persons legally eligible to hold an elective public office will be designated on the ballot and in election communications as its recommended and supported candidate or list of candidates" (Ranney 1981, 75, emphasis in original). Such methods can be classified according to several criteria, but the central criterion is the inclusiveness of the selectorate – who may take part in selecting the party candidates. At the inclusive pole are parties that allow all voters to select the party candidates with hardly any restrictions – similar to primaries in the United States. At the exclusive pole are parties that allow a party leader to single-handedly select the party candidates. In-between are parties that allow the party elite or party delegates to select the party candidates (Hazan and Rahat 2010).

The more inclusive the selectorate, the less control the party has over the process of candidate selection and, as a result, over the behavior of the candidates selected. The inclusiveness of the selectorate thus affects legislative behavior in several ways. First, more inclusive selectorates may infringe on the party's ability to create a united list, due to the fact that the party leadership has less control over the selection process. As a result, the homogeneity of preferences among legislators who belong to parties that use inclusive selectorates is lower than that among legislators who belong to parties that select their candidates by more exclusive methods. Second, inclusive selectorates create a double source of legitimacy for legislators, party and non-party, since legislators are exposed to various pressures which "could be both quite different from, and even contradictory to, that of the party program, and the candidates will have to be responsive to them" (Atmor, Hazan, and Rahat 2011, 25). This may result in lower levels of party unity.[2]

Electoral systems are composed of three main dimensions: district magnitude, electoral formula and ballot structure (Blais 1988; Farrell 2011; Rae 1967; Reynolds, Reilly and Ellis 2005; Taagepera and Shugart 1989). Each of these dimensions has an effect on legislative behavior. *District magnitude* affects the foci of representation, shifting from personal representation in single-member districts (SMD) to party-focused representation in multi-member ones (Bowler, Farrell and Pettitt 2005; Lancaster 1986; Mitchell 2000; Shugart 2001). This distinction is also relevant for the second dimension of electoral systems, the *electoral formula*, since there is a strong correlation between the two – multi-member districts are predominant in proportional representation (PR) electoral systems, while SMDs are predominant in majority/plurality electoral systems. The third dimension of the electoral system is the *ballot structure*, defined as the way in which voters are allowed to express their preference(s) among candidates (Katz 1986; Katz and Bardi 1980). The more open the ballot, the more the electoral system cultivates personal representation and individual accountability, as legislators are not solely dependent on their party for reelection (Carey and Shugart 1995). More open ballots, it is claimed, can damage party unity.[3]

The dimensions of an electoral system can be combined differently to produce a candidate-based electoral system or a party-based one. For example, a plurality/majority SMD electoral system will produce more candidate-based incentives at the expense of party/collective accountability – such as in the U.S. – since greater individual accountability and constituency responsiveness will result in lower levels of party unity (Bowler and Farrell 1993; Stratman and Baur 2002). A PR multi-member district electoral system will do the opposite – such as in the Netherlands – since it is built on responsible parties and collective accountability, which produce higher levels of party unity (Carey 2009; Strøm 1990). This differentiation is based on the extent to which politicians are rewarded for their personal reputation in the elections. In candidate-based electoral systems politicians will cultivate a personal vote by maintaining a close connection with their voters, especially through constituency work, at the expense of party unity (Cain, Ferejohn and Fiorina 1987; Carey 2007, 2009; Carey and Shugart 1995). In party-focused electoral systems the personal incentives are largely absent, legislators are not individually elected, and as a result they must curry favor with the party leadership who can exercise more control over their behavior.

Hypotheses and Method

This chapter examines three hypotheses concerning the effect of candidate selection methods and electoral systems, and the interaction between them, on legislative behavior. The first two hypotheses address either the candidate selection method or the electoral system separately, while the third assesses their joint effect.

> H1: Candidate selection methods have an effect on legislative behavior, whereas the effect of electoral systems on legislative behavior is marginal.

> H2: Electoral systems have an effect on legislative behavior, whereas the effect of candidate selection methods on legislative behavior is marginal.

> H3: Both the candidate selection method and the electoral system have a dependent effect on legislative behavior.

The first hypothesis is counter-intuitive because one expects that legislators will be first and foremost responsive to their wide electorate, not to their relatively small party selectorate. The second hypothesis presents the "conventional wisdom" in the academic literature that focuses on the electoral system as the most important explanation of legislative behavior. The third hypothesis posits that the influence of either the candidate selection method or the electoral system on legislative behavior depends on the nature of the relationship between the electoral system and the candidate selection method. That is, the effect of one depends on the type, or kind, of the other.

Our basic argument is that it is the electoral system that is dependent on the candidate selection method. We first base our argument on the fact that selection mechanisms precede electoral ones: before a candidate can run in a general election, s/he has to survive the selection stage. This enables the candidate selection method to set the ground rules and to shape the arena in which legislators operate. We posit that the electoral system will not have the ability to completely counter the general context set by the candidate selection method, but it certainly has the ability to make significant changes both within, and to, the given framework.

More specifically, we claim that the effect of the electoral system on party unity differs, given different types of candidate selection methods, measured according to their level of inclusiveness. The more inclusive the candidate selection method is, such as U.S.-style primaries, the smaller the effect of the electoral system on party unity. The largest effect of the electoral system on party unity is thus expected when the candidate selection method is the most exclusive.

When the party uses an exclusive selectorate to select its candidates – be that the party leader or a small party caucus – it can select candidates whose ideological preferences are as close as possible to the party's agenda and as a result ensure high levels of party unity. Additionally, since the party controls the most important resource for legislators – their ability to be reselected, and as a result reelected – an exclusive candidate selection method provides clear, party-centered incentives to legislators. Legislators know that if they wish to be reselected by their party they must behave as party team players, demonstrating high levels of party unity.

However, legislators do not only need to be reselected by their party, they also need to be reelected by the voters on Election Day. This is where the electoral system comes into play, affecting the incentives offered to legislators and, as a result, their attitudes and norms of behavior. The electoral system can either reinforce the incentives the candidate selection method offers legislators, or it can contradict them.

When an exclusive party-based selectorate is coupled with a PR party-based electoral system, the two reinforce each other, resulting in high levels of party unity. Unsurprisingly, legislators who are both selected and elected under party-based rules are expected to frequently share the ideological preferences of their party and to demonstrate substantial loyalty towards it. However, when the party-based incentives of an exclusive candidate selection method are coupled with personally focused incentives of an SMD electoral system, legislators are faced with conflicting incentives, pulling in opposite directions. Introducing a candidate-based electoral system to an exclusive selectorate may thus decrease the level of shared preferences the legislator shares with his/her party, as well as create competing principals to whom the legislator must be accountable. Both consequences reduce party unity.

On the contrary, when the party uses inclusive selectorates such as primaries, the nature of the electoral system matters much less. Once a party democratizes its candidate selection method, making it more inclusive, it loses much of its control over the process. Inclusive selectorates offer legislators personally focused incentives and limit, to some extent, the ability of the party to control the identity of the candidates selected. As a result, we claim that once the selectorate becomes inclusive the dynamics of either a reinforcing incentives scenario – when an inclusive selectorate is coupled with an SMD electoral system – or a conflicting incentives scenario – when such a selectorate is coupled with a PR electoral system, becomes largely irrelevant. Given the fact that the dynamics of democratizing candidate selection are so influential (and destructive) to party unity, we argue that the electoral system would not have much of a say on these issues, if any.

In order to test the three hypotheses we used two key variables, one for the candidate selection method and one for the electoral system. We chose to focus on the main characteristic of the candidate selection method that the recent literature points to as the most relevant factor when examining legislative behavior – the inclusiveness of the selectorate (Best and Cotta 2000; Hazan and Rahat 2010; Norris et al. 1990).[4] The inclusiveness of the selectorate is a scale variable borrowed from Hazan and Rahat's (2010) 24-point index. Of the three main characteristics of the electoral system – electoral formula, district magnitude and ballot structure – we chose to focus on the electoral formula as the defining variable of the electoral system (Duverger 1954; Rae 1967; Reynolds, Reilly and Ellis 2005). We dichotomized the electoral formula into a dummy variable:

plurality/majority systems and PR systems. This allows us to distinguish between a candidate-centered SMD electoral system associated with a constituency-based focus of representation and a party-centered PR electoral system associated with a more generalist party-based focus and to test their effect on party unity.

As mentioned above, we expect inclusive selectorates to create an incentive for legislators to demonstrate a more personalized type of representation. The result might be devastating for party unity, since collective representation is, to a great extent, damaged (Bowler, Farrell and Katz 1999; Cross 2008; Katz and Cross 2013). More exclusive selectorates will place the focus on the party, at the expense of personal representation, resulting in increased levels of party unity (Cross 2008; Katz and Cross 2013). As for the electoral system, we expect plurality SMD electoral systems to create an incentive for legislators to engage in constituency service, or pork-barrel politics, and to demonstrate individual accountability to their voters (Carey 2007, 2009). On the other hand, legislators in PR multi-member district electoral systems have an incentive to demonstrate party-focused representation and behave as loyal team players, rather than to engage in active constituency service (Bowler and Farrell 1993; Stratman and Baur 2002).

In order to account for the effects of candidate selection methods and electoral systems on legislative behavior, this chapter relies on the attitudinal data collected for the international PARTIREP project and integrates it with data on candidate selection methods which was gathered from various sources based on party regulations, expert surveys and published articles. The PARTIREP project involved a quantitative cross-national survey carried out among members of 15 national and 58 sub-national European parliaments plus Israel. For the purpose of this analysis only national parliaments were taken into account. Data collection took place between 2009 and 2011. Legislators were asked to participate in either a face-to-face interview, a print questionnaire or a web-based survey.

We analyze cases from 10 countries (out of the 15 included in the PARTIREP project) encompassing a total of 34 political parties. We chose these cases because these are the ones for which we have reliable data on their candidate selection methods. Cross-national data on candidate selection methods is very hard to achieve since it often requires familiarity with local politics and accessibility (Hazan and Rahat 2010). Therefore, this chapter makes use of available data from a variety of sources, including our own extensive data collection.

When analyzing the data we used pooled logistic regression models to assess the effect of the candidate selection method, the electoral system and the interaction between them on party unity. Our models include four control variables: party agreement,[5] parliamentary seniority, government participation and gender. Those were included as they are often addressed in the literature as variables that may affect our dependent variable (see, for example, André and Depauw 2014; André, Gallagher and Sandri 2014; Van Vonno et al. 2014).

Party Unity

We conceptualize party unity as the result of legislators' sequential decision-making processes. In the first stage of the process – party agreement – legislators consider whether or not they agree with their party's position. If they agree, then the result is unity based on shared preferences. If, however, legislators do not agree with the position of their party, they then proceed to the second stage – party loyalty – where they decide whether or not to subscribe to the norm of party unity and vote according to the party line, despite their disagreement. If they disagree but are loyal, the result is unity based on shared norms.

When it comes to party unity, we are interested in the second stage because we feel that party agreement is quite different from party loyalty – focusing on the first will mask much of the relevant dynamics within the party. Clearly the inner dynamics in a party where there is high party agreement are different than the dynamics in a party whose legislators lack party agreement but possess high levels of party loyalty.

We stop before a possible third stage in a legislator's decision-making model. If legislators both disagree with their party and decide not to subscribe to the norm of party unity, a third stage of the process – party discipline – includes the possible use of disciplinary measures, negative sanctions and positive incentives, by the party leadership in order to achieve party unity. We do not include this phase because, once again, the dynamics of party unity based on shared preferences or norms are very different from the dynamics in a party whose legislators lack both and require discipline.

Our conception of party unity thus moves beyond party agreement to legislators' internalized behavioral norms, that is, how legislators believe it is appropriate to behave once they find themselves in a conflict with their party. We believe this stage to be the most important because it evaluates party unity – the legislators' voluntary subscription to the norm that they should not publicly deviate from their party line, even when they disagree with it.[6]

Findings

Table 19.1 shows two models – with and without an interaction term – for the effect of the candidate selection method and the electoral system on party unity. Model 1, which does not include an interaction term between our two explaining variables, shows that both the electoral system and the candidate selection method have an independent effect on party unity. In other words, the candidate selection method has an effect on party unity even when controlling for the electoral system, and vice versa. This brings us to reject hypotheses 1 and 2, according to which only one of the variables has an influence on party unity whereas the other has a marginal effect at best. Model 1 clearly shows that MPs elected by a candidate-centered electoral system are less likely to demonstrate party unity compared to MPs elected by a party-based electoral system (odds ratio of 0.47, $p < 0.01$), and that MPs selected by more inclusive candidate selection methods – primaries being the most inclusive method – are also less likely to demonstrate party unity compared to MPs selected by exclusive methods (odds ratio of 0.9, $p < 0.05$).

Table 19.1 The Effect of Electoral Formula and Selectorate Inclusiveness on Party Loyalty

	Party Loyalty (Model 1)	Party Loyalty (Model 2)
Electoral Formula (SMD)	−0.75*** (.19)	−2.46*** (.71)
Selectorate Inclusiveness	−0.05** (.02)	−0.10*** (.03)
Electoral Formula × Selectorate Inclusiveness		0.14** (.05)
Party Agreement	−0.63*** (.18)	−0.60*** (.18)
Seniority	−0.01 (.01)	−0.01 (.01)
Government Participation	0.59*** (.18)	0.43** (.19)
Gender	0.02 (.21)	0.03 (.21)
Log Likelihood	−341.26	−337.99
Pseudo R²	0.07	0.07
N	553	553

Note: Results are presented as log of odds, robust standard errors in parentheses. *$p < .1$, **$p < .05$, ***$p < .01$.

Model 2 adds an interaction term to the analysis and examines the contingent effect of the electoral system and the candidate selection method on party unity. The fact that the interaction term is statistically significant indicates that there is indeed a meaning to the interplay between the electoral system and the candidate selection method in their effects on party unity. However, since this is an interaction model we cannot interpret these coefficients at face value. Each one of the lower-order terms (the coefficients for the electoral formula and for the inclusiveness of the selectorate) only have a substantive meaning at a specific value of the other (Brambor, Clark and Golder 2006). Therefore, in order to effectively communicate this interaction we use a conditional marginal effect plot, which visualizes the marginal effect of the electoral system at different levels of the inclusiveness of the selectorate.

Figure 19.1 presents the conditional marginal effect of changing the electoral system from a PR system to SMD on the predicted change in the probability of party unity, given different levels of the inclusiveness of the candidate selection method. The figure shows that as the selectorate becomes more inclusive, the difference between PR and SMD electoral systems in their effect on party unity becomes smaller. As was expected, the largest difference found between the two electoral systems is when the selectorate is the most exclusive. That is, under exclusive selectorates electoral systems are most influential in their effect on party unity: the predicted difference in the probability of party unity between PR and SMD systems is about 0.6. As the selectorate becomes more inclusive, the difference between the two types of electoral systems shrinks – hence the ability of the electoral system to influence party unity becomes more limited. Once the selectorate reaches a score of 14 the results become statistically insignificant and therefore we cannot say much about the differences between electoral systems in selectorate scores of 15 and up. Still, we believe this is a strong finding, especially because the vast majority of parties

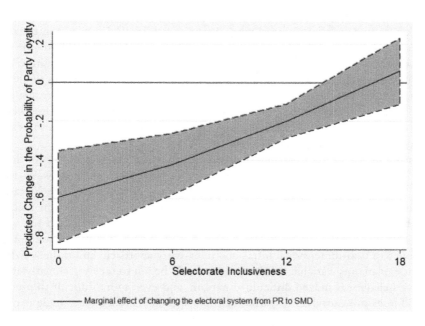

Figure 19.1 The Conditional Marginal Effect of Electoral System on Party Loyalty, at Different Levels of Selectorate Inclusiveness (with 95% CIs)

in our sample (75 percent of the cases), and in the population in general, receive a selectorate score of 0–14.

Figure 19.1 supports our third hypothesis and confirms it: the selectorate conditions the ability of the electoral system to affect party unity. In exclusive selectorates, the electoral system is able to influence party unity, with legislators elected by PR electoral systems demonstrating higher levels of party unity than those elected by SMD electoral systems. In inclusive selectorates, however, the ability of the electoral system to affect party unity is limited.

Conclusion

This research shows that when the party uses inclusive selectorates, such as primaries, then the nature of the electoral system hardly matters for party unity. Once a party democratizes its candidate selection method, making it more inclusive, it loses its control over the process. Inclusive selectorates offer legislators personally focused incentives and limit the ability of the party to control the identity of the candidates selected. It is true that here too we can portray a reinforcing incentives scenario, when an inclusive selectorate is coupled with an SMD electoral system. We can also portray a conflicting incentives scenario, when such a selectorate is coupled with a PR electoral system. We claim, however, that once the selectorate becomes inclusive these dynamics become largely irrelevant. In other words, an inclusive selectorate shapes party unity to such an extent that the electoral system cannot do much about it, whether it is a party-focused PR electoral system, or a personally based SMD one. Once legislators understand that they owe their reselection – which is a prerequisite for their reelection – to someone else other than the party and its leadership, there is no going back. That is, the dynamics of reinforcing and conflicting incentives given the nature of the candidate selection method and the electoral system are relevant, we claim, only for exclusive selectorates.

The interaction between the candidate selection method and the electoral system shows that the key to understanding internal party dynamics lies first and foremost in the nature of the candidate selection method. In other words, the identity of those who control the nomination process has a substantial influence on legislative attitudes and behavioral norms, not only directly, but also indirectly, by conditioning the ability of the electoral system to affect those attributes. The effect of the more inclusive candidate selection methods is thus greater than that of the electoral system; it overcomes and overrides that of the electoral system. In other words, inclusive candidate selection methods such as party primaries are *more* important in explaining legislative behavior than the electoral system.

Our main argument in this chapter has been that one must take into account the effects of both intra-party and inter-party competition, and the interaction between them, in order to better explain legislators' attitudes and norms of behavior. The literature has shown that electoral systems matter, and we posit that candidate selection methods do so, too. But what matters the most is the combination between them and the way they interact with one another. Our research moves us from the traditional unidimensional perspective to a two-dimensional intra- and inter-party approach, and it sheds light on an important explanatory variable that has only recently begun to receive scholarly attention. Legislative behavior is indeed difficult to explain, and even more difficult to predict, but we should not limit ourselves to partial, myopic arguments based on a single explanatory variable.

Appendix

Countries and Parties Included in the Research

Country	Electoral system	Party	Selectorate score	n (party)*
Belgium	PR	MR (Reform Movement)	9	8
		CD&V (Christian Democratic and Flemish)	11	12
		Open VLD (Open Flemish Liberals and Democrats)	9	6
		PS (Socialist Party)	11	10
		SPA (Different Socialist Party)	11	9
		VB (Flemish Interest)	6	7
France	Plurality/ majority	UMP (Union for Popular Movement)	7	21
		PS (Socialist Party)	17	21
Germany	Mixed	CDU/CSU (Christian Democratic Union of Germany/ Christian Social Union of Bavaria)	15	38
		SPD (Social Democratic Party of Germany)	15	33
		Die Linke (The Left)	15	26
		G (Green Party)	15	18
Hungary	Mixed	Fidesz (Hungarian Civic Union)	4	36
		MSZP (Hungarian Socialist Party)	14	48
Ireland	PR (STV)	Fianna Fail	11	14
		Fine Gael	17	10
		Labour	17	6
Israel	PR	Likud	18	4
		Kadima	18	11
		Labour	18	5
		Yisrael Beytenu	0	4
		Shas	0	3
The Netherlands	PR	CDA (Christian Democratic Appeal)	16	21
		PvdA (Labour Party)	9	19
		VVD (The People's Party for Freedom and Democracy)	9	11
Norway	PR	DNA (Labour party)	9	16
		FRP (Progress Party)	7	11
		Høyre (Conservative Party)	9	7
		SV (Socialist Left Party)	9	6
Spain	PR	PP (People's Party)	8	26
		PSOE (Spanish Socialist Workers' Party)	9	68
The UK	Plurality/ majority	Conservative	14	22
		Labour	14	30
		Liberal Democrats	16	7

Note: *To account for differences in the number of respondents across parties we use party weights in all analyses.

Notes

1 The PARTIREP project is a cross-national MP survey aimed at analyzing changing patterns of participation and representation in modern democracies. It includes data on elected representatives from: Austria, Belgium, France, Germany, Hungary, Ireland, Israel, Italy, Netherlands, Norway, Poland, Portugal, Spain, Switzerland, and the United Kingdom. See: http://www.partirep.eu.

2 It is important to note that the inclusiveness of the selectorate is not necessarily correlated with party size. That is, one cannot claim that large parties are the ones that tend to have more inclusive selection procedures and vice versa.

3 Despite the rich theory on the ballot structure and its effect on legislative behavior, our data shows little variation in legislative behavior according to the ballot structure. Moreover, in many instances the effect of the ballot structure on legislative behavior runs in the opposite direction than expected. However, the PARTIREP dataset does not include countries that use open ballots, such as Finland. As a result, we are left with relatively little variation on the ballot structure between countries, such as the variation between countries that have completely closed party lists (Spain, Israel) and countries that have flexible but rather closed party lists (Belgium, Norway). The limited range of ballot structures in our data might be one of the reasons for the aforementioned outcomes; as a result, we choose to focus on the electoral formula as the defining variable of the electoral system in our analysis.

4 The most comprehensive study of candidate selection methods (Hazan and Rahat 2010) elaborates four dimensions of analysis: candidacy; selectorate; decentralization; and voting/appointment. The existing literature does not show a correlation between most of these dimensions and the electoral system. For example: the selectorate might be more or less inclusive despite the fact that the general elections are based on universal suffrage. Similarly, the party might vote or nominate its candidates, while the general elections are based only on voting procedures. Candidacy might be slightly affected by the electoral system since if the election law places limitations on candidacy for public office (such as citizenship or age) then the party can only narrow its candidacy requirements even further, but not the other way around. The only dimension of candidate selection methods where we can see an effect of the electoral system on the candidate selection method is decentralization. That is, it is reasonable to assume that if the electoral system is based on districts, the party will prefer to choose its candidates on the district level as well. We therefore do not address the decentralization dimension of candidate selection in order to avoid problems of multicollinearity.

5 Defined as the extent to which co-partisans share similar policy preferences with one another when voting on legislation.

6 As previously mentioned, there is an intimate connection between party agreement and party unity. In other words, the view that dissent is a reasonable behavior is, at least partially, a function of whether the legislator happens to frequently disagree with the party position or not. Therefore, our analysis of party unity controls for party agreement in order to avoid omitted variable bias. This also allows us to assess whether the source of dissent intentions is the result of a selection effect (presented by party agreement) or the result of the incentives legislators face. Party agreement is added as a control variable to the three controls used in the model. The effect of party agreement on party unity does not diminish the effect of the incentives provided to legislators by both the electoral system and the candidate selection method for unified or disjointed behavior.

References

André, A., and S. Depauw. 2014. "District Magnitude and the Personal Vote." *Electoral Studies* 35(1): 102–114.

André, A., M. Gallagher, and G. Sandri. 2014. "Legislators' Constituency Orientation." In K. Deschouwer and S. Depauw (eds), *Representing the People: A Survey among Members of Statewide and Sub-state Parliaments.* Oxford: Oxford University Press, pp. 166–187.

Atmor, N., R.Y. Hazan, and G. Rahat. 2011. "Moving Beyond the Electoral System: The Influence of Candidate Selection on Personal and Party Representation." In J.M. Colomer (ed.), *Personal Representation: The Neglected Dimension of Electoral Systems.* Colchester: European Consortium for Political Research Press, pp. 21–36.

Best, H., and M. Cotta. 2000. "Elite Transformation and Modes of Representation since the Mid-Nineteenth Century: Some Theoretical Considerations." In H. Best and M. Cotta (eds), *Parliamentary Representatives in Europe 1848–2000: Legislative Recruitment and Careers in Eleven European Countries.* Oxford: Oxford University Press, pp. 1–28.

Blais, A. 1988. "The Classification of Electoral Systems." *European Journal of Political Research* 16(1): 99–110.

Bowler, S., and D.M. Farrell. 1993. "Legislator Shirking and Voter Monitoring: Impacts of European Parliament Electoral Systems upon Legislator-Voter Relationships." *Journal of Common Market Studies* 31(1): 45–70.

Bowler, S., D.M. Farrell, and R.S. Katz. 1999. "Party Cohesion, Party Discipline, and Parliaments." In S. Bowler, D.M. Farrell, and R.S. Katz (eds), *Party Discipline and Parliamentary Government*. Columbus: Ohio State University Press, pp. 3–22.

Bowler, S., D.M. Farrell, and R.T. Pettitt. 2005. "Expert Opinion on Electoral Systems: So Which Electoral System is 'Best'?" *Journal of Elections, Public Opinion and Parties* 15(1): 3–19.

Brambor, T., W.R. Clark, and M. Golder. 2006. "Understanding Interaction Models: Improving Empirical Analyses." *Political Analysis* 14(2): 63–82.

Cain, E.B., J.A. Ferejohn, and M.P. Fiorina. 1987. *The Personal Vote: Constituency Service and Electoral Independence*. Cambridge: Harvard University Press.

Carey, J.M. 2007. "Competing Principals, Political Institutions, and Party Unity in Legislative Voting." *American Journal of Political Science* 51(1): 92–107.

Carey, J.M. 2009. *Legislative Voting and Accountability*. Cambridge: Cambridge University Press.

Carey, J.M., and M.S. Shugart. 1995. "Incentives to Cultivate a Personal Vote: A Rank Ordering of Electoral Formulas." *Electoral Studies* 14(4): 417–439.

Cross, W. 2008. "Democratic Norms and Party Candidate Selection: Taking Contextual Factors into Account." *Party Politics* 14(5): 596–619.

Depauw, S., and S. Martin. 2009. "Legislative Party Discipline and Cohesion in Comparative Perspective." In D. Giannetti and K. Benoit (eds.), *Intra-Party Politics and Coalition Governments*. New York: Taylor and Francis, pp. 103–120.

Duverger, M. 1954. *Political Parties: Their Organization and Activity in the Modern State*. London: Methuen.

Farrell, D.M. 2011. *Electoral Systems: A Comparative Introduction*. Basingstoke: Palgrave Macmillan.

Gallagher, M., and M. Marsh. 1988. *Candidate Selection in Comparative Perspective: The Secret Garden of Politics*. London: Sage.

Hazan, R.Y., and G. Rahat. 2010. *Democracy within Parties: Candidate Selection Methods and Their Political Consequences*. Oxford: Oxford University Press.

Heidar, K.M. 2006. "Parliamentary Party Group Unity: Does the Electoral System Matter?" *Acta Politica* 41(3): 249–266.

Katz, R.S. 1986. "Intraparty Preference Voting." In Bernard Grofman and Arend Lijphart (eds.) *Electoral Laws and Their Political Consequences*. New York: Agathon Press, pp. 85–103.

Katz, R.S. 1997. *Democracy and Elections*. New York: Oxford University Press.

Katz, R.S., and L. Bardi. 1980. "Preference Voting and Turnover in Italian Parliamentary Elections." *American Journal of Political Science* 24(1): 97–114.

Katz, R.S., and W.P. Cross. 2013. "Problematizing Intra-Party Democracy." In W.P. Cross and R.S. Katz (eds.), *The Challenges of Intra-Party Democracy*. Oxford: Oxford University Press, pp. 170–176.

Lancaster, T.D. 1986. "Electoral Structure of Pork Barrel Politics." *International Political Science Review* 7(1): 67–81.

Mitchell, P. 2000. "Voters and their Representatives: Electoral Institutions and Delegation in Parliamentary Democracies." *European Journal of Political Research* 37(3): 335–351.

Narud, H.M., M.N. Pedersen, and H. Valen. 2002. *Party Sovereignty and Citizen Control: Selecting Candidates for Parliamentary Elections in Denmark, Finland, Iceland and Norway*. Odense: University Press of Southern Denmark.

Norris, P., R.K. Carty, L. Erickson, J. Lovenduski, and M. Simms. 1990. "Party Selectorates in Australia, Britain and Canada: Prolegomena for Research in the 1990s." *Journal of Commonwealth and Comparative Politics* 28(2): 219–245.

Rae, D. 1967. *The Political Consequences of Electoral Laws*. New Haven: Yale University Press.

Ranney, A. 1981. "Candidate Selection." In D.B. Howard, R. Penniman and A. Ranney (eds.), *Democracy at the Polls: A Comparative Study of Competitive National Elections*. Washington: American Enterprise Institute, pp. 75–106.

Reynolds, A., B. Reilly, and A. Ellis. 2005. *Electoral System Design: The New International IDEA Handbook*. Stockholm: International Institute for Democracy and Electoral Assistance.

Schattschneider, E.E. 1942. *Party Government*. New York: Holt, Rinehart and Winston.

Sieberer, U. 2006. "Party Unity in Parliamentary Democracies: A Comparative Analysis." *Journal of Legislative Studies* 12(2): 150–178.

Shugart, M.S. 2001. "'Extreme' Electoral Systems and the Appeal of the Mixed-Member Alternative." In M.S. Shugart and M.P. Wattenberg (eds.), *Mixed-Member Electoral Systems: The Best of Both Worlds?* Oxford: Oxford University Press, pp. 25–51.

Stratman, T., and M. Baur. 2002. "Plurality Rule, Proportional Representation and the German Bundestag: How Incentives to Pork-Barrel Differ Across Electoral Systems." *American Journal of Political Science* 46(3): 506–514.

Strøm, K. 1990. *Minority Government and Majority Rule*. Cambridge: Cambridge University Press.

Taagepera, R., and M.S. Shugart. 1989. *Seats and Votes: The Effects and Determinants of Electoral Systems*. New Haven: Yale University Press.

Van Vonno, C., R. Itzkovitch-Malka, S. Depauw, R.B. Andeweg, and R.Y. Hazan. 2014. "Agreement, Loyalty and Discipline: A Sequential Approach to Party Unity." In K. Deschouwer and S. Depauw (eds), *Representing the People: A Survey Among Members of Statewide and Substate Parliaments*. Oxford: Oxford University Press, pp. 110–136.

20

PRIMARIES AND LEGISLATIVE BEHAVIOR

Indriði H. Indriðason and Gunnar Helgi Kristinsson

Interest in more inclusive methods of nominations seems to be spreading in parliamentary systems, which traditionally have relied primarily on relatively exclusive nomination methods. Parliamentary government, as Sartori (1994, 193) put it, "implies party supported government; a support that in turn requires voting discipline along party lines." The temptation to open up the candidate nomination process appears to be spurred by voters growing increasingly skeptical and distrustful of political parties and party elites. Greater openness and broader participation is seen as ways to aid in regaining voters' confidence. But as parties in most parliamentary systems have rather little experience of such nomination methods, there is limited knowledge or understanding of how they actually work. A central concern here is the question whether inclusive nomination methods are compatible with the idea of responsible party government, i.e., do inclusive primaries create havoc within political parties and undermine responsible government or can they be made to work in an orderly fashion within the framework of disciplined party government?

The key question here is which of the many incentives that parliamentarians face are most relevant. A strong tradition in party research is concerned primarily with the electoral motives of politicians (Downs 1957; Rae 1971), who are considered to be interested in maximizing votes in order to secure election. This implies that electoral arrangements are a key ingredient in the structure of incentives affecting legislative behavior. And if electoral arrangements influence behavior, we should expect party primaries to be no exception. In the U.S. there is a longstanding interest in how the "electoral connection" affects legislative behavior (Mayhew 1974). Outside the U.S. there is also a growing interest in how electoral incentives affect such behavior. According to established models of how electoral systems shape the behavioral incentives of politicians, systems with less party control provide incentives to cultivate a personal reputation whereas greater party control may solve the collective action problem of parliamentary groups in favor of more cohesive parties (Sartori 1976; Carey and Shugart 1995). Influential accounts of the likely effects of primaries in parliamentary systems draw a rather gloomy picture of the effects of primary election on the ability of parties to act in a cohesive and responsive manner (Hazan and Rahat 2010). While these accounts are correct in noting that theoretically there is tension between the legislators' incentives and effective party control, not a lot of data exists to evaluate such claims.

Legislators may face non-electoral incentives that are equally important to them as those related to securing reelection. The empirical evidence connecting personalized electoral arrangements with loss of party cohesion is mixed, which suggests that there are more factors at work (Carroll and Nalepa 2013; Depauw and Martin 2009; Sieberer 2006). If members of parliament are not only interested in reelection but also want to influence policy or hold positions of power in the legislature or the executive, their behavior may differ significantly from what theories of electoral motives dictate. Incentives to cultivate a personal vote may, thus, be offset by concerns about how career opportunities are shaped by the opinions and expectations of co-partisans, fellow legislators, and party leaders. Building a personal vote may also be a challenge when voters pay little attention to what their representatives are up to – even highly interested voters are likely to get basic information wrong (Dancey and Sheagley 2013). Party leaders, on the other hand, are likely to observe and to care about their legislators' behavior and to be willing to use the tools at their disposal to encourage behavior that suits party purposes.

The question, then, becomes what party leaders or parliamentary groups want from their members (Kam 2009). In parliamentary systems, the cabinet as a rule controls the legislative agenda to a great extent (Döring 1995). The responsibility for policy making rests primarily with the government. Parties, therefore, place considerable emphasis on their MPs toeing the party line. While most parliaments grant individual MPs some right to initiate legislation, private member bills are rarely adopted. Proposing legislation is the most direct manner of influencing policy but it is, of course, only one manner in which MPs may do so. MPs may, for example, shape the agenda through work in parliamentary committees, by offering legislative amendments, and by shaping the agenda in various ways, such as through debates, committee work, and by effective use of question time.[1] MPs' motivations in engaging in each of these actions may, of course, have more to do with signaling their preferences or legislative effort to their party's selectorate, whether it consists of primary voters or a more narrow segment of party insiders. Thus, the manner in which MPs obtain a place on the party list may affect their legislative behavior but the precise manner in which it does so is likely to depend on how central a role the MPs consider the party to play in terms of achieving their career goals.

Below we examine the degree to which the "electoral connection" affects Icelandic MPs by comparing the legislative behavior of MPs who owe their position to the party leadership with MPs whose path to parliament involved a primary election and was, thus, dependent on the MPs building a personal vote. MPs who contest primaries might thus be expected to approach their work in the legislature with an eye toward building a personal vote, i.e., to try to advance policies that are favorable to their constituencies and, more generally, to signal their commitment to issues of importance to their constituents. We consider a variety of legislative behaviors that may serve these purposes; proposing legislation and parliamentary motions, signaling their preferences via legislative speech, and asking ministers questions to signal commitment to protecting their constituents' interests. Before considering the incentives that MPs face when it comes to their legislative behavior we set the stage by briefly discussing the use of primaries in Iceland and how they are conducted.

Primaries in Iceland

To evaluate the effects of primaries on legislative behavior, variation in both the independent and dependent variables is required. That is, parties must use different forms of nomination methods – that include primary elections – and the rules of parliamentary procedure must be sufficiently lax in order to provide parliamentarians with meaningful opportunities to respond strategically to the incentives that they face. Iceland satisfies both conditions. All the major parties in Iceland have experimented with primaries at one point or another since the early 1970s while none of them has consistently implemented primaries across all the constituencies. Thus, variation in the use of primaries exists both across and within parties. At the same time Alþingi's parliamentary procedures are unusually permissive, e.g., when it comes to offering private member bills and individual parliamentarians having a relatively generous access to the parliamentary agenda.

The Icelandic party system can be described as consisting of four "core" parties. While other parties have contested elections throughout, they have typically been smaller and have played a more marginal role, e.g., when it comes to the formation of government coalitions. The four "core" parties are the ones that have made the most extensive use of party primaries and are, thus, the focus of our analysis here. The Independence Party (IP), a conservative party, has been the largest party for the bulk of the period since Iceland became independent. The Progressive Party (PP) is a center-right party that was originally a farmer's party and, as such, has been particularly successful in the rural constituencies. While the party is typically seen as being closer to the center than the Independence Party on economic issues it is probably more conservative on social issues. On the left there are the Social Democratic Alliance (SDA) and the Left Green Movement (LGM) that can be seen as the descendants of the Social Democratic Party (SDP) and the People's Alliance (PA). The SPD, which merged with smaller parties on the left and the less left-leaning wing of the PA to form the SDA, was a fairly typical social democratic party and the same can be said of the SDA. The PA was a socialist party whose left-wing went on to form the LGM that combined socialist ideology with an emphasis on Green issues.

None of the parties has ever been large enough to form a single party majority government and, thus, the norm has been to form majority coalitions. Government coalitions are typically minimum winning coalitions and minority coalitions are unusual. The composition of government coalitions in Iceland have been structured less along ideological lines than is common in most parliamentary systems – although in more recent times governments have been easier to classify as governments of the left or governments of the right. The IP has been able to leverage its position as (usually) the biggest party to form government coalitions. The PP, however, has also been very successful in joining government coalitions. This is in part because it has often been the median party in the legislature but the PP has also been seen to adopt a more pragmatic, or less ideological, approach to coalition formation.

The primaries originally developed in response to public criticism of too much power being concentrated in the hands of party elites. The parties that initiated the use of primaries, in particular the Independence Party (IP) and Social Democrats (SD), presented them as a democratic alternative to centralized party control and an opportunity for under-represented groups, such as women and young people, to obtain greater political representation. The 1959 electoral reform had also created problems for the parties with large multi-member constituencies replacing a hybrid system of single-, double-, and multi-member constituencies. The system was seen as insulating incumbent MPs from effective competition, combining a high degree of electoral stability with practically no scope for preferential voting. Moreover, competition between different localities within the enlarged constituencies presented problems that threatened party unity within the constituency organizations.

Primary elections are a relatively simple affair where general elections are conducted via majoritarian methods, i.e., in those instances primaries essentially involves selecting a single candidate and there are a number of well-established electoral systems that can be used for that purpose, e.g., plurality rule, alternative vote, or majority run-off elections. Primary elections are, however, uncommon in proportional representation systems where the aim is not just to select a single candidate but a ranked list of candidates. It is, of course, possible to employ simple systems such as plurality rule for the purpose of establishing a party list but doing so has fairly obvious shortcomings. While more sophisticated systems, such as the single-transferable vote (STV), appear well suited for the purpose of establishing a party list, the Icelandic parties

Table 20.1 Seat Allocation under Rank Ordered Plurality Voting, 2013 Independence Party Primary in Northeast District

Votes											
Candidate	*1*	*2*	*1+2*	*3*	*1+2+3*	*4*	*1+ . . . +4*	*5*	*1+ . . . +5*	*6*	*1+ . . . +6*
Kristján Júlíusson	**2223**	151	2374	46	2420	28	2448	23	2471	37	2508
Valgerður Gunnarsdóttir	29	1262	**1291**	324	1615	223	1838	258	2096	206	2302
Ásta Sigurjónsdóttir	11	236	247	911	**1158**	446	1604	307	1911	304	2215
Jens Helgason	16	105	121	261	382	896	**1278**	337	1615	338	1953
Erla S. Ragnarsdóttir	18	357	375	430	805	354	1159	370	**1529**	396	1925
Bergur Benjamínsson	8	82	90	186	276	256	532	778	1310	442	**1752**

Note: Another three candidates that contested the primary are not shown in the figure

nevertheless converged on a unique electoral system that we have termed *rank ordered plurality voting* (Indriðason and Kristinsson 2015).

Ranked ordered plurality voting requires voters, much like STV, to rank the candidates but instead of each voter having a single vote, the ranked ordered plurality voting essentially gives each voter as many votes as there are seats to fill. The first seat on the party list is allocated to the candidate that is ranked first by the most voters (and, unlike STV, there is not quota that needs to be filled). The second seat is allocated to the candidate that was ranked first or second by a plurality of voters – thus, even if your first ranked candidate won the first seat, your vote still counts for your second ranked candidate. This procedure continues until all the seats on the party list have been filled. In the example in Table 20.1, Kristján Júlíusson wins the first seat as he was ranked first by a plurality of the primary voters while Valgerður Gunnarsdóttir gets the second seat with the highest number of votes (1291) for the first (29) and the second seat (1262). The system is quite majoritarian – if a faction constituting a bare majority coordinates its ranking of the candidates then the faction is guaranteed to have total control over the composition of the party list.[2] For our purposes, however, the most important aspect of the primary is simply the fact that voters cast votes for individual candidates. Thus, the success of individual candidates rests on their personal vote, whether through inducing voters to place them higher in the ranking or in terms of mobilizing potential primary participants.

The constituency party organizations typically decide whether to hold a primary or to employ a more restrictive form of candidate nomination – although in some instances the central party organization has presented the constituency organizations with a menu of options to choose from. In addition to choosing whether to hold a primary, the constituency organizations choose whether to hold an open or a closed primary. Thus, there is potentially a lot of variance in terms of the nomination methods employed by each party while in practice it tends to be that the constituency organization that decides to hold a primary adopts similar rules for conducting the primaries.

Primaries and Parliamentary Systems

The study of primary elections, until very recently, has to a large extent been focused on the United States. It is, however, not clear that theories of primary elections in the United States travel easily to other contexts. For one thing, the United States is a presidential system that is characterized by relatively weak and decentralized parties. Parliamentary executives – unlike presidential executives – rely on the confidence of parliament to stay in office. While the "fused power" arrangement that characterizes parliamentary systems may suggest that the legislative branch dominates the executive branch, in reality the opposite appears to be true. That is, strong parties are conducive to maintaining control of the government and, in effect, the vote of confidence encourages parliamentary cohesion (Diermeier and Feddersen 1998). It is, therefore, not clear that personal vote-seeking incentives take the same precedent in parliamentary systems as they do in presidential systems – even in circumstances when winning a seat in parliament depends on the MPs having a personal base of support as it does, for example, in plurality systems, open-list proportional representation systems, or where primary elections are held. While being elected to parliament is clearly important for MPs, the value of a seat in parliament also depends on garnering favor with party leaders who act as gatekeepers to positions of power within the legislature and in the executive. Importantly, the strategies for achieving each of those objectives are not necessarily the same and MPs, thus, face a difficult trade-off. Enhancing one's personal vote, in general, requires the MP to distinguish herself from her party and her co-partisans – doing so is, however, unlikely to endear the MP to party leaders.

To some degree MPs, thus, face a choice between pleasing voters and pleasing party leaders. Below we consider how those choices lead to different expectations about the legislative behavior of MPs. We develop expectations about MPs' legislative behavior under the assumption that electoral incentives dominate and then contrast those with the situation in which MPs are primarily concerned with the fact that the parties hold the keys to positions of power within the legislature and the executive. We then turn to data on legislative activity to examine whether MPs are influenced more by the electoral incentives created by the nomination method or party control.

The incentives to build a personal vote have been shown to depend on factors such as whether the electoral system is an open- or closed-list system, district magnitude, the centralization and inclusiveness of nomination procedures, electoral vulnerability, and the activity of co-partisans (who increase the competition for personal attention). The electoral process in Iceland involves two stages, where the first stage involves the nominations (including primaries) of candidates and the second stage is the parliamentary election. Each of these stages can potentially provide incentives for MPs to build a personal vote. However, as the second stage offers little incentives for personalization, with the general election system being a closed-list proportional representation system, our main focus is on the nomination stage.[3]

Ballot Structure

Following Carey and Shugart's (1995) argument concerning the effects of the ballot structure,[4] the importance of personal reputations ought to be greater where parties hold primary elections. By holding a primary, party leaders hand control over ballot access to the primary voters. There is no vote pooling in the Icelandic primaries since the choice of candidates is conducted ahead of the parliamentary election. The chances for an individual primary candidate to win a seat in parliament are never improved by another candidate receiving more votes.[5] The rank ordered plurality system provides voters with the opportunity to reveal their preferences among different candidates in a relatively detailed manner and places the candidates in a direct competition with one another. Thus, if electoral incentives dominate, we should expect the use of party primaries to increase the incentives to cultivate a personal reputation compared with other methods of candidate selection.

In the party-centered view, however, the incentives to build a personal vote may be offset by the expectations and demands of party leaders. Importantly, those expectations depend on whether the party is in government or in opposition. A government backbencher is unlikely to be encouraged to be active in parliament. Instead, she will be tasked with advancing her party's agenda in the committees and in forum. Parliaments under strong party control, in fact, are likely to restrict the rights of backbenchers to speechmaking or to initiate bills. If government backbenchers want to influence policy or advance their careers they are likely to work through their parties or ministers. Opposition parties, by contrast, have no qualms about undermining government control of the agenda and have little incentive to restrict the legislative activity of their members. They may even encourage their MPs to air popular demands that might pose problems for the government. Moreover, leading members of the opposition can be expected to take a leading role in criticizing the government and actively initiate private member bills, ask questions, and make speeches. In sum, irrespective of the type of nominations method, therefore, more legislative activity is expected from members of the opposition and, in particular, opposition leaders, than government MPs.

District Magnitude and Urban–Rural Differences

Larger district magnitude (that is, a larger number of legislative seats per district) is generally expected to increase the sensitivity of parliamentarians to special interests (Cox 1990; Fujimura 2015). The logic seems to be that with large district magnitude individual candidates may do well by appealing to special interests of various kinds while with smaller magnitude they are more likely to represent a broad cross-section of the community. The opposite conclusion was reached by Lancaster (1986), who maintained that the tendency to boost a personal reputation, e.g. through pork barrel politics, is greater in small districts than in large ones. Several authors, however, envisage a more complicated relationship, in that the impact of district magnitude may be related to features of the ballot structure. Thus, Carey and Shugart (1995) suggest that district magnitude has an impact only where there is no intra-party competition (in closed-list systems the significance of personal reputations grows smaller as the number of candidates on the list grows). Under other allocation formulas on the other hand (i.e., where co-partisans compete for seats), the importance of personal reputation increases with greater district magnitude. This is, at least partly, consistent with Solvak and Pajala's (2015) findings that parliamentary activity under closed-list rules declined as district magnitude became greater.

Primaries are likely to have a similar effect on parliamentary behavior as open-list systems and hence we should expect the importance of a personal reputation to be greater the larger the constituency. On the other hand, the importance of the pork barrel may be greater in smaller constituencies. In Iceland, constituency service in various forms is in greater demand in the smaller rural constituencies than the larger urban ones. If MPs are sensitive to electoral incentives, we should expect the rural ones to be more active than their urban counterparts.

According to the party-centered approach, on the other hand, we should not expect district magnitude to make a great deal of difference. The most effective method of winning approval from the party leadership when in government – irrespective of district magnitude – should be the ability to do valuable work in committees which are unrelated to constituency pork barrel.

Vulnerability

Members of parliament who are insecure with regard to reelection are more likely to cultivate a personal following (Bowler 2010; Herron 2002; Louwerse and Otjes 2016; Bauman 2016; Williams and Indriðason, forthcoming). While much of the literature demonstrating an emphasis on constituency service and other ways of building a personal vote has focused on vote margins in single-member districts, similar logic applies to MPs elected from party lists (Crisp et al. 2013). Members in marginal seats, i.e., those who were among the last ones in off the party list, have an interest in securing a seat higher on the party list in order to insure themselves against fluctuations in their party's electoral performance. MPs who owe their list position to primary voters may, thus, have an incentive to raise their profile with their constituents and one possible way of doing so is by being active in the legislature. While the average primary voter may not pay a great deal of attention to what goes on in the legislature, making speeches, asking questions, and offering private members bills are all ways of documenting the MP's effort that the MP can highlight during her primary campaign. Thus, if electoral incentives are the driver behind MPs' actions, we ought to see greater legislative activity among electorally vulnerable MPs.

However, if members value advancement and influence over reelection, then the electoral connection should be less influential. If MPs see their career advancement as largely being under control of the party, government backbenchers should show low levels of legislative activity and should leave control of the floor to more senior members of their parties. Similarly, leading members of the opposition parties are expected to be in the front line with regard to both legislative initiatives and speech making while more junior backbenchers should be less active so as not to overshadow the leadership although they are expected to be more active than government MPs.

Primary Elections and Legislative Behavior in Iceland

Overall, the two perspectives, emphasizing electoral incentives on the one hand and party control on the other, have quite different implications for the legislative behavior of MPs. The electoral incentives perspective implies that MPs ought to be willing to break away from the party line if they perceive it to be important for their chances of reelection. In the Icelandic context, that means securing a favorable spot on the party list, which requires MPs to build a personal support base where primaries are conducted. Thus, primaries have often been associated with greater independence of legislators from their parties that ought to be reflected in legislative behaviors but also in greater willingness of MPs to vote against the party line in parliament and, more generally, with the weakening of parties.

Whether the primaries constituted a threat to party cohesion at the time they were introduced in the early 1970s is difficult to establish. Roll-call analysis of final votes on bills in Alþingi shows a steady decline in party cohesion during the 1960s, prior to the introduction of the primaries (Kristinsson 2011). The decline continued until the 1980s in the parties which greeted new methods of nominations most warmly (i.e., the IP and the SDP). Indeed, the primaries may have played a role in splits which occurred in both parties during the 1980s, leaving the party leadership with a weak hand in dealing with discontent. During the 1980s, however, two innovations of party management appear to have strengthened cohesion within the parliamentary groups. On the one hand the parties changed the electoral formula in the primaries from *limited voting* (voters vote for a limited number of candidates without ranking them) to one of *rank ordered plurality* (voters rank a fixed number of candidates). While limited voting could produce unpredictable results, the new formula introduced a majoritarian element into the system which may have reduced the likely payoffs from cultivating a personal following. At around the same time (although further research is needed on this) the party leaders appear to have begun using positions at their disposal such as ministerial posts and committee chairs in a more strategic manner. As a result, party cohesion increased. Party cohesion for the Independence Party is shown in Figure 20.1. On the whole, party cohesion in Iceland, despite decentralized and inclusive nomination methods, is comparable to that of the other Nordic countries (Depauw and Martin 2009).

Figure 20.1 Party Cohesion in the Independence Party 1961–2010

Note: adapted from Kristinsson (2011). The figures for 1981–1987 are based on roll-call votes while the period 1991–2010 is based on final votes on bills where disagreement occurred. Data for 1988–1990 are not available. The measure of cohesion is an adapted version of the Rice index taking abstentions into account and projected onto a scale of 0–1.

There are, thus, some suggestions that the adoption of primaries coincided with – or at least did not impede – a decline in party cohesion in Alþingi but that, if present, those effects were temporary as the parties adapted to the changes in the incentives facing MPs.[6] However, the data on party cohesion is at best suggestive as it does not take account of the fact that not all of the parties have used primaries to the same extent and they vary in the degree to which the primaries are open. Thus, in some cases the primaries are open to party members only, in others they are open to members and voters willing to declare support for the party, and in still others they are open to all voters in the constituency. Decentralization of the nomination process within the parties means that there is variation in the method used by the same party across constituencies. Tables 20.2 and 20.3 provide a summary of the nomination processes employed in each electoral district by the main parties ahead of the 1991–2013 elections. The nomination processes have been coded into five categories. "Nomination Committee" means that the local party organization decides or establishes a committee to draw up a list. An "extended committee" refers to processes where it is the local district council with the addition of a select number of additional members who put the party list together. Closed primaries

Table 20.2 Nomination Process by Party

	SDP	PP	IP	PA	SDA	LG	Total
Nomination Committee	11	12	19	8	4	18	72
Extended Committee	0	22	0	0	0	0	22
Closed Primary	0	3	2	8	9	14	36
Semi-open Primary	0	11	24	0	14	0	49
Open Primary	5	0	3	0	5	0	13
Total	16	48	48	16	32	32	192

Table 20.3 Nomination Process by Year

	1991	*1995*	*1999*	*2003*	*2007*	*2009*	*2013*	*Total*
Nomination Committee	14	13	17	12	5	1	10	72
Extended Committee	4	5	3	4	1	2	3	22
Closed Primary	5	4	1	1	4	13	8	36
Semi-open Primary	5	8	6	7	13	7	3	49
Open Primary	4	2	5	0	1	1	0	13
Total	32	32	32	24	24	24	24	192

are restricted to party members, while anyone can vote in an open primary. Semi-open primaries are those where party membership is not required but there is some other requirement for voting in the primary – typically this simply means declaring support for the party. In the period we consider, about half of the party lists were established using a form of primary election. While the use of nomination methods has varied over time there are no clear discernible trends in their use.

In order to test the effects of primaries on parliamentary behavior parliamentary procedure must be sufficiently lax to permit individual parliamentarians to follow their preferences. This is not always the case. Many parliamentary systems have considerable restrictions on the rights of parliamentarians to initiate bills and parliamentary resolutions, question ministers, or make speeches (Döring 1995). In the Icelandic case, with 63 members in the Alþingi, there are very few restrictions of this kind. The right of individual members to initiate bills and resolutions is guaranteed by the constitution (article 38) and the law on parliamentary procedure gives them almost unlimited and equal rights to pose questions to ministers. Speaking time is generously allocated with ministers, committee chairs and initiators of bills and resolutions receiving rather more time than others, but every backbencher has the right, for example, to speak for a total of twenty minutes on a bill's first debate, a total of 30 minutes in their first speech on the second debate and 5 minutes each time after that, and a total of 20 minutes on the third debate (Article 95, Lög um þingsköp Alþingis nr. 55/1991). Different rules apply, however, concerning the opening debate of each session and meetings that are broadcasted where speaking time is divided between parties and the parties select their representatives. Tables 20.4 and 20.5 show these patterns.

Table 20.4 Number of Bills and Parliamentary Motions

Term	*Bills*			*Motions*		
	Ministers	*Government MPs*	*Opposition MPs*	*Ministers*	*Government MPs*	*Opposition MPs*
1991	498	64	110	65	98	128
1995	513	81	88	57	134	66
1999	534	54	199	102	120	210
2003	462	87	185	81	82	248
2007	213	44	76	26	57	74
2009	513	77	180	121	110	234
2013	301	69	72	79	91	125

Table 20.5 Average Number of Questions, Speeches, and Speech Time

Term	No. Questions		No. Speeches			Speaking Minutes		
	Gov't MPs	Opposition MPs	Ministers	Gov't MPs	Opposition MPs	Ministers	Gov't MPs	Opposition MPs
1991	1.6	4.7	150.2	67.1	150.5	575	183	818
1995	1.7	7.8	127.1	67.9	179.8	395	176	894
1999	2.2	10.0	116.6	90.6	170.6	314	191	656
2003	1.7	11.7	130.8	108.2	157.7	326	235	652
2007	1.1	12.3	130.9	103.6	226.6	364	259	818
2009	1.7	10.3	181.2	146.9	293.1	437	275	820
2013	2.6	13.2	181.1	120.5	406.4	407	231	1034

Data and Methods

We examine data on the parliamentary activity of legislators between 1991 and 2016. We focus on the four main parties during this period, which all have made use of primaries to establish their party lists, although their use has varied over time and across districts for each of the parties. The parties are the Progressive Party and the Independence Party, which successfully contested elections throughout the period, along with the Social Democratic Party and the People's Alliance until an attempt at a consolidation of the left led to the formation of the Social Democratic Alliance and the Left Green Movement in 1999.[7] Our sample consists of all members of parliament elected off the party lists in each election from 1991 to 2013. We restrict our analysis to MPs who sat for a full session, as our unit of observation is the legislative activity during each session. Thus, we exclude MPs that only sat for a part of a session as well as temporary and permanent replacement MPs. The electoral term is four years and typically consists of four full sessions in addition to a short (typically, summer) session following parliamentary elections. We exclude the summer sessions from our analysis as they are usually very short and are usually not focused on "regular" parliamentary business. During the period under consideration, changes in government coincided with regular elections with the exception of a new government forming during the 136th session of parliament (2008–2009).[8] As ministerships and government membership are among our independent variables, we exclude the 136th session from the analysis. Finally, we exclude from our analysis MPs who changed party affiliation during a session.

Our dependent variables aim to capture various forms of legislative activity. First, we consider the number of legislative bills and, second, the number of parliamentary motions sponsored by the MP during the legislative session. Most legislation and motions are co-sponsored but we only count legislations and motion where the MP was the "primary" proposer.[9] Third, we count the number of speeches given by the MP during a session as well as the total duration of the speeches given by the MP during the session. Fifth, we count the number of questions the MP asked ministers.

Our key independent variable is whether the MP earned his or her seat on the party list via a primary. The variable *Primary* is coded 1 if the MP's party list was put together using a primary and 0 if otherwise. We argued that the MP's place on the party list was likely to affect her legislative activity. The variable *Seat* is simply the MP's seat on the party list. As the MP's incentives to be active in the legislature may be influenced both by his electoral safety and the need to contest a primary, we also include an interaction between *Primary* and *Seat*. MPs are liable to behave differently with an election on the horizon and the variable *Last Session* is an indicator variable taking the value 1 in the fourth session of the electoral term and 0 if otherwise. Rural district is an indicator variable coded 1 for rural district and 0 if otherwise. The Reykjavík districts, the Southwest district, and the Reykjanes district prior to the last change to district boundaries, are considered urban districts with the rest being considered rural. To account for variation in the length of the sessions we control for *Meeting Days*, i.e., the number of days in which business took place on the floor of parliament during the session. Finally, as ministers and government ministers are likely to face different incentives, the variables *Gov't MP* and *Minister* are indicator variables coded 1 when the MP matches the variable's label.

While controlling for government MPs and ministers may capture some of the differences across MPs of different stripes and stature, it is also possible that the relationship between our dependent variables and our key independent variables depends on whether the MP is a member of the opposition or the government – or is a minister. Thus, for each of our dependent variables we also estimate our models on subsamples of (i) opposition MPs and (ii) government MPs.

As four of our dependent variables are counts of the particular types of legislative activity, i.e., the number of legislative bills, parliamentary motions, speeches and questions, we use count models. To account for the possibility of over- or under-dispersion in the dependent variable, we estimate negative binomial models. When estimating models for the total length of speeches given in the legislature, we use ordinary least squares regression models. In each case we allow the standard errors to be clustered within each party in each district in each election year in order to account for the possibility that the legislative effort of an MP may be correlated with the effort exerted by other MPs. That is, districts may differ in terms of the competitiveness of the selection process (whether a primary or not), for example, leading MPs in highly competitive districts to exert greater effort than in a district exhibiting average levels of competitiveness.

The results are shown in Tables 20.6–20.10. Considering first the number of bills presented by each MP, we find that the method of nomination has a limited effect – at least when considering all MPs together. Primaries do, however, appear to affect the incentives of some opposition MPs. The behavior of opposition MPs elected first on their party list in their district are not affected by the method by which they were nominated but opposition MPs that occupied seats lower on their party list were more likely to present private member bills. The effect is fairly moderate; opposition MPs that didn't head the party list in the district are estimated to propose 2.28 to 3.32 more bills over the four-year legislative term. It is important to emphasize that the variable *Seat* is the MP's position on the party list and not a direct measure of electoral vulnerability. That is, while a party list position is related to electoral vulnerability, there is a big difference between being the first seated MP in a district where the MP is her party's only MP and a district where she is one of the party's five MPs. In some sense, then, *Seat* captures the MP's position within her party rather than vulnerability. In order to examine the effect of electoral vulnerability, we also estimated the models where *Seat* was replaced with a measure of electoral vulnerability. While the results are substantively similar, they are not statistical significant. Thus, it appears that the incentive to propose legislation is more closely linked to the MP's standing within the party than her electoral vulnerability.

Overall, government MPs are less likely to propose legislation, which is in line with the perspective emphasizing the party as a gatekeeper to positions of power and influence. While the coefficient of the interaction between *Primary* and *Seat* is positive and marginally significant, the marginal effect of *Primary* never reaches conventional levels of statistical significance. MPs in rural districts are similarly less likely to propose legislation, despite the fact that MPs in rural districts are generally expected to place greater emphasis on constituency service and pork barrel politics. This suggests that rural MPs focus their energy elsewhere, which is perhaps not surprising given the low probability of members' bills being adopted. The delivery of particularistic policies relies on influencing legislation and, in order to do so, MPs are likely to direct their efforts toward lobbying their party leadership or seeking influence through the legislative committees. Another indicator of whether electoral motives drive parliamentary behavior is the timing of bill introduction. There is little evidence of an increase in bill introduction among opposition MPs during the last session of the legislative term – instead there is a statistically significant decline in the number of bills introduced that suggests, perhaps, that opposition members shift their attention to other activities that they consider more important in electoral terms. The opposite is, however, true of government MPs who are more likely to introduce bills in the last session.[10] One possible explanation of this is that opposition MPs are generally not constrained by their parties throughout the legislative term while government MPs, on the other hand, are, but that those constraints may loosen or become less effective when an election is on the horizon, i.e., maintaining party discipline may become more difficult when there is uncertainty about how long the government will remain in office and, importantly, MPs face uncertainty about their future.[11]

Table 20.6 Number of Bills

	All		Opposition MPs		Government MPs	
	(1)	*(2)*	*(3)*	*(4)*	*(5)*	*(6)*
Primary	0.074	−0.013	0.13	−0.35	−0.027	−0.40
	(0.345)	(0.918)	(0.457)	(0.217)	(0.901)	(0.140)
Seat	0.0047	−0.027	−0.24**	−0.56***	0.042	−0.045
	(0.944)	(0.711)	(0.026)	(0.000)	(0.359)	(0.498)
Primary*Seat		0.048		0.37**		0.13*
		(0.358)		(0.032)		(0.072)
Last Session	−0.054	−0.057	−0.44***	−0.44***	0.31***	0.28**
	(0.300)	(0.299)	(0.000)	(0.000)	(0.001)	(0.039)
Rural Distr.	−0.15***	−0.14***	−0.19	−0.17	−0.42***	−0.43***
	(0.001)	(0.001)	(0.136)	(0.188)	(0.009)	(0.004)
Meeting Days	0.00050	0.00049	−0.010**	−0.0095**	0.0088**	0.0082*
	(0.758)	(0.772)	(0.019)	(0.023)	(0.025)	(0.061)
Govt. MP	−0.89***	−0.89***				
	(<.001)	(<.001)				
Minister	2.72***	2.72***				
	(<.001)	(<.001)				
Constant	0.62**	0.67***	2.15***	2.50***	−1.14**	−0.84
	(0.019)	(0.007)	(<.001)	(<.001)	(0.036)	(0.134)
$\ln(\alpha)$	−0.42***	−0.42***	−0.26**	−0.28**	0.28***	0.26**
	(<.001)	(<.001)	(0.025)	(0.018)	(0.010)	(0.027)
Observations	1231	1231	442	442	548	548
Log Likelihood	−2323.0	−2322.6	−814.1	−812.4	−660.5	−659.1

p-values in parentheses. *$p < 0.10$, **$p < 0.05$, ***$p < 0.01$.

Note: The results with regard to parliamentary motions are fairly similar in substantive terms to the ones for legislative proposals. That is, being nominated through a primary does appear to encourage opposition MPs that didn't occupy the top position to propose more parliamentary motions although the results here fail to reach conventional levels of statistical significance. Government MPs are less likely to propose parliamentary motions as before but none of the other variables are statistically significant although the direction of the estimated effects is generally consistent with the previous results.

Table 20.7 Number of Motions

	All		Opposition MPs		Government MPs	
	(1)	(2)	(3)	(4)	(5)	(6)
Primary	−0.15	−0.25	−0.065	−0.51*	−0.092	−0.14
	(0.3)	(0.3)	(0.8)	(0.06)	(0.3)	(0.5)
Seat	−0.098	−0.13	−0.32***	−0.61***	−0.0039	−0.014
	(0.2)	(0.3)	(<.001)	(0)	(1.0)	(0.8)
Primary*Seat		0.050		0.33***		0.017
		(0.6)		(<.001)		(0.8)
Last Session	0.071	0.073	−0.0083	0.0027	0.0032	0.001
	(0.6)	(0.5)	(0.9)	(1.0)	(1.0)	(1.0)
Rural Distr.	−0.11	−0.11	−0.023	−0.016	−0.096	−0.095
	(0.4)	(0.4)	(0.9)	(1.0)	(0.7)	(0.7)
Meeting Days	0.0034	0.0035	−0.0012	−0.0007	0.0018	0.0018
	(0.5)	(0.5)	(0.8)	(0.9)	(0.7)	(0.7)
Govt. MP	−0.59***	−0.59***				
	(<.001)	(<.001)				
Minister	0.44**	0.43**				
	(0.04)	(0.04)				
Constant	0.77	0.83	1.53**	1.83***	0.055	0.090
	(0.2)	(0.2)	(0.01)	(0.002)	(0.9)	(0.9)
ln(α)	0.35**	0.35**	−0.27	−0.28	0.18	0.18
	(0.04)	(0.04)	(0.5)	(0.4)	(0.2)	(0.2)
Observations	1231	1231	442	442	548	548
Log Likelihood	−2159.3	−2158.9	−880.7	−879.1	−810.9	−810.8

Note: p-values in parentheses. $^*p < 0.10$, $^{**}p < 0.05$, $^{***}p < 0.01$.

Table 20.8 Number of Speeches

	All		Opposition MPs		Government MPs	
	(1)	(2)	(3)	(4)	(5)	(6)
Primary	0.0047	0.063	0.047	−0.022	−0.063	−0.079
	(0.932)	(0.656)	(0.753)	(0.879)	(0.554)	(0.742)
Seat	−0.096***	−0.080*	−0.21***	−0.25***	−0.098***	−0.10**
	(<.001)	(0.079)	(<.001)	(<.001)	(<.001)	(0.020)
Primary*Seat		−0.028		0.049		0.0060
		(0.665)		(0.106)		(0.945)
Last Session	−0.11**	−0.11***	−0.043	−0.040	−0.20**	−0.20***
	(0.011)	(0.003)	(0.697)	(0.712)	(0.025)	(0.009)
Rural Distr.	−0.18***	−0.18***	−0.14	−0.13	−0.34***	−0.34***
	(0.000)	(0.000)	(0.130)	(0.128)	(0.002)	(0.002)
Meeting Days	0.0086***	0.0086***	0.013***	0.013***	0.0047**	0.0047***
	(<.001)	(<.001)	(<.001)	(<.001)	(0.019)	(0.007)
Govt. MP	−0.68***	−0.68***				
	(<.001)	(<.001)				
Minister	0.25***	0.25***				
	(<.001)	(<.001)				

(continued)

Table 20.8 (continued)

	All		Opposition MPs		Government MPs	
	(1)	(2)	(3)	(4)	(5)	(6)
Constant	4.74***	4.71***	4.37***	4.42***	4.60***	4.61***
	(<.001)	(<.001)	(<.001)	(<.001)	(<.001)	(<.001)
ln(α)	−0.97***	−0.97***	−1.04***	−1.04***	−0.75***	−0.75***
	(<.001)	(<.001)	(<.001)	(<.001)	(<.001)	(<.001)
Observations	1224	1224	439	439	544	544
Log Likelihood	−7010.2	−7009.5	−2684.4	−2684.3	−2958.4	−2958.4

Note: p-values in parentheses. *$p < 0.10$, **$p < 0.05$, ***$p < 0.01$.

Table 20.9 Speeches in Minutes

	All		Opposition MPs		Government MPs	
	(1)	(2)	(3)	(4)	(5)	(6)
Primary	−54.8	−57.0	−161.6	−444.4**	−7.23	5.30
	(0.34)	(0.58)	(0.23)	(0.045)	(0.61)	(0.86)
Seat	−34.7*	−35.4	−147.0**	−318.6*	−9.28	−6.58
	(0.088)	(0.23)	(0.039)	(0.056)	(0.11)	(0.38)
Primary*Seat		1.09		199.8		−4.61
		(0.97)		(0.13)		(0.65)
Last Session	−25.3**	−25.3**	−35.9	−30.0	−34.6	−33.9
	(0.017)	(0.018)	(0.60)	(0.65)	(0.17)	(0.17)
Rural Distr.	−42.8***	−42.7***	−58.4	−43.6	−52.5*	−53.1*
	(0.0071)	(0.0080)	(0.35)	(0.49)	(0.063)	(0.065)
Meeting Days	3.54***	3.54***	6.93***	7.28***	0.92	0.94
	(<.001)	(<.001)	(0.003)	(0.0019)	(0.17)	(0.16)
Govt. MP	−521.2***	−521.2***				
	(0.00058)	(0.00058)				
Minister	121.3***	121.3***				
	(0.0024)	(0.0025)				
Constant	525.3***	526.6***	448.0*	634.3*	181.9**	173.1**
	(<.001)	(<.001)	(0.090)	(0.057)	(0.021)	(0.034)
Observations	1224	1224	439	439	544	544
R^2	0.43	0.43	0.20	0.22	0.085	0.086

Note: p-values in parentheses. *$p < 0.10$, **$p < 0.05$, ***$p < 0.01$.

Table 20.10 Number of Questions

	All		Opposition MPs		Government MPs	
	(1)	(2)	(3)	(4)	(5)	(6)
Primary	−0.079	0.27*	0.26***	0.29	−0.25**	−0.035
	(0.46)	(0.067)	(0.005)	(0.22)	(0.021)	(0.87)
Seat	0.054	0.15***	−0.20***	−0.18	0.12***	0.16***

	(0.20)	(<.01)	(<.01)	(0.26)	(0.003)	(<.01)
Primary*Seat		−0.15**		−0.022		−0.079
		(0.014)		(0.89)		(0.24)
Last Session	−0.16*	−0.15**	−0.49***	−0.49***	0.084	0.095
	(0.081)	(0.036)	(<.01)	(<.01)	(0.61)	(0.50)
Rural Distr.	−0.076	−0.093	−0.17*	−0.17*	0.049	0.033
	(0.51)	(0.43)	(0.070)	(0.065)	(0.79)	(0.86)
Meeting Days	0.0033*	0.0028**	−0.0033	−0.0033	0.0055	0.0056
	(0.099)	(0.042)	(0.23)	(0.21)	(0.17)	(0.12)
Govt. MP	−1.40***	−1.39***				
	(<.01)	(<.01)				
Constant	1.99***	1.83***	2.95***	2.93***	0.16	0.037
	(<.01)	(<.01)	(<.01)	(<.01)	(0.74)	(0.94)
ln(α)	0.32***	0.30***	0.039	0.039	0.57***	0.57***
	(<.01)	(<.01)	(0.56)	(0.57)	(<.01)	(<.01)
Observations	983	983	439	439	544	544
Log Likelihood	−2611.3	−2606.6	−1452.5	−1452.5	−1134.4	−1133.7

Note: p-values in parentheses. *$p < 0.10$, **$p < 0.05$, ***$p < 0.01$.

Turning to the speeches made by MPs (Tables 20.8 and 20.9), there is limited evidence for the nomination method mattering in terms of how often MPs make speeches on the floor or for how long they speak. There is a slight suggestion that opposition MPs nominated through primaries give more speeches and that this effect is stronger for MPs lower on the party list but the effect falls short of being statistically significant. With regard to the length of the speeches, MPs that lead their party list spent about six hours less time giving speeches if they were nominated through a primary – for other MPs the effect was not statistically significant (and positive if they were below the second place on the party list).

The lower the MP was on the party list, the fewer speeches she gave and the less time she spent speaking. Again, this suggests that the motives driving MPs to engage in these sorts of activities are not related to electoral concerns but rather the MP's position within the party. Thus, perhaps unsurprisingly, the MPs are not trying to impress voters with their speeches, or other parliamentary activity, but, instead, their audience is their own party. The importance of the party is further supported by the fact that government MPs devote less effort to speechmaking as do MPs in the final session of the electoral term. Rural MPs, who are generally believed to rely more on the personal vote, are also less prone to spend much effort on speechmaking.

Finally, we consider the number of questions MPs ask ministers.[12] Here we do find that MPs nominated through party primaries are more likely to ask questions – although the effect is only statistically significant for the MPs occupying the top two spots on the party list (in the model with the interaction term). Interestingly, government MPs nominated through primaries are less likely to ask ministers questions – this finding does not fit easily with either the party perspective or the electoral perspective. Government MPs are, of course, much less likely to ask ministers questions than opposition MPs are, but it is nevertheless a puzzling finding. The content of the questions may, of course, be relevant; MPs that rely on the party for their list position might, for example, use the question period to "throw the minister a softball" to allow a minister to speak on an issue that she actually wants to talk about or, potentially, to allow the minister to avoid more hostile questions from opposition ministers if time is limited. Or, perhaps, asking questions provides future primary opponents with the ammunition to paint the MPs as disloyal party members.

There are also interesting differences here with regard to the effects of list position on the propensity to ask questions. Among opposition MPs, MPs lower on the party list, and, thus, generally, less secure, ask fewer questions while the opposite is true for government MPs. While the behavior of government MPs fits the electoral perspective, it is not clear that this is the case when the results are taken together. From the electoral perspective it is not clear why the behavior of government and opposition MPs should differ in this manner. The behavior of government MPs can possibly be explained by the party perspective. Government MPs that were low on the party list are more likely to have been looked over in the allocation of positions of influence, may have little to lose with the end of the term drawing close, and, therefore, be more likely to ask questions. And last, opposition MPs ask fewer questions if they come from a rural district and if they are in the last session of the electoral term.

Taken together the results are more supportive of the party perspective than the electoral perspective, i.e., we find limited evidence for an electoral connection even for MPs who are nominated through party primaries. The legislative behavior of government MPs, with the exception of the number of questions asked, is generally neither affected by nomination method nor the position they occupied on the party list in their district. Overall, government MPs are also substantially less active, which suggests that partisanship is the primary factor shaping their behavior. When it comes to opposition MPs, who are less likely to be constrained by their partisanship, we find some indications that electoral concerns shape legislative behavior. In particular we find that opposition MPs nominated through primaries present more legislation and parliamentary motions provided that they did not head the list in their district. There is no clear evidence that nomination method affects their decisions to speak on the floor, but they are more likely to make use of their ability to ask ministers questions.

There are additional suggestions that electoral motives are not the prime determinant of legislative behavior. If anything, legislative activity declines toward the end of the legislative term when MPs would be expected to step up their efforts if the motivation to engage in legislative activity was to improve the chances of reelection. Finally, MPs in rural districts in Iceland have generally been seen as being more engaged in constituency service with a substantial emphasis on the provision of particularistic goods, which suggests that building a personal vote is of substantial importance to them. Yet, we find that across all the forms of legislative behavior we consider, rural MPs are either no different or less engaged than other MPs.

Conclusions

The literature on primaries has tended to focus on the consequences of transferring the power of nomination from party elites to broader sections of party supporters. Seen from the vantage points of the theory of responsible party government, these consequences are often seen as being undesirable, i.e., reducing the ability of the parties to keep their candidates in line, to present a cohesive front, and to reduce accountability. There are good reasons to think this may be the case, i.e., primaries place candidates in direct competition with their co-partisans. Thus, the candidates must distinguish themselves in some manner and seek to build a personal vote, which may involve staking out positions that diverge from the party's policy.[13]

As we noted above, the literature on primary elections has been heavily focused on the United States until very recently and there are reasons to believe that the lessons from there don't travel easily to other political systems. In particular, the incentives to build a personal vote may manifest themselves in different ways in parliamentary systems. Parliamentary systems tend to be characterized by a tight control of the legislative agenda by the government, and the ability of MPs to independently influence policy – or to deliver particularistic goods – is highly limited.

Thus, whether the MP seeks to influence policy or seeks reelection through the provision of pork barrel, achieving those goals generally requires working within her party.

Thus, the question we have sought to address here is whether the incentives to build a personal vote dominate the variety of incentives MPs have to side with their party when it comes to legislative behavior. In the electoral perspective, MPs are assumed to adopt legislative behavior that is conducive to them winning reelection. The key implication of the electoral perspective is that MPs nominated through primary elections, and especially those that are electorally vulnerable, ought to be more active in the legislature in order to build a personal reputation and a record of service for her constituency. In contrast, the party perspective suggests that nomination method ought to have little impact on the MPs legislative behavior, i.e., if the road to a successful political career runs through the party, having success in building a personal vote and in the primaries is only a necessary, but not a sufficient, condition for political influence. It is important to note that the legislative behavior of government MPs is more informative when it comes to evaluating which of these perspectives is a better reflection of MPs' motivations. The reason is that opposition parties and their MPs have similar interests, i.e., to make life more difficult for the government parties. Moreover, as parties tend to be unable to advance their legislative agenda when they are in opposition, the legislative behavior of opposition MPs is not much of threat to the opposition parties.

Overall, our findings suggest that the party perspective describes the legislative behavior of Icelandic MPs better. Apart from reducing the frequency with which government MPs ask ministers questions, being nominated to the party list in a primary election does not appear to affect the legislative behavior of government MPs. We do, however, find that electorally vulnerable opposition MPs that were nominated through a primary are more likely to propose legislation and parliamentary motions. Thus, in a situation where not toeing the party line is less consequential, it appears that the electoral perspective on parliamentarians' behavior gains some relevance. These findings are in line with other findings in the literature on legislative behavior of parliamentarians. Rombi and Seddone (2017) find that the parliamentary behavior of Italian MPs is not affected by the candidate selection methods and Shomer (2009) comes to a similar conclusion in a study of the members of the Israeli Knesset.

A large part of Icelandic MPs' work is concerned with standing committees. This is less transparent than what occurs in plenum and even less visible to the voters. This, by many, is considered the "real" working environment in parliament. Committee meetings, however, with some exceptions, take place behind closed doors. Thus, while the committees may be the main instrument for ordinary MPs for influencing the work of parliament, they do not guarantee them visibility. And in any case, cordial relations with ministers and committee chairs are a far more likely method of obtaining influence than cultivating a personal reputation.

Notes

1 MPs' ability to do so varies, of course, across parliaments. There is, for example, considerable variance in the degree to which committees have oversight functions and in MPs' ability to question ministers (Mattson and Strøm 1995, 249–307; Martin 2011).

2 In contrast, STV tends to produce relatively proportional outcomes. Of course, the meaning of "proportionality" is a little ambiguous in primaries, as proportionality is typically defined in terms of the representation of parties while (most) primaries only involve the candidates of a single party. However, one can instead consider whether the outcome is proportional in terms of party factions or politically relevant subgroups of party members.

3 The Icelandic electoral system is technically a semi-open proportional representation system as voters can change the order of MPs on the party list. Voters, however, make limited use of this option and it is extremely rare for it to affect the outcome of the election.

4 In a discussion of ballot structure, Carey and Shugart (1995) focus on the role of ballot access, vote pooling, and the type of vote cast.

5 At least not directly. The composition of the party list may, of course, affect the party's performance in the parliamentary election, which could be considered a form of vote pooling. Similarly, the fact that the primary voters rank all the candidates provides candidates with an incentive to form electoral alliances, which can be considered a form of vote pooling.

6 Another possible explanation is learning by MPs, in that initially primaries appear to offer MPs a greater independence from their parties that they embraced but then the MPs eventually learn that there are costs associated with deviating from the party line.

7 While most of the parties on the left joined in the formation of the SDA, the left wing of the People's Alliance opted to form the Left-Green Movement.

8 Changes in government are often defined in terms of i) elections, ii) changes in party composition, or iii) change of PM. According to this definition there was also a change in government during the 2003–2007 electoral term when the premiership of the IP-PP was transferred from the IP to the PP in 2004. This change was, however, a part of the parties' coalition agreement and as the composition of the government coalition remained otherwise the same, including these sessions has no implications for our analysis.

9 The primary sponsor, or "frumflytjandi," tends to be the MP who initiated the writing of the legislation or the motion and introduces the legislation in parliament. Moreover, the parliament's website only lists the primary sponsor's name on its website – although the full list of co-sponsors appears on the legislation itself – thus, serving to make the primary sponsor's role far more prominent than that of the co-sponsors.

10 The results for the subsample of government MPs are not shown here but are available upon request. However, comparing coefficient for Last Session in columns 4 and 6 in Table 20.6 suggests that this is likely to be the case.

11 Indeed, when considering changes across all the sessions, we find that government MPs propose more bills in the second half of the electoral term, suggesting that the promise of party patronage declines as the end of the legislative term draws nearer.

12 Ministers are excluded from this analysis for obvious reasons.

13 Scholars have noted that other electoral systems generate similar incentives to those of primary elections. Open-list proportional representation systems, for example, are in effect systems in which a primary election and the general election are rolled into one. Primary systems differ from open-list proportional representation systems in that the primary takes place before the general election, which may allow the party to appear cohesive at election time even after a fractious primary. This may also be important because the distance in time between the primary and general election may serve to raise the intensity of the competition while candidates may moderate their behavior in open-list PR elections for fear of hurting their party's electoral success.

References

Bauman, Markus. 2016. "Constituency Demands and Limited Supplies: Comparing Personal Issue Emphases in Co-sponsorship of Bills and Legislative Speech." *Scandinavian Political Studies* 39(4): 366–387.

Bowler, Shaun. 2010. "Private Members' Bills in the UK Parliament: Is There an 'Electoral Connection'?" *The Journal of Legislative Studies* 16(4): 476–494.

Carey, John, and Matthew Shugart. 1995. "Incentives to Cultivate a Personal Vote: A Rank Ordering of Electoral Formulas." *Electoral Studies* 14(4): 417–439.

Carroll, Royce, and Monika Nalepa. 2013. "When Do Open Lists Matter? The Consequences of the Personal Vote for Party Loyalty." Working paper in SSRN Electronic Journal, April 2013.

Cox, Gary W. 1990. "Centripetal and Centrifugal Incentives in Electoral Systems." *American Journal of Political Science* 34(4): 903–935.

Crisp, B.F., Olivella, S., Malecki, M., and Sher, M. 2013. "Vote-Earning Strategies in Flexible List Systems: Seats at the Price of Unity." *Electoral Studies* 32(4): 658–669.

Dancey, Logan, and Sheagley, Geoffrey. 2013. "Heuristics Behaving Badly: Party Cues and Voter Knowledge." *American Journal of Political Science* 57(2): 312–325.

Depauw, Sam, and Shane Martin. 2009. "Legislative Party Discipline and Cohesion in Comparative Perspective." In *Intra-Party Politics and Coalition Governments*, ed. Daniela Giannetti and Kenneth Benoit. London: Routledge, pp. 103–120.

Diermeier, Daniel, and Feddersen, Timothy J. 1998. "Cohesion in Legislatures and the Vote of Confidence Procedure."*American Political Science Review* 92(3): 611–621.

Döring, Herbert. (ed.) 1995. *Parliament and Majority Rule in Western Europe.* Frankfurt: Campus Verlag.

Downs, Anthony. 1957. *An Economic Theory of Democracy.* New York: Harper and Row.

Fujimura, Naofumi. 2015. "The Influence of Electoral Institutions on Legislative Representation: Evidence from Japan's Single Non-Transferable Vote and Single-Member District Systems." *Party Politics* 2(2): 209–221.

Hazan, Reuven, and Gideon Rahat. 2010. *Democracy within Parties: Candidate Selection Methods and Their Political Consequences.* London: Oxford University Press.

Herron, Erik. 2002. "Electoral Influences on Legislative Behavior in Mixed-Member Systems: Evidence from Ukraine's Verkhovna Rada." *Legislative Studies Quarterly* 27(3): 361–382.

Indriðason, Indriði, and Gunnary Helgi Kristinsson. 2015. "Primary Consequences: The Effects of Candidate Selection through Party Primaries in Iceland." *Party Politics* 21(4): 565–576.

Kam, Christopher. 2009. *Party Discipline and Parliamentary Politics.* Cambridge: Cambridge University Press.

Kristinsson, Gunnar. 2011. "Party Cohesion in the Icelandic Althingi." *Icelandic Review of Politics and Administration* 7(2): 229–252.

Lancaster, Thomas D. 1986. "Electoral Structures and Pork Barrel Politics."*International Political Science Review* 7(1): 67–81.

Louwerse, Tom, and Simon Otjes. 2016. "Personalised Parliamentary Behavior without Electoral Incentives: The Case of the Netherlands." *West European Politics* 39(4): 778–779.

Martin, Shane. 2011. "Parliamentary Questions, the Behaviour of Legislators, and the Function of Legislatures: An Introduction." *Journal of Legislative Studies,* 17(3): 259–270.

Mattson, Ingvar, and Kaare Strøm. 1995. "Parliamentary committees." In Herbert Döring, ed., *Parliaments and Majority Rule in Western Europe.* Frankfurt: Campus Verlag, pp. 249–307.

Mayhew, David R. 1974. *Congress: The Electoral Connection.* New Haven, CT: Yale University Press.

Rae, Douglas W. 1971. *The Political Consequences of Electoral Laws,* 2nd ed. New Haven, CT: Yale University Press.

Rombi, Stefano, and Antonella Seddone. 2017. "Rebel Rebel. Do Primary Elections Affect Legislators' Behaviour? Insights from Italy." *Parliamentary Affairs* 70(3): 569–588.

Sartori, Giovanni. 1976. *Party and Party Systems.* New York: Cambridge University Press.

Sartori, Giovanni. 1994. *Comparative Constitutional Engineering.* New York: New York University Press.

Sartori, Giovanni. 1996. *Parties and Party Systems.* Cambridge: Cambridge University Press.

Shomer, Yael. 2009. "Candidate Selection Procedures, Seniority, and Vote-Seeking Behavior." *Comparative Political Studies* 42(7): 945–970.

Sieberer, Ulrich. 2006. "Party Unity in Parliamentary Democracies: A Comparative Analysis." *The Journal of Legislative Studies* 12(2): 150–178.

Solvak, Mihkel, and Antti Pajala. 2015. "Sponsoring Private Members' Bills in Finland and Estonia: The Electoral Context of Legislative Behavior." *Scandinavian Political Studies* 39(1): 52–72.

Williams, Brian, and Indriði H. Indriðason. Forthcoming. "Luck of the Draw? Private Members' Bills and the Electoral Connection." *Political Science and Research Methods.*

21

PARTY PRIMARIES AS A STRATEGIC CHOICE

The Costs and Benefits of Democratic Candidate Selection

Kathleen Bruhn

A recent political cartoon about the 2016 Republican primary season shows an elephant in a negligee sitting up in bed, remarking "Whoa! I just had the worst nightmare!" In the bed next to the elephant lies Donald Trump, smoking a cigarette.[1] Under any system but one of open primaries, Donald Trump would assuredly not have won the nomination of the Republican Party establishment. The Trump nomination illustrates both the fears and the hopes raised by primary elections: the fear of losing control of the process and selecting a potentially risky nominee, and the hope of selecting a more popular candidate capable of winning the general election. Why do parties choose to subject themselves to primary elections – or not – and what are the consequences for electability?

This chapter examines these two questions through an analysis of primary elections in Latin America and particularly Mexico. I begin with an overview of primary elections in Latin America and their progressive adoption as mandatory requirements in a growing number of countries. Second, I look at the decision about candidate selection procedures through an examination of primaries in Mexico. Finally, I look at the results of primary elections for both the ideological positioning of candidates and their ultimate chances of victory.

Primary Elections in Latin America

In the beginning, as Latin American countries were making the transition from authoritarian to democratic regimes in the 1980s, presidential candidate selection was considered far too important to be left to mere voters. Indeed, the dominant concern in many countries was simply to overcome the barriers posed by the lingering political forces of the outgoing authoritarian government, and a negotiated unified candidacy of all the opposition forces was often seen as the best path forward. The origins of the Concertación in Chile, an alliance among the main leftist parties that has governed nearly continuously since the transition in 1989, date to such an effort to unify the progressive opposition behind a single candidate. In Brazil, the selection of Tancredo Neves as the candidate of the Democratic Alliance in 1985 was meant to improve the chances that a candidate not chosen by the military government would win elections. Even in Mexico, where the transition took place amidst vigorous three-party competition, voices calling for opposition unity were omnipresent (though ignored), and ultimately the transition in 2000 involved a candidate who had not emerged from a primary (Vicente Fox) beating one who had (Francisco Labastida).

Relatively soon after the immediate fears of a coup receded, by the early 1990s, pressures began to mount for parties to democratize internally just as they had democratized the country. Freidenberg (2015, 4) calls internal elections "the queen of reforms," and refers to them as the fulcrum for the modernization of political parties in Latin America. Often the pressure to adopt more democratic candidate selection methods came from within the parties themselves. Even as they acknowledged the risks of primary elections, they sought to gain partisan advantage by adopting them.

Some of the most important benefits of primaries include the potential selection of a candidate with broader popular support than the national party elite, and therefore in a better position to win the general election. Second, in order to win a primary, activists of all of the party's main factions may have to mobilize and even recruit new members to put themselves in a better position. As rivals engaged in competitive mobilization, the result could be significant growth of party membership, activism, and enthusiasm. Third, the party could gain democratic prestige by demonstrating internally what it called for externally. Primaries could thus legitimize parties, especially in a post-authoritarian context where parties are often distrusted and vilified. Finally – and as I shall argue, perhaps most importantly – primaries could serve as a means of resolving internal conflicts and rivalries over prized nominations.

Yet the risks were equally evident. As Brown Arraúz noted in the title of his discussion of primary elections in Panama, primaries can offer a guide, "on how to commit electoral suicide" (2013: 142). Primaries in Panama, he wrote, had

> left as a consequence a party demobilized by lack of money, fatigued, publicly split, confused ideologically, and [with] a series of arguments well established in public opinion against the chosen presidential candidate, that opportunely and successfully would be used by the principal candidate of the opposition during the electoral campaign.
>
> *Brown Arraúz 2013: 145*

One could hardly summarize better the main arguments against the adoption of primary elections. Primary elections ran the risk of dividing the party. During the course of the campaign, rivals within the party would air dirty laundry that, as party insiders, they were in an advantageous position to know about, making these issues public knowledge that could be used against the party in a full campaign. Primary campaigns take resources, sometimes quite a lot of them, which could alternatively have been used in a general election. Sometimes the losing side finds itself so disillusioned and disappointed that they opt out of the general election altogether, or – even worse – split from the party to run an independent campaign. Within the Mexican ruling party, the risk of such splits was seen as perhaps the party's worst fear in most general elections.

Presidential Primaries

When we look at the actual use of primary elections in Latin America, we find a slow but steady trend in their favor. Using published sources (Freidenberg 2015; Alcántara Sáez and Tagina 2013a, 2013b) and online accounts of selection processes, I determined the presidential candidate selection procedure used in the three most recent presidential elections for the continental Latin American countries plus the Dominican Republic for every party/candidate that won at least 5 percent of the vote in the general election. I counted as "primaries" any contests in which either activists or voters more generally were permitted to vote directly for two or more contending candidates. I counted as "conventions" internally competitive processes where voters chose delegates who then voted among at least two candidates. I argue that the actual existence of competition rather than the statutory name for the process is what results in both the risks and benefits of internal elections; a "convention" with only one candidate has a far lower risk of divisions and problems than one with multiple candidates, but also has foreclosed the possibility that the election will choose the best among several potential nominees. I classified all other processes simply as "noncompetitive." One of the most frequent subtypes of this category was self-nomination, the case of candidates who ran as independents or created their own parties in order to launch a campaign for president. In other cases, internal negotiations among party elites resolved any conflicts prior to an openly competitive process, resulting in "unity candidates."

Overall, I found 52 cases of primaries, 13 competitive conventions, and 117 uncompetitive processes. The number of primaries rose from 13 in the earliest of the three elections (usually in the mid-2000s) to 21 in the most recent available election (up to 2016). At the same time, however, parties opted out of primaries at a higher rate than they opted in. The number of relevant parties generally tended to increase over time, with most of these new parties adopting uncompetitive internal candidate selection processes. The number of uncompetitive processes remained relatively stable even as the use of competitive processes increased (see Table 21.1).

One of the most significant causes of the increase in primaries has been the adoption of national laws requiring them. In Argentina, for example, a 2009 law (known as PASO) was passed requiring national parties to select their candidates in primaries. Nevertheless, even after the law, at least one party managed to hold a "primary" with only one candidate; this was the case, for example, in 2011 and 2015 when the governing Partido Justicialista-Frente Para

Table 21.1 Primaries in Latin American Presidential Elections

	Primaries	*Conventions*	*Non–competitive*
Most recent election[a]	21	3	39
Second most recent election[b]	18	4	37
Third most recent election[c]	13	6	41
TOTAL	52	13	117
Prior elections[d]	40	31	64

Notes:

a These elections include Argentina 2015, Bolivia 2014, Brazil 2014, Chile 2012, Colombia 2014, Costa Rica 2014, Dominican Republic 2016, Ecuador 2013, El Salvador 2014, Guatemala 2015, Honduras 2014, Mexico 2012, Nicaragua 2016, Panama 2014, Paraguay 2013, Peru 2016, Uruguay 2014, Venezuela 2012.

b These elections include Argentina 2011, Bolivia 2009, Brazil 2010, Chile 2009, Colombia 2010, Costa Rica 2010, Dominican Republic 2012, Ecuador 2009, El Salvador 2009, Guatemala 2011, Honduras 2009, Mexico 2006, Nicaragua 2011, Panama 2009, Paraguay 2008, Peru 2011, Uruguay 2009, Venezuela 2009.

c These elections include Argentina 2007, Bolivia 2005, Brazil 2006, Chile 2006, Colombia 2006, Costa Rica 2006, Dominican Republic 2008, Ecuador 2006, El Salvador 2004, Guatemala 2003, Honduras 2005, Mexico 2000, Nicaragua 2006, Panama 2004, Paraguay 2003, Peru 2006, Uruguay 2004, Venezuela 2006.

d I draw on Flavia Freidenberg's 2015 classification of presidential selection for elections prior to the third most recent election. I do not count the elections prior to 1990 as many of them were transitional elections and therefore exceptional. There are roughly three elections per country in this group. However, Freidenberg's criteria for conventions are not strictly comparable to mine, as she uses party statutes to determine the selection process rather than the actual existence of competition. The result may be some coding discrepancies between her classification of a "convention" and what I would term an uncompetitive leader-dominated process of selection.

la Victoria (PJ) presented only one consensus candidate (Cristina Fernández de Kirchner and Daniel Scioli, respectively). In the first case, Fernández de Kirchner was a president running for reelection, and in the second, her anointed and endorsed successor sought the nomination of the party that she then dominated. Parties must also hold primaries, by law, in Uruguay, Honduras, and the Dominican Republic, though exceptions occur. In Honduras, for example, parties with only one faction (only one candidate presents himself) do not have to hold a formal primary. In Panama, primaries are only obligatory for the presidential candidate.

Another factor that seems to favor the use of primaries is a political context that discourages the formation of new parties, either legally or de facto, as in the case of traditional party systems where the main parties are long-standing features of the political system. When voters traditionally choose among the same set of parties and it is hard to form a new party, the nomination of existing parties becomes worth fighting over. Colombia, for example, has had until recently an enviable record of holding primaries. Freidenberg (2015) lists the two main historical parties, the PLC and PCC, as holding either primaries or conventions for every election from 1990 to 2014. As new parties began to emerge in Colombia in the 2000s, these new parties were often the vehicle of a particular politician not chosen in an internal contest, but rather "outsider" candidates; President Álvaro Uribe (2002–2010) is a classic example.

Two-round voting, on the other hand, seems to deter the use of primaries by parties. In most of the countries with two-round voting, the first round functions as a de facto "primary" among rivals with similar partisan backgrounds. The ease of registration of new candidates and parties in Peru has led to a situation in which no party feels compelled to hold actual competitive primaries. In Brazil, not even the notoriously organized and pro-democratic Partido dos Trabalhadores (PT) held competitive primaries, due in part to the dominance of its founder, Lula da Silva, during the party's formative phase. And in Argentina, prior to the PASO law requiring primaries, the PJ allowed as many as three candidates to compete under the PJ label, in the 2003 election. In this case, Nestor Kirchner and Carlos Menem, both of the PJ, were the top two candidates that emerged from the first round. Menem dropped out before the second round (*ballotage*), leaving Kirchner the victor.

Subpresidential Primaries

Use of primary elections for positions other than the chief executive is rare. Most countries have adopted a system of closed-list proportional representation for the legislature, which does not lend itself readily to the use of primary elections. Instead, national party leaders (sometimes with local input) tend to dominate the process of selection for these positions. Primaries to select legislative positions have been most commonly used in Argentina (where it has been the law since PASO) and Mexico. The latter has a fairly uncommon mixed system of plurality and proportional representation seats in its legislature. It also does not have any legal requirements regarding the parties' candidate selection process. Finally, Mexico does not allow consecutive reelection for legislative or executive positions. As a result, Mexico's use of primaries varies widely by party and by election, making it an ideal case to analyze the decision to use primaries as well as their consequences.

Mexico presents a valuable case in which to examine candidate selection. Until very recently, the Mexican constitution barred reelection to any political office, meaning that every three years (for local legislatures and the federal Chamber of Deputies) or six years (for the federal Senate, governors, and the presidency) *all* politicians had to find a new job, sometimes within the state bureaucracy, by getting nominated to a different office, or by moving to the private sector. And because the constitution also barred independent candidacies (until 2015), those processes were party-based. The absence of incumbency created ample opportunities to consider candidate selection: every seat, in every election, was an open seat.

In response to these incentives, parties neither adopted primaries wholesale nor rejected them completely. Rather, at all levels of government, parties chose different methods of selection with some care and precision, varying the procedure even within the same party and election. In the case of governors, for example, the long-ruling Partido Revolucionario Institucional (PRI) first experimented with primaries in 1991, selecting its candidates for governor in Colima and Nuevo León but not in other states. These experiments did not work out terribly well; though both candidates were eventually elected, the government's preferred candidate lost the Colima primary and open confrontation between party factions contributed to the rising strength of the conservative opposition party Acción Nacional (PAN) in the state. Nevertheless, particularly after electoral reforms in 1996 provided parties with more funds to support regular internal elections, the use of primaries in the PRI began to rise.

Simultaneously, the PAN continued its long-standing tradition of selecting candidates in state-level conventions, but these conventions became more and more competitive as the PAN's chances of actually winning governors' races increased and more aspiring candidates applied for the nomination. Between 1997 and 2011, over half of all PAN gubernatorial candidates were chosen in some type of internal election, compared to 41 percent of PRI candidates. The leftist Partido de la Revolución Democrática (PRD) also tried its hand at primaries, albeit for only about 24 percent of its gubernatorial candidates (Bruhn 2014, 220–221).

Variation is also evident in the selection of federal legislators. In the 2015 national elections, one-quarter (75) of PAN candidacies for the Chamber of Deputies were decided by direct designation of the CEN, distributed across about two-thirds of Mexico's states (13 states used no designation processes). The PRI relied on designation to select candidates for 173 out of 300 relative majority seats, using conventions to decide the rest. The party showed laser-like precision in naming the districts in which competitive processes would be used. A comparison of the Federal District and the State of Mexico is telling. In the former, the PRI used delegate conventions in only 9 of 27 districts, while in the latter it used them in 19 of 40.

State-level elections show diversity of rules and strategic decision-making as well. In the 2015 elections in Chiapas, for example, the PRI relied on conventions to select candidates in 22 of the 24 local legislative districts in the state and designated candidates in the two remaining districts. Likewise, in 11 of the 27 state-level legislative elections for which we have information about the PAN's selection rules, the PAN used at least two types of rules, with open selection procedures in some, but not all, districts. The PRD has been more likely to use one rule per state, but has also split states into districts with competitive processes and others with designation in some cases.

Choosing to Hold Primaries

Clearly, party leaders make strategic choices about where and whether to hold competitive internal elections. What principles determine this strategic choice? I argue that the main source of pressure to hold internal elections comes from the desire to resolve party rivalries over desirable candidacies, rather than from any deep-seated belief that such elections select better candidates or that voters necessarily reward more internally democratic parties with their support. If such were the case, we would see far more internal elections than we do. Instead, internal elections seem frequently to be held as a last resort, to be avoided if possible by internal negotiations and pressure on weaker candidates to drop out of the race.

Second, internal factionalism plays a complicated role in the choice of selection mechanism. On the one hand, internal ideological homogeneity tends to lower the costs of internal elections by reducing the risk that elections will select a candidate who is out of touch with the preferences of the party elites. The more similar party members are to one another from the top of the party to the bottom, the more likely activist preferences and elite preferences are to resemble one another, and the less likely a "Trumpian" outcome becomes. This should make parties more open to the idea of holding internal elections.

On the other hand, without some internal factionalization, there is less pressure to hold primaries in the first place, and if they are held, they are less likely to be genuinely competitive. De Luca, Jones and Tula (2009, 293) argue that larger and more internally divided parties should choose primaries, in part because they can use primaries as a way to channel internal conflicts. The legitimacy of "democratic elections" can make it harder to reject the eventual nominee; as one PRD leader put it, "people get mad if they feel cheated out of a candidacy by the central organization, but are willing to accept defeat in elections."[2] This argument is similar to that of Kemahlioglu, Weitz-Shapiro, and Hirano (2009) regarding primaries in Latin American presidential elections.

I contend, therefore, that one of the key factors influencing party strategies is the likelihood that the party will win a general election. The prospect of winning the general election, combined with the desirability of the office, will tend to bring potential candidates to the fore. We should expect that, other things being equal, parties are more likely to hold internal elections to select their candidates in districts where they have a reasonable chance of winning. Larger parties should also be more likely to hold internal elections. The more competitive the district, the narrower the margin, the more we might anticipate that parties will do everything in their power to avoid the risk of a divisive primary; however, their ability to maneuver may be constrained by the ambitions of their members. Exceptions to this rule should occur when one party faction has a commanding presence in the district (such as in the case of incumbency) or when the party has sufficient resources to successfully negotiate the creation of a "consensus" candidate by buying off rivals for the nomination. In the case of Mexico, for example, the ruling PRI often had in its safe districts the ability to purchase the loyalty of disappointed rivals for a price, though when negotiations failed the consequences could be a fatal party split.

Gubernatorial Elections in Mexico

We can examine these propositions, first, through analysis of gubernatorial candidacies. In Bruhn (2014), I looked at 265 cases of the choice of election type during a period ranging from 1997 to 2011 in Mexico. This is close to the universe of 267 cases: 89 gubernatorial elections with a decision made by each of the three major parties.[3] For all three parties, although statutes *recommended* the use of internal elections (particularly in the PAN and PRD), party leaders had the authority to determine how each specific nomination would be handled, whether through a competitive internal election, nomination by the party leadership, or negotiations to convince potential competitors to decline in favor of a consensus candidate (*candidato de unidad*).[4]

The models included five factors: whether the state had a governor of the same party (a proxy for incumbency), whether it was a national election year with federal legislative races held simultaneously (which elevates the stakes of the race), the absolute previous margin of victory/defeat (a measure of competitiveness), and whether other parties held internal elections (to measure the significance of pressures for emulation). In addition, I included dummy variables for the main parties, which covers a multitude of internal characteristics including party culture, commitment to internal democracy, and factionalization. Unfortunately, it was not possible to get state-level data on degrees of factionalization. Finally, I included variables for rural population and for the natural log of the number of voters in the state, both of which capture aspects of the logistical challenges of internal elections. I expect state-level elections to be more costly and difficult in more rural states, and in more populous states.

The results indicate a statistically significant effect of election competitiveness. Where the previous election in the district was highly competitive (less than 10 percent margin of victory) we see the strongest likelihood of an internal election. Curiously, parties were less likely to hold internal elections in either very safe or hopeless states. I see this finding as in part an artifact of the contextual conditions of "safe states": the opposition had very few of these, so we are mostly looking at PRI states during an earlier period of competition (before 1997) when the PRI still controlled candidate selection firmly from above in states where it held hegemony and could therefore afford to buy off disgruntled losers in the candidate selection process. As opposition parties became stronger and more capable of winning elections, exit options increased for losing PRI candidates, raising the pressure on the PRI to hold democratic candidate selection processes when multiple rivals for a nomination existed.

Second, we find statistically and consistently significant effects of the party dummies. The PAN was by far the most likely to hold internal elections (competitive conventions) compared to the PRI and the PRD. The PAN was also ideologically the most homogeneous party, as anticipated. The PRI has historically been a catch-all party with wide variation in the ideological positions of its various factions. The PRD owes its foundation to a legal merger between a heterogeneous coalition of leftist parties, urban popular movements, peasant organizations, and former members of the PRI. It has openly solicited members of both the PRI and PAN to run for election under the PRD label. It also presents as few barriers as possible to membership. Although it maintains a member registry, which determines who can vote in internal elections, it has frequently been possible for people to join the party and vote in an internal election moments later.

In contrast, the PAN closely monitors admission to party membership and limits the right to participate in internal elections to a subset of its sympathizers, known as "active members." These members have been sponsored for party membership by a current member, have taken a course in party doctrine, and have served an apprenticeship as "adherents" before being accepted into active membership. The PAN, therefore, should have the smallest gap between the ideological preferences of elites versus likely primary voters. Moreover, although the PAN leans to the right of the PRI on most issues, the party remains quite close to the center and demonstrates substantial internal coherence. A 2006 survey of congressional candidates found that the PAN's median category – center-right – held 48 percent of respondents, while no category held more than 32 percent of PRD respondents (the PRI refused to participate in the candidate survey).[5] On all these grounds, the PAN should be the most likely to hold primaries.

Moreover, the PAN's preferred method of holding an internal election – state-level conventions – posed considerably lower costs and risks than open primary elections; the PRI also preferred conventions to open primaries in most cases when an election had to be held. At a convention, all the actual voting takes place in one location and at one time, enabling easier monitoring of vote counts than when polling stations have to be watched across an entire state. The chances that someone will denounce fraud decrease correspondingly, although they do not disappear entirely.[6]

The interesting thing about this preference is that conventions, while they limit the risks of internal elections, also limit the benefits to be gained from mobilizing large numbers of new activists into a primary. There are still some benefits: packing conventions by recruiting new activists that entitle one to more delegates is a known tactic complained about by some PAN activists (interview with PAN CEN member, 2008). Yet actual mobilization is comparatively limited. It is thus worth noting that primaries and conventions were both more likely in national election years, in two out of three models (Bruhn 2014, 226). The benefit of mobilization must increase when other offices are at stake in the election.

Finally, when we add a variable for previous protests around the nomination process, we find positive and significant effects. If the party in question had previously experienced public protests over its nomination process in the state, it was significantly though modestly *more* likely to hold an internal election to choose its gubernatorial candidate (Bruhn 2014, 227). Instead of avoiding a potentially divisive election where previous problems occurred, parties tended to react by holding more primaries. I read this as evidence that factionalization does contribute to the likelihood of parties being forced to hold internal elections, once we take into account other variables (such as party culture and the type of internal election under consideration). For the most part, these were instances where a prior internal election resulted in public protest: 62 percent of the PRD's primaries resulted in protests, versus just 23 percent of candidate selections when no primary occurred. For the PAN, internal elections culminated in protests 38 percent of the time (versus 30 percent of non-elected nominations), and for the PRI, protests occurred after 31 percent of internal elections (versus 17 percent of noncompetitive processes).

Legislative Primaries

When we look at selection procedures for federal deputies, Bruhn and Wuhs (2016) find that party strength in a state has a positive and significant effect on the likelihood of internal elections in the PRD and PAN, and a significant but *negative* effect on the likelihood of internal competition in the PRI. Likewise, internal elections are more likely for the PAN and PRD in states where the governor was of their own party, but significantly less likely for PRI candidate selection in PRI-governed states. Part of the puzzle is explained to us by Langston (2001, 2003, 2006), who tells us that PRI governors have seized unusual latitude in controlling federal deputy selection since democratization has been underway in Mexico. They seek to lay claim to federal resources by owning as many deputies as they can. The PAN and PRD governors, fewer to begin with than in the case of the PRI, cannot hope to significantly influence the national legislature by dominating the contingent of their own state because they are less likely to logroll successfully with like-minded governors. More pertinently, the PRI's long undemocratic history may give its governors some leeway in insisting on what has been a traditional privilege in the party – the privilege of nominating legislative candidates by *dedazo* (pointing the finger) – where the PAN and PRD's internal commitments to democracy make it harder for them to resist pressures for competitive elections.

Finally, we can look at the selection patterns for local (state-level) deputies (Bruhn and Wuhs 2016). The analysis is based on a sample of cases from the Calderón administration (2006–2012) rather than the full universe of cases due to the difficulty of getting information about selection procedures in local deputy races when compared to governors' races. The sample includes 18 states that vary in terms of their level of economic development, their demographics, and their histories of party competition. We focused our attention on the MR seats rather than the party-dominated PR lists.

What we find is that when we consider all parties, primaries are most likely in "stronghold" states; conventions are most likely in competitive states; and noncompetitive processes are most likely in weak states (see Table 21.2). State party leaders are in fact the most likely body to name local legislative candidates. These overall trends, however, mask significant divergence among the parties in their competitive practices. Most importantly, the PAN and PRD appear to opt

Table 21.2 Local Legislature Selection Procedures

	National Party Designation (%)	State Party Designation (%)	Convention (%)	Primary (%)	N
STRONGHOLD	11.4	35.7	14.3	42.9	14
PRI	33.3	33.3	33.3	0	3
PAN	11.4	33.3	5.3	50	6
PRD	0	40	0	60	5
COMPETITIVE	17.4	35.4	38.7	8.6	31
PRI	7.2	23.3	57.9	11.6	19
PAN	66.7	12.2	16.7	4.5	6
PRD	0	97	0	3	6
WEAK STATE	18.1	30.1	27.9	26.2	39
PRI	6.7	27.7	63.6	20	15
PAN	42	13.6	0	43.6	12
PRD	8.3	63.8	11.1	16.7	12

Source: Bruhn and Wuhs (2016).

out of competitive internal elections in the states where they face a narrow margin of victory in the previous election. They still find themselves holding primaries in their stronghold states, where pressures to do so may be strongest, but party elites (either national or local) attempt to control nominations in cases where primaries might expose them to a risk of defeat. The PAN then reverts to conventions when it has little chance of victory, in accordance with its traditional norms.

The PRI, meanwhile, uses conventions about equally in competitive and hopeless states, but attempts to control nominations more from the center in stronghold states. As in the case of federal deputies, the PRI's behavior in legislative candidate selection diverges from the other two parties and is consistent with its behavior in stronghold states in gubernatorial primaries. Thus, where this historically hierarchical party dominates its competitive environment, it tends to follow historic norms against competitive candidate selection. Only where it faces electoral pressure does the PRI respond by opening up the selection process (see Table 21.2; Bruhn and Wuhs 2016, 828).

This analysis has generally confirmed expectations that external competition tends to motivate parties to choose more competitive internal candidate selection processes, and to validate the significance of internal rivalries. These findings imply, furthermore, that larger parties should have more frequent internal challenges that lead to primaries; small parties are more likely to choose their candidates in less competitive ways. However, parties' political culture also seems to matter in predictable but non-numerical ways. Incumbency should also mitigate the effect on potential rivals of a promising electoral scenario, limiting the number who would decide to challenge an incumbent for reelection. Overall, parties do consider the benefits and costs of primary elections when deciding whether or not to use them.

The Consequences of Primary Elections

Once parties have decided to use primaries to select their candidates, what are the effects on the types of candidates they select? Carey and Polga-Hecimovich argue that presidential candidates in Latin America who emerged from a primary earn what they call a "primary bonus" – that is, other things equal, primary-elected candidates are stronger than those selected by other procedures" (2006, 530–532). The effect is largest when the candidate was the only one to emerge from a primary. However, they do not explain why, if primaries are so successful, more parties do not choose them. Their data cover elections from 1978 through 2004, a total of 826 presidential candidates of whom 47 had been selected in primary elections (Carey and Polga-Hecimovich 2006, 535). Moreover, the effect of incumbency overwhelms the effect of primaries – a 23 percent boost over the party's expected vote share versus a seven percent boost for a candidate nominated in a primary. Finally, in using electoral success rather than candidate characteristics as their dependent variable, they necessarily skip over the question of whether primaries select better candidates, or simply provide parties with democratic credentials – a "stamp of legitimacy" in a post-authoritarian context (Carey and Polga-Hecimovich 2006, 534). In other words, it is not clear *why* these candidates get a primary bonus.

Mexico again offers significant advantages for distinguishing the effects of primaries on candidates, since there is no incumbency effect. In a 2013 article, I examined the ideological characteristics of candidates for the lower house of the Mexican Congress, the Chamber of Deputies, who stood for election in the 300 relative majority seats. I drew upon two surveys of candidates and legislators from the PAN and the PRD.[7] These parties used internal elections to select some but not all of their candidates in 2006; specifically, the PAN chose 52 percent of its candidates in state-level conventions with locally elected delegates, while the PRD chose 36 percent of its candidates in open primary elections. National leaders designated the remaining candidates. We can therefore compare the characteristics of candidates chosen via internal election to candidates chosen by national party elites, holding constant the election year, the party, and the national context.

The first survey took place during the 2006 campaign itself and resulted in 151 completed surveys. A second survey done after the seating of the congress (in order to boost the number of winning candidates and candidates chosen in primary elections) added 40 new legislators. The result was 92 PRD candidates and 96 PAN candidates, a bit less than a third of the total candidates for each party; however, the candidates came from 25 of the 28 states where the PAN elected candidates and from all 25 of the states where the PRD elected candidates, resulting in a generous geographical distribution. Forty-one percent of the PAN members surveyed and 55 percent of the PRD members surveyed lost their legislative race.

I then constructed a dependent variable based on the ideological self-placement of the surveyed candidate on a seven-point scale from Left to Right with one being "very Left" and seven being "very Right." In order to examine the degree to which candidates diverged from the center, I recoded the Left-Right scale as the absolute value of the distance between a respondent's answer and the center of the scale (4). Thus, a candidate who answered with "very Left" would get a score of three, and so would a candidate who answered "very Right." Higher scores indicate more extreme candidates rather than more conservative or liberal ones.

Information about selection procedures was obtained directly from the parties. In addition, I controlled for three demographic variables that might affect ideological position: university education, religiosity, and party identification. University education was coded 1 if the candidate completed college. Religiosity measures the frequency of church attendance, with a 1 indicating that the candidate attended church more than once a week, and 5 indicating that the candidate never attended. I calculated religiosity in terms of the distance from the mean category of once a month. Extreme values on religiosity (either never attending or attending more than once a week) should be associated with more extreme ideological positions. I included party membership (either PAN or PRD) to test whether members of one party were more likely to hold extreme values in general, as opposed to reflecting method of selection. In fact, PAN members had an average extremism score of 1.02 versus 1.81 for the PRD (a statistically significant difference). I also included two district-level variables, on the grounds that extremism might reflect characteristics of the district rather than the selection method. These variables are similar to the individual level characteristics: average level of education, and the strength of the candidate's party in the same district in 2003.

The analysis found that internal elections resulted in significantly *less* extreme candidates than designation by the national leadership. As a result, the predicted probability of extremism varies according to whether there was or was not an internal election. Overall, the predicted probability of a PAN member self-locating as a moderate (value of extremism zero or one) rises from .69 to .81 if she came out of an internal election versus a designation. For the PRD, the predicted probability of moderate self-location rises from .32 to .47 with an internal election versus a designation.

I also found some significant differences in the characteristics of candidates in terms of length of party membership and previous leadership experience by whether or not there had been an internal election. Generally speaking, those elected in a primary were significantly more likely to have been party insiders: they belonged to their party longer (12 versus 4.5 years) and were more likely to have held a prior post in the party leadership. The differences are significant at the .01 level. These positions were almost always local level leadership positions rather than posts in the national leadership (there was no difference between elected and non-elected candidates in terms of the likelihood of prior national leadership experience). Interestingly, there is no significant difference between the two candidate groups based on previous elective office: both internal elections and national party leaders have a tendency to prefer those with local elective experience.

I interpret these results to suggest that far from selecting outsiders with rare charisma, internal elections – at least for federal legislators – tended to select party insiders with the knowledge and networks to mobilize successfully in an internal election campaign. There was very little evidence in Mexican newspapers of public promotion of these primaries, even for the PRD which held the most open primaries. Rather, candidates mostly had to mobilize party insiders and activists in order to win. Turnout was typically low and limited only to the most active party members even when it was technically possible for voters in general to participate.

The insider nature of primaries also explains why I find that the candidates chosen in this way were more likely to have moderate political views. In an internal election campaign, it was usually necessary to mobilize the support of more than one internal faction; this task was easier when the candidate in question was acceptable to a broader variety of people. In contrast, the process of designation by national elites usually involved log-rolling among various factions, such that each faction was able to place its leaders into a number of candidacies (to be negotiated) without having to compromise ideologically. Ironically, party primaries in the U.S. may result in more extreme candidates precisely when they go outside of the party establishment in search of new voters, not because they appeal only to party activists as some of the existing literature would have it.[8]

Electability is a tougher nut to crack. The selection of moderate candidates does not necessarily imply the selection of more electable candidates. At first blush, there seems to be a strong association between having emerged from a primary and winning the general election. In 2006, 70 percent of PRD candidates selected in a primary won their seats, compared to just 19 percent of those chosen by the CEN. Similarly, 64 percent of PAN candidates chosen in a competitive convention won their seats versus 25 percent of those who were not internally elected. These differences are statistically significant at .01. However, we know from our previous analysis that the potential electability of the party in a district is a major driver of the decision to hold a primary in the first place: internal elections are more likely in districts the party expects to win. We therefore have a massive problem of endogeneity to contend with.

This difference cannot be entirely controlled for by projecting the party's expected victory margin based on its vote in the district in 2003 and determining the difference between the expected and the actual vote. In 2006, the presidential election race between PRD candidate Andrés Manuel López Obrador and Felipe Calderón resulted in significant coattail effects, particularly in the case of the PRD, which dwarf any differences that might result from the type of election held. The PRD mobilized its core vote much better in 2006 than in the midterm elections of 2003, and this happened in precisely the areas where it already had more strength. Thus, differences above the expected vote could be attributable to the type of election of the legislative candidate, but could also result from the excitement created by the presidential race itself. Any findings of an above average increase in the vote could well be falsely attributed to the election type.

In any case, the evidence suggests that internal primaries do not boost the performance of parties, and can even hurt it outside the urban areas where parties are better organized. In a previous article (Bruhn 2010), I analyzed the shift in party vote, controlling for the baseline vote from the previous election, in districts with and without internal elections. The analysis controlled for whether the governor of the state was from the same party, on the grounds that co-partisan governors may add extra help to the party's legislative candidates. Second, I controlled for the strength of party infrastructure in the district. For the PAN, I used the party's internal calculations of the percentage of designated "pollwatchers" who turned up on election day to monitor the voting. PAN leaders argued that this variable better measures the party's ability to mobilize activists than mere membership lists. However, this measure is not available for the PRD, so I was forced to use membership lists to calculate a district-level measure of the number of members per one thousand registered voters as an indicator of party organizational density. Finally, I controlled for several contextual variables, including economic growth rates in the state, the percentage of the population living in communities of more than 2,500, and migration rate to the district. Districts with high in-migration rates should be less subject to the influence of past voting patterns, and offer parties a higher percentage of mobilizable new voters who could be won over by an outstanding candidate. Open primaries should thus be more likely in high migration districts.

I ran the models separately by party (since the measures were not entirely commensurate) but the results are similar. For the PAN, internal elections had a positive effect on the PAN vote share after accounting for other factors (albeit only at .1 significance). For the PRD, there was no significant effect of having held an internal election. Unsurprisingly, measures of the party's strength in the district had strongly positive and significant effects on the party's 2006 vote (that is, vote share in 2003 and the measure of party organizational density used). Urban population is significant in both models, though it is negative for the PRD and positive for the PAN. These findings are consistent with general impressions of the voting base of each party: urban and relatively educated for the PAN, and rural for the PRD (with the exception of its greatest electoral redoubt, Mexico City itself).

The conditions under which elections are held seem to matter. Specifically, the effects of internal elections helped the PAN only in districts where 90 percent of the population or more lived in towns of more than 2,500 citizens. At around 86 percent urban, the effect of primaries turned insignificant. For the PRD, the turning point was about 75 percent urban; in districts with 75 percent or more urban population the effects of primaries are negligible. Below 75 percent urban, the impact of holding primaries becomes significant, but is *negative*: primaries actually reduced the expected PRD vote over the baseline. I interpret this result as a consequence of the logistical problems associated with holding elections in rural areas, particularly for a party like the PRD which generally held open primaries rather than conventions. The challenges of setting up polling stations in more rural locations, monitoring the vote, and avoiding the appearance of fraud must have been significant. As the president of the PRD noted at a 2005 meeting to prepare for the 2006 legislative elections,

> unfortunately in the party in all of the processes of direct consultation [primaries] it has meant invariably internal conflict. I would dare to say that if the *compañeros* of Guerrero [a very rural state] had not held primaries for municipal presidencies [mayors], many presidencies that we lost because of internal divisions we would have won as a party.
>
> *PRD 2005, 58*

In 2009, both the PRD and the PAN chose fewer legislative candidates by primaries than in 2006.

Looking at the presidential races discussed at the beginning of this chapter does not offer much positive evidence that primary elections improve electability either. In the last three presidential elections, roughly 31 percent of candidates who emerged from a primary won the presidential race, compared to 33 percent of candidates who emerged from a noncompetitive contest. One of the problems is that a number of countries have now adopted obligatory primaries, reducing the size of any expected "primary bonus" effect (Carey and Polga-Hecimovich 2006) and resulting in the same proportion of winners and losers in every presidential race regardless of the effectiveness of primaries. In the case of noncompetitive selection processes, many of these involved incumbents running unopposed from within their own parties, who as incumbents had a much greater chance of election than challengers (Carey and Polga-Hecimovich 2006). This does not mean that noncompetitive processes in general are better ways of picking candidates.

In short, I find no evidence that primary elections consistently result in the selection of more competitive candidates. We can say that they do not necessarily lead to the selection of extremists, but whether this translates into greater electability is an open question.

Conclusions

This chapter has drawn on data from Latin America to make three general points about the causes and consequences of internal elections. First, primary elections are more likely (absent a legal requirement to hold them) in contexts where the party in question expects to do well in the general election. The prospect of victory excites internal rivalries within the party and encourages ambitious politicians to challenge one another for the nomination. The more ideologically homogeneous the party, the less such internal elections will be seen as a threat to the coherence of the party or the interests of party elites. However, even in such cases primary elections are not seen as the first choice of most parties; rather, they tend to be the result of otherwise irreconcilable internal divisions over the candidate selection.

Second, parties are quite rational in avoiding primaries in the light of the absence of evidence proving they have a systematically positive effect on the chances of success in the general election. They do not necessarily select better candidates, they run the risk of dividing the party just before the election, and their mobilizational impact can be a two-edged sword – mobilizing activists on behalf of alternative candidacies can backfire in the general election if the supporters of the losing candidate cannot be brought back into the fold.

However, the candidates chosen in internal elections are also not systematically worse than candidates designated by party elites. In fact, there is some evidence that they may be more moderate than candidates chosen in uncompetitive ways, precisely because they have had to earn their election by appealing across party factions. The more campaign effects apply (as opposed to mobilization of the party base), the less predictable this outcome becomes, and the riskier internal elections become for the party elites. Small wonder they so frequently prefer to control the nomination process despite the democratic credentials to be gained by holding primaries.

Notes

1 See http://www.wbur.org/hereandnow/2016/05/23/political-cartoonists.
2 Confidential interview with national PRD leader, June 2008, Mexico City. Of course, the risk of protests by disgruntled losers is the other side of the coin, and the reason for party leaders' attempts to negotiate outcomes.
3 I am especially indebted to Joy Langston for generously sharing her data on PRI gubernatorial elections since 1997. Other key sources included *La Jornada, Milenio,* and *El Universal.*
4 This situation is similar to the observation by Serra that, "a large fraction of supposed primaries in the United States end up being uncompetitive one-candidate races," largely based on whether or not party elites decide to endorse a candidate and swing party resources behind him or her (2011: 22).
5 Based on a survey by Bruhn and Greene (2006).
6 Generally, accusations of fraud in conventions related to the selection of delegates and who was qualified to vote on the nomination.
7 The PRI chose none of its 2006 candidates by internal elections and also refused to participate in the surveys. It is therefore necessary to exclude this party.
8 See for example Crotty and Jackson, who summarized the initial findings of researchers on this topic by remarking that "strong partisans turn out for the primary vote at higher rates than the weak partisans or the independents," and that these voters are "ideologically more extreme and take issue positions that are unrepresentative of the parties' mass bases and of the electorate as a whole" (1985, 89). See also Brady and Schwartz 1995; Gerber and Morton 1998.

References

Alcántara Sáez, Manuel, and Maria Laura Tagina, eds. 2013a. *Elecciones y política en América Latina: 2009–2011.* Mexico City: IFE, Cámara de Diputados, Senado de la Republica, Miguel Angel Porrúa.

Alcántara Sáez, Manuel, and Maria Laura Tagina, eds. 2013b. *Procesos Políticos y Electorales en América Latina (2010–2013).* Buenos Aires: Eudeba.

Brady, David, and Edward P. Schwartz. 1995. "Ideology and Interests in Congressional Voting: The Politics of Abortion in the U.S. Senate." *Public Choice* 84(1–2): 25–48.

Brown Arraúz, Harry. 2013. "Panamá: la continuidad del cambio en las elecciones de 2009." In *Elecciones y política en América Latina: 2009–2011*, eds. Manuel Alcántara Sáez and Maria Laura Tagina, Mexico City: IFE, Cámara de Diputados, Senado de la Republica, Miguel Angel Porrúa, pp. 139–162.

Bruhn, Kathleen. 2010. "Too Much Democracy? Primaries and Candidate Success in Mexico's 2006 National Elections." *Latin American Politics and Society* 52(4): 25–52.

Bruhn, Kathleen. 2013. "Electing Extremists? Party Primaries and Legislative Candidates in Mexico." *Comparative Politics* 42(2): 398–417.

Bruhn, Kathleen. 2014. "Choosing how to Choose: From Democratic Primaries to Unholy Alliances in Mexico's Gubernatorial Elections." *Mexican Studies/Estudios Mexicanos* 30(1): 212–240.

Bruhn, Kathleen, and Kenneth F. Greene. 2006. "Mexican 2006 Candidate and Party Leader Survey." Conducted June 2006. Available from the principal investigators.

Bruhn, Kathleen, and Steven T. Wuhs. 2016. "Competition, Decentralization, and Candidate Selection in Mexico." *American Behavioral Scientist* 60(7): 819–836.

Carey, John M., and John Polga-Hecimovich. 2006. "Primary Elections and Candidate Strength in Latin America." *Journal of Politics* 60(3): 530–543.

Crotty, William A., and John S. Jackson. 1985. *Presidential Primaries and Nominations.* Washington, DC: Congressional Quarterly Press.

De Luca, Miguel, Mark P. Jones, and María Inés Tula. 2009. "De internas, aparatos y punteros. La selección de candidatos a diputados nacionales en Argentina, 1983–2005," In *Selección de candidatos, política partidista, y rendimiento democrático*, eds. Flavia Freidenberg and Manuel Alcántara Sáez. Mexico City: Tribunal Electoral del Distrito Federal, pp. 269–298.

Freidenberg, Flavia. 2015. "La *reina* de las reformas: las elecciones internas a las candidaturas presidenciales en América Latina." In *Las Reformas Políticas a las Organizaciones de Partidos*, eds. Flavia Freidenberg and Betilde Muñoz-Pogossian. Mexico City: INE, TEPJF, OEA, Instituto de Iberoamérica y SAAP, pp. 31–91.

Gerber, Elizabeth R., and Rebecca B. Morton. 1998. "Primary Election Systems and Representation." *Journal of Law, Economics, and Organization* 14(2): 304–324.

Kemahlioglu, Ozge, Rebecca Weitz-Shapiro, and Shigeo Hirano. 2009. "Why Primaries in Latin American Presidential Elections?" *Journal of Politics* 71(2): 339–352.

Langston, Joy. 2001. "Why Rules Matter: Changes in Candidate Selection in Mexico's PRI, 1998–2000." *Journal of Latin American Studies* 33(3): 485–511.

Langston, Joy. 2003. "Rising from the Ashes?" *Comparative Political Studies* 36(3): 293–320.

Langston, Joy. 2006. "The Changing Party of the Institutional Revolution: Electoral Competition and Decentralized Candidate Selection." *Party Politics* 12(3): 395–413.

Partido de la Revolución Democrática (PRD). 2005. Meeting of the VI Consejo Nacional, November 5–6. Minutes. *Gaceta* (Mexico City) 1(4): 58.

Serra, Gilles. 2011. "Why Primaries? The Party's Tradeoff between Policy and Valence." *Journal of Theoretical Politics* 23(1): 21–51.

22

PRIMARY ELECTIONS IN NEW DEMOCRACIES

The Evolution of Candidate Selection Methods in Ghana

Nahomi Ichino and Noah L. Nathan[1]

Primary elections are increasingly used to select legislative candidates in new democracies around the world (Field and Siavelis 2008; Öhman 2004). This includes sub-Saharan Africa, where at least one major party in each of the 15 countries listed in Table 22.1 now holds legislative primary elections.[2] These primaries have mainly been adopted as party rules, not legislation, and the rules vary widely across countries and over time.[3] Many involve small groups of local party supporters convening to choose nominees in each district. Other primaries, such as those in Uganda, Botswana, and, recently, in one of Ghana's main parties, are large-scale elections of all rank-and-file party members, similar to primaries in much of the United States. Primaries in Africa have received only very limited attention,[4] however, reflecting the general neglect of primaries outside of advanced industrial democracies in the existing literature.[5] What explains the adoption of democratic candidate selection mechanisms in new democracies? And how do party leaders in these countries decide what rules to use in primary elections?

Most theories of primary elections are based on the experiences of parties in advanced industrial democracies and provide only limited guidance for understanding the adoption of primaries in new democracies. They often begin with the premise that electoral competition takes place in a one-dimensional issue space, usually interpreted as ideology along a left–right dimension (e.g., Gerber and Morton 1998; Jackson et al. 2007), and party leaders are usually assumed to be policy-seeking. From the perspective of the party leader, candidate selection mechanisms differ in their potential trade-offs between the expected performance of a would-be nominee in the general election and the distance between the nominee's and the party leader's policy preferences. A primary election could improve the party's performance by selecting for a nominee with higher valence (Carey and Polga-Hecimovich 2006; Adams and Merrill 2008; Serra 2011). An intra-party competition between potential nominees might also signal to voters that the quality of the nominee will be high, improving electability by enhancing the image of the party in the electorate (Caillaud and Tirole 2002; Crutzen, Castanheira and Sahuguet 2010). In this framework, party leaders balance these potential gains against the potential increase in the distance between the nominee's and party leader's policy preferences in their choice of candidate selection mechanism.

In new democracies in Africa and elsewhere in the developing world, however, elections are less frequently organized around ideological divides (Kitschelt and Wilkinson 2007; Stokes

Table 22.1 Legislative Primaries in African Democracies and Hybrid Regimes

Country	Year	Legislative Body	Political Party with Primaries
Benin	2015	National Assembly	Cowry Forces for an Emerging Benin (FCBE)
Botswana	2014	National Assembly	Bostwana Democratic Party (BDP)
Djibouti	2017	National Assembly	Union for a Presidential Majority (UMP)
			Union for National Salvation (USN)
Ghana	2016	Parliament	National Democratic Congress (NDC)
			New Patriotic Party (NPP)
Kenya	2013	National Assembly	National Alliance (NA)
			Orange Democracy Movement (ODM)
Lesotho	2015	National Assembly	Democratic Congress Party (DCP)
			All Basotho Convention (ABC)
Liberia	2014	Senate/House of Rep.	Unity Party (UP)
			Congress for Democratic Change (CDC)
Malawi	2014	National Assembly	Democratic Progressive Party (DPP)
			Malawi Congress Party (MCP)
Namibia	2014	National Assembly	South West Africa People's Organization (SWAPO)
Nigeria	2015	Senate/House of Rep.	All Progressives Congress (APC)
			People's Democratic Party (PCP)
Sierra Leone	2012	Parliament	All People's Congress (APC)
			Sierra Leone People's Party (SLPP)
Tanzania	2015	National Assembly	Chama Cha Mapinduzi (CCM)
			Party for Democracy and Progress (CHADEMA)
Uganda	2016	National Assembly	National Resistance Movement (NRM)
			Forum for Democratic Change (FDC)
Zambia	2016	National Assembly	Patriotic Party (PF)
			United Party for National Development (UPND)
Zimbabwe	2013	Senate/Natl. Assembly	Zimbabwe African National Union (ZANU–PF)
			Movement for Democratic Change (MDC)

Note: We record all known cases of legislative primaries in the two strongest political parties in the most recent legislative election in any sub-Saharan African country that had a Polity score of 0 or greater or a Freedom House score of "Party Free" or "Free" at any point between 2010 and 2015.

et al. 2013; Riedl 2014). In the African countries in Table 22.1, in stark contrast to advanced industrial democracies, no major parties make a serious effort to distinguish themselves from their competitors along ideological lines.[6] Moreover, most politicians and party activists are not policy-seekers, but instead office- and rent-seekers, which makes party activists vulnerable to vote buying in primaries. The lack of ideological distinction between the parties also means that parties are much more vulnerable to elite defections, as dissociating from a party would not deny a politician the benefit of being affiliated with the party label that best reflects the politician's policy positions.

Leaders of political parties in these new democracies focus on two imperatives other than the location of nominees in an ideological issue space when deciding whether to hold primaries. First, similar to party leaders in all democracies, they need a means to screen for the most electable candidates while avoiding costly intra-party disputes and defections from politicians who do not receive nominations. Second, they must ensure that local party activists are motivated to work on behalf of their party's nominees in the general election – a crucial consideration where parties do not use mass media to communicate ideologically distinct platforms but depend heavily on grassroots campaigning. This alternative approach to primary elections shares a central concern with theories of candidate selection mechanisms that emphasize how primaries address intra-party conflicts among elites (Kemahlioglu et al. 2009) or between leaders and activists (Katz and Mair 1995; Katz 2001).

We examine candidate selection mechanisms in new democracies using the case of Ghana, an emerging democracy in West Africa where the main parties first introduced parliamentary primaries in the mid-1990s. Ghana's extended experience with primaries through multiple elections is instructive in highlighting factors that affect the choice of candidate selection mechanisms in other new democracies, including those where parties are considering primaries for the first time.

It has not been easy for party leaders in Ghana to find candidate selection rules that balance the oft-competing goals of selecting for strong candidates, avoiding elite defections, and motivating grassroots members. Nomination procedures changed several times in each party through trial and error. Party leaders were often unable to predict the consequences of using different nomination procedures and only gradually identified the relative importance of each of these goals to their party's electoral success after facing unanticipated electoral costs created by particular candidate selection rules. Party leaders changed candidate selection mechanisms mainly with the goal of winning the general election, either in response to surprising electoral defeats or in anticipation that defeat loomed if the current system continued. But in so doing, they adjusted the rules to address one set of problems only to inadvertently complicate another, creating a need to further adjust nomination procedures in the future. In particular, steps taken to prevent elite defections have often invited damaging backlash from grassroots members and *vice versa*. One major party – the National Democratic Congress (NDC) – gradually found primary rules that appear to address each of the main imperatives; the other – the New Patriotic Party (NPP) – still has not.

Our exploration of the evolution of candidate selection mechanisms in Ghana deepens understanding of political party development in new democracies in two ways. First, we bring attention to two problems – elite defections and motivating grassroots activists – that are much more serious for leaders of parties in new democracies that lack ideological competition than for party leaders in advanced democracies. These two problems drive the institutional development of parties in new democracies.

Second, we highlight how candidate selection mechanisms are a key tool for party institutionalization, which in turn affects electoral accountability and democratic consolidation. Party institutionalization is the process by which parties develop durable organizations and connections to both voters and elites that persist across elections and are separable from the interests of specific party leaders (Mainwaring and Scully 1995; Riedl 2014). Parties in new democracies compete in what often begins as an unconsolidated political space, in which elites and ordinary voters may choose to forgo parties and pursue their political goals through other, potentially non-democratic, means. In order to become institutionalized, parties must align the incentives of elites and ordinary supporters towards committing to the party in the long-run, crowding out other forms of political mobilization and preventing defections (Hale 2008). The Ghanaian case illustrates how primary elections are a central tool that parties in new democracies can use to align these incentives.

The chapter proceeds as follows. First, we present a theory that explains the likely dynamics of three common types of nomination procedures in new democracies where ideology is not a central feature of elections. We then introduce the Ghanaian case before documenting and analyzing the evolution of candidate selection since democratization in 1992. These sections synthesize material from three empirical papers on primary elections in Ghana (Ichino and

Nathan 2012, 2013b, 2017). The final section concludes, discussing broader implications of primary elections for party institutionalization in new democracies.

Candidate Selection without Spatial Competition

Where ideology is not the main axis of competition between political parties, parties do not invest in building "ideational capital" to attract and motivate members (Hale 2008; Keefer and Vlaicu 2008). Instead, they frequently offer similar platforms as their competitors centered on development issues such as economic growth or fighting corruption, alongside targeted promises to deliver private and local public goods such as jobs and infrastructure (van de Walle 2007; Bleck and van de Walle 2013). Legislative election outcomes are determined not by the candidates' policy positions, which are often very similar, but by a combination of the candidates' financial capacities, their reputations for constituency service, and, in countries with political competition along ethnic lines, their ethnicities. A key element of campaigning in non-programmatic political systems is the pre-election distribution of personal benefits to voters (Stokes et al. 2013; Kramon 2016), and candidates with financial resources will be more competitive. A positive reputation for constituency service, a valence characteristic, improves voters' evaluations of a candidate, and voters also generally prefer co-ethnic representatives.

The *local elites* who form the pool of potential aspirants for legislative office are office-seekers rather than policy-seekers. If they expend personal resources in pursuit of office, they do so in order to obtain ego rents and pecuniary benefits of office. Others involved in politics at the local level also do so to seek personal benefits. Grassroots activists can engage in face-to-face campaigning and mobilize their personal networks of friends and family on behalf of the party. These grassroots activists include *branch-level party leaders* who run local party organizations, as well as rank-and-file *ordinary party members*, who are connected to branch-level leaders by social networks and clientelistic relationships and expect to share in the benefits passed down through the party branch.

Winning elections in new democracies requires *national-level party leaders* to address two related tasks. First, as in established democracies, national party leaders must recruit and put forward the strongest possible candidates. But national party leaders lack good information on which local elites have the financial means and local reputations for constituency service necessary to be competitive in the general election. Moreover, as Caillaud and Tirole (2002) note, party leaders must set up a candidate selection method in which weaker aspirants who are not selected will defer to the nominee and are incentivized to remain committed to the party. This is complicated because local elites are office-seeking and the party's nomination for a particular office is a single, indivisible good.

Second, national party leaders must get branch-level leaders and ordinary members to work on behalf of the party's nominee in the general election. Where parties compete with promises of personal benefits to individual voters and local communities rather than with distinct policy platforms, the mass media cannot substitute for the labor-intensive retail campaigning of grassroots activists to effectively convey the nominee's promises of targeted benefits to voters. Personal interactions and the gifts distributed by these activists are essential components of a viable campaign. Each party's branch-level leaders and ordinary members are thus actors "who hold, or have access to, critical resources that office-seekers need to realize their ambitions" (Aldrich 1995, 20). But because they are active in politics in order to gain personal benefits and not motivated by policy goals, these grassroots agents must be remunerated in some way to encourage them to expend effort on behalf of the party in the campaign.

National party leaders must consider both of these tasks in their choice of candidate selection methods. Different candidate selection methods have advantages and disadvantages with respect to each task, but party leaders often choose among selection methods without being able to fully anticipate many of their implications. Because local elites and grassroots members adjust their own behavior in response to party rules, new nomination procedures can have unintended effects on the party's relationship with local elites and grassroots members, which party leaders may then have to address through further changes to candidate selection rules. Party leaders gradually learn the full implications of different candidate selection mechanisms through trial and error.

We focus on the likely costs and benefits of three candidate selection methods that have been commonly used to choose legislative nominees in the African countries in Table 22.1. The first method is undemocratic – national party leaders select the nominee directly. The downsides of this selection method for each task are clear. Given party leaders' uncertainty about aspirants' attributes, nothing assures that the nominee selected by national party leaders will be a strong candidate or the strongest among the available pool of aspirants. The nominee could be a distinguished and popular politician with significant experience, but could also be someone whose only qualification is that he has close personal connections to the national party leadership. Local elites with the financial means and good reputation for constituency service but who lack ties to party leaders may decline to put themselves forward, resulting in a weaker and smaller overall pool of potential nominees. Moreover, the direct selection of nominees also provides no obvious mechanism to remunerate local party members. This method has some benefits for party leaders, however. It ensures that the nominee will be the person they most prefer by whatever criteria they select, and that the nomination is available to be dispensed as patronage.

The second selection method is a primary election with a small electorate composed of branch-level leaders of the party. Where primary electorates are small, individual primary voters have significant leverage to extract rents from the competing aspirants in return for support. The primary election becomes a vote buying contest. It becomes an indirect mechanism for remunerating branch-level leaders for their participation in the party without party leaders having to do so themselves; vote buying in primaries forces local elites who seek valuable nominations to compensate the party's branch-level leaders from their own funds. In turn, branch-level leaders can share some of these benefits with the ordinary members in their local organization. Primaries with vote buying effectively select for, and attract, aspirants with the necessary financial resources to win the general election. But they will not select for nominees with the best reputations for constituency service nor necessarily the best match between candidate ethnicity and the demographics of a constituency.

Vote buying also raises the prospect of intra-elite disputes after the primary. Local elites who expended considerable resources towards winning a nomination but were outbid may see the process as unfair, feel aggrieved, and leave the party, damaging the party's prospects in the general election. National party leaders have few good options for addressing this disaffection of losing aspirants. They may be able to minimize this prospect by selectively tampering with primaries to ensure that the aspirants who they fear are most capable of damaging the party are indeed nominated, but this is likely to only further aggrieve the other aspirants. Placating losing primary aspirants with alternative appointments to other offices that offer similar pecuniary benefits as a legislative seat is very costly, and not possible at all for the opposition party. Moreover, selectively cancelling primaries after announcing them risks aggrieving the branch-level leaders who expected to be compensated by aspirants during the primary election. These branch-level leaders can punish party leaders by withholding their own effort in the general election campaign and discouraging the effort of the ordinary members who are tied to them.

The third candidate selection method is a primary election in which the electorate comprises both ordinary members and branch-level leaders. Vote buying is a much less effective strategy with a large electorate, so the importance of aspirants' financial resources in the selection process is reduced as compared with the small electorate. The primary can attract aspirants who may be disadvantaged financially but have a strong reputation for constituency service and are a good ethnic match to their constituencies.

Moreover, candidate selection with the larger electorate is less prone to post-primary disputes. Without widespread vote buying, losing aspirants are more likely to see the primary as a fair process. In addition, with a larger primary electorate that more closely mirrors the general election electorate, an aspirant who does not win the nomination will be less likely to conclude that he could defeat the nominee in the general election, weakening the incentives for losing aspirants to defect from the party (Kemahlioglu et al. 2009).

Large-electorate primaries bypass branch-level leaders to directly remunerate ordinary members by including them in the selection process. In doing so, large-electorate primaries reduce the relative power of branch-level leaders by weakening their ability to hold back ordinary members' effort. Whether the personal benefits now directed to ordinary party members in primaries will be sufficient to compensate them for their campaign work, however, depends on the resources of the local elites who seek the nomination and the number of primary voters over which those resources are divided.

The Ghanaian Context

Several features of Ghanaian elections and parties are important for understanding how national party leaders have adapted candidate selection mechanisms for parliament. First, as in many African countries, Ghana's president is by far the most powerful actor in the political system (van de Walle 2003; Barkan 2008). The legislature is weak, exercising little oversight over the executive or influence on policy-making (Lindberg and Zhou 2009; Lindberg 2010). Nevertheless, individual members of parliament (MPs) control constituency development funds from which they can disburse benefits at their own discretion, with little to no oversight on how the money is spent. MPs who are appointed as cabinet ministers also have access to additional resources and opportunities for rent seeking. The returns for being an MP can be large in terms of reputation and prestige, as well as improved business contacts and networks for post-parliamentary careers. Concurrent elections are held every four years for president and the unicameral parliament. MPs are elected from single-member constituencies by plurality rule.

Second, left–right programmatic differences do not distinguish Ghana's two main parties – the National Democratic Congress (NDC) and the New Patriotic Party (NPP) (Riedl 2014). Competition between the NDC and NPP in the 1990s fell mostly along a pro- vs. anti-regime cleavage, and the two parties have since converged on highly similar platforms emphasizing development issues. The parties are now differentiated instead mostly by their ethnic bases. Patronage-based appeals are widespread in election campaigns (Nathan, forthcoming), which feature a mix of ethnic and performance voting (Lindberg 2010; Ichino and Nathan 2013a; Weghorst and Lindberg 2013; Harding 2015).

Third, in the 1990s, both parties built dense, nationwide, grassroots organizations, and today the parties have nearly identical organizational structures, with elected branch-level leadership committees at almost every polling station, as well as higher-level committees of party leaders at the parliamentary constituency, administrative region, and national levels. Election campaigns are labor-intensive, and candidates for president and parliament rely on grassroots members who are key intermediaries in the patronage networks that connect parties to voters between campaigns. The parties provide little financial support for their parliamentary candidates, who must largely finance their own election campaigns (Lindberg 2003).

The Evolution of Candidate Selection Mechanisms in Ghana

Multi-party elections returned to Ghana in 1992 after two decades of nearly uninterrupted authoritarian rule. The Provisional National Defense Council (PNDC) government refashioned itself as the NDC around the candidacy of incumbent ruler Jerry Rawlings. The NPP emerged as the main opposition party. Because the ban on political parties was lifted only a short time before the transition elections of 1992, national leaders of the NDC and NPP selected their respective candidates for parliament (Öhman 2004).

Since that transition election, parliamentary candidate selection methods in Ghana's two main parties have changed several times. Table 22.2 outlines the candidate selection methods used by the two parties in the Fourth Republic (1992–). National leaders of each party wrestled at first with the decision over whether to keep directly selecting nominees or to adopt some kind of limited primary election. By the early 2000s, both parties had decided that the benefits to holding primaries, especially in terms of motivating the grassroots, outweighed the risks of selecting candidates directly. Nevertheless, party leaders continued to struggle with the defection of disgruntled losing aspirants and selection of weak general election candidates. This sparked a new wave of changes to candidate selection methods after the 2008 elections in which national party leaders sought to reduce problems with disgruntled local elites without further sparking a backlash from grassroots activists.

The 1996 Elections

Both parties moved towards a system of delegate-based primaries with small electorates ahead of the 1996 elections. Under the new rules, parliamentary nominees were to be selected at a constituency congress by delegates representing each polling station-level party branch in the constituency.[7] In the NPP, the nominee was to be selected by approximately 100 primary voters, comprising the chairman of each branch, the party's constituency-level executives, and several other local dignitaries. The NDC's constituency congresses were of similar size and composition.

Table 22.2 Main Candidate Selection Mechanisms by Election for the Two Major Parties in Ghana

Year	National Democratic Congress (NDC)	New Patriotic Party (NPP)
1992	Direct selection by national party leaders *NDC wins*	Direct selection by national party leaders
1996	Small-electorate primaries of branch leaders *NDC wins*	Small-electorate primaries of branch leaders
2000	Direct selection by national party leaders	Small-electorate primaries of branch leaders *NPP wins*
2004	Small-electorate primaries of branch leaders	Small-electorate primaries of branch leaders *NPP wins*
2008	Small-electorate primaries of branch leaders *NDC wins*	Small-electorate primaries of branch leaders
2012	Small-electorate primaries of branch leaders *NDC wins*	Small-electorate primaries of branch leaders
2016	Closed primaries of all ordinary members	Small-electorate primaries of branch leaders *NPP wins*

Note: In 2012 and 2016, the NPP held small-electorate primaries but allowed significantly more branch-level leaders to vote per polling station than before.

These small-electorate primaries were unexpectedly characterized by vote buying (Öhman 2004), which had the unanticipated benefit to parties of being a means to compensate branch-level leaders and to motivate their effort without party leaders having to pay them directly. Vote buying turned the primaries into a "cocoa season" for the delegates – an opportunity for branch-level leaders to enjoy a windfall from holding local party positions for which they otherwise were rarely directly compensated.

At the same time, however, important party figures, including some with close ties to President Rawlings, were not re-nominated amid reports that rival aspirants had been able to buy support at the constituency congresses. Some of these aggrieved elites left the party and ran for parliament as independents, siphoning off votes from the NDC.[8] Although the NDC won the 1996 elections, party leaders were concerned that further elite defections would pull the party apart (Öhman 2004; Daddieh and Bob-Milliar 2016).[9]

The 2000 Elections

NDC leaders responded by re-centralizing control over nominations for the 2000 elections, making the party's National Executive Committee the final arbiter for candidate selection. Although direct selection could risk complaints about an unfair process from aspirants who were not selected, NDC leaders believed that they would be better able to placate key party elites and produce intra-elite consensus than would primary voters. NDC leaders claimed they would consult with the grassroots in each constituency before making nominations, but they appear to have largely ignored the preferences of branch-level leaders and ordinary members when selecting nominees before the 2000 elections (Öhman 2004).

The NPP won the 2000 presidential election and gained a majority in parliament for the first time, ending two decades of (P)NDC rule. Shocked by their defeat, NDC leaders attributed their poor performance in part to their centralized control over nominations (Öhman 2004).[10] NDC leaders came to believe that discontent at the grassroots level had reduced local campaign effort and hurt the party's general election performance. Once branch-level leaders learned that they could extract significant personal benefits from aspirants if a competitive primary were to be held, direct selection meant denying branch-level leaders a valuable opportunity to be compensated for their work for the party. Branch-level leaders in many constituencies had responded by protesting against the imposition of parliamentary nominees whom they did not support and threatening to encourage the ordinary members in the local party organization to vote "skirt and blouse" – a Ghanaian expression for split-ticket voting – to block the party's parliamentary nominees. After experimenting with the direct selection of nominees, NDC leaders had realized that direct selection carried significant downsides for their relationship with the grassroots. Consequently, the NDC decided to return to its previous delegate-based primary system for the 2004 elections and kept those rules for 2008.

For the 2000 elections, the opposition NPP kept its small-electorate primary system. At the same time, in selected constituencies, NPP leaders ensured the nomination of their favored local elites by pressuring delegates to pick particular aspirants or manipulating administrative processes to disqualify challengers (Ichino and Nathan 2012).

The 2004 and 2008 Elections

Both the NDC and NPP used small-electorate primaries for the next two elections. Much like the NDC primaries ahead of the 1996 elections, these contests were dominated by vote buying (Ichino and Nathan 2012, 2013b). In a widely repeated characterization, one MP described the primaries as creating a "moneyocracy," instead of a meritocracy, in which financial resources were the main criterion deciding who received nominations.[11] In interviews, primary aspirants described paying tens of thousands of dollars on their primary campaigns – a significant sum in Ghana – with much of the funds directed towards gifts to individual delegates, such as televisions, motorbikes, cash, school scholarships, and other valuable benefits.

Vote buying became the grounds used by several losing aspirants to challenge the outcome of the primary elections. Primaries in the ruling NPP were particularly expensive and problematic, and even winning aspirants in the NPP complained that bidding wars for delegates' votes had spiraled out of control. Some were left scrambling for new campaign funding after the primary to cover general election campaign expenses, having spent their budgets to secure the nomination.[12]

In addition, leaders of both parties continued to intervene selectively to impose favored nominees ahead of the 2004 and 2008 elections, resulting in protests by members and lawsuits by aspirants who had been pushed aside. But they did so in a pattern that demonstrated that party leaders in each party had learned to be sensitive to the risk of backlash from the grassroots. Selective interference in primary elections was less likely in constituencies where it would cause the denial of a large "harvest" for the delegates and was likely to generate greater protests by branch leaders (Ichino and Nathan 2012).

After the 2008 Elections

The main issue confronting leaders of each party after the 2008 election was no longer whether to hold primaries at all. Both parties now considered further democratizing the nomination process by expanding the primary electorate to offset the problems that they had not anticipated when they first introduced primaries: extensive vote buying in primaries that selected for aspirants with financial resources over other merits, and post-primary challenges by losing aspirants upset about vote buying.

With small primary electorates, as a senior NDC leader argued, "You [had] a situation where somebody who has not taken part in party activities for a long time, with moneybag, comes, [and] hijacks the system."[13] Wealthy aspirants who had not worked publicly on behalf of their party in the past and had no reputation for constituency service – and in some cases did not even live in their constituency – could leverage personal wealth to buy their way ahead of local elites who had been working for the party for years. Moreover, some of the aspirants who lost primaries to wealthy outsiders had spent years working on behalf of their party, building up strong reputations for constituency service that made them formidable independent candidates in the general election. Allowing wealthy outsiders to "cut in line" in front of aspirants with more experience risked discouraging local elites from committing to work for a party. The NPP and NDC attempted different solutions to reduce the influence of vote buying. The NPP moved first and failed, while the NDC moved second and appears to have been more successful. We consider these in turn.

After losing the 2008 election, the NPP debated two reform proposals, having attributed the party's loss in part to its candidate selection methods. The first option was to increase from 1 to 5 the number of branch-level leaders who would serve as delegates from each polling station branch. The second option was to dramatically increase the size of the electorate by opening primaries to all rank-and-file party members. With more primary voters, NPP leaders expected that primary aspirants would find it more difficult to buy the delegates' support, forcing primary voters to evaluate aspirants by other criteria such as their reputations for constituency service. Internal talking points circulated among senior NPP leaders advocating for an electorate expansion emphasized that doing so would "lead to election of people who actually . . . work for the party," would "ensure that the selected . . . candidates . . . represent the popular will . . . [and] serve the interests of the party people as a whole," and "reduce expenditure on internal party elections."[14]

The logic behind these proposals is clear. The effectiveness of vote buying depends on the ability to identify, monitor, and enforce exchanges with individual voters (e.g., Stokes et al. 2013). This is possible when the primary electorate is composed of a hundred or so easily identifiable branch-level leaders with whom aspirants can build personal relationships, buy off, and monitor on an individual basis. Enforcement of exchanges with these small sets of voters could be as rigorous as aspirants camping them in hotels before the primary, where they could be kept from soliciting further vote-buying offers from the other aspirants. As the number of voters that need to be bought increases, however, these types of strategies become more difficult. It is impossible for an individual aspirant to monitor and personally interact with thousands of primary voters.[15] Moreover, with a larger electorate, aspirants would have to spread finite budgets over larger numbers of voters, reducing the transfers they can provide to each individual voter.

The NPP adopted the first plan for its primaries ahead of the 2012 elections for several reasons. Some NPP leaders were concerned that organizing primaries among all party members would be too expensive and logistically difficult.[16] In addition, supporters of one of the NPP's main contestants for the 2012 presidential nomination were concerned that he would not be competitive among an electorate of all party members and sought to block the larger reform.[17] Moreover, by keeping branch-level leaders at the heart of the candidate selection process, the smaller expansion plan was unlikely to invite a major backlash from branch-level leaders, even if the expansion led each branch-level leader to receive less from the aspirants.

This reform failed to reduce vote buying in NPP primaries, however. Aspirants reported that there were now simply five times as many branch-level leaders demanding payment for their votes. In a survey of 125 aspirants in the NPP's 2016 primaries, which were held under the same rules as in 2012, the most common complaint about the primary process by far was the pressures created by vote buying (Ichino and Nathan 2017). As one aspirant noted, "We tend to fool ourselves that the larger the electoral college, the less we spend . . . In reality, it is the opposite . . . nobody will come and vote for you if you don't induce him financially."[18]

Although it had won the 2012 elections, NDC leaders were also concerned that contentious primaries had hurt their performance. Aggrieved aspirants and other challenges that the then-incumbent NPP had faced in 2008 had emerged in the now-ruling NDC in 2012. The party's General Secretary identified 15 parliamentary constituencies in which the NDC had won the presidential election but lost the parliamentary seat because of split-ticket voting that could be attributed to a disputed primary or an independent candidacy by a disgruntled primary aspirant.[19]

Despite the NPP's failure to reduce vote buying in 2012, the NDC used a similar logic to decide to eliminate the delegate system and expand its primary electorate. Unlike the NPP, however, the NDC chose to expand the primary to include all ordinary members. Expanding the electorate was intended to "cure moneyocracy in our system."[20] NDC leaders also believed that expanding the electorate would help eliminate complaints from primary losers that they had been denied nominations based on an unfair process that advantaged only the wealthiest politicians. The NDC's General Secretary argued, "the one who will emerge a winner will [now] have the confidence that he has the support of the members of the party at the constituency level and the losers will have a clear message that the whole constituency had decided that it is not their turn."[21] The NDC conducted a biometric registration campaign of all party members in 2015, producing a primary electorate of as many as 8,000 ordinary members per constituency, substantially greater than the several hundred delegates who had voted in each constituency in prior years and an order of magnitude larger than the NPP's expanded primary electorate for 2012.

Unlike the NPP's more marginal reforms in 2012, the NDC's much larger electorate expansion in 2016 seems to have significantly altered the dynamics of the party's primaries. A greater number of local elites sought NDC nominations, including a greater number of women and aspirants from outside the NDC's core ethnic coalition, which increased the diversity of the party's eventual nominees.[22] By contrast, aspirants who had no prior experience in party leadership or government positions but had private sector backgrounds, indicative of having significant financial resources for vote buying but no reputation for constituency service, became significantly less likely to win nominations. These changes are consistent with the reduced influence of vote buying on primary election outcomes (Ichino and Nathan 2017).

This suggests that party leaders in Ghana were correct that expanding the primary electorate had the potential to reduce the influence of vote buying. It is only that NPP leaders had misjudged how large of an electorate expansion was necessary to bring the electorate past the point where vote buying would be very difficult for wealthy aspirants. The expansion of the NDC primary electorate was more successful. With many thousands more primary voters for aspirants to win, vote buying likely became a much less efficient strategy in the NDC primaries, allowing the ethnicity and reputation of aspirants to become more important in deciding nominations (Ichino and Nathan 2017).

At the same time, the reforms raised the possibility that branch-level leaders would revolt at the reduction of vote buying and their lost opportunity for remuneration. But the NDC's 2016 primaries did not generate widespread protests by branch-level leaders, as had occurred in the past. NDC leaders may have averted these protests by including ordinary members in the primary electorate and effectively cutting out the intermediary role of branch-level leaders. Primary aspirants now interacted with ordinary members directly, instead of relying on indirect transfers from the branch-level leaders. Even if branch-level leaders were personally upset at lost rents, they now likely had less influence over ordinary members in their branches necessary to encourage them to join protests or sit out the general election campaign.

Conclusions

Primary elections in new democracies remain understudied, particularly in Africa. This is at least partly an outcome of the difficulty of data collection on internal political party processes in the developing world. For example, Ichino and Nathan (2012, 2013b, 2017) required reconstructing the record of primary elections in Ghana largely from scratch in the absence of reliable official data. But it is also the result of an absence of theoretical frameworks appropriate for candidate selection methods for elections without spatial competition.

Despite these constraints, studying primaries is important for understanding elections in new democracies for several reasons. First, candidate selection mechanisms are a central element of electoral accountability relationships between politicians and voters. Voters can only hold politicians accountable to the extent that they have real alternatives available on the ballot – an outcome determined by candidate selection rules. While a vast literature in the study of African politics investigates the extent to which voters are able to hold local politicians accountable, this research almost never addresses the process by which politicians appear in the voters' choice set. By breaking the direct link between voters and politicians, candidate selection mechanisms may distort politicians' incentives to serve voter interests by making politicians potentially more accountable to actors within parties than to their constituents. In the extreme, as under dominant party rule, candidate selection can be the only stage at which there is any opportunity for electoral accountability (Hyden and Leys 1972; Chazan 1979).

Second, candidate selection rules are a key element of party building. Developing well-institutionalized parties is often seen as an important step towards improving the quality of democratic governance by extending politicians' time horizons, reducing the personalization of politics around specific powerful elites, allowing voters to more easily attribute blame for poor performance, and providing voters with informational heuristics that allow them to select politicians better aligned with their preferences. As parties attempt to become more institutionalized, primaries are a possible tool for preventing intra-elite disputes and efficiently allocating scarce resources demanded by aspiring politicians. We show that primaries can also play an important role attracting grassroots activists into party organizations by creating a mechanism that forces office-seeking elites to compensate local-level agents. Aside from Riedl (2014), few recent studies on party development in the developing world closely examine how internal party institutions can shape the incentives of elites or grassroots activists to commit to pursuing their political goals within a party.

With some of the most well-institutionalized parties in Africa, Ghana is often held up as an exemplary case of party development on the continent, and it is frequently compared with countries with far less stable parties such as Benin, Kenya, or Zambia. The early adoption of primary elections that helped regulate elite conflicts and attract local members is a key part of the explanation for why Ghana has had much greater success in building and sustaining durable party organizations. Some parties in countries where party systems have been far more inchoate, such as Kenya, are now beginning to experiment with primaries as well. The introduction of primaries in these settings should be viewed as a step on the path towards party institutionalization. This chapter proposes a theoretical framework that scholars examining the introduction of primaries in these other cases can use to think about the key trade-offs and imperatives that party leaders will likely confront as they design candidate selection institutions.

Notes

1 We thank Peter Carroll and Lalitha Ramaswamy for their research assistance for this chapter.
2 We searched for any discussion in media reports and secondary literature of legislative primaries held by the two highest-placing parties in the most recent legislative election. We restricted the search to sub-Saharan African countries that are either democracies or hybrid regimes with contested elections, defined as countries with Polity scores of 0 or greater or Freedom House scores of "partly free" or "free" at some point between 2010 and 2015. There are 32 countries that meet these criteria. It is possible that primaries about which no information was readily available are also held in the other 17 African countries. These 17 countries are Burkina Faso, Burundi, Central African Republic, Democratic Republic of Congo, Gabon, Gambia, Guinea, Guinea-Bissau, Ivory Coast, Madagascar, Mali, Mozambique, Niger, Senegal, Somalia, South Africa, and Togo.
3 Primaries are sometimes only selectively implemented in the cases in Table 22.1, with party leaders interfering in the nomination process to handpick some nominees in many parties even after the formal introduction of primary elections.
4 See Ichino and Nathan (2012, 2013b, 2017) on Ghana, however, as well as Izama and Raffler (n.d.) on Uganda, Warren (2016) on Botswana, and Choi (2017) on Kenya.
5 Significant exceptions are Langston (2001), de Luca et al. (2002), Field and Siavelis (2008), and Bruhn (2010). Carey and Polga-Hecimovich (2006) and Kemahlioglu et al. (2009) have also examined primaries for presidential candidates in new democracies in Latin America.
6 In other new democracies, there are sometimes both ideological and non-ideological parties. This includes Latin American countries such as Argentina (Calvo and Murillo 2004) and Mexico (Greene 2007), as well as new democracies in Southeast Asia, such as Indonesia (Slater 2016). In other cases, the same party, such as conservative parties in Chile and Uruguay or India's ruling Bharatyia Janata Party (BJP), simultaneously uses ideological appeals to mobilize voters in some districts and non-ideological appeal in others (Luna 2014; Thachil 2014).

7 In practice, however, party leaders intervened in some primaries, and not all constituencies held primaries (Öhman 2004; Daddieh and Bob-Milliar 2016).

8 Several barriers discourage party switching in Ghana, such that elite defections have taken the form of independent candidacies rather than defeated primary aspirants from one party becoming parliamentary candidates in another. Both major parties require in their party constitutions that a politician be a member of the party for two years before becoming eligible for a nomination. Ghana's constitution also specifies that a by-election be held if an MP leaves his party while in office, deterring party switching by sitting MPs.

9 Interview with former NDC General Secretary, Accra, May 6, 2010.

10 Interview with former NDC General Secretary, Accra, May 6, 2010.

11 Interview with NPP primary aspirant and incumbent MP, Brong Ahafo Region, November 10, 2015.

12 For example, interview with NPP primary aspirant and incumbent MP, Eastern Region, July 19, 2011.

13 "NDC's Expanded Electoral College Will Cure Vote-Buying – Ade Coker," *Citi FM Online*, August 17, 2015.

14 Document obtained from a NPP national executive committee member, August 2011.

15 Primary aspirants could employ clientelistic intermediaries instead, but relying on intermediaries introduces its own inefficiencies, including rent capture by the intermediaries themselves (e.g., Stokes et al. 2013).

16 Mahama Haruna, "Should all NPP Members Elect the Party's Presidential Candidate?," *Ghana Web*, March 28, 2009.

17 Any changes to the parliamentary primary electorate would also have resulted in changes to the presidential primary electorate. Interview with NPP primary aspirant and former MP, Central Region, August 5, 2011.

18 Interview with NPP aspirant and incumbent MP, Western Region, 10 November 2015

19 "NDC to scrap Electoral College: moves for universal membership suffrage," *Daily Graphic*, 10 September 2013.

20 "NDC's Expanded Electoral College Will Cure Vote-Buying – Ade Coker," *Citi FM Online*, August 17, 2015. Also discussed in interview with senior NDC national leader, Accra, October 26, 2015.

21 "NDC to scrap Electoral College: moves for universal membership suffrage," *Daily Graphic*, September 10, 2013.

22 Before the reforms, the woman's organizer, a leadership position set aside for a woman, was typically the only woman among the four delegates voting in NDC primaries from each branch. The gender balance in the primary electorate improved significantly with the reforms since the ordinary party membership has a greater proportion of women

References

Adams, James, and Samuel Merrill, III. 2008. "Candidate and Party Strategies in Two-Stage Elections Beginning with a Primary." *American Journal of Political Science* 52(2): 344–359.

Aldrich, John. 1995. *Why Parties? The Origin and Transformation of Party Politics in America*. Chicago: University of Chicago Press.

Barkan, Joel D. 2008. "Legislatures on the Rise?" *Journal of Democracy* 19(2): 124–137.

Bleck, Jaimie, and Nicolas van de Walle. 2013. "Valence Issues in African Elections: Navigating Uncertainty and the Weight of the Past." *Comparative Political Studies* 46(11): 1394–1421.

Bruhn, Kathleen. 2010. "Too Much Democracy? Primaries and Candidate Success in the 2006 Mexican National Elections." *Latin American Politics and Society* 52(4): 25–52.

Caillaud, B., and Jean Tirole. 2002. "Parties as Political Intermediaries." *Quarterly Journal of Economics* 117(4): 1453–1489.

Calvo, Ernesto, and M. Victoria Murillo. 2004. "Who Delivers? Partisan Clients in the Argentine Electoral Market." *American Journal of Political Science* 48(4): 742–757.

Carey, John M., and John Polga-Hecimovich. 2006. "Primary Elections and Candidate Strength in Latin America." *Journal of Politics* 68(3): 530–43.

Chazan, Naomi. 1979. "African Voters at the Polls: A Re-examination of the Role of Elections in African Politics." *The Journal of Commonwealth and Comparative Politics* 17(2): 136–158.

Choi, Donghyun Danny. 2017. "Instruments of Control: Party Leaders Endorsements and Primary Elections in Africa." Working Paper, University of California, Berkeley.

Crutzen, Benoît S. Y., Micael Castanheira and Nicolas Sahuguet. 2010. "Party Organization and Electoral Competition." *Journal of Law, Economics, & Organization* 26(2): 212–242.

Daddieh, Cyril K., and George M. Bob-Milliar. 2016. "In Search of 'Honorable' Membership: Parliamentary Primaries and Candidate Selection in Ghana." In *Issues in Ghana's Electoral Politics*, ed. Kwame A. Ninsin. Dakar, Senegal: CODESRIA, pp. 13–34.

de Luca, Miguel, Mark P. Jones, and Maria Ines Tula. 2002. "Back Rooms or Ballot Boxes? Candidate Nomination in Argentina." *Comparative Political Studies* 35(2): 413–436.

Field, Bonnie N., and Peter M. Siavelis. 2008. "Candidate Selection Procedures in Transitional Polities." *Party Politics* 14(5): 620–639.

Gerber, Elisabeth R., and Rebecca B. Morton. 1998. "Primary Election Systems and Representation." *Journal of Law, Economics and Organization* 14(2): 304–324.

Greene, Kenneth. 2007. *Why Dominant Parties Lose: Mexico's democratization in Comparative Perspective.* New York: Cambridge University Press.

Hale, Henry E. 2008. *Why Not Parties in Russia? Democracy, Federalism, and the State.* New York: Cambridge University Press.

Harding, Robin. 2015. "Attribution and Accountability: Voting for Roads in Ghana." *World Politics* 67(4): 656–689.

Hyden, Goran, and Colin Leys. 1972. "Elections and Politics in Single-Party Systems: The Case of Kenya and Tanzania." *British Journal of Political Science* 2(4): 389–420.

Ichino, Nahomi, and Noah L. Nathan. 2012. "Primaries on Demand? Intra-Party Politics and Nominations in Ghana." *British Journal of Political Science* 42(4): 769–791.

Ichino, Nahomi, and Noah L. Nathan. 2013a. "Crossing the Line: Local Ethnic Geography and Voting in Ghana." *American Political Science Review* 107(2): 344–361.

Ichino, Nahomi, and Noah L. Nathan. 2013b. "Do Primaries Improve Electoral Performance? Clientelism and Intra-Party Conflict in Ghana." *American Journal of Political Science* 57(3): 428–441.

Ichino, Nahomi, and Noah L. Nathan. 2017. "Democratizing the Party: The Effects of Primary Election Reforms in Ghana." Working Paper, University of Michigan.

Izama, Melina Platas, and Pia Raffler. n.d. "Meet the Candidates: Information and Accountability in Primaries and General Elections." Working Paper, Yale University.

Jackson, Matthew, Laurent Mathevet, and Kyle Mattes. 2007. "Nomination Processes and Policy Outcomes." *Quarterly Journal of Political Science* 2(1): 67–94.

Katz, Richard S. 2001. "The Problem of Candidate Selection and Models of Party Democracy." *Party Politics* 7(3): 277–296.

Katz, Richard S., and Peter Mair. 1995. "Changing Models of Party Organization and Party Democracy: The Emergence of the Cartel Party." *Party Politics* 1(1): 5–28.

Keefer, Philip, and Razvan Vlaicu. 2008. "Democracy, Credibility, and Clientelism." *Journal of Law, Economics, and Organization* 24(2): 371–406.

Kemahlioglu, Ozge, Rebecca Weitz-Shapiro, and Shigeo Hirano. 2009. "Why Primaries in Latin American Presidential Elections?" *Journal of Politics* 71: 339–352.

Kitschelt, Herbert, and Steven I. Wilkinson. 2007. Citizen-Politician Linkages: An Introduction. In *Patrons, Clients, and Policies: Patterns of Democratic Accountability and Political Competition*, ed. Herbert Kitschelt and Steven I. Wilkinson. New York: Cambridge University Press, pp. 1–49.

Kramon, Eric. 2016. "Electoral Handouts as Information: Explaining Unmonitored Vote Buying." *World Politics* 68(3): 454–498.

Langston, Joy. 2001. "Why Rules Matter: Changes in Candidate Selection in Mexico's PRI, 1988–2000." *Journal of Latin American Studies* 33: 485–511.

Lindberg, Staffan I. 2003. "'It's Our Time to 'Chop':' Do Elections in Africa Feed Neo-Patrimonialism rather than Counteract it?" *Democratization* 10(2): 121–40.

Lindberg, Staffan I. 2010. "What Accountability Pressures Do MPs in Africa Face and How Do They Respond? Evidence from Ghana." *Journal of Modern African Studies* 48(1): 117–142.

Lindberg, Staffan I., and Yongmei Zhou. 2009. "Co-optation Despite Democratization in Ghana." In *Legislative Power in Emerging African Democracies*, ed. Joel Barkan. Boulder, CO: Lynne Rienner Publishers, pp. 147–176.

Luna, Juan Pablo. 2014. *Segmented Representation: Political Party Strategies in Unequal Democracies.* New York: Oxford University Press.

Mainwaring, Scott, and Timothy Scully. 1995. "Introduction." In *Building Democratic Institutions: Party Systems in Latin America*, eds. M. Scott and T. Scully. Stanford, CA: Stanford University Press, pp. 1–36.

Nathan, Noah L. Forthcoming. "Does Participation Reinforce Patronage? Policy Preferences, Turnout, and Class in Urban Ghana." *British Journal of Political Science*.

Öhman, Magnus. 2004. "The Heart and Soul of the Party: Candidate Selection in Ghana and Africa." Ph.D. Thesis, Uppsala Universitet, Sweden.

Riedl, Rachel Beatty. 2014. *Authoritarian Origins of Democratic Party Systems in Africa*. New York: Cambridge University Press.

Serra, Gilles. 2011. "Why Primaries? The Party's Tradeoff between Policy and Valence." *Journal of Theoretical Politics* 23(1): 21–51.

Slater, Dan. 2016. "Party Cartelization, Indonesian-Style: The Contingency of Democratic Opposition." Working Paper, University of Chicago.

Stokes, Susan C., Thad Dunning, Marcelo Nazareno, and Valeria Brusco. 2013. *Brokers, Voters, and Clientelism: The Puzzle of Distributive Politics*. New York: Cambridge University Press.

Thachil, Tariq. 2014. *Elite Parties, Poor Voters: How Social Services Win Votes in India*. New York: Cambridge University Press.

van de Walle, Nicolas. 2003. "Presidentialism and Clientelism in Africa's Emerging Party Systems." *Journal of Modern African Studies* 41(2): 297–321.

van de Walle, Nicolas. 2007. "'Meet the New Boss, Same as the Old Boss?' The Evolution of Political Clientelism in Africa." In *Patrons, Clients, and Policies: Patterns of Democratic Accountability and Political Competition*, ed. Herbert Kitschelt and Steven I. Wilkinson. New York: Cambridge University Press, pp. 50–67.

Warren, Shana S. 2016. "Decentralizing Candidate Selection: Preliminary Evidence from Primaries in Botswana." Presented at the 2016 American Political Science Annual Meetings, Philadelphia.

Weghorst, Keith R., and Staffan I. Lindberg. 2013. "What Drives the Swing Voter in Africa?" *American Journal of Political Science* 57(3): 717–734.

23

PARTY PRIMARIES IN CANADA

Scott Pruysers and Anthony Sayers

Personnel selection (i.e., leadership and candidate selection) is among the most important tasks that political parties perform (Kirchheimer 1966; Sartori 1976). Until very recently, parties around the world relied on relatively exclusive selectorates, like the parliamentary party group (PPG) in the case of leadership selection, to make these important intra-party decisions (Pilet and Cross 2014; Kenig 2009). In the last three decades, however, parties in many Western democracies have engaged in an intra-party democracy revolution of sorts, adopting more inclusive and participatory selection procedures, including party primaries. Canadian parties are somewhat anomalous in this regard and have used primaries to select both legislative candidates and party leaders for decades (Cross et al. 2016; Pruysers and Cross 2016).

This chapter explores the development, adoption, and practice of party primaries[1] in Canada. Importantly, we consider primaries for both the selection of legislative candidates as well as party leaders. Although both have resulted in broadly similar processes that invite party members to participate directly in the selection of party personnel, there are several key differences between the two. These differences include a slower path of democratization for leadership selection, as well as institutionalized veto points in candidate selection primaries. We pay particular attention to the inherently self-governing nature of Canadian parties in administering their primaries, considering how the view of parties as private associations allows for frequent rule changes, and even a back-tracking of sorts to less inclusive selection methods. Although the focus is on federal parties, we draw upon the experience of parties at the provincial level throughout the chapter. We end the chapter with a brief discussion of the major challenges that parties face when conducting primary elections, including potential internal divisiveness.

Institutional Context for Party Primaries in Canada

The defining aspect of party primaries in Canada is their self-governing nature. Unlike general elections, which are highly regulated and monitored by the state (i.e., stable electoral rules, wide-reaching financing legislation, spending limits, trained election officers, etc.), parties are generally free to organize and operate as they like. This includes creating (and changing) the rules governing the selection of candidates and leaders. As Pruysers and Cross (2016, 783) write, "parties choose the selectorate, determine when the contest will be held, decide where voting will take place, set eligibility requirements (for both candidates and voters), levy membership fees, and so on." Viewing themselves more as private associations than public utilities (van Biezen 2004), Canadian political parties have been reluctant to use the Canadian state to regulate intra-party affairs. In other words, parties have been hesitant to use state legislation to regulate *themselves*, especially when it comes to how they select party leaders and legislative candidates.[2] Current institutional arrangements allow parties to maintain their preferred balance between central oversight and local input into the selection process without the need for further legislation. As we demonstrate throughout this chapter, this general lack of regulation is a fundamental feature of Canadian primary elections and one that shapes the dynamics of these intra-party elections.

Pruysers and Cross (2016), however, note that there are several caveats to the notion that parties are completely free to conduct their primaries free from state intervention. First, one aspect where the state has been willing to regulate party activities is in their financing. Here party finance legislation has, to some degree, shaped the character of candidate nomination primaries. Introduced into the Canada Elections Act in 1974 (Election Expenses Act, S.C. 1973–1974, c. 51.), limits on spending and provisions regarding reimbursement of candidate expenses marked the first significant regulation of political parties. Administrative demands increased again when in 2004 the Act was amended to outlaw corporate and union donations and placed limits on what candidates could spend in seeking their local nomination (Young and Jansen 2011).[3] Such spending limits were adopted, at least in part, to address concerns regarding the ability of historically marginalized groups to raise adequate funds to be competitive. Even here, however, the state has been hesitant and inconsistent to regulate internal party affairs. While candidate primaries have a state-imposed spending limit, parties are free to set their own spending limits for leadership primaries.

Second, the introduction of party labels to ballots in place of occupation and address in the 1970s formalized the definition and registration of political parties and candidacies. Since Elections Canada could not be in the business of verifying who was the "real" party candidate in every constituency, use of a party label required the candidate to provide a document signed by the leader certifying her candidacy. This statutory requirement developed into a means by which a leader's office could signal who might be acceptable as a candidate. Since then, parties have increasingly required candidates to complete detailed questionnaires and interviews probing their personal and political history in order to avoid selecting a candidate with an embarrassing past. In the last two decades parties have also amended their constitutions, giving the party leader the power to appoint local candidates, in addition to their statutory "veto" (Koop and Bittner 2011). Section 1.2 of the Liberal candidate selection rules, for example, states that: "The Leader has the authority to designate a person to be the candidate in any election, without the need for the conduct of a Meeting" (Liberal Party 2013). Thus, what began as a seemingly mundane legal requirement to allow party labels on the ballot has resulted in considerable central party authority in the selection of local candidates.

Finally, parties have, on occasion, been subject to judicial review. In 2004, for instance, a Calgary judge ordered the provincial Progressive Conservative party to hold a new nomination contest in the electoral district of Calgary-Montrose (Heyman and Wilton 2004). Three years later a group of 11 party activists sought judicial intervention against the federal Conservative party in the district of Calgary West. Although the activists were initially successful, the Alberta Court of Appeal ruled in favor of the party stating that "when arranging for the nomination of their candidate in Calgary West, the Party and the Association were essentially engaged in private activities, and their actions, in this case, are not subject to judicial review" (*Knox v. Conservative Party of Canada 2007*). More recently, an Ontario judge ruled that parties are not immune to judicial scrutiny and oversight:

The decisions that political parties, especially the major political parties, make in terms of the candidates they put forward, the policies they adopt, and the leader that they choose, do have a very serious effect on the rights and interests of the entire voting public . . . The voting public, therefore, has a very direct and significant interest in ensuring that the activities of political parties are carried out in a proper, open and transparent manner.

Perkel 2017

While no clear judicial consensus has emerged, it's clear that there are credible challenges to the notion that parties are purely private associations.

Candidate Primaries

Candidate primaries of the nineteenth century reflected the limited character of the state and franchise along with a cadre form of party organization. The candidate was the linchpin of party politics, connecting voters to government and its largesse, and providing party and government with essential intelligence on local affairs. Notable men were selected by a small group of likeminded individuals bound together by personal connection to the candidate and shared experiences fighting election campaigns. While the franchise may have been limited, the selection of local candidates has been relatively democratic for generations. More than a century ago, for instance, Siegfried (1907, 119) noted that "five or six weeks before voting-day the candidates are nominated by a local convention held in each constituency." This traditional form of candidate primary has persisted for over a century, slowly adapting to the broadening of the franchise and the reformulation of politics in response to the massive growth and formalization of the state. Today, eligible party members in each of the country's 338 electoral districts can cast a ballot for their preferred candidate. Candidate primaries are therefore both inclusive and decentralized (Hazan and Rahat 2010).

As Table 23.1 demonstrates, Canadian parties have taken a very open approach to membership and voter eligibility. Members can often be non-citizens, and as young as 13 years old. The only real barrier to participation is membership, which typically costs a modest fee of about $25 (although this varies by party and sometimes province). Similar to voting eligibility, candidacy requirements are also very modest. In most parties a candidate needs to pay a small deposit, gather a few signatures, and be a party member for a short period of time prior to the nomination. Only in the Conservatives is there a membership requirement that is longer than 30 days. However, as Sayers' (1999) analysis of local campaigns reveals, the New Democrats, despite not having formal rules, have expectations that candidates will have strong ties to the party and considerable party experience.

Candidate primaries in Canadian political parties are somewhat distinctive, marked by local control set against a highly centralized regulatory regime. As Table 23.1 shows, the central party plays a considerable role in what is typically considered a purely local affair. While the party membership of local associations selects most candidates, this choice is subject to scrutiny by the central party. As Pruysers and Cross (2016, 788) write,

The most onerous eligibility requirement is receiving the central party's authorization after passing a strict screening process. With hundreds of individual campaigns, there are considerable opportunities for potential gaffes and controversy. As a result, each party subjects would-be candidates to extensive vetting and rigorous interviews in an attempt to screen out extreme candidates and potential problems before the election begins.

Table 23.1 Candidate Selection Rules Compared

	Conservative	*New Democrat*	*Liberal*
Selectorate	Party members 14 years and older 21-day membership cut-off	Party members 13 years and older 30-day membership cut-off	Party members 14 years and older 2–7-day membership cut-off
Candidate eligibility	Party membership (6 months prior) 25 signatures of members $1,000 deposit	Party membership (30 days prior) No signature requirement No deposit	Party membership (no length specified) 100 signatures of members $1,000 deposit
Candidate approval	All candidates approved centrally	All candidates approved centrally	All candidates approved centrally
Rule–making and administration	Central party sets preconditions for nomination	Central party sets preconditions for nomination	Central party sets preconditions for nomination
Gender and diversity	No formal rules	Freeze nomination until adequate search for women and minorities	Freeze nomination until adequate search for women and minorities

Source: Adapted from Pruysers and Cross (2016).

The Liberal party's "Green Light Committee," for example, conducts background checks, research regarding financial liabilities, history of contribution to the community/party, as well as a lengthy questionnaire. Candidate screening, however, is not the only role that the central party plays in candidate primaries. The central party governs a variety of administrative aspects of the primary, including when the nomination will be opened. The Conservatives, for instance, have strict rules regarding how much money and how many members a local party has before it is able to hold a nomination.

When considering the dynamics and outcomes of candidate selection primaries in Canada there are a few things worth noting. First is the (uneasy) relationship between the central and local party branches. The organizational form that Canadian parties have adopted to manage 338 diverse electoral districts is labelled stratarchical, in that it provides distinct spheres for local and national party operations (Carty 2002; Carty and Cross 2006). The "organizational bargain" between the central party apparatus and local constituency associations provides the center with authority over policy, governance, and branding while the locals have control over the choice of their local candidate (Carty 2004). Not only does voting occur at the constituency level, but local riding associations take an active role in recruiting potential candidates (Cross and Young 2013). However, given that the leader has the authority to approve candidacies by legal statute, and since parties have moved to allow leaders to appoint candidates, the stratarchical bargain does not always work smoothly in practice. Indeed, tension between local autonomy and the central party's veto is a core feature of Canadian parties in the electorate, party organization, and in parliament.

Every election cycle features a variety of news stories about each party regarding the central party disallowing certain candidates after reviewing their paperwork, appointing a preferred candidate, or manipulating the timing and details of a primary to ensure a particular outcome (Cross et al. 2016; Pruysers and Cross 2016). The Conservative party, for instance, disallowed all challengers against its incumbent Member of Parliament in the district of Calgary Skyview in the lead up to the 2015 election (Wingrove 2014). Likewise, despite having considerable support among local activists and having won the party's nomination twice previously, a prominent Liberal was not authorized by the central party to contest a 2014 byelection (Hume 2014). These kinds of intrusions into local party affairs are often met with considerable criticism from local activists who decry central party interference as "sneaky" and "unethical" and it is not uncommon for members of the party and even local executive to publicly cancel their party memberships in protest. While tension between local and national branches is a regular feature of the nominations, overt intervention is still relatively rare and sometimes ineffectual and counterproductive (Carty and Eagles 2005). Despite the tension, the institutionalized veto and the role of the central party in the selection process has allowed parties to meet their core objectives – to avoid embarrassment and place candidates in certain ridings when they must (i.e., when a local association is unable to do so, or when a star candidate needs a district to run in). At the same time, by keeping the interference to a minimum, local associations are able to attract new members, donations, quality candidates, and energy and excitement as a result of the primary election.

The second dynamic of candidate primaries is the large-scale membership mobilization that takes place. The central role of party members in candidate selection primaries and the ability for candidates to shape their selectorate by recruiting new members produces the cyclical pattern in party membership numbers that defines Canadian parties. The mobilization that is necessary for a strong primary showing drives the massive influx of new members and resources to the party that are essential to electoral success – both in the primary and general election. It is not uncommon to see a party's local membership increase by two- or three-fold in contested nominations (Carty, Cross, and Young 2000). Pruysers and Cross (2016) provide an example from the Liberal party where the party's local membership in the Nickel Belt electoral district increased by 1,000 percent, from approximately 200 members after the 2011 federal election to more than 2,000 for the 2015 candidate primary.

There are two important implications to this growth in membership. First, mobilization from ethnic communities is often used as a means of signing up hundreds or even thousands of new members relatively quickly (Cross 2004). Given the modest membership requirements and the influx of new members, long-time party members often complain that their local association has been "hijacked" or taken over in the process. Calling these new members "tourists," long-term and committed party members often view their role as undermined by new members. Second, once primaries and elections are over, there is little ongoing role for party members, and those recruited to participate in the primary retreat in both numbers and engagement (Cross et al. 2016). Indeed, Young and Cross (2002) report that being able to participate in a nomination election is a primary incentive for joining the party for a significant number of party members. Once the nomination is over, however, these members slowly fade from the party, especially those who supported a losing candidate (Cross and Pruysers 2017). The parliamentary leadership is therefore left to manage legislative politics unencumbered by party members and the principles and policies they might champion.

Third, the pool of candidates offered to the voters has never reflected the growing diversity of the voting population (Carty and Erickson 1991). As gatekeepers to elected legislatures, the nomination processes of political parties determine the pool of candidates from which voters can choose on election day and therefore limits who can be elected. In this sense, parties play an important role in the degree to which legislatures are representative of the broader society. The 1967 Royal Commission on the Status of Women encouraged party-sanctioned groups as well as civil society organizations to push for greater inclusion of women. Moreover, growing social diversity since the 1970s has accelerated pressure for a more inclusive slate of candidates.

Despite regular calls for a widening of the types of candidates offered to voters, however, the state has been reluctant to use legislation to regulate party nominations to achieve representational outcomes. Parties have been comparatively slow to respond to these demands, and rather than choosing to regulate primaries more tightly, have used internal, and informal, processes to increase diversity. As demonstrated in Table 23.1, both the Liberals and New Democrats have rules regarding the "freezing" of nominations until a proper search can be done for women and ethnic minority candidates. Section 1.7 (a) of the 2013 Liberal nomination procedures asserts that no nomination meeting shall be issued until:

> the EDA has demonstrated to the satisfaction of the Provincial or Territorial Campaign Chair that the association has conducted an acceptable search for Nomination Contestants, including documented evidence of a thorough search for potential candidates who are female and who are reflective of the demographic and linguistic makeup of the local electorate.
>
> *Liberal Party 2013*

Various provincial parties have rules aimed at increasing both gender and minority representation in their candidate pools. Given the informal and voluntary nature of these approaches, however, it is not surprising that the underrepresentation of women in the candidate pool continues. By the 2015 election, 43 percent of NDP, 31 percent of Liberal, and 20 percent of Conservative candidates were women. Visible minorities made up about 15 percent of candidates overall, about their proportion of the voting population, and at nearly 6 percent, Indigenous candidates did somewhat better than their proportion of the voting population.

The final outcome worth discussing is the "types" of candidates selected – beyond their descriptive characteristics. The intersection of local competitive dynamics and party organizational norms leads to four main types of candidates (Carty, Eagles and Sayers 2003; Sayers 1999) – high profile/incumbents, local notables, party insiders, and stop-gaps.

Sayers (1999, 51), for instance, writes that "in choosing a nominee, nomination meetings are also harbingers of the type of election campaign a party will run in a riding." Stop-gap candidates, those often appointed in undesirable ridings where the local party is moribund and unable to attract a candidate of their own (Pruysers and Cross 2016), have very few resources and receive very little campaign support. When a high-profile candidate wins the primary, however, the campaign that follows tends to be professionalized, run by trusted party strategists, well-funded and staffed, and the recipient of additional news coverage and central party attention.

Leadership Primaries

Like candidate selection, leadership selection in Canada is highly inclusive and participatory. In fact, as Cross et al. (2016, 82) write, "Canadian parties were first among their Westminster counterparts to expand their leadership selectorates beyond those serving in Parliament and to include party members." Despite expanding the selectorate early on, leadership primaries emerged slowly over the course of the twentieth century. For the first five decades after Confederation the Liberal and Conservative parties selected their leaders in a similar fashion as their British counterparts of the time: through caucus (Cross 2014). By 1919, however, the Liberals had moved to a more inclusive selection method in which leaders were to be chosen at a party convention by delegates. The convention process made leadership selection more inclusive as, for the first time, the grassroots of the party had a role. The Conservatives soon followed suit and began selecting leaders at conventions in 1926 (Courtney 1995; Cross 2004).

Selection by convention delegates evolved over a number of decades (more delegates, greater representation of historically marginalized groups, etc.), and this became the norm from the 1920s to the 1980s. When new parties emerged during this period, for instance, they too adopted the convention model. By the 1980s, however, there was widespread criticism of the party convention, especially around the delegate selection process and membership recruitment practices (Carty 2007). The Royal Commission on Electoral Reform and Party Financing recommended the direct election of party leaders via membership ballot as it was viewed as a "credible mechanism for rebuilding public confidence in the leadership selection process" (1991, 280). With mounting criticism of the convention process, Canadian parties began adopting membership ballots for the selection of party leaders in the late 1980s.

Interestingly, the movement towards primaries was pioneered by political parties at the provincial level. In 1985 the Parti Québécois was the first major Canadian party to broaden its selectorate beyond delegates to a party conference. A survey of selection methods in the late 1990s identified a clear trend towards primaries at the provincial level as parties in Alberta, British Columbia, Manitoba, and Ontario had abandoned leadership conventions in favor of closed party primaries (Cross 1996). By 2017 at least one major party in each of the ten provinces selected their party leader through a primary (Cross et al. 2016, 83). Though provincial parties pioneered the move towards primaries, a number of parties at the provincial level continue to select their leaders at delegated conventions (i.e., Nova Scotia Liberals, Manitoba, NDP). Furthermore, several provincial parties have, after selecting leaders through a primary, moved back to the delegated convention format (see Stewart and Stewart 2008, 196). The Nova Scotia Liberals, for example, moved back to selecting party leaders at delegated conventions after conducting four party primaries as did the Nova Scotia PCs and the BC Reform after each conducting one primary. The experience at the provincial level demonstrates that while the trend is towards more inclusive selectorates, change is not completely unidirectional. This speaks to the self-governing nature of Canadian parties and their freedom to change their selection methods quickly and from one election to the next. Without state-imposed rules regarding selection methods, parties are able to completely overhaul their processes, even moving back to less inclusive selectorates.

The adoption of primaries at the federal level began a decade after many provincial parties did so, starting with the Bloc Québécois in 1997. The party primary format was then adopted by the Progressive Conservatives in 1998, the Canadian Alliance in 2000, the New Democrats in 2003, the Conservative Party of Canada in 2004, and the Liberals in 2013.[4] Although considerably slower to adopt primaries than their provincial counterparts, today all of the major federal political parties select their leader through closed or semi-open primaries – either inviting all members or members and supporters to directly cast a ballot. Unlike the adoption of primaries at the provincial level, membership votes have been more firmly established at the federal level, with no significant movement back towards less inclusive selectorates.[5]

Table 23.2 reveals the considerable diversity that can be found in the current rules governing party leadership primaries in Canada. Both the New Democrats and the Conservatives use a closed primary method where participation is limited to dues-paying members. Both parties have relatively modest requirements for participation: for the Conservatives, membership must be obtained 60 days prior to the primary to be eligible to vote whereas this cut-off is 30 days for the NDP. Not all Canadian parties require prior membership. The Alberta PCs, for instance, routinely allowed membership to be purchased on voting day and even between rounds of voting (Stewart 1997). In contrast to the closed primaries used by the Conservatives and New Democrats, the Liberals use semi-open primaries in which members as well as registered supporters are eligible to vote. Although the registration/membership cut-off was initially set to 30 days for the party's 2013 primary, this was changed to 15 midway through the campaign.

Table 23.2 Leadership Selection Rules Compared (Most Recent Primary)

Party	NDP	Conservative	Liberal
Contest year	2017	2017	2013
Selectorate	Party members	Party members	Party members and supporters
Membership cut-off	30 days	60 days	15 days
Ballot type	Ranked ballot; voting occurs once per week until a candidate meets the threshold	Ranked ballot; one member one vote weighted by constituency	Ranked ballot; one member one vote weighted by constituency
Membership fee	$1–25 (depending on province)	$15	$10 for members; no fee for supporters
Spending limit	1,500,000	5,000,000	950,000
Entrance fee	30,000	100,000	75,000
Candidate eligibility	Party membership; 500 member signatures	Party membership of at least 6 months; 300 member signatures	Party membership; 300 member signatures

Source: Compiled by authors.

Membership fees that serve as a prerequisite for participation have often been criticized as a "poll tax" (Cross 2004) that may deter participation from lower income and marginalized Canadians. Interestingly, we have seen some movement towards the lowering of membership fees in recent years and even their complete removal in some cases. During the 2013 Liberal primary, for instance, the party lowered the price of party membership to a modest $10, and implemented an entirely free category of party "supporter" which had the same voting privileges as dues-paying members.[6] While the Conservatives initially raised their fee to $25 for the 2017 leadership primary, the decision was met with widespread criticism that it would dissuade potential participants. Following the criticism, the party lowered the fee to $15. Membership fees in the NDP are somewhat different, given the party's multi-level organizational structure (see Pruysers 2014). As membership in the federal party is obtained provincially (then automatically granted federally), the provincial branches of the party set the rate for party membership. As a result, fees can range from $1 in the province of Alberta to $25 in Ontario. Beyond the minor hurdles of joining in advance and paying a small fee, all of the major parties have taken an inclusive approach to party membership and therefore participation in internal decision-making. In fact, given that non-citizens and those younger than 18 can typically join and vote in a leadership primary, these intra-party elections are in some ways more inclusive than the general election.

Without state-imposed limits, each of the parties is free to adopt its own internal spending limit, although this differs dramatically by party. While the 2013 Liberal primary set a limit of $950,000 per candidate, Conservative candidates are able to spend five times as much with a cap of $5,000,000. This, however, changes with each primary. The previous Conservative primary that was held in 2004, for instance, had a spending limit of $2,500,000. The absence of state mandated rules, however, does more than simply ensure variation among parties. There is good evidence that candidates often spend in excess of the stated limit without any consequences (Cross and Crysler 2009, 2011; Cross et al. 2016). Parties have few incentives to punish a candidate, especially if they happened to win the primary and will be leading the party into a general election. As a result, the enforcement of party rules is relatively lax.

Beyond the difference in the selectorate where the Liberals allow non-members to participate, perhaps the biggest difference in the rules can be found in how the votes are counted. In the New Democratic Party, primaries are conducted using ranked ballots and every member's vote counts equally, regardless of where they live. The Liberals and Conservatives, by contrast, use a uniquely Canadian method that seeks to address the issue of regionalized support. While these parties also use ranked ballots, each member's vote does not count equally in the final decision. Take the Conservatives as an example. In 2017, as in 2004, each electoral district is allocated 100 points in the final decision. Candidates earn a total based on their percentage of the vote in each of the country's 338 electoral districts and require 16,901 points to win. While such a system violates the principles of one-member-one-vote, it ensures that the various regions of the country are represented in the decision. Such an approach may also have practical benefits for the party as it ensures that the winning candidate has a broad base of support across the entire country, which of course is important for the subsequent general election.[7]

It is important to note, however, that had Table 23.2 been created for previous primaries it would look very different. This is because parties routinely change the rules for their leadership primaries with every election (Cross and Blais 2012). When the New Democrats chose their leader in 2003, for instance, the party used a weighted primary (or electoral college) in which the vote was divided between party members (75 percent) and affiliated unions (25 percent). The party has also doubled its entrance fee for every leadership primary since 2003 (starting with $7,500 in 2003, then $15,000 in 2012, and finally $30,000 in 2017). Such changes, of course, are not limited to the New Democrats. Prior to 2013, Liberal leadership elections did not include a supporter category and limited participation to dues-paying members. Changes around spending limits, membership cut-offs, and entrance fees frequently routinely change in all of the parties.

In terms of the campaign dynamics, the defining feature is the recruitment campaign that accompanies every leadership primary.[8] Since the selectorate is not defined at the outset, candidates have the ability to shape and construct a selectorate that is favorable to them by recruiting new members before the deadline. It is not uncommon to see a party's entire membership double during the course of the primary campaign. The Liberals, for instance, witnessed their membership surge from 55,000 prior to their 2013 primary to more than 127,000 members who were eligible to vote by the end of the campaign (and this does not include supporters who also joined to participate). Likewise, the Conservatives recruited 100,000 new members for both their 2004 and 2017 leadership primaries. The potential to shape the selectorate, however, raises a number of concerns regarding how members are recruited and mobilized (discussed below).

The Challenges of Party Primaries

Primaries for candidate and leadership selection offer parties a wide range of benefits. Membership recruitment provides the party with an army of potential volunteers and donors for the general election, grassroots participation provides democratic legitimacy to party decision-making, and the inclusive nature of the contests create excitement and energy for the party in general. There are, however, a variety of concerns associated with primaries in Canada. Since primaries are not administered by the state, parties often lack the resources necessary to meet the standards that are customary for general elections. Although these practices are not limited to Canadian primaries, selection of both leaders and candidates often suffers from a lack of proper oversight, voter fraud, and frequent manipulation of selection rules (Cross et al. 2016).

It is not uncommon, for instance, to have hundreds (and often thousands) of new members signed up to participate in a manner that violates the party's internal rules and sometimes without their knowledge. The 2017 Conservative leadership primary is illustrative in this regard.

More than 1,300 individuals were fraudulently registered as members (Zimonjic 2017). Since primaries are often recruitment/mobilization contests, there are incentives for candidates to recruit thousands of new members using questionable recruitment tactics. Large-scale "ethnic mobilization," for instance, has been a defining feature of candidate and leadership contests for decades. Vote-brokers in hierarchical religious and ethnic communities often mobilize thousands of new members into the party (Cross 2004; Courtney 1995). As Cross et al. (2016, 138) write about candidate primaries, "this can result in a local party association seeing its membership swamped by busloads of new members arriving at their first party meeting for the sole purpose of supporting a particular candidate."

Leading candidates and their supporters also routinely fight over the rules as well. Because Canadian primaries are organized by the parties themselves, they are free to change the rules surrounding leadership elections as frequently as they wish. As such, it is not uncommon to have new rules from one election to the next, even within the same party as demonstrated in previous sections. In recent years, for instance, the New Democrats have removed the vote allocation for union members, and the Liberals have added an entire "supporter" category of voters. While these are examples of large-scale change, more minor aspects of the selection process are routinely changed. Seemingly mundane aspects like the number of polling stations as well as their location can favor one candidate over another. Similarly, membership cut-off deadlines are often the subject of considerable debate as this has the ability to shape the selectorate. Candidates with support from the existing membership prefer to have a longer cut-off whereas outsiders and those with little support from the current membership seek to mobilize new members into the party and therefore prefer shorter cut-offs. Given that the rules of the game can shape the outcome, candidates often position their supporters on the party executive in order to influence the new rules (Cross et al. 2016).

There are also concerns regarding the "divisiveness" of primaries (Johnson and Gibson 1974; Southwell 1986; Ware 1979; Wichowsky and Niebler 2010). Cross and Pruysers (2017) demonstrate that losers of candidate nomination primaries in Canada are significantly less satisfied with their role as members, less active in the general election that follows the primary, and less likely to retain their membership in the future. We provide additional evidence of this "sore loser" effect below. To explore this question, we draw upon financial donor data derived from Elections Canada. In doing so, we utilize a unique and novel operationalization of political support, namely an examination of political contributions during primary elections and the months that follow the internal election. Do party members (or supporters) who donated to a primary contestant continue to donate to the party even if their preferred candidate is defeated in the intra-party election? Public disclosure of political contributions is mandatory at the federal level in Canada. As a result, Elections Canada maintains detailed, publicly available data concerning political donations during both general and intra-party elections. Based on this financial data, donors can be matched to their preferred intra- party contender (i.e., the candidate to whom they donated). We then examine donations after the primary and during the months following the primary to see if those individuals whose preferred candidate lost continue to contribute to the party and how this differs from those who won.[9]

Table 23.3 provides the breakdown of financial contributions for four recent Canadian leadership primaries, highlighting the extent to which supporters of winners and losers made a donation to the party in the following calendar year. While the number of supporters who contributed to both a contestant and the party is relatively small, an identifiable gap between those who donated to the winner and those who donated to a losing candidate is evident in three of the four primaries. Take, for example, the 2012 NDP leadership primary. More than one-third of those members/supporters who donated to Tom Mulcair's primary campaign also donated

Table 23.3 Primary Result and Continued Party Contributions (Recent Canadian Leadership Primaries)

Party	Election result	Donated to the party in the following year	Did not donate to the party in the following year	N
Green (2006)	Supported loser	6% (13)	94% (210)	223
	Supported winner	10% (19)*	90% (170)	189
Bloc (2011)	Supported loser	9% (33)	91% (345)	378
	Supported winner	23% (47)**	77% (157)	204
NDP (2012)	Supported loser	27% (2374)	73% (6412)	8786
	Supported winner	36% (1174)**	64% (2094)	3268
Liberal (2013)	Supported loser	24% (1826)**	76% (5615)	7441
	Supported winner	21% (2493)	79% (9561)	12054
Total	Supported loser	25% (4246)	75% (12582)	16828
	Supported winner	24% (3733)	76% (11981)	15714
				32542

Note: Comparisons in columns between winners and losers. *$p < 0.1$; **$p < 0.$

to the party in the year that followed. By contrast, only slightly more than one quarter of those who donated to one of the losing candidates continued to support the party financially afterwards. This represents a not unsubstantial 9 percent difference. Transforming this into an odds ratio reveals that those who donated to the winning candidate in the 2012 New Democratic Party leadership primary were 1.5 times more likely to continue to donate to the party in the following year compared to those supporters who supported a losing candidate during the internal party election.

Likewise, those who donated to Daniel Paillé during the 2011 Bloc leadership election were more than three times as likely to donate in the following year than those who supported a losing candidate. And while the gap between winners and losers is smaller in the 2006 Green contest, it is evident nonetheless. A challenge for parties conducting a primary election is therefore to keep losing members engaged with the party rather than allowing them to withdraw after their defeat. Only in the 2013 Liberal leadership election do we not find the same general trend. Here those who supported Justin Trudeau are no more likely to remain party contributors compared to those who supported one of the losing candidates. In fact, we find the opposite: losers continue contributing to the party at a slightly higher rate than winners do.

One potential explanation is that the 2013 Liberal primary was not a "divisive" primary at all. In terms of competitiveness of the race, for instance, Justin Trudeau easily won the Liberal leadership on the first ballot with 80 percent of the vote. Indeed, the margin of victory over the second-place contestant was a staggering 70 percent. The other primaries included in Table 23.3, however, were much more competitive. Tom Mulcair, for example, only received 30 percent in the first ballot of the 2012 NDP election. Moreover, the difference between the top two candidates after the first round of voting was only 9 percent – considerably closer than the Liberal contest. Thus, not all primary losses may cause the same disillusionment among members and party supporters. It is likely the case that divisive and highly competitive primaries have greater implications for the health and stability of a party organization compared to internal elections where there is a very clear frontrunner and little meaningful competition between candidates. With that said, more cases need to be added to the analysis before we can draw firm conclusions in this regard.

Beyond differences between winners and losers, Table 23.3 reveals something troubling about party support and the quality of participation in primaries more generally. While these open and participatory primaries allow parties to recruit and mobilize tens of thousands of new members and supporters,[10] this support does not appear to be long lasting. When considering financial contributions, only a quarter of those individuals who were mobilized to contribute to a recent leadership primary continued to donate to the party (regardless of whether they won the internal election or not). In other words, three-in-four individuals who donated to a primary were not active party donors in the following year. The "instant members" who sign up to participate in the primary have very little attachment to the party itself and become inactive quickly after the contest has concluded.[11] The "party" that makes personnel selection decisions is therefore very different than the "party" that continues to exist between these selection events.

Conclusion

Primary elections in Canada are highly inclusive and participatory events. Not only are non-citizens often invited to participate, the age requirements for party membership mean that those who are not yet able to vote in the general election may nonetheless vote for their preferred candidate or leader in the internal party election. As a result of this inclusivity, hundreds of thousands of Canadians routinely cast a ballot in party primaries – more than 130,000 party members, for instance, voted in the 2017 Conservative leadership primary. Although there are concerns regarding the representational outcomes of these internal elections (Pruysers et al. 2017; Rahat, Hazan, and Katz 2008), primaries represent a transfer of meaningful decision-making authority to ordinary grassroots party membership.

While the view of parties as private associations has been challenged in recent years (i.e., minor financial regulations, judicial review, etc.), the defining characteristic of parties, and therefore the primaries that they conduct, is still their self-governing nature. The autonomous nature of Canadian parties to set their own rules and guidelines is illustrated by the fact that each of the federal parties has adopted a somewhat unique leadership selection method that highlights its own organizational ethos: the Liberals invite non-members to vote, the Conservatives weight votes by constituency, and the New Democrats have often provided a special role for organized labor. Evidence of this freedom is further illustrated by the fact that a number of provincial parties have abandoned the use of primaries in favor of less inclusive selection methods. This self-governing nature raises concerns regarding proper oversight and accountability as parties may lack sufficient resources or incentives to conduct internal contests with the rigor expected of general elections. Finally, primaries may come with an organizational cost if sore losers choose to distance themselves from the party.

Notes

1 For a definition and typology of party primaries in parliamentary democracies see Kenig et al. (2015).
2 This, of course, is in contrast to parties in other countries where the state has taken a more active role in the primary process (i.e., the United States) or where the state has broad regulations regarding personnel selection (i.e., German Party Law).
3 The need to meet regulatory requirements along with knowledge of local financial resources has encouraged central parties to pay more attention to local affairs (Coletto et al. 2011). Nonetheless, local associations continue to find ways to act independently of the central party (Currie-Wood 2016) and the removal of state subsidies may well limit the capacity of the national party to intervene in local affairs.

4 In both 2003 and 2006 the Liberals invited party members to vote for their preferred leadership candidate. These votes, however, were translated into delegates who attended a leadership convention. While delegates were bound to vote in the manner specified by the membership on the first round, they were released on subsequent rounds. Given that delegates or members could be decisive, we cannot label these elections as primaries (see Cross et al. 2016). In fact, the membership vote portion was decisive in 2003 as Paul Martin was selected on the first ballot in accordance with the membership's preference but not in 2006 when Stéphane Dion was selected on the fourth ballot by convention delegates.

5 The Progressive Conservatives briefly abandoned the party primary in 2003, only to return the following year. This, however, is the only case at the federal level.

6 There is one caveat. Party members can be as young as 14 whereas supporters had to be 18.

7 Using an example from the 1998 PC primary, Stewart and Carty (2002) illustrate the trade-off between equality of members and regional representation. The party had 1,300 members cast a ballot in the district of Kingston and the Islands compared to eight in Bellechasse-Etchemins-Montmagny L'Islet. In practice this meant that some votes counted 100 times more than others in the final decision (see also Cross (2014) for a discussion of this tradeoff).

8 For a discussion of the outcome of Canadian leadership primaries see Cross et al. (2016, chapter 6).

9 Despite being publicly available, only aggregate results are presented and no data is reported in any form that allows for identification of any individual.

10 For a more detailed discussion of these recruitment patterns see Carty (1991), Sayers (1999), or Pruysers and Cross (2016).

11 See Rahat and Hazan (2007) for a broader discussion of this uncommitted (and often uninterested) layer of party members who are mobilized for a leadership election but become inactive shortly thereafter. Orr (2011, 980), for instance, writes that "parties are considering primaries as a lure, to reach out to supporters who are not interested in joining or committing to the party, with the promise of a say in the party's seminal activity: candidate selection."

References

Carty, Kenneth. 1991. *Canadian Political Parties in the Constituencies*. Toronto: Dundurn Press.

Carty, Kenneth. 2002. "The Politics of Tecumseh Corners: Canadian Political Parties as Franchise Organizations." *The Canadian Journal of Political Science* 35(4): 723–745.

Carty, Kenneth. 2004. "Parties as Franchise Systems: The Stratarchical Organizational Imperative." *Party Politics* 10(1): 15–24.

Carty, Kenneth. 2007. "Leadership Politics and the Transformation of Canadian Parties." In *Political Leadership and Representation in Canada*, eds. H.J. Michelmann, Donald C. Storey and Jeffrey S. Steeves. Toronto: University of Toronto Press, pp. 16–38.

Carty, Kenneth, and William Cross. 2006. "Can Stratarchically Organized Parties be Democratic? The Canadian Case." *Journal of Elections, Public Opinion and Parties* 16(2): 93–114.

Carty, Kenneth, and Munroe Eagles. 2005. *Politics is Local: National Politics at the Grassroots*. Oxford: Oxford University Press.

Carty, Kenneth, and Lynda Erickson. 1991. "Candidate Nomination in Canada's National Political Parties." In *Canadian Political Parties: Leaders, Candidates and Organization*, ed. Herman Bakvis. Toronto: Dundurn Press, pp. 97–190.

Carty, Kenneth, William Cross, and Lisa Young. 2000. *Rebuilding Canadian Party Politics*. Vancouver: UBC Press.

Carty, Kenneth, Munroe Eagles, and Anthony Sayers. 2003. "Candidates and Local Campaigns. Are There Just Four Canadian Types?" *Party Politics* 9(5): 619–636.

Coletto, David, Harold Jansen, and Lisa Young. 2011. "Stratarchical Party Organization and Party Finance in Canada." *Canadian Journal of Political Science* 44(1): 111–136.

Courtney, John C. 1995. *Do Conventions Matter? Choosing National Party Leaders in Canada*. Montreal: McGill-Queen's University Press.

Cross, William. 1996. "Direct Election of Provincial Party Leaders in Canada, 1985–1995: The End of the Leadership Convention." *Canadian Journal of Political Science* 29(2): 295–315.

Cross, William. 2004. *Political Parties*. Vancouver: UBC Press.

Cross, William. 2014. "Party Leadership in Canada." In *The Selection of Party Leaders in Contemporary Parliamentary Democracies*, eds. Jean Benoit-Pilet and William Cross. London: Routledge, pp. 171–188.

Cross, William, and Andre Blais. 2012. *Politics at the Centre: The Selection and Removal of Leaders in the Principal Anglophone Parliamentary Democracies*. Oxford: Oxford University Press.

Cross, William, and John Crysler. 2009. "Grassroots Participation in Party Leadership Selection: Examining the British and Canadian Cases." In *Activating the Citizen: Dilemmas of Participation in Europe and Canada*, eds. Joan DeBardeleben and Jon Pammett. Basingstoke: Palgrave, pp. 173–193.

Cross, William, and John Crysler. 2011. "Financing Party Leadership Campaigns." In *Money, Politics and Democracy: Canada's Party Finance Reforms*, eds. Lisa Young and Harold Jansen. Vancouver: UBC Press, pp. 145–172.

Cross, William, and Scott Pruysers. 2017. "Sore Losers? The Costs or Intra-party Democracy." Forthcoming, *Party Politics*.

Cross, William, and Lisa Young. 2013. "Candidate Recruitment in Canada: The Role of Political Parties." In *Parties, Elections, and the Future of Canadian Politics*, eds. Royce Koop and Amanda Bittner. Vancouver: University of British Columbia Press, pp. 24–45.

Cross, William, Ofer Kenig, Scott Pruysers, and Gideon Rahat. 2016. *The Promise and Challenge of Party Primary Elections: A Comparative Perspective*. Montreal and Kingston: McGill-Queens University Press.

Currie-Wood, Rob. 2016. "Playing in the Margins: Collaboration between Local Party Organizations in the Canadian Party System." Unpublished MA thesis. University of Calgary.

Hazan, Reuven, and Gideon Rahat. 2010. *Democracy Within Parties: Candidate Selection Methods and their Political Consequences*. Oxford: Oxford University Press.

Heyman, David, and Suzanne Wilton. 2004. "Judge Re-opens Tory Nomination." *Calgary Herald*, 31 July.

Hume, Jessica. 2014. "Justin Trudeau Defends Blocking Christine Innes from Running in Byelection." *Toronto Sun*. http://www.torontosun.com/2014/03/26/justin-trudeau-defends-blocking-christine-innes-from-running-in-byelection

Johnson, Donald, and James Gibson. 1974. "The Divisive Primary Revisited: Party Activists in Iowa." *American Political Science Review* 68(1): 67–77.

Kenig, Ofer. 2009. "Classifying Party Leaders' Selection Methods in Parliamentary Democracies." *Journal of Elections, Public Opinion and Parties* 19(4): 433–447.

Kenig, Ofer, William Cross, Scott Pruysers, and Gideon Rahat. 2015. "Party Primaries: Towards a Definition and Typology." *Representation* 51(2): 147–160.

Kirchheimer, Otto. 1966. "The Transformation of the Western European Party Systems." In *Political Parties and Political Development*, eds. Joseph LaPalombara and Myron Weiner. Princeton NJ: Princeton University Press, pp. 177–200.

Knox v. Conservative Party of Canada. 2007. ABCA 295.

Koop, Royce, and Amanda Bittner. 2011. "Parachuted into Parliament: Candidate Nomination, Appointed Candidates, and Legislative Roles in Canada." *Journal of Elections, Public Opinion and Parties* 21(4): 431–452.

Liberal Party. 2013. "National Rules for the Selection of Candidates for the Liberal Party of Canada." *Amended* December, 2013.

Orr, Graeme. 2011. "Party Primaries for Candidate Selection? Right Question, Wrong Answer." *UNSW Law Journal* 34(3): 964–983.

Perkel, Colin. 2017. "Brian Gaff Loses Bid to Join NDP Race, But Judge Rules Parties Subject to Scrutiny." *The Globe and Mail*. https://www.theglobeandmail.com/news/politics/brian-graff-loses-bid-join-ndp-race-but-judge-rules-parties-subject-to-scrutiny/article35283333/

Pilet, Jean-Benoit, and William Cross (eds.). 2014. *Leadership Selection in Contemporary Parliamentary Democracies: A Comparative Study*. London: Routledge.

Pruysers, Scott. 2014. "Reconsidering Vertical Integration: An Examination of National Political Parties and their Counterparts in Ontario." *Canadian Journal of Political Science* 47(2): 237–258.

Pruysers, Scott, and William Cross. 2016. "Candidate Selection in Canada: Local Autonomy, Centralization, and Competing Democratic Norms." *American Behavioral Scientist* 60(7): 781–798.

Pruysers, Scott, William Cross, Anika Gauja, and Gideon Rahat. 2017. "Candidate Selection Rules and Democratic Outcomes: The Impact of Parties on Women's Representation." In *Organizing Political Parties: Representation, Participation, and Power*, Susan E. Scarrow, Paul D. Webb, and Thomas Poguntke (eds.). Oxford: Oxford University Press, pp. 208–233.

Rahat, Gideon, and Reuven Y. Hazan. 2007. "Participation in Party Primaries: Increase in Quantity, Decrease in Quality." In *Participatory Democracy and Political Participation. Can Participatory Engineering Bring Citizens Back In?*, eds. Thomas Zittel and Dieter Fuchs. London: Routledge, pp. 57–72.

Rahat, Gideon, Reuven Y. Hazan, and Richard S. Katz. 2008. "Democracy and Political Parties: On the Uneasy Relationship Between Participation, Competition, and Representation." *Party Politics* 14(6): 663–683.

Royal Commission on Electoral Reform and Party Financing. 1991. *Reforming Electoral Democracy*, Volume 1. Ottawa: Supply and Service Canada.

Sartori, Giovanni. 1976. *Parties and Party Systems: A Framework for Analysis*. Cambridge: Cambridge University Press.

Sayers, Anthony. 1999. *Parties, Candidates, and Constituency Campaigns in Canadian Elections*. Vancouver: University of British Columbia Press.

Siegfried, A. 1907. *The Race Question in Canada*. Reprint 1966. London: Eveleigh.

Southwell, Priscilla. 1986. "The Politics of Disgruntlement: Nonvoting and Defection among Supporters of Nomination Losers, 1968–1984." *Political Behavior* 8(1): 81–95.

Stewart, David. 1997. "The Changing Electorate: An Examination of Participants in the 1992 Alberta Conservative Leadership Election." *Canadian Journal of Political Science* 30(1): 107–128.

Stewart, David, and R. K. Carty. 2002. "Leadership Politics as Party Building: The Conservatives in 1998." In *Political Parties, Representation and Electoral Democracy in Canada*, ed. William Cross. Toronto: Oxford University Press, pp. 55–67.

Stewart, Ian, and David Stewart. 2008. *Conventional Choices. Maritime Leadership Politics*. Vancouver: UBC Press.

van Biezen, Ingrid. 2004. "Political Parties as Public Utilities." *Party Politics* 10(6): 701–722.

Ware, Alan. 1979. "Divisive' Primaries: The Important Questions." *British Journal of Political Science* 9(3): 381–384.

Wichowsky, Amber, and Sarah E. Niebler. 2010. "Narrow Victories and Hard Games: Revisiting the Primary Divisiveness Hypothesis." *American Politics Research* 38(6): 1052–1071.

Wingrove, Jason. 2014. "Resignation of Top Conservative Gives Hope to Blocked Candidates." *The Globe and Mail.* http://www.theglobeandmail.com/news/politics/resignation-of-top-conservative-gives-hope-to-blocked-candidates/article17743978/

Young, Lisa, and William Cross. 2002. "Incentives to Membership in Canadian Political Parties." *Political Research Quarterly* 55(3): 547–569.

Young, Lisa, and Harold Jansen (eds.). 2011. *Money, Politics and Democracy: Canada's Party Finance Reforms*. Vancouver: UBC Press.

Zimonjic, Peter. 2017. "Conservative Party Strikes 1,251 Names off Membership List after Investigation." *CBC News.* http://www.cbc.ca/news/politics/conservative-vote-rigging-investigation-1.4030828

24

THE ITALIAN STYLE OF INTRA-PARTY DEMOCRACY

A Twenty-Year-Long Journey

Marino De Luca

Primary elections are a relatively recent innovation in Europe. Their application is associated with specific circumstances (timing, type of organizing party, democratic regime, etc.), and therefore their adoption is associated with some circumstances that causes a certain level of heterogeneity at the European level. In this perspective, Italy is an important example, since the temporal continuity of its experience with primaries has made it a reference point in the framework of the studies on this topic. The aim of this chapter is to analyze how this instrument became rooted in Italian politics and how it developed. In order to be able to do so, we should focus on the political context before primary elections and understand what the political, social and cultural milieu was that led to the development primary elections.

In the early 1990s, Italian democracy underwent a series of important changes in terms of political system and party system. A number of scandals caused by corruption, as well as judicial investigations, contributed to the demise of the major political parties and to the delegitimization of party leaders (Morlino 1996). Moreover, the new 1993 reform led to a profound reorganization of the party system that altered parties' structure, the relationships among the parties, and voter participation (Katz 1996). Within this context, center-right forces originated from the fusion among post-fascist parties, Christian Democrats, and the ethno-regionalists of the North League (LN), which succeeded in solving the problem of the party leadership that was immediately taken over by Silvio Berlusconi (thanks to his political and economic influence). On the other hand, center-left forces were at the same time facing a decrease in the number of their members and an inability to provide a strong and long-lasting leadership that could counteract Berlusconi (Campus and Pasquino 2006).

In this framework, Italian primary elections took place thanks to three features that were typical of the Italian political system and to two processes that occurred on a larger scale. At a domestic level, institutional, strategic and historical reasons played a key role. Institutional reasons included the above mentioned transformations of the electoral system that – at a municipal level – fostered verticalization and a direct relationship between the representative and the represented party, while – at a national level – led to the bipolarisation of the system through the development of two large and heterogeneous coalitions, with the center-left facing great difficulties in finding a single and commonly accepted representative (Pasquino 2007; D'Alimonte 2008). Moreover, other institutional reasons fostered greater legitimization of such an instrument and its diffusion in that period; in particular, there was greater interest shown in the issue by MPs and there were several attempts at institutional regulation. As for strategic reasons, primary elections in Italy took place, as in other democracies, as a response to the crisis of legitimacy of party leadership experienced by the center-left coalition, which was not able to reach common agreement on a single candidate and to reconcile citizens with politics after the scandals of the early 1990s. Finally, historically contingent reasons indissolubly linked primary elections to a specific political sphere that employed this institutional instrument as a sort of "brand" that had to be defended and further expanded at any electoral level (municipal, political and regional elections for instance), thus affecting the direct selection of party leaders. Furthermore, other political parties also had recourse to such an institutional instrument, even parties far from the center-left coalition; the original structure of this approach was also profoundly changed by the expansion of citizens' participation through online platforms.

As for the two aforementioned processes on a larger scale that allowed the development of primary elections, one was the personalization of politics and the increase in the decision-making process within political parties. As regards personalization, we should consider that people had not only become more visible than political parties (Karvonen 2010), but they had also become more efficient in promoting electoral support (Blondel and Thiébault 2009; Calise 2015; Garzia 2011; Poguntke and Webb 2005; Venturino 2010). As Manin (1997) observed, this dimension of personalization did not correspond to a truly degenerative transformation of the political system, insofar as the nature of representative democracy considers the "personal" element as a basic form of its institutionalization.

The second process affected the decision-making process, leading to an increasingly greater involvement of members and supporters (Cross and Blais 2012; Kenig 2009; Pilet and Cross 2014; Sandri, Seddone and Venturino 2015) with a view to limiting membership decline and providing new opportunities for participation (Cross and Katz 2013; Hazan and Rahat 2010). From this perspective, there were two main goals: improving the public image of parties by promoting new inclusive methods to involve citizens, and re-defining the relationship of the party with members/supporters who had a new incentive for their involvement (Scarrow 1999; 2000).

This chapter will focus on the historical and political evolution of intra-party democracy processes. Specifically, the second section will give space to the causes of the transition to a more inclusive party system; the third will discuss the rules and arrangements of these processes in the various parties; the fourth will look at the primaries for the prime minister's choice; the fifth will cover the primaries for the selection of parliamentary candidates; in the sixth, local primaries (regional, provincial and municipal) will be described and in the seventh section, finally, the processes for the party leader's selection will be analyzed.

It's a Long Italian Story

In Italy, before the collapse of the party system, but also subsequently in the transition period, the selection of candidates was organized based on an apparent intra-party agreement at a central and local level. Such a negotiation was *de facto* more oriented toward a national level – suffice it to say, the shares of central national bodies (Wertman 1988; Bille 2001). In practice, before the changes of the 1990s, four large national parties existed: the Communist Party (PCI), the Socialist Party (PSI), the Christian Democrats (DC) and the Italian Social Movement (MSI). Other smaller parties, such as the Liberal Party (PLI) and the Republican Party (PRI) were organized in a few areas and strongly anchored to groups and associations such as the association of entrepreneurs (Bardi and Morlino 1992, 1994). In all those parties the role and importance of members was very limited.

The 1993 reform and the reorganization of the party system did not allow any amendment in the selection of candidates and party leaders, at least immediately. In fact, a more inclusive candidate selection and open methods leadership selection increased the level of intra-party democracy in Italy only towards the mid-2000s.[1] Primary elections became central in the public debate in 2005, thanks to two events that magnified their success and increased people's enthusiasm and participation. The first event was the regional primary elections of the center-left coalition in the Puglia region, won by Nichi Vendola, the most extremist candidate, who unexpectedly defeated a more moderate candidate of his own coalition and was able to succeed over the center-right coalition candidate at the general elections. The second event, in contrast, marked the debut of national primary elections promoted once again by the center-left coalition to select the candidate for the Presidency of the Council to the general elections in 2006. That was a less competitive example of primary elections organized to strengthen the leadership of Romano Prodi, who was facing criticism and objections raised by other representatives of the center-left coalition. The participation of four million voters was a unique event and it represented an innovation in the system of candidate selection. In fact, the primary elections, won by Romano Prodi, who then became prime minister of the Italian government, had a positive impact on the parties' image and organization and started a long period of prosperity that subsequently had an influence on the selection of candidates at any level (municipal, provincial and regional levels).

At the national level, after the early elections in 2008, primaries were held in 2012 and they introduced a new aspect. Pier Luigi Bersani was selected as the candidate for the Presidency of the Council by means of two-round primary elections characterized by a high level of competition between Bersani and the other candidate Matteo Renzi. However, the 2013 general elections marked an element of novelty also in terms of MPs' selection. The two parties that had promoted the primary elections won by Bersani, namely the Democratic Party (PD) and Left Ecology Freedom (SEL), decided to select candidates to the Parliament and their political lists based on primary elections. Moreover, another party, the Five Star Movement (M5S) simultaneously decided to choose its candidates for Parliament by means of online closed primary elections (Lanzone and Rombi 2014). Such an important aspect of the Italian system of selection of candidates for the government could be attributed to the 2013 general elections, the so-called *Porcellum* method, according to which national political parties organized their lists by means of a pre-stated list of candidates, without the possibility of expressing any preference.

However, the greater inclusiveness of the system of candidate selection also had a positive impact on the selection of party leaders, thus revolutionizing the method for the selection of party leaders. Indeed, since 2007, on the occasion of its establishment and as subsequently stated in its charter, the Democratic Party started a multi-level approach of greater inclusiveness in the selection of its leaders; the most important step was the employment of a system similar to that of the 2005 primary elections for the selection of the leader of the center-left coalition. The model promoted by the Democratic Party for the selection of its leader that was subsequently employed in 2009, 2013 and 2017, was also employed by other parties. In 2013, two completely different political parties – Italy of Values (IdV) and North League (LN) – which had been long led by their founders, started a process of leadership selection through this new approach. After the exit of Antonio di Pietro, the main judicial figure of the investigation team of *Mani Pulite* in the early 1990s, Italy of Values opted for an (online and offline) direct election of the member of the party, while in the North League its founder, Umberto Bossi, was defeated by the new party leader, Matteo Salvini, in primary elections open not only to party members. In 2014, Brothers of Italy – National Alliance (FdI-AN), a center-right coalition – also chose its leader based on uncompetitive and open primary elections where Giorgia Meloni, the only candidate, was elected as the president of the party.

This brief overview highlights the most important steps of the Italian parties towards an intra-party democracy. The national media's emphasis on this phenomenon served to increase its popularity. However, the majority of such elections were held at a local level, and very often far from the spotlight. In any case, in Italy they represented a fundamental step in the development of new forms of participation and greater inclusiveness in the choices made by political parties.

The Italian Rules of Intra-Party Democracy

The first element to be analyzed in the context of new intra-party democracy processes is related to rules. The "private" nature of Italian primaries allows parties to self-regulate the process of selection of candidates or leaders. This implies that intra-party democracy processes are often tailored on specific organizational needs (or events) promoted by the parties themselves. This approach, which was subsequently affected by a series of attempts to advertise the system,[2] has determined small regulation differences, above all at a local level. However, the procedure of national primary elections is premised on some well-defined and common features among all types of selection, apart from some exceptions that will be subsequently reviewed.

The primary elections won by Romano Prodi in 2005 set some general rules that were formalized only in 2008, after the drawing up of the statute of the Democratic Party. Such an initial regulation was directly and indirectly transposed into the primary elections promoted both by the center-left parties and others. In the initial 2005 rules, two main regulations governed the sphere of selection and candidacy. As for the selection of candidates, citizens entitled to vote for the Chamber of Deputies were permitted to vote, upon the signing of the "Progetto" and payment of a voluntary donation of minimum 1 Euro coverage for expenses. The electorate was highly inclusive, since immigrants legally residing in Italy for at least three years and the so-called *potential* voters, i.e. young people who were to be 18 by the end of the legislation, were also permitted to vote. The regulations also held that voters had to give their consent to enter their names in a list of participants to the election which the public could consult.[3] As for the selection of candidates to the party leadership, candidacy was admitted provided that at least 10,000 (up to a maximum of 20,000) voters' signatures were submitted. Finally, in order to be entitled to participate in the system, candidates could not have been involved in any political activity in support of the center-right coalition in the previous legislation.

The PD statute, as previously stated, was the main regulatory element in terms of participation in primaries, thus better outlining rules and introducing some important novelties (Venturino 2015). The statute set forth that electors, and not only party members, could decide on the selection of candidates for public posts of party leaders. The two categories are listed in a register of members and in a register of voters based on some requirements. In both cases, the Democratic Party admitted the participation of all Italian citizens and citizens of EU Member States, as well as non-EU citizens residing in Italy. Among other things, the statute ruled that to be entitled to be a member of the party or acquire the status of voter in primary elections promoted by the party itself, citizens must be 16 years old. Moreover, participation in primary elections required the payment of a donation, which in a certain number of cases was not requested of party members. As for candidacy, the statute establishes two different criteria, one employed for the selection of party leaders, and the other for the selection of candidates for other posts. In the first case, leaders' selection criteria depend upon requirements such as being a party member and candidacy being supported by at least ten percent of the members of the outgoing National Assembly, or by party members numbering between 1,500 and 2,000 people. In contrast, candidates for monocratic roles (e.g. Mayor, President of the Provincial Government, or President of the Regional Government) are selected by means of primaries promoted by the party or the coalition. In the first instance, candidacy can be promoted with the support of ten percent of the members of the Assembly of the referring territorial district concerned, i.e. with a number of signatures equal to at least three percent of party members in a territorial district. In the second case a shared regulation among the coalition forces is established and PD party members can submit their candidacy provided that it has been supported by at least 35 percent of the members of the Assembly of the territorial district concerned, in other words, that it corresponds to at least 20 percent of the party members in the territorial district concerned.

In contrast, center-right parties and coalitions rarely employed such processes for the selection of candidates and leaders and, instead, they avoided them in many cases. In the House of Freedoms (CDL), the adoption of primary elections was promoted by the leader of the Union of the Center (UDC), Marco Follini, at the time of the 2005 primaries of the center-left coalition, however, the proposal was abandoned when Berlusconi was suggested as a candidate. Similarly, another attempt promoted by the Secretary of the People of Freedom (PDL), Angelino Alfano, in respect of the 2013 general elections failed. In this case, rules based on the primaries promoted by the center-left coalition were proposed and, upon payment of a donation of two Euros and signing of the Charter of Values, citizens registered on electoral rolls could take part in the selection of the candidate proposed for the leadership of the center-right coalition. Such entitlement was extended to citizens aged 16, but denied to foreign citizens. As for candidacy, at least 10,000 signatures were necessary, with a limit of 2,000 signatures in each Region.

Another party of the center-right coalition, the North League, organized an inclusive selection both in 2013 and in 2017 to elect the federal secretary of the party (in both cases Matteo Salvini was appointed). Participation was limited to party members with at least one year's membership,[4] while candidacy was limited to people who had been LN party members for at least 10 years, upon the support of at least 1000 signatures collected among party activists.

Finally, even in 2014 another party of the center-right coalition – Brothers of Italy - National Alliance – experimented with primary elections at a national level to appoint its president, Giorgia Meloni, and this experience was extended to all EU citizens from the age of 16.

Primaries were also adopted by another important Italian political party, the Five Star Movement, on several other occasions: to select parliamentary candidates in the 2013 general elections; candidates for the European Parliament in 2014; candidates for regional ministers and regional president; and candidates for municipal elections, both for the office of mayor or municipal commissioners in many cases. The initial attempt, in the general elections of February 2013, was an opportunity to test the use of an online platform, that has since then become the distinctive feature of intra-party democracy processes of the party. The M5S experience was a clear example of closed primaries, accessed only by a section of party members.[5] Candidacy criteria were also very stringent, since only non-elected party members of previous elections were entitled to participate. Generally speaking, the online platform is still the "environment" par excellence where primary elections of the party take place, apart from some exceptions when the M5S organized traditional primaries ahead of municipal elections, between 2013 and 2015. Such a peculiar selection mode implies several consequences in terms of participation, results, list formation and more broadly on the party organizational structure.

The Selection of the Prime Minister

This section, along with the subsequent ones, will take into account intra-party democracy processes, analyzing them based on party typology and territorial level of reference. More specifically, this section will focus on the primaries held by the center-left coalition in 2005 and 2012 to select a candidate for the party leadership.

The peculiarity of 2005 primary elections, which were held one year before the general elections upon initiative of the center-left coalition called then "The Union," lay in the fact that

Romano Prodi's victory was taken for granted and that the elections only aimed at strengthening his leadership (Hopkin 2006). In fact, the center-left coalition was trying to avoid the mistake that had been made by Prodi himself in 1996 when, not having been directly supported by the parties, he had faced many difficulties in holding the parliamentary majority intact (Corbetta and Vignati 2013). Internal divisions in the center-left coalition lasted a long time, and almost ten years late, the former Italian prime minister, despite his non-adherence to any political party, but enjoying an enhanced reputation thanks to his experience as the President of the European Commission, seemed again to be the only political figure that could have united the multi-faceted center-left coalition. In 2005 other candidates were competing for the leadership along with Prodi: Fausto Bertinotti (Communist Refoundation Party), Clemente Mastella (Union of Democrats for Europe), Antonio Di Pietro (Italy of Values), Alfonso Pecoraro Scanio (Federation of the Greens), Ivan Scalfarotto and Simona Panzino (independent). The was an extraordinary participation that peaked to over 4 million[6] voters. The results showed that Prodi had reached over 74 percent of votes, while the first of his competitors reached only 15 percent (see Table 24.1).

Therefore, rather than complying with an increasing need for intra-party democracy, the first attempt of primary elections in Italy was introduced to settle a dispute among the parties of the center-left coalition and to legitimize its leadership. However, the success of this experience led to several consequences. The first result, since the origins of the Democratic Party in 2007, was the choice to include both party members and voters in the procedure of the party leader selection. In the same year, the direct election of the democratic Walter Veltroni made him the natural candidate for the post of prime minister in the 2008 general elections, thus avoiding the need for further primaries (Bordandini et al. 2009; Lazar 2008; Hanretty and Wilson 2010). Despite the good results for the PD in 2008, the center-right coalition, led by Silvio Berlusconi won the election. Simultaneously, the PD adopted a statute with open primaries as a tool to select candidates at any level; the statute also established that the selection of the leader was to be based on a multi-phase process similar to the 2005 open primaries that had played a key role in the process.

After the 2008 elections, the center-left coalition had recourse to open primaries also in 2012 to select the candidate for the coalition "Italy. Common Good" (Vassallo and Passarelli 2016). However, based on the statute of the PD, only the then-leader Pier Luigi Bersani – selected in 2009 by means of open selection – was entitled to participate in the primaries as a representative of the PD. Objection to this rule and its postponement allowed two other PD candidates to take part in the primaries of the coalition. One was Matteo Renzi, who had been asking for a party leadership replacement for a long time, and the other was Laura Puppato, a regional minister of the PD and the only woman candidate. Besides the three PD candidates, other competitors participated in the primaries, such as Nichi Vendola of the post-communist Left Ecology Freedom left wing, who became the Governor of the Puglia Region by means of the regional primary elections

Table 24.1 The 2005 Center-Left Coalition Primary

Candidate	Party	Votes	%
Romano Prodi	The Olive Tree	3,182,686	74.2
Fausto Bertinotti	Communist Refoundation Party	631,592	14.7
Clemente Mastella	Union of Democrats for Europe	196,014	4.5
Antonio Di Pietro	Italy of Values	142,143	3.3
Alfonso Pecoraro Scanio	Federation of the Greens	95,388	2.2
Ivan Scalfarotto	Independent	26,912	0.6
Simona Panzino	Independent	19,752	0.5
Total		*4,294,487*	*100*

system, and Bruno Tabacci, the leader of the Democratic Center (CD). So, while in 2005 the other parties of the coalition were more numerous and influential, in 2012 the central role played by the PD, as compared to the two smaller parties, was evident. The 2012 primaries, in fact, were initially perceived as a competition to decide on the leader of the PD: the main aim was to solve a problem within the party itself, which was divided between a wing led by Matteo Renzi – who was then the mayor of Florence – and a wing led by the leader of the party Pier Luigi Bersani.

The plurality system, adopted in 2005, was abandoned in favor of a second ballot system aiming at 50 percent plus one of the votes. This system and some of its rules, had an impact on participation. In the first ballot, in fact, the turnout was three million voters with a ten percentage-point deviation between the two candidates. The second ballot saw a decreased number of voters, since only participants voting in the first ballot had been admitted, thus excluding potential new voters. This choice practically prevented Renzi from achieving a comeback. The attitudes of the defeated candidates also had an impact on the final result: the majority of Nichi Vendola's voters in the first ballot, in fact, voted for Bersani in the second ballot, thus allowing the latter to reach over 60 percent of the consensus (See Table 24.2).

Once these data have been analyzed in descriptive terms, it is worth focusing on one of the most debated topics in the European literature, the impact of primaries on electoral performance and on party membership (De Luca and Venturino 2015, 2017). Starting from electoral results, the general elections held one year after the primaries of 2005 and 2012 were characterized by a series of extraordinary events that affected their results. In the general elections of 2006 the change in the electoral system by means of a controversial law, the so-called *Porcellum*, which was subsequently considered unconstitutional, had a substantial effect on election results in terms of parliamentary representation. In 2013, however, the highest volatility ever was registered. The most important political parties collapsed and the M5S reached 25 percent of the consensus in its first electoral campaign, thus becoming the first political party in Italy. By taking into account such external conditions, it could be observed that between the parliamentary elections of 2001 and those of 2006 (close to the primaries in 2005), the center-left coalition led by Romano Prodi obtained about three million votes more (Table 24.3), thereby winning the elections by a large margin against the center-right coalition led by Silvio Berlusconi. However, the Prodi government lasted only two years, and in the subsequent elections in 2008, as already pointed out, the center-left coalition led by the PD representative Walter Veltroni was defeated by Berlusconi's center-right coalition. As for the general elections in 2013, primaries played a key role in the public image of the political party. In fact, soon after the 2012 primaries, the candidate Bersani registered a peak in the consensus and was on top of all the polls. However, the advantage gained by the center-left representative decreased just before the elections. This event implied a considerable loss of consensus (about 3.5 million votes) and the creation of a three-pole parliamentary

Table 24.2 The 2012 Center-Left Coalition Primary

Candidate	First Round			Second Round		
	Party	Votes	%	Candidate	Votes	%
Pier Luigi Bersani	Democratic Party	1,395,096	44.9	Pier Luigi Bersani	1,706,457	60.9
Matteo Renzi	Democratic Party	1,104,958	35.5	Matteo Renzi	1,095,925	39.1
Nichi Vendola	Left Ecology Freedom	485,689	15.6			
Laura Puppato	Democratic Party	80,628	2.6			
Bruno Tabacci	Democratic Centre	43,840	1.4			
Total		3,110,211	100		2,802,382	100

Table 24.3 Votes in the General Elections of the Party Promoters of the 2005 and 2012 Primary Elections

Primaries	Before primary	After primary	Difference
2005	16,019,388[a]	19,002,598[b]	+2,983,210
2012	13,689,330[c]	10,047,808[d]	−3,641,522

Source: Ministry of Interior.

Note: a The Olive Tree, 2001 parliamentary election; b The Union, 2006 parliamentary election; c Democratic Party and Italy of Values, 2008 parliamentary election; d Democratic Party, Left Ecology Freedom, Democratic Center and South Tyrolean People's Party, 2013 parliamentary election.

representation (center-left, center-right and M5S) that made a parliamentary majority more difficult. After long negotiations, a government led by the PD vice-secretary Enrico Letta was formed and supported also by the center-right coalition. Such a choice caused a fracture in the center-left coalition, since Left Ecology Freedom decided not to support the new government. Therefore, after an initial success of the primaries, a disastrous situation affected the left-wing parties and, more in general, Italian political life.

To sum up, in terms of electoral performance, both primary elections were a partial success for the center-left coalition. In 2005 they provided an increase in votes and allowed the creation of a center-left government that, however, did not last long. Despite the collapse in terms of votes, in 2012 they allowed the center-left coalition to create a government supported by political forces other than those of the center-left coalition.

As for membership, there were two different effects on the numbers of party members. When parties employ closed primaries, generally adhesion increases immediately before primaries and new party members either quit after them or they remain within the party as relatively inactive members (Cross and Rahat 2012). The situation is different when open primaries, where citizens can vote for their candidate without becoming party members, are adopted. Therefore, in regard to open primary elections, no considerable increase in members should be registered. In contrast, the number of members could increase after open primaries as a consequence of a better image of the political party. In Italy, data on membership was influenced by the transformations undergone by political parties over the last two decades. That having been said, while in the 2005 primaries data on membership of the two main parties, that created the PD, registered an increase of about 56 thousand members, in the 2012 primaries the parties that promoted primary elections after a general collapse registered a slight diminution of about one thousand members (Table 24.4). Thus, while in the first case the increase seems to be connected to the primary, in the second no effect seems to be connected to the primary; instead, a general collapse of membership occurred. This aspect will be better addressed in the section on intra-party democracy processes in the choice of leader.

Table 24.4 Membership of the Party Promoters of the 2005 and 2012 Primary Elections

Primaries	Before primary	After primary	Difference
2005	815,481[a]	872,414[a]	+56,933
2012	578,191[b]	577,169[b]	−1,022

Source: Democrats of the Left, Daisy, Democratic Party and Left Ecology Freedom.

Note: a Democrats of the Left and the Daisy; b Democratic Party and Left Ecology Freedom.

Parliamentary Primaries

Until 2013, primaries were almost exclusively employed to select people for prime minister and other leadership roles. However, as already pointed out, the adoption of the so-called *Porcellum* system with pre-selected lists of candidates appointed by the party, encouraged some political parties to have recourse to primary elections to select their candidates for parliamentary elections (Pasquino and Valbruzzi 2013; Regalia and Valbruzzi 2016). In the 2013 general elections, two parties, PD and SEL, after selecting Pier Luigi Bersani as a leader candidate in national primary elections, decided to organize elections all over Italy to appoint candidates for the Parliament. These were "semi-open" primaries; only party members or supporters who had already voted in the primary elections of the coalition for the appointment of Bersani were entitled to participate. More than three million voters took part in the selection of the premier candidate, while subsequently about two million voters participated in the primaries to appoint candidates to the Parliament (Musella 2014).

However, PD and SEL were not the only parties which adopted this type of selection and – before them – the M5S had organized online "closed" primaries to select their candidates to the Parliament (Bordignon and Ceccarini 2013; Lanzone and Rombi 2014; Tronconi 2015). As compared to what happened in the PD and SEL, parliamentary primary elections, called *"parlamentarie"* by Beppe Grillo to distinguish his own party from the others that were adopting the same procedure, were different for a number of reasons. First, votes were expressed online only by means of a pluralistic system and each participant could express up to a maximum of three votes. Second, these primaries took place over four days and third, only "certified" voters as at 30 September 2012 were entitled to participate, i.e., 31,612 voters, of which only 64.1 percent participated. Finally, unlike the PD and SEL, the M5S was the only party that had selected the whole set of candidates to the Parliament.

Table 24.5 shows selection based on some socio-graphic and political features of primary candidates. Starting from the example of the PD and SEL primaries, overall, no specific differences emerge among candidates and winners. Generally speaking, gender balance was maintained among those who were candidates and the winners. This element is not surprising: the electoral system devised by the two parties imposed the double gender preference. Also, in regard to age a certain coherence could be observed between the two groups: 46 percent of candidates and elected members of the PD and about 50 percent of the SEL belonged to an over-50 age group. In terms of education, candidates of both parties displayed higher education levels with over 70 percent in the PD. As for the incumbency factor, in the PD the share of candidates without any administrative role passed from 41.9 to 37.9 percent, while in SEL it was 77–78 percent, with no parliamentary representation, since the party had not reached the quorum required to have access to the distribution of the constituencies in the previous legislation.

In the case of the M5S, Table 24.5 shows that the most important feature was candidates' gender. In the primaries of M5S, no shares for women had been envisaged, nor had electoral systems imposing a gender balance been devised. Results indicate a percentage of men above 80 percent among both candidates and winners. In terms of age, under-50 candidates are the largest number among both primaries candidates and winners. Also, educational levels are interesting: among the candidates who won the primaries there is a certain balance between those who have a final diploma and graduates. In terms of incumbency, no previous administrative posts were registered at either a local or a national level. This confirms the novelty of the leadership proposed by the M5S.

However, with regard to the impact on the general elections, among the three cases the most important difference is the choice of M5S not to include candidates who had not been elected

Table 24.5 Candidates and Winners in the Parliamentary Primary for the 2013 General Elections

	Democratic Party		Left Ecology Freedom		5 Star Movement	
	candidates	*winners*	*candidates*	*winners*	*candidates*	*winners*
Woman	49.5	49.6	47	48.1	14.9	18.8
Man	50.5	50.4	53	51.9	85.1	81.2
20–29 years	4.6	3.8	5.1	4.8	9	10.2
30–39 years	20.6	20.4	18.9	19.1	30.4	30.7
40–49 years	29.3	30.2	27.8	28.8	39	37.9
50–59 years	34.0	35.3	33.3	32.5	17.3	17.1
60–74 years	11.5	10.3	14.9	14.8	4.3	4.1
Primary/middle school diploma	0.8	0.9	1.5	1.4	6.4	5.7
Secondary school diploma	23.9	25.5	28	29.4	49.6	46.8
Degree	74.1	72.5	63.2	63.2	43.4	47.4
N.a.	1.2	1.1	7.3	6	0.6	0.1
None	41.8	37.8	78.1	77	100	100
Municipal level	26.9	26.7	16.6	17.5	0	0
Provincial level	9.3	9.7	3.3	3.6	0	0
Regional level	4.9	5.7	2	1.9	0	0
National level	17.1	20.1	0	0	0	0
	885	663	457	418	1242	775

Source: C&LS-Candidate and Leader Selection.

by online primaries. As Table 24.6 shows, the leaders of the two center-left parties reserved some shares of nominees so as to be able to put their own trusted candidates in the lists. This led the PD to elect 27.9 percent of its candidates to Parliament directly co-opted by the Party Secretariat, while the share was 29.5 percent for the SEL.

More generally, data on the 2013 general elections indicate a renewal of the political class with a decrease in the percentage of outgoing MPs among newly elected members (De Lucia 2013). New parties, such as M5S and SEL, were most responsible for this change; however, the PD also contributed: 262 MPs were elected for the first time, in comparison to more than 400 who already sat in Parliament. Another very important aspect, beside the aforementioned changes, is the increase in the percentage of women elected (10 percent more), which brings the share of women in the Parliament to 30.8 percent. Among the parties with the highest percentage of women were the parties that promoted primaries: PD and M5S (38 percent), and SEL (27 percent).

Table 24.6 Candidate Selection Procedures of Elected MPs in the 2013 General Elections

	Democratic Party		Left Ecology Freedom		5 Star Movement	
	N	*%*	*N*	*%*	*N*	*%*
Primary election	287	72.1	31	70.5	163	100.0
Party appointment	111	27.9	13	29.5	0	–
Total	*398*[a]	*100*	*44*	*100*	*162*[b]	*100*

Note: a Nine people elected in the foreign district should be added; b One person elected in the foreign district should be added.

To sum up, the experience in primary elections for Italian MPs shows some clear elements. The gender composition of Parliament was more balanced when it was imposed by the parties themselves (as in the PD and SEL primaries) through the "double preference" approach. When this factor is not taken into account (e.g. the M5S primaries) or no leading criterion is adopted (due to the choice of both parties to select a share of candidates directly appointed by the party) men are numerically superior. However, an important consequence of MPs' election was the increase of women among the elected. Finally, another element in common is the larger presence of younger candidates, which contributed to a transformation of the political class.

Regional, Provincial, and Municipal Selection

Over the last decade Italian primaries have become a distinctive feature of center-left parties, and a consolidated practice in the Italian political system. Despite much media attention at a national level, intra-party democracy in Italy has developed and stabilized above all at a sub-national level. As a whole, in Italy over 1,000 primary elections took place and, among these, over 90 percent were held at a municipal level.

In this regard, this section analyzes open primaries held between 2004 and 2005 at the regional, provincial and municipal level to select candidates for executive positions such as the president of the Regional Government, of the Provincial Government, or the Mayor. A common element in these cases was voters' participation, which constantly made primary elections an innovative tool for the selection of candidates. While previous studies have extensively investigated this aspect, this section of the chapter will focus on local primaries in terms of distribution, number of candidates and impact on general elections.

Regional Primaries

Primary elections to select candidates for the post of President of Regional Governments have increasingly played a key role in Italian politics (Massetti and Sandri 2013; De Luca and Rombi 2016). As already stated, the first relevant primaries were held in the Puglia Region with Vendola as a candidate in 2005, and they had a great impact both on the party system and on the media. As shown in Table 24.7, while in the 2003–2006 elections only two primaries were held, and four in the 2008–2011 period, in the 2012–2015 period 11 primaries were held, comprising over 50 percent of all Italian regions. Most such competitions took place in southern Italy and the Italian islands (11 primaries) as compared to northern and central regions, which were characterized by three primary elections each. Moreover, if we look at the promoting parties, 14 primary elections out of 17 cases were promoted by the center-left parties to select a leader for the coalition, while they were held to settle intra-party issues in the PD in only three instances. However, in the coalition primaries, the PD candidate won in 10 cases out of 14. In two cases, formally independent candidates won, but they were supported by the main parties of the coalition: Rita Borsellino in the 2005 primaries in Sicily and Umberto Ambrosoli in 2012 in Lombardy. In conclusion, the only candidate who defeated moderate candidates was Nichi Vendola, who was appointed for the first time in 2005 as a representative of RC, and was then re-confirmed after five years, supported by the SEL.

Initially, regional primaries featured competition between two candidates and this was confirmed in the five primaries held between 2005 and 2010; an exception to this was Calabria. Subsequently, the competition took place with the participation of three candidates. Only in Basilicata were there four candidates competing for the post of President of the Region, while five candidates were competing in Molise and Sardinia.

Table 24.7 The Italian Regional Primaries, 2005–2015

Region	Year	Promoter	Number of candidates	Winner	Winner's party	Regional election victory?
Apulia	2005	center-left	2	Nichi Vendola	RC	Yes
Siciliy	2006	center-left	2	Rita Borsellino	Independent	No
Apulia	2010	center-left	2	Nichi Vendola	SEL	Yes
Umbria	2010	PD	2	Catiuscia Marini	PD	Yes
Calabria	2010	PD	3	Agazio Loiero	PD	No
Molise	2011	center-left	5	Paolo Frattura	PD	No
Lombardy	2013	center-left	3	Umberto Ambrosoli	Independent	No
Basilicata	2013	center-left	4	Marcello Pittella	PD	Yes
Sardinia	2014	center-left	5	Francesca Barracciu	PD	Withdrawn
Abruzzo	2014	center-left	3	Luciano D'Alfonso	PD	Yes
Emilia Romagna	2014	PD	2	Stefano Bonaccini	PD	Yes
Calabria	2014	center-left	3	Mario Oliverio	PD	Yes
Apulia	2015	center-left	3	Michele Emiliano	PD	Yes
Veneto	2015	center-left	3	Alessandra Moretti	PD	No
Liguria	2015	center-left	3	Raffaella Paita	PD	No
Campania	2015	center-left	3	Vincenzo De Luca	PD	Yes
Marche	2015	center-left	3	Luca Ceriscioli	PD	Yes

Source: C&LS-Candidate and Leader Selection.

As for gender differences and their impact on the general elections, women prevailed in only five cases, and among these only one (Catiuscia Marini in Umbria) became the President of the Region. In the remaining 12 cases the male nominees were able to win the following regional elections, in nine cases with a higher percentage in terms of success in comparison to the last electoral cycle.

Provincial Primaries

Table 24.8 shows the primary elections held in Italy between 2006 and 2013 to select candidates for the post of President of the Provincial Government. The time-span under consideration is smaller as compared to other primaries at the local level, since Provincial Governments in Italy have been profoundly reformed by the Decreto Salva-Italia (Save-Italy decree) approved by Monti's government in December 2011. Subsequently, Law No. 56 of 2014 transformed the provincial government of ordinary regions into second-level administrative entities with a restricted suffrage election of their bodies. Such a change altered the institutional layout and downsized their electoral and political importance.

If we look at the data in Table 24.8, it is evident that provincial primaries, like regional ones, organized only by center-left parties, were mainly coalition primaries, except for those promoted in the early years of the PD, which – under the leadership of Walter Veltroni – opted for a strategy of non-alliance with other parties.

These primaries were held in southern provinces only in five cases, mainly concentrating in central and northern Italy. As for the number of candidates, the data in the table indicates an average range between two and four; a few cases with five candidates and just one case with six candidates are reported. The winners of the primaries, all men, except for three women, were representatives of moderate parties: Democrats of the Left (DS), Democracy is Freedom – The Daisy

Table 24.8 The Italian Provincial Primaries, 2006–2013

Province	Year	Promoter	Number of candidates	Winner	Winner's party	Provincial election victory?
Gorizia	2006	center-left	4	Enrico Gherghetta	DS	Yes
Lucca	2006	center-left	4	Stefano Baccelli	DL	Yes
Imperia	2006	center-left	2	Fulvio Vassallo	DS	No
Ancona	2007	DS	2	Patrizia Casagrande	DS	Yes
La Spezia	2007	center-left	5	Marino Fiasella	DL	Yes
Vercelli	2007	center-left	3	Francesco Carcò	SDI	No
Vicenza	2007	center-left	3	Pietro Collareda	DL	No
Asti	2008	PD	2	Roberto Peretti	PD	No
Caltanissetta	2008	PD	4	Salvatore Messana	PD	No
Fermo 1	2009	PD	2	Renzo Offidani	PD	Not candidate
Ascoli	2009	PD	3	Emidio Mandozzi	PD	No
Cuneo	2009	PD	3	Mino Taricco	PD	No
Savona	2009	PD	6	Michele Boffa	PD	No
Taranto	2009	center-left	2	Gianni Florido	PD	Yes
Arezzo	2009	center-left	2	Roberto Vasai	PD	Yes
Pistoia	2009	center-left	3	Federica Fratoli	PD	Yes
Siena	2009	PD	3	Simone Bezzini	PD	Yes
Firenze	2009	center-left	3	Andrea Barducci	PD	Yes
Grosseto	2009	center-left	3	Leonardo Marras	PD	Yes
Prato	2009	center-left	2	Lamberto Gestri	PD	Yes
Fermo 2	2009	center-left	2	Fabrizio Cesetti	Left	Yes
Pordenone	2009	PD	2	Giorgio Zanin	PD	No
Napoli	2009	center-left	3	Luigi Nicolais	PD	No
Isernia	2009	center-left	5	Antonio Sorbo	Left	No
Avellino	2009	center-left	3	Alberta De Simone	PD	No
Brescia	2009	PD	5	Diego Peli	PD	No
Verona	2009	PD	3	Diego Zardini	PD	No
Ravenna	2011	center-left	4	Claudio Casadio	PD	Yes
Trento	2013	center-left	5	Ugo Rossi	PATT	Yes

Source: C&LS-Candidate and Leader Selection.

(DL), Italian Democratic Socialists (SDI), Democratic Party (PD), and the Trentino Tyrolean Autonomist Party (PATT); only in two cases did candidates belong to the so-called extreme left-wing, while the PD has always played a key role since its creation. The nominees were elected president in 14 provincial elections, i.e. half of the cases. This figure, however, does not completely portray the fact that primaries promoted the electoral success of the candidates.

Municipal Primaries

Between 2004 and 2015, 952 open primaries were organized to select candidates for the post of mayor. Table 24.9 shows the distribution of primaries over the period analyzed. More specifically, in 2004 and 2005, before the so-called "Prodi's primaries," the lowest number of primaries was held; by contrast, almost half of the municipal primaries were concentrated in 2009 and 2014. The table shows the number of municipalities that employed primaries for the selection of the mayor every year. Generally speaking, primaries were more frequent in the years showing a

Table 24.9 The Italian Mayoral Primaries, 2004–2015

Year	Number of municipalities with mayoral elections	Number of mayoral Primary elections
2004	4,518	4
2005	1,097	2
2006	1,328	29
2007	1,020	48
2008	616	37
2009	4,292	177
2010	1,071	36
2011	1,343	58
2012	1,009	117
2013	719	88
2014	4,105	297
2015	1,108	59
Total	22,226	952[a]

Source: C&LS-Candidate and Leader Selection

Note: a The number of municipalities with mayoral primary elections is 920.

higher number of municipal elections. In this respect, we should also take into account that citizens of over 8,000 municipalities normally vote at the end of the five-year legislation period, or in case of crisis of the town council; such events, starting from the direct election of the mayor introduced in 1993, automatically imply anticipated elections.

Another interesting element, underlined by several scholars (e.g., Sandri and Venturino 2016), is that the larger the municipality, the higher the probability for primary elections. This is fairly evident in provincial capitals where both traditional and new parties deploy more developed organizations, made up of party leaders, members and activists working in territorial establishments or organized in basic units such as the meet-up groups adopted by the M5S. Both territorial establishments and organizational power make it easier to promote primaries in larger municipalities as compared to smaller ones. Moreover, another hypothesis, which can account for the diffusion of primaries in provincial capitals, is the final reward: being the mayor of a large municipality is not only more profitable for candidates, but it can also be an important step forward for a higher level political career. Large municipalities are often a springboard and a higher number of candidates for the post of mayor ultimately leads to primary elections.

Another important aspect of municipal primaries is that, starting from 2012, several political forces promoted more primary elections. In fact, while almost all primaries at the national, regional, and provincial level were organized by left-wing parties or coalitions, primary elections for the selection of mayors were characterized by the presence of other political groups. As Table 24.10 shows, this approach was sporadically used by some center-right parties and coalitions, civic parties, regional/autonomous parties and by the M5S. However, as shown in the table, the vast majority of these primary elections – 866, accounting for 91 percent of the total – were organized by center-left parties or coalitions.

As far as competitiveness is concerned, however, Table 24.11 shows a distribution of primaries based on the number of candidates.[7] The first datum focuses on the limited number of primaries with one candidate only, organized in two cases by the center-left coalition and in other two cases by the PD, while in the remaining three cases they were organized by two minor

Table 24.10 The Italian Mayoral Primary Elections by Promoting Party/Coalition, 2004–2015

Promoter	N	%
Center-left coalition	542	56.9
Democratic Party	305	32.1
Civic list	32	3.4
Center-right coalition	22	2.3
Center-left civic list	18	1.9
5 Star Movement	14	1.5
The People of Freedom	7	0.7
Center-right civic list	3	0.3
Center coalition	2	0.2
Future and Freedom for Italy	2	0.2
South Tyrolean People's Party	2	0.2
Brothers of Italy - National Alliance	2	0.2
Democrats of the Left	1	0.1
Total	*952*	*100*

Source: C&LS-Candidate and Leader Selection.

parties of the center-right coalition: Future and Freedom for Italy (FLI) and Brothers of Italy – National Alliance (FDI). The events that led to this choice are different. In the center-left coalition the presence of a single candidate was due to the retirement of the candidates because of personal reasons or as a result of intra-party/coalition conflicts, while in the second case, the presence of a single candidate for the center-right coalition was the outcome of a decision made by organizers.

The multi-candidate model in Table 24.11 shows that over 90 percent of municipal primaries was held with between 2 and 4 candidates. In contrast, primaries with five or more candidates accounted for only seven percent of the total. It is not easy to affirm that an excessive number of candidates could be a "pathology" of the system; however, primaries for the selection of the mayor ensure fair competition: citizens are aware of the candidates' programs and can choose based on their own information collection.

Table 24.11 Number of Candidates Running in the Italian Mayoral Primaries, 2004–2015

Number of candidates	N	%
1	7	0.7
2	437	46.0
3	304	32.0
4	126	13.3
5	51	5.4
6	15	1.6
7	8	0.8
8	1	0.1
9	1	0.1
Total	*950*	*100*

Source: C&LS-Candidate and Leader Selection.

Table 24.12 Number of Candidates Running in the Italian Mayoral Primaries by Promoting Party/
Coalition, 2004–2015

Promoter	Percent of candidates	N
Civic list	3.3	30
The People of Freedom	3.3	7
Center-left coalition	3.1	542
Center-right coalition	2.8	22
Center-left civic list	2.7	18
Center-right civic list	2.7	3
South Tyrolean People's Party	2.5	2
Democratic Party	2.4	305
Democrats of the Left	2.0	1
Center coalition	2.0	2
Brothers of Italy – National Alliance	1.5	2
Future and Freedom for Italy	1.0	2
Average	*2.5*	*936*[a]

Source: C&LS–Candidate and Leader.

Note: a Only primaries where it was possible to find the total number of candidates.

Table 24.12 shows competition in primaries for the selection of mayors based on the promoting party. The average number of candidates in these elections is 2.5; higher numbers of candidates are found in competitions organized by civic parties (3.3). The most interesting example is, again, the experience of center-left parties. When center-left parties are organized in coalition the average is 3.1 candidates, while in the main party of the coalition, (namely the PD) the average is 2.4. This suggests that in coalition competitions, internal pluralism leads to representation candidacies, while in the case of the PD the lower average reflects the different nuances of the party and intra-party competitiveness.

As for the format of the competition, further analysis should focus on the presence of female candidates. Of the 928 primaries for the selection of mayors where data is available,[8] 519 cases featured only male candidates (55.9 percent). In the remaining 409 primaries, between one and three candidates were women.[9] There were only 127 cases in which a female candidate won in the subsequent municipal elections (13.3 percent).

In regard to the consequences of primaries, one of the most explored aspects is the performance of candidates in the subsequent elections. In particular, the main element of observation is the "primary penalty," the potential for high level of division caused by the primaries that negatively affects the result of general elections; this mainly occurs at a local level (Ichino and Nathan 2013). However, if we look at the whole *corpus* of local Italian primaries, candidates selected by means of open primaries were defeated in 393 local elections (41.3 percent), but they succeeded in 533 municipal competitions (56 percent).[10] In order to be able to provide final results, a comparison between the results of the elections for the candidates chosen for the first time and the results of the candidates chosen though other methods is necessary; however, it appears that no marked "primary penalty" exists for local elections.

To conclude, as compared to other kinds of primaries, local primaries organized for the selection of mayoral candidates are characterized by two peculiarities: they were held regularly over a period of time and displayed a high number of cases; and the diffusion of inclusive methods at a territorial and party level seems to suggest a "contagion effect." To be sure, open primaries are a peculiarity of center-left parties; however, their use was increasingly extended to center-right, regional and M5S parties.

Leadership Selection

Within the Italian political system, the PD is the only political organization that has strengthened intra-party democracy both through primaries for the selection of candidates and through the direct election of its leaders (Sandri, Seddone and Venturino 2013; Sandri and Seddone 2015a). Despite the statute of the PD that entitles only its members to choose its leaders at a provincial and municipal level (art. 15.4), the selection of regional secretaries is organized based on a complex process, very similar to the selection of its national secretary, allowing all citizens to participate, based on the model of open primaries (art. 15.8). Between 2007 and 2017, the PD party organized 69 selections of regional secretaries. In 60 cases, the selections took place by means of open primaries, while in the remaining nine cases, the Regional Assembly selected them (Venturino 2015). In the same period the PD had five national secretaries, three of whom were selected through the participation of party members and voters, while two secretaries were appointed by the National Assembly to replace resigning, outgoing secretaries.[11] The party statute establishes different roles for members and voters. Indeed, the selection of leaders is pivoted on two stages. The first stage is similar to the OMOV system, or "one-member-one-vote," and involves enrolled members. The second stage is similar to the OPOV system, or "one-person-one-vot," involving also supporters.[12]

By considering more inclusive selections of party leaders, the three PD secretaries were elected by party members and voters in four elections: in 2007 when the party was founded and over 3.5 million voters elected the first secretary Walter Veltroni; in 2009, when over three million people took part in the selection of Pier Luigi Bersani; in 2013 when about 2.8 million voters participated in the election of Matteo Renzi as the party secretary; and then in 2017 when Renzi was re-elected by about 1.8 million voters (Table 24.13). Therefore, in just ten years, the PD changed leaders five times and, so far, Renzi's tenure is the longest-running. Moreover, the inclusion of supporters and general voters in the selection blurred the intra-party boundaries

Table 24.13 Leadership Selection of the Democratic Party, 2007–2017

Party leader	Period	Selection system	Selectors	Number of candidates	Winner (%)	Runner–up (%)
Walter Veltroni	October 2007– February 2009	OPOV	3,541,917	5	74.8	13.2
Dario Franceschini	February 2009– November 2009	National Assembly	1,258	2	91.9	8.1
Pier Luigi Bersani	November 2009– April 2013	OMOV + OPOV	3,102,709[a]	3	53.8	34.3
Guglielmo Epifani	May 2013– December 2013	National Assembly	593	1	85.8	–
Matteo Renzi	December 2013– February 2017	OMOV + OPOV	2,805,775[a]	3	65.8	20.5
Matteo Renzi	May 2017–present	OMOV + OPOV	1,838,938[a]	3	69.2	19.9

Note: The participation data refers to the OPOV system.

further, thus placing the party in a less institutionalized sphere (Fasano and Seddone 2016). However, this high level of inclusion was never perceived by party members as an attempt to downsize their intra-party role (Sandri and Seddone 2015b). It rather served to reinforce participation over time, rendering this an intrinsic characteristic of the PD.

Table 24.14 shows participation levels in the four selections at the regional level. When one considers aggregate national data, a remarkable element is the decrease in participation in elections. Over the last ten years the initial spur seems to have been exhausted and the number of voters has shrunk considerably. In 2007, for instance, when the party was founded and Veltroni elected, a turnout of 74.8 percent was reached, while the direct competitors, i.e., Rosi Bindi and Enrico Letta, reached only 13.2 percent and 11.9 percent respectively. Two extra candidates took part in that election, Pietro Giorgio Gawronski and Mario Adinolfi, who both collected a few thousand votes (0.3 percent). In that selection, the low level of competitiveness was counteracted by the large participation in celebration of the party foundation.

Table 24.14 Participation in the OPOV System Selection of the Democratic Party, 2007–2017

Regions	2007	2009	2013	2017
Valle d'Aosta	3,345	2,345	3,569	1,889
Piemonte	162,949	158,208	164,578	89,379
Liguria	79,895	88,234	81,870	47,972
Lombardy	351,144	357,970	377,806	226,359
Northwest	*597,333*	*606,757*	*627,823*	*365,599*
Trentino Alto Adige	29,849	26,477	27,955	14,023
Veneto	176,917	176,476	177,621	86,756
Friuli–Venezia Giulia	53,363	52,276	46,928	25,536
North East	*260,129*	*255,229*	*252,504*	*126,315*
Emilia–Romagna	421,325	391,087	405,505	215,958
Tuscany	311,869	285,221	393,513	210,753
Umbria	77,329	75,074	71,176	40,339
Marche	101,217	85,918	93,486	47,106
Center (Red Zone)	*911,740*	*837,300*	*963,680*	*514,156*
Lazio	348,865	316,745	252,523	173,195
Abruzzo	111,452	60,563	54,144	40,052
Molise	17,191	18,697	12,385	11,936
Campania	456,081	300,949	192,463	156,808
Apulia	247,866	174,220	123,178	156,197
Basilicata	68,457	66,647	32,541	41,568
Calabria	208,968	144,671	89,580	81,926
Sicily	183,854	201,577	128,992	112,445
Sardinia	111,301	106,755	59,098	47,203
South and Islands	*1,754,035*	*1,390,824*	*944,904*	*821,330*
Abroad	18,680	12,599	16,864	11,538
Italy	*3,541,917*	*3,102,709*	*2,805,775*	*1,838,938*

Source: Democratic Party.

With the election of Pier Luigi Bersani, in 2009, the PD introduced the "multi-stage" selection procedure described above, involving party members and voters in different steps. This approach allowed access also to non-members and the selection through the so-called primary election system played a key role. On that occasion the most competitive selection in the history of the PD took place and Bersani won with 53.2 percent of the votes, followed by Dario Franceschini (34.3 percent) and Ignazio Marino (12.5 percent). However, in 2009 participation plunged; in fact, in all areas of the country, except for the northern and western regions (led by Liguria and Lombardy) participation decreased.

The decrease continued in the subsequent primary elections of 2013, despite some interesting aspects: notwithstanding the decrease of about 300,000 electors, some differences emerged. The decrease was more marked in the central and southern regions, as well as in the Islands, while in northern and western regions, along with central regions, participation increased considerably. This occurrence is mostly a consequence of the transformation in the PD and the participation of Renzi in the competition. The latter, in fact, after having been defeated by Bersani in the coalition primary elections of 2012, had always been presented as the leader candidate aiming at a makeover of the party. In the 2013 competition, three candidates were running for the post: the frontrunner Renzi; Gianni Cuperlo, representing the post-communist party tradition; and Giuseppe Civati, a young MP who had already served as regional minister. Actually, in the OMOV competition another candidate was present: the European MP Gianni Pittella, who had been put aside after the OMOV voting. The final result saw Renzi heading the competition with 67.5 percent of the vote, followed by Cuperlo (18.2 percent) and Civati (14.2 percent).

Slightly more than two months after his election and the collapse of Letta, Renzi became prime minister. For the first time, the overlap between party leadership and premiership (mentioned in the PD statute) occurred, thus moving the PD towards a "presidential" party structure (Musella and Webb 2015).

When he became prime minister, Renzi initiated a series of reforms, among which was a reform of the constitution of the Italian Republic. The prime minister anchored his premiership to this event; in fact, after the defeat of its political wing in the constitutional referendum of 4th December 2016, Renzi resigned. Paolo Gentiloni was then appointed as prime minister and he did not alter the government structure much, leading the country in line with the approach of Renzi's government. After this, his leadership was also questioned and this led to a new electoral campaign for the national secretariat. After less than five months, then, and in defiance of all forecasts, the former prime minister regained the party leadership with 69.2 percent of the votes, almost a total consensus, far ahead of his opponents Andrea Orlando (19.9 percent) and Michele Emiliano (10.9 percent). However, as shown in Table 24.15, participation dropped substantially, by more than one million votes, from the previous primary elections. Thus, less enthusiasm was shown for the latest primaries, also because the favorite candidate was competing in a more institutionalized role characterized, for better or worse, by his double incumbency (leader of the party and of the government). Renzi, thus, appeared less as the young politician who had promised to "scrap" the old political system and more as someone attempting to reconfirm the good things made by his government.

If there was a collapse in the number of participants voting for the leadership, it is important to understand what happened to the PD membership. Like many other parties of western Europe, the two founding parties of the PD (the DS and DL) had already experienced a significant decrease in their membership. However, despite the decade-long decrease in membership, the creation of the new party led to an increase in members (about one million) of the founding parties. To understand the size of the new party it is necessary to examine the number of new members in the 2008/2009 period, when the party had 820,000 members. Since then, there

Table 24.15 Party Membership of Democratic Party (before and after its Foundation), 2005–2017

Year	Political party significant events	Members	Difference	Var (%)
2005	Center–left primary for Prime Minister candidate	800,907[a]	−14,574	−1.8
2006	General Elections	872,414[a]	+71,507	+8.9
2007	PD foundation and party leader selection	1,000,229[a]	+127,815	+14.7
2008/2009[b]	General Elections/ European elections and Party leader selection	820,607	−179,622	−18.0
2010	–	618,768	−201,839	−24.6
2011	Monti premiership	537,757	−81,011	−13.1
2012	Center–left primary for Prime Minister candidate	500,163	−37,594	−7.0
2013	General Elections/Party leader selection	542,890	+42,727	+8.5
2014	Renzi premiership and European elections	378,669	−164,221	−30.2
2015	–	395,574	+16,905	+4.5
2016	Renzi resignation and Gentiloni premiership	405,041	+9,467	+2.4
2017	Party leader selection	449,852	+44,811	+11.1

Source: Democratic of the Left and DL (2005-2007); Democratic Party (2008–2017).

Note: a Data derived from the sum between DS and DL members; b Biennial Membership provided by the party.

has been a substantial decrease in participation, resulting in a membership of about 500,000 in 2012. In 2013, when Renzi was selected, the party registered a slight trend reversal which led to 42,727 more members as compared to the previous year. However, in the following year a further decrease (over 30 percent) left the PD at a historical low. Since 2015, there has been a slow growth, and membership peaked again (over 11.1 percent) in the last selection of the party leader.

In general, considering the membership, the party accounts for about six percent of its electors, in line with other European parties (Scarrow and Gezgor 2010; Van Biezen, Mair and Poguntke 2012). However, the increase in members and the swift decrease after its foundation and the primaries for the party leader confirm the hypothesis of the "instant members," members of the party who were initially attracted by this event and abandoned the party immediately afterwards (Hazan and Rahat 2010).

The generally positive assessment of intra-party democratic processes in public discourse has triggered a "contagion" effect in the other parties, as previously stated. Notable among these parties has been the North League, which – after the resignation of its founder Umberto Bossi after 20 years and a brief mandate of Roberto Maroni – selected Matteo Salvini as the party leader both in 2013 and 2017, by means of a sort of closed primary election where all party members were entitled to participate. As anticipated in the section on the regulations, participation in the primaries was even more exclusive, since only members with at least 12 months' membership were entitled to vote. In both cases, as shown in Table 24.16, Salvini obtained a result of over 80 percent of the votes, thus transforming the party congress into an event legitimating his leadership.

Table 24.16 Leadership Selection of North League, 2013–2017

	Participation	*Number of Candidates*	*Winner (%)*	*Runner-Up (%)*
2013	10,221	2	81.7	18.3
2017	8,024	2	82.7	17.3

Source: North League.

More recently, the small right-wing party Brothers of Italy – National Alliance organized an uncontested primary election to select its new party leader (Giorgia Meloni), to choose the new party logo, and to measure the voters' positions on some Italian political events. A total of 249,380 people participated in the election and 225,532 voters expressed their preference in the polling stations scattered all over Italy, while 23,848 people voted online through the system organized by the party.

Therefore, the "contagion" seems to be a feature of the current Italian political scene even if the organizational impact of the primaries has been controversial, in that their positive effects in terms of political communication, inclusion, transparency and democratization have made primaries an effective tool in reacting to the current situation of low faith in politics and a widespread anti-party attitude.

Conclusion

The intra-party democratic processes developed in Italy have become a unique feature of the Italian model of politics. The reasons previously outlined – the change in the electoral system, which fostered a verticalization of the relationships between citizens and representatives; the crisis of leadership legitimacy in the center-left coalition; the "brand" of a model to select candidates and party leaders; and the contagion of non-center-left parties – illustrate this.

The private nature of such processes has allowed parties to self-regulate their introduction in relation to the special needs of the promoting party. In this perspective, we could consider the system employed by the PD as the main reference of the Italian model. However, in regard to inclusiveness, the process of selection in Italy can be differentiated based on the greater/lower criteria of inclusion. As shown in Table 24.17, this allows us to further differentiate between *closed models* (where only party members were entitled to vote) in the M5S for the selection of candidates and in the LN for the selection of the leaders, and *open models* typical of the center-left coalition and, in particular, of the PD.

More specifically, intra-party democracy models for the selection of candidates have affected different territorial levels. Prodi's national primaries in 2005, which paved the way for other experiences, were originally created to reinforce Prodi's leadership in a dispute among the promoting parties. The subsequent primaries for Bersani's elections in 2012 were characterized

Table 24.17 Typology of the Italian Candidate and Leader Selections

	Candidate selection	*Leader selection*
Closed (party members)	5 Star Movement	North League
Open (voters and supporters)	Center-left coalition, Democratic Party	Brothers of Italy – National Alliance, Democratic Party

by greater competitiveness. In this manner, primaries have become a competition tool rather than a legitimization tool, and in both cases they have been characterized by a high level of participation. The 2005 primaries allowed organizers to build the government and to increase consensus in the general elections. In 2012, despite the collapse in terms of voters, primaries started a process to build the government, based on a "great coalition" system with the support of center-right forces.

As for other territorial levels (regional, provincial and municipal), primaries have been used frequently to select candidates. An initial difference of this type of primaries is that while all the primaries at a regional and provincial level were organized by center-left parties or coalitions, municipal primaries were rather characterized by the presence of other parties. Municipal primaries, even though not being under the spotlight, were (and still are) for figures and importance the core of the process of democratization of parties in Italy. They are the most regular and most competitive primary elections that bring candidates for the post of mayor close to citizens and have a positive impact on municipal elections, if we consider the "victory" factor.

However, Italian primaries in 2013 also had an impact on the choice of candidates for Parliament. In that case, thanks to a system that gave advantage to parties that used a centralized selection process, the most important parties of the center-left (PD and SEL) as well as the M5S had recourse to primaries to select MPs and senators. In the first case, they were semi-open primaries and in the second case they were online closed primaries. In both cases, however, primaries were able to renew the political class and to create a territorialization of the vote to the advantage of more "rooted" candidates.

Finally, intra-party democracy processes have also affected the selection of leaders. In this case, the PD reintroduced the open primaries model to select both national and regional leaders. The inclusion of both supporters and voters in the selection of the leaders on one side blurred the boundaries of parties and on the other allowed a contamination between members and electors, which – over time – reinforced participation as a typical feature of the PD.

Participation, despite the decrease in the number of participants (as compared to previous experiences) is still one of the most distinctive features of the Italian model. In fact, even if in some cases such democratic processes revealed weakness or contradiction, so far they have represented one of the few moments of true participation of citizens in the political life of the country, and they continue to do so.

Notes

1 Actually, the first primary elections had already been held in the 1990s. In 1998, a center-right party, the National Alliance (AN), experimented with open primary elections to select candidates for the provincial council in Rome, while primary elections for the selection of the candidate to the City Council were held in 1999. In that case, these were (closed) primary elections held to select the candidate for the Municipal Elections in Bologna (a historical stronghold of the left-wing party); the candidate of the center-left coalition Silvia Bartolini was a representative of the Democrats of the Left (DS), and she obtained 79.9 percent out of 21,688 participants. Such an attempt, quickly organized and in the framework of a severe crisis of the center-left coalition in the city, remained famous for the unexpected defeat of the center-left coalition, which was unable to elect a left-wing mayor for the first time in the post-war period.

2 In 2004 the Regional Government of Tuscany passed a law (Law No. 70, repealed in 2014) allowing parties to hold official primaries to select their own candidates for the regional council. This law was employed in regional elections in 2005 by DS and TF parties and in 2010 by PD and SEL. In 2009 another region, Calabria, passed a law, although never used, which formally allowed parties to hold primary elections to select their candidates running for the presidency of the regional council.

3 The general system remained in the subsequent primaries of the coalition in 2012, held to select the candidate for the leadership of the party: participation was open to all adult citizens – even citizens of the European Union residing in Italy and to non-EU citizens having a resident permit – upon payment of a donation of two Euro, by signing the public appeal of support (*Appello di sostegno*), the charter of intents and their enrolment in a Voters List.

4 The LN party makes a distinction between "supporting members" and "activist ordinary members." The former have specific duties, however they cannot vote in congresses, nor submit their candidacy. The latter are members with the right to vote and the right of representation in the party. Such qualification can be acquired only by adult individuals who have been supporting members for at least one year and have participated in political activity or propaganda, upon previous application by the interested party and upon approval.

5 Minors and non-EU citizens are not entitled to vote; they cannot access the online platform, because they are non-members of the M5S. Moreover, in order to be able to access the online voting platform, a minimum membership period is required. It may vary and it is officially indicated on the website every time there is a vote announcement.

6 An interesting aspect of this was the ability of the parties to mobilize voters during primaries. Based on the coalition parties' membership figures some scholars assume that a plausible participation threshold was 1.3 million voters. This further explains why the participation of four million voters in the 2005 primaries was an extraordinary event.

7 Two cases are missing in the global calculation: those organized by Civic Parties in small municipalities where the final number of competing candidates could not be inferred.

8 In the remaining cases, most of which are primaries organized by Civic Parties in small municipalities, it was not possible to find data on the gender of all candidates.

9 In 354 primaries, there was one female candidate, in 50 primaries, two female candidates and in 5 primaries, three female candidates.

10 In 26 cases (2.7 percent) nominees withdrew their candidacy, thus not participating in the subsequent municipal elections.

11 Dario Franceschini replaced Walter Veltroni in 2008, and Guglielmo Epifani replaced Pier Luigi Bersani in 2013.

12 If the winner of the second stage does not obtain an absolute majority, the National Assembly selects the party candidate.

References

Bardi, Luciano, and Leonardo Morlino. 1992. "Italy." In *Party Organizations: A Data Handbook on Party Organizations in Western Democracies, 1960–90*, eds. Richard S. Katz and Peter Mair. London: Sage, pp. 458–618.

Bardi, Luciano, and Leonardo Morlino. 1994. "Italy: Tracing the Roots of the Great Transformation." In *How Parties Organize: Change and Adaptation in Party Organizations in Western Democracies*, eds. Richard S. Katz and Peter Mair. London: Sage, pp. 242–77.

Bille, Lars. 2001. "Democratizing a Democratic Procedure: Myth or Reality? Candidate Selection in Western European Parties, 1960–1990." *Party Politics* 7(3): 363–380.

Blondel, Jean, and Jean-Louis Thiébault. (eds.). 2009. *Political Leadership, Parties and Citizens: The Personalization of Leadership*. London: Routledge.

Bordandini, Paola, Aldi De Virgilio, and Francesco Raniolo. 2009. "The Birth of a Party: The Case of the Italian Partito Democratico. *South European Society & Politics* 13(3): 303–324.

Bordignon, Fabio, and Luigi Ceccarini. 2013. "Five Stars and a Cricket. Beppe Grillo Shakes Italian Politics." *South European Society and Politics* 18(4): 427–449.

Calise, Mauro. 2015. "The Personal Party: An Analytical Framework." *Italian Political Science Review/Rivista Italiana di Scienza Politica* 45(3): 301–315.

Campus, Donatella, and Gianfranco Pasquino. 2006. "Leadership in Italy: The Changing Role of Leaders in Elections and in Government." *Journal of Contemporary European Studies* 14(1): 25–40.

Corbetta, Piergiorgio, and Rinaldo Vignati. 2013. "The Primaries of the Centre Left: Only a Temporary Success?" *Contemporary Italian Politics* 5 (1): 82–96.

Cross, William P., and Andre Blais. 2012. *Politics at the Centre: The Selection and Removal of Party Leaders in the Anglo Parliamentary Democracies*. Oxford: Oxford University Press.

Cross, William P., and Gideon Rahat. 2012. "'The Pathologies of Party Primaries and their Possible Solution." Presented at the workshop on 'Party Primaries in Europe: Consequences and Challenges', European Consortium for Political Research's Joint Sessions of Workshops, University of Antwerp, Belgium, 11–15 April.

Cross, William P., and Richard S. Katz. (eds.). 2013. *The Challenges of Intra-Party Democracy*. Oxford: Oxford University Press.

D'Alimonte, Roberto. 2008. "Italy: A Case of Fragmented Bipolarism." In *The Politics of Electoral Systems*, eds. Michael Gallagher and Paul Mitchell. Oxford: Oxford University Press, pp. 253–275.

De Luca, Marino, and Stafano Rombi. 2016. "The Regional Primary Elections in Italy: A General Overview." *Contemporary Italian Politics* 8(1): 24–41.

De Luca, Marino, and Fulvio Venturino. 2015. "Democratising Candidate Selection in Italy and France." In *Party Primaries in Comparative Perspective*, eds. Giulia Sandri, Antonella Seddone, and Fulvio Venturino. London: Ashgate, pp. 129–144.

De Luca, Marino, and Fulvio Venturino. 2017. "The Effects of Primaries on Electoral Performance: France and Italy in Comparative Perspective." *French Politics* 15(1): 43–56.

De Lucia, Federico. 2013. "The 2013 Parliament: New and More Gender-balanced." In *The Italian General Election of 2013: A Dangerous Stalemate?*, eds. Lorenzo De Sio, Vincenzo Emanuele, Nicola Maggini and Aldo Paparo. Roma: CISE, pp. 93–96.

Fasano, Luciano M., and Antonella Seddone. 2016. "Selecting the Leader, Italian Style." *Contemporary Italian Politics* 8(1): 83–102.

Garzia, Diego. 2011. "The Personalization of Politics in Western Democracies: Causes and Consequences on Leader–Follower Relationships. *The Leadership Quarterly* 22(4): 697–709.

Hanretty, Chris, and Alex Wilson. 2010. "The Partito Democratico: A Troubled Beginning." In *Italian Politics 2009: Managing Uncertainty*, eds. Marco Giuliani and Erik Jones. New York: Berghahn Books, pp. 76–92.

Hazan, Reuven Y., and Gideon Rahat. 2010. *Democracy Within Parties: Candidate Selection Methods and their Political Consequences*. Oxford: Oxford University Press.

Hopkin, Jonathan. 2006. "From Federation to Union, from Parties to Primaries: The Search for Unity in the Center-Left." In *Italian Politics 2005: The End of the Berlusconi Era?*, eds. Grant Amyot and Luca Verzichelli. New York: Berghahn Books, pp. 67–84.

Ichino, Nahomi, and Noah L. Nathan. 2013. "Do Primaries Improve Electoral Performance? Clientelism and Intra-Party Conflict in Ghana." *American Journal of Political Science* 57(2): 428–441.

Karvonen, Lauri. 2010. *The Personalisation of Politics: A Study of Parliamentary Democracies*. London: Routledge ECPR Press.

Katz, Richard S. 1996. "Electoral Reform and the Transformation of Party Politics in Italy." *Party Politics* 2(1): 31–53.

Kenig, Ofer. 2009. "Classifying Party Leaders' Selection Methods in Parliamentary Democracies." *Journal of Elections, Public Opinion and Parties* 19(4): 433–447.

Lanzone, Maria Elisabetta, and Stefano Rombi. 2014. "Who Did Participate in the Online Primary Elections of the Five Star Movement (M5S) in Italy? Causes, Features and Effects of the Selection Process." *Partecipazione e conflitto* 7(1): 170–191.

Lazar, Marc. 2008. "The Birth of the Democratic Party." In *Italian Politics, 2007: Frustrated Aspirations for Change*, eds. Mark Donovan and Paolo Onofri. New York: Berghahn Books, pp. 51–67.

Manin, Bernard. 1997. *The Principles of Representative Government*. New York: Cambridge University Press.

Massetti, Emanuele, and Giulia Sandri. 2013. "Italy: Between Growing Incongruence and Region-Specific Dynamics." In *Regional and National Elections in Western Europe. Territoriality of the Vote in Thirteen Countries*, eds. Regis Dandoy and Arjan Schakel. Basingstoke: Palgrave, pp. 142–162.

Morlino, Leonardo. 1996. Crisis of Parties and Change of Party System in Italy." *Party Politics* 2(1): 5–30.

Musella, Fortunato. 2014. "Parlamentarie PD under the Microscope." *Representation* 50(2): 245–258.

Musella, Fortunato, and Paul Webb. 2015. "The Revolution of Personal Leaders." *Italian Political Science Review/Rivista Italiana di Scienza Politica* 45(3): 223–226.

Pasquino, Gianfranco. 2007. "Tricks and Treats: The 2005 Italian Electoral Law and Its Consequences." *South European Society & Politics* 12(1): 79–93.

Pasquino, Gianfranco, and Marco Valbruzzi. 2013. "Prime Minister Primaries: Candidate Selection between Innovation and Manipulation." In *Italian Politics 2012: Technocrats in Office*, eds. Aldo DiVirgilio and Claudio M. Radaelli. New York: Berghahn Books, pp. 112–132.

Pilet, Jean-Benoit, and William P. Cross. (eds.). 2014. *The Selection of Political Party Leaders in Contemporary Parliamentary Democracies: A Comparative Study.* New York: Routledge.

Poguntke, Thomas, and Paul Webb. (eds.). 2005. *The Presidentialization of Politics: A Comparative Study of Modern Democracies.* Oxford: Oxford University Press.

Regalia, Marta, and Marco Valbruzzi. 2016. "With or Without Parliamentary Primaries? Some Evidence from the Italian Laboratory." *Contemporary Italian Politics* 8(1): 42–61.

Sandri, Giulia, and Antonella Seddone. 2015a. *The Primary Game. Primary Elections and the Italian Democratic Party.* Novi Ligure: Epoké.

Sandri, Giulia, and Antonella Seddone. 2015b. "Sense or Sensibility? Political Attitudes and Voting Behaviour of Party Members, Voters, and Supporters of the Italian Center-Left." *Italian Political Science Review/Rivista Italiana di Scienza Politica* 45(1): 25–51.

Sandri, Giulia, Antonella Seddone, and Fulvio Venturino. 2013. "The Selection of Party Leaders in Italy, 1989–2012." In *The Selection of Political Party Leaders in Contemporary Parliamentary Democracies. A Comparative Study,* eds. Jean-Benoit Pilet and William P. Cross. London: Routledge, pp. 93–107.

Sandri, Giulia, Antonella Seddone, and Fulvio Venturino. (eds.). 2015. *Party Primaries in Comparative Perspective.* Farnham: Ashgate Publishing.

Sandri, Giulia, and Fulvio Venturino. 2016. "Primaries at the Municipal Level: How, How Many and Why." *Contemporary Italian Politics* 8(1): 62–82.

Scarrow, Susan E. 1999. "Parties and the Expansion of Direct Democracy: Who Benefits?" *Party Politics* 5(3): 341–362.

Scarrow, Susan E. 2000. "Parties without Members? Party Organization in a Changing Electoral Environment." In *Parties Without Partisans: Political Change in Advanced Industrial Democracies,* eds. Russell J. Dalton and Martin P. Wattenberg. Oxford: Oxford University Press, pp. 79–101.

Scarrow, Susan E., and Burcu Gezgor. 2010. "Declining Memberships, Changing Members? European Political Party Members in a New Era." *Party Politics* 16(6): 823–843.

Tronconi, Fillipo. (ed.). 2015. *Beppe Grillo's Five Star Movement. Organization, Communication and Ideology.* Farnham: Ashgate.

Van Biezen, Ingrid, Peter Mair, and Thomas Poguntke. 2012. "Going, going, . . . gone? The Decline of Party Membership in Contemporary Europe." *European Journal of Political Research* 51(1): 24–56.

Vassallo, Salvatore, and Gianluca Passarelli. 2016. "Centre-Left Prime Ministerial Primaries in Italy: The Laboratory of the 'Open Party' Model." *Contemporary Italian Politics* 8(1): 12–23.

Venturino, Fulvio. 2010. "Italy: From Partitocracy to Personal Parties." In *Political Leadership, Parties and Citizens. The Personalization of Leadership,* eds. Jean Blondel and Jean-Louis Thiébault. New York: Routledge, pp. 172–189.

Venturino, Fulvio. 2015. "Promoting Internal Democracy. An Analysis of the Statute of the Partito Democratico." In *The Primaries Game. The Case of the Italian Democratic Party,* eds. Giulia Sandri and Antonella Seddone. Novi Ligure: Epoké, pp. 35–50.

Wertman, Douglas A. 1988. "Italy: Local Involvement, Central Control." In *Candidate Selection in Comparative Perspective: The Secret Garden of Politics,* eds. Michael Gallagher and Michael Marsh. London: Sage, pp. 145–168.

PART VI

Primary Election Reform

As previous chapters of this book have shown, there are many components to primary elections that can be changed. Although it is not always clear who will benefit – that is, which types of politicians, which parties, which types of voters, which sorts of political values – there is still much potential for reform. There have at times been organized efforts to change primaries or to establish them in places where they did not exist. Yet it is difficult to speak of a reform "agenda" or to link any such agenda to larger political ideologies or perspectives. This section explores two reform ideas – one which has been implemented and has received much attention, and another that has yet to be taken seriously by politicians but may ultimately prove to be of consequence.

In the United States, the closest thing there is to a reform agenda is the effort over the past two decades in some western states to establish a nonpartisan "top-two" primary. The idea has been proposed in several states, but it has only been implemented in three: California, Louisiana, and Washington. J. Andrew Sinclair and Ian O'Grady explore the consequences of California's establishment of the top-two primary, and the bibliography to their chapter lists other studies of California's experiment. It remains difficult to determine what consequences California's new primary law will have, in part because the state has simultaneously pursued other electoral reforms, such as a new nonpartisan redistricting plan, and in part because the political culture of the state may be sufficiently different from that of other states, in that what "works" in California may not work elsewhere. Yet California's new primary is likely to play a role in guiding primary reforms in years to come.

Also in this section, Michael Kang and Barry Burden explore the effect of "sore loser" laws in American elections. Most states prohibit primary losers from running in the general election as independents or as the nominee of a rival party. As Kang and Burden show, these laws may ultimately discourage competition and yield suboptimal results. In many instances, a primary loser may be the strongest general election opponent for the primary election winner, and the general electorate may be more hospitable to the primary loser than it is to the winner. Kang and Burden explore the history of these laws, and their chapter leaves us with the possibility that, despite the lack of attention it has received, the abolition of sore loser laws might be a reform worthy of consideration.

25

BEYOND OPEN AND CLOSED

Complexity in American Primary
Election Reform

J. Andrew Sinclair and Ian O'Grady

In many respects, American political institutions are the outliers among Western democracies. The formal rules of political interaction reflect the age of the Constitution and uniqueness of its initial federal design. Comparative scholars of election rules often struggle to place the United States in the context of other countries because it relies on a complex separation-of-powers structure rather than electoral rules, like proportional representation, to drive policy bargaining (see Powell 2000, 41).[1] Furthermore, these institutions evolved alongside an unexpected development: the Constitution's framers did not envision a role for the type of political parties which swiftly – and, critically, endogenously – developed (see Aldrich 2011, 71). American electoral institutions serve as an arbiter of conflict both between and within political parties. The story of primary election reform – more than just the specialized and unique area of presidential primary elections – is fundamentally a story about political actors seeking policy change by altering institutions within America's comparatively malleable and strongly localized framework (as in North 1998).

The combination of single-member districts (for most – but not all – legislative offices, as discussed below), a single (mostly) directly elected national chief executive, and aspects of historical accident have generated a stable arrangement in which two national parties obtain almost all of the votes cast in most elections (see Cox 1997). Although there have been realignments, these two great parties have been stable enough for voters to develop a personal "party identification" with substantive meaning in common across states (see Campbell et al. 1960). Nationally, both major parties are competitive: between 1945 and 2017, there were six Democratic Party presidents and seven Republican Party[2] presidents; recently party control of the U.S. House of Representatives flipped after the 1994, 2006, and 2010 elections; and filibuster-proof majorities in the U.S. Senate are rare. The electoral machinery serves to select candidates for office and regulate the manner and extent in which a contest for votes influences conflict over policy. Although the institutions drive participants into a two-party *system* (see Aldrich 2011, 310–312), the policy space is clearly multi-dimensional. Aldrich's argument about the development of parties describes them as "driven by the consequences of majority instability, that is, by the social choice problem" (Aldrich 2011, 71). The result is often reasonably simplified into a single dimension, which helps explain the enduring usefulness of the Downsian (1957) spatial model.

The relative competitiveness of the two major parties nationally does not imply local competition. In many individual states, one party or the other dominates. Figure 25.1 displays

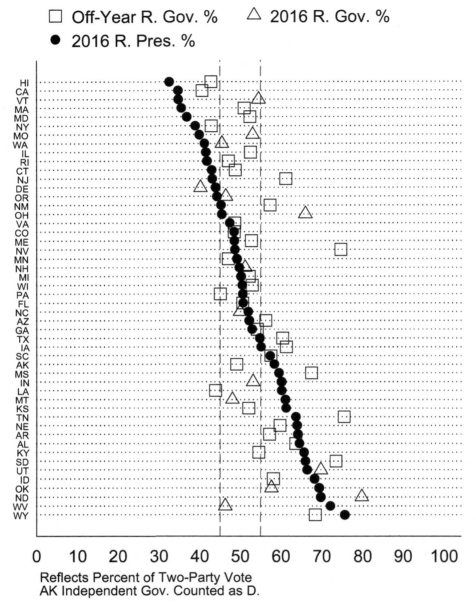

Figure 25.1 Party Strength by State; Republican Two-Party Vote Share in the 2016 Presidential and Most Recent Gubernatorial Election

the vote share of current governors in their last election and the most recent state presidential vote share. Uncompetitive states are not new; V.O. Key wrote at mid-century:

> In only a dozen states do the two major parties compete on a fairly even basis . . . the net effect of the overwhelming attachment of many states to one or the other of the national parties means that, in reality, no party system exists within such states for state purposes.
>
> *Key 1958, 318*

Of course, most states operate a two-stage election procedure: a *primary* resolving intra-party conflict followed by a *general* election resolving inter-party conflict. Key famously remarked that "the Democratic primary in the South is in reality the election" (1949, 407).

While it is broadly understood that Democracy means "rule by the people," there is not universal agreement on how to operationalize this principle. Powell (2000, 8) organizes a large literature into concepts arranged on two dimensions: the voter's time perspective (retrospective, prospective) and the target of a voter's choice (representative agents or collective government). The four resulting combinations – accountability, mandates, trusteeship, or representative delegates – do emphasize different ideal qualities and, Powell argues, are associated with different institutional arrangements. Nevertheless, some level of contestation, if not close competition, is necessary for any of these. Key wrote that "[politicians] are keenly desirous of public office, an honorable ambition, perhaps the most honorable of ambitions. Only through the clash of such ambitions can the ideals of democracy be approached" (1949, 297). Riker (1982) saw the liberal interpretation of democracy, one functionally about accountability, as resting on the ability to remove public officials for perceived poor performance.[3] There are many reasons to believe that even Riker's minimal requirement is difficult to obtain: Bertelli (2016) observes that only if it is clear who is doing the policy work and what the worker is doing can retrospective accountability be obtained in public administration; Achen and Bartels (2016) are quite pessimistic about a voter's ability to do this under any circumstances. Many of the challenges scholars identify even in settings with high voter information and competitive parties, like presidential elections, are more problematic for lower offices like the U.S. House, state lower houses, and state upper houses.[4] As Key wrote, absent meaningful cross-party competition, the existence – or absence, or extent – of genuine meaning to democracy relies on the functioning of the primary election institutions.

Do primary elections help mitigate these concerns? Merely holding an election is generally understood to be insufficient: "the American political tradition caps decisions made by popular vote with a resplendent halo of legitimacy," although this may be fictional both for reasons Key addressed (the small necessary electorate in many primaries; Key 1956, 133) and for reasons he did not emphasize (the social choice problem better addressed by others). Riker's concerns (grounded in Arrow 1951) about a "populist" interpretation of elections still leave room to evaluate whether some types of election systems seem to perform better than others on average. For those willing to contemplate the existence of mandates in certain circumstances, the lopsidedness of some districts is not as concerning: a mandate, after all, means that "a clear majority of voters chooses a package of policies they desire" (Powell 2000, 70). In that vein, the questions relating to the diverse primary institutions operated in different states largely must try to answer Key's concern that "so few votes determine the party nomination that aspirants for office need only command the loyalties of a relatively small following" (1956, 140–41). Bueno de Mesquita and Smith (2011) observe that for all politicians, in democracies and non-democracies alike, the fundamental concern is really how many people have to be provided with a return in exchange for support and how easily those partners can be replaced. The persistent concern with the operation of primary elections is that the size of the (meaningful) winning coalition may be so small as to upset the always tenuous relationship between rulers and the mass of the ruled.

Given the diversity of types of primary election laws, and the number of parameters one could manipulate, primary reform has long been a subject of interest for both practitioners and scholars. While Arrow's Theorem and the other theoretical results (see Riker 1982) indicate that there will be no perfect electoral institution in all circumstances, some types of rules might at least produce some outcomes more often than others in a statistically reliable way. The naïve expectation here would be to at least be able to choose off a menu of primary types with well-defined tradeoffs. Diversity of preferences and political endowments would explain why some groups seem interested in "reform" and others more interested in maintaining the status quo. There is one small problem: scholars have not come close to reaching a consensus on the information required to guide such a choice.

In 2012 Arizona voters rejected Proposition 121, a version of a nonpartisan top-two primary procedure, by a wide margin (nearly 2:1).[5] The proposition was largely backed by former Mayor of Phoenix and Democrat-turned-Independent Paul Johnson, although no notable additional faction of either the Republican or the Democratic Party signed on to support it (Khan 2012; Lemons 2012; Wyloge 2013). This came up again in 2016 but the campaign failed to qualify for the ballot (Pitzl 2016). In Arizona, the minority party (the Democrats) did not favor this reform, while in California, only a few years earlier, several key figures in the minority party (the Republicans) did. In Arizona, why did both major political parties – and traditional opponents – unite to oppose this reform?[6] In other words: did someone make a mistake? North (1998) suggests it is reasonable to believe the standard assumption of many game-theoretic models – that the players "know what they are doing" – may not hold in many complex policy processes; players may not perceive all available opportunities until policy "entrepreneurs" find them.

One reason to study politics is to produce useable information – information participants could use to inform the choices they make. The literature in political science on primary elections is growing and benefiting from many of the new methodological developments. Nevertheless, basic questions like what different factions of the Arizona Democratic Party should have expected from a nonpartisan primary remain as subjects of considerable controversy. Our goal in this chapter is to offer a slightly different way of conceptualizing primary "reform" and use three contrasting recent cases – a change in Idaho, a change in California, and the retention of the status quo in Arizona – to better frame the choices parties make.

What Is a "Primary Reform"?

To explain our case selection, it is necessary to consider more broadly the question of what a primary election reform actually is. Contemporary reform proposals are best understood as reforms-of-reforms. Direct primaries date back about a century and altered existing nomination procedures. No form of direct primary is described in the Constitution of the United States for any office. States have broad authority granted in Article I, subject to modification, to determine their own election procedures. The direct primary is largely the endogenous creation of political processes within states (Ware 2002), with the design of the laws in each state likely influenced by the dynamics of policy diffusion and thus often working similarly within some broad outlines.[7] While diffusion is not always geographic (see Shipan and Volden 2012), there often appear to be components of the development of primary election laws that have regional or temporal similarities.

And why do the rules change? American states have adopted and modified their election procedures through the complex interaction of party conflict at the state level, the interaction of national politics with state institutions, citizen initiatives and "good government" advocacy, and the intervention of the courts (see Ware 2002). The election rules interact with other unique state institutional arrangements, including specific items often minimized or ignored in the primary elections literature, like the availability of direct democracy to get around the legislature or the existence of supermajority rules in the state legislature.[8] The rules states use to elect candidates to office are diverse, endogenously generated, and subject to change and ongoing controversy.

Changes to primary laws are nested within the larger universe of election procedures as well. The set of institutions most directly relevant to the primary laws include: the ways voters are registered and what information is retained about them; the way parties and candidates get on the ballot, including ballot fees or signature requirements; the rules in both the primary and general phase by which candidates get on the ballot or may be written in – including "sore loser" laws, the procedures parties use to endorse candidates (if they do; formal or informal), and the timing of those procedures; the voting technology; the extent of the connection between presidential and non-presidential nominating rules; which voters may vote for which candidates, who gets to decide this, and how that decision is made; and the way primary results are mapped into the configuration of the general election contest. The approach in much of the primary election literature is to try to collapse all of the variation of electoral institutions into perhaps four or five types for analysis; although in some settings this may be appropriate, it is important to keep in mind that there is considerable potentially meaningful variation from state to state even within the broad classifications.

The typical classification system used in the study of primary elections places the institutions along a scale of "openness." This approach (most notably: Gerber and Morton 1998; Kanthak and Morton 2001; McGhee et al. 2014; Rogowski 2013) focuses on the options available to voters at the first, primary, stage. A *closed* primary requires voters to affiliate with a party to have access to that party's ballot; a *semi-closed* primary also allows independent voters to pick a party for the entire primary election ballot; a *semi-open* primary allows any voter to pick a party for the election in some public fashion; and an *open* primary allows voters to choose a party on election day in private. At the extreme, there are several types of primaries (*blanket, nonpartisan top-two,* and related) which allow voters to pick any candidate for any office. McGhee et al. (2014, 340–341) present the best summary of this standard view, building on Gerber and Morton (1998).[9] McGhee et al. (2014) also point out that the formal theory literature provides weak and sometimes contradictory guidance in terms of what to expect from these different rules.

Several influential papers, including McGhee et al. (2014), use some version of this classification scheme, applied to data collected for U.S. states across time, to examine the impact of primary type on some measure of legislator ideology. Effectively, this is an application of a simple spatial model, reflecting the conventional wisdom: the more open the primary, the more centrist the median voter, and thus the more centrist the winner.[10] The results of this intuitive approach have been inconsistent; McGhee et al. argue "states' political economy, political culture, demographics, or other political institutions" may be driving polarization but that "primary elections [types] are not among the most important factors" (2014, 348). They further note, to explain variation in the findings, some limitations in both the data and methods of earlier work, in particular "the inability to compare polarization both pre- and post-treatment for a wide range of states" (2014, 348). In many ways, this remains a challenge for this type of approach, no matter how competently executed.

The primary laws are not randomly assigned and change in an identifiable pattern over time. Due to a series of court decisions, followed by modifications to the laws in some circumstances, a number of states went from having a traditional closed primary to a "party choice" rule, in which each party can decide to hold a closed or semi-closed primary. This accounts for many of the changes, as illustrated in Figure 25.2, between 1980 and the present – the period most extensively studied in the literature. In general, states are either in a universe in which party registration is required (closed, semi-closed, party choice) for administering the rule or a universe in which it is not (semi-open, open, blanket, nonpartisan).[11]

Why focus on the three states we describe in the next sections? Very few states make changes across the major categories, largely separated by the existence and role of party registration. California is one of the few with multiple changes: it goes from a closed primary to the blanket primary (1998, 2000); adopts a semi-closed system (2002–2010); and then ends up with a

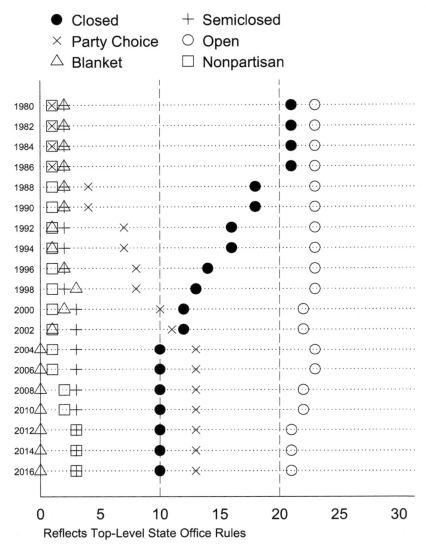

Figure 25.2 Use of Primary Election Types Since 1980

nonpartisan system (2012–2016). Idaho is the rare case of partially leaving the open primary to adopt partisan voter registration (beginning in 2012), so the Republicans could close their primary. Arizona is more typical: the state passed by voter initiative a switch to go from pure closed to semi-closed in time for the 2000 elections (Berman 2016) but this does not require large changes in other aspects of election administration.[12]

The drift from closed primaries to semi-closed or party-choice primaries is a consequence, at least in part, of a series of judicial decisions giving parties a greater ability to make these choices, even if existing state law forbids it. In *Tashjian v. Republican Party of Connecticut* (479 U.S. 208, 1986), the Republican Party sued the state to obtain the right to allow nonpartisan voters to vote in the (previously closed) Republican Party primary.[13] Courts subsequently limited this ruling to unaffiliated voters in *Clingman v. Beaver* (544 U.S. 581, 2005). Nevertheless, a state-mandated closed primary existed in any state after *Tashjian* only by the sufferance of both parties (and not just the party in the majority, capable of passing a new state law). Although one could argue all closed states should be coded "party choice" after *Tashjian*, we have retained the closed coding in Figure 25.2 for any state that did not formally change its laws or challenge the ruling in court.[14] Even so, several party-choice states have held mostly closed primaries, although the mechanism is in place for them to do otherwise. Nevertheless, adjusting these rules – from a closed primary to a party-choice (closed, semi-closed) primary – represents one of the major shifts in the laws between 1980 and 2016.

The other major decision of this era driving institutional change is *California Democratic Party v. Jones* (530 U.S. 567, 2000). Persily (2002, 306) observes: "after *Tashjian*, it was clear that the state could not force a party to restrict participation in its primary to party members. The precise question in *Jones*, however – whether a state could force a party to *expand* participation in its primary – remained unanswered." Several California political parties, including both the Republicans and Democrats, had sued to stop the blanket primary, a rule passed by initiative in 1996. This type of primary, long used in both Alaska and Washington, allowed any voter to choose any candidate. Candidates of each qualified political party competed for the nomination of that political party; voters effectively could switch between parties as they moved down the ballot. In *Jones* the Court found that the blanket primary infringed too much on a party's associational rights. This had several consequences: the three states with blanket primaries replaced them with other rules (as analytically exploited in McGhee et al. 2014); California and Washington both ended up with a nonpartisan "top-two" primary as a consequence of a suggestion included in the *Jones* decision; and Idaho's Republican Party tried what Persily (2002) suggested was a logical extension and sued to close a traditional open primary (see Alvarez and Sinclair 2015, 26–27).

The blanket primary has a slight, but legally critical, difference from the nonpartisan primary procedure (the "top-two") now used in California and Washington: in these nonpartisan primaries, the first-round primary does not purport to select the nominee of a political party for the second-round general election runoff. McGhee (2010, 3) effectively illustrates this selection process by drawing lines separating candidates by party and voters by party for a traditional partisan primary, separating only candidates by party for the blanket primary, and separating neither candidates by party nor voters by party for the nonpartisan top-two. While it is common for the blanket and the nonpartisan top-two to be lumped together, the blanket primary remains a partisan primary for the candidates and the general elections are structured like other partisan systems; the nonpartisan top-two, however, impacts both the primary and the general election by potentially changing the general election field.[15]

As we will describe, Idaho is a rare case of a state moving from an open primary to at party-choice system based on partisan registration. This too is a consequence of the *Jones* decision, although of considerably lower profile than the changes in California. In the opinion, the United States District Court observed in *Idaho Republican Party v. Ysursa*: "recognizing the difference between blanket and open primaries, this Court nevertheless finds the Supreme Court's analysis in *Jones* instructive . . . choosing ideologically extreme candidates is precisely what a political party is entitled to do in asserting its right of association under the First Amendment" (765 F. Supp. 2d, 2011, 8, 17). Idaho had previously operated an open primary; after the decision, the state began allowing registration by party and, per the Party's request, closed the Republican primary.

Idaho's story differs from Utah's, another Republican-dominated western state, and one of the other few states to leave an open primary system. This serves to illustrate the advantage of considering individual cases, given the unsatisfying results in the national studies. Utah's rules were complicated (as noted in McGhee et al. 2014, who decided to count it as closed for this reason) by the presence of a strong pre-primary party convention system sufficiently power-ful recently to deny incumbent Governor Olene Walker (Askar 2011) and incumbent Senator Bob Bennett (Catanese 2010) the opportunity to even run for reelection.[16] Nevertheless, in the lead-up to the 2000 election Utah switched from having open to party-choice primaries; the Republicans closed theirs while the Democrats kept theirs open. This only applies, of course, when a primary actually occurs, which was still only if there was sufficient competition but insuf-ficient agreement in the party convention.[17] The Utah legislature, dominated by Republicans, passed a primary reform bill (SB 54) in 2014 that both provided for an alternative path to the ballot around the convention and re-adopted open primaries; the Republican Party sued and lost in the District Court on the path around the convention but won on the open primary issue (Romboy 2016). The Utah story helps to illustrate how the various pre-primary ballot access and endorsement procedures (McNitt 1980) complicate the coding of primary election types; even simple pre-primary approval endorsements can have a meaningful impact on election outcomes (Kousser et al. 2015) and of course these will vary from state party to state party.[18]

Despite the changes in a handful of open primary states, it is still the case that most observable primary changes happen between closed, semi-closed, and party-choice systems.[19] Identifying effects is further complicated by other institutions which could interact with the primary rule type or overwhelm the effects; in some cases, these rules are systematically associated with one type of primary because states share other common historical origins. Some of the southern open primaries also have a second primary for some offices (potentially requiring three election stages) that operates as a runoff between the two highest vote-getting partisan candidates (see Bullock and Johnson 1992; Kousser 1984).[20] Furthermore, in some states the party still has a right to hold a convention instead of a primary for some offices; although this seems to be a right rarely exercised, it has been recently contentious among (for example) Virginia Republicans (see Geraghty 2015). The Virginia Republican Party only arrived at the decision to hold a primary to select their 2017 statewide candidates by a 41:40 vote of the state party's Central Committee (Vozzella 2016). Of course, differing rules across multiple levels can have impacts on participa-tion at all levels: one has to wonder if the unusual rules for other offices in the 2014 campaign influenced Republican House Majority Leader Eric Cantor's defeat (see Sherman 2014).

Other related election laws could also be important. For example, the available means of vot-ing (early in-person, early by mail, and election day[21]) and the particular rules about the admin-istration of the vote can increase or decrease the size of the electorate (Burden et al. 2014). The extensive use of mail voting – and in some places, only mail voting – creates not only a "rolling deadline" (Pirch 2012) for election day but also dramatically different conditions under which voters may fill out ballots – privacy of party ballot choice (where applicable) works differently, as might the role of information on the ballot if voters have their home computer close at hand.[22] These rules could meaningfully interact with primary types.[23] Typically in states in which voters may choose a primary, if those voters are also voting by mail they must make a request about which party ballot they desire in advance of the election; raising the cost of meaningful partici-pation. Overall, a decrease in the use of closed primaries, an increase in the forms of conveni-ence voting available, falling cost of information search and a fragmenting media environment, and increased campaign mobilization technology have all changed together over time. While scholars have made reasonable efforts to identify the impact of changes in primary election laws, the conditions for observing an impact are far from ideal. As McGhee et al. note: "endogeneity is a difficult problem to address, since we cannot randomly assign primary systems by state and observe the result" (2014, 345). Furthermore, the coding of the laws themselves is subject to meaningful measurement error, as with any exercise of trying to group alike but not identical items into categorical bins.

Ultimately, it appears scholars have developed some skepticism that primary election laws matter at all, at least when it comes to ideology ("we should expect little from open primary reform in the modern political age," McGhee et al. 2014, 349). There are good reasons to believe political parties have a large influence over the outcomes, if merely from the perspective of understanding sources of political power (Bachrach and Baratz 1962) or the attributes of the "guardians of the formal agenda" (Cobb and Elder 1971). This fits more modern theories of political parties (Cohen et al. 2008; Masket 2011), in which parties are best understood as organizations of policy demanders able to guide resources and provide opportunities to those who will be effective agents for those policy priorities. Other authors have focused on different attributes of primary elections (beyond ideology) and pointed in a valuable direction: for example, Hirano and Snyder (2014) find that primary elections can help select higher quality candidates in places absent meaningful cross-party competition.

If primary election laws do not matter, why do some participants seem to go to such great lengths to change them? One possibility is that the participants who have made changes have made them in error – as discussed below, there is an ongoing and robust debate about this in California. At least a reasonable starting place, though, is to look at a few recent changes in primary election laws, the political situations coincident with those changes, and to closely examine what sorts of outcomes the participants driving the change might count as success. This is not, by any means, the end of the story; it is simply a good place to begin the process of better understanding how primary reforms might work.

Policy Entrepreneurs and Party Factions

The conversion of most states to direct primary elections took place shortly after the turn of the last century and the resulting rules were very much creatures of their time, place, and institutional context; the direct primary developed from a combination of reformist zeal and party-insider interest, particularly in terms of trying to leverage the benefits of legal regulation (Ware 2002).[24] A rigid story of reformers-against-parties does not work well for the origin of primaries (as Ware 2002 argues, although this is the popular perception) and a healthy skepticism of this dynamic seems appropriate in evaluating recent reforms as well. "Good government" is only part of the reform story. Institutional change comes from successful policy entrepreneurs: someone or some group both interested in shifting the outcomes and able to see a path to do so. We should expect different types of choices from different kinds of participants – and, given some of the dynamics outlined in Ware (2002), we should also expect that any successful institutional change will require the assistance of at least some faction of a relevant political party.

We should not expect the same reforms in all cases, nor the same groups pushing for them. Figure 25.3 illustrates both the Republican partisan strength and the ideological position of the majority (using the Shor and McCarty 2015 state legislative scores) for Idaho, California, and Arizona. If each party can be divided into its Haves and Have-Nots,[25] and there is a majority and a main minority party, this describes a four-faction universe in each state. It is a simplification, but a useful one:

- If one party is dominant: it matters by how much, and which faction controls the formal party apparatus. In general, we should expect parties with very large majorities to have a higher chance of seeking to close the primary, and shrink the meaningful electorate, if ideological purists manage to take control of the party machinery. Idaho serves as an example of this dynamic. In these circumstances the minority party is generally so helpless as to have limited capacity to change the rules.[26]

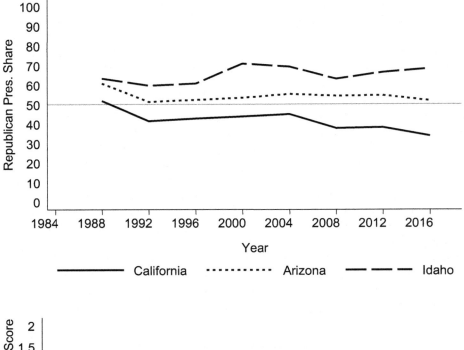

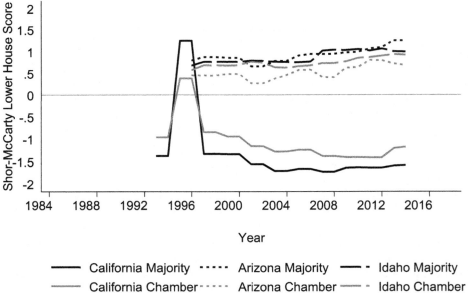

Figure 25.3 Republican Two-Party Vote Share 1988–2016 and Shor-McCarty Legislative Scores

- If there is a dominant party but the minority party retains some bargaining leverage, we should see interest in primary reform aimed at moderation or opportunities for influence provided that a moderate faction of the minority party can gain control and that the prospects of future victory are low. This is the case of the California Republicans and the non-partisan primary. These conditions should also be relatively rare.

- If the partisan balance is close or likely to become close, the participants who in other circumstances might push for either vastly shrinking the (effective) electorate or moderating the party for the sake of electability are more likely to try to balance reaching centrist voters with maintaining some cohesion. We may be more likely to see symmetric approaches across both parties. This turns out to be the story in Arizona.

The Idaho, California, and Arizona cases each contribute to our understanding of these circumstances. As shown in Figure 25.3, Republicans dominate Idaho in terms of vote share and the policies of the legislature are correspondingly right-ward; Republicans are headed towards extinction in California, having last held a majority in the legislature in the mid-1990s and steadily dwindling since; and in Arizona, Republicans hold a narrow vote share lead but have been able to translate this into ideological positions not so far different from Idaho's legislature. Idaho shifts to closed primaries for the Republican Party but the Idaho Democrats keep theirs open. California's centrist Republican wing, leveraging their last relevance in the state legislature, manages to obtain nonpartisan primaries by negotiation in the legislature, followed by a ballot measure. In Arizona, a similar rule to California's failed to capture the interest of any sizeable faction of the state's Democrats, the most likely insider-group to favor such a rule.

Idaho: The Monopolists

Idaho looks like Key's one-party South – a state where the primary is the election.[27] The recent change from an open to party-choice system, as one should expect, emerged out of the factional politics in the dominant party. The push to close Republican primaries (the "reform") originated with a small group of political Have-Not Republicans. Since the Idaho reform required the intervention of the courts (in *Ysursa*), this was not likely something readily accomplished in the legislature itself, even though the Republican Party held large majorities. As elsewhere, it matters which type of person controls the key legislative, executive, and party offices in each party.[28] In Idaho, when the change was first proposed, prominent party figures opposed it,

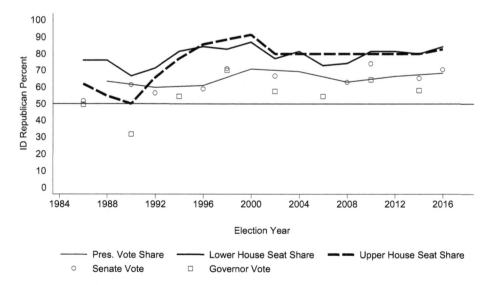

Figure 25.4 Time Trends in Idaho Politics

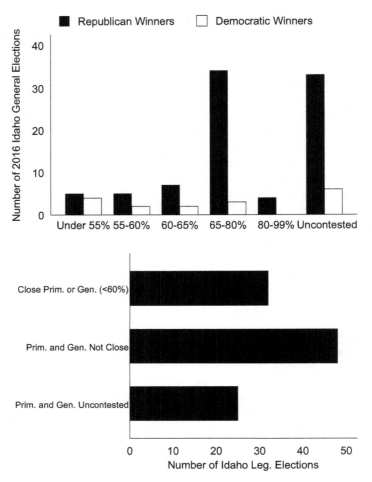

Figure 25.5 2016 Idaho Snapshot

including Idaho's Republican Party Chair and Republican Governor (see Andersen 2007 and Russell 2008a).[29] The insurgents eventually obtained enough support in the state party organization to bring the lawsuit. It appears that the insurgents convinced the "intense policy demanders" that the party could get away with acting more like a political monopolist.

Figure 25.4 shows the Idaho Republican Party's dominance over time. Since the mid-1990s, the Republicans have held substantial majorities in both chambers of the legislature and routinely win statewide elections. In the 2016 election, only six of 35 legislative districts elected a Democrat to the state legislature – to the Senate or either one of two House seats per district. Four of the six Democrat-electing districts are located around Boise, Idaho's most populous city. Put differently, out of 105 Republican primary winners for the state legislature in 2016, 88 went on to win the general election.

Beyond holding large majorities in the legislature, Idaho Republicans also tend to win both rounds of the elections by large margins (see Figure 25.5). In the general elections, most winners were either unopposed or won greater than 65 percent of the vote. Only a very small handful won with under 55 percent of the vote, and even had the Democrats won all the (relatively) close contests, they would not have captured a majority in the legislature. The lower-half of Figure 25.5 focuses on Key's question about whether accountability can be imagined at any stage; in this sense, it matters if either the primary or the general election was close. A quarter of current legislators ran unopposed at both levels; only in about a third of the races did the winner face either a close primary or general contest (defined very loosely: winning by less than 60 percent of the vote).

We should not presume failure. As Erikson and Wright argued about U.S. House elections:

> Candidates, generally desirous of attaining and staying in office, heed their electorate's wishes and work to give them what they want. Elections bring about much higher levels of policy representation than most observers would expect based on the low levels of citizen awareness.
>
> *2013, 113*

But who are the necessary constituents in different primary systems? Suspicious that non-party members were adulterating the nominating process, former Idaho State Senator and Majority Leader Rod Beck – who himself lost in the state's open primary system to another Republican for U.S. Senate in 1992 – began his campaign for closed primaries (see Russell 2008a).[30] At the 2007 GOP Central Committee Summer Meeting, he successfully lobbied members to vote for closing Republican primaries; the motion was passed 88 to 58 (Russell 2007a). He then rallied more than 70 other Republicans, some in elected office, to join him in his lawsuit against Republican Secretary of State Ben Ysursa, demanding that he bring state law into compliance with the Central Committee's wishes (Andersen 2007). The lawsuit stalled when then-Party Chairman Kirk Sullivan signed an affidavit stating that the party members' lawsuit did not represent the interests of the Party (Russell 2007b). With Sullivan's affidavit in hand, the state filed a motion to dismiss, arguing the Central Committee vote did not necessarily imply Party support of the lawsuit; the court agreed and dismissed the suit (Andersen 2007). Sullivan's actions enraged Beck and his allies (Andersen 2007). As a consequence, Sullivan pushed Republicans in the legislature to enact a solution into law. Legislators, however, ran into constitutional concerns regarding an imposed closed primary for the Idaho Democratic Party. Without a solution by the end of the 2007 Session, Beck looked elsewhere (Popkey 2014).

Beck worked with allies at the following GOP Central Committee meeting to again pass a closed primary resolution. This resolution authorized party members to sue on behalf of the Party, reinitiated the original lawsuit, and tied the hands of Sullivan and other party "elites" (Russell 2008a).[31] At the June 2008 State Convention just six months later, Beck helped oust Sullivan as Chair, dealing Governor Otter, who backed the moderate Sullivan, an embarrassing loss in the process (see Russell 2008b; Hoffman 2008; and Popkey 2014).[32] Beck may have defeated Sullivan himself if Norm Semanko – another politically experienced conservative – had not jumped in days before the party convention as a compromise choice. When asked why he sought the chairship, Semanko responded, "I made no bones about it that I didn't think Rod Beck would have been a good chairman . . . When I was convinced that Rod was going to beat Kirk [Sullivan], that's when I had to make a decision . . . " (Hoffman 2008). As Chairman, Semanko would join the lawsuit against Ysursa for closed primaries in his capacity (see *Idaho Republican Party v. Ysursa*, 660 F. Supp. 2d 1195, 2009).

In 2011, *Idaho Republican Party v. Ysursa* decided the issue in favor of the party's request to close the primary. The state legislature passed HB 351 to alter law to comply with the court's ruling.[33] Provisions included adding partisan registration, allowing parties to "open" and "close" primaries to voters of their choosing, and improvising for the 2012 election, where voters would be allowed to formally affiliate with a state political party for the first time up to election day. Republicans have maintained closed primaries since, while Idaho Democrats have left their primaries open to participation from both unaffiliated voters and registered members of other political parties.

Although much of the news coverage of Idaho's intraparty struggle centers on Rod Beck, it is quite possible that someone else would have fought for the same thing.[34] Functionally, this is following the spatial logic: the reason to close the primaries is to shrink the electorate, removing the chance of Democrats adulterating their primaries and supported by the opposition of "moderates" like Sullivan and Otter (Russell 2008b). Even without the spatial considerations, shrinking the electorate would seem to reduce potential opportunities for entry and limit the size of the constituency to which an incumbent must provide value (in the spirit of Bueno de Mesquita and Smith 2011). The Republicans should not care very much if nominating more conservative candidates comes at some risk of defeat (as in Hall 2015) since they can afford to lose a few seats now and then without giving up control of the legislature. Furthermore, the Democratic Party was so weak that it is not obvious they would be in a position to take advantage of the spatial asymmetry; in some parts of Idaho, how many Democrats are willing to pay the cost of running for office with such a low expected return on the effort?

The interesting question in Idaho is what to expect and measure from this reform. On one hand, if the result is the nomination of ideologically more extreme candidates (even more conservative), Hall (2015) would predict some defeats – possibly in the long run moderating the legislature (the opposite of the inferred intended consequence). The asymmetry means some voters, who under the old system may have chosen to join the Republicans, can now only join the Democrats, possibly making the Democratic electorate more conservative. The smaller electorate might help protect right-wing candidates against accountability for overall performance while also being more accountable to right-wing constituents.[35] Additional years in the operation of the new primary will also produce more data to use to examine changes in the rate of primary challenges, incumbent defeats and retirements, and voting history, and so on. Some of the outcomes may be less obvious and reflect resource distribution that may have little to do with stated policy preferences on "big picture" and high-profile issues.

Given the current state of the literature, we should not expect the shift in Idaho's law to change much about polarization in the legislature. So why did they do it? As with the other states, it is possible that individual or anecdotal experience, or the same sort of back-of-the-envelope theory, generated an expectation about moderating effects of open primaries that is otherwise not supported by more rigorous analysis – that is, the faction advancing this made an error and paid a cost to change the law for no ideological return. It has not yet been very many years in Idaho with the new rule, and this is a shift that is somewhat rare in the data in a state that is an outlier in other respects, so this likely deserves further analysis in this regard. In any event, it may also be the case that the proponents will derive other benefits from having a smaller coalition unrelated to ideology. What is clear is that the situation in Idaho does match a fairly simple idea about many bargaining games: winners should construct coalitions out of the minimal number of participants in order to maximize their share of the benefits. The California Republican Party in 2009–2010, covered in the next section, had no such luxuries.

California: The Rear-Guard

In 2009, California Republicans were solidly in the minority in the state legislature: nevertheless, they were not irrelevant. Republican Governor Arnold Schwarzenegger, a well-known action film actor, was elected in 2003 as part of a recall election of an unpopular Democratic governor. Schwarzenegger won again in 2006, maintaining a tenuous Republican hold on the state executive branch. In 2010 and 2014, no Republicans would capture a statewide office while the Republicans continued to lose strength in the legislature. Overall, the Republican Party had been in a decline at least since the mid-1990s (see Figure 25.6; also see Sinclair 2017). Part of what kept the party relevant, though, was a supermajority requirement for the state budget. In 2009, Democrats found themselves in a position in which some bargaining had to take place with Republicans. Schwarzenegger and a few key allies in the legislature used this leverage to advance a political reform agenda, including a change to the primary elections.

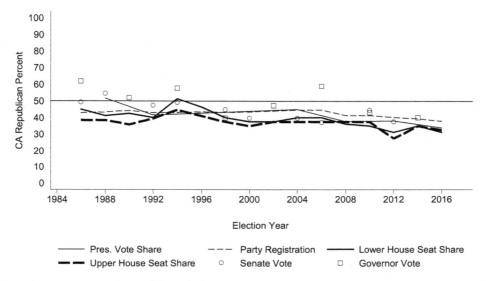

Figure 25.6 Time Trends in California Politics

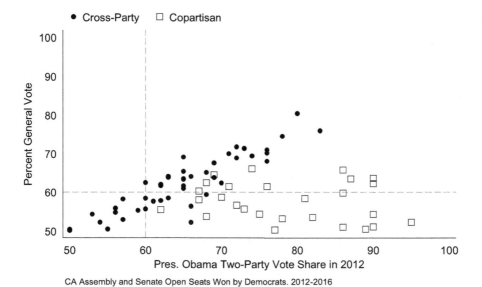

Figure 25.7 2012–2016 California Snapshot

Although the nonpartisan primary election system is often viewed as an "anti-party" reform, that risks falling into the intellectual trap Ware (2002) describes. Certainly some voters were very frustrated with the actions of political parties and ultimately voted for the initiative in that spirit (Alvarez and Sinclair 2015). Proposition 14, though, was a legislatively referred amendment, sent to the ballot as a deal for the vote of then-State Senator Abel Maldonado and five others. This was an act of political courage because it involved agreeing to solve a budget hole through a combination of budget cuts and tax increases. Although the *Los Angeles Times* pronounced that "Maldonado . . . walked away a huge prize winner" from the deal (Skelton 2009) and he would soon be made Lt. Governor, the deal was unpopular with conservatives. Running for a U.S. House seat in 2012, he struggled to gain the endorsement of his own Party Central Committee (Bartowski 2012) and went on to lose the general election. He pulled out early from an effort to run for Governor in 2014. At the time, some thought Maldonado supported the nonpartisan primary to make it easier for center-right Republicans like himself to win public office; at least judged by his own case, if that were the motivation, it failed.

The involvement of the moderate wing of the Republican Party, temporarily empowered by holding the governorship and a few key votes in the legislature, demonstrates the relevance of Ware's observations about earlier reforms. Ware writes: "Party politicians were not the 'victims' of anti-party reformers who somehow imposed a debilitating reform on them" (2002, 257). Schwarzenegger, Maldonado, and the interest groups and party elites supporting them – Charles Munger, Jr. most notably – engaged in a reform that enlarged the potential pool of voters, and scrambled the way in which candidates competed, for some reason. Although the formal organization of the Republican Party did not support the measure when it went to the ballot as Proposition 14 in 2010, the adoption of the new rule involved a powerful faction of the Republican Party in alliance with angry voters and "good government" groups. So we ask again: why did they do it?

One reason was certainly that it had the potential to elect more moderate legislators, or at least allow them to get through the primary; as McGhee (2010) observed, this was the most commonly cited goal for the reform. For centrist Republicans, the Republican brand in California was becoming a problem; as Figure 25.6 illustrates, the fortunes of the party were sinking, in part because of the policy positions taken by the national version of the party.[36] Having candidates for office espouse more moderate policy positions could potentially help revive the party as a whole. For legislators in Sacramento it would also be possible to take riskier votes on governing the state with less fear of retaliation in subsequent primary elections (or so the theory went). As the state's voters drifted left, the moderate (or, at least, willing to compromise in order to win) wing of the party wanted to shift as well.[37] This was not successful; the party's fortunes have continued to fall, in part because the state Republicans are not entirely in control of their own destiny. President Donald Trump only captured 32 percent of the California vote, illustrating how even a nationally successful campaign can act as a liability for the state party.

Centrist Republicans had another reason to support the nonpartisan primary. Even if they failed to improve the Party's fortunes, in 2009–2010, they at least had the opportunity to act as an effective rear-guard for its retreat, seeking to inflict the most policy damage possible on the Democrats. The moderating effect was not only aimed at their own party but also at the Democrats (perhaps more so); even if the Republican candidates were irrelevant in the future, primary reform gave Republican voters a chance to matter. Charles Munger Jr., a major backer of moderate Republican campaigns noted that "our role as Republicans for a while will be to choose the best Democrat" (Alvarez and Sinclair 2015, 42; citing York 2010). This comes in two flavors, outlined as different visions of democracy in Powell (2000): a retrospective angle, focused on the ability to reward or punish incumbents, and a prospective angle, focused on selecting Democrats with more moderate positions.

The debate about the success or failure of the nonpartisan primary continues in California. Mirroring differing opinions on primaries more generally, a clear picture does not emerge from the scholarly literature. Ahler, Citrin, and Lenz (2016) argue voter behavior in the primary stage was unlikely to generate ideological moderation. Nagler (2015) raised the possibility of considerable roll-off among voters without a candidate of their own party on the ballot in November. Evidence for only limited amounts of strategic voting behavior in the primary can also be found in Alvarez and Sinclair (2015) and Sinclair (2015). Hill and Kousser (2016) conducted a field experiment to see if it was possible to turn out unlikely voters; although they find this possible, it is not clear that the candidates and parties have been sufficiently "entrepreneurial" to do this on a large scale. That is consistent with Hill's earlier argument that primary laws do not seem to shape the composition of the electorate (2015).

There are corresponding concerns that the nonpartisan primary did not quickly deliver on some key promises, including ideological moderation. Kousser, Phillips, and Shor examine if the joint impact of the redistricting reforms and the adoption of the nonpartisan primary produced better congruence with district preferences and find "the clear message of the data . . . is 'no, not yet'" (2016, 13). Along with several other authors making early examinations of the nonpartisan primary, they are careful to highlight the early nature of the results; in their case, a focus on comparing 2010 to 2012. McGhee (2010) also argues that while there may be some differences in the success of the California Chamber of Commerce's agenda, it is difficult to attribute these to the electoral reforms. Grose (2014) was more positive but similarly cautious. It is commonly asserted that the nonpartisan primary has not achieved the objectives of the moderate Republican faction or the interest groups and voters who backed Proposition 14. The comfortable victory of U.S. Senate candidate Kamala Harris, with the endorsement of the state's Democratic Party, over (at least nominally) "Blue Dog" Democrat Loretta Sanchez in 2016's first statewide copartisan election would seem to confirm this view.[38]

There are some reasons to suspect that the nonpartisan primary has changed the dynamics of California politics to some extent. Figure 25.7 illustrates the vote share for Democratic winners of the general election (2012–2016) in open-seat elections for the California legislature relative to the district's (two-party) vote share for President Obama in 2012. The hollow squares represent copartisan, Democrat-vs.-Democrat elections; the solid dots represent all the other elections in which a Democrat won. There is a fairly linear relationship with a bivariate slope not far from one for the traditional election configurations: the lower-tier candidate, subject to some noise, more or less tends to get about the same amount of the vote that Obama obtained in 2012. The slope is much flatter for the copartisan elections; there are some that are still relatively uncompetitive (with the winner getting more than 60 percent of the vote) but several that are very close (Alvarez and Sinclair 2015, 58, produced a version of this figure for 2012 only). In competitive copartisan elections, the Republican voters are potentially important.

What are the consequences of having close copartisan general elections between two Democrats in places otherwise unlikely to competitive elections in November? One possibility, of course, is "no effect." If these copartisan general elections are merely delaying the result of what a partisan primary would have produced at the primary stage, then the elections would appear more competitive without necessarily producing any new (small-d) democratic meaning. It also could be the case that the other institutional incentives – within the party, within the legislature, etc. – are so strong as to render any electoral incentive inadequate in comparison. To borrow from *Yes, Minister*: "the principle of democratic accountability requires the occasional human sacrifice," although for this to be more than just a randomized risk of the job, it must be the case that the other institutional actors are unable to enforce party discipline.[39]

Alvarez and Sinclair (2015), in their surveys in five specific Assembly Districts, do see more centrist candidates prevailing in copartisan elections (echoed in Sinclair 2015). Sinclair and Wray (2015) find voters are engaging in more information search in copartisan elections, at least suggesting a logical pathway by which copartisan elections could produce moderation. Furthermore, Alvarez and Sinclair (2015) advanced the argument that the most important institutional innovation in the nonpartisan primary is not the availability of strategic voting opportunities in the primary round but the reduction of the final choice to two candidates. Given only two options, a voter in that case is most likely to pick a candidate attempting to offer something – if not necessarily ideological moderation, at least more effective constituent services or competent policymaking.

It seems that so far the nonpartisan top-two has reserved for the Republican voters some potential relevance, although the jury is still out on whether this is more than mere untapped potential. The California case also highlights how these rules conceivably could have decidedly nonlinear effects, depending on a state's partisanship. As in Idaho, at some point the majority faction can afford to lose some seats – whether to the other party (probably a greater risk in Idaho) or to a policy nonconforming centrist of the same party (probably a greater risk in California) – and that should impact the incentives of a number of participants; California may be nearing that point, at least in the short term. There is still much to learn about the nonpartisan top-two primary. For our purposes, though, they key observation is that a powerful enough faction of the minority party thought this would help their cause to invest resources in its passage.

Arizona: The Aspirants

Nonpartisan primary reform encountered a very different political environment in neighboring Arizona in 2012 than it had in California in 2010. While both political parties opposed it (see Khan 2012), the key difference was that no significant faction of the minority party, the Arizona Democratic Party, supported it in the same way as Schwarzenegger and company in California (Wyloge 2013). One way to explain the choice is that the Arizona Democrats are anticipating having a reasonable chance of becoming the majority party.

Former Mayor of Phoenix and Democrat-turned-Independent Paul Johnson chaired the pro-reform campaign, but was unable to garner the political support needed to pass the initiative.[40] This did not represent a substantial faction of the Democratic Party; Johnson later commented, "We had almost no candidates outwardly supporting it." Leading the way, Democratic (and Hispanic) State Senator Steve Gallardo and Maricopa County Supervisor Mary Rose Wilcox joined with conservative Republican Maricopa County Attorney Bill Montgomery and long-time U.S. Senator Jon Kyl in opposing the ballot measure (Wyloge 2013).

There is a palpable sense in Arizona that "demographics are destiny" and that the state will ultimately have political geography more like New Mexico's (Nagourney 2012), or even California's (see Badger 2017). Figure 25.8 illustrates the partisan dynamics in Arizona, with Republicans holding a slight advantage persistently over time. Nevertheless, anticipation of a shift is certainly part of the public perception of the state's politics and the lower half of Figure 25.8 illustrates the application of a naïve bivariate regression on presidential vote share over the most recent elections; in some way, the Republican share trends downward (if one is adequately selective with the data). In the final stretch of the 2016 presidential election, Hillary Clinton's campaign decided to "aggressively compete in Arizona, a state with a growing Hispanic population that has been ground zero for the country's heated debate over immigration" (Flegenheimer and Martin 2016). While that bet did not pay off in 2016, it still represents a common belief about the state's future: "destiny" is just a bit further off. Figure 25.9 illustrates

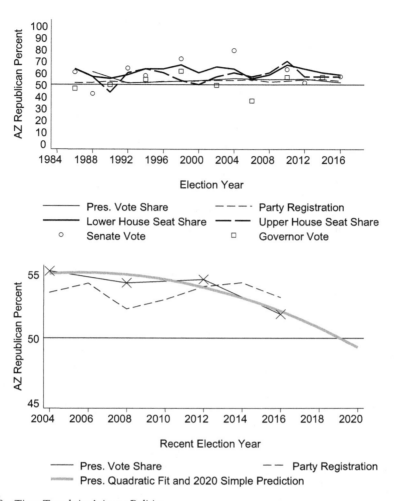

Figure 25.8 Time Trends in Arizona Politics

the Democratic Party vote share in 2016 by legislative district. To really compete in the state, Democrats will have to make some serious gains in a few additional districts or hope for a more favorable redistricting in the next cycle. It is possible for the Democrats to take the majority in the relatively near future, but it seems likely at this point to be a close thing if they should.

Despite Arizona's history as a Republican state and setbacks in the 2010 election (as for Democrats in all parts of the country), the 2012 Arizona Democratic Party sensed indications that their party was on the cusp of a political breakthrough, including recent successful candidacies for statewide office and promising demographic trends (Fitz, Goldenberg, and Kelley 2012; Nagourney 2012). As a result, there was a smaller incentive for elected Democrats, even the most moderate, to prefer a nonpartisan system, for the direction of state politics favored more Democratic, or less conservative, outcomes, without major institutional change – unlike the situation for their Republican counterparts in neighboring California. Moreover, preserving partisan primaries not only advantaged them when, someday, more winners of Arizona Democratic primaries would go on to hold office, thus exerting more partisan control of state governance; it also possibly disadvantaged the Republicans in the short term, as candidates of narrow, extreme

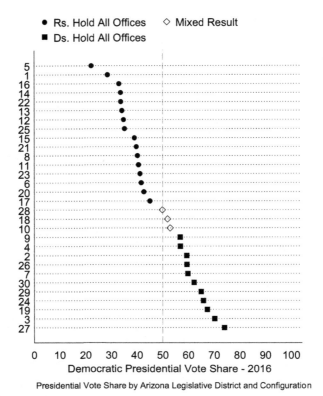

● Rs. Hold All Offices　　◇ Mixed Result
■ Ds. Hold All Offices

Democratic Presidential Vote Share - 2016

Presidential Vote Share by Arizona Legislative District and Configuration

Figure 25.9　2016 Arizona Snapshot

ideologies continued to hold office and pursue fringe legislation (Sterling 2012). It is possible that Republican nomination of an ideological extremist, resulting in an additional Democratic victory in a competitive district (via the mechanism outlined in Hall 2015), could be what flips control of the legislature as Democrats become increasingly competitive over time. Democrats could have their cake (have a tighter partisan hold in their brighter electoral future) and eat it too (allow Republicans to continue to fall victim to the whims of their own primary electorate[41]). This would generate some kind of stability so long as the Republican primary electorate and party officials either sufficiently prioritized ideology, were willing to take on the risk, or were simply placing different bets on the uncertain ability of each side to adapt within the constraints of partisan primaries.

The nonpartisan primary would have also potentially interacted in a different, and unclear, way with Arizona's unusual district and member arrangement in the legislature. Arizona uses multi-member districts in the lower house of the legislature (2 seats), elected from the same geographic region as the upper house. Although other states have a similar arrangement, as in Idaho, these are often simply two single-member district elections happening at the same time within the same district; while that may have interesting consequences for candidate entry-choice, after that stage the elections are functionally distinct. Not so in Arizona, where the semi-closed primary allows each party to nominate two candidates in the primary and then voters cast up to two ballots in the general election stage, although no more than one per candidate. The consequence in most cases is not surprising: in nearly all districts (represented by solid dots in Figure 25.9) both lower house seats and the upper house seat go to members of the same party;

only in a handful do the voters split them. A common electoral strategy appears to be taking a "single shot," for the weaker of the two major parties to run only a single candidate in the hope that anyone wishing to split their ticket will concentrate on that one candidate. Bertelli and Richardson (2008) test, among other hypotheses, and then support the assertion that the spatial incentives for differentiation (rather than the centralizing tendency of Downsian two-candidate reasoning) should have generated more legislative extremism and greater ideal point dispersion in the lower house. The nonpartisan primary would have been a "top-four," not a "top-two," for the lower house[42] and, in that event, very little of the evidence from the other states applies to how this might work.

Democrats may have had ideological or representational concerns as well. A chief concern among Arizona's Democrats was diluting Latino votes, especially in districts where the Latino population was substantial, but less than majority.[43] In districts that were competitive between the state's Democrats and Republicans, and where Latinos were a plurality of the population, Latino voters had a strong chance of driving their candidate of choice through the Democratic primary and into a competitive general election. Under a nonpartisan system, Democrats feared that the Latino Democratic candidate (or candidates) would be eliminated in the system's first-round free-for-all; similar concerns have been raised about southern-style run-off primaries (Kousser 1984), although Alvarez and Sinclair (2015) found little evidence for this in California's nonpartisan primary. Politically, under a partisan primary system, the Democrats could maintain ranks in strong Democratic (and Latino) districts, as opposed to having to possibly redirect funds to intraparty fights in a nonpartisan system, and focus resources on competitive districts for marginal gains in the legislature; meanwhile, they could also continue to protect and develop Latino candidates and officeholders, the future of the state and their party.

In Arizona especially, the Democrats seemed to have bet on their future success. While they kept the door open for future advantages as a majority party, they may have sacrificed opportunities for greater policy relevance in the short term. The Arizona Republicans have won a relatively disproportionate number of seats in the legislature (relative to its performance at the presidential level and in Congress), and the next politically reachable districts are still some distance away.[44] There does not seem to be so much a "right" answer, as there is the one carrying more or less risk for different types of outcomes. At least for the moment, it appears that both parties will fight it out under their old primary election rules.

Into the Unknown: Research Offers More Questions than Answers

Primary reform is not a simple matter of choosing between open and closed primary rules. It is not merely the case that the web of formal and informal institutions is intricate but also that the conditions for study are typically poor: endogenous institution selection, analytically challenging patterns of variation, and relatively small numbers of events organized along a common time continuum. An underlying tension remains between the nuance this field of study requires and the simplicity of the answers demanded by practitioners, unable to wait for more data to come in – what rules should a given player want now? For the practitioners, the question and the timescale is often clear: what benefits my cause and will this happen for election day? Scholars, meanwhile, are not beholden to such timescales and requirements and are thus free to evaluate choices made by political actors with the benefit of hindsight as well. Even retrospectively, in the cases of Idaho, California, and Arizona, it is not easy to judge if the participants made the best decisions available to advance their goals. The choices made in each state, though, reveal something about the beliefs of each party faction. They are making choices consistent with a facially plausible theory of how these rules might impact their interests.

Future study will need to carefully strike a balance between considering all of the potential factors, and their interactions, that explain relevant outcomes and finding something practically evaluable. The field of primary election reform is bedeviled by complexity; while a simple model might treat both the California Republican Party and the Arizona Democratic Party as long-suffering minority parties, as we argue in this chapter, it is particularly important for the respective factional actors that the California Republicans seem to be on their way down while the Arizona Democrats are on their way up. Furthermore, even a nominally similar primary rule would have to work differently in both states because of Arizona's multi-member district lower house. Furthermore, the specific details of which type of faction has the greatest influence in state party politics at the moment influences both which institutions are selected and to what end, as illustrated in Idaho. The statistical noise generated by these sorts of individual judgments may be relatively large compared to the signal strength given the small (effective) sample size of state observations and the number of things changing in all of these places all the time.

Despite some challenges for the study of primary election reform in the United States, this remains a compelling area for research. First, it is an area of American politics in which there is considerable institutional variation, enabling the many advantages of comparative research; if studying state primaries is difficult, research on the rare presidential nomination process is even more challenging. Second, this is an area of both considerable substantive importance and ongoing change. As Key wrote, in many places the primary is the election. As these recent changes in Idaho and California, and the near miss in Arizona, illustrate, states and parties do change their rules, and may adopt rules that have not yet been used anywhere. Research into primary election reform can greatly add to our understanding and practice of democracy.

Notes

1 In evaluating the constitutional designs of twenty different democracies, Powell writes: "The United States is constitutionally unique in this group. Having very strong independent powers in both the executive and the legislature and a host of other points featuring possible sharing of power, it does not imply strong majoritarianism in its decision rules. The executive has a hard task in implementing its policy commitments even when it has congressional majorities. On the other hand, the United States uses single-member district election rules . . ." (Powell 2000, 41).

2 Counting those sworn in: Democrats Truman, Kennedy, Johnson, Carter, Clinton, and Obama; Republicans Eisenhower, Nixon, Ford, Reagan, G.H.W. Bush, G.W. Bush, and Trump. Several were very close: Kennedy (1960) and Nixon (1968) each won the popular vote by less than 1 percent; W. Bush (2000) and Trump (2016) lost the popular vote but won in the electoral college; and Johnson (1964) and Nixon (1972), with the largest margins, still only captured around 60 percent of the popular vote. Compared to many state legislative elections, even the "landslides" at the national level are relatively competitive in terms of the popular vote.

3 Riker's views also profoundly influenced Powell's notions of accountability. Powell (2000, 11) wrote: "William Riker put this very plainly: 'the essence of the liberal interpretation of voting is the notion that voting permits the rejection of candidates or officials who have offended so many voters that they cannot win an election.'"

4 Nebraska operates a unicameral legislature and is the general exception to the rule; see Masket and Shor (2015). The structure and composition of state legislatures provides for interesting variation; interesting for our analysis, both Idaho and Arizona have lower houses with multiple members representing the same geography, although selected in different ways in each state. More generally, district size also varies tremendously: New Hampshire's lower house has 400 members, with each legislator representing only several thousand constituents. California's lower house has 80 members with districts only slightly smaller than a U.S. House District. Scale should matter: even if New Hampshire used *precisely* the same rules as California, there is no reason to believe that the consequences would be unaffected by the enormous differences in scale.

5 Official election results are available here: apps.azsos.gov/election/2012/General/Canvass2012GE.pdf

6 Republicans and Democrats gave a joint press conference "United in Opposition to Top-Two," currently available via YouTube: https://www.youtube.com/watch?v=xo9xQbCzhfg. The video description reads: "Published on Oct 15, 2012. The Save Our Vote committee holds a press conference in opposition to Arizona Proposition 121, the 'Top Two' proposition. Representatives from all corners of the political spectrum speak in opposition. Speakers include Senator Jon Kyl, County Attorney Bill Montgomery, State Senator Steve Gallardo, Maricopa County Supervisor Mary Rose Wilcox, Arizona Libertarian Party Communications Director Barry Hess, Arizona Green Party co-Chair Angel Torres, and Alice Stambaugh representing the Arizona League of Women Voters."

7 To the extent that primary procedures are ever exogenously imposed, this tends to happen through the courts. Although scholars have made some effort to use court decisions as exogenous shocks to the system to better understand the way primary laws work (see McGhee et al. 2014, 345–346), courts have limited ability to create (see Persily 2002); thus whatever the states adopt if a current rule is struck down is still rooted in the state's own political processes.

8 An argument made in Sinclair (2017) about the joint impact of California's top-two election procedure and a change in the majority requirement to pass a state budget.

9 Gerber and Morton reflected common uses of these terms in politics at the time, although these words are often used in conflicting and confusing ways. In particular, it is commonplace to see the term "open primary" to describe something other than the partisan open primary most frequently given this name in the academic literature.

10 Gerber and Morton (1998, 311) point out that it is actually quite difficult to map the consequences of different types of open primaries into expected outcomes because voters will not necessarily vote for their ideological first-preference; instead, they may behave strategically and "crossover" into another party for a variety of tactical reasons: "we therefore note the possibility for both sincere and strategic crossover voting in open primaries but cannot anticipate, on the basis of our theory, which will be more important." This problem is difficult to resolve, leaving many scholars to test the standard predictions; McGhee et al. (2014, 340), sixteen years later: "the political science literature has provided little consistent guidance on what to expect from this variation." It seems unlikely to do so convincingly in the near future as well, for the reasons that McGhee et al. outline.

11 Numerous sources were required to construct Figure 25.2. This data is an update based on Sinclair (2013), which re-examined many of the sources listed in Gerber and Morton (1998), Kanthak and Morton (2001), and early versions of McGhee et al. (2014). These include Bott (1990), Lubecky (1987), McNitt (1980) and Jewell (1977). For southern states, see Bullock and Johnson (1992). As in McGhee et al. (2014), the rest of the database was constructed using a combination of direct examination of state laws, review of current state websites, telephone and email conversation with state and party officials, and published news reports. The appendix in McGhee et al. (2014, 349) is a useful illustration of the coding challenges and "judgment calls for borderline cases," required here as well. For example, we treat Utah (for the purposes of this figure) as "open," although McGhee et al. treat it as closed because it had (until very recently) a strong pre-primary convention. The critical difference between this version and McGhee et al. is that McGhee et al. code the "party choice" results as simply the choice of each party (without considering the choice of the other party).

12 Berman (2016) nicely outlines the connectedness of a series of reforms: term limits (passed in 1992), changing the primary process (passed in 1998), public funding of elections (also in 1998), and an independent redistricting commission (passed in 2000). This makes the 2012 defeat of the nonpartisan primary initiative much more notable as other initiatives for changing the process had been successful.

13 This took too long to resolve; the key proponent of the change, Senator Weicker, lost a general election challenge to a Democrat, Joe Lieberman, who obtained the support of some Republicans. Weicker would later go on to be a third-party governor of the state (see Weicker 1995, 180).

14 The reason for this: it is still somewhat more difficult to change the rule in a state out of compliance (involving changing the party rule to establish harm and then going to court) than it is in states with a procedure in place for the party to choose.

15 Louisiana has used a version of this, although the history of the reform, timing of the elections, and procedure for advancement are different; Nebraska has nonpartisan elections for its state legislature (but not higher offices; see Masket and Shor 2015).

16 Connecticut also at one point operated a similar strong convention system paired with a direct primary in absence of agreement, as have other states in some capacity at some time for some offices; McNitt (1980) lists: New York, Connecticut, Utah, New Mexico, Rhode Island, North Dakota, Colorado, Delaware, Idaho, Massachusetts, and Nebraska.

17 For example, in the Utah Democratic Party: "In 2014, we only had one state house primary, in House District 38 located in Kearns & West Valley City, and only 260 people voted in that primary. It was open to any registered voter" (Lauren Littlefield, electronic mail, March 22, 2017).

18 And many are simply unique: see McGhee et al. (2014) for commentary on coding Colorado's precinct caucus system.

19 This is true tracing the history even farther back than 1980; recent studies seem to focus after this point because data is more easily available for some of the other variables. Sinclair (2013, 154) shows a general pattern of type stability back through 1946.

20 As an example of the potential interaction between multiple components of an institutional design, consider the case of Republican Senator Thad Cochran of Mississippi, elected in 1978. Faced with a "tea party" opponent in 2014, Chris McDaniel, Cochran failed to win the primary. McDaniel also failed to win the primary: although McDaniel was half a percent ahead of Cochran, a third candidate had captured about 5,000 votes, enough to deny either a majority. This required a second runoff primary under Mississippi's runoff rules. Mississippi also had open primary elections and it appears that Cochran managed to win the second round by increasing the total number of voters: "Cochran's campaign explicitly tried to increase his turnout in the runoff by bringing Democratic-leaning African-Americans to the polls" (Enten 2014). Cochran won. There seems to be a good reason to believe that these voters tipped the scales in his favor (Enten 2014; Hood and McKee 2016). This is not just an impact of having an open primary but also, and necessarily, an impact of having a runoff. The first round was open too but McDaniel still came in ahead – so the runoff was critical. And, had the runoff been closed, it is not likely Cochran could have won it – so the openness was also critical.

21 There are several more relevant dimensions to this as well. For mail voting: is it the only way to vote? Do states allow for permanent registration to obtain mail ballots? Do the states require an excuse in order to obtain one? For early voting: is an excuse required? And how many days, for what length of time, and in how many locations will early voting be offered? For more discussion of these types of alternatives, see Alvarez, Levin, and Sinclair (2012).

22 Reilly, Richey, and Taylor (2012) analyze the connection between Google search data and roll-off and find that greater searching corresponds with lower levels of roll-off, suggesting that if voters do search for information they are more likely to participate. It seems quite possible that some of the primary types which afford voters greater choice could only have an impact if voters also have convenient access to information.

23 Ware argues much the same thing for an earlier period: "changes in campaign technology fundamentally shifted the balance between candidates and parties. Moreover, without the widespread use of the direct primary, the technological advances – television, computer-analyzed opinion polls, and so on – would not have had the effect that they did" (2002, 244).

24 Ware's larger point adds depth to the usual reformer-vs-party story: if the parties were so powerful, why did they let the direct primary through? Ware writes "the conventional account is about as implausible as claiming that the driving force behind the direct primary was a large invisible rabbit called Harvey" (2002, 16). Ware's counterargument is that political parties "institutionalize because a sufficient number of politicians within those parties come to understand that their own interests are affected by present arrangements . . . the direct primary was not an isolated reform that happened to be enacted when parties were sufficiently weak that their opponents could overcome them ('heroically'). It was a reform that had its origins in changes in American society that, by the 1880s, were starting to pose severe problems for party politicians" (2002, 22).

25 Although these are generic terms, we mean them in the sense of Alinsky (1971).

26 And the primary rules may matter very little for the minority party – if the party is particularly helpless, it may struggle to obtain more than one candidate per seat in any case, generating few contested primaries.

27 Recent observers have deemed the Idaho Republican primary the "de facto" or "real" election (Trillhaase 2014; Pierce 2016).

28 Utah is an interesting contrast. In Utah, the Republican legislature changed the rules and the party sued to stop the changes in court. In Idaho, the legislature did not change the rules and the party sued to change them.

29 Governor Butch Otter expressed his concern regarding the "potential damage" of closing the Republican primary (Andersen 2007).

30 Beck was known for his support for Paul as late as June 2008, months after John McCain clinched the Republican primary for president: http://www.idahopress.com/news/beck-ron-paul-supporter-join-

in-bid-to-oust-id/article_421234d2-2431-511f-8706-1f76976a53b5.html; Beck would later serve as Donald Trump's Idaho campaign chair in 2016 (Russell 2016).

31 Beck's opponents described as "elites" in a local political blog, see Fischer (2008).

32 Otter is otherwise a successful politician; he served in various roles: State House from 1973 to 1979, Lieutenant Governor from 1987 to 2001, U.S. House from 2001 to 2007, and Governor since 2007.

33 Text of House Bill 351 is available online: https://legislature.idaho.gov/sessioninfo/2011/legislation/H0351/

34 Delegates at the Idaho Republican Party's state convention twice voted on the issue of closed primaries, passing in 2006, but then losing just narrowly in 2008, 199 to 192 (Miller 2008).

35 Navigating this electorate can be difficult, even so: Raul Labrador and Mike Simpson, the two Republican House members, took different initial approaches to the 2017 efforts to repeal the Affordable Care Act (Johnson 2017).

36 Take, as an example, support for same-sex marriage: it was on its way to becoming a clear majority position among California independents (by 2013: 67 percent in favor) and voters overall (61 percent in favor); an accelerating upward trend in support in favor of same-sex marriage coincided with these procedural battles (Petek 2014); and the 2008 Proposition 8 ban only passed with 52 percent of the vote.

37 One of the Republican candidates interviewed in Alvarez and Sinclair (2015, 163), Brad Torgan, explained that he was willing to run for office in part because it would give him a greater ability to help write the social issues out of the California Republican Party platform.

38 A dynamic noted in the national coverage of the race (see Drusch 2015). The *National Review* endorsed Sanchez, including this sub-headline on the article: "Better the Blue Dog Democrat than the contemptible, corrupt, repulsive Democrat" (Gelernter 2016).

39 *Yes Minister*, episode 7, April 7, 1980. The line is Sir Humphrey's.

40 In a 2012 story, *Phoenix New Times* names Johnson as a political independent: http://www.phoenix newtimes.com/blogs/russell-pearce-conqueror-jerry-lewis-endorsed-by-eddie-basha-paul-johnson-democratic-lies-denounced-6500747.

41 Consider, for example, the bind in which Senator Jeff Flake (R-AZ) found himself for the period 2016–2018.

42 The text reads: "for any office to which more than one candidate will be elected, the number of candidates who will compete in the general election shall be the number of candidates to be elected times two" (see: http://apps.azsos.gov/election/2012/info/PubPamphlet/Sun_Sounds/english/prop121.htm).

43 Republicans and Democrats gave a joint press conference "United in Opposition to Top-Two," currently available via YouTube: https://www.youtube.com/watch?v=xo9xQbCzhfg.

44 Currently, Democrats represent four out of nine of Arizona's congressional districts; Democrats represented five out of nine, which is notable compared to the strength of the Republican majority in state legislature.

References

Achen, Christopher, and Larry Bartels. 2016. *Democracy for Realists: Why Elections Do Not Produce Responsive Government*. Princeton, NJ: Princeton University Press.

Ahler, Douglas J., Jack Citrin, and Gabriel S. Lenz. 2016. "Do Open Primaries Improve Representation? An Experimental Test of California's 2012 Top-Two Primary." *Legislative Studies Quarterly* 41(2): 237–268.

Aldrich, John. H. 2011. *Why Parties? A Second Look*. Chicago: University of Chicago Press,.

Alinsky, Saul D. 1971. *Rules for Radicals: A Practical Primer for Realistic Radicals*. New York: Vintage Books, reprinted 1989.

Alvarez, R. Michael, Ines Levin, and J. Andrew Sinclair. 2012. "Making Voting Easier: Convenience Voting in the 2008 Presidential Election." *Political Research Quarterly* 65(2): 248–262.

Alvarez, R. Michael, and J. Andrew Sinclair. 2015. *Nonpartisan Primary Election Reform: Mitigating Mischief*. New York: Cambridge University Press.

Andersen, Shea. 2007. "The Primary Problem – Idaho's Dominant Party Struggles with Success and Change." *Boise Weekly*. Aug. 21, http://www.boiseweekly.com/boise/the-primary-problem/Content?oid=933446

Arrow, Kenneth J. 1951. *Social Choice and Individual Values*. New Haven, CT: Yale University Press.

Askar, Jamshid Ghazi. 2011. "Olene Walker: Legacy without an Heir." *Deseret News*, July 10, http://www.deseretnews.com/article/700150803/Olene-Walker-Legacy-without-an-heir.html

Bachrach, Peter, and Morton S. Baratz. 1962. "Two Faces of Power." *The American Political Science Review* 56(4): 947–952.

Badger, Emily. 2017. "Immigrant Shock: Can California Predict the Nation's Future?" *The New York Times, The Upshot.* February 1, https://www.nytimes.com/2017/02/01/upshot/strife-over-immigrants-can-california-foretell-nations-future.html

Bartowski, Steve. 2012. "Abel Maldonado Dividing Point among Republicans." *calcoastnews.com*, June 28, https://calcoastnews.com/2012/06/abel-maldonado-dividing-point-among-republicans/

Berman, David. 2016. "Building and Rebuilding an Election System in Arizona: Where We've Been, Where We're Going." Monograph, Morrison Institute for Public Policy, March. https://morrisoninstitute.asu.edu/sites/default/files/content/products/Berman_Elections.pdf

Bertelli, Anthony M., and Lilliard E. Richardson. 2008. "Ideological Extremism and Electoral Design. Multimember versus Single Member Districts." *Public Choice* 137(1/2): 347–368.

Bertelli, Anthony M. 2016. "Who Are the Policy Workers, and What Are They Doing? Citizen's Heuristics and Democratic Accountability in Complex Governance." *Public Performance & Management Review* 40(2): 208–234.

Bott, Alexander J. 1990. *Handbook of United States Election Laws and Practices.* New York: Greenwood.

Bueno de Mesquita, Bruce, and Alastair Smith. 2011. *The Dictator's Handbook: Why Bad Behavior is Almost Always Good Politics.* New York: Public Affairs.

Bullock III, Charles S., and Loch K. Johnson. 1992. *Runoff Elections in the United States.* Chapel Hill: University of North Carolina Press.

Burden, Barry C., David T. Canon, Kenneth R. Mayer, and Donald P. Moynihan. 2014. "Election Laws, Mobilization, and Turnout: The Unanticipated Consequences of Election Reform." *American Journal of Political Science* 58(1): 95–109.

Catanese, David. 2010. "Sen. Bennett Loses GOP Nomination." *Politico*, May 8. http://www.politico.com/story/2010/05/sen-bennett-loses-gop-nomination-036960

Campbell, Angus, Philip E. Converse, Warren E. Miller, and Donald E. Stokes. 1960. *The American Voter.* Chicago: University of Chicago Press.

Cobb, Roger W., and Charles D. Elder. 1971. "The Politics of Agenda-Building: An Alternative Perspective for Modern Democratic Theory." *The Journal of Politics* 33(4): 892–915.

Cohen, Marty, David Karol, Hans Noel, and John Zaller. 2008. *The Party Decides: Presidential Nominations Before and After Reform.* Chicago: University of Chicago Press.

Cox, Gary W. 1997. *Making Votes Count: Strategic Coordination in the World's Electoral Systems.* New York: Cambridge University Press.

Downs, Anthony. 1957. *An Economic Theory of Democracy.* New York: Addison-Wesley.

Drusch, Andrea. 2015. "Loretta Sanchez Places a Bet on a Democrat-Versus-Democrat Senate Race in California." *The Atlantic*, October 20. https://www.theatlantic.com/politics/archive/2015/10/loretta-sanchez-places-a-bet-on-a-democrat-versus-democrat-senate-race-in-california/435141/

Enten, Harry. 2014. "It Looks Like African-Americans Really Did Help Thad Cochran Win." *Five ThirtyEight.* June 25. https://fivethirtyeight.com/datalab/it-looks-like-african-americans-really-did-help-thad-cochran-win/

Erikson, Robert S., and Gerald C. Wright. 2013. "Voters, Candidates, and Issues in Congressional Elections." In *Congress Reconsidered* (10th ed.), eds. Lawrence C. Dodd and Bruce I. Oppenheimer. Thousand Oaks: CQ Press, pp. 91–117.

Fischer, Bryan. 2008. "Guest Post: Time for a New Chairman of the Idaho GOP?" *TrishAndHalli.com.* May 29. http://www.trishandhalli.com/2008/05/29/idaho-legislature/guest-post-time-for-a-new-chairman-of-the-idaho-gop/

Fitz, Marshall, Jonathan Goldenberg, and Angela Maria Kelley. 2012. "The Top 10 Things You Should Know About Arizona's Latinos and Immigrants." Center for American Progress. Feb. *24.* https://www.americanprogress.org/issues/immigration/news/2012/02/24/11077/the-top-10-things-you-should-know-about-arizonas-latinos-and-immigrants/

Flegenheimer, Matt, and Jonathan Martin. 2016. "Showing Confidence, Hillary Clinton Pushes Into Republican Strongholds." *The New York Times.* October 17. https://www.nytimes.com/2016/10/18/us/politics/hillary-clinton-campaign.html

Gelernter, Josh. 2016. "Don't Ignore California's Vital Senate Race: Better the Blue Dog Democrat than the Contemptible, Corrupt, Repulsive Democrat." *National Review.* September 24. http://www.nationalreview.com/article/440353/california-senate-race-loretta-sanchez-blue-dog-democrat-over-kamala-harris.

Geraghty, Jim. 2015. "Virginia's Primary Problem." *National Review*. March 12. http://www.national review.com/article/415337/virginias-primary-problem-jim-geraghty

Gerber, Elisabeth R., and Rebecca B. Morton. 1998. "Primary Election Systems and Representation." *Journal of Law, Economics, & Organization* 14(2): 304–324.

Grose, Christian R. 2014. "The Adoption of Electoral Reforms and Ideological Change in the California State Legislature." *USC Schwarzenegger Institute*, Working Paper.

Hall, Andrew. 2015. "What Happens When Extremists Win Primaries?" *American Political Science Review* 109(1): 18–42.

Hill, Seth J. 2015. "Institution of Nomination and the Policy Ideology of Primary Electorates." *Quarterly Journal of Political Science* 10(4): 461–487.

Hill, Seth J., and Thad Kousser. 2016. "Turning Out Unlikely Voters? A Field Experiment in the Top-Two Primary." *Political Behavior* 38(2): 413–432.

Hirano, Shigeo, and Games M. Snyder, Jr. 2014. "Primary Elections and the Quality of Elected Officials." *Quarterly Journal of Political Science* 9(3): 473–500.

Hoffman, Nathaniel. 2008. "Norm Semanko." *Boise Weekly*. Jul. 16. http://www.boiseweekly.com/boise/norm-semanko/Content?oid=937353

Hood III, M. V., and Seth C. McKee. 2016. "Black Votes Count: The 2014 Republican Senate Nomination in Mississippi." *Social Science Quarterly* 98(1): 89–106.

Jewell, Malcolm. 1977. "Voting Turnout in State Gubernatorial Primaries." *The Western Political Quarterly* 30(2): 236–254.

Johnson, Dean. 2017. "Idaho's Congressional Delegation Respond to President Trump's Health Care Bill." KTVB.*com*. March 24. http://www.ktvb.com/news/politics/idahos-congressional-delegation-respond-to-president-trumps-health-care-bill/425408972

Kanthak, Kristin, and Rebecca Morton. 2001. "Congressional Primaries." In *Congressional Primaries and the Politics of Representation*, eds. Peter F. Galderisi, Mami Ezra, and Michael Lyons. New York: Rowan & Littlefield, pp. 116–131.

Key, V.O. 1949. *Southern Politics in State and Nation*. Knoxville: University of Tennessee Press, reprinted 1984.

Key, V.O. 1956. *American State Politics: An Introduction*. New York: Alfred A. Knopf.

Key, V.O. 1958. *Politics, Parties, and Pressure Groups*, 4th ed. New York: Thomas Y. Crowell Co., first edition 1942.

Khan, Natasha. 2012. "Political Parties United in Dislike of 'Top Two' Primaries." *Cronkite News* (online), Oct. 1. http://cronkitenewsonline.com/2012/10/arizona-political-parties-united-in-dislike-of-top-two-primaries-proposition-121/

Kousser, Morgan. 1984. "Origins of the Run-Off Primary." *The Black Scholar* 15(23): 23–26.

Kousser, Thad, Scott Lucas, Seth Masket, and Eric McGhee. 2015. "Kingmakers or Cheerleaders? Party Power and the Causal Effects of Endorsements." *Political Research Quarterly* 68(3): 443–456.

Kousser, Thad, Justin Phillips, and Boris Shor. 2016. "Reform and Representation: A New Method Applied to Recent Electoral Changes." *Political Science Research and Methods*, doi:10.1017/psrm.2016.43

Lemons, Stephen. 2012. "Russell Pearce-Conqueror Jerry Lewis Endorsed by Eddie Basha, Paul Johnson; Democratic Lies Denounced." *Phoenix New Times* (Online). Nov. 5. http://www.phoenixnewtimes.com/blogs/russell-pearce-conqueror-jerry-lewis-endorsed-by-eddie-basha-paul-johnson-democratic-lies-denounced-6500747

Lubecky, David. 1987. "Comment: Setting Voter Qualifications for State Primary Elections: Reassertion of the Right of State Political Parties to Self-Determination." *University of Cincinnati Law Review* 55: 799–830.

Masket, Seth. 2011. *No Middle Ground: How Informal Party Organizations Control Nominations and Polarize Legislatures*. Ann Arbor: University of Michigan Press.

Masket, Seth, and Boris Shor. 2015. "Polarization without Parties: Term Limits and Legislative Partisanship in Nebraska's Unicameral Legislature." *State Politics & Policy Quarterly* 15(1): 67–90.

McGhee, Eric. 2010. "At Issue: Open Primaries." With contributions from Daniel Krimm. *San Francisco: Public Policy Institute of California*, February. http://www.ppic.org/content/pubs/atissue/AI_210EMAI.pdf

McGhee, Eric, Seth Masket, Boris Shor, Steven Rogers, and Nolan McCarty. 2014. "A Primary Cause of Partisanship? Nomination Systems and Legislator Ideology." *American Journal of Political Science* 58(2): 337–351.

McNitt, Andrew D. 1980. "The Effect of Preprimary Endorsement on Competition for Nominations: An Examination of Different Nominating Systems." *The Journal of Politics* 42(1): 257–266.

Miller, John. 2008. "Semanko Promises Unity as Idaho GOP Leader." *Times-News* via MagicValley.com. June 15. http://magicvalley.com/news/local/semanko-promises-unity-as-idaho-gop-leader/article_03375770-e3d1-59f5-a5bc-231b17aa1f0f.html

Nagler, Jonathan. 2015. "Voter Behavior in California's Top Two Primary." *California Journal of Politics and Policy* 7:(1). Online at https://escholarship.org/uc/item/89g5x6vn

Nagourney, Adam. 2012. "Obama Camp, Seeing Shift, Bets on Long Shot in Arizona." *New York Times*. April 15. http://www.nytimes.com/2012/04/16/us/politics/obama-campaign-turns-attention-on-arizona.html

North, Douglas C. 1998. "Five Propositions about Institutional Change." In *Explaining Social Institutions*, eds. Jack Knight and Itai Sened. Ann Arbor: University of Michigan Press, pp. 15–27.

Persily, Nathaniel. 2002. "The Blanket Primary in the Courts: The Precedent and Implications of California Democratic Party v. Jones." In *Voting at the Political Fault Line: California's Experiment with the Blanket Primary*, eds. Bruce E. Cain and Elisabeth R. Gerber. Berkeley: University of California Press, pp. 303–323.

Petek, Sonja. 2014. "Californians' Attitudes Toward Same-Sex Marriage." Monograph. *San Francisco: Public Policy Institute of California*, July. http://www.ppic.org/main/publication_show.asp?i=1012

Pierce, Jim. 2016. "Idaho's Unaffiliated Should Declare for GOP and Vote in Primaries." *Idaho Statesman*. Mar. 3. http://www.idahostatesman.com/opinion/readers-opinion/article63938772.html

Pirch, Kevin A. 2012. "When Did the Campaign End? An Examination of the Timing of Vote Returns in the 2008 General Election in Washington State." *PS: Political Science and Politics* 45(4): 711–715.

Pitzl, Mary Jo. 2016. "Election-Reform Campaign Suspended after Major Backer Pulls Out." *The Arizona Republic*, March 10. http://www.azcentral.com/story/news/politics/arizona/2016/03/10/arizona-dark-money-disclosure-and-open-primary-drive-put-on-hold/81591964/

Popkey, Dan. 2014. "Nothing Personal: Beck Hopes Otter Names Him to Idaho House." *Idaho Statesman*—Blogs.Jan. 10. http://blogs.idahostatesman.com/nothing-personal-beck-hopes-otter-names-him-to-idaho-house/

Powell Jr., G. Bingham. 2000. *Elections as Instruments of Democracy: Majoritarian and Proportional Visions*. New Haven, CT: Yale University Press.

Reilly, Shauna, Sean Richey, and J. Benjamin Taylor. 2012. "Using Google Search Data for State Politics Research: An Empirical Validity Test Using Roll-Off Data." *State Politics & Policy Quarterly* 12(2): 146–159.

Riker, William H. 1982. *Liberalism against Populism: A Confrontation between the Theory of Democracy and the Theory of Social Choice*. New York: W.H. Freeman, reprinted 1986.

Rogowski, Jon C. 2013. "Primary Systems, Candidate Platforms, and Ideological Extremity." Working Paper, Washington University (St. Louis, MO).

Romboy, Dennis. 2016. "Federal Judge Upholds Controversial Utah Election Law." *Deseret News*. April 15. http://www.deseretnews.com/article/865652353/Federal-judge-upholds-controversial-Utah-election-law.html

Russell, Betsy Z. 2007a. "Republicans Close Doors to Primary." *The Spokesman-Review*. Jun. 3. http://www.spokesman.com/stories/2007/jun/03/idaho-republicans-close-doors-to-primary/

Russell, Betsy Z. 2007b. "Republicans v. Republicans." *The Spokesman-Review*. Aug. 3. http://www.spokesman.com/blogs/boise/2007/aug/03/republicans-vs-republicans/

Russell, Betsy Z. 2008a. "Idaho Republicans Seek Closed Primary." *The Spokesman-Review*. Jan. 27 http://www.spokesman.com/stories/2008/jan/27/idaho-republicans-seek-closed-primary/

Russell, Betsy Z. 2008b. "New GOP Chairman Has His Work Cut Out." *The Spokesman-Review*. Jul. 22. http://www.spokesman.com/stories/2008/jul/22/new-gop-chairman-has-his-work-cut-out/

Russell, Betsy Z. 2016. "Rod Beck on Why He's Chairing Trump Campaign in Idaho. . ." *The Spokesman-Review*. Mar. 8. http://www.spokesman.com/blogs/boise/2016/mar/08/rod-beck-why-hes-chairing-trump-campaign-idaho/

Sherman, Jake. 2014. "Cantor Loses." *Politico*, June 10. http://www.politico.com/story/2014/06/eric-cantor-primary-election-results-virginia-107683

Shipan, Charles M., and Craig Volden. 2012. "Policy Diffusion: Seven Lessons for Scholars and Practitioners." *Public Administration Review* 72(6): 788–796.

Shor, Boris, and Nolan McCarty. 2015. "Aggregate State Legislator Shor-McCarty Ideological Data, June 2015 update." https://dataverse.harvard.edu/dataset.xhtml?persistentId=doi:10.7910/DVN/K7ELHW

Sinclair, Betsy, and Michael Wray. 2015. "Googling the Top Two: Information Search in California's Top Two Primary." *California Journal of Politics & Policy* 7:(1). Online at https://escholarship.org/uc/item/1fg8b858

Sinclair, J. Andrew. 2013. "Of Primary Importance: American Primary Elections 1945–2012." Ph.D. diss., California Institute of Technology.

Sinclair, J. Andrew. 2015. "Winning from the Center: Frank Bigelow and California's Nonpartisan Primary." *California Journal of Politics & Policy* 7:(1). Online at https://escholarship.org/uc/item/9vb15608

Sinclair, J. Andrew. 2017. "Democratic Accountability and Institutional Reform: Lessons from California's 2010 Angry Electorate." Working Paper, New York University.

Skelton, George. 2009. "Sen. Maldonado Comes Out a Winner in Budget Brawl." *Los Angeles Times*. February 20. http://articles.latimes.com/2009/feb/20/local/me-cap20

Sterling, Terry Greene. 2012. "How GOP Overreach Put Arizona Back in Play." *Rolling Stone*. Feb. 22. http://www.rollingstone.com/politics/news/how-gop-overreach-put-arizona-back-in-play-20120222

Trillhaase, Marty. 2014. "Go Ahead. Make Rod Beck's day; Get Unaffiliated." *Lewiston Tribune* via *The Spokesman-Review*. March. http://media.spokesman.com/documents/2014/03/Go_Ahead.pdf

Vozzella, Laura. 2016. "In Establishment-Friendly Flip, GOP Picks Primary over Convention for 2017." *The Washington Post*. August 27. https://www.washingtonpost.com/local/virginia-politics/in-establishment-friendly-flip-va-gop-picks-primary-over-convention-for-2017/2016/08/27/f87275c6-6bb9-11e6-8225-fbb8a6fc65bc_story.html

Ware, Alan. 2002. *The American Direct Primary: Party Institutionalization and Transformation in the North*. New York: Cambridge University Press.

Weicker Jr., Lowell P. 1995. *Maverick: A Life in Politics*. With Barry Sussman. New York: Little, Brown & Co.

Wyloge, Evan. 2013. "Failed Top-Two Primary Measure Had Most Support among Independent Voters." *Arizona Capitol Times*. Jan. 22. http://azcapitoltimes.com/news/2013/01/22/failed-top-two-primary-measure-had-most-support-among-independent-voters/

York, Anthony. 2010. "Proposition 14 Passes, Bringing Open Primaries to California." *Los Angeles Times PolitiCal*. June 8 http://latimesblogs.latimes.com/california-politics/2010/06/do-not-publish--propositon-14-passes.html

26

SORE LOSER LAWS IN PRESIDENTIAL AND CONGRESSIONAL ELECTIONS

Michael S. Kang and Barry C. Burden[1]

Sore loser laws – which restrict candidates who lose primaries from running in general elections – are a virtually ubiquitous feature of American politics, but are almost never studied seriously by political scientists or election law scholars. In this chapter, we build on our earlier studies of sore loser laws (Burden, Jones, and Kang 2014; Kang 2011) in two new ways. First, we expand on our findings on the polarizing influence of sore loser laws as applied to congressional and state legislative candidates by looking at the actual incidence of sore loser candidates where they were permitted by law. Second, we survey the state-by-state application of sore loser laws to presidential candidates.

By comparison with general elections, primary elections display greater variety in the rules and processes that govern them across the states. Primaries differ in whether voters must be registered with a party to participate, whether the winning candidate must surpass a threshold to avoid a runoff, and even the date on which the elections take place. Scholars have rightly sought to understand the consequences of these permutations but have largely neglected one aspect of primaries that also affects general elections: the sore loser law.

Sore loser laws make the primary outcome even more important because they restrict candidates who fail to win party primaries from getting ballot access in the general election. The term "sore loser" implies a candidate who is angry at losing a primary and seeks to get back in the game by appearing on the general election ballot as an independent or under a different party's label. Once a relative rarity, sore loser laws have been steadily adopted over the decades until a version is now in place in almost every state.[2] These laws are important because they raise the stakes of candidates' decisions about whether and how to run for office. When a sore loser ban is in place, insurgent and nontraditional candidates face more pressure to run for a major party nomination than as an independent or third-party candidate in the general election. This incentive might help to shore up the two-party system, but it also has the potential to reduce competition and foster party polarization.

Consequences of Variation in State Sore Loser Laws

All sore loser laws restrict candidates who lose party primaries from running in the general election against the party whose nomination they previously sought. However, states impose their restrictions in different ways, some of which are quite circuitous.

When it comes to congressional and most state offices, we have previously reported that nearly every state restricts a primary loser from subsequently filing to run as another party's nominee simultaneously, or as an independent candidate on the general election ballot for the same office in the same election cycle. We reported in 2010 that 15 states specifically disqualified any candidate who has lost a party primary from running in the general election for the same office. Twenty-five other states achieved the same result by effectively prohibiting any primary candidate from running in more than one party primary or running as an independent candidate at all. That is, 40 of 50 states made winning their party's primary election the exclusive route to the general election ballot for primary candidates. Five states opened this door only slightly wider by allowing candidates to cross-file as an independent candidate in addition to a party primary, or to file for more than one primary, but their deadlines required candidates to cross-file well before the elections such that their dual affiliations would be known to the primary electorate. In two other states with nonpartisan primaries only the top two vote-getters proceed to the general election, effectively eliminating sore loser opportunities. In sum, only three states allowed primary losers subsequently to file to appear on the general election ballot as another party's nominee or as an independent.

We have argued that sore loser laws contribute to polarization of the political parties. When combined with ballot access laws that encourage candidates to seek a party's nomination as a means to office, sore loser laws effectively discourage moderate candidates who would have difficulty winning primaries decided by conservative Republicans or liberal Democrats. As a result, theory suggests that nominees who emerge in a system where sore losers are banned will be more ideologically polarized than those who run in a system where sore losers are permitted (Kang 2011).

We found that restrictions on sore loser candidacies contributed to party polarization in Congress and state legislatures (Burden, Jones, and Kang 2014). Taking advantage of the fact that nearly half the states adopted their sore loser laws between 1976 and 1994, we compared the ideological positions of congressional candidates, measured by two different survey sources, in states with and without sore loser laws. We demonstrated that candidates under sore loser restrictions were more ideologically extreme, particularly so for Republicans, such that the gap between Republican and Democratic candidates was about 10 percent greater in states with sore loser laws. We yielded similar results when we compared congressional roll call voting, using NOMINATE data on ideological positions, for legislators in states with and without sore loser laws. We again found that sore loser laws widened polarization between Republicans and Democrats, and that this result survived robustness checks for endogeneity. Whatever benefits sore loser laws might provide, theory and evidence suggest that they contribute to party polarization.

Sore Loser Candidates in Congressional Elections

One question unaddressed in our earlier research is how prevalent sore loser candidates actually are. Although our theory did not require sore losers to actually materialize, the bite of sore loser bans would seem sharper if we see evidence they actually screen out candidates.

We now investigate several years of congressional elections to see if sore loser candidates actually emerge in states that permitted them or somehow sneak through in states that did not permit them. To put this inquiry more starkly, we intend to measure the frequency of two kinds of cases. First are "positive" cases where a candidate who lost a primary in a state that prohibits sore losers nonetheless appears on the general election ballot. Second are "negative" cases where primary losers in states without limitations on sore losers appear on the general election ballot.

If we are interpreting statutes correctly and they are being enforced properly, there should be no "positive" cases. Any candidates who do sneak through a ban would indicate that the statute does not have the meaning we have ascribed to it or that executives and courts have not noticed or cared about end-runs around the sore loser restrictions.

Expectations about the frequency of "negative" cases are far less clear. On the one hand, we have argued that sore loser bans discourage entry by some candidates who would otherwise run in a party primary if they had assurance in law that they could run in the general election despite failing to win the nomination. The number of such candidates should not be zero because that would suggest that sore loser laws have no impact on who runs, a reality that would be contrary to our theory and the intentions of many state legislators who enacted them. But given the low levels of overall competition in congressional primaries (Ansolabehere et al. 2010; Boatright 2014), we would not expect many sore loser candidates to run in the general election due to the small candidate pool that exists in the primary and the physical, financial, and reputational costs of running again after losing a party nomination.

Because sore loser bans are nearly ubiquitous today, we went back in time to investigate whether sore losers appeared when they were allowed to do so. We chose to analyze several election cycles in the 1970s, the last time that half of the states still permitted sore losers. To avoid the peculiarities caused by redistricting, we analyzed U.S. Senate elections. Due to the staggering of Senate classes, we covered the three consecutive election cycles of 1974, 1976, and 1978 meaning that we have data on every state and all 100 Senate seats.

Tracking down sore loser candidates in elections that took place decades ago is not an easy task, so we adopted a systematic but multifaceted approach to data collection. We began with official election returns from the Clerk of the House of Representatives for a complete record of non-major party candidates who won votes in the general election. We then worked backwards to discern if any of those candidates had run in a Democratic or Republican primary that same year. This information was often available through resources such as the *CQ Guide to U.S. Elections* and the website ourcampaigns.com. These resources were verified and augmented using mostly local newspaper coverage of primary elections.

We acknowledge that party politics in the 1970s were different than the contemporary era because the major parties were more ideologically diverse. The Democrats in particular still contained a large conservative wing based largely in the South (Poole and Rosenthal 2007; Rohde 1991). One might expect more intraparty competition due to the heterogeneity of the party, but there is little evidence that "getting primaried" was more common in the 1970s (Boatright 2013). We nonetheless cannot guarantee that a roll back of sore loser laws in the twenty-first century would have precisely the same impact as it did several decades ago.

As Table 26.1 indicates, of the 100 seats we studied, 52 were up for election in states with sore loser bans while 48 took place in states where sore losers were permitted.[3] The average number of major party primary candidates was slightly higher in the sore loser law states (5.9 per seat versus 5.5 per seat), which might suggest that the laws did not deter candidates from running in primaries even though they lacked the opportunity to run in the general election if they

Table 26.1 Sore Loser Candidates in U.S. Senate Elections 1974–1978

Seats Up	Major Party Primary Candidates	Major Party General Election Candidates	Non-Major Party General Election Candidates	Sore Loser Candidates on Ballot	Sore Loser Candidates among Counted Write-In Votes
52 (sore loser laws)	305	98	79	0	1
48 (no sore loser laws)	264	92	75	3	5

failed to win party nominations. The total number of candidates on the general election ballot was indistinguishable between the two kinds of states: 3.4 per state in states banning sore losers versus 3.5 in states that permitted them.

The key finding is that no "positive" sore losers appeared in states where they were banned (as we expected) and a small number of "negative" cases appeared in states where they were permitted. We identified zero such cases in one year, one in another year, and two in another year, for a total of three out of about 48 Senate races, or 6 percent of the time. Thus, when they were permitted, sore losers appeared in about one out of 20 elections.

Sore loser candidates also sometimes received write-in votes in the general election in states where they are officially tallied. Write-in candidates are unique because they may earn votes despite not being listed on the ballot.[4] In the three election cycles we examined, we found five cases of this in the states without sore loser bans and one case in states with such bans. Although this case does not violate our coding of state laws because we only counted states as having sore loser laws if they prevented primary candidates from appearing on the general election ballot, this seemingly "positive" case deserves some discussion.

The write-in case involved a candidate named Jason Boe, Oregon State Senate President, who ran for the Democratic nomination for U.S. Senate in Oregon in 1974. He lost that primary to former Senator Wayne Morse by just under 10 percentage points. In an extra complication, Morse died two months after winning the nomination. The party's central committee chose a different candidate (i.e., not Boe) to replace him on the ballot. Boe nonetheless earned 5,072 write-in votes in the general election (totally about .66 percent of the total vote cast). This was not a typical congressional primary.

To ensure that the results were not limited to the Senate, we also explored House elections in two large states. Focusing on two of the same three election cycles – 1974 and 1978 – we collected data on New York (which banned sore losers) and California (which allowed them). We used a similar methodology as above to track down all non-major party candidates who earned general election votes in these two states.

Table 26.2 reports the results. We identified eight "negative" cases out of 78 seats up for election. That is a rate of 10 percent, slightly below the 6 percent rate we calculated in U.S. Senate races during the same era. This higher rate translates to a sore loser candidate in about one out of every ten elections where they were permitted. In the eight New York cases where sore loser candidates ran, five sought the Democratic nomination and then appeared as Liberal Party candidates in the general election while two sought the Republican nomination and then appeared as Conservative Party candidates in the general election, while one ran for both Conservative and Republican nominations and then ran as a Conservative in the general. These particular combinations reflect the uniqueness of political parties in New York that have been shaped in part by the availability of usage of "fusion" tickets, in which multiple parties endorse the same candidate (Scarrow 1986).

Although sore loser candidates are somewhat infrequent, this does not necessarily mean that sore loser laws are unimportant. They might affect candidate behaviors, such as whether/when

Table 26.2 Sore Loser Candidates in California and New York U.S. House Elections in 1974 and 1978

States	Seats Up	Sore Loser Candidates on Ballot	Sore Loser Candidates among Counted Write-In Votes
California (sore loser law)	86	0	0
New York (no sore loser law)	78	8	0

to run and what positions to take, that we cannot easily observe. But there are also some real cases of sore loser candidates running in general elections where they are permitted to do so. Based on our examination of elections from an era when many states lacked sore loser restrictions, about between one in 10 and one in 20 elections with a ban would have seen additional candidates on the general election ballot had the prohibition on sore loser candidates not been in place. Courts and lawmakers need to decide whether the benefits of sore loser bans in congressional elections outweigh the downsides of screening out these additional candidates for office and contributing to partisan polarization.

Application to Presidential Candidates

Although the application and effects of sore loser bans are clear in congressional elections, how they apply to presidential elections is much less clear. Consider one example from the 2016 presidential campaign. Soon after Donald Trump began his campaign for the Republican presidential nomination in the summer of 2015, he suggested he might run as an independent or a minor party candidate if he was not "treated fairly" by the party in the primary process. Even before Trump had participated in the Ohio presidential primary election, Ohio Secretary of State Jon Husted fired back that Trump could not legally make the suggested sore loser run under Ohio law and that Husted would block Trump from making one in his state.[5] There was a great deal of public argument and uncertainty about whether Ohio's sore loser law even applied to presidential candidates, but because Trump ultimately won the Republican nomination for president, Husted's claims and Ohio law were never put to the test.

In fact, it is difficult to determine whether a state's sore loser law applies to presidential candidates. Why is the legal picture less clear at the presidential level? First, unlike congressional representatives, the party nominee is chosen at the national, rather than state level. Most states hold their own presidential primary elections that decide only the allocation of a state's respective party delegates in this larger national process. As a result, the eventual party nominee may win the national nomination without winning every single state's primary election or other selection process. For example, Hillary Clinton and Donald Trump were the 2016 winners of their party primary process despite finishing behind other candidates in a number of states. Clinton won the Democratic presidential nomination by receiving 55.2 percent of the national primary vote and a plurality of party delegates in 34 states, but runner-up Bernie Sanders won primary elections in 11 states and a plurality of party delegates by caucus in another 12 states. Similarly, Republican presidential nominee Donald Trump won a plurality of delegates in 37 states but finished behind another primary candidate in 13 states. Even when Clinton and Trump failed to win a plurality of delegates in a state, they typically were able to win some proportional minority of delegates in the state despite "losing" the state to a rival. The primary is for allocating delegates rather than for selecting candidates directly.

The mismatch between the national scale of the presidential election and the state-limited scope of any state sore loser law complicates the application. State sore loser laws typically restrict primary losers from running in the subsequent general election. But if the intent of sore loser prohibition is to keep a "sore loser" in the primary from getting a second chance at the general election, then it makes little sense to bar a presidential candidate who happens to have lost a state's primary election but nonetheless went on to win the national party's nomination from running in the general election. As an example, both Clinton and Trump lost the Oklahoma primary election in 2016 but still won their respective national primary processes and earned their parties' nomination for the general election. It would be nonsensical for Oklahoma to bar either from the presidential general election as sore losers because they failed to win Oklahoma's primary election.[6] They were losers of the Oklahoma primary, but more importantly, winners of the national nomination process. Express sore loser prohibitions that apply, if at all, against presidential candidates therefore should be limited to those who have failed to win their parties' national nomination, rather than applied generally to losing candidates of any specific state primary. To construe sore loser prohibitions otherwise, a federal district court once explained, "might preclude the ultimate nominee at the [national party] convention from appearing on the general election, if he lost the [state's] primary election" (*Greaves v. Mills*).

Second, while the vast majority of states have sore loser restrictions for most elective offices, those statutes often carve out a special set of different rules for presidential candidates. The result is fewer sore loser restrictions for presidential elections. For one thing, many states do not even hold a primary election at the presidential level. As of 2016, 15 states used caucuses rather than primaries to allocate presidential delegates for at least one of the major parties, even if primary elections are nonetheless used to decide party nominations for other offices.[7] None of these states attempted to apply sore loser restrictions to caucus losers. In addition, there were two states (Connecticut and New York) that hold presidential primaries but do not have sore loser laws. And five more states held presidential primaries and had sore loser restrictions applicable to congressional candidates that do not apply to presidential candidates, made clear either by statute or court decision.[8] In sum, there were 22 states (depending on the party) where presidential candidates clearly do not face a sore loser prohibition.

In our judgment, there are 11 other states where the state sore loser restrictions for congressional candidates also appear to apply to presidential candidates. We are not necessarily claiming this as our preferred policy but instead that the sore loser provisions for congressional candidates in these 11 states likely apply to presidential candidates as a matter of statutory interpretation and other applicable law. In seven of these 11 states, either specific statutory language or a court decision makes explicitly clear that the state sore loser restrictions for congressional candidates apply equally to presidential candidates.[9] In the other four states, the sore loser restrictions appear to apply generally to all elections, even if not expressly specified for presidential elections, and there are no exceptions carved out for presidential elections in the statute.[10] In short, it is reasonably clear that at least 22 states do not have a sore loser prohibition for presidential candidates and at least 11 states do.

Determining sore loser restrictions for presidential candidates in the remaining 17 states is more challenging. In most of these states, the question is whether general sore loser restrictions for congressional candidates apply to presidential candidates despite the fact that the regulation of presidential elections is separated into a distinct statutory chapter, or otherwise differentiated in the code from other elections.

To be specific, 15 of these 17 states break out regulation of presidential elections but in doing so do not specify a sore loser prohibition for presidential candidates. However, these 15 states prohibit sore loser candidacies by candidates for other offices. The question is therefore whether this general sore loser prohibition applies to presidential candidates in the absence of any clarifying language. As an example, Arkansas specifies its conduct of "Elections" under Title 7 of its annotated state statutory code and then "Nominations and Primary Elections" under Title 7, Chapter 7. Within Chapter 7, Arkansas Code § 7-7-204, titled "Candidacy for multiple nominations prohibited," contains Arkansas's sore loser prohibition. It makes clear that a candidate in a party primary shall not be eligible to be the nominee of any other party nor run as an independent or write-in candidate for the same office during the following general election. But Arkansas's process for presidential elections is separated into a different Chapter 8, titled "Federal Elections." Chapter 8 contains no separate sore loser provision that it applies to the presidential election. Careful interpretation of the state's specific statutory language and structure is required to determine whether

Arkansas's sore loser provision under Chapter 7 applies to the presidential elections regulated separately under Chapter 8.[11]

In our view, four of these 15 states – Delaware, New Jersey, Vermont, and Virginia – have general sore loser restrictions on congressional candidates that do *not* apply to presidential candidates. Although these four states separately regulate presidential candidates, they do not impose specific sore loser restrictions on presidential candidates within that separate regulation, nor is there any statutory indication that the general sore loser restrictions are intended to reach presidential candidates.[12] As one court explained, the sore loser restrictions in these states do not extend to presidential candidates because the separate regulation of presidential elections neither "contains its own 'sore loser' provision nor incorporates the provisions found elsewhere in the Election Code."[13]

By contrast, we think it is fair to infer that the general sore loser restrictions apply to presidential candidates in the remaining 11 states, notwithstanding the fact that regulation of presidential elections is separately codified. In eight of these 11 states, the regulation of presidential elections is separately codified, but the statutory language nonetheless incorporates general restrictions and requirements from the rest of the election code and expressly clarifies that general rules applicable to primary elections apply to the presidential candidates unless otherwise stated.[14] These states thus incorporate their sore loser restrictions into their regulation of presidential elections in some explicit manner. As a result, it appears that these eight states extend their sore loser restrictions to presidential candidates despite the fact that regulation of presidential candidates is separately provided, at least in the absence of an express exception from the sore loser provisions.

In three states – Arizona, Missouri, and Tennessee – there is no explicit incorporation of the sore loser restrictions to presidential candidates, but we believe the state sore loser restrictions are implicitly incorporated to apply to presidential candidates based on the canon *expressio unius est exclusio alterius*. This canon of statutory interpretation provides that the expression of one thing implies the exclusion of all others not expressed. In these three states, the separate regulation of presidential candidates provides expressly for exceptions from general election rules when applied to presidential candidates and elections. For instance, Missouri does not allow a candidate to file as a party candidate for more than one office per election cycle but specifically exempts presidential candidates from this requirement.[15] Missouri, however, makes no such explicit exception for presidential candidates from its sore loser restrictions. Because Missouri makes explicit exception from general election rules for presidential candidates in certain instances, but does not do so for its sore loser restrictions, the implication under *expressio unius* is that Missouri law does not exempt presidential candidates from its sore loser restrictions.

Finally, there are two remaining states where it seems unclear whether state sore loser restrictions apply to presidential candidates: Montana and Rhode Island. Statutory interpretation of the relevant law in these states is especially murky because they do not clarify the applicability of the sore loser restrictions and the statutory language is otherwise ambiguous enough to make imputation one way or the other difficult. Reference to defined terms such as "presidential preference primary" or "independent presidential candidates," distinct from "primary elections" or "independent candidates" subject to sore loser provisions, makes it hard to tell whether the legislative design includes the former within the sore loser restrictions covering the latter.

The underlying problem, of course, is that the legislative design for sore losers likely did not specifically consider the question of presidential candidates. The applicability of sore loser restrictions even to congressional candidates seems somewhat incidental to the timing of filing deadlines in several states. So it is no surprise that many states do not address the still more esoteric question whether they apply to presidential candidates every four years.

Based on our statutory review, Table 26.3 summarizes sore loser laws across the states as we interpret them. To recap, we estimate that sore loser restrictions apply to presidential candidates in 22 states (marked as CF or SL), do not apply in 26 states (marked as None or Caucus), and may or may not apply in two states (marked as uncertain). We offer no view about these laws' constitutionality and set aside for purposes of this analysis the possibility of a successful constitutional challenge in court. Our final assessment differs considerably from Richard Winger's (2015) conclusion that only two states, South Dakota and Texas, had sore loser laws that apply to presidential primaries. We diverge from Winger's estimate for two principal reasons. The first is that we identify sore loser laws more expansively than Winger. While Winger focuses on express sore loser prohibitions, we include as a sore loser law not only the express prohibitions on sore loser candidacies, but also any combination of cross-filing prohibitions, disaffiliation requirements, and filing deadlines that make it effectively impossible for a candidate to lose a party primary and then subsequently file as an independent candidate or nominee of another party for the general election. For reasons explained in Kang (2011), we believe that such less direct restrictions on sore loser candidacies nonetheless prevent effective sore loser candidacies almost as well as express prohibitions.

Table 26.3 Sore Loser Laws for Presidential Candidates 2016

State	Type of Sore Loser Restriction	State	Type of Sore Loser Restriction
Alabama	CF	Montana	Uncertain
Alaska	Caucus	Nebraska	Caucus
Arizona	CF	Nevada	Caucus
Arkansas	SL	New Hampshire	CF
California	None	New Jersey	None
Colorado	Caucus	New Mexico	None
Connecticut	None	New York	None
Delaware	None	North Carolina	SL
Florida	None	North Dakota	Caucus
Georgia	CF	Ohio	CF
Hawaii	Caucus	Oklahoma	CF
Idaho	Caucus	Oregon	SL
Illinois	CF	Pennsylvania	CF
Indiana	None	Rhode Island	Uncertain
Iowa	Caucus	South Carolina	SL
Kansas	Caucus	South Dakota	CF
Kentucky	Caucus	Tennessee	CF
Louisiana	CF	Texas	SL
Maine	Caucus	Utah	Caucus
Maryland	None	Vermont	None
Massachusetts	CF	Virginia	None
Michigan	CF	Washington	Caucus
Minnesota	Caucus	West Virginia	CF
Mississippi	CF	Wisconsin	CF
Missouri	CF	Wyoming	Caucus

Notes:
CF = cross-filing prohibition
SL = express ban on sore loser candidates
Caucus = caucus state
None = no limitation on sore loser candidates

Second, Winger categorizes a state as not having a sore loser restriction on presidential candidates – even if the law is clearly in the affirmative – when the state has not enforced the restriction against at least one presidential candidate in the past. Winger's notion of administrative precedent in the application of sore loser laws sensibly acknowledges past administrative practice, but we stick to the statutory text and judicial interpretation of the text in our classifications. It is not clear that a state is legally bound by its previous *administrative* applications of its sore loser restrictions, particularly when many years have passed since the last test of the statute, whatever the normative case for binding the state to its previous practice. A state's past practice may be probative of the statutory purpose and proper interpretation, but new election administrators have their own interpretations of their state's regulations that do not necessarily agree with with their predecessors'. Indeed, interpretation of these state laws is hardly straightforward, as we would readily admit of our own analysis. As a result, subsequent judicial and administrative interpretations of these laws will not always coincide, even when made in good faith.

A state's past administration of its sore loser restrictions is therefore not a reliable guide to its future enforcement under what may be quite different circumstances. Not only do new decision makers take office with potentially very different views of state law, but the political circumstances of presidential sore loser candidacies that would trigger the sore loser restrictions are likely to be highly idiosyncratic and salient to enforcement. During the 2016 Republican presidential primaries, primary candidates were pressured to sign a party loyalty pledge that would putatively have required them to support the eventual party nominee. In this context, Donald Trump was repeatedly asked about the possibility that he would run as an independent candidate if he did not win the party nomination, as was widely expected at the time. A Trump sore loser candidacy as then contemplated, splitting the ballot with a mainstream Republican nominee, would have raised the political stakes dramatically for the Republican Party compared to the more typical sore loser candidacy by Lyndon LaRouche in 1992 or Gary Johnson in 2012. The typical sore loser run by LaRouche or Johnson, even Ron Paul in 2008, presents little threat of siphoning off decisive numbers of votes in any state. But Trump's much greater popularity as a sore loser candidate, had he not won the nomination himself, would have presented a serious threat to the Republican nominee in the 2016 election such that pressure would have been intense on Republican state officials to wield sore loser restrictions to bar Trump. As a consequence, the fact that a state earlier permitted a sore loser candidacy by a fringe candidate, with no chance of disrupting the general election, is no guarantee that the state would similarly permit a sore loser run by a more viable candidate under different political circumstances.[16]

Conclusion

Our analysis has provided new insights into the operation of sore loser laws in both congressional and presidential elections in the United States. At the congressional level, we have shown that sore loser bans are now ubiquitous but that they were in place in only half of the states as recently as the 1970s. Examining Senate and House primaries from that earlier period, we found that sore loser candidates did in fact run in general elections between 6 percent and 10 percent of the time when they were permitted. Sore loser laws are thus consequential because they inhibit electoral activity that would otherwise have taken place. At the presidential level, we assessed the applicability of sore loser laws in the states. We discovered substantial ambiguity in statutory language and determined that sore loser bans apply in only about half of the states. The general election activity of primary losers that is generally impossible in congressional elections is thus widely permitted in presidential elections.

Although sore loser provisions are seldom studied by scholars, they are potentially important restrictions that draw tighter connections between primary and general elections. In particular, we contend that they make both types of elections more consequential. A sore loser ban limits the general election to candidates who have won party primaries or who opt to run outside the party apparatus. Because of the endorsement of a party and the ballot line that the party offers in the general election, sore loser laws effectively encourage insurgent and nontraditional candidates to pursue office through a major party in the primary rather than against it in the general. This inconsistency between the two levels of federal elections – not to mention variation that might exist at the state and local level – suggests that lawmakers and scholars ought to give more consideration to the operation of sore loser provisions across the states.

The normative desirability of sore loser laws reflects tradeoffs among a variety of goals and will depend on which of these values gets priority. We have shown here that sore loser laws do squelch electoral competition in general elections to some degree and our previous research showed that they contributed to party polarization. We regard these as real liabilities. But sore loser restrictions might be attractive to those who wish to maintain the dominance of the two-party system, believing that the major parties are the right vehicles for channeling most policy disagreements. There might also be benefits for those who prioritize order and stability in the political system.

Notes

1 We thank Evan Crawford and Brian Saling for indispensable research assistance.
2 A smaller number of states have laws that require candidates who previously ran under a party label to disaffiliate before running as independents or minor party candidates in subsequent elections (Chamberlain and Klarner 2016).
3 We excluded Connecticut and Delaware in 1976 because they did not have conventional primary systems at the time, thus reducing the sample size to 98. However, due to death or retirement, Alabama and Minnesota had both of their Senate seats up for election in 1978, bringing the total back up to 100.
4 Some states require write-in candidates to register with the state to earn votes while others will count votes for any candidate whose name is written in. The most notable recent case of a sore loser candidate winning on write-in votes is Lisa Murkowski's 2010 Senate re-election victory in Alaska.
5 Paul Singer, "A Trump Independent Run Got Harder Thursday Night, *USA Today*, August 7, 2015; Jeremy Pelzer, "Donald Trump Can't Run as an Independent in Ohio, Secretary of State's Office Says," *Cleveland Plain Dealer*, December 14, 2015.
6 The U.S. Supreme Court explained that the state's interest in political stability thus makes less sense in support of a sore loser law applied to presidential candidates. See *Anderson v. Celebrezze*, 460 U.S. 780, 804 (1983) ("The State's interest in regulating a nationwide Presidential election is not nearly as strong; no State could singlehandedly assure 'political stability' in the Presidential context.").
7 The caucus states were Alaska, Colorado, Hawaii, Idaho (Democrats only), Iowa, Kansas, Kentucky (Republicans only), Maine, Minnesota, Nebraska (Democrats only), Nevada, North Dakota, Utah, Washington (Democrats only), and Wyoming. Several territories also used caucuses to select delegates.
8 The five states are California, Florida, Indiana, Maryland, and New Mexico. Kentucky also would fall into this category when it holds primary elections.
9 The seven states are Illinois, Louisiana, Michigan, North Carolina, Ohio, Oklahoma, and Texas.
10 The four states are Oregon, Pennsylvania, South Dakota, and Wisconsin.
11 We ultimately classify Arkansas as applying its sore loser law to presidential candidates. See below.
12 For one complicated example, New Jersey prohibits a general election candidacy by "a candidate who unsuccessfully sought nomination of a political party to that office in the primary election held in the same calendar year." N.J. Stat Ann. § 19:13-8.1. However, New Jersey law refers to presidential candidates for the general election not as nominated by "primary election" but instead as "nominated by the political parties at state convention," N.J. Stat Ann. § 19:13-1, which arguably exempts presidential candidates from the aforementioned sore loser prohibition.
13 *Anderson v. Hooper*, 498 F.Supp. 898, 903 (D. N.M. 1980) (interpreting New Mexico's similar statutory language and structure).

14 The eight states are Alabama, Arkansas, Georgia, Massachusetts, Mississippi, New Hampshire, South Carolina, and West Virginia.

15 Mo. Ann. Stat § 115.351.

16 A good example of just such a state change in position is Tennessee Secretary of State Tre Hargett's insistence in 2016 that his state's sore loser law would prevent a general election candidacy by Trump. See Mary Troyan, "Some Question Whether Tenn. 'Sore Loser' Law Would Affect Trump Independent Bid," *USA Today*, Feb. 18, 2016. The state of Tennessee actually had permitted Gary Johnson's sore loser candidacy just four years earlier in 2012, but Hargett's office dismissed that previous position as an anomalous result from "minor party litigation."

References

Ansolabehere, Stephen, John Mark Hansen, Shigeo Hirano, and James M. Snyder, Jr. 2010. "More Democracy: The Direct Primary and Competition in U.S. Elections." *Studies in American Political Development* 24 (1): 190–205.

Boatright, Robert G. 2013. *Getting Primaried: The Changing Politics of Congressional Primary Challenges*. Ann Arbor, MI: University of Michigan Press.

Boatright, Robert G. 2014. *Congressional Primary Elections*. Florence, KY: Routledge.

Burden, Barry C., Bradley M. Jones, and Michael S. Kang. 2014. "Sore Loser Laws and Congressional Polarization." *Legislative Studies Quarterly* 39 (2): 299–325.

Chamberlain, Adam, and Carl Klarner. 2016. "Spoilers? Evaluating the Logic Behind Partisan Disaffiliation Requirements for Independent and Third-Party Candidates." *Election Law Journal* 15 (2): 330–350.

Kang, Michael S. 2011. "Sore Loser Laws and Democratic Contestation." *Georgetown Law Journal* 99: 1013–1075.

Poole, Keith T., and Howard Rosenthal. 2007. *Ideology and Congress*. New Brunswick, NJ: Transaction Publishers.

Rohde, David W. 1991. *Parties and Leaders in the Postreform House*. Chicago, IL: University of Chicago Press.

Scarrow, Howard A. 1986. "Duverger's Law, Fusion, and the Decline of American 'Third' Parties." *Western Political Quarterly* 39 (3): 634–647.

Winger, Richard. 2015. "Chart on Page 3." *Ballot Access News*, 2–3, September 1.

INDEX

Reilly, Shauna, et al. 450n22
religion *see* voter demographics
Renzi, Matteo 401, 404–5, 415, 417–18
Repeal the Direct Primary (Freyd) 4
Republican Majority Campaign 249
Republican Party (Italy PRI) 400
Republican Party (US): 2016 presidential debates of 314; 2016 presidential primaries of 253–57, 265–72, 274, 285, 290–305; 2016 vote share of *428*; coalition of 241–42, 247–50, 280–81; competitiveness of presidential primaries of 279–83; conservative members of 294–97, **298**, **300**, 305n3; control of debates by 315–16; ideological segmentation of 293–97, 305n2; moderates and liberals of 294–97, **300**, 305n2; PAC donations to 238–41; party loyalty pledge of 464; reform-oriented factions in 435–37; in southern states, 103–6, 111–15; Tea Party wing of 191, 195, 213, 217–18, 224nn3–4, 256, 266, 280; very conservative members of 294–99, **300**, 305n2
research on primaries 5–11; on candidate characteristics 9; comparative perspective in 7–8; on consequences 8–9; on motivations 8; during the Progressive Era 5, 8, 15; on spending 8; state- and region-specific focus of 5, 9, 11n3; on voter characteristics 8
Reynolds, John F. 3, 8, 15–16, 162
Rice, Tom W. 178, 185, 190
Richardson, Lilliard E. 447
Riker, William 195, 429, 448n3
Rockefeller, Nelson 293
Rogers, Steven 11, 73
Rohde, Stein 69
Rombi, Stefano 351
Romney, Mitt: 2008 primaries of 270; 2012 primaries of 215, 259–60, 274, 308, 313; competitiveness of primaries of *281*; conservative record of 307; crossover voters and 119, 126–29; endorsements of 259, 282; voter ideology and 294, 304
Roosevelt, Franklin D. 49
Roosevelt, Theodore 50, 52
Rosenblum, Nancy 10
Rosenstone, Steven J. 134
Rosenthal, Howard 150
Royal Commission on Electoral Reform and Party Financing (Canada) 390
Royal Commission on the Status of Women (Canada) 388
Rubio, Marco 267–71, 278, 285, 315; debate performance of 317–18; ideological campaign of 297–300, 304; political ideology of 291
rules and regulations of primaries 3, 10, 16; on campaign finance 52–53, 256; on certification of winners 51; competitiveness

and 189–90; of direct primaries 39, 46, 49–53; in foreign primaries 30–36; impact on outcomes of 96; on mandatory primaries 164–65; McGovern-Fraser Commission reforms of 195, 209n5, 256–59, 264, 266, 273; moderation of nominees and 190; origins of 21–24; on primary schedules 253; on sore losers 425, 431, 456–65, 465n6, 465n12; state-level variations in 4, 10, 37, 41, 68–69, 189, 456–57, 465n6, 465n12; on types of primaries **130**, 151; voter ID laws and 134, 137, 144n8; voter turnout and 134–44
run-off primaries 4, 28–30, 37nn11–12, 51
Rusk, Jerrold G. 172n14
Ryan, Paul 224

safe districts 69n5
Salvini, Matteo 401, 418
same-day registration 134
Sanchez, Loretta 443, 451n38
Sanders, Bernie 26, 176, 316; crossover voters and 126, 128, 129; debates of 316; endorsements of 263–64; presidential primaries of 255, 257, 260–65, 271, 274, 283–85, 460
Sandri, Giulia 321
Santorum, Rick 119, 260, *268*, 278, 291, 295, 297
Sartori, Giovanni 335
Sayers, Anthony 9, 322, 389
Scala, Dante 9, 253–54
Scalfarotto, Ivan, 404
Scandinavian democracy 2
Scanio, Alfonso Pecoraro 404
Scarrow, Susan 33
Schiffer, Adam J. 313
Schumer, Charles 226
Schwarzenegger, Arnold 440–44
Scioli, Daniel 357
secret ballot *see* Australian ballot
Seddone, Antonella 321, 351
segmented partisanship 120–21, 294–97
selectorates 18, 37n1
Sellers, Patrick 190
Semanko, Norm 439
semi-closed primaries **130**, 431–34; partisan identity and 120, 129; voter eligibility in 150; *see also* hybrid primaries
semi-open primaries 35, **130**, 431; candidate ideology and, 147–55; partisan identity and 120, 129; voter eligibility in 150, 152–53; *see also* hybrid primaries
Senate primaries: divisiveness in 175, 178–85, 190; party coalitions in 237–50; sore loser laws and 457–60, 464–65; voter turnout in 135, 139, 144; *see also* general elections